BY BRIAN JAY JONES

Washington Irving: An American Original
Jim Henson: The Biography

JIM HENSON

JIM HENSON

The Biography

BRIAN JAY JONES

BALLANTINE BOOKS

NEW YORK

Published in the United States by Ballantine Books, an imprint of The Random House Publishing Group, a division of Random House LLC, New York, a Penguin Random House Company.

BALLANTINE and the HOUSE colophon are registered trademarks of Random House LLC.

LIBRARY OF CONGRESS CATALOGING-IN-PUBLICATION DATA

Jones, Brian Jay.

Jim Henson : the biography / Brian Jay Jones.

p. cm.

Includes bibliographical references and index.

ISBN 978-0-345-52611-3

eBook ISBN 978-0-345-52613-7

1. Henson, Jim. 2. Puppeteers—United States—Biography. 3. Television producers and directors—United States—Biography. 4. Muppet Show (Television program) 5. Sesame Street (Television program) I. Title.

PN1982.H46J66 2013

791.4302'33092—dc23

[B] 2013024039

Printed in the United States of America on acid-free paper

www.ballantinebooks.com

9 8 7 6 5 4 3 2 1

FIRST EDITION

Book design by Carole Lowenstein

For Barb and Madi

CONTENTS

BLUE SKY

1973

JIM HENSON SLOWLY FOLDED HIMSELF INTO A COUCH INSIDE REEVES Teletape Studio, sliding down, as he often did, until he was nearly horizontal, his shaggy head against the back cushions and his long legs stretched out in front of him. As always, Jim was the calm in the middle of the chaos, sitting quietly as studio technicians and crew members whirled around him, adjusting lights and bustling about the background sets for *Sesame Street*'s Muppet segments. Jim simply lounged, hands folded across his stomach, fingers laced together. Draped limply across his lap was the green fleece form of Kermit the Frog, staring lifelessly at the floor, mouth agape.

Jim and Kermit were waiting.

In the five years *Sesame Street* had been on the air, many of its most memorable moments involved children interacting with the Muppets. And while all of the Muppet performers were good with children, most agreed that it was Kermit children believed in and trusted completely—mostly because they completely believed in and trusted Jim Henson. Jim—and therefore Kermit—had a natural sweetness, a reassuring patience, and a willingness to indulge silliness—and the resulting interaction could be pure magic. Even as Jim sat waiting, then, there was, as always, a buzz of anticipation.

Sesame Street director Jon Stone—a warm bear of a man with an easy smile—strolled the set, the end of a chewed pencil sticking out of his salt-and-pepper beard. "Blue sky!" he said loudly—a signal that a child was present on the set, a coded reminder that the normally boisterous Muppet performers and crew should watch their language. There was actually little chance of Jim himself swearing—normally his epithets were nothing stronger than "Oh, for heaven's sake!"—but with the cue that his young costar, a little girl named Joey, had arrived, Jim slowly unfolded himself and rose to his full six-foot-one height.

Casually, Jim pulled Kermit onto his right arm, slightly parting his thumb from his fingers as he slid his hand into the frog's mouth, then smoothed the long green sleeve from Kermit's body down over his elbow. He brought the frog's face up toward his own, tilting the head slightly—and suddenly, Kermit was magically alive, sizing up Jim with eyes that seemed to widen or narrow as Jim arched or clenched his fingers inside Kermit's head.

While *Sesame Street*'s Muppet sets were usually elevated on stilts some six feet off the floor—making it possible for puppeteers to perform while standing—no child would ever be placed at such a perilous height. Instead, Joey—in a pink striped shirt, with her long blond hair tied at the top of her head—was moved into position on a stool while Jim knelt on the floor next to her. Slowly he raised Kermit up beside her, eying the Muppet's position on a video monitor in front of his crouched knees. Joey's eyes locked immediately on Kermit. The frog was no mere puppet; Kermit was *real*.

"*Rolleeoleeoleeyo!*" called out Stone—and as tape began to roll, Joey was already patting and petting Kermit lovingly.

"Hey, can you sing the alphabet, Joey?" asked Kermit.

"Yes," said Joey, nodding earnestly, "yes, I could."

"Let's hear you sing the alphabet."

"*A B C D . . .*" sang Joey, and Jim bopped Kermit along in time to the familiar "Twinkle, Twinkle, Little Star" melody, bouncing the frog's head back and forth. "*E F,*" continued Joey—then instead of G, she substituted "*Cookie Monster!*" and giggled at her own joke.

All eyes in the studio were on the frog, waiting to see what Jim would do.

Jim reacted instantly, arching his long fingers inside Kermit to give him a surprised expression. Then he turned the frog, in a classic slow burn, toward the still-giggling Joey. "You're not singin' the alphabet!" Kermit said cheerily, and began the song again. Joey sang along eagerly, this time gliding past the letter G without incident, and stumbling only slightly through the troublesome quintet of *LMNOP.*

Joey patted Kermit lightly, unable to keep her hands off the slightly fuzzy Muppet. "*Q R Cookie Monster!*" she sang, and broke down in another fit of giggles.

Jim pressed his thumb and fingers tightly together inside Kermit's head, giving the frog a brief look of mock irritation. Then he arched his hand back upward, returning Kermit's expression to one of mild surprise. Joey tilted her head slightly and giggled directly into Kermit's eyes. She believed in him completely.

"Cookie Monster isn't a letter of the alphabet!" said Kermit helpfully. "It goes, *Q R S . . .*"

"*T U Cookie Monster!*" Joey exploded into giggles, clenching her hands in front of her.

For a moment, Jim nearly broke character. He snickered slightly. "Yuh-you're just teasing me!" he finally said in Kermit's voice, and the two of them began singing together again. "*W X Y and Z . . .*"

Joey briefly placed her hand on Kermit's shoulder as they entered the refrain. "*Now I've sung my ABCs . . .*" the two of them sang.

"*. . . next time Cookie Monster!*" Joey erupted, and broke down in giggles again.

"Next time, Cookie Monster can do it with you!" griped Kermit. "I'm leaving!" Jim pulled Kermit's face into a mild grimace—and with a groan of exasperation skulked the frog away, out of camera shot.

Joey stared after him. "I love you," she said, matter-of-factly.

Jim bounced Kermit eagerly back toward the little girl. "I love you, too," he said warmly.

"Thanks," said Joey.

And she draped an arm around Kermit and kissed him on the head.

JIM HENSON

CHAPTER ONE

THE DELTA

1936–1949

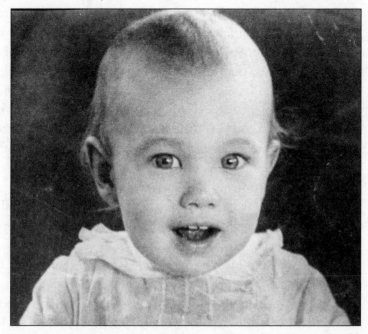

James Maury Henson in 1937, at about six months old.

DEER CREEK WINDS CASUALLY, ALMOST LAZILY, THROUGH THE MUGGY lowlands in the heart of the Mississippi Delta. Its point of origin—near the little town of Scott, in Bolivar County—lies roughly ninety miles north of its terminal point at the Yazoo River three counties away. But Deer Creek takes its time getting there, looping and whorling back and forth in a two-hundred-mile-long amble, looking like a child's cursive scrawled across the map.

The town of Leland, Mississippi, straddles Deer Creek just as it twists into one of its first tight hairpin turns, about ten miles east of Greenville. Established before the Civil War, the sleepy settlement, sprawled out across several former plantations, had taken advantage of fertile soil and regular steamboat traffic on Deer Creek to become one of the wealthiest in the Delta region. In the 1880s came the Yazoo and Mississippi Valley Railroad, along with an influx of grocers and landlords and innkeepers—but even with the growing merchant class and increasing gentrification, it was still land that mattered most in Leland, and in the Mississippi Delta. In 1904, then, the state legislature called for the creation of an agricultural experiment station in the Delta region, preferably "at a point where experiments with the soil of the hills as well as the Delta can be made." That point turned out to be two hundred acres of land hugging Deer Creek, in the village of Stoneville, putting the state's new Delta Branch Experiment Station just north of—and practically butted up against—Leland. By 1918, the facility in Stoneville was housing researchers and their families from the U.S. Department of Agriculture, carrying out research on crops, soil, and animal production for the federal government; by 1930, its findings on animal feed and insect control were particularly welcome to planters and sharecroppers doing their best to scratch out a living from the swampy Delta soil during the Great Depression.

Paul Ransom Henson—Jim Henson's father—was neither a planter nor a sharecropper. Nor had he come to the Delta region to work a family farm during the Depression or satisfy a random pang of wanderlust. Paul Henson was a practical man, and he had come to Leland in 1931 with his new wife, Betty, for a practical reason: he had accepted a government post at the Delta Branch Experiment Station in Stoneville.

Paul Henson came from a line of similarly sturdy and clear-minded men who sought neither to offend nor agitate, a trait that Paul's famous son would inherit as well—and, in fact, Jim Henson would always be very proud of his father's rugged, even-tempered Midwestern lineage. On one side of his father's family were the Dolton and Barnes lines—good-natured, nonconfrontational, and accommodating almost to a fault—while on the other were the Hensons—practical, rugged, and imperturbable.

One of Jim's favorite family stories involved his great-great-grandfather, a strongly pro-Northern farmer named Richmond

Dolton who, during the Civil War, had been living in a small Missouri town in which most of the residents were Southern sympathizers. Rather than offend the Confederate sensibilities of his neighbors, the amiable Dolton simply swapped his farm—in a typically equitable and businesslike exchange—for a similar one in a town in Kansas where the residents shared his own Union tendencies. The move would come to be particularly appreciated by Dolton's teenage daughter, Aramentia, though for reasons more prurient than political—for it was here in Kansas that Aramentia Dolton met Ransom Aaron Barnes, a New Jersey native who had settled in the area. In 1869, she and Barnes were married; less than a year later, they would have a daughter, Effie Carrie Barnes—Paul Henson's mother.

On the Henson side, Jim could trace his pedigree back to colonial-era farmers in North Carolina whose descendants had slowly pushed west with the expanding American frontier, setting up farms and raising families in Kentucky and Kansas. One of those descendants was Jim's paternal grandfather, a sturdy Kansas farmer named Albert Gordon Henson, who, in 1889, had married Richmond Dolton's levelheaded granddaughter, Effie Carrie Barnes. After an ambitious though unsuccessful effort to stake a claim during the Cherokee Strip land run—where he had rumbled into the dusty Oklahoma countryside in a mule-drawn buckboard—Albert and Effie would eventually settle in Lincoln County, just east of Oklahoma City. It was here that Paul Ransom Henson—the name Ransom was borrowed from Effie's father, Ransom Aaron Barnes— would be born in 1904, the youngest of Albert and Effie's nine children.

Each morning, Paul Henson would be awakened at first light to do his chores and walk the half mile to school, a one-room building crammed with fifty children and presided over by two teachers. While Albert Henson never had much formal schooling, he was determined to make education a priority for the children in the Henson household. With that sort of parental encouragement, Paul graduated from high school in 1924 at age nineteen, and immediately headed for Iowa State College—now Iowa State University, a school recognized then, as now, for the quality of its agricultural programs. Over the next four years, Paul was a member of the agriculture-oriented Alpha Gamma Rho fraternity, participated on the Farm Crops Judging Team (the team would place third nationally in 1927), and even discovered a knack for performance as a member of the Dramatic Club. In July 1928, he received his BS in Farm Crops and Soils, completing a thesis on the hybridization of soybeans.

Following graduation, Paul began work on his master's degree at the University of Maryland, enrolling in courses covering plant physics, biochemistry, genetics, statistics, agronomy, and soil technology. One afternoon, while eating his lunch, he caught sight of an attractive young woman walking toward the campus restaurant—when pressed, he would later admit his eyes had been drawn mainly to her legs—and was determined to win an introduction. The legs, as it turned out, belonged to Elizabeth Brown—Betty, as everyone called her—the twenty-one-year-old secretary to Harry Patterson, dean of the College of Agriculture.

Elizabeth Marcella Brown was born in Washington, D.C., and raised in Maryland, but had lived in Memphis and New Orleans long enough to pick up both the lilting accent and genteel demeanor of a Southern belle. The accent and the manners were fitting, for Betty had a refined, distinctly Southern, and generally artistic pedigree. In fact, it was through Betty's side of the family that Jim Henson could trace his artistic ability, in a straight and colorful line running through his mother and grandmother back to his maternal great-grandfather, a talented Civil War–era mapmaker named Oscar.

Oscar Hinrichs—a swaggering Prussian who had immigrated to the United States in 1837 at the age of two—began working as a cartographer for the United States Coast Survey at age twenty-one, reporting directly to Alexander Dallas Bache, head of the survey and a great-grandson of Benjamin Franklin. When the Civil War began in 1860, Oscar enthusiastically enlisted with the Confederacy—even smuggling himself into the South with the help of Confederate sympathizers in Maryland—and loaned his valuable mapmaking skills to the Southern cause even as he survived battles at Antietam, Gettysburg, and the Wilderness. After the war, Oscar married Marylander Mary Stanley—whose father had helped him sneak into the Confederacy—and moved to New York City. Over the next ten years,

Mary bore Oscar six children, including one daughter, Sarah—Betty Brown's mother, and Jim Henson's grandmother. It was Sarah who inherited Oscar Hinrichs's innate artistic streak, and she would learn not only how to paint and draw, but also how to sew, carve, and use hand tools—talents that Jim Henson would wield just as skillfully two generations later as he sketched, carved, and sewed his earliest Muppets.

The Hinrichs family eventually settled in Washington, D.C., where Oscar unhappily bounced between jobs, convinced employers were discriminating against him because of his service to the Confederacy. Compounding his misery, Mary became ill with uterine cancer and died in 1891 at the age of fifty-two. Less than a year later, a grief-stricken Oscar Hinrichs took his own life, leaving an orphaned fourteen-year-old Sarah to tend to two younger brothers. Dutifully, Sarah dropped out of the art school into which she had just been accepted and moved with her brothers into a Washington boardinghouse. For the rest of their lives, neither Sarah nor her siblings openly discussed Oscar Hinrichs's sad demise—a penchant for maintaining a respectful silence about unhappy circumstances that her grandson Jim Henson would also share.

In 1902, twenty-four-year-old Sarah Hinrichs was introduced to Maury Brown, a lanky, thirty-four-year-old clerk and stenographer for Southern Railway. Born in Kentucky on the day after Christmas in 1868, Maury Heady Brown—Jim Henson's grandfather—was a self-made man with a rugged Southern determination. Raised by a single mother who was totally deaf, Brown had run away from home at age ten and learned to use the telegraph, supporting himself by reporting horse-racing scores for a Lexington racetrack. A voracious reader and quick learner, he next taught himself typewriting and shorthand, eventually becoming so proficient at both that he was hired as the full-time private secretary to the president of Southern Railway. When he met Sarah Hinrichs in the winter of 1902, Brown fell in love immediately—and on their second date, as they ice skated on the frozen Potomac River, Maury Brown presented Sarah Hinrichs with an armful of red roses and asked for her hand. While the newspapers in 1903 may have noted the marriage of Maury and Sarah Brown, to each other—and to the rest of the family—they would always be "Pop" and "Dear."

For the next few years, Pop and Dear bounced around with the Southern Railway, landing briefly in Missouri, Washington, Memphis, and New Orleans, and all while raising three daughters, Mary Agnes, Elizabeth, and Barbara—better known as Attie, Betty, and Bobby. Perhaps because they moved around so often, the Browns were an exceptionally close and good-natured family. "I just thought we had the happiest home that ever was," Bobby said later. "And I remember what a shock it was when I would go to other people's houses to sleep over and found out that all families weren't as fun and nice to each other as ours!"

At some point in his youth, Maury Brown embraced Christian Science, a relatively new faith that had been formally established in 1879. Consequently, the daughters were all brought up as Christian Scientists, though moderate in their practice, likely through the influence of Dear. While the daughters might forgo most medical care in favor of prayer or homeopathic treatments—as a girl, Betty was dunked in alternating hot and cold water baths to combat a case of whooping cough—more serious injuries were almost always attended to by physicians. When Attie was badly hurt in a car accident one winter, the family immediately called for a doctor—and far from being concerned about compromising her faith, Attie remembered being more embarrassed that the doctor had to cut away her long underwear to set her broken leg.

Eventually, the Browns returned to the D.C. area for good, living first in a "perfectly awful" place near the railroad tracks in Hyattsville, Maryland—the house would shake violently as trains roared past—before settling into the much quieter Marion Street in 1923. Attie and Betty were expected to help pay the mortgage each month, and shortly after high school both found work as secretaries—Attie at an express company, and Betty at the nearby University of Maryland, where she, and her legs, soon caught the eye of Paul Henson.

Paul would woo Betty for the better part of two years, studying genetics and plant biology at the university during the week and attending regular tennis parties hosted by the Browns on weekends—

and Paul quickly came to adore not just Betty, but the entire Brown family. It was easy to see why; Dear and Pop were devoted to each other, while the girls, both then and later, had distinct, almost Dickensian, personalities. Attie was the serious and straitlaced one and became a devoted Episcopalian. Betty was considered practical and no-nonsense, though she could show flashes of a slightly silly sense of humor, while Bobby was the happy-go-lucky one who worked to ensure that everything was "upbeat all the time." All three, too, were excellent tennis players, having been taught to play at a young age by their dashing uncle Fritz Hinrichs, who also taught the girls to dance. Attie later admitted she "could've cared less" about tennis, but the parties kept the Browns in the center of a wide social circle, and their names on the society pages of *The Washington Post*.

In the spring of 1930, Paul completed work on his master's thesis—on the "effect of starchy endosperm on the distribution of carbohydrates in the corn plant"—and received a master of science degree in June. He and Betty married on December 27, 1930—the same day Attie, still recovering from her car accident, married Stanleigh "Jinx" Jenkins, a good-natured high school teacher and Episcopalian minister. Although Paul was graduating during the first difficult years of the Great Depression, with his advanced degree and his background in soybean research, he found employment almost immediately as an agronomist with the U.S. Department of Agriculture. In early 1931, the USDA decided to post him not to the research facility at nearby Beltsville, Maryland, as perhaps Betty had hoped, but rather at the Delta Branch Experiment Station in Mississippi. The newlywed Hensons were off to Leland.

Despite the distance from home, even Betty Henson had to admit that Leland was an attractive place to start a family. The surrounding landscape was lush and green, brimming with wildflowers almost year-round. Cypress trees lined Deer Creek, keeping the shores shady and relatively cool even in the humid summer. The population was just large enough—hovering around three thousand—to support movie theaters, drugstores, and several churches and restaurants, while still being small enough to provide a small-town feel. Further, with the steady flow into Stoneville of college-educated scientists— most of them, like Paul Henson, with advanced degrees—the school in Leland was one of the best in Mississippi. The town, in fact, seemed immune to the Depression infecting the rest of the country. Near record harvests of cotton were ginned at Stoneville and packed into the railroad cars that regularly chugged through the Delta region. Construction was booming, and businesses were doing so well that local police fretted about the best way to manage the traffic that was snarling Broad and Main Streets on Saturday evenings.

Further, the government had gone out of its way to make the relatively remote Stoneville facility as attractive as possible to its scientists and staff. Most employees lived on the grounds of the facility itself—and, in fact, a home had been built specifically for the Hensons in early 1931, a four-room house just southeast of the new main administration building, erected at a cost of $3,093. Milk was delivered daily, free of charge, courtesy of the on-site dairy, and each year the facility would sponsor a Delta Days celebration where families would come from miles around to eat from enormous pits of barbecued chicken and pork and take part in pickup baseball games and other contests.

The Hensons would be in Leland only a little more than a year before they added their first child. In the autumn of 1932, with Dear and Bobby close at hand, Betty bore a son they named Paul Ransom Henson, Jr.—a small, sad-eyed boy on whom Betty doted. For the next four years, Betty would make regular and extended trips back to her parents' place in Maryland—where the rest of the family could coo and fuss over their firstborn—while Paul Sr. settled into his position at Stoneville, escaping the stifling heat of the administration building each day by tromping the nearby fields of soybeans stretching steadily upward toward the Mississippi sun.

Four years later, the week of September 20, 1936, was an unseasonably hot one for the Delta region. Cotton plants wilted under a scorching sun, while a few scattered rain showers lamely soaked into the dry, brittle ground. On Wednesday evening—the 23rd—with thunderstorms still rumbling across the Delta, Paul Henson drove his pregnant wife the nine dusty miles from Stoneville to Greenville and checked her into King's Daughters Hospital, a stern-looking building the locals called simply "The Hospital," since it was the only one in the region. The following morning—at 11:40 A.M. on Thursday, September 24, 1936, with a Dr. Lucas attending—Betty Henson gave birth to her second child, an eight-pound, eleven-ounce, round-faced son with a shock of sandy hair. While their first son had been named for her husband, for their second child Betty looked to her side of the family—and perhaps intentionally employed the same trick Paul Henson's own mother had used when naming him—using her father's first name as her new son's middle one. Betty and Paul Henson's younger son, then, would be James Maury Henson—though his family would almost always call him Jimmy.

Only a little more than a year later, in early 1938, the Hensons moved back to Maryland, taking a house at 4012 Tennyson Road in Hyattsville. Founded just before the Civil War and straddling railroad tracks and the Baltimore and Washington Turnpike, Hyattsville was at an ideal location to funnel traffic and commerce between Baltimore and the nation's capital. By the late 1930s, it was a bustling streetcar suburb with a thriving downtown—including a brand-new Woolworth's—and like Leland, was already struggling with traffic and parking problems.

For the next five years, between the constant bustle of bridge and tennis parties at the Browns' a few blocks away, Paul Henson would make the short daily commute up Baltimore Avenue to the Beltsville Agricultural Research Center and its newly established Bureau of Plant Industry. In 1940, he completed a course in cytology at the University of Maryland, and began researching alternatives for beef cattle feed, eventually publishing his findings in the respected *Journal of Animal Science*.

For his younger son, however, those first years in Maryland were a blur—no surprise, really, considering that Jim's colleagues would later laugh that his ability to recall the past was almost nonexistent. "Jim hardly ever gets the past straight," Muppet writer Jerry Juhl said. "That's because he's completely future oriented." Jim did recall seeing *Snow White and the Seven Dwarfs* and *The Wizard of Oz* at this time—and while he would later cite *The Wizard of Oz* as his favorite film, given that he would have been barely three at the time of its 1939 release, it's little wonder that what he remembered most was being terrified of the roaring MGM lion before the film's opening scene.

Perhaps one of the most important and lasting impacts of these early Maryland years, however, was on Jim's way of speaking. While Southern-born, Jim learned to talk in the D.C. region, where he was more likely to hear the slightly fronted vowels of the mid-Atlantic accent than the Southern drawl of the Delta. Although Jim may have continued to hear Betty's gentle Southern lilt at home, it was Paul's flat, slightly nasal, Midwestern twang, as well as his almost whisper-quiet way of speaking, that Jim ultimately adopted. As he grew older, too, Jim developed a particular quirk in his speaking that, to many, would be as identifiable with him as his bib of a beard: when deep in thought, Jim would *hmmm* quietly as he considered a question or comment—and colleagues would learn to gauge Jim's mood from the length or tenor of a particular *hmmm*.

At the end of Jim's first-grade year, the Hensons returned to Leland, moving back into government housing on the Stoneville campus. The Henson home edged up against an orchard of pecan trees, planted for research and hybridization studies, but raided regularly by Jim and Paul Jr., who would bring in sackfuls of nuts for Betty to bake into pecan pies. Chickens ran in a small fenced-in area in the side yard, while the back of the house faced a fountain and circular drive leading up to the three-story, red-brick administration building. Just beyond the road that ran in front of the Henson house, the lawn sloped sharply down to Deer Creek.

Deer Creek, for all its beauty, wasn't a creek for swimming. Already shallow and swampy, cypress trees crashed regularly down into the murky water, creating makeshift dams that backed up with a mess of mud and debris. "None of us were allowed to swim in that creek," recalled Gordon Jones, Jim's best friend at the time. It was still their primary spot for playing, though instead of swimming or fishing, Jim and his friends generally preferred romping along the sloping banks. But "there were snakes all along the creek bank," recalled Tommy Baggette, another Leland friend, "and everybody had to be careful where they walked." To Jim, the snakes were all part of what he later recalled fondly as "an idyllic time." "I was a Mississippi Tom Sawyer," he said later. "I had a BB gun, and I'd shoot at the water moccasins in the swamp just to wake them up."

When he wasn't romping on the banks of Deer Creek or startling snakes with his gun, Jim was an avid bird-watcher, squinting into the high grass near the fields on the Stoneville compound, or peering up into the tops of the cypress trees with a pair of binoculars, then thumbing through his thick book of birds to try to identify what he'd seen flutter past. Baggette remembered being impressed by a reference book Jim had made himself by pasting in pictures of birds cut from books and magazines, and filling the margins with his own drawings. When pressed, Jim would name the blackbird as his favorite, not only for its spunky personality, but also because he delighted in the sound of the bird's less formal name: the grackle. It was the sort of deliciously sharp-sounding nonsensical word that Jim loved—a meaningless word that just *sounded* like it meant something.

Jim and Paul Jr. were enrolled at the Leland Consolidated School, an elegant high-ceilinged, single-story brick building that backed onto the creek. Here Jim joined the Cub Scouts, and picked up with a regular group of friends, including the bookish Jones, the rascally Baggette, the colorfully named Royall Frazier, and a strapping young man named Theodore Kermit Scott. While the Hensons still referred to their youngest son as Jimmy, to Jones, Frazier, and most of Leland, he was hailed by the groan-inducing *James,* thanks to a fourth-grade teacher who needed a way to distinguish between three boys in her class with similar names. "Jimmy Childress was going to be Jimmy," said Frazier later, laughing. "Jim Carr was going to be Jim and that meant Jim Henson was going to be James!"

Sundays in Leland were for church—and even with its relatively small population, Leland had a number of churches, with Methodist, Catholic, Presbyterian, Baptist, and several separate black churches all represented by their own imposing brick or stone structures. Paul Henson was, for the most part, a nonpracticing Methodist, while Betty and her sons were among the few Christian Scientists in the entire Delta region—before the arrival of the Hensons, a religious survey of the town had located exactly two Christian Scientists—but Jim's unusual faith was never cause for much conversation between him and his friends. Discussing his religious views years later, Jim was deferential to faith in general, a courtesy friends and colleagues deeply respected. "Over the years, I've evolved my own set of beliefs and attitudes—as we all have—I feel work for me," Jim wrote later. "I don't feel particularly comfortable telling others how to think or live. There are people who know more about these things than I do." "He was not an evangelical at all," agreed Gordon Jones, "and I wondered if it wasn't more of an intellectual thing, something that his parents had put on him, because it wasn't something that he seemed to really enjoy talking about or feel like he had to talk about."

Still, Jones, a Baptist, was curious enough to ask Jim about his religion at least once. "I remember he had pretty good answers," Jones said. "I wanted to know 'What happens when you get sick?' and 'Don't you go to the doctor?' And he let me know that a Christian Scientist's faith would handle that kind of thing." When it came to more serious illnesses, Jones said, Jim informed him that these were due to "a temporary lapse of faith." At that point, "they would go to the doctor," Jones said. "But generally, they depended on their faith to heal them."

With no real organized church of Christian Science in the area, Jim participated to some degree in the social opportunities provided by Leland's many other churches. Some weekends, Kermit Scott and his family would pick Jim up in Stoneville and attend services at the white Spanish Mission–style Methodist church in Leland. Other times, the Fraziers would bring him to the brick Presbyterian church on the corner of Willeroy and Broad Streets, where Jim would attend Sunday school classes. Here the basement classroom was presided over by a local osteopath named Dr. Cronin, whose lessons were remembered more for their entertainment value than for instruction in the gospels. Cronin delighted in engaging students with trivia questions and awarding prizes for the quickest correct answer, and for one particular contest announced that the student with the first correct answer would receive a softball bat while the runner-up would get a softball. "Jim found it just before I did and so Jim had first prize and I had second," Frazier recalled. "But Jim already had a bat

[so] he went ahead and said, 'No, I'll take the ball,' and he let me have the bat, just because I wanted it so badly." That was character-istic of Jim, said Frazier warmly. "He was a good friend."

If Sundays were for church, however, Saturdays were for Temple.

On the corner of Broad and Fourth in downtown Leland stood the town's sturdy brick movie theater, the Temple, built by the local Masons who used its spacious upstairs rooms for meetings. The name was appropriate, for here an eight-year-old Jim Henson would spend countless Saturdays sitting with his eyes cast reverently up-ward in the darkened theater, engrossed in the flickering images on the screen. "We'd always go on Saturday to watch the double feature cowboy movies," Baggette said. For fifteen cents, Jim and his friends could each get a bag of popcorn and spend an entire day soaking up serials, newsreels, cartoons, and the latest comedies or action films. Jim particularly liked films with exotic locations and costumes, whether it involved the American West or the Far East, and he and his friends would spend the rest of the week reenacting what they'd seen on screen, stalking each other through the pecan trees near Jim's house, building elaborate props, and putting together costumes from old clothing and materials salvaged from linen closets.

Sometimes neighbors would see Jim sitting swami-style on the front lawn of the Henson house, bunched up in a sheet with his head wrapped in a makeshift turban, pretending to snake-charm a garden hose. That was typical; whether it was figuring out how to make clothespin guns that fired rubber bands or building miniature sling-shots, Jim could almost always come up with a clever or creative way to make their games more fun. "A child's use of imagination and fantasy blends into his use of creativity," Jim explained later. The trick, he said, was to "try out whole new directions. There are many ways of doing something. Look for what no one has tried before." As he would demonstrate many times throughout his life, sometimes the cleverest solutions to a problem were also the simplest—and usu-ally lying in plain sight, provided you could see a thing differently.

Jones, for example, remembered being fascinated with the 1944 Columbia serial *The Desert Hawk,* a swashbuckling Arabian adven-ture in which Gilbert Roland played twin brothers, one good, one evil. "The good guy had a birthmark. It was a black star on one of his wrists," Jones recalled. "So Jim brought me a little cork he had made—he had cut it out and made a star and charred it so that I could make a little black star on my wrist if I wanted to, which I thought was just absolutely great. It hadn't occurred to me to make that thing or even figure out how to do it . . . but he was always coming up with simple little things that others didn't." Even at eight years old, Jones said, Jim "had something the rest of us didn't have—an unusual degree of originality."

But Jim had something else, too. He had Dear.

Even with her daughter Betty living more than a thousand miles away, Dear continued to make regular trips from Maryland to Mississippi, usually traveling by train, with daughter Bobby for company. Perhaps because Betty tended to indulge the more fragile, less independent Paul Jr., and often left Jim to entertain himself, Jim was exceptionally close to Dear—they even shared the same birthday—and on her arrival, Jim and Dear would immerse themselves in paint and pencils and crayons and glue. Like her mapmaking father, Dear was quick and sure with a pencil, and she encouraged Jim in his own drawings—which were often of loopy-eyed birds or wide-mouthed monsters—as Jim discovered how the placement of two dots for eyes could convey emotion, or how a slash could make an angry mouth. It was the same simplicity that he would later bring to his sense of design for the Muppets.

Dear was equally certain with a paintbrush—she had oil-painted a picture of the roses Pop had given her when he proposed, for example, which remained a family heirloom until it fell apart in the 1970s—and had a knack for crafts and delicate woodwork, including carving and sculpting, all skills she had also learned from Oscar Hinrichs. "[He's] the one who taught our mother to do the handwork things she did," said Attie of her grandfather—and Dear nurtured the same talents and enthusiasm in her grandson.

Apart from her considerable painting and drawing skills, Dear excelled with needle and thread. Her sewing ability, in fact, was the stuff of family legend. Enormous quilts and needlework decorated her home, and Dear had made not only all of her own clothes, but all of her daughters' clothes as well. Attie recalled with awe Dear's ability to sew with nearly any material, including a coat she had sewn from a heavy, scratchy army blanket. "How she sewed that material," Attie said, "nobody knows." This skill, too, Dear would cultivate in Jim, who would later build, sculpt, and sew his puppets out of nearly any materials he could find lying around.

Perhaps most important, Dear was Jim's best audience. She encouraged Jim in his play and in his dressing up and prop making, coaxed stories from him and indulged his fondness for puns and practical jokes. A voracious reader, Dear also inspired a love of reading in Jim, whether it was L. Frank Baum's *Wizard of Oz* books or the comics pages of the newspaper. And with her proud Southern heritage—"the Brown girls were never allowed to forget they were Southerners!" said Bobby—Dear instilled in Jim a similar sense of genteel self-importance. It wasn't arrogance, but simply a conviction that he could do and be anything he wanted—a confidence and self-awareness that, for the rest of his life, family and colleagues admired and found reassuring. "He was convinced he was going to be successful," his wife, Jane, said later. "I think he knew he was extraordinary. But it was in a quiet way where he just quietly knew that he knew things."

With such encouragement at home, it was no surprise Jim found school relatively easy. While he wasn't the best student in class—that distinction fell to Jones, who later became a physicist—Jim was ranked in the top three. Jim's classmates remember him as being very clever, but never seeking the spotlight. No one could recall Jim taking an interest in school productions, apart from obligatory supporting roles in chorus or Christmas plays. It was perhaps just as well, for Jim was so soft-spoken that audience members would likely have had to strain to hear him.

While Jim was taller than most boys his age, he was neither gawky nor an athlete, though Kermit Scott admitted that Jim was "a little bit more of a nerd" than the rest of the gang. Still, Jim could surprise his classmates by exhibiting the same brand of toughness that had sent his paternal grandfather rumbling wildly into the Cherokee Strip. One evening out at Jones's farm, Jim and his friends took part in a boxing match—a sport at which the well-built, and slightly older, Tommy Baggette excelled. The boys took turns putting on the gloves and fighting one-on-one, but when it came time to find an opponent to take on the good-natured but solid Baggette, all eyes went downward. Finally, Jim stepped forward. "[He] would do things like that," Jones remembered. "He had guts . . . if somebody else wouldn't do it, he would—and . . . he'd just go ahead and make the best of it." The result? "Tommy hit him with an uppercut and knocked him down," Jones said. "But I just remember thinking how much nerve it took for [Jim] to put himself in that spot."

Still, there were no hard feelings between Jim and Baggette, whose mother, Jessie Mae, served as one of the den mothers for their Cub Scout troop. It was in Cub Scouts, in fact, that Jim got his first taste of performing, putting on a kind of pantomime with Gordon Jones as part of a troop skit night. As Jones stood with his hands clenched behind his back, giving a short speech in a deadpan manner, Jim stood pressed up behind him, poking his arms through the crook of Jones's arms to perform the speaker's hands. "He'd reach out his handkerchief and pat [Jones's] forehead, doing all these kinds of things which we all thought was hilarious," Frazier remembered. It was no accident, Jones said later, that Jim performed the expressive hands, which was the part of the skit "calling for originality and showmanship. . . . Jim was the showman."

Betty Henson also served as a den mother for Jim's Cub Scout troop. As it turned out, the Henson home was a favorite gathering place, not only because Betty was known to serve warm pecan pies at Scout meetings, but also because the Henson household was a genuinely warm one. Everyone liked each other and a good sense of humor mattered. The Hensons, said Jones, "were very quiet people. . . . But they all had a sense of humor and they would say things that were funny. But there was no loud-voice laughing. Everybody was very merry, and they did a lot of wordplay and things of that nature."

While Paul Sr.—"Dr. Henson," as the boys respectfully called him—was perhaps the quietest member of the family, he was known around the Stoneville compound for his way with a story. During the almost weekly summer fish fries at the Experiment Station, a crowd would gather around Paul as he launched into one funny story after another. As for Betty Henson, she was "absolutely delightful," said Jones, with "a bright, witty sense of humor." She took great delight in gently teasing the boys, pouring a glass of milk to overflowing, for example, if the boys didn't literally say "when." "I'd say 'Okay, that's enough,' and she'd keep pouring!" laughed Jones. "His mother was great for jokes," agreed Frazier, who recalled Betty trying to convince him that a blurry baby picture actually showed Jim with six toes. "She said, 'You never noticed he had six toes?' . . . And I kept saying, 'Take off your shoe, Jim!' "

Jim, it seemed, could see the humor in almost any situation. For a while, the Hensons owned a horse named Peggy, a volatile creature that Jim and Kermit Scott would attempt to ride among the pecan trees near the Henson house. Instead, Peggy would bolt for the low-hanging branches to knock Jim, or anyone else, off her back. While Jim howled with laughter at the nerve of the horse, Scott was less amused. "Both of us nearly got killed," he grumbled.

Wild horses aside, Jim and Paul Jr. were always tinkering with something. While Paul was more mathematically inclined, working on detailed projects with small parts, Jim was the more ambitious of the two brothers, often taking on big, messy projects that required a great deal of space. While Jim and Paul were four years apart, they remained close—given his slight build, Paul was more comfortable playing with Jim and his friends than boys his own age (Paul Henson would, in fact, remain of slight build for the rest of his life)—and he and Jim would spend hours together in their side yard, hunched over model airplanes and crystal radio sets. Jim would always be a gadget freak, a passion he had likely inherited from his great-uncle Ernie, Dear's younger brother, who had built his own crystal radio in the 1920s so he and Dear could listen to *Two Black Crows* together on the radio's earpiece. To Frazier's delight, Jim's radios worked, too. "You could get one radio station very faintly," said an impressed Frazier. "But it worked!"

As much as Jim liked building radios and knowing how they worked, he loved listening to them even more. "Early radio drama was an important part of my childhood," Jim said fondly. "I'd go home at four-thirty or five in the afternoon to hear shows like *The Green Hornet, The Shadow* and *Red Ryder* . . . and of course I loved the comedians." Fibber McGee and Molly was one of Jim's favorites, as was Jack Benny. But most of all, Jim lived for Sunday evenings, when NBC radio aired *The Chase and Sanborn Hour,* featuring ventriloquist Edgar Bergen and his dummy Charlie McCarthy.

Bergen was that oddest of phenomena—a ventriloquist who had rocketed to success on the radio, where no one could see the performance. Those watching Bergen live in the studio might have argued that was for the best, as Bergen's ventriloquism skills could often get sloppy, his lips visibly moving when he spoke through his dummies. It was a charge Bergen shrugged off; to Bergen, the technique was secondary to the characters—and Bergen excelled both at creating memorable characters and bringing them to life almost purely through the sound of his voice. Bergen engaged his characters in rapid-fire banter so nimbly—rotating flawlessly between his own voice and the voices of his impish sidekick Charlie McCarthy or dimbulb Mortimer Snerd—that radio listeners were convinced they were real people. Jim Henson, for one, was certain of it. "I wasn't thinking of any of those people as puppets," he said. "They were human to me."

But it went even further than that, as Jim would explain years later; using a dummy allowed Bergen to do something indefinable. "Edgar Bergen's work with Charlie and Mortimer was magic," Jim enthused. "Magic in the real sense. Something happened when Edgar spoke through Charlie—things were said that couldn't be said by ordinary people." As Jim would discover, there *was* a kind of magic, a wonderful kind of freedom, involved in letting a character at the end of your arm give voice to sentiments one might not feel comfortable expressing while wearing the guise of, as Jim called them, "ordinary people."

In 1948, the U.S. Department of Agriculture sent the Henson family back to Maryland, where Paul returned to work at the Beltsville Agricultural Research Center. The family purchased a cozy new 1,500-square-foot house at 4002 Beechwood Road in the recently incorporated town of University Park, only a little more than a mile from the University of Maryland. It had been hard leaving Leland, not only for twelve-year-old Jim, but for his circle of friends as well. "I was really sad and upset that he was getting ready to move," said

Gordon Jones, who would also move from Leland a short time later. But being back in Maryland did bring with it one major blessing: it meant being close to Dear, who still lived with Pop in the house at 4306 Marion Street in Hyattsville, less than ten minutes away. Now, instead of gathering as a family perhaps once every three months, the Hensons and the Browns could get together every week to eat large family dinners around Dear's meticulously set table, then retire to the porch to talk and tell stories as they rocked in rhythm on squeaking metal gliders. Those gatherings would always be some of Jim's fondest memories. "There was so much laughter," he said, "because everyone was always telling jokes and saying funny things."

It was easy to see where Betty Henson had gotten her sense of humor, for both Pop and Dear were funny, though in different ways. Where Dear tended toward the silly, Pop had a more "keen, subtle sense of humor." But "he never laughed in ridicule," Attie explained. "He didn't think ridicule was funny at all." In fact, Pop would never allow conversations to veer toward anything remotely unpleasant or disagreeable—a trait that would define Jim as well. "If the dinner conversation seemed to be getting out of hand," recalled Paul Henson, "he'd get a *Reader's Digest* and read to us!" Many times, Pop would come to the table with a joke or funny story already in mind, fully prepared if necessary to seize control of a wandering conversation or glum mood.

Things could get even livelier at the holidays when Attie and Bobby and their families were added to the mix. "Fifteen or twenty people would be there, sitting around the dinner table," Jim remembered, "and my grandparents would have stories to tell—usually stories from their childhood. They would tell a tale, and somebody would try to top it. I've always felt that these childhood experiences of my family sitting around the dinner table, making each other laugh, were my introduction to humor." In fact, Jim's own sense of humor was a heady mix of every kind of humor seated around the table—a touch of Dear's laugh-out-loud sensibility, a bit of Paul's quiet joy in storytelling, a dash of Betty's twinkling delight in wordplay, then seasoned with Pop's more subtle edge that always laughed *with* an audience, never *at* them.

But by 1949, there was something else that had perhaps an even more pronounced effect on Jim. Always the gadget freak, there was a new device that had him absolutely fascinated. It was an obsession that would direct his focus, shape the artist he would become, and change the very course of his life.

It was a television. And Jim was going to make certain he "drove 'em all crazy" until he had one.

CHAPTER TWO

A MEANS TO AN END

1949–1955

Jim's first Muppet, Pierre the French Rat.

THE STORY OF TELEVISION BEGINS—LIKE ANY GOOD AMERICAN SUC-
cess story should—with a birth in a log cabin.

More precisely, it begins in a log cabin near Beaver, Utah, where
Philo Taylor Farnsworth—or Phil, as nearly everyone would call
him—was born on August 19, 1906. A precocious child, everyone
around him was certain Phil was a genius—and he didn't disappoint.
In 1919, at age thirteen, Phil invented a burglarproof ignition switch
for automobiles, earning him an award from *Science and Invention*
magazine. At seventeen, he entered Brigham Young University, spe-
cializing in chemistry and electronics. By age twenty, he was running
his own business.

But it was an idea that came to him at age fourteen—allegedly with one of those remarkable *Eureka!* moments that are probably too good a story to be entirely true—that would ensure Phil a place in the pantheons of both popular culture and history. In 1920, while tilling a potato field in a monotonous back and forth pattern with his horse-drawn plow, Phil imagined that an electron beam might scan an image in exactly the same way, moving across the image line-by-line.

He was right—and on September 7, 1927, in a makeshift laboratory in a San Francisco loft, Philo T. Farnsworth transmitted the world's first electronic television image: a straight white line scratched into a piece of black-painted glass. When the glass slide was slowly rotated ninety degrees, so, too, did the image on the screen. "There you are," Farnsworth said with typical aplomb, "electronic television."

Farnsworth would become increasingly irritated with his best-known invention over the next twenty years—he even prohibited his own family from watching it—but his annoyance was definitely not shared by an eager viewing public. Even with little on television to watch in 1950, such scant fare had little effect on the public's enthusiasm for the remarkable machine. As one historian later put it, "the simultaneity of television overrode all defects; when people could see things happening far away, they couldn't get over the wonder of it."

For Jim Henson, that simultaneity was more than just exciting, it was practically magic. To the boy who had sat spellbound in the movie theater watching exotic tales of the Far East, this was like a genie's sorcery. "I loved the idea that what you saw was taking place somewhere else at the same time," Jim recalled. "It was one of those absolutely wonderful things." After watching television at a friend's house in late 1949, Jim was convinced his family had to have a television set of their very own. Now.

There was one problem: as a relatively new and rare commodity—in 1948, there were an estimated 350,000 television sets in use, compared with 66 million radios—televisions were expensive. In 1950, a sixteen-inch black-and-white television—like the boxy Admiral, with an "Automatic Picture Lock-In" guaranteed to "bring you steady, clear reception even in hard to reach areas"—would set a family back $250, the equivalent of about $2,000 today. Fancier televisions with footed cabinets or, for the big money, those with a radio and record player built in, could run as much as $399, about $3,500 today.

Despite the costs, Jim was determined. "I badgered my family into buying a set," he later admitted somewhat sheepishly. "I absolutely *loved* television." It was a battle of wills Paul Henson, Sr., had little chance of winning. In 1950, Jim Henson had his television. And he watched it. Religiously.

There were four television channels available in the Washington, D.C., area in 1950—not bad, considering that only two years earlier there were fewer than forty television stations broadcasting in only twenty-three cities nationally. In fact, by 1950, it was reported that people in the Baltimore-Washington area already spent more time watching TV than listening to the radio. As stations played with the new technology and different formats, local shows came and went, some wildly experimental, some mundane, and most lasting only a few weeks before being pulled from the air, never to be heard of again. Jim watched them all, and as he did so, one thing quickly became clear: "I immediately wanted to work in television."

Doing exactly what, he wasn't certain—but in the meantime, Jim soaked up all television had to offer, including the conventions and formats that he would lovingly parody later in life, and the technical tricks he would master, then reinvent. He was especially intrigued with variety shows, one of the staples of the early television era, many with ensemble casts featuring comedians, singers, orchestras, magicians—and all performed live, with comedy sketches, songs, monologues, and performances of every kind boomeranging off each other at a breakneck pace. And more often than not, presiding over the show was a host or emcee, who was usually just as much a part of the chaos around him despite his best efforts to keep things moving smoothly. It was a format Jim found irresistible.

In the evenings, for example, Jim found Milton Berle, whose madcap performances on *Texaco Star Theater* did much to popularize TV and make it a must-have gadget. Spinning the television dial over to *Your Show of Shows,* front man Sid Caesar could often be found careening wildly off-script, ad-libbing madly, dropping into different voices and accents, even incoherent double-talk, all in the name of a laugh. But Caesar's show was also home to some of the smartest comedy writers around—including Carl Reiner and Mel Brooks—giving Caesar solid material from which he could vamp and improvise. It was a smart show that didn't mind looking silly— a kind of humor Jim could appreciate.

As inspired as Caesar's performances could be, they were nothing, as far as Jim was concerned, compared to those of Ernie Kovacs. More than just a master of deadpan comic delivery, Kovacs inherently understood the new TV medium like few others. Kovacs appreciated that it was the image on the TV screen that mattered the most, not what a live audience might see in studio—and he delighted in routines using visual tricks that only worked when seen on a television screen. Some involved bits of technical wizardry that Kovacs used to enhance sight gags, like superimposed or reversed images. But one of his best and most memorable tricks—in which items removed from a lunchbox seem to roll horizontally across a table and into someone's lap—had a deftly simple solution: Kovacs sharply tilted the entire set, then tilted the camera at the same angle, making the on-screen image appear perfectly horizontal. Jim may have roared with laughter at the gag, but it also taught him an important, if obvious, lesson: look through the eyepiece and know exactly what your camera is seeing—because that's your audience's reality. It was a lesson Jim would come to appreciate, and apply masterfully, in only a few short years.

There were plenty of kids' shows to watch as well—*Howdy Doody*, in fact, had been one of the very first shows broadcast on television nationally, starting in 1947. Young Marylanders could take their pick not only of *Howdy*, but also of shows like *Life with Snarky Parker*, a cowboy piece featuring the marionettes of Bil and Cora Baird, and *The Adventures of Lucky Pup*, with puppets by Morey Bunin. "I don't think I ever saw [*Snarky Parker*]," Jim admitted later—little surprise, considering he was well beyond the age group of its target audience. He did, however, remember seeing the Bairds perform their marionettes on other shows. "What I really knew of Bil and Cora Baird's work was their variety show stuff," Jim said. "They were doing a CBS morning show, in opposition to the

Today show. They were just [performing to] novelty records and little tiny short bits and pieces."

He was more familiar, however, with the work of a talented puppeteer whom he would later count as a friend: Burr Tillstrom, who performed the puppet stars of NBC's enormously popular *Kukla, Fran and Ollie*. There were few people, in fact, who *weren't* fans of Tillstrom's work. Launched as a kids' show in 1947, *Kukla, Fran and Ollie* had quickly attracted more adult fans than children—it counted among its admirers John Steinbeck, Orson Welles, and James Thurber—and by 1949 it had already been featured in *Life* magazine.

The brainchild of the Chicago-born Tillstrom, *Kukla, Fran and Ollie* featured two of Tillstrom's puppets—the well-intentioned Kukla and the rakish dragon Ollie—interacting with the show's sole human cast member, Fran Allison, a former schoolteacher with a quick wit and no small amount of charm. The real magic was in the genuine chemistry between Allison and her puppet costars as they bantered, conversed, sang, and laughed together—and all without a script, ad-libbing the entire show. Tillstrom's artistry was so endearing, in fact, that when Tillstrom had an ill Kukla blow his nose on the curtain of his puppet theater, hundreds of concerned fans mailed in handkerchiefs.

But there was much more going on for Jim in 1950 than just television. In March of that year, *The Christian Science Monitor* published one of the many cartoons he had submitted, a major source of pride for the thirteen-year-old Jim and his family—and especially to Dear, who had encouraged Jim with her own pencils, pens, and paints. The cartoon—credited to Jimmy Henson—shows two chefs pondering a large soup pot on a table in front of them. "Shall we toss it and call it salad?" asks one chef of the other, pointing down at the mess of ingredients, "or cook it and call it stew?" One chef is rail thin—almost looking as Jim himself would look in several years—while the other is plumper, his hat slightly crooked, setting up the study in contrasts that Jim always found hilarious and would use to great effect later in designing characters like Ernie and Bert or *The Muppet Show*'s Bunsen Honeydew and Beaker.

Cartoons and comics were, in fact, another important part of

Jim's creative life. Like most young people, Jim would open the newspaper almost instinctively to the comics section each day. While *The Washington Post* contained plenty of comics, Jim preferred the selection offered in the Washington *Evening Star* for one reason: it carried Walt Kelly's comic strip *Pogo*.

Only a little more than a year into its remarkable twenty-seven-year run—and, in 1950, carried in only a handful of daily newspapers—*Pogo* had already charmed its way to a position of prominence at the top of the *Evening Star*'s left-hand comics page. Set in the Georgia portion of the Okefenokee Swamp—and probably looking to Jim like an idealized version of Leland—*Pogo* starred an amiable possum whose kind nature frequently, and sometimes unwillingly, wrapped him up in the lives and machinations of a colorful cast of supporting characters, ranging from a wisecracking alligator named Albert to the self-important *faux* intellectual Dr. Howland Owl.

Jim was an enormous fan of *Pogo*, buying the paperback reprints of the daily strips almost as fast as Simon & Schuster could print them, and would remain a fan the rest of his life. With its calm-at-the-eye-of-the-hurricane main character and colorful ensemble cast, it is no great leap to see Kelly's fingerprints on what Jim would later create with his cast of Muppets. Indeed, Jim would always willingly and cheerily cite Kelly as an inspiration:

> Walt Kelly put together a team of characters. And it started with Pogo as the central character . . . a fairly normal, ordinary person . . . and all around him, he had Albert Alligator and a bunch of comedy characters bouncing off him. We use a very similar chemistry. Kermit is the Pogo. You have one normal person who represents the way people ordinarily think. And everything else, slightly crazier comedy characters are all around that person.

But beyond the dynamic of his cast of characters, Kelly performed a clever sleight-of-hand with *Pogo*—a trick Jim would also master and which would, in some ways, sum up his charm as an entertainer. A skilled satirist, Kelly often used *Pogo* to comment on social and political issues, tweaking religion and eggheads, presidents, and politicians. It was snarky and sometimes subversive, but when coming out of the mouths of Kelly's entertaining, disarmingly cute, funny animals, readers were inclined to let him get away with it. It was snuggly satire, a deliciously dangerous combination of art and writing—and younger readers could be entertained by the antics of the cute characters while their parents smiled over the more adult humor and themes.

What it taught Jim Henson is that, done right, you can have it both ways. You can entertain younger audiences while still playing to adult viewers—a practice that would make Jim's contributions to *Sesame Street* so powerful and memorable. Perhaps more important, it also showed that you could get away with being a little dangerous, provocative, or just plain deep if you did it with a smile on your face and remembered that entertainment always came first. When done right, it's possible to be silly and subversive at the same time.

For Jim, who had come to appreciate in Leland that he need look no further than his own backyard for excitement, Hyattsville, Maryland, was a wealth of entertainment. Blended almost seamlessly with the neighborhoods of northeastern Washington, Hyattsville was a fully realized suburb that could reap the benefits of its urban neighbor—good roads and mass transit, easy access to museums and Washington's touristy attractions—and still manage to feel almost as rural as Mississippi, with plenty of woods and open spaces where Jim could bird-watch or just lie on his back and stare dreamily into the sky.

Jim particularly loved bike riding with Paul in Rock Creek Park in Washington, speeding down the tree-shaded pathways on their bikes or, at times, laughing and shouting as they pedaled a tandem. As they rode, Jim would snap pictures, usually capturing Paul only as a blur as he sped past, but delighting when he managed to keep Paul in focus by riding alongside him with the camera, keeping Paul sharp against the blurred background of trees and pedestrians. On rainy weekends, the brothers would ride in the park with their cousins Will and Stan—Attie's boys—and Jim would position himself near one of the deep puddles in the path to try to capture on film the exact moment when Will's front wheel entered the puddle, spraying water in a deep V around the bike. Even at thirteen, Jim took great joy in seeing the world as the camera saw it.

In the evenings, the Hensons would sit on their back porch and talk well into the evening—Jim would always love good conversation—or would gather around an old pump organ in the parlor that Jim and Paul Jr. had rescued from a junk pile and repaired back to playability. As Betty Henson pumped and pounded the keyboard for all she was worth, the family sang songs from the A. A. Milne songbook and, later, Walt Kelly's pun-filled *Songs of the Pogo,* which Jim adored. Indeed, twenty years later, Jim would use songs from both songbooks—including Kelly's "Don't Sugar Me" and Milne's "Halfway Down the Stairs"—on *The Muppet Show.*

In the fall of 1950, both Jim and Paul Jr. were headed for new schools—Paul to the University of Maryland, and Jim to Hyattsville High School, where he was starting his freshman year. While Paul was ostensibly studying teaching—likely at the behest of Betty Henson—he had different career ambitions. In Hyattsville, as they had in Leland, Paul and Jim had continued to tinker with engines and small machines. While Jim had developed a fascination with cars—an affinity that would continue for the rest of his life—Paul was absolutely transfixed by airplanes. "He always wanted to fly," remembered Tommy Baggette. If Paul had his way, then, he was going to be a pilot.

Jim, meanwhile, would attend classes at Hyattsville High until 1951, when the crumbling school would be closed for good. For the next three years, Jim attended the sparkling new Northwestern High School, the pride of the Hyattsville community—Maryland governor T. R. McKeldin himself had spoken at its dedication in November—just around the corner from the Henson home. At Northwestern, Jim joined the tennis team, where he quickly became one of the best players on the squad. Like his parents and grandparents, Jim took the game seriously, and teammate Joe Irwin—who would remain a lifelong friend—remembered the tennis court as one of the few places he ever saw Jim's temper flare. During a game of doubles, recalled Irwin, "I hit a bad lob, and this guy crushed it right at Jim and hit him." Jim and Irwin locked eyes, "and I knew the game had changed," Irwin said. On the next volley, "Jim crushed it right back at this guy," Irwin remembered. "That was about as much anger as I've ever seen Jim put out. There was this need to get even, and Jim did. And then they played nicer." Playing nice would always be important to Jim.

Off the court, Jim participated in high school drama, mostly designing posters and painting sets, but every once in a while taking on small acting parts. He also joined the school's new puppetry club, most likely because its sponsor, Miss Dawson, announced they would be performing a show based on Jim's beloved *Pogo*. But just as with the drama club, Jim was far more interested in designing and building sets than in doing any of the performing.

In September 1952, Jim Henson turned sixteen. As a budding car enthusiast, getting his driver's license was a definite thrill, but Jim was even more excited by the prospect that he was now old enough to work. He was determined, however, that his first job would not involve busing tables or washing dishes; television was still where he wanted to be. As Jim recalled, "When I was old enough to get a job—sixteen—I went out and approached all these little studios in Washington" eager to fill any opening that might be available. But the enthusiastic teenager was out of luck—either none of the local television studios was hiring, or none was willing to take a chance on a passionate but unproven young man. Jim would have to wait more than a year for his opportunity.

It would be hard to wait. By March 1954—Jim's senior year—television would provide Americans with a window on a riveting real-life drama, as the United States Senate Subcommittee on Investigations began televising hearings to look into conflicting accusations between Senator Joseph McCarthy and the U.S. Army regarding the treatment of McCarthy's former aide David Schine. In the Washington area, the tumultuous hearings were broadcast live on two channels, making them unavoidable, must see television. Even under the impartial gaze of the black-and-white television cameras, McCarthy's true colors were soon obvious. "You're not fooling anyone," Senator Stuart Symington warned McCarthy—and Symington's disgust was shared by millions of television viewers. It was the end for McCarthy, but for television, it was a beginning—a new and unexpected flexing of muscles. Simply by broadcasting the hearings live, television had created An Event. It was Jim's first real experience with the power of television not only as entertainment, but as informer and educator. Jim would never forget the power of the glowing image on the small screen as an agent for change.

Less than a mile from the Henson home was Baltimore Avenue, considered the main drag in Hyattsville, and crammed with plenty of diversions like the orange-roofed hamburger joint called Hot Shoppes, the bowling alley, and the thousand-seat Hyattsville Theatre, built in 1938 in a flashy Art Moderne style. The theater was only a little more than a mile from the Henson home, a quick sprint down Baltimore Avenue, and was always a good place to catch a movie, along with the latest *Looney Tunes* cartoon that always showed before the main feature.

The Hyattsville Theatre was also a good place to bring prospective girlfriends. While his quiet way of speaking often led many to think he was shy, Jim was actually popular among the girls and had little trouble getting dates. Unusually tall for his age—he would eventually top out at six foot one, though he was so lanky everyone would always swear he was taller—Jim's height gave him presence, and even standing still, with one foot slightly forward and one hand resting lightly on his hip, he could exude the casual charm of his Southern forebears.

Like many young people, Jim struggled with acne for most of his teenage years, his condition eventually becoming so severe that he pleaded with his mother for a medical treatment. Betty Henson, standing firm in her Christian Science beliefs, refused to allow Jim to take medication to clear his skin. It was a point of considerable friction between mother and son; but while Paul Henson, Sr., might wilt under Jim's persistent badgering, Betty Henson would not. Even though his *gee whiz* Jimmy Stewart looks made him more striking than he often gave himself credit for, Jim's acne would leave him scarred and somewhat self-conscious about his looks. As he got older, he would hide his pocked cheeks behind a beard.

While Jim was, for the most part, a gentlemanly date—outgoing, slightly silly, with an engaging Southern gentility—he could be, as one former girlfriend put it, *a little fast*. Joe Irwin, who frequently double-dated with Jim, could only shake his head in amusement at his friend's boldness as they parked with their dates on Maryland's rural back roads. "I would have a nice little proper date sitting up [front] next to me and Jim would be disappearing into the back seat," Irwin laughed, then arched an eyebrow coyly as he chose his words carefully: "Jim was more . . . adventurous."

Meanwhile, Jim had made a name for himself at Northwestern High School with his artwork, turning in cartoons for student publications and silkscreen-printed posters promoting plays in the theater department. Even early on, Jim had already learned how to get the most out of simple shapes; his poster for the murder mystery *Nine Girls* shows eight lollipop-headed stick figures with surprised white eyes gaping nervously as the ninth casts a glance sideways with suspicious, slitted eyes—more of the stylized simplicity he would bring to his early designs for the Muppets. Just as important, Jim almost intuitively understood that it was the eyes that gave characters focus and life, even when those characters were drawn simply. *Especially* when those characters were drawn simply.

With high school graduation approaching, Jim was still considering ways to break into television. He was already planning to enter the University of Maryland in the fall, hoping to study stage and television design with an eye toward securing a job in television—or, barring that, in theater. But he was also still on the lookout for any opportunity to get his foot in the door of any television studio as quickly as possible.

In the late spring of 1954, toward the end of Jim's senior year, he suddenly found his chance. In May, the local CBS affiliate, WTOP, announced that TV personality Roy Meachum was seeking "youngsters twelve to fourteen years of age who can manipulate marionettes" for Meachum's upcoming *Junior Morning Show,* which WTOP was planning to launch in June as a children's version of CBS's successful *Morning Show*. Despite his regular membership in Northwestern's puppetry club, Jim considered himself more of an artist and designer than a puppeteer. But if puppetry was what it was going to take to get into television, Jim would sell himself to the network as just the right puppeteer for the job.

Unfortunately, Jim knew very little about puppetry. "When I was a kid, I never saw a puppet show," he said later. "I never played with puppets or had any interest in them. It was just a means to an end." But with his opportunity to get into television on the line, this particular means to an end was going to require Jim to learn about puppets and puppetry—and fast. Fortunately, help was as close as Northwestern's library, where Jim checked out two books that would change his life: Marjorie Batchelder's 1947 puppetry handbook *The Puppet Theatre Handbook,* and *My Profession,* the 1950 autobiography of the versatile Russian puppeteer Sergei Vladimirovich Obraztsov. With Batchelder's practical advice on puppet building, and Obraztsov's inspired suggestions for performing—and with only a week or so before the audition—Jim immersed himself in a self-taught crash course in puppetry.

Jim enlisted the help of friend and fellow drama club member Russell Wall, and together they built what we can fairly call the ancestors to the Muppets in the living room of Jim's home on Beechwood Road. While it is likely that Jim and Wall built at least two puppets, one for each to perform, we only know that one was a puppet called Pierre the Rat, based on a cartoon Jim had drawn for Hyattsville High School's student publication *Wildcat Scratches.* Pierre was a small, skinny hand puppet with a rat head carved of plastic wood, wearing sunglasses and a beret with a white-tipped plastic cigarette glued to a hinged mouth—primitive, but an impressive first effort. Equipped with their new puppets, Jim and Wall headed over to WTOP studios in D.C. and auditioned.

They got the job.

In early June 1954, shortly after Jim's graduation from Northwestern High School, Jim and Russell Wall made the short drive to WTOP television studios to begin several days of frantic rehearsals before the *Junior Morning Show*'s debut the following week. Days later, inside one of WTOP's cramped studios, a voice called for silence, a camera whirred silently to life, and an indicator light glowed dully, signaling that the *Junior Morning Show* was now on the air. Just like that, seventeen-year-old Jim Henson was finally in television.

There was only one problem. While Jim and Russell Wall were each of legal working age, three of their fellow puppeteers were not. On June 25, the *Evening Star* reported that the *Junior Morning Show* would be canceled after only three weeks for violating child labor laws. "Three of the program's participants were under fourteen," the *Star* tut-tutted, "and consequently could not get work permits."

For a moment, it appeared Jim's television career might be over before it had even begun. But despite his relative inexperience as a puppeteer, Jim had already impressed Roy Meachum, who generously continued to scout for work for Jim and Russell Wall on WTOP. Meachum even landed them a spot on his own *Saturday* show, where their puppets lip-synched to records. However, Meachum's *Saturday* show was also doomed, running only through August.

At that point, Jim was just beginning to attend classes at the University of Maryland, and perhaps considered the demise of the *Saturday* show as a blessing in disguise—with *Saturday* canned, he was free to concentrate on his studies and learn all he could about television design and production. This, with his brief appearances on WTOP, might, in time, lead to a different opportunity in television—one that hopefully didn't involve puppets. "It was interesting and kind of fun to do," Jim later said, "but I wasn't really interested in puppetry then."

But whether Jim thought he might be done with television for the moment, he was too good—too talented—for television to be done with him. Unknown to Jim, during one of his *Saturday* appearances, his performance had caught the eye of James Kovach, a program director from the local NBC affiliate, WRC-TV. Kovach had come to the WTOP studio with the hope of luring the versatile Meachum from channel 9 over to the higher-rated channel 4, but had also liked what he had seen of Meachum's young puppeteer. Meachum declined Kovach's offer to jump ship—but weeks later, with *Saturday* facing cancellation and Jim facing unemployment, Meachum phoned Kovach and enthusiastically encouraged him to find a place for Jim over at NBC.

The offer was unexpected, and seemingly out of nowhere—and Jim jumped at it, though he was still put through a brief audition before Kovach formally offered him the job. "I took the puppets over to NBC," Jim recalled, "and they started putting me on these little local shows," mostly performing in short segments alongside WRC in-house talent like Mike Hunnicutt, a jovial former radio personality with a loopy sense of humor. Hunnicutt would stammer and giggle his way through sketches in a manner much like Red Skelton, and Jim adored him, often hanging around to watch the host banter with technicians long after the cameras went dark.

Another show to feature Jim's puppetry—though he had been hired first as a set designer—was a weekend children's show called *Circle 4 Ranch,* hosted by Joe Campbell, a singing cowboy who told stories of frontier heroes and folklore between snippets of old westerns. When the show was lengthened from thirty minutes to a full hour in the fall of 1954, Campbell was anxious to fill the additional time with skits and songs, and thought it might be interesting to add puppets to chat with, in the same way Buffalo Bob Smith interacted with his marionette costars on NBC's powerhouse kids' show *Howdy Doody.* That suggestion sparked an idea in *Circle 4* director and producer Bob Porter, who introduced to Campbell the "scrawny teenager" laboring in set design Porter had seen performing puppets with other WRC personalities. "The three of us had lunch and decided how to proceed," Campbell recalled. "Jim agreed to make some puppets that I had in mind." Campbell provided Jim with a drawing of two cowboys he called Longhorn and Shorthorn, which he asked Jim to build and perform for the show. Sadly, Campbell's show would only last another six months—yet Campbell would soon come to play an important, somewhat controversial, and largely unknown role in the creation of the Muppets.

By his own account, Jim would work solo for the next eight months—Russell Wall, as far as anyone could remember, left the area after graduation—making random appearances on various NBC shows as needed, usually lip-synching his puppets to records. In the meantime, he was attending the University of Maryland full-time, while still living at home, less than two miles from campus. With Paul Henson, Sr., as a role model, as well as the active enthusiasm for knowledge shown by his extended family, education—or perhaps more particularly, *learning*—was something that would always be important to Jim, and he took school seriously, maintaining a B average. He continued his active involvement in drama and theater, again discovering that he preferred the technical aspects and the behind-the-scenes maneuverings to the onstage performing. "I was very interested in theatre, mostly in stage design," Jim said. "I did a little bit of acting [in] the first year of college and then fairly soon thereafter I settled into the backstage scenery."

For most of his college career, then, Jim would design and build sets. He would serve as the University Theater's publicity director for several years, and just as he had for Northwestern's drama department, he designed and printed posters for student drama productions and other university events. He would, in fact, turn his talent for silkscreen posters into a side business, running a print shop out of the university's student union building.

He also quickly became aware that the university's college of fine arts wasn't where he wanted to be. "My first year I started off planning to major in art because I was interested in theater design, stage design or television design," Jim said later. "But at that particular college, the advertising, art, costume design, interior design, layout—all of that stuff was part of Home Economics, for some strange reason. . . . And puppetry was a course that was given there that was also in Home Economics."

The Home Economics department—or Practical Arts, as it came to be called—was no haven for aspiring homemakers, as it was so often derisively described. Instead, it housed a wide variety of art and education programs, including several commercial art courses coveted by those wanting to be advertising executives. As Jim soon discovered, there was another reason, more prurient than academic, to switch to Home Economics. "[My] puppetry teacher said, you switch over to Home Economics, you don't have to take all of the math and sciences that you do in Fine Arts, so you can take more art courses," Jim recalled. "So I switched over to Home Economics on that basis and also ended up in classes [where] I think there were about six guys and 500 girls. Oh, it was marvelous!"

One of those five hundred girls was a twenty-year-old art and education major named Jane Nebel, now in the first semester of her senior year. Artsy and talented and with a dry sense of humor as edgy as Jim's was playful, Jane was versatile in arts and crafts—and, as Jim would soon discover, a capable puppeteer.

Born in St. Albans, Queens, on June 16, 1934, Jane was the third and youngest child of Winifred and Adalbert Nebel, an insurance salesman with an interest in astrology. Shortly after Jane was born, however, Adalbert—who, as Jane remembered, always "had a bit of a temper"—abruptly quit his job at the insurance company and found himself without work at the height of the Depression. Jane's practical-minded mother—who had been perfectly happy living as the wife of an insurance man—firmly reminded her husband of their mortgage and three children and insisted Adalbert find work immediately, despite the hard economic conditions that made jobs scarce.

Dutifully, Adalbert took odd jobs, selling cosmetics and stocking candy machines, while taking astrology classes in the evenings. Money continued to be scarce, but Adalbert would always manage to earn one reprieve after another from the family's softhearted landlord by displaying a remarkable flair for the dramatic that his daughter would inherit. After learning the landlord was on his way over to collect the rent, Adalbert would meticulously place Jane on her mother's lap and dress her brother in his finest clothes, brushing the boy's hair until it shone. He would then answer the door, making certain to open it far enough to allow the landlord to see Mrs. Nebel and the children, looking every inch the picture-perfect storybook family—and quite impossible for the sympathetic landlord to eject into the street over back rent.

Eventually, Adalbert became experienced enough at astrology to earn his living as an astrologer, adopting the professional persona of Dal Lee and becoming well known as the editor of the popular and highly successful publications *Astrology Guide* and *Your Personal Astrology.* As Dal Lee, Adalbert loved writing the editorials for his magazines, his two-finger typing clattering away loudly at all hours of the night. To Jane, awakened by the noise, it was one of the most reassuring sounds in the world. "I could depend on going downstairs at two in the morning and having a good talk with him," she said. Jane adored their conversations, and while she never became a strong believer in astrology, she did come to appreciate their shared stubborn streak and wickedly skeptical sense of humor. *Listen to what people have to say,* Adalbert told his daughter, *even if what they're saying may not be true.*

As a teenager, Jane moved to Salisbury, Maryland, in the state's Eastern Shore region, but spent the next several years more than three hundred miles away in a boarding school in Lexington, Virginia. While Jane referred to her own grades as "not so great," with her Maryland residency they were sound enough for admittance to the University of Maryland in 1951. Enrolling as a practical art major, Jane had initially chosen the arts and crafts program under the Home Economics department, then moved to the College of Education to become an art education major. As part of that particular curriculum, students were still required to take classes from the arts and crafts program—including puppetry.

The puppetry course at the University of Maryland was a new addition to the Home Economics curriculum—so new, in fact, that the university hadn't yet hired a teacher who could be said to be a proficient puppeteer. Instead, the job had fallen to Ed Longley, a young teacher out of New York's Columbia University. At the time of his hiring, the university had informed Longley—a master silversmith who taught jewelry making—that teaching the new puppetry course would be a condition of his employment in the Home Economics department. "He was a very good guy," Jane said, "but he didn't know puppetry." As a result, Longley was still feeling his way in the fall of 1954, working with a class composed mostly of seniors—and mostly women—none of whom had ever taken a puppetry course, but who were now using the class to complete their coursework before graduation and looking to Longley for guidance.

Guidance they would get—but not necessarily from Longley.

Heads turned when Jim Henson entered Longley's classroom in the autumn of 1954. He walked, Jane remembered, "like Abe Lincoln," flat-footed with long strides. And while the fashionably short pea coat he wore that winter made his legs look longer and lankier than usual, it wasn't his height that raised eyebrows; it was his youth. "Most of us had known each other for quite a few years," Jane said. And to a class full of seasoned seniors, a freshman, barely eighteen years old, was regarded as little more than an interloper. Yet Jim carried himself with confidence; he had grown up just down the road from the university, making this essentially home territory. Further, while Jim had been performing puppets on television for less than a year, that was still more practical puppetry experience than anyone, including Longley, could claim. In no time at all, recalled Jane, "Jim took over the class."

For one of the major projects that semester, Longley divided his class into two groups and asked them to write, perform, and build all the puppets and props for two shows, one using hand puppets, and the other using marionettes. While Jim was in the hand puppet group, he eagerly suggested the marionette group adapt a favorite story of his, James Thurber's fairy tale *The 13 Clocks,* about a wily prince who, with the help of a clever, enigmatic character called the Golux, outwits the coldhearted duke for the hand of the duke's daughter. In his own group, Jim eagerly wrote the script and oversaw the puppet building and set design. Jane remembers being "totally impressed" with the way Jim worked. "He'd just look at the situation, and look at what he thought needed to be done," said Jane, "and he'd just do it." On the day of the show, Jane performed the role of the Golux in the marionette group, giving a performance so nimble that Jim was impressed. So impressed, in fact, that Jim decided to ask for her assistance.

In early 1955, WRC program director James Kovach and director Carl Degen were putting together a new variety program called *Afternoon* that would air daily at 2:15 on WRC. "Back in those days in television," Jim said, "most local stations had a midday show for housewives that had a series of things. It was like a variety show for midday." Kovach had at the helm two reliable personalities; besides Mac McGarry, a bespectacled local disc jockey and television announcer getting his first real on-camera break, there was also an enthusiastic twenty-one-year-old American University student named Willard Scott, feeling his way years before finding fame on the *Today* show. But Kovach wanted something new and different to add to the mix, and recommended to Degen that they hire Jim to join the *Afternoon* lineup. As Jim later described it, "They would have a cooking segment, they'd have news, they'd have a local combo, and they'd do fashion shows with models, so it was a fairly large operation—and we were part of that."

Afternoon debuted on WRC on Monday, March 7, 1955—a significant date in that it not only marks the true beginning of Jim and Jane's professional partnership, but also because of the following notice, which appeared under the "TV Highlights" section of *The Washington Post and Times Herald:*

> 2:15 P.M.—Afternoon: A new variety program features Mac McGarry and Willard Scott as co-hosts; fashion information from Inga; music by Mel Clement Quartet; vocals by Jack Maggio; and special features by the Muppets, who are puppeteers.

This is the first time the term *Muppets* appears in print, helpfully but incorrectly glossed by a copy editor at the *Post,* who applied the term to Jim and Jane rather than to the puppets. At age eighteen, Jim had already coined the term that would become his legacy, his own brand, as indelibly linked to his name as Microsoft with Bill Gates or, perhaps more appropriately, Walt Disney with Mickey Mouse.

Interestingly, Jim was already using the term *Muppet* as early as December 1954, while working for Joe Campbell at *Circle 4 Ranch.* After receiving two cowboy puppets he had asked Jim to build, Campbell scrawled out a receipt, using the back of a cue sheet for the December 18, 1954, installment of *Circle 4 Ranch.* The receipt granted Campbell, for the cost of one dollar, "51% ownership of muppetts [*sic*] known as 'Shorthorn' and 'Longhorn.'" Further, a number of acetate disc soundtracks prerecorded by Campbell for Jim's puppets to perform to—some dating as far back as November 10, 1954—were labeled by studio engineers with stickers reading "Campbell Muppets" or "Circle 4 Muppets." Clearly, then, the term *Muppets*—with or without an extraneous T—was already in use at that time.

"It was really just a term we made up," Jim admitted later. "For a long time I would tell people it was a combination of marionettes and puppets, but, basically, it was really just a word that we coined," he added, pointing out correctly that, "we have done very few things connected with marionettes."

Could something else have inspired the term, though? It's possible that *muppet* was a play on the word *moppet,* a term for a small child. Dating back to the seventeenth century—and likely tracing its origins to the word *moppe,* a Middle English word for rag doll—the word was cutesy and archaic, even in 1955. But it was also a word Jim Henson, along with nearly every newspaper reader in Hyattsville, would have seen practically every day—for running on channel 5 each weekday from 6:00 to 7:00 P.M. was *Hoppity Skippity with Moppet Movies,* a local children's show that had been a fixture in the D.C. area since 1948. Given that it was broadcast during the dinner hour, it is likely that Jim was familiar with it. But whether Jim ever watched the show, he would certainly have seen its name as he scanned the television listings in the newspaper.

It takes no real stretch of the imagination, then, to picture Jim—perhaps trying to come up with a catchy name for the puppets he was handing over to Campbell—coming across the word *moppets* and, with a mere change of a vowel, almost magically blending the words *puppet* and *moppet.* Like *grackle,* it was one of those words that already sounded like it should mean something. Whether intentional or not, the association with the word *moppet* is serendipitous, as the childlike innocence of the Muppets would, to Jim, always be one of their most endearing qualities. "As I try to zero in on what's important for the Muppets," Jim said years later, "I think it's a sense of innocence, naiveté—you know, the experience of a simple person meeting life."

The newly christened Muppets, as part of the *Afternoon* lineup, would be going out live over the air each day, and Jim and Jane were expected to come prepared with new pieces to perform. There was little time for rehearsals from one show to another, but Jim—as he would for the rest of his life—seemed to thrive on the spontaneous, seat-of-the-pants performing. According to host Mac McGarry, Jim was able to work out his routines "just by sitting down and thinking for a few minutes."

As its talented cast began to learn to play off of each other's strengths, *Afternoon* quickly built a following. *Washington Post* reviewer Lawrence Laurent elegantly described the show as "integrated chaos," which seemed to be the kind of atmosphere in which Jim would flourish. But looking back, Jim wasn't happy with what he called his "little entertainment pieces," which mostly involved having the Muppets lip-synch to novelty records. "The work I did in those days is not stuff that I'm creatively very proud of," Jim said later. "That stuff was really experimenting and it was just stuff that I did as a lark. I was going to college and so I was doing this and it was a way of working my way through school."

Jim was so uncertain about his performance, in fact, that he approached a WRC reporter who was rumored to have an inside line with Kovach and asked "in his stumbling unsure way" if the reporter could talk with Kovach about getting Jim a job with the floor crew. The reporter—or so the story goes—told Jim to stick with his Muppets and "get very rich."

The *Afternoon* crew were dazzled not only by the Muppets, but by their quiet, unassuming creator. "Jim Henson was a very nice young guy. Thoughtful. Obviously a genius in the making," remembered host Mac McGarry. "Everybody loved his characters. . . . He subdued his own being and made his characters come to life. It was not too long on the show before I realized I was not talking to Jim Henson. These characters were there, independently. They have their own being." But it was *Afternoon* producer-director Carl Degen who most neatly summed up the consensus around the studio: "The kid is positively a genius," Degen told *The Washington Post*. "He's absolutely amazing."

As Jane recalled, she and Jim were originally put on *Afternoon* "to do spots for children. But we were college students amusing ourselves, and we did these wild things with the puppets, lip-synching to Stan Freberg records—like his takeoff on 'Banana Boat'—and things like that." The madcap recordings of Stan Freberg were, in fact, a favorite not only of Jim's, but also of other performers and sometime puppeteers like Soupy Sales, who often used Freberg's songs for his puppets Pookie and Hippie to clown to. Freberg had a sense of humor very similar to Jim's, as both adored bad puns, non sequiturs, deadpan delivery of a punch line, and silly songs. But what made Freberg's records especially useful was that his recordings were fully realized routines—three frantic minutes filled with jokes, sound effects, conversations, and commentary that made them perfect for several Muppets to lip-synch and perform to.

Other times, Jim would choose tamer and more straightforward material, like contemporary songs, which made for routines that were often funnier than those using novelty records simply because Jim would make them so waggishly ridiculous—dressing characters in wigs, concluding the songs with an explosion, or having one creature devour another, just the kind of absurd ending Jim loved. "We very often would take a song and do strange things to it . . . that nobody could understand," Jim said. "I always enjoyed those!" Looking back, Jane, too, could only shrug and laugh. "I guess it had a quality of abandon and nonsense and of being somewhat experimental," she said. *Afternoon*'s music director Mel Clement—who remembered absolutely "falling down" with laughter at the Muppet sketches—was impressed. "Those kids," Clement said admiringly of Jim and Jane, "knocked us all out."

They were knocking out plenty of others, too. In the spring of 1955, after a little less than two months of performing on *Afternoon*, Jim and Jane were offered the chance to create their own five-minute show on WRC, in a prime piece of TV real estate: 11:25 P.M., the five-minute slot between the local evening news and the *Tonight* show with Steve Allen. "A choice time slot," Jane remarked.

It was indeed—one that Jim would make the most of. The Muppets were on their way.

CHAPTER THREE

SAM AND FRIENDS

1955–1957

Jim with the cast of Sam and Friends, *1961.*

ON MONDAY, MAY 9, 1955, NINE WEEKS TO THE DAY AFTER THE DEBUT of *Afternoon,* Jim and Jane's five-minute romp *Sam and Friends* premiered on WRC-TV. There was actually little fanfare; there was no brief mention in the "TV Highlights" section, as had marked *Afternoon*'s first appearance, only a single word inserted after the hyperabbreviated TV listings for WRC's 11:00 P.M. news broadcast with anchorman Richard Harkness: "Harkness; Wthr. Sports; Muppets."

Despite its initial quiet appearance in the TV listings, there was nothing calm or serene about *Sam and Friends.* Unshackled from *Afternoon*'s variety show format, Jim and Jane were free to create their own manic world for their Muppets, giving them their own slightly skewed reality. For their Muppet cast, Jim turned to the growing collection of Muppets he had built, many of which he had already been using on *Afternoon*. For his new show's point man, Jim had decided on Sam, a bald, bulb-nosed human character, with knobby ears that stuck straight out from his head and wide-open eyes that gave him a perpetually surprised look. "I made him originally to use with Phil Harris records," Jim said, "but he proved the most popular Muppet of all. That gave us the idea for *Sam and Friends*."

The "Friends" of *Sam and Friends*, however, were more abstract, hazily defined and colorfully named: Harry the Hipster, a snakelike beatnik in sunglasses; Yorick, a prune-colored, skull-like creature that was *id* incarnate; the beak-nosed Hank and Frank; the squashed-looking Mushmellon. Considerable thought had gone into both the concept of the show and the design of the Muppet cast. The title was no mere throwaway; there was actual method to the show's madness. At its core, *Sam and Friends* was all about the quiet, amiable Sam making his way through life with the help of his Friends—"abstract companions" who egg him on, move him forward, and encourage him through their own loony behavior, even if that behavior was still nothing more than lip-synching to records. The Friends, while real to Sam and to viewers, explained Jane, "are actually within him, within Sam." A rather high-brow conceit for a show that got its biggest laughs from characters exploding, but it was typical Jim: even a five-minute comedy romp, no matter how absurd, had to mean *something*.

There was another abstract Muppet in Sam's cast who, while still only relegated to mostly small parts—and usually getting devoured at the end—already had a special place in Jim's heart. It was a puppet Jim had built while passing several long sad days tending to his grandfather Pop, who was slowly dying of heart failure—a puppet that, even early on, Jim would always call his favorite.

It was a milky blue character named Kermit.

Maury Brown had always been frail—his daughters remember him demanding quiet in the house to ease his nerves—and in 1955, a doctor had insisted that he and Dear move from their two-story home on Marion Street into a smaller, single-story apartment. The move had depressed Pop—"he intended to die in that house" on Marion Street, Attie said—and his health had deteriorated rapidly, as Pop grew increasingly senile even as his heart failed. Jim was shaken by the impending death of his grandfather—he had, after all, been partly named for him—but Jim would do as he always did in the face of grief: he would build and create. Foraging for any suitable materials, Jim settled on his mother's old felt coat, and as he leaned over the table in the Hensons' living room he sewed a simple puppet body, with a slightly pointed face, out of the faded turquoise material. For eyes, he simply glued two halves of a Ping-Pong ball—with slashed circles carefully inked in black on each—to the top of the head. That was it. From the simplest of materials—and, perhaps appropriately, from a determination to bring a bit of order from darkness—Kermit was born.

Those who knew Jim as a boy would often wonder if he had named his most famous creation after his childhood friend Kermit Scott. The answer—according to both Jim and Kermit Scott—was no. The name Kermit, while quirky, was by no means uncommon in 1955; President Theodore Roosevelt had named his second son Kermit in 1889, which made the name somewhat faddish in the first half of the twentieth century. To Jim, though, as with *grackle* or *Muppet,* it was all about the sound of the word; with its hard K, pressed M, and snapped T, the name Kermit was memorable and fairly funny.

As a relatively no-frills puppet, Kermit was the epitome of elegant simplicity, which made him that much more fun for Jim to play with. "Kermit started out as a way of building, putting a mouth and covering over my hand," Jim later explained. "There was nothing in Kermit outside of the piece of cardboard—it was originally cardboard—and the cloth shape that was his head. He's one of the simplest kinds of puppet you can make, and he's very flexible because of that . . . which gives him a range of expression. A lot of people build very stiff puppets—you can barely move the things—and you can get very little expression out of a character that you can barely move. Your hand has a lot of flexibility to it, and what you want to do is to build a puppet that can reflect all that flexibility."

If Kermit was one of the most flexible of Muppets, one thing he was not—at least not yet—was a frog. While it is nearly impossible for viewers today to watch Kermit on *Sam and Friends* and think of him as anything but a frog, viewers in 1955 saw him as simply another of the silly supporting cast. Oddly colored—"milky turquoise" Jim called it—with padded oval feet, Kermit was still as vague a being as the fuzzy Mushmellon, or the wide-mouthed Moldy Hay. "I didn't call him a frog," Jim said. "All the characters in those days were abstract because that was part of the principle that I was working under, that you wanted abstract things."

For Jim, that abstraction was also, in some ways, an exciting way of challenging his audience—of making them an active part of the performance. "Those abstract characters I still feel are slightly more pure," Jim later explained. "If you take a character and you call him a frog . . . you immediately give the audience a handle. You're assisting the audience to understand; you're giving them a bridge or an access. And if you don't give them that, if you keep it more abstract, it's almost more pure. It's a cooler thing. It's a difference of sort of warmth and cool."

It wasn't only their abstract quality that made Jim's Muppets—and *Sam and Friends*—unlike anything on television. Until Jim and the Muppets, puppetry on TV had essentially looked like filmed puppet shows—on *Kukla, Fran and Ollie,* for instance, Burr Tillstrom performed his puppets while standing behind a puppet stage, poking his characters out underneath a gauzy curtain as he stood concealed behind the proscenium. Jim had sometimes performed in a similar manner on *Afternoon,* squatting down behind low walls or maneuvering puppets up through openings in sets when the show required the Muppets to interact with the human cast members. But that was really still just a puppet show on television, and not a puppet *television* show.

Like Ernie Kovacs before him, who understood that a mutual tilt of the camera and the set could playfully manipulate an audience's perception, Jim, too, was intuitively aware that he could use the eye of the camera—and the four sides of a home viewer's television screen—to create his own reality. Now that there was no need for his Muppets to coexist with live actors, Jim saw that no puppet theater was needed at all—that, in fact, the space between the four sides of the TV screen *was* his puppet theater. Jim had learned Kovacs's lesson well; namely, a television audience can only see what you choose for it to see. No walls were needed to conceal the puppeteer when he or she could kneel down just out of sight of the camera, giving the Muppets the entire viewing area in which to perform and exist.

But Jim understood that it went even deeper than that. Jim knew that for all its technical prowess, the television camera is, in a sense, blind. It has no peripheral vision, and it doesn't get distracted by what's taking place just beyond the range of its lens. All it sees is what is visible through the eyepiece, no more, no less—and Jim instinctively appreciated that if the eye of the camera defines your performance, then you'd better make certain you know exactly what the camera is seeing. The only way to do this, then, was to watch the performance on a television monitor.

At first, it was merely a matter of spot-checking their performance, making sure heads were out of sight and the Muppet was centered on a screen, similar to a habit Burr Tillstrom had developed on *Kukla, Fran and Ollie,* where Tillstrom would often keep a TV placed off to one side to keep an eye on how his puppet theater looked on camera. Soon Jim and Jane had monitors placed in opposite corners of the studio, so no matter which way a performer was facing, a monitor was visible. Eventually, Jim had one small monitor placed on the floor directly in front of the performers, where he and Jane could closely scrutinize the performance from their knees. But Jim's approach to the use of the monitor differed from Tillstrom's in a significant way. For Tillstrom, the monitor was passive, merely relaying the performance, which remained confined by the puppet theater. But for Jim, the monitor *was* the puppet theater— as such, it *defined* the performance.

Moreover, using the monitor to watch themselves perform on screen made the show that much better. Unlike other television actors, who can't see their own performance as it happens, "you can actually see what you are doing as you do it," Jim explained, "and have the opportunity to modify your performance for better effect." It also allowed the puppeteer to share the viewing experience with the audience at home—a dynamic Jane found particularly thrilling. "You'd perform but you'd also be the audience," said Jane. "I think that's a big difference, because the people at home watching are seeing a very intimate, internal thing that's happening with that performer."

While the use of the monitor was a brilliant innovation, it required one real bit of mental gymnastics: since the performer is facing the camera, what he sees on the monitor in front of him is essentially his own image in reverse. So, while the performer might be moving a Muppet to his or her own left, on the television monitor, it moves to the right—a bit of reverse orientation that takes some getting used to. But for Jim, the effort was worth it to get the performance exactly right. "After you go through working with the monitor for a particular period of time," said Jim, "then it's totally automatic and you never even think about it."

Now that Jim had removed the need for a puppet theater—and, through the use of the monitor, given the performer the ability to watch and modify his performance—the Muppets themselves suddenly, almost magically, had a life of their own. In the eyes of the camera, it was as if they were simply actors being filmed. "What Jim came to love right away was how convincing the reality is on a television screen," Jane said. "It's not like going from a [puppet] stage at all; the reality was extraordinary." So long as Jim and Jane were careful to remain out of the shot, the Muppets could move freely anywhere in the viewing area, even approaching the camera—and the audience—for an intimate close-up, something that could *not* happen with a traditional puppet theater. This was something brand-new: it was puppetry made expressly for the medium of television, making TV's strengths and weaknesses work for the performer.

For Jim, it had all been a matter of problem solving—and his relative inexperience in both puppetry and television allowed him to look for solutions that might not have occurred to more seasoned performers, even when, as in the case of the television monitor, that solution was lying in plain sight. "Many of the things I've done in my life have basically been self-taught," Jim admitted later. "I had never worked with puppets . . . and even when I began on television, I really didn't know what I was doing. I'm sure this was a good thing, because I learned as I tackled each problem. I think if you study—if you learn too much of what others have done—you may tend to take the same direction as everybody else."

There was little danger of Jim doing that—he was already too far ahead of everybody else. Still, for all his success and innovation, Jim was always respectful of the work of his predecessors in television. The differences in their approaches both to puppetry and the television medium, were, he thought, simply generational—a matter of when you learned the craft and what media were available when you began performing. "Burr Tillstrom and the Bairds had more to do with the beginning of puppetry on television than we did," Jim explained. "But they had developed their art and style to a certain extent before hitting television."

Jim's puppets, however, were born in and made for the television generation—and as such, they had to look good on TV. "We pretty much had a form and a shape by that time—a style," Jim said of his early days on television, "and I think one of the advantages of not having any relationship to any other puppeteer was that it gave me a reason to put [the form and shapes of the Muppets] together myself for the needs of television." Jim would have no marionette strings in the shot, or painted wooden heads frozen into perpetual grins, breaking the illusion. With the TV camera allowing for close-ups, Jim wanted his puppets to breathe with a life of their own, with working mouths and hands, capable of expression and personality. "Very early on we discovered what you could do with the flexibility of the faces," Jim said. "It was a question of combining that with what you could do with the hand in order to get the expressions to work. Most puppeteers at that time still worked with absolutely rigid faces, and generally no expression at all, because—before television—puppets were generally meant to be seen at a distance of fifteen to twenty feet," he explained. "I think we were among the first to design puppets specifically for television, where you're relating to the camera and working with what you can do with the face seen from very close." "[They were] puppets that didn't look like puppets had *ever* looked," recalled Muppet veteran Jerry Juhl. "It was the mobility of the faces, and the total abstraction of them. . . . They were just *mind-blowing,* certainly to puppeteers."

While Sam was made of plastic wood—and was, in Jim's hands, still remarkably expressive (so much so, in fact, that only three months after making his debut, Sam was named "the most brilliant newcomer to the Washington scene" by the TV critic at *The Sunday*

Star)—puppets made of nonpliable materials would quickly become the exception. Instead, Jim discovered that foam rubber was an ideal material for sculpting puppet heads, which he could then cover with fabric, fleece, or whatever else might be on hand, whether it was pieces of carpet, yarn, twine, or his mother's coat. This allowed for less clunky, more expressive puppets, giving the puppeteer the ability to turn in a performance—through the tilt of the puppet's head, a slight elongation of the face, or a scrunching of the mouth—that made the character that much more alive.

Just as important, from his lifelong love of drawing and cartooning—and perhaps with the lessons of his poster for *Nine Girls* in mind—Jim intuitively understood the critical importance of the placement of a character's eyes, as well as the location of the pupils in those eyes. Early on, Jim discovered that by almost imperceptibly crossing the eyes, he actually gave the eyes focus, giving his Muppets a look of keen attentiveness rather than a vacant stare.

As for the operation of a Muppet's hands, in the early years, Jim manipulated his characters' arms with long rods attached close to the Muppet's wrist, a device that owed more to the old-style rod puppets than to marionettes. It was simple but effective—and it would be the template for the basic Muppet structure. Jim was not yet building "live hand" puppets in which he could move the mouth with his right hand and use his own left hand up inside the Muppet's left hand—as he would with Muppets like Rowlf the Dog, or Ernie on *Sesame Street*—likely because with only him and Jane performing, they often needed to work with a Muppet on each arm.

But what work it was. Left on their own now, Jim and Jane put together a madcap four-minute show—the last minute was left to sponsors like Esskay meats—that was over much too quickly for D.C. audiences ("It was so short that it was over as soon as it began!" was a typical lament). According to Jim, the name of the game on the early *Sam and Friends* was still pantomiming and lip-synching to comedy records and novelty songs, which Jim raided from the WRC music library or plumbed from his own extensive collection—by his own count, he had over five hundred records. The lip-synching approach meant that Jim did not have to provide voices for any of his Muppets—something he was still nervous about doing—and it was also, as Jim said, "a way that one could do entertaining pieces rather safely and easily."

Actually, it *wasn't* always easy. Jim had worked hard to perfect his lip-synching technique, figuring out quickly that there was more to lip-synching than mere timing. Jane compared it to pushing the words out of the puppet's mouth, rather than snapping the mouth open and closed, "like catching flies"—a habit that often plagued even an experienced performer like Burr Tillstrom, who often opened and closed Ollie's mouth with an audible *clack*. Jim would practice in front of a mirror, sometimes for hours, working to master little nuances, like moving the puppet slightly forward and down as it spoke, and opening the mouth by moving his thumb rather than his fingers, which looked more natural and less like the Muppet's head was coming unhinged and flapping open backward.

Jim also thrived on collaboration—and so did Jane. If Jim was the energy and brilliance of the act, then Jane was the ideal performing partner, responding to and interacting with Jim's characters naturally and intuitively. She also had a masterful sense of comic timing, and Jim continually encouraged her performances with his own sense of fun and camaraderie—a liberating combination that would similarly inspire other colleagues and collaborators in the years to come.

The two of them worked so well together, in fact, that he was determined to keep their professional partnership going even after her graduation from the University of Maryland in 1955. Jane enrolled in a master's program in art at Catholic University in Washington, D.C., that fall, but promised Jim she would continue their work together, tweaking her own course load to accommodate their filming for *Afternoon* each day, and *Sam and Friends* each night—no small sacrifice.

Besides Jane, another graduate of the University of Maryland that year was Jim's brother, Paul. It had taken Paul an additional year to complete his studies, due to a brief two semesters at Principia, a school for Christian Scientists in Elsah, Illinois, but in June 1955, Paul received his bachelor's degree in mathematics. Now engaged to be married, Paul had decided on a career as a navy pilot, and would be commissioned in October 1955. From there, he would be stationed in Florida to undergo training, on his way to his lifelong dream of becoming a pilot.

As the Muppets grew in popularity, Jim was being asked to make appearances on more and more local shows—and as he began his sophomore year in autumn 1955, Jim was astonished at the money he was being paid. "When I first started working, it was $5 a show," Jim said later. "It was probably a little higher by the time I got to my own show, but I remember that they put me under contract at $100 a week, which to me was really an astronomical price."

It was indeed. At a time when most college students were making a minimum wage of seventy-five cents an hour busing tables or pumping gas, nineteen-year-old Jim Henson was being paid roughly $5,200 a year to perform on television—the equivalent of about $40,000 today. Jim was expected, however, to use that money to design, build, and paint all his Muppets and the sets for *Sam and Friends*—an obligation that never bothered him one bit. "I was a kid and it was fun," Jim said with a shrug. "And also there wasn't much money in television in those days anyhow." When he was finished with his sets, Jim was happy to spend what money was left over on friends and family, purchasing a color television and a brand-new electric organ for his mother. There would be no more puffing at the pump organ for Betty Henson.

While the Muppets were gaining a following and their creator was earning a considerable amount of money, Jim remained unfazed by the attention and income. Those who knew Jim only through his work on *Sam and Friends* were often surprised to learn, on meeting him in person, that the creator of the manic Muppets was actually a soft-spoken, gentlemanly young man who was still called Jimmy by friends and family. But looking closer, it was also easy to see the twinkle in the eye and the slight grin that gave away the madcap sense of humor. "He had a warm glow," remembered Rudy Pugliese, who taught drama at the University of Maryland. "He's just looking at everyone to see what kind of humor he can find in them. . . . His wit was very apparent, very sharp and very clever. And it appeared more clever because of his shyness. . . . He had charisma, a warmth that made you comfortable when talking to him." And it was during one of their regular talks, Pugliese admitted later, that he asked Jim, "Why are you wasting your time with those puppets?"

While Jim never considered his work a waste, it was, nevertheless, a question he had often asked himself. "All the time I was in school, I didn't take puppetry seriously," Jim said. "I mean, it didn't seem to be the sort of thing a grown man works at for a living." Rather, it was a placeholder until a better opportunity came along. Just as an aspiring college journalist might take a summer job writing obituaries hoping that the experience and connections will lead to a permanent, proper press job, so, too, did Jim continue to view the Muppets as a preface to what he considered a real job in television, whether it was art and stage design, direction, or production. "I had assumed at that point that I would probably end up in scenic design or advertising art," he said.

Sam and Friends continued to gain a following, but in the summer of 1955, WRC—never one to be content with a good thing— began to fidget with its late evening lineup, and announced that it was canceling *Sam and Friends*. To Jim's surprise and delight, angry phone calls and letters poured into WRC studios, and WRC executives immediately backtracked, putting *Sam* back on the air after missing only one night. Still, as the *Evening Star* was quick to point out, it was only a partial victory, since Sam would now air only three nights a week instead of five. "Don't be too grateful to WRC," sniffed the *Star.* "Just nod politely."

Even the three nights wouldn't last long, as a twitchy WRC bounced its newscast from 11:00 to 10:00 P.M., then back again. Jim moved with it at first, performing each evening at 10:25, until mid-October when WRC inexplicably handed *Sam and Friends'* evening time slot over to guitar virtuoso Les Paul and his wife, Mary Ford. For the next seven months or so, then, Jim would devote his time mostly to *Afternoon,* where he had proven his ability to draw viewers. Wisely, Sam would be featured prominently in WRC's newspaper ads, grinning from the pages of *The Washington Post* to promote the station's afternoon lineup. Even with Sam's shifting schedule, Jim was delighted with all he had accomplished.

Then, in the spring of 1956, tragedy struck.

On Sunday, April 15, 1956, Jim's brother, Paul—now serving as an ensign in the U.S. Navy and undergoing his pilot training in Pensacola, Florida—was riding in a car with two other young men when the driver suddenly lost control. The car veered off the road and rolled four times, instantly killing the driver and critically injuring Paul Henson. After receiving the phone call informing them of the accident, Betty and Paul Henson, Sr., sped for Florida, but too late: twenty-three-year-old Paul Henson, Jr., passed away later that afternoon.

For the Henson family, it was a devastating loss. While there was some solace to be found through Christian Science—in the belief that spiritual development actively continues even after death, and that death is simply another state in which a person may attain the love of God—Betty Henson "never got over" Paul's death. The silly, joking Betty Henson—the one who would pour milk to overflowing—was still pleasant and loving, but her family—including Jim—always thought a part of her died along with Paul. As much as he might try, Jim would never really get over Paul's death, either—and for the rest of his life, during quiet moments, Jim would often remark that he still missed Paul terribly. Unlike Betty, however, Jim would channel his sorrow into silliness, his anxiety into art.

Partly, it was a typically Henson way of coping; just as Dear had rarely allowed discussion of the suicide of her father, Oscar, the Hensons simply soldiered on, remaining pleasant and sociable, and rarely speaking of Paul's death with outsiders. "The way of carrying on would be to keep a smile on your face" said one Henson family member. "The idea of being sociable, and conversational, and fun in conversation, is very highly valued." In fact, one of the highest compliments a Henson could administer would be to declare that someone was "good company." For Jim, then, art was part of his way of carrying on, of being good company.

But Paul's death was, to Jim, more than just the sense of loss. Suddenly, the nineteen-year-old who already seemed to work harder than everyone else was aware that the clock was ticking. Years later, Jim's oldest daughter, Lisa, would speak of Jim's sorrow as an almost "repressed sadness" that motivated Jim's work. "He shared so much with his brother as a young kid, and then to have that survivor crisis—thinking, 'Now I have to be him and me'—and he had rocket fuel in his career from then on." Said Jim's friend and longtime collaborator Frank Oz, "When his brother died, he felt like he maybe didn't have enough time. Not like he was feeling his mortality or a premonition that he would die young or anything like that—but he realized that he just didn't have an infinite amount of time to do all the things he wanted to do."

As he had done at the time of Pop's death a year earlier, Jim turned to work for release, applying himself—if that was possible— even harder. "His intention of working [was] probably increased by Paul's death," said Jane Henson. "And I think he was very aware that he then became the only child and was responsible to be not only what he was going to be, but what Paul would have been as well. And it was heavy on him." There would always be, said Jane, a touch of "sublime, sweet melancholy" in Jim's work.

Melancholy wasn't necessarily a bad thing. For Jim, whose Christian Science faith had been tinted and colored by his own creative enthusiasm and singular sense of humor, there was "a rightness" in the ups and downs in life, a comfort in the consistency of its joys and sorrows. While Paul's death may have driven Jim to work harder than ever and make the most of his own life, it may also have helped Jim to more fully clarify and appreciate his own unique outlook on our existence. "I believe that we form our own lives, that we create our own reality, and that everything works out for the best," Jim said later. "I know I drive some people crazy with what seems to be ridiculous optimism, but it has always worked out for me." Jim's optimism and enthusiasm for life, even in the face of hardship or sadness, would remain one of his most endearing and inspiring qualities.

Working out from under the shadow of Paul's death that summer, Jim's "ridiculous optimism" would be justified—for professionally, things were suddenly working out for the best. WRC was continuing to tinker with its scheduling, this time fiddling with its afternoon lineup, and had decided to cancel *Afternoon*. However, unlike the previous winter, when Jim had forfeited his time slot to another, the producers had worked overtime to find a new way to spotlight Jim's talents.

In May 1956, the Muppets were made a regular part of the newest incarnation of the WRC staple *Footlight Theatre,* serving as supporting players to guitar strummer Paul Arnold, who was expected to keep things moving between installments of banal singing cowboy films like *Rainbow over the Rockies* ("that whole Footlight Theatre was *so* contrived," Jane groaned). That usually involved bantering with Sam and the Muppets, who, truth be told, were probably attracting more viewers than Arnold. But Jim collaborated with the versatile Arnold with typical gusto, even adding a new member to the Muppet cast, a vaguely camel-like pirate named Omar, whom Arnold voiced. Jim worked hard that spring, rehearsing and performing for *Footlight Theatre,* making public appearances with the Muppets, and continuing to run his silkscreen poster business out of the student union building at the University of Maryland. The work continued to pay dividends. In 1956, the car lover finally purchased a gorgeous, gleaming sports car of his very own, the first of many sleek-lined cars Jim would own in his lifetime.

When it came to cars, Jim's love was practically genetic: Jim's great-uncle Fritz—one of Dear's fun-loving younger brothers—was also a car fanatic, and had purchased a car in the early 1920s without even knowing how to drive. ("He just drove it home," laughed Betty Henson, who had tagged along. "It was a wild ride!") Even Betty had the car bug, as she had been the first of the Browns to purchase a car, buying "a little gray box" the year before she married Paul Henson. Jim's particular affinity, going all the way back to his tinkering days in Leland, was for sports cars, the more streamlined the better—and in 1956, Jim snagged a gleaming white 1956 convertible Thunderbird. It wasn't his first car; he had previously owned a Ford, but that car had been purely functional, where this was a thing of beauty, low-slung with whitewall tires and fender vents, and Jim adored it. A photo from the time shows Jim parked in his driveway in Hyattsville, sitting in the car with Sam, pointing gleefully at something off-camera as Sam responds enthusiastically. Jane said Jim's family, always one of his best audiences, was probably looking on cheering. "After all," she added, "Sam had made it all possible."

Almost immediately, Jim decided to take an extended road trip across the country, piling into the Thunderbird with Joe Irwin and a week's worth of clean clothes for what turned out to be a three-week trip. Jim loved driving, and he especially loved driving without any schedule or destination. During the day, he and Joe would split the time behind the wheel, speeding across the countryside with the top down until their sunburned noses peeled, then all night as the mountains of Albuquerque or Las Vegas loomed up against the stars. Jim took great delight in stopping when anything caught his attention, which was just as likely to be an oddly worded sign as it was an unusually gnarled tree. "He posed himself beside these signs," said Irwin later, laughing. During a stop near the Grand Canyon, Jim had himself photographed blatantly disregarding a sign reading STAY ON TRAIL, while outside the Triangle X Ranch in Wyoming, Jim posed himself against a sign advertising the DUDE FOR DAY RANCH, standing with one leg forward and one hand cocked on his hip, and looking—despite his loafers and collared shirt—every inch a gunslinger.

Returning to Maryland later that summer, Jim was thrilled to hear the news that his hard work was getting noticed beyond the D.C. region. In New York, producers for Steve Allen's *Tonight* show were hearing more and more about their lead-in down in Washington. "Producers got in touch with the Washington station and said, 'tell us about these puppets,'" recalled Jane. And suddenly, in late August, she and Jim were climbing into Jim's Thunderbird on their way to New York City to audition for NBC at WRCA studios. "Producers were impressed," reported Lawrence Laurent in *The Washington Post*—and two months later, on October 11, the Muppets would make their first appearance on the *Tonight* show with Steve Allen. "This could be their big break," enthused the *Evening Star*.

Until now, the Muppets had never been seen outside the Washington, D.C., market. The *Tonight* show, with its national audience, would give Jim and Jane an enormous amount of exposure—and they were determined to give viewers a good dose of Muppet madness. Jim decided to use a relatively new but reliable sketch, featuring Rosemary Clooney's rendition of "I've Grown Accustomed to Your Face" from the recent Broadway hit *My Fair Lady*. Following Steve Allen's enthusiastic introduction, Jim performed Kermit—wearing a blond wig—lip-synching the song as he earnestly serenaded a squatty figure with its face concealed by a mask with a cutesy, doe-eyed face drawn on it. As the song reached the first musical interlude, the mask was slowly devoured from behind, revealing the deadpan Yorick beneath. Nervous laughter came from the live studio audience. What *was* all this?

As the song continued, a stunned Kermit tried gamely to keep singing, even as Yorick—in a wonderfully creepy performance by Jane—meticulously made his way toward Kermit, determined now to devour him. As Kermit scooted away and slapped frantically at Yorick, the purple skull continued to nibble at Kermit's arms and legs, before finally dragging a flailing Kermit offstage. The audience roared its approval. The Muppets were a hit.

Despite the growing success of the Muppets, back in D.C. an antsy WRC was still shuffling its afternoon lineup. After several weeks of jumbling, *Sam and Friends* was integrated into the final ten minutes of each evening's newscast, airing nightly at 6:50. It was a plum position in the lineup—and, given Jim and Jane's successful appearance on the *Tonight* show, a well-deserved one. Before the end of 1956, they would make several other national appearances, including a performance on *The Arthur Godfrey Show*. It had been a good year—and things would get even better in 1957.

Beginning in January 1957, Jim was given his old 11:25 P.M. time slot, just after the late evening news and before the *Tonight* show, which was trying to find its way following the recent departure of host Steve Allen. Jim now had the 6:50 P.M. slot after the early news, and the 11:25 P.M. spot following the late news, making him responsible for ten shows a week. Add to that the increasing number of guest spots on countless other variety shows and the requisite public appearances, and Jim's schedule quickly became grueling. "There were times that I had three shows a day," Jim said later. "So it kept me busy."

So busy, in fact, that in February 1957, Jim decided to withdraw, at least briefly, from the University of Maryland. Schoolwork itself was really no problem for Jim; as a mostly A or B student, he excelled in courses in puppetry, design, stagecraft, art history, illustration, and even a year in ROTC. His only low grades were in typewriting, economics, and physical education. The decision to withdraw, then, was not to be made lightly. But Jim was perhaps astute enough to recognize that he had been given an enormous opportunity: he had not one, but two daily shows, over which he had almost complete creative control. For an aspiring artist, it was a unique chance to learn by doing—and all things being equal, Jim had perhaps decided his best classroom was not up the road at the university, but down the hill at WRC studios. Jim already had a full-time job lined up at WRC working in the studio's scenic art department, designing and building sets. Through this job and his nightly work on *Sam and Friends,* Jim was determined to learn all he could about what went on both in front of and behind the camera. He would become a student of television.

That didn't make his schedule less hectic—in many ways, it was even crazier. There was his full-time job in WRC's art department, but even on the days he wasn't working, Jim was taking his *Sam and Friends* routines more seriously now, spending the mornings sorting through and listening to records, hoping for the spark of an idea for a Muppet performance—it was his intention, he said, not to repeat a song for at least two months. Once inspired, he would write brief routines, sometimes scratching them out like cartoons on a yellow pad, though Jim would often write on any piece of paper he could find. Meanwhile, Jane would rise early to attend morning classes at Catholic University, then make the six-mile drive to Jim's family home in University Park. Over a late lunch, the two of them would review Jim's routines, select the music, discuss any sets that might need to be built, and toss around other ideas. Then it was time to head into the District to WRC studios to rehearse the *Sam and Friends* segment for the evening newscast, which would be performed live at 6:50.

After the early evening performance, Jane would return to her place in Northeast Washington to do homework, while Jim went back to University Park to have dinner, build and paint sets, or touch up and repair any Muppets showing signs of wear. At 10:30, he and Jane would meet back at WRC for an hour of rehearsal before going live at 11:25 with the five-minute installment of *Sam and Friends.* Even after they'd finished filming for the evening, Jim would sometimes stay for hours afterward, talking with cameramen and technicians. "In his spare time he'd be in the control room, trying to understand what was going on," Jane recalled. "And the technicians loved teaching him because he really learned his lessons well. He couldn't wait to try out the things he was learning on *Sam and Friends*."

Early on, Jim learned simple camera tricks that could enhance their performance. "At that time, all those television cameras were equipped with turrets [of lenses] and we would ask for the widest angle lens and experiment with moving in and out of the camera," said Jim. "You could do really interesting things in terms of depth." He discovered, for instance, that by holding the character back only a few feet, then moving forward, a wide-angle lens made the Muppet appear to rush the camera, covering a seemingly huge distance in a flash. It was unsophisticated but effective, and Jim encouraged the floor crew to freely offer suggestions on other technical tricks that might punch up their performance. "The atmosphere in the studio was very relaxed because in the beginning, we were lip-synching to records," said Jane. "There was no live sound . . . so there was no need to be completely quiet. We could talk as we worked, and if something went especially well, the crew would applaud. If something went wrong, we'd laugh anyway!"

The majority of their performances still involved lip-synching and pantomiming to novelty records—which, fortunately, Stan Freberg and others were continuing to produce regularly. "We'd use a lot of records," Jane remarked later. "If it didn't go well, we wouldn't use it again, but if it did go well, we'd save it and use it again." In the free-for-all atmosphere of early television, there was never any thought given to clearing the records for usage, which likely would have involved paying royalties. "I think we were working with something that was setting a precedent," Jane offered later, coyly suggesting that their use of the records may have fallen under the same "fair use" rules of live radio. "The whole business was much more cottage industry—it wasn't the way it is now."

In fact, remembered Jane, some of the artists whose records had been used on *Sam and Friends* grumbled at first, noting the lack of royalties or the use of an otherwise serious performance for a laugh and a punch line. When any wounded artists brought their concerns to Jim's attention, however, it was always easier to ask forgiveness than permission—and most crumpled in the face of Jim's charm. Stan Freberg, in fact, admitted he had been irritated when he learned his records were being used without attribution or recompense, and went storming down to WRC in April 1957 to issue a personal cease and desist. Once he had the opportunity to actually see Jim and Jane perform, however, Freberg melted—and shortly thereafter sent the two an enthusiastic telegram with his blessings. "I take it all back," gushed Freberg. "This is one of the greatest acts I have ever seen [and I] am honored to let you use my records for ever and longer."

Jim reenrolled at the University of Maryland in the fall of 1957, following a brief summer vacation in Mexico. The break, if you could call it that, had done him good. He introduced a new character, the cigar-shaped, brush-mustached Professor Madcliffe, "who has a knack," Jim explained, "for not being able to repair things he's helped put out of order." He would also be the first Muppet Jim would perform in his own voice—mostly interacting with Paul Arnold as he introduced segments—instead of lip-synching to records.

Creatively, Jim's sketches for *Sam and Friends* were growing more and more outlandish, juxtaposing bizarre behavior—in which his Muppets usually pummeled, blew up, or devoured each other—with earnest, sappy songs. Jim relished every moment. "In the early days of the Muppets, we had two endings," Jim said. "Either one creature ate the other, or both of them blew up. . . . I've always been particular to things eating other things!" It was a sense of humor you either got, or you didn't; it was as simple as that, and Jim wasn't about to tone down his act. "We'd try some really way-out things," Jim said later. "I remember one strange thing we had on the show— a puppet made from the skull of a squirrel. We used to take this slightly macabre thing and make it talk, and also we used it to lip-synch to this terrible song called 'There's a New Sound' . . . it has only one chord and it would drive people crazy. . . . I was convinced no one else at the station ever watched the show because there was never a complaint or any attempt at censorship of any kind."

And still WRC couldn't seem to leave well enough alone. In September 1957, the network scratched *Sam and Friends* from its 6:50 P.M. spot, and cleared out its evening programming as the network struggled with lackluster ratings from the *Tonight* show. As they had in 1955, *Sam*'s fans responded angrily. "We have so few local shows that are worthwhile that when we do get something good, let's fight to keep it on and going strong," declared one letter to the *Star*. "Sam, Yorick and Kermit are a lot more entertaining than *Death Valley Days* and *Last of the Mohicans*." "This is one case where I'm certain that WRC regretted cancellation of the show," agreed the *Star*'s editors. Responding to the uproar, *Sam* was quietly returned to its regular spots in the WRC lineup.

The Tonight Show, too, would right itself shortly thereafter, determining at last that it would officially be called *The Tonight Show* and installing Jack Paar as host. In fact, as the lead-in to the newly energized *Tonight Show, Sam and Friends* had become a local late night powerhouse. But it was a final bit of tinkering in the WRC schedule—this time courtesy of parent company NBC—that would give Jim not just one, but two of the most desirable time slots in television.

Initially, WRC execs had likely hoped that Jim's 6:50 performance of *Sam and Friends* would lure in and keep viewers tuned to NBC for the next hour, gently persuading them to sit through *Superman* or *Nat King Cole,* until the 7:45 broadcast of a new fifteen-minute, national nightly news show NBC was working hard to promote: *The Huntley-Brinkley Report. The Huntley-Brinkley Report* had been inserted into the NBC lineup on October 29, 1956, to replace John Cameron Swayze's flailing *Camel News Caravan,* which had sunk slowly beneath CBS in the ratings. For its new newscast, NBC had gambled on a unique two-man format, with Chet Huntley broadcasting from New York City and David Brinkley from the WRC studios at Wardman Park in Washington—but the wager was proving slow to pay off.

However, in September 1957—as part of the strategy that would eventually make *Huntley-Brinkley* the nation's most respected and critically acclaimed news broadcast—NBC had decided to move *Huntley-Brinkley* out of its relatively late 7:45 P.M. slot and start the show an hour earlier, having it come on right after most local newscasts so viewers wouldn't have to wait an hour between local and national news. WRC obligingly shortened its own 6:30 newscast to fifteen minutes, and gave Jim—and *Sam and Friends*—the final five minutes before WRC cut away to the national feed of *Huntley-Brinkley* at 6:45.

It was an unbelievable break, and nearly fifty years later, Jane was still shaking her head in amazement at their luck. "We got the *Huntley-Brinkley* audience, *and* the [*Tonight Show*] audience!" Jane laughed. "I mean, what could be better? . . . You'd have national news, international news, weather, sports . . . and Kermit!" As David Brinkley began his broadcasts each evening at 6:45 at Wardman Park, Jim and Jane were several doors down, packing up their Muppets and preparing to return to the studio in five hours for the 11:25 broadcast. WRC anchorman Bryson Rash, who had the opportunity to watch *Sam and Friends* in the studio as he wrapped up the evening news, never ceased to be amazed by Jim's performance. Jim was "very shy, a retiring sort of person," recalled Rash. "But he was vigorous and he had a great imagination, of course, and he did a wonderful show."

Even as the Muppets grew in popularity, so, too, did their performers. *The Washington Post,* for example, was happy to let its readers know that Jane designed most of her own clothes, studied German three nights a week in an adult education course ("because it's free," she explained), and lived with a roommate in an apartment with no television. Jim appreciated such press, and teased Jane about the countless photographs that seemed to appear of her with the Muppets. "Why are you having *your* picture taken with all *my* puppets?" Jim would ask in mock annoyance. Likely it was because Jane was the more press-savvy of the two of them; when faced with an interviewer, Jim would usually slouch way down on a chair, his arms folded and long legs crossed in front of him, content to let Jane do the talking. Indeed, of the two of them, Jane was the more bohemian and worldly, the one who lived in an apartment in the District, making pottery, chatting with artists, and cooking for herself, very much grown up and on her own. Jim, meanwhile, still lived rent-free with his parents in the house on suburban Beechwood Road, still sleeping in the same bedroom he had shared with Paul.

Despite their obvious personal chemistry, Jim and Jane's relationship remained collegial and strictly professional, likely to the confusion of friends who wondered how two people could work together so intimately, arms often tangled together overhead as they worked from their knees, and yet remain merely co-workers. In fact, both Jim and Jane were involved with other people, with Jane engaged to Bill Schmittmann, a student from American University she had been dating since 1955, and Jim seeing Anne Marie Hood, a vivacious teaching student, three years younger—a "cheerleader type," said Jane flatly, "but a nice girl"—to whom he would be engaged later that year. For the moment, then, the only relationship Jim and Jane were interested in having with each other was a professional one—and they made it official in 1957, agreeing to become business partners and sealing their deal with a handshake.

Almost immediately, the new partners would have a remarkable opportunity. That summer, the Ver Standig advertising agency of Washington, D.C., had been approached by one of its clients, the John H. Wilkins Company, about producing a series of catchy ten-second spots for their coffee. The company wanted something innovative, memorable, and, if possible, funny. Helen Ver Standig, a fan of *Sam and Friends,* thought she knew exactly whom to call.

CHAPTER FOUR

MUPPETS, INC.

1957–1962

Wilkins (right) and Wontkins.

THE JOHN H. WILKINS COMPANY WAS ONE OF WASHINGTON'S SCRAP-
pier and more successful local businesses. John H. Wilkins, Sr., had
started the firm in 1900 as a tiny specialty coffee shop in the downtown area, where one of his regulars had been the respected politician William Jennings Bryan, who was not only fond of the coffee,
but was also known to scarf down any food left sitting out on open
trays or half-empty plates. In 1917, Wilkins had gone into the coffee
wholesale business, joined in 1921 by his son, John H. Wilkins, Jr.
The younger Wilkins had taken over the company with the passing
of his father in 1947, and by the 1950s, the firm was one of the most

successful businesses in the area, selling 11 million pounds of coffee annually, supplying two thirds of the coffee used in area hotels and restaurants, and over a quarter of that used in D.C. area homes—including the White House. "Use Wilkins coffee," was Wilkins Jr.'s personal sales pitch and mantra, "it's a wonderful way to start the day."

Helen Ver Standig approached Jim to discuss a new advertising campaign for Wilkins, which would involve filming fifteen ten-second coffee commercials, with an option to create more, based on demand. Jim would have only about eight seconds for each ad—the last two seconds were needed to show the product itself—so the ad would have to make the point quickly and effectively. There had been some skepticism about using puppets to sell coffee, but for Ver Standig, Jim was more than just Muppets. While she conceded that she thought the humor on *Sam and Friends* was "really pretty corny," she still felt there was something there, an edgy sensibility that she thought would make the Wilkins campaign memorable.

It was a challenge, but it didn't take Jim long to accept the offer—and he already had an idea of how he would handle the project. "We took a very different approach," he explained. "We tried to sell things by making people laugh." Unlike most commercials at the time, which simply showed a product and described it in voice-over, Jim wanted to make fun of advertising itself, using an over-the-top, mock-heavy-handed approach. For his commercials, then, Jim would take John Wilkins's mantra and give it a Muppet twist. No longer would Wilkins coffee be merely a wonderful way to start the day; it would be, "Use Wilkins coffee . . . or else!"

In that "or else!" clause lay Jim's particular expertise.

Jim set to work drawing out his ideas for the Wilkins project, storyboarding his spots in pencil on lined yellow paper. For the commercials, Jim created two new characters, the skinny, rounded, excitable Wilkins, who *will* drink Wilkins coffee, and the squatty, triangular, grumpy Wontkins, who *won't*. It was the same Laurel and Hardy study in contrasting characters that Jim got such a kick out of—only this time, that conflicting dynamic was the defining premise of the commercials, all of which worked in the same way: Wilkins asks Wontkins to try Wilkins coffee, Wontkins refuses, so

Wilkins lets Wontkins have it. But it was the increasingly absurd and sometimes shocking forms of punishment that Wilkins would dish out that would make Jim's Wilkins spots some of the most memorable, and successful, commercials of the era, with the skeptical Wontkins being clubbed, shot, egged, blown up, run over, stomped on, or decapitated for his refusal to sample Wilkins coffee.

In fact, it was almost *too* easy for Jim to come up with increasingly ridiculous scenarios for punishing Wontkins—for Jim really *didn't* like Wilkins coffee, or coffee of any kind for that matter. To Jim, the Wilkins commercials were a playful way of working out what it *would* take to get him to drink coffee—and the answer was: quite a lot. (Jim would, in fact, later politely gag down a sip of Wilkins coffee at a formal dinner at the Wilkinses' home, much to the delight of Jane, who knew of his aversion to the stuff.) For the commercials, then, Jim would always perform the crotchety Wontkins, while Jane performed Wilkins, lip-synching the puppet to Jim's prerecorded voice.

Jim's early segments capitalized on his fondness for ending sketches with explosions—or, at least, on explosive variations. In one of the first spots Jim produced, Wilkins points a cannon at Wontkins and asks, "Okay, buddy, whattaya think of Wilkins coffee?" "I never tasted it," Wontkins admits. Wilkins fires the cannon, blasting Wontkins off-screen, then turns the cannon toward the viewer. "Now what do *you* think of Wilkins?" he asks calmly. Quick cut to a shot of Wilkins coffee, commercial over, point made. In another, Wilkins and Wontkins stand at a microphone, as if aware they're recording a commercial. "Care for a cup of Wilkins coffee?" asks Wilkins. "No, I don't like coffee," Wontkins growls—and a hand holding a pistol emerges from off-screen and shoots him point-blank. "This has been a public service!" Wilkins says to the viewer.

For Jim, this was an opportunity to gleefully indulge in near chaotic humor. And at only eight seconds, it all went by so quickly viewers hardly knew whether to shriek or laugh. As it turns out, they did *both*, exactly as Jim expected. In Wilkins and Wontkins, Jim had created the kind of silly and endearing characters that were already becoming his trademark—the kind of characters that could even let him get away with being a little dangerous. And as Jim had learned from Walt Kelly's *Pogo*, your audience was willing to let you be a little subversive when you were giving them something fun to look at and, more important, when they were being entertained.

The ads were enormously successful, sending sales of Wilkins coffee soaring by 25 percent, and winning for Jim and Jane—and the Ver Standig advertising firm—local awards for excellence in advertising. "The commercials were an immediate hit and they made a big impact," Jim recalled. "In terms of popularity of commercials in the Washington area, we were the number one, most popular commercial." Many viewers, in fact, confessed that they were merely "sitting through" afternoon westerns or quiz shows in hopes of catching the latest commercial.

The Wilkins Company was delighted—"This is the biggest thing that has ever happened to Wilkins Coffee," exclaimed John Wilkins—and for Helen Ver Standig, her confidence in Jim had been vindicated. "He had the creative ability of being able to get his audience to identify emotionally with his Muppets," she said. "Everybody in the morning feels like killing their husband or wife anyway. . . . People went mad for these puppets." So mad, in fact, that they spawned the first bit of Muppet-related merchandise, a pair of Wilkins and Wontkins "Hand Muppets" that fans could get by sending in a dollar and "the last inch of winding band on Wilkins Coffee." Made of "soft but durable vinyl," more than 25,000 pairs of Wilkins and Wontkins puppets sold during the 1958 Christmas season. Despite the use of the Muppet name in the promotion, Jim and Jane saw none of the profits—which at the time didn't bother them much. "I'm sure it cost them more to make than they ever sold," Jane said.

Jim and Jane would end up filming nearly 180 commercials for Wilkins coffee over the next several years—filmed mostly at Rodel Studios in Washington—coming up with new and more creative scenarios in which Wilkins could torment poor Wontkins. Some ads let Jim indulge in his delight for puns ("I shoulda saw this coming!" says a tied-up Wontkins as he inches toward a roaring buzz saw. "He always was a cutup!" Wilkins says, one-upping his partner for the punch line), play with nonsensical endings (Wontkins gets crushed by a falling Washington Monument), or indulge in good old-fashioned pie-in-the-face humor. Perhaps due to their obvious, almost aggressive glee, there were surprisingly few complaints about their cartoonish violence—in fact, most viewers understood exactly what Jim was up to. "The funniest thing we have seen in many a moon," wrote one viewer. "[It] has a message that gets across to people in a most unusual way."

Jim's Wilkins commercials also caught the attention of other coffee companies across the eastern seaboard, who wanted the Muppets selling *their* coffee, too. "[The commercials] got a lot of talk, and so then the advertising agency started syndicating them and they would sell them to a coffee company in Boston, another coffee company in New York," Jim recalled. "We had up to about a dozen or so clients going at the same time," Jim said, including Community Coffee of Louisiana, La Touraine Coffee of Boston, Nash's Coffee of Minnesota, and even the carbonated drink CalSo in California. "At that point, I was making a lot of money," Jim said. That was typical understatement—in 1958 and 1959, Nash's Coffee alone would pay Jim a total of $20,000 (about $150,000 today) for eight commercials. But it was also a lot of work, as Jim preferred to reshoot old Wilkins commercials using the names of the other products. For the perfectionist Jim, it would have been cheating, for example, to dub in the five syllables of "La Touraine Coffee" over Wilkins mouthing the four syllables for "Wilkins Coffee."

Apart from their phenomenal marketing and financial success, the Wilkins spots marked another kind of personal victory for Jim. "That was almost the first voice stuff I did," he noted proudly. Up until now, he had, by his own admission, done only "a couple of little tiny things" with voices on *Sam and Friends*. Now he was doing all his own voices, giving Wilkins, after a bit of experimentation, a slightly quavering voice pitched just a bit higher than his own, and Wontkins a gruff rasp, similar to the voice he would later use for Rowlf the Dog.

The Muppets were becoming wildly successful—in 1958, *Sam and Friends* would win an Emmy for Best Local Entertainment Program—and yet, Jim was still uncertain whether there was a future for him as a puppeteer. While the Muppets were still paying the bills—and, with their new foray into advertising, paying remarkably well—Jim was still looking toward a future as a painter or as a set designer, while Jane was hoping for a career in commercial art or fashion. In a profile of Jim in a 1958 issue of the University of Maryland's *Old Line* magazine, Jim would only promise to "continue with the Muppets as long as there is a demand for them."

Privately, in fact, Jim was ready to quit *Sam and Friends* altogether. "I decided to chuck it all and go off to be a painter," Jim said. "I was an artist, you see, so I was going to take the shows off the air, just quit for a while." Jim's decision sent WRC executives scrambling for a way to keep their twenty-one-year-old ratings magnet on the payroll. "The station prevailed upon me," Jim said later, laughing. "They said, 'Look, we'll pay you money and you can put somebody else doing the show,' and so I realized I can get money and at the same time be off painting."

To take over his performing duties on *Sam and Friends,* Jim engaged the services of a friend he had known since Northwestern High School, a fellow University of Maryland student named Bobby Payne. Payne, a quiet and somewhat shy young man, was awed by the supremely confident Jim. "He already knew what he was wanting!" Payne said with amazement. Late that spring, Jim picked up Payne in his convertible and drove to WRC's new studios on Nebraska Avenue in Northwest Washington to give Payne a crash course in the Muppet style of performing.

Payne quickly came to appreciate the sheer strength and stamina Jim brought to the job. Performing Sam, Payne recalled, could be a workout. "He had this bar inside him that you could [use to shrug Sam's shoulders]," said Payne. "It would kill you to do a whole number. He was made of plastic wood in his hands and head—he was just heavy!" But even as precise and as demanding as he could be, Jim was always patient and encouraging. "Jim more or less said, 'You should be able to do anything,'" Payne said. "And so he really challenged me to try to do those things."

In June 1958, then, with the Muppets in good hands—in addition to hiring Payne as a performer, he had left the general management of the Muppets in the capable care of Jane—Jim "wandered over to Europe," as he casually described it, with no real plan but to travel the continent and study painting. It would turn out to be a critical journey for Jim and his development as an artist—though not as the painter he had initially aspired to be.

Initially, Jim traveled in Europe with Joe Irwin, who was more than happy to continue in the same aide-de-camp role as he had for their cross-country trip, snapping pictures of Jim as he stood in front of the Eiffel Tower, stretching himself as tall and dignified as he could get, or gleefully leaping onto railroad tracks in Germany to pretend to push a freight train. As a twenty-one-year-old on his first European adventure, Jim was a whirlwind of activity, weaving through museums in France, scrambling over rocks in Lucerne, and craning his neck at barmaids in Germany. Irwin, who had enlisted in the military, finally had to leave Jim in France after a few weeks to report for active duty. "But I know the kind of adventures he had while in Paris," Irwin said later, laughing. It was, as Irwin characterized it, " 'Sex on the Seine' . . . I'm surprised he came back!"

For weeks, Jim simply roamed, attending the World's Fair in Brussels, and gazing at paintings and sculpture in Switzerland, France, or Germany. But to his surprise, there was another art form Europeans enjoyed, and that they took just as seriously as painting or sculpture. "In Europe," said Jim with amazement, "everyone goes to puppet shows." As Joe Irwin recalled, Jim was particularly fascinated by the countless amateur Punch and Judy shows—and was even more intrigued with the reaction of the audiences, who hooted and hissed and actively engaged with the puppets, often throwing out story suggestions or having shouted conversations with the characters. It was one of the first times Jim had ever been an active audience member, and he "absolutely marveled" at how completely an audience could get caught up in the performance. "[Audiences] were very involved," said Irwin. "These puppets became live entertainers, [especially] to the children."

Jim traveled more deliberately now, seeking out puppet shows of every kind, and talking with puppeteers, puppet makers, even audiences. What he saw was craftspeople who took real pride in their work, painting elaborate wooden heads and sewing beautiful cloth puppets. He saw puppet theaters and sets that rivaled opera houses, while others were equally as gorgeous in their stark minimalism. "That was the first time I'd ever met any other puppeteers. . . . When I traveled around, I saw the work of a number of people," Jim said. "They were very serious about their work. I thought that what they were doing was really interesting."

It was a turning point. Until now, no matter how good or ground-breaking his own work might have been, Jim had always had Rudy Pugliese's question burning in the back of his head: *Why are you wasting your time with those puppets?* Now he finally had his answer: he wasn't. As he headed for home in August 1958 after six weeks abroad, he had made his decision. "It was at that point I realized the puppetry was an art form, a valid way to do really interesting things," Jim remarked. "I came back from that trip all fired up to do wonderful puppetry." He also came back with a beard, a variation on the European-style Vandyke, making a brushy circle around his mouth and trimmed to a slight point. It was both fashionable and, in Jim's opinion, functional, as it covered the acne scars that were always more visible to himself than to others.

It was as if those few weeks in Europe had opened a creative floodgate—for what followed would be a period of enormous experimentation and artistic growth as Jim pursued a wide variety of interests and began to play with other forms of media. Many projects would never make it beyond the idea phase, drawn into Jim's sketchbooks with elaborate notes, while others would result in wonderful bits of animation or recordings that Jim would keep privately to himself, satisfied merely with the act of creating and imagining. He was reaching out, exploring new ways to tell stories and create worlds, the ideas coming almost faster than he could scribble down or carry out.

That autumn, Jim took no courses at the University of Maryland. Invigorated by both the puppetry and the literature of his European trip, he was determined to stage a European-style production of *Hansel and Gretel,* and spent the fall filling pages of his sketchbooks with set designs and rough story outlines. Jim's pencil drawings for *Hansel and Gretel* alone justify his initial enthusiasm for a career in set design; his sketches of a haunted forest are alive with energy, filled with smiling trees that twist themselves into thorny, gnarled knots, and grimacing tree stumps with spooky, blank, jack-o'-lantern eyes. It's just the kind of place in which a fairy tale should exist, and Jim clearly had a sense of the look and feel of the world in which his story would take place—the same design mentality he would bring to *The Dark Crystal* two decades later. Working with

Bobby Payne, Jim got as far as building several sets for *Hansel and Gretel*, as well as several puppets—including a witch with light-up eyes—but in the end Jim shelved the project, calling it "ridiculously overcomplicated." Still, the writing and design work had been good experience. Jim was becoming a storyteller.

Even without *Hansel and Gretel*, there was plenty to keep Jim busy. First and foremost, Jim returned to school full-time in 1959, determined to complete his degree. On the work end of things, during Jim's absence, WRC had made the Muppets a regular part of *In Our Town*, a half-hour daily variety show airing at 1:00 each afternoon, giving the Muppets *three* regular spots in the daily lineup. Jim also arranged for more appearances on Jack Paar's *Tonight Show* and continued to film commercials for Wilkins and other coffee companies at the rate of about one a week.

With a steady income and the Muppets increasingly in demand, Jim and Jane were ready to take their business to the next level. Moving beyond a mere business partnership, they decided to create their own company—and in 1958, Jim and Jane officially established Muppets, Inc. While Jim always described them as equal partners in the business, Jane would always refer to Jim as the boss. Jim replied that if he was, indeed, the boss, it was "just a little bit." In truth, it was more than just a little bit; Jim had drawn up the papers for Muppets, Inc. so that he owned 60 percent of the company to Jane's 40.

But there was another relationship Jim wanted to make official as well. "When he came back from Europe, he had it in his mind that we were supposed to get married," Jane said later. "He said, 'We're going to do this with the puppets and then we're going to get married.'"

The proposition wasn't entirely out of the blue. In the four years the two of them had been working together, they had developed an ability to speak without talking, each almost intuitively understanding what the other was thinking. It made for great puppetry, and lately it had made for some interesting moments for Jim's fiancée Anne Marie, and Jane's fiancé, Bill. "I remember an elevator ride at WRC one night, when Jim had gone up to get Anne Marie from school," Jane said. "And we're all [four] in the elevator . . . and Jim and I were like, 'You know, we're here and that's important but those other two people don't need to be here.' It was that kind of feeling about it. We had a kind of permanency about us."

And so the engagements were broken off, and Jim and Jane had gone out a few times—dinner at a Mexican restaurant where Jim was more interested in the murals than the meal, going ice skating, or attending outdoor performances by the Kingston Trio or Harry Belafonte—but mostly, said Jane, "they weren't dates, they were working situations." Their courtship was part of Jim's life plan, the next logical step after forming Muppets, Inc. toward becoming Jim Henson. Jim and Jane's relationship was based on passion—passion for art, for performance, and for each other—but it was more a business proposal than a marriage proposal. "It was like, 'Do I have a choice in this?'" Jane recalled, laughing at first about their unusual courtship—but then grew more reflective about their complex thirty-year relationship. "Every marriage comes with an agreement, and our agreement was that we would support his work," she said firmly. "So, in many ways, the work came first. That's not necessarily a good agreement. This isn't against Jim—I just think that the general agreement of the whole marriage and family thing was that the work was primary. Where that came from I'm not really sure. I guess it's because Jim and I were working [when we] got married, but that wasn't always a good agreement . . . and it really was not supposed to be questioned.

"I can say this about Jim and me," she said finally. "He is totally a natural leader. And I am absolutely a follower. I really am. I'm pretty good at allowing things to happen when they're supposed to rather than being a leader. But Jim was always a leader. *Always.*"

To those who knew of Jim's penchant for "the cheerleader type," the artsier Jane didn't seem, on the face of it, to be Jim's sort. But Joe Irwin, who knew them both, thought he understood. Jane had one thing to which Jim would always be attracted: *talent.* She was also warm and "had an artistic bent," Irwin explained, which Jim found compelling. But there was also, he thought, a mutual sexual attraction that Jim couldn't deny. Jane was three years Jim's senior, and older—and more experienced—than most girls Jim had dated. "She was mature," Irwin said delicately, "and probably more adventurous."

Jane couldn't deny there was an intense intimacy there—that "permanency" that Jane had sensed during their elevator ride at WRC. "We were very fond of being with each other," Jane said. "There was a love there. Quite honestly, I can't remember *falling* in love; it was more like a recognition of 'Look, this is what's been happening.'" It had been, as many would say later, admiration at first sight.

And so, on May 28, 1959, at Jane's family home in Salisbury, Maryland, Jane Nebel and Jim Henson were married in a small ceremony presided over by the family minister, Jim's Uncle Jinx, with Joe Irwin serving as Jim's best man. (Irwin, in fact, had nearly missed the wedding, having run into bad weather during his flight into D.C.—but Jim had paid for a private plane to pick up his best man the moment he landed at National Airport to whisk him to Maryland's Eastern Shore.) There was only one condition imposed on the match, and that had come from Betty Henson, who insisted her son shave off his new beard for the wedding. Jim dutifully obliged, putting the shearings in an envelope and mailing them to Jane just before the wedding with a playful note reading, "From Samson to Delilah." In celebration of the nuptials, *Sam and Friends* went on a short honeymoon hiatus—the Hensons themselves would make a quick honeymoon sprint to the beach at Delaware's Rehoboth—with loyal *Post* reporter Lawrence Laurent tipping readers off to the cause of *Sam*'s brief absence from the WRC lineup.

The newlywed Hensons settled into a new home in the suburb of Bethesda, Maryland, buying a sprawling ranch on woodsy Nevis Road—not only the first home Jim would own, but the first time he had ever lived away from his parents—filled with modern furniture, purchased with Muppet money. In the basement, Jim set up the first Muppet workshop, a comfortable space crammed with cabinets and tables strewn with fabric, paints, foam, glue, and art supplies. Here Jim would come to scribble ideas in his sketchbooks and manage the affairs of Muppets, Inc., with a Siamese cat named George Washington curled at his feet.

He had another new toy in the workshop: a Bolex 16mm movie

camera—an ideal camera for an aspiring animator, as it had a side release button, which made it possible to film just a few frames at a time. Jim excitedly set to work creating what he called "animated paintings." "I started painting on a sheet of paper placed under the lens of the animation stand," Jim recalled. "I would just paint a couple of strokes and take a frame or two of film, and I would be able to watch this painting evolve and move. From that time on I lost interest in easel painting as such because the movement concept was just so much more interesting. I was really very excited about it." Jim would later put his animated paintings to notable use in many of *Sesame Street*'s colorful counting sequences.

Perhaps instilled with a new sense of self-confidence in his writing skills from his experience with *Hansel and Gretel*, Jim was beginning to write more original pieces for *Sam and Friends* at the rate of "about two or three" a week, banging out his skits on a typewriter or scribbling in pencil on lined yellow notebook paper. He was also doing more of his own voices for his Muppets, experimenting to come up with just the right sound for each of *Sam*'s cast members. For Professor Madcliffe—the first character Jim would voice—Jim settled on a higher-pitched, manic game show host voice. Harry the Hipster was easier; Jim had this kind of character down pat, speaking in the same sort of gruff hepcat voice he would later give to Dr. Teeth. And perhaps appropriately, given his connection with the character, Kermit was closer to Jim's own voice, though slightly more nasal and—in these early days, at least—with just a hint of a swampy Mississippi twang.

When performing his own sketches, Jim would drive to WRC early to record all of his voices, music, and sound effects to tape, which he and Jane—and sometimes Bobby Payne—would then edit and revise, creating a four-and-a-half-minute soundtrack for their performance. For the rest of the afternoon, they would listen to the track over and over, memorizing the vocals and sound effects to ensure they could lip-synch the Muppets seamlessly to Jim's own voices. For her part, Jane would remain the silent partner, though that had not necessarily been her decision. "Jim never had me do voices," Jane said later, with only a hint of regret. "I don't think it was my choice, I think it was Jim's. That probably *was* a disappointment, but in the long run it was fine, because I didn't really want to be doing that [for a living]."

One of the earliest *Sam and Friends* episodes Jim wrote was "Powder Burn," a pun-filled parody of TV's *Gunsmoke* that could have been lifted directly from Stan Freberg or the pages of the new *MAD* magazine, filled with the kind of winking puns, clever plays on words, and silly names that Jim loved—the "stage coach" everyone is expecting at noon, for example, turns out to be a drama teacher, played enthusiastically by Jim with Professor Madcliffe. Another sketch poked fun at *Meet the Press,* satirizing the news show with a bit of *Pogo*-esque political commentary on organized crime. Television parodies were always fun for Jim—he particularly enjoyed lampooning game shows, a habit that would continue on *Sesame Street.*

One of Jim's most ambitious pieces, however, was a skit he called "Visual Thinking," a sketch that reflected Jim's growing mastery of the television medium, his love of animation, and his increasing fascination with the workings of the mind and imagination. As the sketch opens, Kermit tells Harry he's learning to visualize his thoughts—and to make the point, he says the letter Q, then looks up to watch as the letter writes itself in the air over his head. "You're a beginner," responds Harry. "I'm an old hand at this stuff. Watch!"— and on cue, an animated stopwatch appears over Harry's head. As the skit progresses, Harry talks about music—as musical notes dot themselves across the screen—then scats for a bit, creating animated scribbles that Harry erases by scatting backward. But when Harry scats again—and then can't recall what he said well enough to say it backward—more and more scrawls make their way across the screen, eventually whiting out the entire space as Kermit calls weakly for help. In his script for the piece, Jim was careful to indicate where on the screen all the effects were located, as well as their length of time down to the fraction of a second, ensuring he could have his characters respond perfectly to the on-screen animation. The bit worked perfectly, and Jim would keep it in the routine for several years—and it, too, would show up in a slightly modified form on *Sesame Street.*

It was obvious to anyone watching *Sam and Friends* that Jim and Jane were having fun—so much fun, in fact, that their enormous success was almost incidental to them. Interviewing the Hensons for *The Christian Science Monitor* in late 1959, reporter Ursula Keller speculated that Jane and Jim had earned over $100,000 in 1959—nearly three quarters of a million dollars today, and an enormous sum for a young man not yet even in his mid-twenties. But Jane bristled at such talk. "Money cannot measure success or happiness," she told Keller matter-of-factly. Those who knew the young couple at the time weren't surprised by their attitude toward the material. "My impression of [Jim] and his wife was that they were totally unspoiled by their success," one friend remarked. "He was just so simple, so unspoiled. They were so unimpressed with themselves."

That's not to say Jim didn't have his moments of flashy, well-deserved pride. In May 1960, he graduated from the University of Maryland with a degree in home economics. At this point in his career, a college degree was probably not a requirement for life after graduation, but Jim clearly valued education, and had returned to school after his extended absence, completing his degree in six years. Jim was rightly very proud of the accomplishment, and attended his graduation driving a Rolls-Royce Silver Cloud he had purchased used for a dizzying $5,000. But there was something else even more wonderful that spring—something he was even prouder of: in early May, Jane had given birth to their first child, Lisa Marie Henson.

Two months after graduation, with eight-week-old Lisa in tow, Jim and Jane piled into the Rolls-Royce and drove to Detroit to attend the 1960 Puppeteers of America convention. The decision to make a thousand-mile round-trip drive with an infant says much about Jim's newly realized commitment to his chosen profession. He had immersed himself in the company of puppeteers while in Europe, but lacking Europe's widespread devotion to the craft in the United States, Jim was going to have to actively seek out those who shared his passion. That meant joining the Puppeteers of America, an organization founded in 1936 to, among other things, "encourage and promote puppetry as a means of communication, an extension of human expression, and as a performing Art." That was just the sort of enthusiasm Jim could get behind.

The convention turned out to be everything Jim hoped it would be, with performances of every type of puppetry and the opportu-

nity to talk with every kind of puppeteer. He even struck up a friendship with the one puppeteer with whom he probably had the most in
common, fellow TV performer Burr Tillstrom, who was attending
the convention with his talented puppet builder, Don Sahlin. Besides
puppetry, Tillstrom and Jim had other interests in common, too—
both had a background in Christian Science—but even with their
different approaches to humor—where Tillstrom was pensive, Jim
was explosive—Tillstrom would turn out to have the same impish
streak as Jim. One afternoon, with only a little prodding from Tillstrom, the two puppeteers drove through the streets of Detroit in
Jim's Rolls-Royce, with Jim enthusiastically working Kermit through
the car's sunroof while Tillstrom drove, barely able to contain his
laughter. Jane—who admits to hiding in the backseat—could only
shake her head in mock disbelief. "What with the Rolls and the new
baby," she said later, "we made quite an impression—without particularly intending to." It was clear to Tillstrom he had a comrade in
arms, just as silly, and just as talented, as he was.

It was through Tillstrom that Jim would make the acquaintance
of another gentleman who shared their devilish sense of humor—
although by his own admission, *gentleman* was probably not the
right term to describe twenty-nine-year-old talent agent Bernie Brillstein. *Player* was more like it.

The son of Russian Jewish immigrants and nephew of a vaude-
villian, the streetwise, ambitious Brillstein had leapfrogged his way
up the ladder at the renowned William Morris Agency, moving in five
short years from the mailroom to the publicity department to the
head of the commercial office. A bear of a man with a large libido
and an even bigger taste for talent, Brillstein was also a master of the
art of the deal. He was accustomed to working hard for his clients
and determined never to take no for an answer. Brillstein would
eventually become one of the most powerful and respected agents,
managers, and producers in show business, with an A-list roster of
celebrity clients, including, it seemed, nearly the entire cast of *Saturday Night Live.*

In 1960, however, as head of William Morris's commercial office,
his job was recruiting and representing talent for television commercials. Brillstein, an early fan of television, quickly put to rest the

showbiz aphorism that television commercials were for has-beens or the hard up, assembling a stable of top-tier clients like Zsa Zsa Gabor, Harpo Marx . . . and Burr Tillstrom. At the Detroit puppetry convention, Jim mentioned to Tillstrom that he, too, was looking for an agent—that it was becoming increasingly difficult to secure bookings on the variety show circuit, and that an agent was the best way to get a foot in the door. Sometime later, Tillstrom phoned Brillstein in New York and asked if he would do him a favor and meet with a puppeteer friend of his.

Brillstein groaned. "Burr, give me a break, will ya please?" the agent said. "I love you . . . but you're one in a million. I'm into nightclub comedians and comedy. I don't really want to handle puppeteers."

Tillstrom was persistent. "Bernie, this guy's something special, and he's a really nice guy."

"I didn't want to," Brillstein said later, "but I said okay."

Jim diligently made the trip to New York where he was waved into Brillstein's office—and Brillstein would never forget his first impression of twenty-three-year-old Jim Henson. "In walked this guy who looked like a cross between Abe Lincoln and Jesus," Brillstein recalled. "He was so gentle and unpretentious that he never spoke above a whisper." Jim had brought with him a box of Muppets and proceeded to put on a show for Brillstein. "It was magic," Brillstein said forty years later, still amazed at the performance:

> When Jim performed, I *understood* it. I got it. . . . I don't know what I saw in him, but I saw something. I realize that at first, before we became close friends, Jim appealed to my perverse sense of humor. *Sesame Street,* which was still a few years off, was for kids, but Henson was not a kids' act. He was hip and slightly dark. He had cute little creations—and he liked to blow them up.

Shortly after Jim left the office, Brillstein's phone rang. "Bernie," his boss asked from the other end, "have you heard of Jim Henson and the Muppets?" Brillstein roared with laughter. "Heard of him?" Brillstein howled. "I just signed him!" (While Brillstein liked to claim that the two of them never entered into a formal agreement, doing business solely on the strength of a handshake, the two did, in fact, sign a contract.)

That summer, the Muppets made their first appearance on Dave Garroway's *Today* show, with Jim and Jane broadcasting on a live feed from WRC studios while Garroway chatted with them from New York. Jim was still an enormous fan of variety shows like *Today* and had performed on enough of them by now that he felt certain he could write and produce a variety show of his own—one that would allow him to develop his own characters, write longer sketches, and indulge in a bit of chaos every once in a while. He was also certain that the Muppets could keep a viewer's attention for longer than just five-minute segments. As Jim saw it, the Muppets could more than hold their own for a full half hour—they could even headline their own show. It was a dream Jim would pursue for more than fifteen years.

With this in mind, Jim began sketching ideas for a Muppet variety show he called *Zoocus*—a melding of *zoo* and *circus*—developing characters that reflected his own interests and sense of humor. There was Carburetor Jones, a streamlined Muppet with flying hair who shared Jim's love of cars, and a character known simply as the Cat, who personified Jim's interest in jazz culture and shared Harry the Hipster's beatnik syntax. And then there was a favorite character type of Jim's: the stuffed shirt academic who doesn't get the joke. "Acts as oracle to whom others ask questions," Jim wrote of a character called the Philosopher. "Quotes quotes, usually wrong or inappropriate, doesn't know anything practical."

Elements of *Zoocus* would show up later on *The Muppet Show*, with Dr. Teeth as a hipper descendant of the Cat, and Sam the Eagle channeling the Philosopher in his plea for higher culture. Just as interesting, even in 1960, Jim had a clear vision of the stage design that, in many ways, directly influenced the set he designed for *The Muppet Show* in 1976. Already there were the kinds of colonnades through which the Muppets would appear in *The Muppet Show*'s opening credits, and a wall of windows of varying heights where humans could interact with puppets.

Zoocus would never move beyond the pages of Jim's notebooks, most likely due to a lack of time to pursue the project. Time, in fact, was on Jim's mind more and more—the ticking clock, that feeling of disappearing time, that had seemed to haunt Jim immediately following his brother's death, was suddenly ticking again. Still performing two, sometimes three shows a day, making live appearances, and now with his responsibilities as a husband and new father, there were days when Jim likely wondered if there would ever be time enough to do all the things he wanted to do—time enough to turn the ideas into reality. Typically, Jim took his own inner strife and turned it into art.

In late 1959, Jim had mentioned in an interview with *The Christian Science Monitor* that he had been thinking about starting a recording company. In 1960, perhaps as a dry run, Jim recorded a single for Signature Records featuring two songs he had written, "Tick-Tock Sick" and "The Countryside." Both allowed Jim to indulge his love of jazz and comedy records—and "Tick-Tock Sick" in particular gave Jim an opportunity to playfully comment on his own busy state of mind in busy 1960.

Jim performed "Tick-Tock Sick" in a whispery, hepcat style reminiscent of a beatnik poet at an open mike in a coffeehouse, singing over a walking bass line and the sound of a steadily ticking clock. The song starts off as a celebration of the sound of a ticking grandfather clock, but becomes a more sinister set of "calculated clickings" as more and more clocks measure out the days with their ticking. Finally, an alarm clock clangs loudly, and Jim chucks it out the window, then cathartically smashes the rest of his clocks, vowing never to let the rhythm of his life be determined by the ticking and ringing of clocks. For the twenty-three-year-old Jim, while time could never be truly conquered, it could at least be controlled by slowing down, getting away from deadlines from time to time, and savoring the simpler things. It was advice he would strive to live by— successfully, for the most part—for the rest of his life.

While Jim may have been vowing in "Tick-Tock Sick" to slow down, that would have to wait—for he was now busier than ever. *Sam and Friends* was at the height of its popularity, and WRC was wisely using Sam prominently in its promotional materials for the channel's evening lineup. "Sam is back!" crowed WRC in a September 1960 ad in *The Washington Post*, as it announced a time change for its newscast, with Sam's shocked face staring out at readers.

There were more appearances on the *Today* show—along with countless other appearances on nearly every other variety or talk show of the day—with Jim and Jane again piped in to Dave Garroway's New York studio on a live feed from WRC in Washington. In one notable *Today* show appearance—in which Garroway introduced Jim and Jane as "two of the most interesting people ever"— Jim and Jane gave two particularly spirited performances. The first had Kermit and a vaguely-humanoid Muppet named Chicken Liver lip-synching to "Yes, We Have No Bananas," with Jim as Kermit turning in a rollicking and very convincing banjo solo, while Jane enthusiastically performed Chicken Liver pounding away on an old piano. The next piece was one of their regular crowd-pleasers—Jim had a growing selection of proven Muppet performances he would use regularly—performing to Louis Prima and Keely Smith's "That Old Black Magic," with Kermit vamping it up in a dark wig and Sam miming to the lead vocal. It was another whopping success.

In early 1961, Jane learned she was pregnant with their second child. Jim was delighted—and he and Jane decided the time was right to make a difficult but crucial decision: following the birth of their next child, Jane would retire from performing. For now, she would remain an active performer for as long as she could—and would always stay involved with the company even as she devoted herself nearly full-time to the children. But with the Muppets showing no signs of waning in popularity—and Jim increasingly anxious to expand into other media—Jim was going to need help sooner rather than later.

That summer, Jim, one-year-old Lisa, and a very pregnant Jane made the trip to the Puppeteers of America convention in Asilomar, California, driving out this time in a much more comfortable but significantly less flashy station wagon. While Jim didn't necessarily regard this as a recruiting trip, he was always interested in watching others perform and making contacts. His trip to the Detroit convention had sparked a professional friendship with Burr Tillstrom and led him to Bernie Brillstein. The journey to California, however, would mark the beginning of an even more extraordinary relationship.

Arriving at the convention, Jim immediately attached himself to

Mike Oznowicz and his wife, Frances, two talented performers he had met briefly at the Detroit convention in 1960. The Dutch-born Oznowicz had fled Nazi-occupied Europe with his family in the late 1930s, taking refuge first in North Africa and then England, where Frances bore two sons—her second, Frank Richard Oznowicz, would be born in Hereford, England, on May 25, 1944—before immigrating to the United States in 1951. Arriving in New York, Oznowicz spent his last dollar putting his pregnant wife and two sons safely on the train for their new home in Montana, where the family who had sponsored their immigration were waiting, then hitchhiked the rest of the way himself. After a short stay in Montana, the family moved to Oakland, California, living briefly in an attic until Mike found employment as a window dresser for women's apparel stores. A lifelong puppetry enthusiast, Mike and his wife had become active members of the Puppeteers of America and were, in Jim's opinion, "marvelous, very outgoing" people and terrific performers.

Jim was just as intrigued by their son Frank, now a quietly intense teenager approaching his senior year in high school, and already a gifted performer of marionettes. But despite his talent, for the young Frank Oznowicz—he would later shorten it to Oz—puppetry was only a hobby, and an almost incidental one at that, placing a distant third behind girls and sports. "I never wanted to be a puppeteer," Oz said. Still, it was difficult to ignore puppetry in the Oznowicz home—"Our house was like a salon for puppeteers and performers," Oz said later—and by his own admission he had "latched on to" puppetry both as a way of pleasing his parents and to raise money for a planned trip to Europe. At age fourteen, then, he had joined Lettie Schubert's traveling Vagabond Puppets team at the Oakland Recreation Department, then performed regularly—and without pay—at Fairyland Amusement Park, where he struck up a friendship with a young man named Jerry Juhl, five years his senior, and an equally talented performer who had lately become a regular in the Oznowicz home "salon."

Oz had come to the Asilomar convention mainly to perform with Juhl and another Vagabond puppeteer in a show Juhl had written called *The Witch Who Stole Thursday;* he also wanted to participate in a talent contest, which, predictably, he won. While his parents had met Jim in Detroit a year earlier, Oz knew nothing about him, though he was slightly familiar with the Muppets, thanks to the Wilkins and Wontkins commercials Jim had produced for the regional carbonated drink CalSo. Those ads had impressed him, Oz remembered, because "they weren't like anything else!" When he finally met Jim in person, Oz couldn't help but be enchanted by the soft-spoken twenty-four-year-old who could suddenly become a manic force of nature once a puppet was placed in his hands. "He was this very quiet, shy guy," Oz said, "who did these absolutely fucking amazing puppets that were totally brand new and fresh, that had never been done before."

Once in Jim's presence, it was easy to get caught up in the excitement, and Oz—who admitted that puppetry was a good way for a self-described "shy, self-effacing boy" to express himself—performed several short routines with his father, including a sketch called "Sunday Painter," in which a painter sets out to paint a picture of an uncooperative flower, which sags and rights itself, much to the painter's frustration. Afterward, Jim pulled Oz aside to discuss the performance. "He said, 'The ending is weak!'" Oz recalled, still laughing at the comment five decades later. "That was very Jim. My ending was a bit arty, whereas Jim liked things to be blown up or eaten!"

Despite the ending, Jim was impressed enough with the young man's skills to discuss with Mike and Frances Oznowicz the possibility of their son coming back east to join him at Muppets, Inc. But Oz was barely seventeen, and still in high school. "He was really still at home and not ready to come east," Jim remembered, "but we talked about it as an idea." And with that idea, a seed had been planted—one that would grow and blossom into one of the finest, and funniest, creative and productive partnerships in entertainment.

Years later, Jim would admit that there were moments in his life when he felt that "somebody or something" was guiding him. This felt like one of those moments—and he would later chalk up his lifelong partnership with Frank Oz to a fortunate bit of serendipity. "I think it was an accident," Jim said years later. "I don't think I was consciously looking for somebody." Instead, somebody or something had found them for each other. Oz might have agreed: it was only by chance that he had even been at the convention in the first place. "I never used to go to [puppetry conventions] ever . . . except for this one I went to when I was seventeen years old, and Jim happened to be there."

For now, Oz would remain in California to finish high school. But Oz thought he knew someone else who might work well with Jim, and recommended Jim speak to his fellow Vagabond puppeteer, Jerry Juhl.

Juhl, unlike Oz, *did* want to be a puppeteer. Born Jerome Ravn Juhl in St. Paul, Minnesota, the twenty-one-year-old Juhl had been building and performing puppets since the age of eleven—and after moving to Menlo Park, California, had founded the Menlo Marionettes while still in high school. After graduating from San Jose State College with a degree in speech and drama, he had joined, then headed, the Vagabond Puppets—where he tapped the young Frank Oz as his assistant—and co-created and performed the puppet Pup on the local children's television show *Sylvie and Pup.* With his thick glasses and neatly coiffed hair, Juhl looked more like an insurance salesman than a puppeteer. But behind the businesslike demeanor was a wit as rapier sharp as Jim's, and the same sense of playful fun.

Juhl was familiar with the Muppets through their various television appearances, and found their unpredictable edge strangely fascinating. "The Muppets already had a cult following," Juhl said, "with a reputation for bizarre, slightly dangerous comedy." Juhl was unprepared, then, for his first glimpse of the man responsible for such outlandish humor. "Jim seemed so utterly *normal*," Juhl recalled. "He had driven across the country in a shiny new station wagon with his wife, Jane, and baby Lisa. They looked as average and suburban as actors in a Chevrolet commercial."

Jim invited Juhl out to the parking lot where he had parked his station wagon with the large black box of Muppets in the back. In a scene that would have been familiar to Bernie Brillstein, Jim opened the box, took out his Muppets one by one, and began to perform. And like Brillstein, Juhl never forgot what he saw that afternoon:

The things he brought out of that box seemed to me to be magical presences, like totems, but funnier. An angry creature whose whole body was a rounded triangle; a purple skull named Yorick; a green froglike thing. One after another, Jim pulled them from the box, put them on his hand and brought them to life. Who was this Henson guy? These things weren't puppets—not as I had ever seen or defined them.

Juhl was speechless. "This guy was like a sailor who had studied the compass and found that there was a fifth direction in which one could sail." There was no doubt in his mind as to his decision. "When he offered me a berth on that ship, I signed on," making Juhl the first official full-time employee of Muppets, Inc.

Shortly after returning to Maryland in August, Jane gave birth to their second child, Cheryl. The newly hired Jerry Juhl took over Jane's performing duties on *Sam and Friends,* which was still one of WRC's most popular programs after more than six years. Jim, however, was again growing tired of the five-minutes-twice-a-day routine of *Sam and Friends.* The show had succeeded beyond his wildest dreams—but Jim was dreaming even wilder now, and was looking for opportunities to try something new.

He would have his chance sooner than expected, thanks to a fortuitous invitation from the U.S. Department of Agriculture—an invitation so out of the blue that it may have come about, in part, through Paul Henson's contacts inside the USDA. In mid-November 1961, the USDA would be hosting a weeklong U.S. Food Fair in Hamburg, Germany—part of the U.S. government's effort to "develop and expand the sale and use of U.S. foods and agriculture products and commodities" throughout Europe—and fair officials were wondering if Jim, and *Sam and Friends,* might be interested in providing entertainment at one of the pavilions.

Jim agreed to participate—but not with *Sam and Friends.* For Jim, this was the opportunity he had been looking for to try something different—and, better yet, it could be done far away from a home crowd that still expected Sam and Kermit to lip-synch to Stan Freberg records. He and Juhl set to work writing a number of skits that would allow them to showcase several new kinds of puppets, and even tapped the brilliant young beat comedian Del Close—

whose work Jim was likely familiar with through Close's 1959 comedy record *How to Speak Hip*—to write a sketch for the show. If the Hamburg fair was a trial run for the next stage of Muppets, Inc., Jim was taking the opportunity seriously, diligently typing up a formal presentation for government officials, renewing his passport, and corresponding politely with USDA employees who were convinced they knew better than Jim what was funny. For Jim, it wasn't just about being funny; it was also about gauging the audience's response to new kinds of puppetry and performances and figuring out what worked and what didn't. "If . . . one or two of these bits either doesn't live up to expectations, or doesn't perform well with the audiences," Jim assured his hosts, "I will withdraw that particular bit and double up one of the others."

One of the first sketches presented in Hamburg was "The Drill Team," featuring, as Jim explained, "a rather ingenious set of mechanical puppets"—a military drill team made of wood, each with moving arms and painted, smiling faces, mounted to a rolling rack so the figures would move in unison. The piece—which mainly involved their commanding officer barking inarticulate orders as he put the drill team through their moves—was full of little surprises: the drill team fired guns that emitted smoke—usually just powder blown through a straw—and when at the end of the skit the team trained its fire on their captain, the figure's nose lit up. But the audience responded with only polite enthusiasm. While Jim would haul the routine out from time to time over the next few years, he would eventually shelve it.

Much better received was "The Chef's Salad," an improv piece featuring Omar as an inattentive chef who crazily cuts up food—and everything else—as he prepares a salad. For the first time, Jim performed with a "live hand" puppet, in which the main puppeteer performs the puppet's mouth and inserts his other hand—usually the left, since most right-handed puppeteers prefer to operate the character's mouth with their dominant hand—into the puppet's left glove hand. Meanwhile, a second performer, in this case Juhl, operates the puppet's right hand. This setup requires a great deal of coordination to ensure the puppeteers work seamlessly—the right hand needs to know almost instinctively what the left hand is up to—but when done well, it allows the puppet to handle objects deftly and turn in a much more believable performance. In this case, Jim and Juhl performed the character flawlessly, with Jim ranting in mock German as they hurled cheese and eggs into a bowl, blew Omar's nose into a handkerchief—which was thrown in the bowl as well—then stirred the mix with gusto. Jim still couldn't resist ending the sketch in true Muppet fashion—the concoction exploded in Omar's face—and the crowd roared its approval. The piece would stay, and fifteen years later, Jim would use almost exactly the same setup—all the way down to the mock foreign dialect—for *The Muppet Show*'s Swedish Chef.

One of the most ambitious and weirdly odd pieces was a lip-synch performance to Marlene Dietrich's "Time on My Hands," performed by a new puppet Jim called Limbo the Floating Face. Limbo, as Jim described it, was "a very flexible face"—mostly just a mouth and eyes—performed by tugging on an elaborate rigging of nearly invisible fish line at the bottom of a frame that caused the foam rubber mouth to open and close and the eyes to widen or crinkle shut. It was a complicated puppet, and Jim was proud of it, calling it "revolutionary." The Hamburg crowd greeted the performance warmly, though with some confusion—but Jim was pleased with it and would perform variations on the piece for the next decade, unveiling it on talk shows and, in an ambitious computer-animated form, on *Sesame Street*.

The USDA was thrilled with Jim and Jerry's performance, hailing it as "a spectacular feat of entertainment," and Jim must have been pleased as his plane touched down in New York at the end of November. For the most part, the performances had been a departure from his more familiar style of Muppets, but the crowd had responded favorably. With some more work, he could start introducing these more experimental forms of puppetry in front of American audiences.

First, however, it was time to close up shop on *Sam and Friends*. *Sam* would make his exit quite literally with a bang, as the final episode—broadcast at 11:25 on Friday, December 15, 1961—would conclude with what was becoming a Muppet kind of ending, with the *Sam and Friends* set exploding and falling to pieces around the cast.

There was an uproar from *Sam*'s fans over its demise, but Jim was too busy to notice. In February 1962, he and Jerry Juhl headed for Europe again, this time to take part in a "Green Week" show in Berlin, hosted by the U.S. Information Agency. Jim chose to perform many of the same skits he and Juhl had used in the Hamburg show, with one major addition: he was determined, after the lukewarm reception of the "Drill Team" piece in Hamburg, to come up with a mechanical puppet performance that worked.

He succeeded, for the most part, because the new performance was so funny. Lampooning "the average European impression of the average American tourist," Jim's new mechanical puppets were based on the stereotype of the ugly American, featuring a cigar-chomping loudmouth in a Hawaiian shirt who demands he be sold one of the Alps so he can build a hotel, and an abrasive, gum-smacking woman who patronizingly advises audiences to always learn a few words in a foreign language "to make the natives feel more at home." The audience loved it, and Jim went home satisfied with his early experiment in animatronics—a field he would come to redefine decades later in his highly successful and always innovative Creature Shop.

In June 1962, Jim and his team—including Jane, Jerry Juhl, and Bobby Payne—traveled by train to Atlanta, Georgia, to tape a half-hour pilot Jim and Juhl had written, called *Tales of the Tinkerdee*. *Tinkerdee* was Jim's opportunity to work with the conceits of folklore and fairy tales, still of great interest to him since his visit to Europe, and to put to work—in a pared-down manner—some of the "overcomplicated" storytelling elements of the unrealized *Hansel and Gretel* project. Instead of adapting an existing story, however, *Tinkerdee* allowed Jim to create his own magical kingdom, populate it with his own characters, and tell a story in his own unique madcap style without the need to be deferential to source material. It would also be a chance to introduce a number of live hand Muppets, the first Jim would use in an American production following their successful Hamburg debut.

The plot of *Tinkerdee* revolves around King Goshposh and his plans to throw a birthday party for his daughter, Princess Gwendolinda, and the parallel efforts of Taminella Grinderfall, "the witchiest witch of all," to crash the party, conk the princess on the head, and make off with the gifts. With the help of Charlie the Ogre, Taminella uses a variety of disguises to infiltrate the castle, where she is finally caught and imprisoned by the king. "It was really just half-an-hour of one-line jokes," said Juhl later. "We'd done those kind of gags before, on *Sam and Friends* . . . but this was the first time we'd stretched them to fill thirty minutes."

Stretched was a rather unfair assessment, for *Tinkerdee* is a gal-lopingly fast-paced piece. At no time does the camera linger or the pace sag, and with only six speaking characters, Jim makes all their moments count. Jim's King Goshposh is the kind of clueless author-ity figure Jim loved to play, dispensing nuggets of dopey advice while gnawing on a cigar (in a masterful bit of puppet design and crafts-manship, the cigar seeped real smoke). Jim himself even makes a cameo appearance, of sorts, as Taminella's dimwitted sidekick, Charlie the Ogre, visible only from the waist down, his bare legs spattered with mud.

Serving as *Tinkerdee*'s narrator and Greek chorus is Kermit, dressed as a minstrel and strumming a lute. "You'd see him on little grassy knolls singing the narration we had written in the form of quatrains and god-awful puns and hideous rhymes," said Juhl. More significantly, with his crenulated minstrel collar on, Kermit suddenly looks every inch a frog—or close enough so that from here on out it would be a no-brainer to definitively call him one. "We frogified him," Jim said later, only slightly lamenting the loss of the abstrac-tion. "He just slowly became a frog."

Despite the more nimble live hand Muppets, rock-solid perfor-mances, and some laugh-out-loud moments (typically, Jim couldn't resist ending the episode with a pie in the face), *Tales of the Tin-kerdee* failed to pique the interest of any TV network. Perhaps the humor was too similar to *Rocky and Bullwinkle*—an admitted influence—for executives to fully appreciate its originality. More likely, the networks simply didn't share Jim's confidence that the Muppets could hold their own for thirty minutes—or, barring that, attract a demographically desirable audience. While Jim had never billed himself as a kids' act, network suits simply couldn't see puppets as anything but entertainment for children, in spite of Jim's hard work to the contrary. Just as *The Flintstones*—or, later, *The Simpsons*—would demonstrate that cartoons could transcend a stereotypically young audience and hold their own with adult viewers, so, too, would Jim have to decisively prove that the Muppets could attract and hold a decidedly more grown-up audience.

In less than a year, Jim would make his point—and the Muppets would become a national phenomenon. But it would be a dog, not a frog, who would lead the way.

CHAPTER FIVE

A CRAZY LITTLE BAND

1962–1969

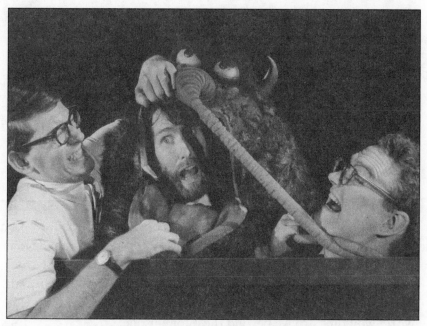

Frank Oz, Jim, and Jerry Juhl wrestle with Muppet monster Big V.

IN JUNE 1962, AROUND THE TIME JIM WAS COMPLETING WORK ON THE *Tinkerdee* pilot in Atlanta, the Puppeteers of America—this time holding its annual festival in Oxford, Ohio—announced that it had elected Jim Henson as president of the organization. That made Jim, at twenty-five, the youngest performer to hold the position. Considering both his youth and the fact that he had been a member of the organization for only a little more than two years, Jim's election as its leader says much about his increasing importance and influence on puppetry.

To Jerry Juhl and other puppeteers who understood how far Jim had advanced their craft beyond traditional puppetry, Jim's ascension within their ranks was no surprise. "For puppeteers, [watching the Muppets] was just absolutely startling," Juhl said. "[They were] puppets that didn't look like puppets had ever looked. It was just phenomenal. . . . It was the mobility of the faces, and the total abstraction of them."

While puppeteers may have appreciated how different and sophisticated the Muppets were, television executives didn't. The lack of interest in *Tinkerdee,* while disappointing, was, Jim thought, typical of those who didn't understand the craft. "When you try to sell anyone on puppets, it's the old problem," he told the *New York Post.* "They automatically say, 'Puppets are for kids.'"

While network executives may not have been willing to greenlight a regular Muppet television show, booking agents were still more than happy to have the Muppets appear on variety and talk shows. In late spring, the Muppets were asked to be regulars on *Mad, Mad World,* a new sketch show satirizing news and current events, and co-written by Larry Gelbart, whose *A Funny Thing Happened on the Way to the Forum* had just opened on Broadway. On paper, it seemed it couldn't miss, and Jim and Jerry Juhl gamely performed the Limbo bit, as well as "Visual Thinking." But the show sagged when the Muppets weren't on-screen, bogging down in stale political humor and *faux* man-on-the-street interviews. *Mad, Mad World* wouldn't survive beyond the pilot episode.

A better opportunity began in the fall, when the Muppets began appearing regularly on the *Today* show, with Jim and Jerry Juhl making the trip from Washington to New York at a pace of about once a week to be ready for the 7:00 A.M. broadcast. Apart from the more familiar sketches—there was "Visual Thinking," as well as variations on the "Chef's Salad" piece—Jim was anxious to introduce skits featuring characters from *Tinkerdee.* He was proud of the advances he had made with live hand puppets, and considered the Taminella Grinderfall Muppet a genuine breakthrough. "We have a witch who is delightful," Jim said of Taminella. "The gestures and expressions she can get are wonderful. I consider her probably our best character to date." So pleased was Jim with the live hand performances, in fact, that he would take the first available opportunity to perform one for a commercial.

In late 1962, Jim was approached by Ralph Freeman, an ad man for the James Lovick & Company advertising agency of Toronto, about putting together a series of Purina Dog Chow commercials for Canadian television. While Purina wanted its ads to have the same edge as the Wilkins coffee commercials, it didn't want the ads to feature Wilkins and Wontkins. Instead, Freeman helpfully passed along several ideas from Purina, most featuring two dogs bantering about Purina Dog Chow. Jim likely groaned at the material from Purina—here was someone trying to tell him how to be funny again—but agreed to produce seven commercials for Purina, and set to work designing new characters for the ads.

In his sketchbook, Jim drew several different kinds of dogs, finally deciding that the two he liked best were a small dog with a pointy nose and fluffy ears, and a larger one with a round head, wide mouth, floppy ears, and wide eyes. The smaller dog, in a nod to the Sherlock Holmes story, Jim decided to name Baskerville. As for the other, Jim had written up a list of possible names—Barkley, Woofington, Howlington, Boundwell—but most of those were a mouthful. A better name, it seemed, was signed at the bottom of each letter Jim received from his contact at the Lovick advertising agency: Ralph Freeman. Ralph it would be, then—or Rowlf, as Jim would later spell it—much to the delight of the Lovick firm.

For the first time, Jim decided not to build his Muppet himself, handing the character sketches off instead to Burr Tillstrom's master puppet builder, thirty-four-year-old Don Sahlin, whom Jim had met at the Puppeteers of America convention in Detroit in 1960. Using Jim's sketches, Sahlin drew his own design for Rowlf, noting the height and relative scales of the puppet, then set to work building the puppet. Sahlin—a talented marionettist and puppeteer who had also created special effects for films like *Tom Thumb* and *The Time Machine*—had a remarkable ability to translate Jim's sketches into three dimensions, a bit of artistic symbiosis Jim appreciated. "I would generally do a little scribble on a scrap of paper, which Don would regard with a certain reverence as being the 'essence' which he was working toward," said Jim. "Don had a very simple way of working—reducing all nonessential things and honing in on what was important."

In particular, Sahlin understood—as did Jim—that the place-

ment of the eyes was critical. "That single decision seemed to finalize the character more than anything else," Jim said later. Part of the
trick was to pay careful attention to an area Sahlin came to call
"The Magic Triangle"—the zone defined by the relative position of
the character's eyes to its nose and mouth. So important were the
eyes, in fact, that Sahlin would always ask that Jim be present when
he placed any character's eyes. "He always wanted me there, to make
sure it was right for both of us, making sure the eyes had a point of
focus," Jim said. "Because without that, you had no character."

The Ralph/Rowlf Muppet that Sahlin delivered to Jim definitely
had character—a beautifully constructed, live hand puppet that almost magically seemed to embody Jim's initial sketches. He was also
a deceptively simple puppet, not much more than the wide mouth,
floppy ears, and wide eyes Jim had drawn—and yet something in
Sahlin's nearly abstract design gave Rowlf an expressiveness, a twinkle that Jim would spark to life. Impressed, Jim quickly hired Sahlin
as the Muppets' chief designer and puppet builder, where his sense
of expressive abstraction—as well as his ability to sew an almost invisible seam that came to be known as "the Henson Stitch"—would
define the look of the Muppets for more than a decade. Indeed, it
was Sahlin, Jim said, who "had more to do with the basic style that
people think of as the Muppets than anybody else."

Jim billed Purina $1,500 for the costs of building Rowlf and
Baskerville, then shot seven quick commercials for the company. Bernie Brillstein later recalled—though he was never certain if the offer
came from Purina or another client—that Jim was offered $100,000
for the company to own Rowlf outright. Brillstein nearly leapt at the
offer, but Jim immediately squashed the deal. "Bernie," warned Jim,
"*never sell anything I own.*" "He knew then," said Brillstein. "He
has this whole business side. He had these *sides* to him that were so
complex, and when I least thought he'd understand something, he
understood it better than I did. So he taught me a long time ago,
don't sell what you create." (Frank Oz thought Jim's determination
in this regard was rooted in his business dealings with the Wilkins
company, where Jim had often struggled—not always successfully—
to maintain clear ownership, and marketing, of his characters.) With
Rowlf still safely in Jim's ownership, work was completed on the

commercials and Rowlf, said Jim, was "tossed into a cupboard with a dozen other puppets and nearly forgotten." "We were never told whether the commercials sold the dog food or not," Jim said with a shrug, then—quite literally—moved on.

On Wednesday, January 23, 1963, a moving truck pulled away from the Henson home in Bethesda, bound for New York City. The family—and the Muppets—were moving to New York, a decision that had prompted little discussion or hesitation on Jim's part. "Anyone in this business of television has to live in Los Angeles or New York," said Jim plainly.

The Hensons and Juhl began their drive to New York later that afternoon, with Jim and Jane traveling with the kids in the station wagon and Juhl driving Jim's newest sports car, a glimmering Porsche. It was so bitterly cold that the rear window of the Porsche shattered, leaving Juhl shivering at the wheel and coming down with the flu as he drove. Eventually the car broke down, stranding Juhl at a roadside hotel.

While Juhl was marooned, Jim and Jane managed to continue driving through the night toward their new apartment, arriving in Manhattan around 5:00 A.M. The Muppets were scheduled to make an appearance on the *Today* show that same morning—and rather than cancel or reschedule after the exhausting drive, Jim and Jane simply headed to the NBC studios at 30 Rockefeller Center, arriving just in time to rehearse and perform two pieces live—and without Juhl. It was chaos, but it was "totally typical of the way Jim worked," laughed Juhl. "He was moving his entire family, his entire life, *and me,* from Maryland to the middle of New York City. His whole life [was] in total upheaval." Yet, Jim's attitude, said Juhl, was "we might as well do the *Today* show!"

The Hensons moved to Beekman Place on Manhattan's East Side, taking up residence on the eleventh floor of the same "wonderful old apartment building" as Burr Tillstrom, who had helped them find the place. While it had two good-sized bedrooms and large living spaces, it actually wasn't much bigger than their place in Bethesda. But with its stern facade and an apartment that afforded spectacular views of the city, it was definitely more exciting and glamorous than Maryland. The Hensons were moving up.

So were the Muppets. At the same time, Jim set up headquarters for Muppets, Inc. just around the corner from the Beekman Place apartment, renting out the second floor of a townhouse at 303 East 53rd Street, above a trendy nightclub called Chuck's Composite. In the small front room overlooking 53rd Street, Jim set up a workshop for Don Sahlin—who officially began his employment with the Muppets in February 1963—cramming Don's sewing table and workbench alongside Jim's animation stand. As a final touch typical of both Jim and Sahlin, an oversized version of Yorick gaped out the window at the street below.

In the main room, just across from the front door, sat Jerry Juhl at a desk next to the Ampex tape machine, on which Jim would still prerecord some voice tracks for Muppet performances. Against the opposite wall was a long workbench and a small closet door on which Jim hung a dartboard—and, above that, a light-up, papier-mâché moose head. In the back corner, directly in front of the sliding glass door that led out to the rear balcony, Jim set up his desk, with a big black padded Eames chair and matching ottoman. "[Our] spaces never looked like offices," Juhl said. "We did it up as a kind of lovely, pleasant living room."

For the next few months, Jim and Juhl continued their regular routine of weekly *Today* show performances and filming more explosive coffee commercials, even as Jim—actively embracing his role as president of Puppeteers of America—presided over the organization's annual festival in Hurleyville, New York. Following a family vacation to the Olympic Peninsula near Seattle in July, Jim returned to New York in early August to hire a secretary to handle correspondence and answer the phone. He also readied a space in the offices for another performer he had recently hired: nineteen-year-old Frank Oz, who had graduated from high school in Oakland in late spring.

Following Oz's graduation, Jim had called Mike and Frances Oznowicz to have a "very serious" conversation about their son moving to New York to join the Muppets. "Having your young son move across the country . . . I mean, they knew I wasn't coming back. It had to be hard," Oz said. "But my parents knew Jim. They knew he was a good person." And so the Oznowiczes had said yes—and in August 1963, Frank Oz formally joined the Muppets, bounding up the narrow stairway at the townhouse on 53rd Street and entering the living-room-like space that would change his life. "This is the room where Jim, wearing his bright flowered ties and speaking just above a whisper, would hold meetings with clients," Oz recalled fondly. "This is where Jim and I and Don and Jerry would hear that Kennedy had been shot. This is where we'd eat the deli sandwiches with those funny-tasting East Coast pickles. For the kid from Oakland, everything here was new and strange and exciting and adult."

While the kid from Oakland had committed to moving to New York to work, he was hired at first only part-time, mostly performing Wontkins in commercials, and earning $100 a week. When Oz wasn't working, he was taking classes at the City College of New York, mainly to appease his parents, who wanted him to get an education. "But I didn't come to New York to go to school," Oz said. "I came to work!"

Regular work would come shortly. That summer, the Muppets were asked to make an appearance on the first seven episodes of a new version of *The Jimmy Dean Show*, a variety show featuring the popular country singer, which was set to debut on ABC in early fall. The timing was ideal: Jim and Juhl had wrapped up their weekly *Today* show appearances in late June, and no new appearances had yet been scheduled. The offer from Dean was definitely worth considering.

Tall, lanky, and goofily handsome, the talented, Texas-born Jimmy Dean had an easygoing manner—and matching drawl—that belied a hardscrabble determination. A high school dropout who had been raised by a single mother, his first real break came in 1953 at the age of twenty-five with the small hit "Bummin' Around." That opened up a career for Dean as an on-air personality in Washington, D.C., working first on radio and then, in 1957, as host of *Country Style* on WTOP-TV—a show so popular that it was picked up and syndicated nationally by CBS.

In 1961, Dean had a monster hit with the song "Big Bad John," which camped at number one for several weeks and won Dean a 1962 Grammy. Riding high on the single, Dean made numerous television appearances, including a successful stint as a guest host of *The Tonight Show*, which racked up impressive enough ratings that several networks, as Dean put it, "began looking at ol' JD with dollar signs in their eyes." The winner of the bidding war was ABC—and now that he was at the helm of his own show, Dean was searching for guests for his first few weeks. In particular, Dean recalled an act he had seen on television while living and working in D.C. in the late 1950s, and asked producer Bob Banner to "check out a particular act . . . that I remembered doing Wilkins Coffee commercials," Dean said. Jim, and the Muppets, were tracked down by producers and immediately hired.

On August 29, 1963, as videotape rolled at ABC's Studio 51, Dean introduced the Muppets as "one of the most talented groups I've ever seen." Jim, Jerry Juhl, and Frank Oz launched into "Cool Jazz," one of their artier pieces in which gloved hands "dance" to various kinds of music, a reliably solid piece that Jim had recently put into their variety show rotation. For the Muppets' next segment, Jim and Oz performed Rowlf—only just rescued from the cupboard at the Muppet workshop where he had been retired after the Purina commercials—singing "Moon River" with the Willis Sisters. This, too, was a solid performance, though there was little indication that something special was happening. That changed the following week, when Rowlf was given the opportunity to participate in a sketch with Dean himself. The two chatted amiably for several minutes, then sang a spirited duet of the old Bert Williams song "Nobody," which Dean had recorded the year before.

The performance sparkled. With Jim giving a charming and entirely convincing performance—and Dean believing in Rowlf completely—there was a chemistry that "turned out to be the hit of the show," said Dean. ABC was bombarded with fan mail for Rowlf, and the following week, as he introduced Rowlf as his "old hound dog buddy," Dean acknowledged that they'd "had all kinds of people asking us to have him back again." The two then launched into a lively duet of "Side by Side"—and with that, what was initially to be a seven-week stint turned into regular weekly appearances on the show for the next three years, with Jim and Oz performing Rowlf for twenty-seven straight weeks in the first season alone.

Performing Rowlf on *Jimmy Dean* was a different experience from previous Muppet performances. For one thing, Jim wasn't directly involved in the writing of Rowlf's sketches. While Rowlf and Dean's banter sounded casual and ad-libbed, it was actually tightly scripted, all the way down to Rowlf's double-takes and slow-burn reactions—and Jim had to put himself, and his character, in the hands of Dean's writing staff. It was a creative leap of faith, but Jim was fortunate in that Dean had surrounded himself with seasoned comedy writers like Buddy Arnold, who'd written for Milton Berle, and John Aylesworth, Will Glickman, and Frank Peppiatt, who wrote regularly for countless variety shows. "These were old-school guys," Oz said, and Jim—who had been willing to learn camera tricks and production techniques from old hands at WRC—was equally as thrilled by the opportunity to immerse himself firsthand in this old school of comedy writing. And so, Jim would sit in the writers' room as Aylesworth and his staff hashed around ideas and punch lines. "We would spend all week working on this little dialogue until it was honed to perfection," Jim said. "They would work with me in terms of performance and the delivery of punch lines. . . . It's amazing the little things the audience is not aware of—things that affect their response in terms of a laugh."

Jim also had to adjust to working live; since he and Dean would be playing off of each other, there would be no prerecorded soundtrack for lip-synching, as Jim had done for *Sam and Friends*. Instead, Dean would chat with Rowlf live in the studio, usually seated on a bench against a low wall over which Rowlf would appear. Jim and Oz would crouch together behind the wall, Oz pressed up under Jim's right armpit as he operated Rowlf's right hand, and both of them intently watching their performance on a small monitor. It might have looked like a tangle, but Jim claimed performing the live hand puppet was "really quite simple. The only complicated gestures are things like trying to applaud." As for performing the right hand, the trick, Oz said, "is not to do too much." It was physically tough work, squatting with their arms over their heads for over seven minutes, but the results were remarkable. The performance was so convincing, in fact, that Jim would often catch the cue card man holding up cards for Rowlf to read, while other times the microphone boom operator would swing the microphone over Rowlf's head, forgetting that Jim was actually speaking on a miked headset behind the low wall.

"As we first had Rowlf set up, he was a deep thinker, a dog who went into monologues," Jim said. "Working with Jimmy suddenly transformed Rowlf into a most human thing. . . . None of my Muppets had ever worked with humans before, and Jimmy Dean . . . turned Rowlf into a perfectly believable human kind of dog." Indeed, Dean believed in Rowlf so completely that he would sometimes genuinely break up when Rowlf delivered one-liners, laughing so hard that he was unable to sing. "I treated Rowlf like he was real, but he *was* real to me," Dean said, "and I think that's one of the reasons he made such an impression on everyone." For many, the impression continued even after the cameras stopped rolling. Dean's secretary, for one, could easily lose herself in the illusion. During a particularly boisterous rehearsal in Dean's office, Dean gave Rowlf a playful cuff on the ear that sent his eye flying off his head and across the room. Horrified, the secretary screamed and ran. Dean's secretary wasn't the only believer; viewers were sending Rowlf over two thousand fan letters each week, more than even Dean himself received. "It's been interesting for me to watch people come to believe in a puppet so completely," Jim remarked.

The Jimmy Dean Show was so successful that Dean took it on the road, performing an extended version of his television show before live audiences in a wide variety of venues across the country, from Las Vegas and Carnegie Hall to Purdue University and the Louisiana State Fair. Jim and Dean got along well both onstage and off. Besides being a top-notch performer, Dean had a working style very similar to Jim's. "He's free-form. He's quick on his feet and he knows what he wants," said one producer, describing Dean much the way Bob Payne had described Jim (*"He already knew what he was wanting!"*). Yet, even as the boss, Dean got on famously with his writers, producers, and other performers. He was a good time as well—"a rascal," Oz called him—hosting regular parties at his home in New Jersey, where he proudly showed off a large collection of dainty crystal champagne flutes. Oz was charmed. "That was completely unexpected" of a cowboy, Oz said.

Dean also paid generously. In 1963, Jim earned $1,500 per show for the first seven weeks—about $10,000 today—then $1,750 per show for the rest of the first season. By the third season, Dean would pay them $1,800 per week. More important to Jim than the money, the enormous success of Rowlf on a program aimed at an adult audience had proven that puppets weren't just for kids.

Capitalizing on that success, however, would continue to prove difficult. With Rowlf's popularity soaring, Jim proposed a television series featuring Rowlf traveling around the galaxy in a homemade spaceship. The proposal met with some enthusiasm, but Jim was up against the usual puppetry prejudice: no one could see Jim's idea as anything more than a kids' show, which was *not* where Jim wanted to be. "He was not interested in kids' stuff," stressed Juhl. "Puppetry was so pigeonholed as a children's medium, particularly on television, and that just wasn't what he did."

Juhl also admitted that, despite their regular appearances on *Jimmy Dean*—which only meant regular pay for about half of each year—there were many times he felt the Muppets might not make it. "I probably felt a lot more uncertain about it than I think Jim did," Juhl said, but "it all did seem fairly like we were just hanging in there."

Actually, they were more than just hanging in there; when they weren't working on *Jimmy Dean*, Jim had his crew back at Muppets, Inc. to continue working on commercials, which were still the company's most reliable source of income. The Wilkins ads continued to be hugely popular, and Jim was still fielding offers from coffee, tea, milk, and bread companies around the country who wanted to make use of the Muppets. Initially, Jim allowed the Ver Standig advertising company, which still managed the Wilkins account, to handle the negotiations for these transactions, leaving most of the legwork to Ver Standig's creative director, James W. Young. Unfortunately, as Jim soon discovered, Young had a tendency during tough negotiations to openly bad-mouth Jim, as if doing so would earn him sympathy from potential clients. "I would have been just as happy if we had not gotten into the muppet business," Young griped to one coffee company, while complaining to another that "it's taken years off my life to deal with them."

Finally deciding that enough was enough, Jim hired his own business director, tapping Alden Murray, a former attorney for NBC, to manage "business operations, including supervision of productions, client contract negotiation and administration, sales development and presentations, public relations . . . billing and collection." Murray, however, would last less than a year. Jim finally decided he could retain greater creative control, and better relationships, if he handled most of the business himself.

Now it was up to Jim to deal directly with Wilkins and other clients, explaining the finer points of union wage scales and costs of videotape, pitching new ideas for commercials, negotiating contracts, writing reams of correspondence, and running down cans of film that had gone astray in the mail. Errant film cans, in fact, were a major source of headaches. Most of the time, Jim used Memphis Picture Laboratories in Tennessee to develop and print his commercials, and the firm had an unfortunate tendency to deliver materials late or at the very last minute. Other times, Jim would mail copies of his commercials—many times the *only* copy—to a potential client for review, only to scramble to get the film canisters back. "Could you please return that last film that was sent to you?" Jim wrote in near panic to one executive. "I had just spliced that film together . . . before I could have it duplicated—so that's the only copy in existence."

"It was slapdash," Frank Oz said, but one had to remember that there was really "[no] company behind Jim where he could call upon the resources of various departments to help him with the high quality. . . . The resources were Don . . . and Jerry and me. . . . There was no art department, there was no merchandising . . . it was just kind of us guys and Jim the leader."

As it turned out, those resources were more than enough to produce some remarkably memorable, and profitable, commercials. One advertising executive noted that when the Muppets were hired to do ads for Kraml milk in Chicago, Kraml leapfrogged from twenty-third in sales among fifty Chicago dairies to an astounding *fifth*. "Until we had the Muppets nobody had heard of us outside a five-mile radius of the dairy," said an amazed Jim Kraml. "Today everyone within 50 miles of Chicago knows Kraml dairy." With those kinds of results, Muppets, Inc. would end up producing commercials for more than fifty companies in less than ten years.

When it came to filming the commercials, Jim's studio of preference was still Rodel Studios in Washington, a warehouselike facility in the Foggy Bottom District where Jim and Jane had produced some of the first Wilkins spots. Typically, Jim would make the trip down to D.C. with Oz, Juhl, and Sahlin. "We'd usually stay in this little hotel in Rosslyn [Virginia], right across the river," Oz recalled, "only we couldn't afford rooms for four people, so we'd get two rooms and flip a coin to see who would share a room with who."

The team wasn't sharing hotel rooms because Jim was being tight-fisted. While the Muppets were being paid well for their commercials—Claussen's Bakeries, for example, laid out $7,500 for eight spots—shooting them could be expensive. Studio time at Rodel could cost as much as $3,500 a day, bringing the costs for a four-day shoot to $12,000. Consequently, there were times the Muppets were barely breaking even for their efforts. But Jim was determined to stay at work, racking up countless hours of studio time, until he was happy with the results. "Part of what makes the Muppets work," said Oz, "is that we do lots and lots and lots of takes until we get it right."

That kind of commitment made shooting even one ten-second commercial a time-consuming process. There were the usual problems associated with any kind of filming—"false start" noted the camera report sheet for one spot—but filming puppets presented its own unique set of challenges that had to be worked around. "Jim's head in shot," one report sheet noted, while another take was scratched because "[Wilkins] looks wrong." Then, of course, shots could break down due to "very crazy horeseplay" among the performers. Oz recalled filming one spot where Wontkins was to get hit with eggs, only to find the rest of the Muppet crew too happy to oblige, chucking egg after egg at Wontkins as the cameras rolled. Oz gamely remained hunched beneath for shot after shot, wearing a raincoat dripping with yolk.

Other spots required more elaborate special effects, and Jim was just as determined to keep filming until he was happy with the results. One particular Wilkins ad, for instance, called for Wontkins to be set on fire, an effect achieved through the use of cold flame, a generally harmless substance that burns away quickly and cleanly without actually setting the underlying object on fire. But "they *soaked* Wontkins in it," Oz recalled. "I was nervous about it, but Jim said, 'you'll be fine,' which he *always* said when one of us had to do something crazy!" As the cameras rolled, a match was touched to Wontkins from below, and the puppet suddenly erupted into a flaming ball of blue and white, dripping and splattering burning cold flame down on Oz, scorching the hair on his arm. Oz plunged his arm—and the still burning Wontkins—into a bucket of water. "*Hmmm,*" said Jim as Wontkins and Oz smoldered. "Let's do it again."

While Jim was still drafting many of the commercials himself—neatly typing out proposals or scripts on fine milled paper with an orange bar across the bottom that read *Muppets Script*—he was turning more and more to Jerry Juhl to do the writing. It was a task Juhl was happy to take on; while he had been hired as a performer, it didn't take long for Juhl to realize that with Oz around, he had "some pretty high-powered" competition for performance time. Consequently, said Juhl, "I thought I'd better do something else if I'm going to make a living here. . . . We were getting more and more things that needed script material so I just sort of drifted slowly over to become a writer." As it turned out, writing was Juhl's true forte.

Following the birth of their third child and first son, Brian, in November 1963, Jim and Jane had begun to run out of space in their Manhattan apartment. In April 1964, then, Jim moved his growing family out to Greenwich, Connecticut, choosing a charming nineteenth-century farmhouse on busy Round Hill Road. The house had a distinguished pedigree, having once been owned by the American Impressionist painter John Henry Twachtman, and later remodeled by Stanford White, the New York architect who designed the iconic Washington Square Arch in 1889. Over the next ten years, Jim and Jane would add their own touches as well, colorfully painting many of the house's built-in fixtures and tiling the bathroom in a vibrant mosaic of fish and flowers. "The house in Greenwich was a special kind of home," Lisa Henson recalled. "I think it must have felt really great to buy a home like that, and to have that piece of property. It was beautiful."

The surrounding property had personality as well. A picturesque stream ran near the rear of the house—it had shown up on several of Twachtman's canvases—where the Hensons would play and skip rocks. Over the garage was an old studio, likely abandoned by the painter, crammed full of old furniture and half-finished paintings, with a dangerously rotten floor. One of the closest neighbors was the creaky, cranky Colonel Twachtman, the son of the painter, who had a parrot that spoke and squawked in the voice of his dead wife. The Henson children would creep up near the house only "close enough to be shooed off by him," then run back down the hill, shrieking, to the safety of their own yard. "We were always terrified of him!" Brian Henson said later, laughing.

Most mornings, as Jane drove the children to school in the station wagon, Jim would drive his Porsche the thirty miles from Greenwich into the city, where he was often the first to arrive at the Muppet workshop. One spring morning, Jerry Juhl opened the office door to find Jim sprawled out at his desk, "sitting with a storyboard pad, drawing this idea out." It was an idea for a film, said Jane Henson, which "came just completely full-blown out of his mind."

Jim had been working in television for nearly a decade now, and while he had done remarkable work, redefining the way puppets looked and acted on television, he was beginning to feel as confined by the four sides of the television screen as one of his Muppets. *The Jimmy Dean Show* had provided some welcome national exposure, proving not only that Jim could create a fully formed character but also that puppets could be for adults. But while puppetry had provided Jim with an entry into television—that handy means to an end—television itself was no longer the endgame. Jim was ready to move beyond the confines of the television screen, and he was determined to show that he could do it without puppets. That was no surprise to Juhl, as he watched Jim sketching away at his storyboards. "Jim wasn't a puppeteer," Juhl stressed. "He got into puppetry because it was a way of getting into television and film . . . that was really his passion."

So Jim was going to make a movie. Not a full-length feature, or at least not yet; at the moment, that would take too much time. And time was, in fact, exactly what this short film would be about—*Time to Go,* Jim called it for several weeks, before finally deciding on *Time Piece,* "the story of an Everyman, frustrated by the typical tasks of a typical day," as Jim described it. While the Muppet crew would be called on to assist with some of the props or setups, *Time Piece* would be almost entirely a one-man production, with Jim serving as the film's writer, producer, director, animator, and lead actor. He would even write the music, most of it percussion, with a bit of help from Don Sebesky, who served as Jimmy Dean's musical director. And for the first time, there wouldn't be a single puppet in sight.

While there was no script—only the storyboards Juhl had seen—Jim's notes, it seemed, were everywhere. Lists of props were jotted on yellow pads. Across the back of a large envelope, Jim had scribbled LITTLE THINGS, followed by a cryptic checklist: CLOCK BLOW-UP. MARCHING. STAMP PADS. TICKER TAPE. Beneath that was BIG THINGS, with an equally odd list of items: FACTORY. DUNE AREA. FLYING. TOILET FLUSH. On a newspaper-sized sheet of white paper, Jim had drawn up a calendar with his shooting schedule, describing exactly what he or his team would be filming on a given day. Inside the square for Thursday, June 11, 1964, for example, Jim had written:

SHOOT

WHISTLER'S MOTHER

+

MARTINI TABLE

SAWING WIFE IN HALF

SONG + DANCE

BATHROOM

It may have looked like an avant-garde haiku, but to Jim it all made sense—which was more than the rest of the team could say. "We didn't know what was going on," Oz said later. "I didn't know what the hell the movie was." "There was this storyboard and Jim pointed and we did it," agreed Juhl, who remembered spending the summer of 1964 tromping around mud flats in Newark, "dropping clocks in mud and having to wade into the mud to get them back."

For the next eight months or so, between appearances on *Jimmy Dean*, trips to D.C. to film commercials, and a puppetry conference in Miami (Jim would step down as president of the Puppeteers of America for 1964, though he would remain on the board), Jim would grab any opportunity to shoot even a few seconds of footage for his film. "We were all over the place," remembered Oz. "We were doing [a show in] Vegas and Jim and I went out in the desert and I just [shot a] handheld camera roll. He was running along the mountains in silhouette." Other days, Jim would have himself filmed strolling down a New York sidewalk in a loincloth, or shoot several minutes of Oz pogo-sticking in a gorilla costume. "All those *Time Piece* shots were so bizarre," said Oz.

Whether the rest of the Muppet staff understood what Jim was up to, it was, they knew, clearly "a personal piece." "It came totally from Jim," Juhl said. "I don't think there was ever a project that came more specifically." Thematically, it was a subject Jim had explored before in "Tick-Tock Sick": the incessant, relentless, perpetual passage of time. Creatively, it was an opportunity, as Jane said, for Jim to tap "all [the] different places in his artistic thinking."

Time Piece opens simply enough, with Jim—the Everyman—in a hospital bed being examined by a doctor. The sound of Jim's heartbeat and blinking eyes become the percussive rhythm of drumbeats and machinery clicks, and over the next eight minutes the main character's everyday routine—going to work, eating dinner, going out to a nightclub with his wife—unfolds rapidly through a series of "repeated cuts from realistic scenes," as Jim described it, "to wild dream sequences that seem to comment on the reality they interrupt." Each shot, Oz recalled, "was maybe about a second or four seconds long," but Jim made every second count, even tracking in a notebook precisely how many frames of film each shot would take up. Looking at it today, *Time Piece* plays like an extended alternative music video, cutting quickly from shot to shot—sometimes almost quicker than the eye can register—under a frantic percussion soundtrack.

"I was . . . playing with a kind of flow-of-consciousness type of editing," Jim said later, "where one image took you to another and there was no logic to it, but your mind put it together." That was true enough, as even the most casual of viewers can't help but feel they've gotten . . . well, *something* from it. But the plot is beside the point. The real star is Jim's strong visual sense, which carries the film forward on one memorable image after another: Jim as a gunslinger shooting the *Mona Lisa*. Jim as a factory worker pulling levers as a conveyor belt carries rusty cans. Jim painting a real elephant pink. "Richard Lester did *A Hard Day's Night* at about the same time I was doing *Time Piece*," Jim said later, "and I just loved what one could do with the montaging of visual images."

Through it all, Jim's Everyman is in constant motion, strolling down sidewalks, swinging Tarzan-style through the jungle, leaping from a diving board, flapping on makeshift wings, or dodging through a cemetery in top hat and tails. It's a race against time, and every sound in the film—Jim's tapping fingers, a cough, a nightclub drummer, a woman's high heels clacking—vibrates with the regular rhythm of a ticking clock. Perhaps tellingly, Jim's Everyman speaks only one word of dialogue, repeating it four times in eight minutes: *"Help."*

"*Time Piece* is about time and a man running, and I understand that about Jim," Juhl said later. "Jim was always running from time. . . . There never would've been enough time, and I think he knew that really early." Perhaps it was Jim once again coping with the loss of his brother, Paul, and the feeling that there would never be enough time to do all the things he hoped to do—but then again, maybe it wasn't. "A lot of people want to say something," Jim said. "But I don't start out to say things. I try to keep it first of all entertaining, and then humorous." For the most part, Jim would remain coy about whether he was really trying to make any kind of statement with *Time Piece*, remarking that he was simply exploring "the possibility of filmic stream of consciousness."

After completing the film in May 1965, Jim hosted a premiere party for his "rather weird little movie" at the Museum of Modern Art, renting out the fourth-floor screening room and running the film continuously for several hours. Oz, who had initially been unsure exactly what to make of the snippets of film they were shooting, was enthusiastic about the final product: "It was Jim pushing the form." Following the premiere, Jim held a reception at the Muppets headquarters on 53rd Street, drinking champagne with friends and mulling over ways to put the film into a nationwide release, a task he assigned to Bernie Brillstein.

The agent aggressively made the rounds with copies of the film, which baffled several potential distributors. ("I don't think there's anything we can do with it," wrote a confused representative at United Artists, adding that "the short does show a certain talent, but I think it's a gimmicky sort of a talent.") Eventually, Brillstein landed a deal that would distribute the film nationally with French director Claude Lelouch's acclaimed *A Man and a Woman*. That put *Time Piece* squarely in art house circles, including a highly successful eighteen-month run at the Paris Theatre in New York—an unexpected and distinguished venue for a twenty-eight-year-old whose previous film work had mostly been ten-second commercials with creatures exploding or devouring each other.

While *Time Piece* had been Jim's pet project for nearly a year, there was still plenty going on at Muppets, Inc. During the summer of 1964, following a performance in Las Vegas with Jimmy Dean, Jim and his team had made a trip out to San Francisco to film another *Tinkerdee*-based pilot, this time at the behest of the Quaker Oats company, which was interested in working with the Muppets on a Saturday morning television series. While Jim would normally have bristled at the idea of straitjacketing himself into a children's puppet show, with *Time Piece* under way, he perhaps felt he had a project in the works that would help him define himself as more than just "a puppet guy."

Still, this new pilot, *The Land of Tinkerdee,* was far less ambitious than the earlier *Tales of the Tinkerdee*. Clocking in at less than ten minutes and filmed only in black-and-white, the *Land of Tinkerdee* pilot was limited to one set—a tinker's workshop—and featured appearances by only two Muppets, King Goshposh and a new live hand sheepdog puppet named Rufus. It's not subpar work, but it does appear that Jim's heart was elsewhere at the time—which it was—and in a December meeting with Quaker Oats, the company opted not to pick up the show. What makes *The Land of Tinkerdee* memorable, however, is its setup: *Land* featured a live performer (Darryl Ferreira, a friend of Oz and Juhl's from Oakland) as a tinker who interacts with a Muppet dog in a workshop at the gateway to a magical domain—nearly the same setup as *Fraggle Rock* twenty years later.

As the Muppets took on more and more projects, Jim was looking at adding several more employees, at least on a part-time basis, to the Muppet offices. The most notable addition was a bearded thirty-one-year-old performer named Jerry Nelson, a gifted puppeteer who, like Jim and Oz, initially had no interest in puppetry. Born in Oklahoma and raised in Washington, D.C., Nelson had served in the army and, after briefly attending college, moved to New York to become an actor, taking walk-on roles in shows like *The Defenders* and *Naked City*. In 1964, while out of a job, he learned that puppeteer Bil Baird was looking for performers to work marionettes for a New England tour. Nelson, who hadn't touched a marionette in twenty years, nevertheless ad-libbed his audition with Baird, performing a tough-talking, trench-coated mobster, and landed the job. Later that same summer, while performing with Baird's troupe at the New York World's Fair, Nelson met Jim's old friend Bobby Payne, who suggested Nelson give Jim a call. "He thought our senses of humor would mesh very nicely," recalled Nelson.

At Jim's request, Nelson submitted a recording of himself performing some character voices, "mostly just Stan Freberg impressions," Nelson said later, laughing. At the moment, Jim was the only performer providing voices—and with Oz insisting that he would "never" do a voice (a vow he would stick to only another year), Jim was likely looking at ways to give the Muppets a more diverse sound. If that was indeed the case, Nelson was an ideal find. With his acting background and love of music, Nelson provided not only a wide range of voices, but he could sing—and sing beautifully—as well. Jim listened to the recordings and liked what he heard, then brought Nelson in for a quick audition. The two fell in together immediately; hiring him would be an easy decision.

Jim's professional family wasn't the only one that was growing. In April 1965, shortly after returning from a vacation in Puerto Rico, Jane gave birth to their fourth child, a son they named John Paul.

That left Jane—with the help of a young au pair—to manage a house with two young girls, a toddler, a newborn, and a new Great Dane puppy named Troy, which Jim had rather cluelessly presented to the already swamped Jane. (Troy, in fact, would prove to be more than *anyone* could handle and would soon be given away.) With her hands full, and Jim's schedule changing daily, things could get frantic at the Henson household, once with frightening consequences. One June afternoon, Lisa, nearly five, and Cheryl, just shy of four, were playing in the gravel driveway of their Greenwich home when Jane—turning quickly into the short driveway out of the speeding traffic on Round Hill Road—accidentally ran over them with the station wagon.

When the phone rang at Muppets, Inc., both Juhl and Oz remember watching Jim as he learned what had happened. One of Jim's strengths as a father, said Cheryl later, was his ability to "approach things in a calm and kind way," but Jane's news shook him deeply. "He just went ashen," Oz recalled, then hung up the phone and rushed from the room without saying a word. "A terrible day," remembered Juhl with a shudder. Although Lisa had been pinned by the car, she wasn't badly hurt, but Cheryl's ankle had been fractured. To Jim's and Jane's relief, both Cheryl and Lisa would be running through the woods by autumn as if nothing had happened—though Lisa would be haunted by nightmares for some time—with Jim trailing behind them, movie camera rolling, getting the footage he would use later in a charming short film called *Run, Run*.

Jane could still be found at the downtown offices from time to time, often sitting in front of a mirror with Frank Oz, helping him perfect his lip-synching. "I sat in front of that mirror for *hours*. Jane was really good at lip-synch," said Oz appreciatively—but he thought he understood why Jane had gotten out of regular performing, for reasons that went beyond motherhood. "A great puppeteer needs to be aggressive and selfish," Oz said—qualities, he thought, the artsier Jane lacked. "It's also important to be uncomfortable. You should be prepared and ready at all times," Oz continued. "If you're comfortable, you're doing it wrong."

If discomfort was truly the mark of a great performer, then when it came to filming a series of commercials for Southern Bread, Jim and his team were definitely doing things right. For the Southern Bread campaign, Jim had asked Sahlin to create a live hand puppet resembling the company's mascot, a white-mustached Southern colonel in a starched white suit and hat. Jim filmed most of the commercials on location, requiring him and Oz or Nelson to squeeze and mash themselves into odd places, lying on railroad tracks, hunching down in cars, or squatting on the pavement outside Yankee Stadium.

More perilous, however, was a Southern Bread spot Jim had dreamed up that required an arrow to fly in from off-screen and puncture an apple on top of the colonel's head. Jim decided to film the ad in his backyard in Greenwich—this time performing the character with Jerry Nelson—and hired a professional archer, a young woman of about twenty-five, to shoot the arrow through an apple balanced on the puppet's head. "The gal started walking away to do this," Nelson recalled, "and Jim said 'Oh, you don't have to go *that* far. You can come up close because the camera won't see it.' And she said, 'No, I have to get a certain distance away, because when the arrow leaves the bow, it waffles.' " As the archer moved into position twenty yards away, Jim and Nelson knelt on the ground, Jim with his hand up inside the puppet's head, and Nelson crouched under Jim's armpit. "Jim was fearless," Nelson said, but Nelson was *terrified*— and ducked his head as low as he could as the young woman drew back the bow and took aim.

"She shot it and hit the apple and knocked it off . . . [and] I said 'Oh, great!' " laughed Nelson. But Jim—just as he had with Oz and the flame-engulfed Wontkins—was determined to get the shot right. "No, that's not what we want," Jim insisted; the arrow had to stay *in* the apple. "When he had a vision in his mind, he would *chase* it," said Nelson. With cameras rolling, the archer nocked another arrow and fired again and again, finally nailing the apple on the fifth take. As Jane said later, "That's one of the times I thought, 'Oh my God, he's crazy!' Jim was so fearless at things like that, and [yet] he was so afraid of spiders in the shower!"

That was life with the Muppets: a kind of fearless craziness that pervaded nearly every aspect of the business. "Working at the Muppet office was always fun," said Oz, "especially when Don Sahlin was around." While all the Muppet staff enjoyed pranks and jokes, Sahlin was an especially notorious trickster, with the added advantage that he could invent and build nearly anything, which made him particularly potent as a prankster. "I loved the way Don played," said Jim. "Throughout his life he would play—pick up some bit of feathers and attach a long rubber band to it, stretch it down the hall, and release it as you came into the room. Or he'd put a puppet on the john. He had this sense of playfulness that he actually used, and inspiration would come out of these free-release moments."

Where Jim was involved, too, nothing was ordinary. Even the official letterhead for Muppets, Inc. had a ragged colored bar angling across the page so that letters had to be oddly formatted—a task that fell to secretary Carroll Conroy, who had taken on responsibilities as a bookkeeper in addition to her tasks as Jim's executive secretary. Conroy brought her own sense of fun to Jim's formal correspondence, writing pithy letters to Brillstein or bantering with clients on Jim's behalf ("With typical speed and efficiency of the broadcasting industry," begins one note, "we just got your letter"). She also managed to resist the urge to correct the countless clients who constantly misspelled Jim's last name as "Hensen."

The confusion was probably understandable; after all, it wasn't Jim's name on the door or the company letterhead, but rather THE MUPPETS. Booking agents hired the Muppets, not Jim Henson. "The Muppets were known," Brian Henson said later, "but he wasn't." With their plentiful commercials, countless appearances on variety shows, and Rowlf's continued prominence on *Jimmy Dean,* it may have looked from the outside like the Muppets was a large organization. Even Jerry Nelson admitted as much; after being hired, he had headed up the stairs of the townhouse of Muppet Studios with stars in his eyes only to discover, to his surprise, that "it wasn't all that big."

"We were just kind of this crazy little band at that time," Oz said later. "We would go into *The Tonight Show* . . . with these black boxes and Jim'd have this beard. We'd be these guys and they'd think we were rock musicians. . . . We were *The Muppets,* like an act." In fact, in an era when rock groups had names like the Troggs or the Animals, being booked into hotels as "The Muppets" could sometimes lead to confusion. Once, following a Muppet performance in Los Angeles, a hotel manager refused to give the team their rooms. "They thought the Muppets were a rock group," Juhl said, and were concerned the performers would trash the hotel. Jim managed to smooth things over by having "a serious conversation" with the hotel management, though Oz added that Jim "didn't look very clean cut either!"

Actually, in the mid-1960s, Jim looked more like a beatnik businessman, wearing slacks and crisply starched shirts with brightly colored ties, his brown hair cut short and his beard neatly clipped close to his face. After arriving at the workshop, Jim would roll up his sleeves, then sink down into his black Eames chair, scrunching down until he was almost lying on his back, one long leg on the desk or crossed over the other as he sketched in his notebook or jotted story ideas on yellow notepads. From this position, too, he would discuss story or commercial ideas with the rest of the Muppet team, *hmmmm*ing or laughing as he considered each suggestion. "Someone would have an idea, and we'd laugh out loud at it and throw it around some more," said Oz.

One of Jim's more playful ideas—which was thrown around, then finally deposited squarely on the shoulders of Oz—was a spirited ad campaign for La Choy Chinese food. For the first time, Jim designed and built a full-sized walkaround character: a fluorescent pink-and-orange-colored dragon named Delbert who, with the help of some Don Sahlin sorcery, breathed real fire. For the La Choy commercials, Oz lumbered around in the gigantic dragon costume, surprising Boy Scouts and housewives as he knocked over rows of food in a supermarket, crashed through walls, and shattered a television. "I hated those costume things, and Jim knew it," Oz said. "That's why he reveled in me doing it!" The problem, Oz explained, was that once he got into the dragon costume, "I was blind . . . I counted steps to figure out where to walk and listened to voices so I would know which way to turn." It was a dry run for the kind of large walkaround characters that Jim would refine for *Sesame Street*'s Big Bird, then perfect for sweeping fantasy projects like *The Dark Crystal*.

Just as ambitious were a number of short films that Jim would produce for IBM at the behest of a charismatic and forward-thinking

IBM executive named David Lazer, who was hoping to inject Jim's "sense of humor and crazy nuttiness" into short "coffee breaks" to be shown at IBM business meetings. Briskly written and enthusiastically performed and edited, some of these films were to promote new products, while others were simply intended as "icebreakers" for business meetings and staff retreats. Jim reported that IBM was "ecstatic" when it received the first four short films in early 1966—and Jim, too, was delighted with the opportunity to work with the company, forging a friendship with Lazer that would eventually extend beyond their work for IBM.

As a gadget enthusiast, Jim was intrigued by the company's constant stream of new contraptions. For most of his IBM films, Jim chose to use the versatile Rowlf, in part because as a live hand puppet he could pick up and fiddle with each new machine—such as an electric guitar from the "Hippie Products Division"—but also because Lazer was a fan of the character. "We made Rowlf a . . . bungling salesman," Lazer said, and "everyone just went crazy over him." Jim also created a number of artsy films for the company, such as *Paperwork Explosion,* a rapid-fire appraisal of IBM's technology set against a background of electronic music by Raymond Scott, in which Jim cautioned viewers to remember that "Machines should work; people should think."

Lazer loved escaping his "dinky little offices" at IBM to come brainstorm with Jim and Jerry Juhl at Muppets, Inc. "There was this aura of calmness, gentleness," Lazer recalled. "Everybody was so nice. It was a nice warm feeling. It sounds trite now, but it was true." As with much of the commercial work, Jim was barely breaking even on the IBM films. But Lazer came to appreciate that, for Jim, it was usually more about fun than profit. "I knew that he was taking a beating [financially]," Lazer said later. "Something about Jim—it's not the money. It's got to feel right for him. It's got to click for him. . . . I liked that about him very much." The affiliation with IBM would also give Jim the opportunity to take short working vacations to perform Rowlf at a number of IBM's high-powered meetings, traveling with Jane to Florida and with Juhl and Nelson to Nassau, where Jim was excited to win $75 gambling—a new pastime that agent Bernie Brillstein claimed was due to his influence.

Jim was still traveling across the country with Jimmy Dean, too, though the appearances at enormous nightclubs and open-air venues were more work than vacation, especially since the members of the Muppet team were responsible for serving as their own stagehands, setting up and taking down the puppet stage for Rowlf's appearance in complete darkness. "We'd do our little bit," Nelson recalled, "and then the lights would go out and we'd pick up our little stage in the dark and find our way out." During one intermission, Jim stepped out of the darkened theater with Rowlf still on his arm, and was immediately mobbed by fans. "Next thing you know," said an amused Dean, "they'll be calling the *dog* the star of this here ol' show." After a show in Anaheim, Jim dodged around fans and dashed immediately to the airport, to arrive back home in Connecticut just in time for Lisa's sixth birthday party. No matter how hectic his schedule, Jim would always take the time to be an active, attentive parent.

To Jim's delight, *Time Piece* was continuing to attract audiences—and awards—not only in the United States, but overseas as well. In August 1965, he was notified that the film had received the Plaque de St. Mark ("whatever that is," Jim wrote dryly in his journal) at the Venice Film Festival, as well as several smaller prizes, including recognition in Berlin at the XII Oberhausen Film Festival. Reactions to the film still varied, as Jim noted, "from 'A frightening look at modern living' to 'A very funny movie,' to 'What the hell is it?'" In early 1966, Jim learned *Time Piece* had been nominated for an Academy Award in the Best Short Subject, Live Action category. He and Jane attended the awards ceremony in Los Angeles in April, where the film lost to Claude Berri's French comedy *The Chicken*. Nevertheless, the Hensons, Jane remembered, still had "such fun!"

While Jim could shrug off losing the Oscar, there was one potential loss that wouldn't be so easy to shake. In early 1966, Frank Oz, now twenty-one, was notified that he had been drafted and was being asked to report for duty in February. Oz vacated his New York apartment and Jim, trying to make the best of the situation, informed Jerry Nelson that he would now be hired full-time to take over Oz's performing duties—welcome news for the recently divorced Nelson, who was caring for a daughter with cystic fibrosis and looking for more than just part-time jobs. Oz was working to secure placement in a unit to entertain troops, rather than serving in combat, "which lessened the dramatic impact of my leaving," Oz said, but the team was still determined to send him off with a flourish. On February 18, the Muppet staff and their families threw a goodbye party for their youngest performer, waving to him from the second-story window as his cab sped toward Whitehall Street, all but certain they had lost Oz for at least the next two years.

As it turned out, they lost him for barely an hour. "I reported for duty," Oz recalled, "and was let go because of a minor heart condition." Oz excitedly climbed back into a cab and ordered the driver back to the Muppet offices, where his own farewell party had only just ended. "I came back up the stairs to the office, and there was Jerry Nelson, sitting by himself on the couch," Oz said, laughing. "And he looked up at me with this blank look on his face and just said, 'Shit!'" Jim was delighted. "FRANK OZ is not drafted!" Jim wrote in his journal, with near palpable relief.

Nelson's job, meanwhile, would remain secure for most of the year, as Oz decided to take some time visiting relatives in England and Belgium; indeed, Jim and Nelson would perform Rowlf for the final episode of *Jimmy Dean* on March 25, 1966. On Oz's return, Nelson would remain on staff as a part-time performer, splitting his time between Jim and Bil Baird. According to Nelson, "Jim would call me up and say, 'Are you able to do an *Ed Sullivan*? And I would check with Bil to make sure it was okay—he always said 'yeah, sure.' He liked Jim a lot and respected his work."

Fortunately for Nelson, the appearances on *Ed Sullivan* or *The Tonight Show* would continue with an almost rhythmic regularity. Jim was writing more and more new material for these appearances, honestly appraising the relative success of each in his private journal. Jim was unhappy, for example, with a Thanksgiving-related appearance on Johnny Carson, scrawling BOMB in his journal entry in all capital letters ("Johnny is not one of those people who is really comfortable talking to the puppets," Juhl offered helpfully). Better were two sketches on a live New Year's Eve appearance six weeks later, though Jim was only willing to call the appearance "fair," perhaps realizing that one sketch had gone on a bit too long. For a Perry Como Christmas special, the Muppet team performed a piece involving five of Santa's reindeer trying to make it snow for Christmas—a skit Jim decided was "Fairly good," and it truly was, getting laughs in all the right places and enthusiastic applause from the audience.

Despite insisting that he would never perform voices, Oz had made his vocal debut in July 1965 performing half of a confused two-headed monster on trumpeter Al Hirt's *Fanfare*. The same show featured another new skit involving two Oz-designed abstract Muppets—basically flexible tubes with wide eyes and fuzzy feet— who danced to Hirt's chart-topping "Java." The "Java" sketch, which became one of the Muppets' most popular, was a throwback to the earliest Muppet performances, essentially a game of one-upmanship that ended with the smaller character blowing up the larger one. "Our material does have a certain similarity," Jim good-naturedly admitted.

Jim, it seemed, could find inspiration anywhere. In late 1964, Jim—along with Juhl, Oz, and Sahlin—arrived at NBC studios at 10:00 A.M. for a morning rehearsal for *The Jack Paar Program*, only to be told they weren't needed until 4:00 that afternoon. As the Muppet performers lounged around the dressing room with nothing but time on their hands, someone pulled open a door at the other end of the room, "expecting it to lead somewhere," said Juhl, "but instead it was just this shallow closet with a maze of pipes." Where others might see twisting pipes and valves and spigots, Jim saw monsters and faces and noses. The rest was easy. As Juhl explained:

> We had nothing to do, and Don had brought paints because we were performing something that needed touch-ups, so one thing led to another and we started decorating the pipes. It was Jim's idea—a typical Jim idea—and as the whole thing got more elaborate, one of us hopped in a cab and brought more material from the workshop.

Soon the team had the pipes and valves decorated with colored paint, fake fur and hair, googly eyes, and grinning or roaring mouths—a shrine to the Muppets' brand of "affectionate anarchy," as Oz said later. Even as the team worked, Juhl said, "people at the studio began to hear about this crazy closet and started stopping by, asking if they could take pictures." By the time of their 4:00 performance, even Paar had heard what the "crazy Muppet people" were up to and sent a cameraman to film the closet for his television audience to see. "What's interesting is that Jim never intended for those pipes to be discovered that quickly," Diana Birkenfield remembered later. "He wanted it to be a surprise for the next person who might open that closet door."

During the summer of 1966, the Muppets spent a week cohosting *The Mike Douglas Show,* which gave Jim the opportunity to perform several quirky pieces, such as feathers dancing to the Young Rascals' recent hit "Good Lovin'" (soldiering on even as one feather puppet accidentally wrapped around the blades of a spinning fan) and yet another variation of the Limbo character. Jim was increasingly fascinated by Limbo, which gave him the opportunity to explore his own interests in how the brain processed information and imagination. To produce one memorable sequence, Jim maneuvered a camera slowly through a tangle of materials he had strung throughout the Muppet workshop—webs of yarn, scraps of paper, wads of plastic wrap—then projected the final film behind Limbo as a representation of various regions of the brain.

While Limbo's somewhat surreal style may have baffled fans expecting to see Rowlf, Jim was unapologetic about giving audiences something new. "Good puppetry has a broad range," Jim said. "It appeals to the children, the squares, and sophisticates." So appealing were the Muppets, in fact, that in early 1966 Jim accepted an offer from the Ideal Toy Company to produce Rowlf and Kermit puppets, the first merchandising Jim had allowed since the Wilkins giveaways seven years earlier. Naturally, Jim produced the commercials for the toys, poking a little fun at himself by having two Kermit puppets plead with viewers to "buy us . . . [or] we'll bite you in the leg."

As the decade passed, Jim would let both his hair and his beard grow out and begin wearing soft suede or leather jackets with flowered shirts, looking very much the hippie many thought he was, despite the fact that his age—he turned thirty in September 1966—put him at the edge of what the hippies themselves would derisively tag as "The Establishment." But Jim, by his very nature, defied such easy labels. By 1967, certainly, he had attained a degree of financial success—though with four children, it would still be a while before he would approach the domain of the truly wealthy—with the attractive house in Greenwich and, in August, a brand-new Porsche Targa. "He always had those fancy new cars," recalled Lisa Henson. "But he also really, really liked things to be nice. He had fantastic taste, whether it was clothing, or homes, or furniture, whatever." Jim's style, in fact, was almost directly opposite Jane's, who liked simpler things and would always feel somewhat "conflicted" about wealth or possessions.

But while Jim's financial success may have made him look like one of the "squares or sophisticates," by 1967—that acid-soaked, Day-Glo year of *Sgt. Pepper* when psychedelia went mainstream—Jim entered one of the most experimental and creative phases of his career, motivated largely by a desire to become something more than just Muppets. "Except for *Jimmy Dean,* there were just commercials and guest spots on other people's shows—and in the end these were frustrating because they provided no opportunity for character development," said Jane. "The Muppets were pretty well liked by then. All of the big shows were ready to at least listen to our ideas, and when they had an opening they'd put us on. But nobody was prepared to give the Muppets a show of their own, and Jim began to feel maybe he should be looking in another direction." Over the next three years, then, Jim would pursue a wide variety of projects in various media, very few of which involved a single puppet.

One of the most ambitious projects was not a television or movie-related project at all, but rather "a new concept in total entertainment," a themed nightclub Jim was calling Cyclia. "The idea began during the first wave of psychedelia," recalled Jane. "Jim went to see Jefferson Airplane and he was very intrigued with it—the light shows and the psychedelic graphics." To provide his potential guests with "the entertainment experience of the future," Jim envisioned that the walls, floor, and ceiling of his nightclub would be broken into faceted, crystal-like shapes onto which films would be projected—completely immersing dancers in a sea of images, choreographed precisely to the volume and type of music being played. When the music was quiet, for example, there would be images of trees or water; when the music got loud, there would be traffic, machinery, and explosions. And once an hour, a woman in a white leotard would rise from a pedestal in the center of the floor to have film projected on her body as she danced. It would be, Jim proposed, a very fashionable place, with "a definite prestige atmosphere, and as such [the cover charge] will not be inexpensive."

While senses-soaking, high-tech themed nightclubs would become fashionable by the late 1970s, in 1967, Jim's idea for Cyclia was clearly ahead of its time—so far ahead, in fact, that finding the necessary space, materials, and technology to make it happen was a major challenge. To take care of the legwork, Jim hired Barry Clark, an enthusiastic West Coaster who had experience managing musicians and clubs, and asked him to scout possible locations as well as potential investors. Meanwhile, Jim and the Muppet team would take care of the films that would be projected on Cyclia's faceted surfaces and dancing girls.

Jim had been shooting film for Cyclia as early as 1965, dispatching Frank Oz and Jerry Nelson to Shea Stadium in August to film the crowd screaming and reacting during the Beatles' landmark concert. Other times, as they had with *Time Piece,* footage would be shot whenever there was a spare moment, filming city streets from the back of a motorcycle, or rain rippling through puddles as they stood on a corner on Broadway. "I shot thousands and thousands of feet of sixteen-millimeter film for Cyclia," recalled Oz. "It's where I got the first experience that enabled me to become a movie director." But "you couldn't shoot just random stuff," continued Oz. "Jim was actually thinking thematically. Since there would be sixteen projectors showing images, they had to be thematically sound—like sixteen screens of people screaming at the Beatles." In fact, Jim had thirteen themes in mind—including "Woods," "Junk," "City at Night" "India," and "Nude"—all of which would then be edited together into an hour-long film called *Cataclysm* that would project constantly on walls and bodies throughout the evening.

For most of 1966, Jim was seriously considering purchasing and converting ABZ Studios, a set of buildings at 266-268 East 78th Street in Manhattan, to house his club. Local zoning ordinances were a bit vague, allowing for a restaurant—though not "a cabaret"—and for music, "as long as there were no more than three instruments used, excluding any brass instruments." Despite the limitations, Jim was prepared to purchase the property, and its two mortgages, outright for $200,000—about $1 million today, and an astronomical sum for a company that could barely afford to keep five full-time employees on its payroll. However, when legal difficulties arose regarding the original owner's certificate of occupancy, Jim formally rescinded his offer. "Nearly bought ABZ," he noted in his journal with a touch of regret.

Following the breakdown of the ABZ negotiations Jim looked at several other locations, including buildings at West 60th Street, just off Central Park, a site in Santa Monica, California, and a large vacant lot on Second Avenue in New York City, at the foot of the Queensboro Bridge, where Jim proposed building a geodesic dome or even dropping in an inflatable structure. None of these ambitious ideas, however, moved much beyond the discussion phase.

More promising, it seemed, was a joint venture agreement with the El Morocco club on Broadway to take over the famous club's Garrison Room—but that, too, proved to be a dead end. "We went to the El Morocco," Oz said, "[and] Jim and I went to [the dance club] Electric Circus just to look at it . . . [but] it just wasn't selling." Still, Jim remained almost defiantly committed to the project, incorporating Cyclia Enterprises in the fall of 1967, running endless cost analyses, piecing together a rough cut of *Cataclysm,* and handing out fluorescent-colored brochures to potential backers. "It could well be that he was toying with a dream," said Jerry Juhl later, "[but he was] enjoying the process tremendously." Oz agreed. "Jim went where the excitement was." Eventually, the nightclub idea was abandoned, though Cyclia Enterprises—perhaps a testament to Jim's ridiculous optimism—would not be formally disbanded until 1970.

Even as he spent late evenings sketching Cyclia floor plans, painting concept art, or editing *Cataclysm,* Jim would still return home each night to Greenwich where he would join the family in the latest crafts or art project—and there was always some project spread out at the Henson household, whether it was wooden boxes to be dabbed with acrylic paints or materials to construct custom dollhouses. "You would think that he would be tired of making things by the time he came home at night, but it wasn't the case," said Lisa. "Even on weekends, he was still working on the art projects with us." "There was a lot of making things," said Cheryl, "and there was a lot of respect for childhood."

"Jim loved to come home and be with the kids," said Jane. "He'd just come up with all these different projects. If we were driving along and we saw high grass, Jim would say, 'Oh! Let's do a film with you coming in and out of the grass and popping up over the grasses!' So we'd stop the car and out comes the Bolex [camera] and they'd do a film. In the spring, he would get photographs of little teeny ferns opening up. What was very basic to his work is that he was really in love with life. He was really intrigued with how all these little pieces of life worked and he was equally as intrigued with his children. He loved just watching them be children and doing the things they enjoyed doing."

While the Henson children all knew their father worked with puppets, they were never encouraged to believe that any of the Muppet characters were living, breathing creatures. To Jim, puppets were merely one of the tools of his trade, a part of his act, to be thrown into a cabinet when they were worn out or no longer needed—an attitude he imparted to his children, who found more than a few discarded Muppets in their toy boxes. "He was very matter-of-fact about it," said Lisa. "His attitude was, 'None of this stuff is really precious—you can make it and then you can take it apart and make something else with it.' He even had some of the old *Sam and Friends* Muppets lying around the house and they became rags because we played with them. Chicken Liver was a particular victim of our playing!" (In 2010, Chicken Liver would be rescued and restored and now resides in the Smithsonian Institution.)

All three school-age children had been enrolled briefly in the Whitby Montessori School, then the North Street School in Greenwich, before entering Mead School, where Jane became actively involved in the school's dynamic art program. It was an activity that required even more of her already precious time but gave her "an embracing environment," recalled Cheryl, and a much needed creative outlet. To keep things in order at home, then, Jane had help from a savvy nanny named Lillian Soden, who would take over the household, usually on each Tuesday and Wednesday, to give Jim and Jane the chance to spend the evening together, heading into New York for dinner and a movie or music in a nightclub. Though she was only in the house briefly each week, Lillian's presence was pervasive in the Henson household. In some ways, Lilly served for Lisa and Cheryl the same role that Dear—who passed away in August 1967—had for Jim, encouraging and inspiring the girls with her own particular skills and talents. "There were times when Lilly just really held it all together in terms of her incredible cooking and her great values," Cheryl said later. "Lilly was just amazing." To Lisa, Lillian "was like my surrogate grandmother. She taught me everything I know about etiquette, whether it's sending thank-you notes or how to set the table. She was incredible."

During the days, when he wasn't working on Cyclia with Barry Clark, Jim was writing regularly with Jerry Juhl, pitching ideas for countless television series and specials almost constantly from 1967 through 1969. "Jim and I would sit and think up anything, from hourlong [specials] down to five minute sketches for *The Ed Sullivan Show*," said Juhl. The ideas were becoming wilder and more far out, with Juhl writing down the proposals nearly as fast as Jim could spin them. In April 1967, for example, Jim pitched *Moki,* a gender-bending case of mistaken identity in which a long-haired, androgynous young man is mistaken for a female fashion model. Brillstein shopped the proposal, but the subject matter was too touchy, even to those who recognized the brilliance behind it. "This guy Henson's obviously got a nutty visual mind," one potential director told Brillstein, "[but] this story scares the bejesus out of me. It's not exactly dirty—it just ain't quite clean . . . the guy is very talented and it's a funny idea, but I guess I'm just old fashioned."

Another innovative pitch was *Inside My Head,* which was basically a live-action version of the Limbo sketch in which a conversation between a man and woman is played out inside the man's brain. Jim envisioned the brain as a set made up of "strange electronic pulses and rhythms . . . a maze of fibers, membranes, and convoluted openings" and the same kind of quick-cut montages Jim had used for Limbo. The visual representations for how the brain works, Jim explained earnestly, "would be based on all the known facts about the brain which are not only fascinating, but more amazing and wondrous than anything a science fiction writer would invent." To his disappointment, as with *Moki,* no television network expressed interest in *Inside My Head.* And still there were a few Muppet-related proposals—all of which went nowhere—including the sur-realistic *Adventures of the Snerf-Poof from Planet Snee* and the even more bizarre *Johnny Carson and the Muppet Machine,* which Jim illustrated in a style that could have been ripped from the trippy pages of the fledgling underground comix scene.

If Jim was having a hard time finding a network willing to take a chance on some of his wilder projects, he soon found a receptive audience at NBC, which had recently launched *NBC Experiment in Television,* a series that catered to the more avant-garde or experi-mental filmmakers. Hyping its specials as "Off the Beaten Path," the hour-long *Experiment* ran without commercials on Sunday after-noons, spotlighting eclectic pieces like *A Coney Island of the Mind,* performed by students at the University of Southern California School of the Performing Arts, or *Movies in the Now Generation,* a collection of short student films hosted by George Plimpton.

For *Experiment,* Jim put aside dramatic and comedic pieces like *Moki* and *Inside My Head,* and proposed instead a documentary he called *A Collage of Today* "to communicate the ideas of Youth in the forms they understand," as Jim explained, "employing film and video media in new and exciting ways to best convey not only the substance, but the mood of the young." With the okay from NBC on February 15 and a budget of $100,000, Jim sent Barry Clark—who was still enthusiastically but unsuccessfully pitching Cyclia—on a quick sprint to scout out college campuses and clubs in San Fran-cisco, Los Angeles, Houston, Miami, and Omaha.

Jim burrowed into the project for the next two months, poring through books and magazines with Juhl for quotes and snippets of poetry or dialogue, filming one-on-one interviews in late February, and editing by mid-March. On Sunday, April 21, 1968, Jim's one-hour documentary—now titled *Youth 68: Everything's Changing . . .*

Or Maybe It Isn't—was broadcast on NBC, only a little less than four months after receiving the initial okay from the network—a remarkable pace. "We worked twenty hours a day for eight weeks," said Barry Clark.

Utilizing the same rapid-fire editing Jim had first used in *Time Piece*, *Youth 68* truly was a multimedia collage. Music overlaps with spoken commentary, and many times the screen is split into multiple images, resembling a monitor in a psychedelic film editing room. Jim was determined to aggressively use television technology—particularly chromakey, in which two images are composited together—to flood the viewer with sounds and images. Through chromakey, for example, the darkened silhouettes of dancers could be filled with film images, finally giving Jim the projected-on dancers he had envisioned for Cyclia.

At its core, *Youth 68* features interviews with young men and women around the country—including extended commentary from a charming Cass Elliot of the Mamas and the Papas and Marty Balin of Jefferson Airplane who too casually waves around a pistol—as they earnestly discuss music, drugs, education, the draft, religion, and the future. Perhaps reflecting Jim's own equivocal political viewpoint, *Youth 68* doesn't come down strongly on any position, preferring to allow each side to have its say—with, perhaps, one exception: as an army recruitment brochure was read aloud, Jim showed images of soldiers carrying their wounded, pushing back protesters, and wielding flamethrowers. But while Jim may have been antiwar, he had little interest in using his art to make a political statement. Still, Jim's apolitical stance was actually a kind of statement in itself, and Jim couldn't resist ending the program with one long-haired young man declaring that, "Nothing will be changed. The people who watch a broadcast like this aren't going to learn anything."

In fact, Jim's main motivation for *Youth 68* was neither political nor social, but technical. "Back in the sixties . . . I thought of myself as an experimental filmmaker," Jim said. "I was interested in the visual image for its own sake—different ways of using it—quick cutting and things of that sort. . . . I loved what one could do with the montaging of visual images, so I was playing with that in several experimental projects." Juhl put it more bluntly. "We got into [*Youth*

68] . . . because of the look and the technology that [Jim] had available to play with," Juhl said. "It was so typical of Jim to start from that point of view."

Critics responded favorably to Jim's experimental documentary—and many were even quick to recognize the technical wizardry involved. "Visually the program was a nearly continuous light show with images overlaid on image . . . so there were sometimes three things to watch," said the *Seattle Post-Intelligencer*, while the respected columnist Ralph J. Gleason enthused that "No television program on a commercial network that I have seen utilized the possibilities of the TV camera to the extent this show did." *Variety* declared it simply "one of the most inspired programs of this season." Viewers, however—who were more inclined to focus on content rather than Jim's technical prowess—were split. Some thought it "excellent," "brave," or "courageous," while others viewed it "with alarm and more than a little disgust," and demanded that NBC apologize for "some of the great damage you have done to our children and their future generations."

By summer, however, even those alarmed by what they saw as "the Hippies and drug addicts" of *Youth 68* would agree its outlook seemed benign, even quaint, against the background of the tumultuous summer of 1968. Two weeks before the debut of *Youth 68,* Martin Luther King had been assassinated in Memphis, sparking riots across the country. Six weeks later, Robert F. Kennedy was gunned down in Los Angeles. In early July, racial violence rocked Glenville, Ohio, leaving seven dead. A month later, police and protesters clashed outside the Democratic convention in Chicago. Jim's hopeful but naive "communicat[ion] of ideas" blew away with the same wind that dispersed the tear gas at the protests in Chicago.

That summer in New York, Jim had decided to change both the address and the name of his organization, moving Muppets, Inc. out of its 53rd Street address, and over to 227 East 67th Street, taking over the top two floors above an Italian restaurant. The new offices were accessible from the street entrance by a stairway so long, said one visitor, that it looked like the first steep hill of a roller coaster—and

Jim would buzz visitors in from the street, then stand at the very top of the steps just outside his office, gleefully shouting "Keep coming!" as visitors trudged up the long staircase.

With the new offices came a new name: Henson Associates, or HA! as Jim would winkingly abbreviate it. In the spirit of Henson Associates' playful acronym, Jim would later give the other divisions of his company similarly structured names, creating HO! (Henson Organization), HE! (Henson Enterprises), HIT! (Henson International Television), and HUM! (Henson Universal Music). With the name change, Jim was making a point: his company was about more than Muppets. He wanted to be considered more than just "a novelty act," said Jerry Nelson. It was his name over the door now, not Muppets—though Jim typically couldn't resist a bit of self-effacing silliness, as the sign outside the door at 227 greeted visitors with:

Henson Associates and Muppets Inc. This sign will be replaced with a nice expensive one some day—maybe.

Jim was still mulling over "a few larger projects," explained Barry Clark—who would leave the company that summer—and hoped to "attempt a feature film before the public's current infatuation with film declines." What those "larger projects" might be, however, even Jim didn't know. Since 1962, he and Jerry Juhl had been drafting an ambitious non-Muppet-related movie script called *Tale of Sand,* a dark western in which the main character learns he's the Chosen One. It had "a weird kind of dark ritual look to it," Juhl said later, like "a bad dream, except that most if it was very funny." Jim was floating the script around Hollywood—he wanted to play the main character, so he was pushing hard—"but nothing ever happened to it," said Juhl flatly. "It was not a very Hollywood idea . . . it was such a bizarre piece of work there wasn't much hope for it." Still, Jim and Juhl would tinker with it for years.

Finally, in late 1968, Jim dusted off an experimental piece he and Juhl had scripted and circulated unsuccessfully two years earlier, a one-hour special called *The Cube*—an "original, surrealistic comedy," as Jim described it, that "dramatizes the complex, baffling problems of reality versus illusion." *Baffling* was putting it mildly; when Brillstein had shopped the script in 1966, most executives had no idea what to make of it. "I see no hope for it in prime time," wrote one confused producer, "unless [the networks] turn out to be far more courageous and experimental than I expect them to be."

By 1968, that experimental network would turn out to once again be NBC—still looking for projects for its *Experiment in Television,* and still enthusiastic about Jim's work following the success of *Youth 68.* On December 30, 1968, then, the network gave Jim the go-ahead for the project; by February 8, 1969, he was already filming the special in Toronto. For the first time, Jim would be producing a serious full-length feature, using professional actors—and no puppets—and he was determined to ensure it looked exactly as he envisioned. "After *Time Piece,* Jim often got frustrated when directors couldn't give him what he wanted," said Oz, who had seen Jim patiently, but firmly, try to articulate his vision to other directors and filmmakers.

For *The Cube,* there would be no intermediaries who needed explanations; Jim would again step behind the camera himself. "[Jim's] inspiration for *The Cube* came more from exploring the possibilities of television," Juhl said. "We were just reaching the point with videotape editing where you could play with it and get novel results. . . . It was really a matter of shooting film-style on tape, but the possibilities seemed exciting to us, and especially to Jim." For the five days it would take to shoot *The Cube*—a whirlwind pace made only slightly easier by the fact that the entire production used only one set, the eponymous cube—Jim would issue directions to his actors in a near whisper, *hmmmm* quietly as he considered their input, then stand patiently in his black leather jacket, arms folded, as the cameras rolled. The taping went smoothly, and Jim edited the film on February 16 and 17 to have a cut ready to show the network on the 18th. Five days later, *The Cube* was on the air.

Deliberately vague and defiantly artsy, *The Cube* perhaps most closely resembles an avant-garde episode of *The Twilight Zone.* The main character—played by comedic actor Dick Schaal and identified only as "The Man in the Cube"—is trapped in a white, cube-shaped room, with no idea how he arrived there or who he is. As furniture, props, and characters move in and out through the room—including two Gestapo-type policemen, a rock group, and a critic who informs

the Man that he is actually in a television show—it becomes difficult, even for the viewer, to determine what, if anything, is real.
Growing increasingly paranoid, the Man finally exits the Cube to
the sound of applause, then enters a psychiatrist's office where he
accidentally cuts himself . . . and bleeds jam. Everything fades, and
he's trapped back in the Cube.

"Congratulations," wrote one viewer to NBC, "we're not just
sure what we learned from it but it was quite a relief from the usual
TV fare." Even co-writer Jerry Juhl wasn't sure what it was about.
"We were in an era where . . . everybody had a paranoid streak," Juhl
explained. In a way, it was *Time Piece* again, with the main character
trying to make sense of the world around him—but even that was
probably reading too much into it. More than anything, Jim was
playing with the form, spinning a circular tale with a shock ending in
an artistic way. "When [Jim] got into the experimental film mode,
that was the story he tended to tell," said Juhl, "one of those 'repeat
stories.' "

Response to *The Cube* was mixed—and viewers and critics either loved it or hated it, with very little middle ground. "A dramatic
highlight of the season," proclaimed critic Ben Gross in the New
York *Daily News,* while other viewers thought it "excellent," "provocative," or "a challenge and a pleasure." Many disagreed. "The
people who wrote it must be weird," one viewer wrote flatly. *Variety*
groaned that "it must have been intended for what is called egghead
ghetto time [meanwhile], the lower strata of TV viewers must still be
wondering what it was all about."

One viewer—a Mr. Dionne from California, who likely *didn't*
consider himself part of the "lower strata"—fired off an angry, rambling letter, complaining haughtily that "the most disciplined attention I could give [*The Cube*] was a belch from the grave of Marcus
Aurelius, occasioned, I might add, by the dead weight of its own dust
caving in on itself." Two weeks later came Jim's one-sentence response:

Dear Mr. Dionne:
What the fuck are you talking about?

Yours truly,
JIM HENSON

Reading the letter forty years later, Frank Oz roared with laughter. "That's actually very Jim!" It was uncharacteristic of Jim to swear—his strongest epithet was usually "Oh, for heaven's sake!"—but that was the difference, Lisa Henson explained, between "work Jim" and "home Jim." "That isn't something in *our* lives he would say," agreed Jane, "but he would certainly talk that way to Frank!"

If *The Cube,* or even *Youth 68,* left critics and audiences baffled, Jim didn't mind a bit; he was pursuing his own interests, regardless of success—and besides, he still had Muppet commercials and appearances on variety shows to pay the bills. "I used to always think in terms of having two careers going, two threads that I was working with at the same time," Jim said later. "One was accepted by the audience and was successful, and that was the Muppets. The other [experimental films] was something I was very interested in and enjoyed. It didn't have that commercial success, but that didn't particularly frustrate me because I enjoyed it."

Still, Jim was looking for a major project—something larger than scattered one-hour specials, psychedelic nightclubs, or experimental films. For a brief moment, there was the prospect of a collaboration with the cartoonist Johnny Hart, who had proposed developing a series based on his popular comic strip *The Wizard of Id.* Jim met with Hart and agreed to prepare a short pilot to "demonstrate the technique and approach of its proposed television special" for a total cost of only $1,500. Don Sahlin masterfully built puppets and sets closely resembling Hart's original drawings, and the Muppet team performed the sketches with enthusiasm, even working in an explosion at the end. But the project went nowhere, due largely to lack of interest on Hart's part, who "just decided he didn't want to do it," recalled Jerry Nelson. For Jim, there were no hard feelings; in fact, he would continue to circulate the pilot among the major networks for another year.

Even as Jim remained on good terms with Hart, he was struggling in a recent relationship with the Frito-Lay company, which had approached Henson Associates about producing several commercials for Munchos potato crisps. Things got off to a shaky start when the Young & Rubicam ad firm, representing Frito-Lay, sent over a contract adding a clause to take ownership of any characters created for the ads. "This is completely wrong," Jim scrawled in his looping cursive on a note stapled to the contract. "We always insist on ownership of the characters." *Never sell anything I own,* Jim had warned Brillstein six years earlier—and he still meant it, even if it meant scuttling a relationship with a client. The offending clause was removed, and Jim would shoot three commercials for Munchos, memorable mostly for their antagonist: a snack-stealing monster that Jim had originally created for an unaired ad campaign for General Foods back in 1966.

Frito-Lay was delighted with the spots and requested several more commercials. Jim, however, was no longer interested—at last, he had found his next big project. It wouldn't be long before the monster from the Munchos commercials would no longer crave and eat potato chips, but would devour cookies instead.

"Tape Pilot Shows," Jim wrote in his journal entry for July 9, 1969, then two more words: *"Sesame Street."*

CHAPTER SIX

SESAME STREET

1969–1970

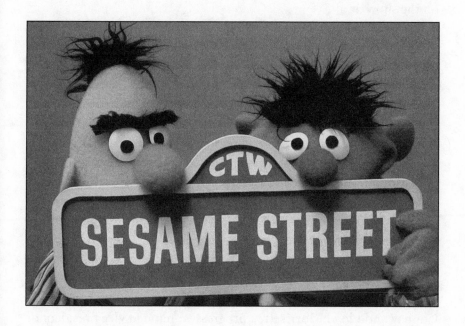

"I THINK THERE WAS A KIND OF COLLECTIVE GENIUS ABOUT THE CORE group that created *Sesame Street*," Children's Television Workshop co-founder Joan Ganz Cooney once remarked, "but there was only one real genius in our midst, and that was Jim."

That was high praise, considering the caliber of the team Cooney and her CTW colleague Lloyd Morrisett had put together to develop the show. Besides music maestro Joe Raposo—a swaggering, Harvard-educated virtuoso who could knock off a tune about happiness or itchiness over lunch—Cooney had landed several veterans of the well-regarded children's show *Captain Kangaroo*, including a brilliant, Yale-educated writer and producer named Jon Stone. Yet, while the Muppets would come to practically define the overall look and feel of *Sesame Street,* Jim had been among the last to join CTW's creative team. It had been Stone, in fact, who had not only recommended Jim to Cooney, but had also strongly suggested that if CTW couldn't secure Jim's services, they'd be better off with no puppets on the show at all.

Jon Stone had first become acquainted with Jim in 1965, when the two of them had been practically thrown together by CBS producer Fred Silverman for a pilot Stone was developing, a Cinderella spoof combining live actors and puppets. The finished pilot had gone nowhere, but Jim and Stone struck up a friendship, founded on their mutual regard for each other's talents. "We discovered we had a tremendous empathy for each other's work styles and sense of humor," Stone said. "I just loved what he was doing." The two got on so well, in fact, that Jim hired Stone several years later to direct *Youth 68,* and the two vowed to continue looking for another project to work on together. By July 1968, with only a little nudging from Stone, they had found that next project.

That summer, both Jim and Stone were deeply involved with the Children's Television Workshop, a nonprofit organization created in March 1968 by a young television producer named Joan Ganz Cooney and Lloyd Morrisett, a progressive-minded vice president of the Carnegie Corporation. Their goal, said Cooney, was simple: "to create a successful television program that would make a difference in the lives of children, in particular, poor inner-city children, and help prepare them for school."

They were wading into choppy waters. Previously, educational television had consisted largely of stone-faced educators either staring directly into the camera lecturing, or writing on a blackboard— essentially a filmed classroom lesson, neither of which made for terribly compelling television. On the other hand, educational shows aimed solely at children—like *Romper Room* or *Captain Kangaroo*— were fun and well intentioned but were guided by no true pedagogies. Cooney envisioned a show that would take the best of each approach: a fun, fast-paced kids' show with content steeped in the latest pedagogies and education research. "I want this show to jump and move fast," Cooney told *The New York Times.* "[Kids] like commercials and banana peel humor and avant-garde video and audio techniques. . . . We have to infuse our content into forms children find accessible."

If that was the critereon, Jim Henson was clearly her man. For the moment, however, Cooney admitted she had "blanked" on Jim's name when putting together her creative crew, and was now hunting elsewhere for her team by poaching from the best children's television staff available: the team at the highly successful *Captain Kangaroo,* where the Captain himself, Bob Keeshan, knew how to assemble talent. Immediately, Cooney lured away Dave Connell, one of Keeshan's executive producers, as well as Sam Gibbon, another *Kangaroo* veteran who was put in charge of curriculum development. Her real catch, however, was the versatile Stone, who had to be persuaded out of a freelancer's relatively quiet existence to take on the responsibilities of directing and writing for a daily show again. ("I talked to [Joan Cooney] for fifteen minutes," recalled Stone, "and I was hers for life.")

Next came a series of five seminars in Cambridge and New York over the summer of 1968, providing, on the face of it, an opportunity to develop the goals and direction of the still unnamed show, but mostly allowing the academics and the creative talent their first real chance to stare each other down and learn to work together. After the first workshop in June, Stone invited Jim to sit in on the next series of meetings, to be held July 25 and 26 at Harvard. Jim traveled to Cambridge and sat in on the discussions, rarely speaking, but listening intently. Stone and Cooney's project had his attention; he'd be back for the next meeting in August, this time to be held in New York at the Waldorf-Astoria hotel.

Several weeks later, Jim entered the conference room at the Waldorf and took a seat near the back—slouching down, as usual, until he was nearly horizontal—and sat so quietly that he finally had to be pointed out to Cooney, who had heard Jim's praises sung by Stone and others but had yet to meet him in person. Even then, it still took a moment for Cooney to register. "I hadn't remembered the name at first," Cooney admitted later, but then "a lightbulb went on" and she remembered seeing a compilation of Jim's commercials over at the

Johnny Victor Theatre in New York earlier in the year. "I was on the floor," Cooney said. "I couldn't believe puppets could be so hip and funny." Once she realized the slouching, bearded figure was the puppeteer Stone had recommended—the same one whose commercials had made her "fall over laughing"—"I was thrilled," she said. Stone and his creative team were more than just thrilled; they were united in their determination to hire him.

Getting Jim, and the Muppets, wouldn't necessarily be easy. Always fascinated by any opportunity to push the boundaries of television, Jim was intrigued by the concept of a new kind of children's educational program that would use television as a positive force. But he initially resisted Stone's and Cooney's entreaties to join the CTW creative team, largely because after spending the last decade expanding into film, animation, documentaries, and experimental television, he didn't want to be thought of mainly as a puppeteer again. Even worse, if he were to begin performing regularly on a children's show, he would be slapped with the dreaded label *children's puppeteer*. "There was a huge ambivalence there," said Jerry Juhl, "because one of *the* things that he would say most often and most strongly about the puppet work . . . was that this was *adult puppetry*."

Fortunately, the new show offered Jim creative opportunities beyond just puppetry. At the moment, in fact, with the first show still more than a year away, the Muppets weren't even needed; instead, CTW was interested in putting together short films, no more than one or two minutes long, to teach children letters, numbers, or other concepts like body parts. These short pieces were to be inserted like advertisements—and, in fact, would always be referred to as "inserts"—at regular intervals throughout each show, repeated two, sometimes even three times per hour. This was just the sort of thing Jim could get excited about. With his rat-a-tat editing style that had defined *Time Piece* and *Youth 68*, his bold animation techniques, and his knack for quickly and effectively driving home a point— a skill honed from making commercials in which he had only eight seconds to get his message across—Jim was uniquely suited to take on the task of creating CTW's first "educational commercials." "Jim got involved right away because he loved making short films so much," said Jon Stone. But Jim also had one other significant vantage point: as the father of four children under the age of ten, he had spent countless evenings painting, gluing, talking with and listening to his own kids—and had come to appreciate just how perceptive, interesting, and receptive an audience of children could be.

And so, Jim agreed to join CTW's creative team—but there was one bit of business to resolve first. While Jim was committed to producing Muppet segments for the new show, he insisted, as usual, on owning his characters. That determination caused some grumbling among CTW lawyers, who pointed out that CTW would ultimately be providing the facilities and doing the filming, editing, and production work. Jim stood firm, but eventually agreed that while he would maintain ownership of the characters—and could approve the merchandise in which any of his characters were used—Henson Associates and CTW would split the profits from any Muppet-related merchandise associated with the show.

Before a single frame of film had been shot, Jim and CTW had negotiated—as part of the contract that would acquire Jim's services—the outline of the agreement relating to merchandising that would ensure, well beyond the wildest dreams of either party, the future financial success of Henson Associates—and, for that matter, for CTW. For Jim, it had been about protecting his work; clearly, neither Jim nor anyone else could have foreseen the merchandising juggernaut they were creating. In fact, after the first CTW meetings in Cambridge in June 1968, Jim wouldn't even mention CTW in his personal journal until early 1969. However lofty the goals of CTW might be, there were no guarantees the show would last beyond one season. "This was an educational children's show," remarked Jerry Juhl, summing up the consensus at the time. "The thought was 'thirteen weeks, and it'll be over.'"

Regardless, once Jim was on board, his commitment was complete, and he quickly set to work producing short films for "this future amorphous television show that was still a year-and-a-half away." One of the first films Jim created was a short piece he called "Body Parts vs. Heavy Machinery," comparing the movements of the body to similar movements in machines, and featuring several boys—including five-year-old Brian Henson—playing in a sandbox, scooping up fistfuls of sand, intercut with shots of a working steam shovel clawing at mounds of earth.

While the film and its lessons wouldn't be seen or appreciated by preschoolers for nearly a year, for Brian Henson, the educational benefits were immediate: at breakfast the morning after completing work on the film, Jim presented Brian with his first paycheck, a compliment, and a gentle lesson in fiscal responsibility. "He said, 'So Brian, you've done a good week's work and you've earned this,'" Brian recalled later. "He gave me a check for fifty dollars and . . . then he said, 'So here's what we're going to do: you earned that money so now we're going to take that to the bank, and you're going to open a bank account and you're going to deposit your fifty dollars and you're going to get a bank book and then it will earn interest and you can add money.' . . . In that moment, he taught me how people earn a living and how the world works. I probably learned more from that experience than anything else in my life." It was Jim in what Brian would affectionately call "full-blown father mode," providing gentle guidance and educating in short, easy-to-understand terms—just as he would for millions of other children with his short films.

The next order of business was to produce a "pitch reel," to be shown on closed-circuit television to public television stations in the spring, giving them ample opportunity to learn more about the show before episodes became available in the autumn. On January 22, 1969—two weeks before he would sprint to Toronto for the whirlwind taping session for *The Cube*—Jim taped the Muppet portions of the twenty-five-minute pitch reel, using Kermit and Rowlf, who was still the best-known Muppet, as emcees. Between short films and earnest explanations about the research behind the show, Jim wove a running gag about the difficulty in coming up with a name for the show, with assorted Muppet ad men sitting around a smoky boardroom table, hashing through possible names. "We'll call it *The Itty Bitty Farm and City Witty Ditty Nitty Gritty Dog and Kitty Pretty Little Kiddie Show*," suggests the chairman—only to have a monster angrily devour his chair. Finally, one ad man has an epiphany. "Hey, these kids can't read or write, can they? Then howzabout we call the show *Hey, Stupid!*" Exasperated, Rowlf breaks up the meeting and announces he'll come up with the name himself.

Actually, Jim's rambunctious Muppet meeting was bitingly close to reality—for the CTW team *hadn't* come up with the show's name until practically the moment before Jim began rolling tape on the pitch reel. In late 1968, Stone had suggested *123 Avenue B,* a title that held until mid-January 1969, when it was decided the name sounded too much like a real address. At that point, Stone turned to his writing team for suggestions, poring over lists with everything from the boring *Fun Street* to the uninspired *The Video Classroom.* Nothing really leapt off the page until a writer named Virginia Schone submitted a list containing two alliterative words: *Sesame Street.*

"I fought like hell—I thought it was an awful name," Stone said later. "I thought the E at the end was bad education—it looks like a silent E, so it'd be '*See-same Street*' if you're trying to read—and I thought it was too cute." Producer Dave Connell, however, issued a directive that "if nobody came up with a better idea, as of Monday we [are] going to call the show *Sesame Street.*" By Monday, the name had stuck—and as Jim began filming on Wednesday, it was Kermit who was shown coming up with the name on-screen, casually explaining that the reference to the phrase *open sesame* "kinda gives the idea of a street where neat stuff happens."

CTW intended to have pilot episodes of *Sesame Street* ready by June 1969, so Jim began sketching out a few new Muppets for the show early that spring, handing Don Sahlin a felt-tip drawing, little more than a doodle, of two characters. The first had surprised eyes set in a tall, banana-shaped head, topped by a shock of dark hair, while the other—looking rather like Moldy Hay from *Sam and Friends*—had a head like a football, a large nose, and even larger ears, with shaggy dark hair covering his eyes. Typically, Sahlin captured the spirit of Jim's drawing—highlighting the features that defined the characters and discarding those that didn't—and produced two Muppets that manifested the study in opposites, both in design and personality, that Jim always found wonderfully funny. "The design was so simple and pure and wonderful," said Oz. "You had somebody who is all vertical and somebody who is all horizontal." In the talented hands of Oz and Jim, those vertical and horizontal characters would quickly become, in the minds of many, one of the funniest comedy duos anywhere, providing teachable moments for millions even as they poked, prodded, teased, and taunted each other: Ernie and Bert.

It took some trying for Jim and Oz to decide which performer would take which puppet. "We played with who did what using the mirror in the workshop," recalled Oz, with each taking a turn performing Ernie then Bert. Ultimately, the design of the puppets triggered their personalities. "The design really reflects the character and affects the kind of voice you do," Oz said. "Ernie is expansiveness, while Bert is this rigid, uptight guy." With that as the basis, it was easy for Jim to finally assume the more laid-back Ernie, and Oz the serious Bert. Still, it would take a bit more tinkering before everything would fall into place with the characters—it even took Jim awhile to find the right voice for Ernie, at first giving the character a voice similar to Rowlf's. But with the creation of Ernie and Bert, Jim had made his first iconic contribution to *Sesame Street*. It would be far from his last. (Contrary to popular rumor, Ernie and Bert were *not* named for the similarly named cop and taxi driver in the film *It's a Wonderful Life*—"it's a total coincidence," said Stone—though it should perhaps be noted that Jim *did* have a great-uncle named Ernie.)

Another of Jim's most endearing contributions to *Sesame Street* were the short films and animations he would supply to be used as inserts, many of which were completed before the first episode aired. Following the completion of the body parts film in January 1969, Jim began working on a series of storyboards for ten short pieces of film and animation that would be used to teach children to count. While Jim would label his March 1969 storyboards *Numerosity*— and CTW would invoice them under the labels "Henson 2" or whichever number Jim featured in his film—for a generation of viewers, they would always be known simply as "the baker films."

Each film began with a colorfully animated counting sequence, followed by a number of short live-action clips in which human actors counted aloud various objects (including, in one segment, Jim as a juggler who counts three balls). At the end, a neatly pressed baker carrying a precariously balanced armful of the appropriate number of desserts appears at the top of a short flight of stairs, dramatically announces his culinary creation ("Ten . . . chocolate layer . . . cakes!"), and immediately falls down the stairs—Jim's educational television equivalent to ending a sketch with an explosion. "I don't like it," said Cooney of what she called "banana peel humor." "Younger children—two-year-olds—they think he's hurt." But it would stay. With the films completed, Jim sent his usual thank-you notes to his actors, then billed CTW an even $40,000, well below the actual costs for producing the films—especially since Jim had estimated his expenses based on producing ten one-minute films, when the completed films actually ran nearly two minutes in length. In the spirit of the project, however, Jim refused to bill CTW for the overages.

On July 9, 1969, only a little more than a month after the *Numerosity* work sessions, Jim and Oz—stocked with Ernie and Bert and a handful of generic puppets with interchangeable eyes, noses, and hair that Jim called "Anything Muppets"—spent nine days in Philadelphia taping five pilot shows for *Sesame Street*. The pilots were to be shown to test audiences in Philadelphia and New York, a group that included the toughest critics of all: the preschoolers who were *Sesame Street*'s target audience. As it turns out, the responses of this key group would result in an important change in the show's format.

In its original pilot format, *Sesame Street* moved from segment to segment in a deliberate, self-aware manner, with the human cast members introducing many of the short films or animations. The Muppets would then be seen in their own segments, often referencing prior inserts, and serving as the links from one piece to the next. This gave the show the magaziney *Laugh-In* feel Cooney had originally envisioned, but such a format meant the Muppets were completely isolated from *Sesame Street*'s human cast. This had been done deliberately, and with the best of intentions. "We had been told by all our advisors that preschoolers have difficulty in differentiating between fantasy and reality," Stone said. "So the first idea was that you would have the street—a very real-looking set with real people on it—and then you would cut away to puppets, to animation, to all the things that make up the fantasy.

"We did the test shows that way," Stone continued, "and we realized right away that we had a problem, because the people on the street couldn't compete with the puppets. We had children watching these shows and their attention span just went way down when we cut to the street. . . . So the information we got from these test shows demonstrated that we needed a transition from the fantasy to the reality."

The solution to this unforeseen hitch, then, was simple: Muppets were needed on the street.

Jim thought about it, and after taking his family on a quick vacation to Barbados and St. Lucia at the end of July, returned to Jon Stone with several ideas. One of his thoughts was "to have a character that the child could live through," a Muppet who was representative of the audience. "Big Bird, in theory, is himself a child," said Jim, "and we wanted to make this great big silly awkward creature that would make the same kind of dumb mistakes that kids make." To make things even more interesting, Jim and Stone decided on another character that was nearly the antithesis of the wide-eyed, innocent Big Bird: a cynical, complaining grouch named Oscar. "Oscar is there because we didn't want a bland kiddie show," said Stone. "We didn't want to let it get too sweet."

The remaining issue, at least for Jim, was one of personnel. Doing brief Muppet sketches and inserts on tape was one thing; appearing regularly on a daily show was another. Performing Big Bird and Oscar would be a time-consuming task that would require the puppeteer to be present for all 130 shows CTW anticipated filming each year—and Jim, who intended for both characters to be performed by the same puppeteer, was not inclined to devote himself to full-time puppeteering. The versatile Oz was briefly considered for the task, but Jim had envisioned Big Bird as a full-body, walkaround puppet, and Oz, after his experience in the stuffy La Choy dragon costume, was remaining steadfast in his refusal to perform any more large characters—and besides, Oz was too valuable to spare for 130 shows. With the first episodes of *Sesame Street* going before the cameras in less than four months, then, Jim needed to quickly hire a puppeteer specifically for the job of performing Big Bird and Oscar.

Fortunately, Jim already had a recruiting mission on his calendar—

and in August 1969, he traveled to Salt Lake City for several days to attend the annual conference for the Puppeteers of America. There he attended a performance by a thirty-five-year-old puppeteer named Caroll Spinney, who advertised his performance as "an experimental production" of live puppetry interacting with an animated background. It would have been an impressive combination of media had it actually worked. But as Spinney began his performance, an errant spotlight shone down on his movie screen, completely washing out the animated background. "I couldn't see my films to synchronize my movements," Spinney lamented. "It was an immediate disaster. I lost the whole bit." Spinney managed to salvage the performance through a bit of ad-libbing, then slunk offstage. To his surprise, Jim greeted him backstage in his near-whisper way, and asked Spinney if he could meet with him later to talk.

That invitation sounded familiar to Spinney, who had met Jim several years earlier at a puppetry convention in Sturbridge, Massachusetts. There, Jim had suggested Spinney come to New York "to talk about" working for the Muppets—but Spinney hadn't followed up on the suggestion, failing to realize that "Jim never just wanted to chat. If he said he wanted to talk about something, it meant that he wanted to *do* it." This time, Spinney wouldn't make the same mistake.

Spinney stashed his gear, then ran to the lounge where Jim was already waiting, slouched down on a couch. "I saw your show," Jim told Spinney. "I liked what you were *trying* to do." Spinney laughed, relieved. Jim understood—and when offered another chance to "join the Muppets," Spinney eagerly accepted. As usual, Jim had a knack for choosing the right people for the job—and despite Spinney's disastrous live show, Jim had seen the performer's talent.

Even as Jim was finding his puppeteer, the workshop at Henson Associates was bustling with activity. With production on *Sesame Street* ramping up, Jim had employed several more designers to work alongside Sahlin, including Caroly Wilcox—a talented puppeteer with a penchant for design—and the serendipitously named Kermit Love, a marionettist and former Broadway costume designer with a Santa Claus beard who excelled at crafting full-body puppets. Meanwhile, in the administrative offices upstairs, Jim had recently hired

Diana Birkenfield, a former production assistant on *The Jimmy Dean Show,* to act as his first full-time producer, reviewing and vetting potential projects.

One office, however, sat empty. In June, Jerry Juhl had approached Jim and amiably informed him that he and his wife, Susan, were planning to move to California, where Jerry hoped to make it as a freelance writer. "I wasn't in California very long at all before I got a call from Jon Stone," recalled Juhl. "They actually had a really hard time finding writers [for *Sesame Street*]." Like many, Juhl was skeptical about whether *Sesame Street* would last more than a season—and he didn't want to relocate to New York to find the worthy experiment had failed after three months. But Stone, and Jim, were persistent; when it came to the Muppets, Jim was certain Juhl knew their temperament and rhythms better than anyone—Jim wanted and needed him. So Stone tried again, offering Juhl the option of remaining in California and working long-distance. With that, Juhl agreed to become one of Stone's most important *Sesame Street* writers, mailing in Muppet scripts from California—and commuting into New York when necessary—for the next five years.

As fall approached, the Muppet builders were putting the finishing touches on both Big Bird and Oscar, readying them for the first full day of street shooting on October 13, 1969. Jim wanted Big Bird to be the next phase in full-body characters, an improvement over earlier efforts that had limited facial expressions and squatty arms that inhibited arm and hand movements. Jim wanted Big Bird to have a more expressive face, with eyes that blinked, and a flexible body that allowed the performer to more easily move and react. Sahlin, then, was eagerly at work on Big Bird's head and the whirl of gears that would allow the performer to open the puppet's eyes, while Kermit Love, with his flair for the dramatic, assembled the body. Apart from the drawings he had provided, Jim had inspired Big Bird's design in other ways. "When Big Bird was being developed, I kept the image of Jim Henson in mind," said Love. "I always thought of Jim's stature—he was well over six feet tall, and that loping gait he had when he walked down a hallway. Somehow or other, that was what stuck in my mind." For a moment, Jim had even considered constructing a puppet in which the performer walked backward, to more closely simulate the actual bend of a bird's leg. "Fortunately," said Spinney, "Jim abandoned that idea, or I could have spent over thirty years walking around backward."

There was nothing overly complicated about Oscar, however—he was a Muppet typical of Jim's ferocious yet somehow nonthreatening monsters, originally an orange shag rug with a wide mouth and angry eyebrows. Oscar had been partly inspired by regular lunches at a seafood restaurant just around the corner from the Muppet workshop called Oscar's Salt of the Sea, where the grumbling, growling owner often reduced Jim and Jon Stone to fits of giggles. As initially envisioned by Jim and Stone, Oscar was supposed to be a grouch that lived in the sewers, accessible through a manhole cover. "It would lift up and you'd see these little eyes looking at you, and you'd [go] down through the dripping water in the sewers [and] here would [be] these scruffy little things in half darkness that were picking things out of the water and eating them," recalled Stone. It was an idea he and Jim found hilarious, but ultimately, "we decided that was too gross." Oscar would live in a much more easily accessible—and far less gross—garbage can.

On Monday, September 29, 1969, Jim and Oz began filming their first set of Muppet inserts at Reeves Teletape at 67th and Broadway, just a short cab ride across Central Park. The first segment, written and directed by Stone, featured Ernie and Bert riffing on what would be one of the themes for *Sesame Street*'s first episode: the letter W and the word *wash*. The very first look preschoolers would have of Ernie and Bert, then, featured Ernie singing in the bathtub, asking an already annoyed Bert to toss a bar of soap "into Rosie."

"I call my bathtub Rosie," explained Ernie.

"Ernie, why do you call your bathtub Rosie?" asked Bert.

"Because every time I take a bath," responded Ernie, "I leave a ring around Rosie!"—and then came what would quickly become a signature sound from the show, mimicked by countless four-year-olds across the nation to the exasperation of preschool teachers everywhere: Ernie's trademark laugh, a rapid-fire series of guttural, slightly slurpy gunshots: *kkkkhi-kkkkkhi-kkkkkhi-kkkkhi-kkkkhi!* A star was born.

A little less than two weeks later, on Friday, October 10, Jim went to the Teletape facility at 81st and Broadway—residing in an old RKO movie theater that had been converted for television—and strolled the recently completed *Sesame Street* set with Sahlin and Spinney, inspecting the various nooks where the Muppet performers would be kneeling, crouching, or lying as they worked. The area around Oscar's trash can was immediately problematic: it had been constructed in such a way that the right-handed Spinney couldn't wedge his arm into the trash can's opening. Spinney would have to perform Oscar left-handed until the set could be adjusted. "Left hands are much stupider than your right if you're right handed," Spinney explained. Still, Jim was anxious to see how Oscar would look on the set and asked Spinney to perform the character anyway, regardless of the difficult setup.

Even without the contorted trash can, Spinney was nervous about debuting Oscar in front of Jim. He had only just decided that morning on the voice he would use for the character—based on a gruff Bronx cabdriver who had driven Spinney to the studio and growled, "Where to, Mac?"—and had yet to find out if it met with Jim's approval. "I hoped I had the right voice," Spinney said later. Jim waited patiently as Spinney pulled Oscar onto his left arm and twisted himself awkwardly behind the cutaway can. After a moment, Jim rapped on Oscar's trash can; the lid banged open and the dingy orange Oscar emerged to glare at Jim. "Get away from my trash can!" Spinney snarled in his cabdriver's voice.

Jim smiled and nodded appreciatively. "That'll do fine."

Beginning Monday, October 13, Jim would spend a few days on the *Sesame Street* set performing Kermit and Ernie, but for the most part the fall of 1969 was business as usual at Henson Associates, with continued appearances on variety shows and work on commercials. For Jim and his team, *Sesame Street* was, for the moment, just another assignment to add to the already lengthy list of projects Jim was either working on or had in development. In fact, when the first episode of *Sesame Street* aired nationally on November 10, it didn't even merit mentioning in Jim's private journal. That may have been due, in part, to a stinging review of the first two weeks' worth of *Sesame Street* episodes by *New York Times* critic Jack Gould, which Jim later admitted had bruised his feelings. In his review, Gould sneeringly referred to the Muppets as "stocking puppets" and thought them "distressingly bland." "One yearns for Burr Till-strom," Gould concluded. It would not be the last time Gould would claw at Jim.

Still, Gould's harsh review was decidedly in the minority—for it was clear almost immediately that Jim had helped create something extraordinary. In the October 31, 1969, issue of *Life*—which hit newsstands several weeks before the first episode of *Sesame Street* aired—Jim and the *Sesame Street* Muppets were featured in a full-page photo and story. In November, the Washington, D.C., City Council approved a resolution renaming a local road "Sesame Street" for a week. By December, Big Bird was already making a featured appearance on *Ed Sullivan,* dancing with chorus girls in a piece by noted Broadway choreographer Pete Gennaro. That same month *Woman's Day* featured sewing patterns readers could use to make their own Muppets—and then perform them to an original routine written by Jerry Juhl. "It's clever and witty and charming," enthused the *Detroit Free Press.* "It's integrated. It's non-violent. It's fun. It may even be educational." Before the end of the year, even Jack Gould had to finally admit *Sesame Street* was "an undisputed hit." "I didn't know what success meant, but I knew we had it," Joan Cooney said later.

Even with *Sesame Street* building momentum, Jim continued writing new pieces for variety show appearances. On November 30, he and Oz performed a musical skit on *The Ed Sullivan Show* using several new Muppets, including a crazy-haired puppet in sunglasses who would come to be known by the name of the song performed that evening, a bit of nonsensical scat by the Italian composer Piero Umiliani called "Mah Nà Mah Nà." Jim had found the song in a location about as far away from *Sesame Street* as possible: a 1968 Italian sexploitation film called *Sweden: Heaven and Hell,* which premiered in New York in August 1969. Oz felt sure that he and Jim had probably both seen the film when it played at the Avco Embassy Theatre five minutes away from the Henson offices, but "only Jim," Oz said, laughing, "would have recognized its potential so quickly!"

As sung by Jim—with Oz performing two vaguely bovine backup singers known as Snowths—"Mahna Mahna" (as Jim would always spell it) seemed custom-made for the Muppet brand of madness. Jim took great delight in playing with the four sides of the television screen, zipping his character in sideways, rushing the camera from upstage, or even backing in from downstage. It was an affectionate nod to the simpler days of *Sam and Friends*—while there was no explosion at the end, the sketch concluded with the puppets smashing into the camera, blacking it out—and the *Sullivan* crowd went wild, laughing and applauding spontaneously several times during the three-and-a-half-minute performance.

In early 1970, with *Sesame Street* officially a success, ABC-TV expressed interest in reviving a Muppet project that had been languishing, unaired, for nearly two years: a fairy tale satire called *Hey Cinderella!* that Jim had taped in the fall of 1968, using the basic outline of the failed Cinderella pilot he and Jon Stone had collaborated on back in 1965. Jim was delighted with ABC's decision to pick up the hour-long special; he was hoping to make *Hey Cinderella!* the first in a regular series he was calling *Tales from Muppetland,* and set to work filming several short spots with Kermit that could be inserted into *Hey Cinderella!* just before each commercial. That seemingly innocuous decision would lead to unexpected headaches.

Following the April 10 airing of *Hey Cinderella!,* Jack Gould—the same critic who had already dismissed Jim's work on *Sesame Street* as "distressingly bland"—took a swipe at Jim again, this time taking great umbrage with the use of Kermit in the filmed lead-ins to each commercial break. "Apparently, the Children's Television Workshop . . . is not adverse to cashing in when success strikes," lamented Gould. "*Sesame Street* last night lost a little of its luster as Kermit broke the faith and became one more pitchman."

That was too much for Jim. It didn't seem to matter to Gould that although the production team included Jim and Jon Stone, *Hey Cinderella!* had absolutely no affiliation with CTW or *Sesame Street.* Further, Kermit was the furthest thing from a pitchman; Jim had been very careful not to show Kermit actually endorsing any products. Frustrated, Jim appealed to Gould in writing, trying, without much success, to set the record straight. "For the past ten or twelve years, approximately half my income has been derived from producing Muppet commercials," Jim explained. "Since the advent of *Sesame Street*, and my own interest and concern for television . . . I have become a great deal more selective, and have turned down many lucrative offers that seemed to be trying to capitalize on *Sesame Street*." Rightly pointing out that "it is my income from commercial TV that makes my participation in educational TV possible," Jim assured the critic that he would continue "to work with a degree of integrity and responsibility to the children of the country."

Commercials would remain Henson Associates' primary source of revenue, at least for a while, but Gould's criticism, however unfair, had stung. In August 1970, Jim refused to renew his contract to film additional commercials for the Frito-Lay company, citing both his time commitment to *Sesame Street* as well as Henson Associates' "extreme sensitivity to commercialization of the Muppet characters." As he had assured Gould, Jim was indeed becoming more selective in the kinds of projects he took on, preferring to produce short sales or promotional films for internal use by companies rather than major advertising campaigns. In a sense, he was lying low.

One of the most successful of those internal campaigns was another series of short films with Rowlf for IBM. Working with IBM meant Jim could continue to work with David Lazer, who impressed Jim with his energy and enthusiasm. Jim and Lazer could sit talking for hours in Jim's office or even huddled together in the editing room while Jim cut film or dubbed sound effects. Some evenings, Lisa or Cheryl—or sometimes both—would join Jim and Lazer in the workshop, giving Lazer the opportunity to observe Jim with his children—and Lazer immediately understood why Jim could so effortlessly produce segments for *Sesame Street* that resonated with children.

"We were really checking the clocks to finish the edit," Lazer said, "and either Cheryl or Lisa asked a question, and he turned around—and I was going crazy—and he turned around as calm as could be and gave her a straight, honest adult answer. And I learned a lesson then: he had such respect for his children. . . . They asked him a question, and he took the time to answer it."

"The attitude you have as a parent is what your kids will learn from more than what you tell them," Jim said later. "They don't remember what you try to teach them. They remember what you *are*." As Lazer had noticed, Jim valued the views of his children and, in fact, frequently asked for their opinions of his work, gauging their reactions to performances and asking questions. "Jim was intrigued with his children," said Jane. "They had a great sense of humor and so he immediately started using them to find out what was funny, what worked. He really respected their opinions." Generally, if the children laughed, the routine stayed in. If they didn't, ten-year-old Lisa was often the first to pipe up with a critique. "Lisa has great taste," Jim told *The Philadelphia Inquirer.* "She can tell you specifically if something is working, or if you're doing a punch line above children's heads. If she feels they won't understand it, we make it simpler."

With countless newspaper interviews and his Muppets peering out from the cover of *TV Guide,* Jim and the Muppets were quickly becoming the public face of *Sesame Street.* As such, his time was more and more in demand for participation in various education conferences, attending CTW seminars with Jane at the stately Arden House in Harriman, New York, or spending several days in Aspen at a symposium discussing education on television. Jim was continuing to feel boxed in by being thought of primarily as a children's performer, and reminded readers in one interview after another that he considered his success on *Sesame Street* "odd, because we're really not kid oriented. About 95 percent of all the things I've ever done [have] been for adults."

Jim was still working hard to get several non–*Sesame Street*–related Muppet projects off the ground, including a Christmas special that Jerry Juhl had been writing as far back as 1963, about Santa Claus being kidnapped and replaced by an impostor who plans to burgle homes around the world. Jim had been trying to sell the show for the last seven years, rewriting the script and pitching all the major networks—including a few in Canada—until finally, in June 1970, Ed Sullivan, long impressed with Jim and his appearances on his show, agreed to produce the script as the hour-long feature *The Great Santa Claus Switch.*

Once again, there were personnel issues. While Santa would be played by a live actor—Jim had suggested Zero Mostel and Phil Silvers, before landing Art Carney—there would be countless new Muppet monsters and walkaround characters, which would require performers Jim didn't have. Instead of scouting for talent at puppetry conventions, this time Jim decided to bring the potential talent to him by hosting a series of auditions at the Muppet workshop. Before a single session could be set up, however, Jim found his first performer in an old friend and colleague: Jerry Nelson.

In late 1969, Nelson was performing small acting roles and taking odd jobs while devoting himself nearly full-time to the needs of his nine-year-old daughter, Christine, who had cystic fibrosis. While attending a Christmas party that winter, he had seen *Sesame Street* playing on a television in another room. "I forgot about the party and just sat and watched the rest of *Sesame Street*," Nelson said. After Christmas, Nelson called Jim excitedly. "I told him I'd seen *Sesame Street*—and I was just flabbergasted and thought it was a really wonderful show. He asked me if I would be interested in a spring workshop that he was putting together to find people, because he needed a very large team for the [*Great*] *Santa Claus Switch*. So I said yes."

For two weeks beginning June 15, 1970, Jim—along with Nelson and Oz—oversaw his first series of auditions for Muppet performers, a practice that would become a habit over the next twenty years. Jim was both pragmatic and idealistic about recruiting puppeteers. "Puppetry is different, say, from making movies where you can just go out and hire people," he explained. "In puppetry, you have to grow them yourself. You have to breed them. In other words, ours is very much a team effort." He was also careful to point out that there was more to being a puppeteer than the ability to lip-synch a puppet. "We look for a basic sense of performance, a sense of humor," said Jim—and therefore Muppet auditions had a tendency to attract not just puppeteers, but also actors, mimes, impressionists, and voice actors. "You have to find people who put their whole performance into their hand," Jim explained, "and that's a very specific talent that a lot of performers don't have. A lot of very funny performers will never be good puppeteers."

One unlikely performer was a twenty-three-year-old actress and voice-over artist named Fran Brill, who responded to the call for

Muppet performers thinking she'd be hired merely to dub voices. Brill's voice indeed caught Jim's ear, "but puppeteers do their own voices," Brill said, "[so] I ended up doing the two-week workshop to learn the basics of puppetry." Brill would prove to be a talented puppeteer—and it was fortunate for Jim he had found such a proficient female performer, for both Jim and Joan Cooney had been under fire from women's organizations for a lack of female Muppets, and Muppet performers, on *Sesame Street.* "That was very much criticized," Cooney recalled. "We had a terrible time."

Ultimately, hiring Brill turned out to be more than meeting a mere quota. "She brought a sharpness" to the Muppets, said Oz, "a sense of craft. . . . She wasn't always funny, but that didn't matter. She knew our rhythms." After performing in *The Great Santa Claus Switch,* Brill would cross over to *Sesame Street,* at first performing Ernie's right hand, then working her way into characters of her own, including the forthright Prairie Dawn, a character she would perform for the next forty years. Jumping into the mix with Jim and the Muppet team, Brill said later, was "analogous to a family of boys acquiring a female sibling. The family remained a 'boys club' but the dynamic changed when I as the younger 'sister' arrived. . . . I got kidded but I had to earn their respect. I had to keep up. It was challenging but an enormous amount of fun."

The June workshop found another puppeteer who bounced perfectly to the Muppet beat. If Brill was more sharpness than spontaneity, then eighteen-year-old Richard Hunt was her polar opposite. A fan of the Muppets since their early appearances on *Ed Sullivan,* the gap-toothed, wild-haired, and openly gay Hunt was enthusiasm incarnate, with the gusto of a game show host, who was always grabbing a puppet to stick in someone's face. "When I was eighteen, *Sesame Street* had just started, and I thought, 'Oh, this might be a good way to do something,'" Hunt said. "I thought, 'The Muppets are nuts!' and I felt I would fit right into that." Right from the beginning, Jim and the Muppet team knew they had found someone special. "God, he was a comedic force," said Oz. "His craft actually wasn't great but he was such a force it just didn't matter."

The Great Santa Claus Switch was Jim's most ambitious Muppet-related project yet, utilizing nearly twenty performers and taxing the

Muppet workshop to produce rows and rows of elves and monsters—
including several gigantic walkarounds—in a short amount of time.
"It was one of the most exhausting times I ever had," said Muppet
designer Caroly Wilcox. With the workshop crammed with designers, costumers, builders, and work-in-progress puppets, the team
was practically falling over each other. Sahlin, nearing his wit's end,
could be found at his workbench loudly blaring classical music to
soothe his fraying nerves.

With the bulk of the work on *Santa* complete, Jim began work
that autumn on another set of number films for the second season of
Sesame Street, this time romping in various kinds of media, including short live-action films, computer animation, stop motion, and
the "moving paintings" Jim loved creating. "He'd be in the back
working for hours, until three in the morning," Oz said, storyboarding, writing, painting, composing music, and editing with the same
intensity as the baker films of a year ago. Among the pieces were two
memorable stop motion films featuring the King of Eight and the
Queen of Six, a computer animation featuring Limbo counting to
ten, and a beautiful short film in which two cats invade a tea party in
a dollhouse. The primary prop for this particular film was something very close to Jim's heart, for he had borrowed nine-year-old
Cheryl's dollhouse, a charming replica of their own Greenwich home
that Jim had constructed to fit Cheryl and Lisa's Madame Alexander
dolls. "My dad made the whole thing himself, which is a really big
project," Lisa recalled. "You can imagine how busy he is," and yet he
still found time "to make this entire dollhouse from scratch—and it's
beautiful."

Jim also worked closely with writer and illustrator Maurice Sendak on two short animated pieces he had in mind for the numbers
seven and nine. In September, Sendak sent Jim his storyboards and
sketches. "I like both a lot," Sendak wrote Jim in his crabbed hand-
writing, "but won't be hurt if you don't." There was little danger of
that—the sketches Sendak sent over were just the kind of playful
chaos Jim adored: one featured a collection of seven colorful monsters who terrorized a village, while the other showcased a group of
nine pigs who dropped in on a birthday party for a boy named Bum-
ble Arty. Jim coordinated the projects with relish, working closely

with the animators and editing the two pieces. The final films were exciting and vibrant, with deliciously dark undercurrents . . . and ultimately deemed inappropriate for young audiences due to the presence of cannons in one film and wine in the other. "Yanked by the suits at CTW," Jon Stone told Jim wistfully.

Production on the second season of *Sesame Street* began in early September 1970. In the off-season, CTW had at last modified Oscar's trash can to allow Spinney to perform right-handed—but there were several other changes, some more subtle than others, taking place on the street as well. "Jim never considered anything to be 'done,'" Spinney said—and in the past months, Kermit Love had slightly redesigned Big Bird, adding more feathers to the top of his head, which made him look less dimwitted, while Don Sahlin had tinkered a bit with the eye mechanisms to allow for more expressiveness. Spinney, and *Sesame Street*'s writers, had also gotten a better handle on the character, no longer playing him like a country bumpkin, but rather as a four-year-old—a preschooler in plumage. As originally envisioned by Jim and Jon Stone, Big Bird was intended to be "the representative of the audience." At last, he truly was.

Oscar had undergone a facelift, too. Three months earlier, while preparing Big Bird and Oscar for an appearance on *The Flip Wilson Show,* Jim had taken the opportunity to rework the puppet, slightly altering the shape of the head and changing his color from radioactive orange to a mossy green. That was all news to CTW head Dave Connell, who didn't see the revised Oscar until after the *Flip Wilson* taping, exploding "What the hell is that?" But Jim wanted Oscar green. He would stay that way.

The only other disagreement regarding Oscar had to do with the character's personality. Spinney was convinced Stone and the other writers had Oscar all wrong. "He's not a villain, not horrible," Spinney insisted. "He fundamentally has got a heart of gold." It was a thesis with which Jon Stone strongly disagreed. "There's no heart of gold," Stone said. "The guy is a shit, right to the core." It would remain a point of contention between Spinney and the writers for years, even as Oscar became more and more popular.

Jim and other members of the Muppet team would continue to perform characters on the street set from time to time, but for the most part Spinney was on his own, the lone representative of "Muppets West," as Jim would affectionately call him. During the first season, Spinney had sometimes worked with Jim and the rest of the team on the Muppet inserts, performing right hands or the so-called Anything Muppets—Muppets that could be dressed with different eyes, noses, and hair as needed—but "he didn't really enjoy it," said Jerry Nelson. "That sort of ensemble playing was not Caroll's forte . . . and so eventually he stopped doing it." In the opinion of Oz, Spinney lacked the aggressiveness to work within a group dynamic; his performing style was better suited for single character sequences.

Even without Spinney, with the addition of Nelson, Hunt, and Brill—and, at times, Jane Henson—the rest of the Muppet team was starting to hit its stride. The team would work Fridays at Reeves Teletape where, for the first time, Jim had his Muppet sets built up on stilts, elevating the sets more than six feet off the ground—a brilliant though obvious innovation that allowed puppeteers to perform standing up rather than on their knees or in rolling chairs. For the most part, the scripts for *Sesame Street* were written weeks in advance—"they're just handed to me," Jim said—but before passing them to Jim, many sketches had been punched up by Jerry Juhl, still working dutifully from California to incorporate a bit of madness into the Muppet sketches being written by *Sesame Street*'s writing staff.

It wasn't always easy. "There was a big three-hole binder," said Juhl. "It was the writers notebook that came from the educational consultants on the show with all the goals and things." Many times, Juhl would think of something gloriously silly and worthy of the Muppets, "then ransack this notebook trying to find [an educational] justification for the piece!" Once Juhl's Muppetized scripts arrived, the Muppet performers would do a quick read-through— while Jim delighted in telling reporters, with an absolutely straight face, that the Muppet team rehearsed for "two weeks to a month," in truth, he preferred a more spontaneous style of performing—then would pull their Muppets onto their arms, ready to roll tape.

Once tape began to roll, the real work—and the real fun—began. "Jim was an extraordinarily serious, yet silly man," said Brill. "He would encourage you to be as crazy as possible, because when you're inhibited as a performer, you can't be creative. Because he would be silly, everyone else would be silly." Oz could be very serious, almost stern, as he prepared to perform—until the cameras came on, at which point he became a comedic virtuoso, creating characters and situations almost at will. There was always a playful irreverence for their craft, as if Oz—unlike Jim—had never really decided if this was something a grown man should do for a living. "Ready to wiggle some dolls?" Oz would ask cheekily, as the performers settled into place.

Jim was also fortunate to have Jon Stone in the director's seat, where he reveled in, and encouraged, the Muppet brand of silliness. For Stone, who spent all week writing segments or overseeing *Sesame Street*'s live actors, directing the Muppet inserts on Fridays was "like a day off . . . that was my holiday." A Yale-trained actor and dramatist, Stone preferred to direct from the studio floor rather than from the control booth, stroking his salt-and-pepper beard and grinning broadly as Jim and the puppeteers moved into place, then signaling the booth to start rolling tape by calling out "Rolleeoleeoleeyo!"—the cue to the performers it was time for action to begin. "He loved the one-on-one aspect of directing," Oz said. "Everything enhanced the spirit of the show."

For Jim, that spirit—like that direct eye contact with his own children that had impressed David Lazer—mattered almost more than the message. *They remember what you are,* Jim had said. The Muppets, then, were Jim's conversation with millions of children, spoken directly to them in a language they could understand: complete and utter silliness and abandon. And what about their parents who might be watching? Jim never doubted for a moment that it was their language, too. "The most sophisticated people I know . . . inside, they are all children," Jim said.

There were times, though, when even Juhl's efforts weren't enough to liven up an otherwise well-intentioned *Sesame Street* script. "Often, the material that we were given was kind of dry," said Jim, "but Frank and I would play with it and improvise and bring in gags until it worked for us. Sometimes you can make a line funny just by having your character do a double take. But always we did this while staying true to the spirit of what we had been given in the first place." The years Jim had spent in the company of joke writers on *The Jimmy Dean Show* had served him well—for Jim understood not only what was funny, but also how to take material provided by others and *make* it funny.

Jim and Oz could be particularly uproarious when performing Ernie and Bert, wildly tossing jokes back and forth and improvising in character. "Performing the Ernie and Bert pieces with Frank has always been one of the great joys of doing the show," Jim said. "It's really a unique way of working in television, because . . . about half the time when Frank and I are working, we decide not to use the script. Instead, we'll take the basic concepts of it, and if it has a punch line or two, we'll circle around and hit those lines. But other than that, we'll just talk the piece and so we're really working spontaneously and just sort of playing off of each other. It's a lot of fun."

"We respected the writers' jokes and we knew we had to hit the educational aspect," agreed Oz, "but we'd meander around all that." Sometimes that meandering took them widely off-script, and Jim and Oz would get so wrapped up in their ad-libbing that Jim would break down into a fit of his high-pitched giggles, laughing until tears ran down his face. "The best thing of all," Oz said warmly, "was to watch Jim laugh until he cried." Finally, as Jim and Oz composed themselves, someone would ask in mock professorial tones, "And what are we teaching?"—to which Stone would playfully respond, "Who cares?" Educators and child psychologists might have scratched their heads trying to figure out how sneezing one's nose off into a hanky could possibly be educational . . . and yet as Jim and Oz played it, somehow it was.

So completely had Jim and Oz wrapped themselves in Ernie and Bert that it was hard to imagine that it had taken a bit of experimenting before the two of them decided who would perform which character. "I can't imagine doing Bert now, because Bert has become so much a part of Frank," Jim said later. In Jon Stone's view, however, it should have been obvious all along. "They're Jim and Frank," Stone said. "Their relationship *is* the relationship with Jim and

Frank. Jim just loved to play tricks on Frank . . . and Frank is Bert. Frank is very buttoned-up and uptight and compulsively neat, and Jim was just wild and off the walls and funny." "There are certainly elements of our own personalities in Bert and Ernie," agreed Jim. "We play each other's timing and we play off each other very well. And that's what a good comedy team does."

While Ernie and Bert—and therefore Jim and Oz—would come to be almost universally hailed as a comedic duo on the same upper stratum as Abbott and Costello, Laurel and Hardy, or Burns and Allen, Oz never really thought of Jim and himself as a comedy team. "We were two people so in tune with each other that we didn't have to say anything to communicate," Oz said. "We'd get done with a take and we'd look at each other and we both knew without saying anything that we'd have to do it again, and we both knew why. That was the special bond we had." They didn't make comedy, said Oz; instead, "we created a kind of aliveness." Whatever it was, "it was a magical coming together of a couple of characters," said Jon Stone. "Frank and Jim were yin and yang. . . . They were this inseparable couple. It was a beautiful love affair, in the best sense of the word."

Besides Ernie, Jim was regularly performing Kermit for the *Sesame Street* inserts, though he had scaled back the frog's appearances somewhat following Gould's confusion over Kermit's appearance in *Hey Cinderella!* The incident had left such a bad taste in his mouth, in fact, that Jim took Kermit off *Sesame Street* altogether for nearly a year. Trying to fill the void, the writers introduced Herbert Birdsfoot, a nice guy lecturer performed by Jerry Nelson, "to be a kind of Kermit spokesperson," said Stone. It was an experiment doomed to fail from the beginning. "It never really took off," Stone said. "Trying to follow Kermit is like trying to follow Will Rogers."

Actually, it was like trying to follow Jim Henson—for the more Jim performed Kermit, the more the two of them seemed to become intertwined. While Jim always described Kermit as somewhat "snarkier" than himself—as Jim had discovered from Edgar Bergen, a puppet could say things that couldn't be said by ordinary people—it was becoming harder to tell where the frog ended and Jim began. Over the past few years, Kermit had become a more rounded, more refined character. "Kermit is the closest one to me," Jim said later.

"He's the easiest to talk with. He's the only one who can't be worked by anybody else, only by me. See, Kermit is just a piece of cloth with a mouthpiece in it. The character is literally my hand."

Jim's other regular character was the excitable game show host Guy Smiley, a performance Joan Cooney always thought was Jim's funniest. Whether he was hosting game show parodies like "Beat the Time" or "Here Is Your Life," Guy was an amped-up version of Jim's own personality, brimming with enthusiasm, rooting for contestants, and always convinced that whatever game they were playing was pretty much the greatest game ever. "I live kind of within myself as a person, so my outlet has always been the Muppets; therefore, I tend to do sort of wildly extroverted characters," said Jim. The only downside to performing Guy was that his higher-pitched, nearly shouted manic voice could be hard on Jim's vocal cords; at times, Jim would finish taping Guy Smiley segments with his voice nearly ragged.

Oz had nearly the same problem performing a character who was one of Guy Smiley's regular contestants, a furry blue monster with a rumbling voice who, like other characters Oz would perform, moved from being a face in the background to front stage, where he became a break-out star: Cookie Monster. The voice, Oz said, was "an explosion of energy" that could "absolutely rip" his throat, and took some time for Oz to master without shredding his larynx.

Monsters had been a Muppet staple for nearly as long as there had been Muppets—Yorick had devoured Kermit on national television as early as 1956—making it all but inevitable that Jim would introduce monsters on *Sesame Street*. Oscar, despite his appearance, somehow seemed to defy the label *monster*—he was a *grouch*, which seemed to give him a status all his own. Cookie, on the other hand, was unapologetically a monster—but if educators were worried that Jim's monsters would give preschoolers nightmares, Jim was already one step ahead of them, saliently explaining the educational aspects of his monsters even as he acknowledged educators' concerns. "On *Sesame Street*, the monsters are kind of soft and cuddly and fuzzy, but for a three- or four-year-old child, they might be rather frightening things," Jim said sympathetically. "At the same time, the child can get to know these monsters and understand that they are not things to be frightened of. It's a scary image, but the child can learn to handle it."

Cookie could trace his roots back to a prototype built by Don Sahlin for a 1966 ad campaign for General Foods, when Jim had sketched three different monsters to each steal one of three shaped snacks called Wheels, Crowns, and Flutes. Cookie's ancestor, the Wheel Stealer, was a fuzzy, twitchy, googly-eyed fanged monster who grabbed and gobbled handfuls of wheel-shaped chips. When General Foods opted not to use the ad, Jim recycled the Wheel Stealer for one of his IBM Coffee Breaks, where the monster devoured a talking coffee machine, then exploded—a sketch Jim enjoyed so much he re-created it for *The Ed Sullivan Show* in 1967. The monster was used again in 1969, this time with his fangs removed, for the Munchos potato chips commercials. That defanged version eventually made his way onto *Sesame Street,* where he first appeared among a crowd of monsters. At the end of Oz's skillful right arm, Cookie—referred to in early publicity simply as "Blue Monster"—slowly worked his way to the front of more and more inserts, devouring not just cookies, but salt shakers, telephones, and letters of the alphabet.

Another Oz-performed monster would become almost as synonymous with *Sesame Street* as Big Bird—and if Big Bird, as Jim and Jon Stone hoped, was the "representative of the audience," then the fuzzy, lovable Grover was the audience's devoted best friend. As with many of *Sesame Street*'s most memorable characters, it had taken some time before the character finally clicked. Like Cookie Monster, Grover had been simply one in a crowd of previously used monsters, having first appeared as a monster named Gleep in a 1967 Christmas sketch on *The Ed Sullivan Show.* In his first *Sesame Street* inserts, the still unnamed Grover was more monsterlike, with darker, matted fur and slightly sinister eyes.

By the second season, that would change. Part of the transition had to do with design—the monster was given a brighter, bluer fur, and wider eyes. But Oz had also begun to get a handle on the character, finally arriving at a name as he played with the puppet between takes, and developing a better understanding of Grover's motivation, thanks to some help from his dog, a devoted mutt named Fred. Watching Fred romping buoyantly in the park one afternoon, Oz said, "I noticed the purity of the dog." It was suddenly clear. "There's a purity in Grover," said Oz. "He wants to please." Grover had arrived.

Finding a character to act as Grover's primary foil fell largely to Jerry Nelson, who started on *Sesame Street* in 1970 just as he had on *The Jimmy Dean Show* in 1965: performing right hands. As he began taking on more characters, Nelson developed the first major straight man for Grover with the eternally annoyed Mr. Johnson, a blue, round-headed Anything Muppet who seemed to constantly dine in restaurants where Grover served as his waiter, and received perpetually poor—though enthusiastic—service. Acting as a foil for Grover "really enabled me to get a real feel for that kind of ongoing, day-to-day playing in an ensemble manner," said Nelson. Nelson would become one of *Sesame Street*'s most versatile and valued puppeteers, performing Herbert Birdsfoot, Sherlock Hemlock, Herry Monster, and, by the fourth season, the number-loving vampire Count Von Count.

Nelson also served as the lead puppeteer on Snuffleupagus, one of Jim's first two-man, full-body, walkaround Muppets, unveiled in 1971. "Jim *loved* complicated puppetry," said Cooney, though Jim admitted that the success of Snuffy was largely through trial and error. "Every time we built [a full-body Muppet], we would learn a lot about what to do and not to do next time," said Jim—and Snuffy was a true feat of engineering, requiring two performers to work cooperatively beyond merely right and left hands. Such cooperation required enormous intuition between two performers, and Nelson quickly learned that he and Richard Hunt could communicate just as silently, and just as seamlessly, as Jim and Oz. Into the rear of Snuffy Hunt went. "It wasn't much fun for Richard," Nelson admitted later, but their performance, all the way down to Snuffy's dancing, was flawless. "Richard was good and gave him good movement," said Nelson.

For Hunt, it was all an adventure. "He was like a puppy . . . really bouncy and eager," said Nelson. "So we had to sit on him a lot." It didn't seem to matter. Assigned largely right-hand (and tail-end) work and background Muppets, Hunt threw himself into any assignment with zeal and without complaint. Jim, too, quickly appreciated Hunt's ability to fall into sync with other performers, though Hunt admitted there was a bit of a trick to performing a right hand with Jim. "I always used to do Jim's right hand as Ernie," Hunt said later, "and I would hold one of his belt loops with my left hand so that I was with him literally. Otherwise you're being dragged along . . . by grabbing his belt loop, the minute he moves, I'm feeling him move—with the first real spasm of the first twitch, I just immediately move with him."

Many of *Sesame Street*'s most memorable moments involved children interacting with the Muppets, a brilliant decision that was driven more by idleness on the part of the writers than inspiration—when bits were ad-libbed, no scriptwriting was necessary. (When children were on the set, Stone would call out "blue sky!"—code that a child was present and performers and crew members should refrain from swearing.) Instead, said Stone, "we'd give the puppeteer a concept or a problem . . . and have them just talk it over with the kids. And we found early on that certain puppeteers—Jerry, Frank, and Jim—were wonderful at it." Even more surprising, said Stone, the team found that "as soon as the puppet goes up on somebody's arm, the puppeteer ceases to exist." Jim was delighted. "I'm working with Ernie, [who] has no bottom half or legs or anything like that. He ends at the waist," Jim explained. "Yet, the kids will look right at Ernie and me—this strange, bearded man—standing right there, talking for the puppet, and there's no question the kids believe Ernie is a real personality."

Jim was proud of his involvement with *Sesame Street,* and knew early on he was involved not only with something that could make a difference in the lives of children, but might also give his bruised-but-beloved television what he saw as a much needed sense of purpose. "Family, school and television are the most important factors in raising children," Jim remarked to *TV Guide* in 1970. "Of these, television has the least sense of responsibility." Elsewhere, he complained candidly that "TV is frustrating. It is an exciting art and communications form capable of contributing so much, but it just isn't set up to do it. It's geared to sell products—the whole reason for being against all other things which are neat and innovative."

Still, if his hope for a higher calling for television was destined to disappoint, Jim was committed to making his corner of television as bright as possible. "Kids love to learn, and the learning should be exciting and fun," he said. "That's what we're out to do." Echoed Juhl, "It's why the show is a success. The show is obviously done to be entertaining and everybody has a wonderful time." And no one, said Cheryl Henson, was having a more wonderful time than her father. "He loved to perform with Frank and Jerry and all the puppeteers," she said. "When we were little kids watching *Sesame Street,* we often felt as if my father was performing just for us—but I think that he was really just having a good time with his friends."

As *Sesame Street* began its second season, it was clear the show had become a full-blown phenomenon, endlessly discussed and analyzed by everyone, including television critics, educators, psychiatrists, clergymen, physicians, and writers like George Plimpton, who confessed that his addiction to the show had "destroyed God knows how much writing I could have done." In November 1970, Big Bird appeared on the cover of *Time,* fronting an extensive article that discussed *Sesame Street*'s "profusion of aims, [and] confusion of techniques," then asked rhetorically, "how could such a show possibly succeed? Answer: spectacularly well." Already the show was broadcast in fifty countries—though not yet England, where the BBC's chief of children's programming called the show "nondemocratic and possibly dangerous for young Britons"—and was seen by seven million American children each day.

Through it all, everyone acknowledged that the Muppets were instrumental in *Sesame Street*'s success. "Jim's contribution was absolutely essential," said Jerry Nelson. "I mean, the show never would have had the success it has without Jim's contribution to it." Even Jim's tormentor at *The New York Times,* Jack Gould, became a grudging cheerleader. "Jim Henson's Muppets . . . is still central to the success of *Sesame Street.* They are fun for youngsters and intriguing to adults in the imaginative ways in which he uses them."

The success of the show, in fact, became nearly overwhelming for Jim and quickly came to define the creative direction of Henson Associates, despite Jim's best efforts. The company that had produced such avant-garde, experimental fare as *Youth 68* and *The Cube* over the last two years was now all Muppets, all the time—but Jim was optimistic, even grateful, for the opportunity to devote his time to the Muppets again. "I think it wasn't until *Sesame Street* that the Muppets took over most of my creative energy," Jim said later.

> It was what the audience wanted and so I felt I should be putting my time and energy into that. The Muppets have always had a life of their own and we who do the Muppets serve that life and the audience. This entity called the Muppets is something that I don't dictate at all. The audience doesn't dictate it either—but the response of the audience is all part of it. It has a natural flow of life that one goes with. It's been fun and rewarding—just wonderful—and I hope that will continue.

The success of *Sesame Street* affected more than just his ability to develop other film projects; it was also the final impetus toward Jim pulling the plug on commercials altogether. "When *Sesame Street* came on . . . we were too busy to do commercials," said Jim. And, he had to admit, "it was a pleasure to get out of that world. . . . It's a world of compromise." While Jim would continue to produce ads intermittently for the rest of his career, the creative thrill was gone. "I just stopped doing that stuff," he explained later. "At that point, I was at the level where they respect you and your opinion and all that sort of thing. But even then . . . every meeting is a meeting with a dozen people who all have opinions and the whole process is really not easy on a creative person."

So Jim was determined to get out of advertising—"my goals have changed, and are taking me farther away from the commercial area," he told a disappointed Quaker Oats—but doing so would mean shutting off a major source of revenue for Henson Associates. Jim never liked discussing money; he had angrily scratched out a paragraph in his copy of a *TV Guide* interview that speculated he had "hauled in $350,000 in '69" and earned about $25,000 per commercial. While the article had actually been fairly accurate, for Jim it had been rude to bring the matter up; talking about finances, he told another reporter, was "really ugly." And yet the dilemma remained: Jim had given up most of his outside projects to commit himself to *Sesame Street*—and that commitment had impeded his ability to pursue the other projects he needed to stay in business. Clearly, another source of revenue was needed.

Children's Television Workshop also understood that finding that revenue stream was critical to its continued existence. The organization—which relied almost solely on taxpayer funding and contributions from social-minded companies—knew it couldn't count on such largesse forever. "Foundation support is impermanent," CTW co-founder Lloyd Morrisett said plainly. "Governmental funding is uncertain. Every organization needs a stable financial base in order to attract talented people."

Jim had actually made just such an argument at an October symposium hosted by Action for Children's Television, where he laid out the critical need for money in public television, addressing his comments to educators and possible benefactors in the same clear language he used when speaking with his own children. "If I have a song to sing, it is about money," Jim wrote, "because I think good children's television is more a money problem than anything else. . . . Good shows cost money, and if you want to have a lot of programs for kids, it costs a lot of money and someone has to pay for it."

Both Jim and CTW, then, had the same problem. And they found their mutual answer in the most unlikely of places: the *Billboard* charts. At the end of *Sesame Street*'s first season, Columbia Records had issued *The Sesame Street Book and Record,* which sold half a million copies, peaked at number 23, and would eventually win a Grammy Award—not bad for a year in which it had to jockey for position with albums by the Beatles and Led Zeppelin. Even more impressive, a single from the *Sesame Street* record—the catchy "Rubber Duckie," sung by Jim as Ernie—had reached number 16 in September 1970. Clearly, there was a market for *Sesame Street*– and Muppet-related merchandise.

It had been Bernie Brillstein who had first broached the subject with Jim, calling on him at the house in Greenwich to make the case. "I told him, '*Sesame Street* is now *boom,*'" Brillstein said. "And Jim was very peculiar about merchandising, because he usually didn't like what people did. And I'm saying, 'Jim, you have to merchandise those characters. It's insane! It's the most popular show in America!'"

And yet, Jim was skeptical. While he was always careful to make certain he owned his characters, that principle, to the frustration of toy manufacturers everywhere, had translated into little merchandise; in the last decade, he had permitted very few Muppet-related items beyond a series of Kermit and Rowlf puppets and a few promotional giveaways. "You can't take advantage of the love the kids have for these characters," Jim would say time and time again. Oz, too, noted that bags of money had already been waved under their noses, to no avail. "If Jim or the Muppets wanted to go only after money," said Oz, "we could have truly cleaned up. I can't tell you how many cookie manufacturers wanted Cookie Monster to pitch their product."

But Brillstein was persistent. "Here's what you have to do," he told Jim. "First of all, you have to do it for the fans, for the kids. Second of all, you'll have complete control of it, and you control the quality. Third of all, if it works like I think it's gonna work, you will be financially independent and you can use the money for your own independence and creativity and no one will ever tell you what to do again."

With Brillstein's enthusiastic advice still ringing in his ears, Jim met with Joan Cooney to discuss the possibilities of merchandising *Sesame Street*. Jim brought with him Jay Emmett, head of the Licensing Corporation of America, which had managed marketing for organizations like the National Football League and handled the merchandising of Superman and Batman for National Publications. It was Jim's intention to have Emmett independently coordinate all the *Sesame Street*–related marketing—meaning he would be an employee of neither Henson Associates nor CTW. Cooney, however, had other ideas.

"I said no," said Cooney, who wanted merchandising controlled inside CTW, "and Jim and I had one of our little tiffs. . . . Jim could actually do no wrong for me, and I think that was true for him with me. I very seldom said no to him." But in this, Cooney stood firm— and Jim eventually agreed that merchandising for *Sesame Street* would be managed at CTW, in a new division headed by twenty-nine-year-old Christopher Cerf, a former senior editor at Random House. The basic agreement that Jim and CTW had negotiated in 1969—in which Jim would continue to retain ownership of his characters, and split any merchandise-related profits with CTW—would remain in place. The mechanics of that agreement, however—

including exactly how those profits would be split—was another matter.

Both Jim and CTW agreed that quality and value should drive the product. "Our bottom line consideration," stressed Jim, "is to stay cost conscious and make sure the product remains a good value." On CTW's end, any contract Cerf negotiated required that merchandise "receive the widest possible distribution" and be "available at the lowest possible prices." Further, Jim's approval would be required for any *Sesame Street* products that used Muppet images—which was practically everything.

The first *Sesame Street* merchandise Jim and CTW agreed to allow—mostly puppets, books, Colorforms, and puzzles—shipped in the fall of 1971 from Random House, Western Publishing, and Topper Toys. Topper in particular had lobbied hard for the merchandising rights, adding 110,000 square feet to its plant in Elizabeth, New Jersey, to meet anticipated demand, allocating $400,000 to marketing, and paying an advance to CTW of $250,000. In the first year alone, Topper estimated it had generated more than $5 million in *Sesame Street*–related sales, splitting its profits evenly with CTW.

When it came to profit sharing between CTW and Jim, however, things were less well defined. For the first few years, it was a complicated math problem, as lawyers from Henson Associates and CTW huddled almost weekly to argue over whether a product had "more Muppets or more educational value" and then divided the royalties accordingly. Eventually, the two companies negotiated an agreement that outlined broadly defined categories—music, puppets, stuffed animals—with preset percentages for each company, a structure that remained in place for thirty years.

The money began to flow faster and deeper than anyone anticipated. Western Publishing's *The Monster at the End of This Book*, for instance, featuring Grover in a story written by Jon Stone, sold more than two million copies within a year, with Henson Associates being paid a "designer's percentage" for the use of Grover. By Jim's own estimate, *Sesame Street*'s Muppet merchandising had earned nearly $10 million by the mid-1970s.

As was his habit, Jim invested most of the money back in the company. While Jim's percentage from the profits would never be enough to put the company on autopilot, it was sufficient enough for him to start investing in what he jokingly called "research and development," gradually adding new performers and Muppet designers. The revenue would also provide Jim, as Brillstein had predicted, with the freedom to pursue other projects without worrying about whether they would immediately be profitable. "Jim was incredibly proud of *Sesame Street* and very protective of it," said Jerry Juhl. "[But] once that show was established, he suddenly found himself being called *Mr. Children's Television*. He was perfectly happy to accept that—but he really wanted to do something else."

"His means of expression were always more than just one thing," said Oz. "He went with the flow, allowed it to happen to him, and then would diversify along the way. . . . He enjoyed *Sesame Street,* but he was always doing new things." At the moment, however, no one knew exactly what this particular new thing was. And neither, really, did Jim.

CHAPTER SEVEN

BIG IDEAS

1970–1973

Jim gives a rooftop performance of the gigantic Boss Man Muppet. Trying to shake his image as a children's performer, Jim tried for years to stage an elaborate all-puppet Broadway show, with increasingly larger and more complicated puppets.

THE WEEK BEFORE THANKSGIVING 1970, JIM FLEW TO LOS ANGELES with Frank Oz and Don Sahlin to tape several short segments with *Laugh-In* ingenue Goldie Hawn for her first solo television special, *Pure Goldie*. "We can do anything you like," Jim had helpfully told Hawn's producer, but the Muppet moments would be brief—Hawn had crammed her hour-long special with five other supportive guest stars jockeying for time. And yet, the Muppet appearance would be memorable, for it was the first time non–*Sesame Street* viewers would have the opportunity to hear Kermit perform a song that had quickly grown close to Jim's heart and, within a few years, would be well on its way to becoming a standard.

During the months they were taping *Sesame Street,* director Jon Stone and composer Joe Raposo would meet each week at a bar just across the street from CTW headquarters, where the two would discuss the music needed for upcoming episodes. "I'd sit there, and I would give [Joe] just a list of tunes I needed music to," Stone said. Halfway through *Sesame Street's* first season, Stone sat down across from the tunesmith and laid down a requirement for the coming week: "We need a song for a frog." From that seemingly simple request came one of Raposo's most endearing tunes: "Bein' Green," an anthem for tolerance and self-acceptance that seemed tailor-made as a hymn for the new decade, still struggling with the turbulent civil rights reform, political skepticism, and sputtering idealism that had marked the end of the 1960s. Given the cynicism of the era, then, what makes Raposo's tune so remarkable—especially as sung by Jim—is its sheer sincerity, never cloying or overly sentimental.

Jim had first performed the song for a March 1970 episode of *Sesame Street,* in a quiet moment featuring Kermit sitting alone in a darkened forest. Raposo's lyrics, while slow and sweet, had a deceptively complex, syncopated structure, at times requiring a bit of verbal gymnastics to make some of the longer phrases fit the music:

> *It's not easy being green—*
> *It seems you blend in with so many other ordinary things.*
> *And people tend to pass you over 'cause you're*
> *Not standing out like flashy sparkles in the water,*
> *Or stars in the sky.*

In the first take for *Sesame Street,* Jim was still feeling his way around the song, half singing and half talking his way through it, at times arriving at the end of the lines slightly ahead of the music. The performance was heartfelt, but Jim would make a better pass at the song for the *Sesame Street* record later that year, turning in a slightly more upbeat, better-structured performance. As time went on and as Jim performed the song more and more, he would figure out how to get the most from it, slowing it down slightly to give it a more humble, introspective feel, which made the turn into the final verses one of quiet celebration. It was the song's resolution in the last verse, said Cheryl Henson, that truly fit her father best:

When green is all there is to be,
It could make you wonder why.
But why wonder? Why wonder?
I am green—and it'll do fine. It's beautiful,
And I think it's what I want to be.

Jim immediately appreciated the universal appeal of the song—Frank Sinatra had already recorded it for his 1971 album *Sinatra & Company*—and suggested Kermit sing the tune with Hawn. As it turned out, Kermit—and the Muppets—provided the only notable moments in an otherwise flat hour. Hawn wasn't surprised at all by the chemistry critics had noticed between her and Kermit. "I really found it so difficult not to believe the Muppets were real," she said. "They came alive to me and I guess I related to them. It's amazing. Kermit is a ball of string and felt, yet there is life in that."

That Thanksgiving, Jim and his family celebrated the holiday with his parents in Albuquerque, New Mexico, where Paul and Betty Henson had moved after Paul's retirement from the Department of Agriculture. Jim was worried about the effect mandatory retirement might have on his father—"one day he was working, and the next day he had nothing to do," Jim said sadly—while Betty, meanwhile, was struggling with health issues. In the minds of many, including Jim, the death of Paul Jr. nearly fifteen years earlier had had a corrosive effect on her physical and mental well-being; she was no longer the smiling hostess remembered by Jim's friends and cousins. Concerned for the health of both his parents, Jim would make an extra effort to visit them regularly, often permitting the Henson children to remain with their grandparents in New Mexico for several weeks at a time.

As Christmas approached, Jim returned to the editing room to put the final touches on *The Great Santa Claus Switch*, which was finally scheduled to air on Sunday, December 20. Jim was cutting it close; he was working on the final mix all the way into Saturday the 19th, and was finally pulled from the editing room to celebrate the arrival of an early Christmas present: his fifth and final child, a baby girl he and Jane named Heather. Jim raced to the hospital to visit Jane and his new daughter, passing a walkie-talkie to the rest of the Henson children in the parking lot so they could speak with their parents—and their new sister—as they waved from the hospital window.

The airing of *The Great Santa Claus Switch* in December 1970 marked the end of a seven-year effort to bring the show to television—and while the show would never become the holiday standard Jim had hoped, the reaction from critics was warm, even enthusiastic, calling it a "delightful visual treat for the kids . . . which had adult appeal as well." Reviewers were particularly fascinated with two new gigantic walkaround Muppets Jim had created for the show, a team of fuzzy monsters named Thog and Thig. "It was their show, no mistaking it," enthused one critic, while *Variety* noted, "Henson deserves credit for the new Muppets he devised, especially dullard Uglies Thig and Thog."

Jim was particularly pleased with the lovable Thog, and would spend the next few years grooming the character for stardom, pushing him out in front of several live shows and television appearances. But *Santa Claus Switch*'s most lasting character wouldn't be Thog, but rather one of its nearly anonymous smaller monsters, a purple, hooked-nose creature named Snarl, who lived in a cigar box. Five years later, the same Muppet would be recycled and slightly remodeled as *The Muppet Show*'s stunt-loving Gonzo. Just as significantly, the sidekick monsters in *Santa Claus Switch* were referred to as "frackles"—a word Jerry Juhl would come back to more than a decade later as Muppet writers tried to come up with a name for a new species of Muppet characters.

Jim spent most of the spring of 1971 working on *The Frog Prince,* another installment of the *Tales from Muppetland* series he had started with *Hey Cinderella!* It was a project Jim was committed to producing quickly, though with *Sesame Street* taking up much of his time, completing the script had taken longer than he and Juhl had hoped. "Time is slipping away," wrote producer John T. Ross, who had agreed to co-produce with Diana Birkenfield, "and we don't have a fortune to work with." By March, however, with the script approved, Jim was making regular trips from New York to Toronto to oversee the construction of several platformed sets at Robert Lawrence Studios. These were slightly different from the elevated backgrounds of *Sesame Street* in that entire sets were elevated on struts, where they could be pulled apart and moved around, giving performers and Muppets the freedom to move easily in and out of them.

In late March, three days after completing work on the second season of *Sesame Street*, Jim spent nine days directing and performing in *The Frog Prince,* a relatively faithful adaptation of the classic fairy tale. Unlike the heavily populated *Great Santa Claus Switch,* which had exhausted the Muppet workshop, *Frog Prince* relied on a smaller cast, including Kermit and a number of pre-existing Muppets, such as King Goshposh, Taminella Grinderfall, and Featherstone from *Tales of the Tinkerdee.* Jim also introduced several new characters, including two who would become Muppet regulars, Robin the frog and Sweetums the ogre, an enormous walkaround puppet with working eyes and a gigantic, floppy bulldog mouth.

In the seven months since Jim's last visit to Toronto to film *Santa Claus Switch, Sesame Street* had become an enormous hit in Canada—and when word got out that the Muppets would be filming at Robert Lawrence Studios, Ross was flooded with requests from fans asking if they could come to the studios to watch. "We just can't get into that, we don't have the room," an exasperated Ross told the *Toronto Telegram.*

Jim worked quickly, often directing from his knees with the Goshposh costume still pulled over his head. Other times, as his performers rehearsed, Jim would stand slightly off to the side in one of his colorful silk shirts, arms folded, laughing and *hmmmm*ing supportively. Jim was willing to rehearse a scene for as long as it took to get it right—and once he was ready, he would roll tape as long as needed. Finally, he would simply say "Lovely"—a sure sign to the Muppet performers that he had what he wanted.

With editing completed in early April, *The Frog Prince* aired barely a month later, premiering on CBS on May 11. The production was slick, with strong performances, good songs by Juhl and Joe Raposo, and a clever script—and critics were rightly impressed. "Jim Henson's Muppets are so humorously conceived, we've become terribly fond of them," said the New York *Daily News,* while *Variety* lauded the show for having "both kid and adult appeal," a sentiment echoed by *The Christian Science Monitor.* "Jim Henson's Muppets are so good," said the *Monitor,* "they may actually justify the cliche 'for children and adults alike.'"

Reading his reviews, Jim likely breathed a sigh of relief: in the media, at least, he was beginning to be seen as more than just a children's entertainer—but that didn't mean he had to stop continually explaining himself. "Good, solid entertainment is funny for young and old," he patiently told one reporter. "There is a tendency to think of *children's entertainment* versus *adult entertainment.* It's possible to have an identical level for both." Still, he admitted it was difficult to convince adults that puppetry wasn't just kids' stuff. "People don't tend to like [puppets]," Jim said. "They turn off at the idea, but that's because puppets are generally not well done."

That summer, he would have the chance to show just what puppets were capable of in perhaps the most adult venue of all: throbbing, glittering Las Vegas. In May 1971, Jim spent several days in Las Vegas meeting with the vivacious Nancy Sinatra, who was hoping the Muppets could help her make her mark with a show of her own in a town already conquered by her famous father. Jim was excited about the idea of performing in a live show in a large venue—and the location Sinatra had chosen was huge indeed: the newly opened Hilton International, at that time the largest hotel in the world and featuring a showroom that seated more than 1,500. A room that size would require larger puppets, which could be more easily seen than regular-sized Muppets. With that in mind, Jim had set to work putting together new puppets and a new show designed specifically for a sizable Vegas audience in an equally sizable room.

It was hard work. Each evening, Jim, Oz, and Jerry Nelson would rehearse until nearly 2:00 A.M., then return to their hotel rooms, exhausted, to sleep until noon. Once the novelty of hitting the casinos or the spas wore off, Jim grew restless during the day and called Jerry Juhl in California to beg for his company—a request Juhl was happy to oblige. "Jim was going crazy," said Juhl. "The days stretched before him endlessly." With the sun scorching down on them, Jim and Juhl would sit poolside at the Hilton, tinkering with the enigmatic *Tale of Sand* screenplay they had begun in the early 1960s or bouncing ideas off each other for further *Tales from Muppetland* specials.

"Jimmy Henson" as an elementary school student in Leland, Mississippi, in 1946. "I was a Mississippi Tom Sawyer," Jim said.
(COURTESY OF HENSON FAMILY PROPERTIES)

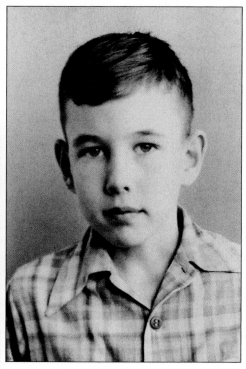

LEFT: *Betty and Paul Henson, Sr., with sons Jim (center) and Paul Jr., circa 1940.*
(COURTESY OF HENSON FAMILY PROPERTIES)

All in a day's play: a young Jim— swaddled in a makeshift turban and robe—attempts to snake-charm a garden hose.
(COURTESY OF HENSON FAMILY PROPERTIES)

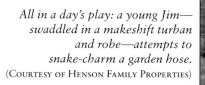

Jim credited family gatherings at the dinner table—like this one in 1956—with shaping his sense of humor. "There was so much laughter," he recalled, "because everyone was always telling jokes and saying funny things." From left: Jim's aunts Attie and Bobby, Uncle Jinx (with back to camera), Jim's grandmother "Dear," Paul Sr., unidentified, Jim, and Betty Henson.
(COURTESY OF HENSON FAMILY PROPERTIES)

Jim was nineteen when his brother, Paul Henson, Jr., a navy ensign (shown at right in 1953), was killed in an automobile accident at age twenty-three. The effect on Jim, recalled Frank Oz, was profound. "He realized that he just didn't have an infinite amount of time to do all the things he wanted to do."
(COURTESY OF HENSON FAMILY PROPERTIES)

The birthplace of the Mup Jim in front of the Henson home on Beechwood Road Hyattsville, Maryland, in 1
(COURTESY OF HENSON FAMILY PROPERTIES)

Jim touches up the paint on Kermit's mouth. Made from Betty Henson's milky-blue coat, with Ping-Pong balls for eyes, the eventual star of the Muppet realm was only an abstract thing, and not yet a frog.
(COURTESY OF THE JIM HENSON COMPANY.
KERMIT THE FROG © DISNEY)

sketches of Kermit and Sam, 1960.
URTESY OF THE JIM HENSON COMPANY.
MUPPETS © DISNEY)

Jim and Jane Nebel—first his performing partner and later his wife—with Sam, Kermit, and Yorick. The enormously popular Sam and Friends *earned Jim his first Emmy at the age of twenty-one.*
(COURTESY OF THE JIM HENSON COMPANY. MUPPETS © DISNEY)

*Jim on the day of his graduation f[rom the]
University of Maryland in 1960. T[he fa-]
mous success of* Sam and Friends [made it]
*possible for Jim to drive to the ce[remony]
in his own Rolls-Royce Silve[r...]*
(COURTESY OF HENSON FAMILY PR[OPERTIES])

*Newlyweds Jim and Jane Henson dance as Jim's
mother plays the piano. Betty Henson had insisted
her son shave off his new beard for the wedding.*
(COURTESY OF HENSON FAMILY PROPERTIES. PHOTO: DEL ANKERS)

*Family affair: Jim, adjusting Limbo, checks on Jane
as she tends to both Sam and daughter Lisa,
the first of the Hensons' five children.*
(COURTESY OF THE JIM HENSON COMPANY.
MUPPETS © DISNEY. PHOTO: DEL ANKERS)

*Jim—in a typical position—u[p]
from his Eames chair in the fi[rst]
Muppets, Inc., offices, located [above]
a nightclub on East 53rd Stree[t in]
New York in the early 1960s. "[The]
spaces never looked like office[s,]*
said Muppet writer Jerry Juhl[.]
(COURTESY OF THE JIM HENSON CO[MPANY])

The first three employees of Muppets, Inc. Left to right: performer/writer Jerry Juhl, performer Jerry Nelson, and Muppet designer/builder Don Sahlin.
<small>(COURTESY OF THE JIM HENSON COMPANY. PHOTO: DEL ANKERS)</small>

While a brilliant performer, Jim was ~~eq~~ly as talented behind the camera— ~~a~~nd spent much of the 1960s in the ~~dir~~ector's chair, overseeing everything from ten-second commercials to hourlong television specials.
<small>(COURTESY OF THE JIM HENSON COMPANY. PHOTO: DEL ANKERS)</small>

~~Fra~~nk Oz was nineteen years old and just out of ~~hig~~h school when he joined Muppets, Inc., in ~~196~~3 and was given the job of "right-handing" ~~as J~~im performed Rowlf the Dog on The Jimmy ~~Dean~~ Show. It was the beginning of one of the ~~close~~st, and funniest, creative partnerships ~~in e~~ntertainment.
<small>(~~CO~~URTESY OF THE JIM HENSON COMPANY. ~~MU~~PPETS © DISNEY. PHOTO: DEL ANKERS)</small>

Jim soars across the screen in his 1965 Academy Award–nominated short film Time Piece. *"Back in the sixties . . . I thought of myself as an experimental filmmaker,"* Jim said. *"[Those films] didn't have that commercial success, but that didn't particularly frustrate me because I enjoyed it."*
<small>(COURTESY OF THE JIM HENSON COMPANY)</small>

Jim's Muppets were pivotal to the succ[ess] of Sesame Street, *making the education[al]* show an overnight sensation and an American institution. Jim was fiercely devoted to the show, and he and Frank Oz *(shown here in 1969)* would regularly perform Ernie and Bert together until Jim's death. (COURTESY OF SESAME WORKSHOP)

A manic Muppet monster devours a machine in one of Jim's short films for IBM from the late 1960s. The monster would be defanged and used again as Sesame Street's *ravenous Cookie Monster.*
(COURTESY OF THE JIM HENSON COMPANY. MUPPETS © DISNEY)

Jim with Sesame Street *co-creator Joan Ganz Cooney in the 1980s.*
(COURTESY OF THE JIM HENSON COMPANY. PHOTO: MATTHEW MAURO)

[T]he Henson family in the late 1970s.
[Lef]t to right: Cheryl, Jane, Brian, Jim
(with Heather on shoulders),
John, and Lisa.
(COURTESY OF THE JIM HENSON
COMPANY. PHOTO: NANCY MORAN)

Jim at the editing table in 1972[;]
[p]erformer John Lovelady, designer
[An]nie Erickson, builder Faz Fazakas,
and designer Don Sahlin look on.
([C]OURTESY OF THE JIM HENSON COMPANY)

Attorney Al Gottesman deftly negotiated the profit-sharing deal that divvied up the millions from Sesame Street *merchandising between Henson Associates and Children's Television Workshop. Gottesman became one of Jim's most valued legal advisors.*
(COURTESY OF THE JIM HENSON COMPANY.
PHOTO: JOHN E. BARRETT)

Jim's hand-drawn cover to one of his earliest proposals for
The Muppet Show, *from the late 1960s.*
(Courtesy of The Jim Henson Company. Muppets © Disney)

Sinatra's show, which opened on a baking hot June 8, was acclaimed by critics as "big, busy, colorful, exciting and highly entertaining." But it was the Muppets—jostling for time alongside Frank Sinatra, Jr., and the flamboyant boxer Sugar Ray Robinson—who most reviewers agreed "brought down the house." "We tried to put together material we thought would work in terms of large movement and color," explained Jim. "There is that whole feeling of brotherhood and kindness and gentleness beneath it all but the idea here is to entertain."

The Muppets were given the plum position of opening the show, launching into the popular "Mahna Mahna" routine, featuring oversized versions of the Muppets he had used on *The Ed Sullivan Show*. Between musical numbers and sketches, Jim also took the opportunity to unveil one of his most ambitious puppets yet: a two-story, vaguely insectoid figure that appeared to be made of giant pipe cleaners, who danced and sang to the Luther Dixon and Al Smith blues tune "Big Boss Man." The character—which Jim would forever refer to simply as "Boss Man"—was essentially a gigantic rod puppet that Jim strapped himself into, standing onstage visibly harnessed to the puppet as he danced it around the set—a peek behind the puppetry process that one reviewer found "jarring."

Jim was delighted with the Vegas show and with the experience of performing live again. Yet although the Sinatra show was hailed as family entertainment, appealing to more than just the preschool set, Jim was still finding it hard to escape from the shadow of *Sesame Street* and had to continually steer reporters away from talking solely about his work for CTW. "I don't particularly like people to think that is all we do," he told one reporter somewhat impatiently. "We have always worked in the realm of adults. Maybe that's why we are here [in Vegas]."

In fact, the Sinatra show had been a trial run, an opportunity not only to try out some new kinds of puppetry, but also to learn what would and wouldn't work on a darkened stage in a large room. "Working here [in Vegas] appealed to us in many ways," he explained—then announced a surprising new project: "I have in mind doing a stage show," he continued, "a full Broadway show with puppets. This [Sinatra show] enabled me to try a few things I wanted to try onstage."

With the Sinatra show running smoothly, Jim opted to take a quick vacation, handing his Las Vegas performing duties over to Oz and Nelson. In late June, Jim piled Jane and the five kids into the station wagon for a long, leisurely drive—Jim *always* loved to drive—from New York to California, sleeping at motels, and stopping every now and then to take pictures of amusing signs and sights. In early July, they joined Jerry and Sue Juhl at the Wilderness Trails ranch in Colorado, spending nearly a week horseback riding and hiking.

While Jim enjoyed vacationing, he had a tough time staying in one place for very long—and just as he had in Las Vegas, he would become increasingly fidgety as the days passed, thinking about projects and scribbling ideas in small notebooks or yellow pads. Predictably, then, after only a few days in Colorado, Jim and Jerry Juhl stole away together to write—they were still passing pages of the screenplay for *Tale of Sand* back and forth—and kick around ideas. "We spent half our time riding around on horses, and of course the other half Jim and I sat working somewhere, which was always the standard pattern," said Juhl. "[Jim was] not a vacation kind of guy." Still, when the children were around, Jim lavished them with attention, and Cheryl would always recall their vacation at the ranch as one of her favorites.

The Hensons closed out their trip with a swing through Las Vegas, where Jim returned to perform with Nancy Sinatra for closing night on July 18, then finished up with three days at Disneyland—"a great success," Jim said. By early August, Jim was back in New York, just in time to turn around and travel to Nashville to attend the latest Puppeteers of America conference.

Jim's continued membership in Puppeteers of America wasn't just a show of good faith to his profession. "My dad . . . always remained faithful and involved with the serious puppeteers," said Lisa Henson. "Jim was loyal to puppetry and to Puppeteers of America because he believed in the value of the art as a form of expression," said Oz. "When you're a puppeteer, you act with the end of your arm. Your arm is your trade, and Jim appreciated that." That attitude was in direct conflict with Oz's, who never got comfortable with identifying himself as a puppeteer. "The more I was associated with puppets, the harder it was for me to be associated with the other things I wanted to do," Oz said, "or, at least, that was my own neurosis speaking. But Jim didn't have such apprehensions."

In fact, since his eye-opening trip to Europe in 1958, Jim had learned all he could about the long history of puppetry, reading about puppets in ancient Indonesia and Java, or studying the subtle differences in performance styles across European countries. Still, Jim refused to approach puppetry too intellectually. "When I hear the art of puppetry discussed, I often feel frustrated in that it's one of those pure things that somehow becomes much less interesting when it is overdiscussed or analyzed," he said later. "I feel it does what it does and even is a bit weakened if you know what it is doing. At its best, it is talking to a deeper part of you, and if you know that it's doing that, or you become aware of it, you lessen the ability to go straight in." More than anything, he was a fan, often collecting puppets for display in his home workshop. He was particularly pleased with a Sicilian rod puppet he had picked up, a four-foot knight in full armor with a detachable head ideally suited for losing in sword fights.

That autumn, between daytime work on inserts for *Sesame Street*'s third season and late night recording sessions for *The Muppet Alphabet Album*—an ambitious *Sesame Street*–related project that featured a song for every letter of the alphabet—Jim and Jane moved their family from the relatively secluded neighborhood in Greenwich to a more suburban home near Bedford, New York. "That was a big difference," said Lisa, "because we moved from this very historic building with a lot of personality to a brand-new home on a cul-de-sac suburban neighborhood. . . . We could ride bicycles and get out and walk to the bus and everything."

"It's nice for the children to be living in a neighborhood like this and going to the [local public] schools," Jim said. "Jane and I are both essentially loners. . . . I don't think children should be isolated, but we don't get involved with the neighbors." That wasn't quite true—some days, Brian would cut through the woods to visit a nearby horse barn, managed by a single mother with ten kids who allowed even her youngest children to rake their horse track by towing a large rake behind a converted milk truck. Brian was quick to lend a hand at the wheel. "I was driving early," he said diplomatically. As Brian got older, Jim would permit him to drive their own cars from the street down their long curving driveway to the garage—a task the twelve-year-old Brian "absolutely adored."

As usual, the Henson home bustled with projects and activity. Jim and Lisa set to work building a highly detailed dollhouse inspired by a real Manhattan townhouse they had scouted out and photographed—an ambitious project that took several years to complete. Brian built elaborate contraptions that would allow him to roll a marble from their bedrooms on the second floor all the way through the house down to the basement, while John would speed around the yard on his bike. Cheryl would ferry toddler Heather around the house and yard, painting Easter eggs in the downstairs playroom as Heather banged on a toy xylophone. Assorted pets, including cats, rabbits, guinea pigs, and a ferret, freely roamed the property, and Jane decorated the house with handmade crafts and pottery. "At home, we had all kinds . . . of creative things going on," said Jane. "So if there were puppets, they were made in the kitchen out of wooden spoons and paper cups and things like that. . . . Just a general feeling of creativity was always around the house."

Still, there were times when even such quiet pleasure was too loud for Jim, particularly when there were projects to brainstorm, scripts to be written, or times he just needed to think. "He loved to take a chair out into the garden and sit quietly, away from the hustle and bustle of the home, and just be," said Cheryl. "He needed to find quiet time to hear himself."

On Thanksgiving Day 1971, Jim was the featured guest for all ninety remarkable minutes of *The Dick Cavett Show,* performing several sketches—including old standbys like "I've Grown Accustomed to Her Face," newer skits like "Mahna Mahna," as well as new *Sesame Street* pieces—and demonstrating how Muppets were built and performed. It was a fun and fascinating appearance, yet Jim looked uncomfortable, loping onstage in black pants and buckled boots with a slightly too short woven tunic pulled over a beige turtleneck. Slouching down next to Cavett on the couch and crossing his long legs in front of him, a bit of bare calf was slightly visible above his boot line. As he spoke, his hands played with his beard; Jim was visibly nervous. He had never really gotten comfortable on camera—even the few times he had been called out onstage by Ed Sullivan after Muppet performances, Jim would shake hands and exit rapidly, saying as little as possible. "It took him a while to get comfortable in his own skin," said Oz.

Jim admitted as much. "I've . . . sat on the panel as myself just talking, not performing with the Muppets," he said later. "I liked it, sort of. I was comfortable, but not really comfortable. It's not what I was meant to be here for. Frankly, I'm a lot more comfortable if I'm wearing a puppet." For this appearance, however, Jim, Oz, and Nelson would be performing their puppets as they sat next to Cavett on the couch, visibly interacting and ad-libbing in character. "He was nervous about going on a live situation, unlike Frank, who kind of glories in that sort of thing," said Jerry Juhl. "Frank really loves to go in, to work live and work dangerously and ad-lib. . . . Jim was always nervous about it." And yet Jim bantered gamely with Cavett, and even the few times things went wrong—several tapes wouldn't cue up, and Ernie's sunglasses wouldn't stay on in one sketch—Jim always recovered, using self-deprecating humor. But if Jim was nervous about his ability to match wits with the clever Cavett, the host himself was in awe of Jim. "No matter how much you know about how this works," Cavett told his audience, "the minute you see them again, they're completely convincing. It's amazing." As Jim performed Kermit from the couch, Cavett was captivated. "It's hard to tell where Kermit leaves off and you begin!" said Cavett.

"Yes, I've noticed that," Jim responded, smiling.

Jim spent most of the Christmas holiday working out ideas for his Broadway show, a project he was determined to stage sooner rather than later. Despite his recent work in more adult venues and more sophisticated puppetry, the label reading *children's performer,* Jim feared, was beginning to stick. "It's something I've always faced, this slight condescension toward puppets," said Jim. "Well, my kids like puppets, certainly, but so do adults." The problem, as he saw it, was that adult audiences—at least in the United States—had never had the chance to see what good puppetry was capable of. The Broadway show Jim envisioned would finally give adult audiences that opportunity; more important, in the process, it would help him shed the stifling image the media was creating of Jim, and the Muppets, as purely sugarcoated kids' entertainment.

"Puppeteering covers a wide range of stuff," Jim explained to *The San Diego Union* patiently. "The nice thing is, you do it all—you can write it, stage it, build the sets, the puppets. It's a complete thing. Puppetry has been around for thousands of years. It's a part of theater in which small wooden figures serve to represent people. In theater, people represent things. And with puppets, you can deal with subjects in a way that isn't always possible with people. I think of puppetry as expressing one's self through charades."

In the four months since he had publicly announced his intent to pursue a live show, Jim had filled page after page in his yellow pads with ideas for skits and draft scripts, scribbling them out as he always did with a black felt-tip pen, then handing the pages over to his assistant to type. In early December, in fact, he felt he was far enough along with the project to meet with representatives of Lincoln Center about staging the show in one of their theaters, eventually reserving the elegant, and practically brand-new, Alice Tully Hall.

There was good reason for Jim to assume the time was right for a live stage show for puppets. Sid and Marty Krofft had recently produced a traveling show—basically a live version of their Saturday morning television hit *H.R. Pufnstuf*—the success of which was noted at Henson Associates a bit enviously. Additionally, in early 1971, puppeteer Wayland Flowers—with his outrageous, wisecracking puppet Madame—had opened a successful off-Broadway show called *Kumquats*, billed as the "World's First Erotic Puppet Show." Jim wasn't proposing anything quite that bawdy, though one of his first notes for the show—called *In Uffish Thought* in its earliest drafts—stressed that "it would not be supposed that the show is for children. It is intended to be an adult presentation." But perhaps realizing that aiming at a primarily adult audience might limit the show's commercial appeal, Jim had scrapped that idea and started over. While he still wanted to address more grown-up themes and write more sophisticated material, "We know that many people will bring children, just because of the . . . Muppets," he wrote, "so at no time will we do material in bad taste." Still, he assured potential investors, "This will not prevent this from being strong theatre."

Jim would write countless drafts and proposals for his show—pitched variously as *An Evening with the Muppets, The Muppets Get It Together,* and *The Muppets in Concert*—submitting presentations containing beautifully colored illustrations, drafting complete show outlines, hiring songwriters, and continually filling notebooks with new ideas and character sketches. While proposals could vary depending on whom Jim was pitching—whether potential funders, television executives, or Broadway producers—they all had one thing in common: "This is a very unusual evening of theatre," Jim would write in one pitch after another. "It is puppetry—but puppetry unlike any you've ever seen before."

One of the earliest and more intriguing sketches was a piece written by Juhl, based on an idea that Jim and Oz had regularly considered, but never carried out, during their days of performing Rowlf live with Jimmy Dean. "We loved the idea of Rowlf sitting there on a huge podium, and then it collapses and you see Jim and me performing him," Oz said. "We *loved* the idea of being seen. That was one thing I loved about Jim—he was never precious with the puppets." This progressive attitude toward puppetry was well ahead of its time; forty years later, puppeteers would routinely be visible to audiences as they performed their characters onstage in shows like *The Lion King* and *Avenue Q.* In 1971, however, such an approach challenged nearly every expectation American audiences had for a puppet show.

Juhl's script, then, began with Rowlf alone onstage addressing the audience. "I'm not a real dog," Rowlf says earnestly. "Where real dogs have hind legs, do you know what I've got? Puppeteers!"—at which point the podium hiding Jim and Oz would be pulled away, exposing the puppeteers, and shattering the barrier between reality and illusion. It was a theme that fascinated Jim—*The Cube* had practically been built around it—and the concept would run through several sketches in yet another proposal, this time featuring a gigantic puppet named Clyde, who would be visibly operated onstage by five puppeteers. "You will pay no attention to them," Clyde insists, "because that is our illusion—and that illusion is our reality, and the reality is the illusion." (Typically, Jim refused to end the piece on such a cerebral tone, noting that immediately after delivering this speech, Clyde "explodes in all directions.")

In other pieces, there was a new sociopolitical edge Jim hadn't shown with the Muppets before. Unlike Walt Kelly in *Pogo*, however, Jim was never comfortable aiming his satirical punches at individuals; instead, he took on higher concepts like technology, science, the generation gap, and, in one particularly biting piece, greed and the economy. That particular sketch—in which a giant, rolling face ingested stock funds and tax shelters—was one of Jim's favorites; he had even gone so far as to have the Muppet builders construct a gigantic face, and took great delight in allowing reporters to take photographs of him being gobbled up by it. Ultimately, the show, as Jim saw it, was designed to "present a series of contrasting moods and scale, showing the full range of what puppetry is capable of doing." It was clearly something new and unique: a puppetry *tour de force*, cleverly written and ambitiously designed—so ambitious, in fact, that Jim was finding it increasingly hard to hold it together.

In early 1972, Jim was back in Toronto to oversee preliminary work for a new installment of *Tales from Muppetland* called *The Muppet Musicians of Bremen*, adapted from the Grimm fairy tale. Many of the Muppets in *Bremen* would have a slightly different look from puppets in previous specials, thanks to the addition of a new designer named Bonnie Erickson, whose sense of design was a bit more cartoony and less abstract than Sahlin's. Where Sahlin designed and built in flat abstractions, sewing soft, malleable Muppets from fabric and stuffing, Erickson thought and worked in three-dimensional textures, carving Muppet heads out of enormous squares of polyurethane that could be easily mooshed and mashed and manipulated by performers to give the puppets a dynamic range of expression. Erickson's most notable contribution to *Bremen* would be the malleable foam heads carved for its hillbilly villains, giving each a look so bizarrely lifelike that one Hollywood special effects artist asked Jim how it had been done. "He thought that we were applying the foam directly to people's faces," laughed Jim.

To give the foam heads a softer, fuzzier appearance, Jim had recently adopted a process called *flocking,* commonly used in lining the interior of jewelry boxes. Flocking involved coating the Muppet's foam surface with an adhesive, then shaking fine synthetic fibers— the so-called *flock*—through a screen onto the glue. When an electrical charge was run through the wet, sticky surface—and for Muppet heads, this was usually done by sticking a pin into the puppet's face and electrifying it—the flock would stand up perpendicularly and then set in place. It was flocking that gave the interior of jewelry boxes their velvety feel; when applied to the Muppets, it gave each puppet a fuzzy look. As an added benefit, it also caught the light in a manner Jim loved, lighting the puppet beautifully on television. From here on, the flocking of Muppet heads would become a regular practice, giving Muppets like Miss Piggy or Statler and Waldorf their soft, slightly stippled appearance.

Still, the process for designing and building Muppets was always the same. "The character comes first," Jim said, "then I do a bunch of sketches and one of those will have an essence of the character." The workshop staff was small enough in 1971 that Jim was still able to oversee the development and building of nearly every Muppet himself. "[Jim] was the art director," said designer Caroly Wilcox, "so at least once a day he would make comments on how things were progressing." Sometimes, Jim would hand the designers a piece of yellow paper with nothing more than a squiggle with eyes and ears. "It was fun to play with that," said Wilcox, "the individual puppet builder designer had a lot more to put in."

With a growing staff, increasing revenues from merchandising to manage, and more and more contracts and legal agreements crossing his desk, Jim decided it was time to bring in a full-time business manager and administrator to keep an eye on the fine print and the bottom line. In March, he hired Al Gottesman, an attorney with a bit of showbiz savvy—as a young man, he had served as a page for Sid Caesar's *Your Show of Shows*—who had earlier impressed Jim with his level head and steady hand during the negotiations that produced the complex math formula that divvied up merchandising revenues between Henson Associates and Children's Television Workshop. That made Gottesman ideally suited for his first task: protecting the Muppets from copyright infringement.

The enormous success of *Sesame Street* had created a demand for Muppet merchandise that went beyond those officially licensed by Jim and CTW, which, in turn, had the unfortunate side effect of spawning an underground market of poorly made Muppet knock-offs. Public television stations, looking for gifts to give to donors, simply copied Muppet images onto watch faces; grocery stores, unable to hire the real Big Bird, threw together sloppy homemade costumes instead. "[Jim] felt concerned about kids and the public being misled into believing that Big Bird looked the way some costumed Big Bird [did] in front of a supermarket," said Gottesman. "It came from the integrity of the characters and of Jim."

With work completed on *The Muppet Musicians of Bremen* in March—it would air in April to generally good reviews—Jim was filing away ideas for future installments of *Tales from Muppetland,* such as adaptations of *Aladdin* and *Jack and the Giant Killer.* He was also interested in adapting several books that were personally meaningful to him, including *The 13 Clocks* ("the one property I've wanted to do with the Muppets for twenty years," Jim wrote) and Margery Williams's sentimental *The Velveteen Rabbit,* which Jim briefly considered producing with Raymond Wagner at MGM Studios. None of these projects, however, would advance much further than his notebooks.

In late April, Jim took the family on a short vacation, this time making the relatively short drive from New York up to Cape Cod. As Jim flew kites in the brisk ocean air, the Henson children would chase along behind him, clambering up and down the sand dunes. When the inevitable snarl of kite string occurred, Brian Henson would patiently work apart the knots and roll the untangled string into a tight ball. "I was very good," Brian laughed. "I found it therapeutic . . . I don't know why. . . . It was pretty chaotic at home. My brother was certainly quite chaotic."

For some time now, seven-year-old John Henson had been behaving erratically and recklessly, roughly handling the Henson pets or suddenly locking his gaze on some invisible focal point; of greater concern, he would sometimes pedal his bicycle madly in circles before wrecking intentionally. "I was a strange kid," John admitted later. Mostly, he was struggling with the frustrations of being severely dyslexic, though John attributed much of it to "an endless energy. If you look at the old home movies, everyone's around and every once in a while you'd see this little blond blur just careen through the frame; that was me. I was just always going—and the faster the better." At times, recalled Jane, Jim found his youngest son slightly frustrating. "[He and John] certainly cared for each other very much but I think they had probably a harder time understanding each other." Despite the bang-ups on his bike, John was convinced that he could never be badly hurt because a guardian angel was looking out for him—an idea that Jim found fascinating. Jim and Jane consulted doctors and sent John for testing, hoping to help him overcome some of his difficulties with dyslexia and looking for advice that might help ensure their dreamy son didn't hurt himself.

Most likely it was John's situation—as well as Jim's own continued fascination with the brain—that fueled Jim's interest in *The Affect Show,* a weekly program being developed by CTW with the New Age goal of "increas[ing] a child's psychological awareness of his own thoughts and feelings as well as his understanding of the thoughts and feelings of others." Gathering in June at the Arden House in Harriman, New York—the same location where CTW had conducted many of its reading seminars—CTW's cluster of child development specialists, psychologists, and educators excitedly discussed the potential for such a series, eventually suggesting that the show reflect "a family mood with characters, probably puppets, who encounter situations that call for different types of personality or emotions." CTW agreed to hold another meeting in late July, "by which time it is hoped some rough pieces of program material might be produced for reactions from the group"—a thinly veiled appeal that was aimed clearly at Jim.

Jim was intrigued by the premise, jotting down on lined yellow paper ideas for several skits that he thought might illustrate higher psychological concepts, such as a "character that always sees things in abstract symbols" or a "character that summarizes." It was a show, he told producer Diana Birkenfield, that was "meaningful" and "ought to be done." Birkenfield, however, was unimpressed. As Jim's producer, it was her job to look for projects that would be good for Jim and for Henson Associates—and she didn't think this was one of them.

Telling Jim no—especially when he was excited by an idea or project—was never an easy task. Over the years, only a few friends, acquaintances, and employees would ever really learn how to gently and diplomatically tell Jim if something was a bad idea or couldn't be done. One of those who could, and did, was Frank Oz, who left diplomacy at the door when it came to giving Jim his opinion. "I'd say to him, 'this doesn't fucking work!'" Oz said, laughing. "But if he felt strongly about something, it was tough to get him to back down. Anyone could say no to Jim, but you had to do it in a certain way, and you couldn't argue too much. You had to know when to step back."

Stepping back, however, was not Birkenfield's style. A loyal and savvy producer with a sharp eye for quality, Birkenfield took her job as the first line of defense against unworthy projects almost personally. If she felt Jim was considering projects that were unworthy of his name or reputation, she would "stand up to him and get angry at him and not talk to him for a while," recalled Gottesman. "She was totally devoted to him and devoted to his work."

In the case of CTW's proposed *Affect Show*, Birkenfield put her thoughts on paper, pounding out a blistering memo warning Jim that the show was an ill-advised idea that would not only take up too much of his time, but move his career in the wrong direction. "In my opinion," she wrote, "[the] Muppets should be working toward making it independently" rather than tying themselves to CTW. Attaching the Muppets to yet another CTW project, she warned, was only fueling the limited perception of Jim as a children's performer. "Adult TV has not been cracked, nor feature films, nor live presentation . . . [the] big thing that people can talk about . . . has yet to come." Birkenfield thought the proposed Broadway show might be the turning point in Jim's career—but only if he dedicated himself full-time to getting it done, rather than allowing himself to be distracted by projects like *The Affect Show*. "In the overall picture of what [Henson Associates] has done, is doing, and should be doing,"

she concluded, "I do not see your specific reasons for becoming involved with this series . . . [but] you make the decision . . . and let's
go."

Birkenfield was right, and Jim knew it; after producing two admittedly "poor" sample pieces, he chose not to pursue the project,
and the program never got off the ground. But that sort of aggressive
approach grated on Jim. "Diana was just a bit too relentless for
Jim," said Oz. "She would go after him." Jim never got angry or
upset; he never erupted or lost his temper; instead, he would get very
quiet—"powerfully silent," Oz called it—and he and Birkenfield
likely spent several hours in icy silence at the Muppet offices until
smoothing things over. The following year, at a meeting in California, there would be a similarly heated confrontation between Birkenfield and the outspoken Bernie Brillstein as Jim looked on in stony
silence. "DIANA VS. BERNIE," Jim wrote wearily in his journal. Several months later, she and Jim would have a very frank and private
conversation. "Talked to Diana Birkenfield," Jim wrote matter-of-
factly in his journal, "—ended her employment." Still, despite the
difference in the communication styles, Jim admired and respected
Birkenfield's talents, and would bring her back to the company in the
1980s. "These things were never personal," said Oz.

Sesame Street–related projects took up much of the summer, as
Jim spent the end of July working on the *Bert & Ernie Sing-Along*
record, and August taping *Sesame Street* inserts at Reeves. Still, Jim
took time off in mid-August to head to Oakland for the annual Puppeteers of America conference—and in September, he and Jane spent
more than a week in Europe attending the festival for UNIMA, the
Union Internationale de la Marionette, an international organization "devoted to the cause of international friendship through the
art of puppetry." Jim had helped found the American branch of
UNIMA in 1966, and in 1972 was serving as its American chairman.
Jim was delighted with the opportunity to mingle with more than
two thousand puppeteers from around the world, though perhaps
the biggest thrill of the trip was meeting Russian puppeteer Sergei
Obraztsov, whose book *My Profession* had been pivotal in helping
Jim learn puppetry in 1954.

On October 21, amid a particulary hectic meeting and travel schedule—including a Los Angeles meeting to discuss the Broadway show with writer Larry Gelbart and musician Billy Goldenberg—Jim learned that his mother had died in Albuquerque. The precise cause of Betty's death would remain a mystery; some thought she had simply pined away since Paul Jr.'s death more than fifteen years earlier. "I think it's fascinating that Jim and the whole family were content to live with that mystery," said Lisa Henson. "It was the religion, partially, but also an acceptance of certain unanswered questions." Jim flew immediately to New Mexico to be with his father—but a typically packed schedule demanded that he turn around less than twenty-four hours later to go to Los Angeles to tape a Perry Como Christmas special. He returned to Albuquerque on the morning of October 23 to oversee his mother's funeral and spend several days tending to his father. Only Jane was with him; the children had been left in Bedford. "My parents weren't really big on funerals," said Cheryl.

Betty Henson's death affected Jim perhaps more deeply than he let on to others. "Mom passed on," he confided privately in his journal, giving his mother three words more notice than he had given even to his beloved Dear after her death in 1967. In December, Jim immersed himself in Ruth Montgomery's recently published book, *A World Beyond,* an "account of life in the next stages of existence" that Montgomery had purportedly written while channeling a deceased psychic. Montgomery's reassuring message—that death is only a step toward a new level of existence—was closely in tune with Jim's own unique brand of spiritualism: a belief in a higher consciousness, a higher calling, and a higher, inherent order to the universe. It was a message brimming with hope for a son coping with the loss of a parent.

While afterimages of his Christian Science upbringing would remain part of his personal convictions, when it came down to it, Jim was more spiritual than religious, though he always remained "very respectful" of religion. "My dad would never, ever be snippy about somebody else's beliefs," Cheryl said. If Jim had a guiding ethos, then, it was *optimism*—a faith that human beings lived their lives for a purpose, and everything would come out all right in the end. As Jim later wrote:

I've read and studied about various other ways of thinking and I like the way most religions are based on the same good underlying principles. . . .

I believe in taking a positive attitude toward the world, toward people, and toward my work. I think I'm here for a purpose. I think it's likely that we all are, but I'm only sure about myself. I try to tune myself in to whatever it is that I'm supposed to be, and I try to think of myself as a part of all of us—all mankind and all life. I find it's not easy to keep these lofty thoughts in mind as the day goes by, but it certainly helps me a great deal to start out this way. . . .

Despite this discussion of things spiritual, I still think of myself as a very "human" being, I have the full complement of weaknesses, fears, problems, ego and sensuality. But I think this is why we're here—to work our way through all this and, hopefully, come out a bit wiser and better for having gone through it all.

But Jim's faith in the order of things—"the innocence and the simple optimism," said Jerry Juhl, that he "really loved"—also entailed a balance between darkness and light. "There was that dark side that he dealt with," said Juhl, "and I think he kept searching into spirituality, looking for ways to synthesize what was happening, for ways to explain the dark side." Jim felt "very strongly" about reincarnation as one opportunity to balance the universe and atone for mistakes in this and past lives, said Richard Hunt—but added that Jim "wasn't some looney spiritualist type character. He just would look into *everything*."

Muppet performer Fran Brill, too, was impressed with Jim's willingness to explore new ideas and new ways of thinking.

One of the extraordinary things about Jim was that he was a perpetual student of life. Genius that he was, he was always searching, questioning, exploring. When I first met Jim, in the early years of *Sesame Street,* he was . . . going to psychics and palm-readers, experiencing transcendental meditation, doing *est*—whatever was out there. He was judgmental about nothing—open to almost everything. I think he felt that all these "journeys" were the means to the same end—raising his level of consciousness, deepening his understanding of how all things on earth were related one to another, that every action had a reaction. He told me that for him there was no one right way, but that he took a little something from all of them.

Ultimately, said Jim, "I believe that life is basically a process of growth—that we go through many lives, choosing those situations and problems that we will learn through." For now, that was enough.

As Jim coped with his mother's death, there was a business-related problem to deal with as well. For nearly a year, Topper Toys—one of the busiest producers of *Sesame Street*-related merchandise—had been hemorrhaging money, due largely to an ill-advised decision to try to compete with the highly popular Barbie with a lower rent doll called Dawn. After posting nearly $10 million in losses, there was an "awkward mess" between CTW and Topper over continued licensing rights to *Sesame Street,* with Henson Associates squarely in the middle. In sticky cases like this, the lawyers for both CTW and Henson Associates would usually appeal to Jim and Joan Cooney to try to resolve the matter personally. "We've got to stay together for the children," Cooney would earnestly say to Jim—which was usually all that was needed for her and Jim to resolve the matter quickly. In the case of the problematic Topper, the licensing agreement would be terminated in January 1973, with Ideal and Fisher-Price swooping in to pick up the merchandising opportunity.

Just after the New Year, Jim took the family to Stratton, Vermont, for his first try at skiing. Despite his prowess on the tennis court, Jim never considered himself much of an athlete; even his own family would giggle when Jim tried to do anything physical—when he once tried scuba diving, Lisa had nearly hyperventilated with laughter. ("I looked underwater, and I saw him all lanky, with his arms and legs flailing, and I just died laughing!") Nonetheless, he gamely accepted Jon Stone's offer to join him at his Vermont home for a few days in

January to take some skiing lessons and try out some of Stratton's gentler, sloping ski trails.

"Like every other first-day skier, he spent a lot of time on his backside until he was absolutely covered with snow," recalled Stone. "It was all over his clothes, in his beard, [and] in his hair." At the end of the afternoon, Stone remembered waiting for Jim at the bottom of the mountain when he suddenly saw "this skinny snowman coming at me down that gentle little hill, standing straight up, arms straight out to the side, poles dangling. I remember telling him he looked like Christ of the Andes, and we both sat down in the snow, laughing."

Jim loved learning to ski alongside his children. "He really didn't like to do something with the kids where he was already good at it, because he didn't have the patience of them not knowing anything," said Jane. "So his approach to skiing was, 'I have never skiied, so I'm going to learn to ski with the kids.'" The kids loved it, too; part of the fun was having their father struggling and laughing right next to them. "We were all about the same level," said Brian, "which was fun."

On their many regular return trips to Stratton, the family would rent a house near the mountain and ski all day in a group—except for Jane, who was often stranded back at the cabin taking care of Heather. Admittedly, spending all day skiing—or scuba diving or horseback riding—wasn't Jane's idea of a vacation. Just as Jane had simpler, earthier tastes in décor, so, too, were her tastes in vacations. She preferred casual, low-key family drives or visits to Cape Cod rather than the galloping, diving, rowdy vacations favored by Jim. "[Driving] across country . . . that was more her style of thing," said Lisa. "He liked a more active, kind of luxury trip . . . [while] my mom would stay home."

Apart from his new pastime, Jim was taking an interest in the burgeoning environmental movement, participating in a spring 1973 ecology special called *Keep U.S. Beautiful* where he performed a musical number with monsters made from garbage—ancestors of *Fraggle Rock*'s Marjorie the Trash Heap. Typically, Jim downplayed his activism. "I'm not an ecology nut, but I do have my own personal cause," he told the *Los Angeles Times*. "People are messing up the cities something awful. . . . The aim of the program is not to tell people what to do, but to bring the problem out into the open so that hopefully they will think twice before they dirty up the streets and the roads again." In other words, there would be no heavy-handed messages; as he told his children time and time again, *They remember what you are.* The Muppets would lead by example.

Jim was continuing to hire new designers and builders for the Muppet workshop, bringing in two craftsmen who, in different ways, would have a lasting impact on the Muppets. The need for additional designers and builders was due partly to the recent reduction in Don Sahlin's hours, a difficult but necessary decision prompted by Sahlin's increasingly slow method of working. One new designer was the bespectacled and slightly eccentric Franz "Faz" Fazakas, a former employee of Bil Baird's who could out-gadget and out-tinker even the versatile Sahlin. While Fazakas had performed some minor puppetry on *The Frog Prince* and *The Muppet Musicians of Bremen,* his real strength was in designing and inventing intricate mechanisms that gave Muppets more versatility. It was Fazakas, for example, who would improve the eye mechanisms on Big Bird and Sweetums, giving both characters a much broader range of emotions.

The other craftsman brought into the workshop was a brilliant, bearded, twenty-six-year-old Californian named Dave Goelz, who had a degree in industrial design and an almost instinctive sense for puppetry—though an often painful lack of confidence in his skills as a performer. Goelz, who had designed for John Deere and Hewlett-Packard, had seen the Muppets on *Ed Sullivan* and *Sesame Street* and became "fascinated with the design process" he saw on-screen. After watching Oz perform at a show at Mills College in Oakland—Goelz later admitted he had stalked Oz "like an assassin," meticulously watching the performance through a telephoto lens—Goelz was determined to get involved with the Muppets.

At Oz's invitation, Goelz spent a week watching the Muppet performers taping *Sesame Street* inserts at Reeves Teletape, bringing with him a number of homemade puppets to show Jim. Unfortunately, Goelz had chosen to be on-set during the week Jim was in France for the UNIMA conference—but Bonnie Erickson, with an eye for design talent, was impressed enough by Goelz's work to recommend that Jim follow up with a phone call. Two conversations later, Goelz found himself in New York working at a bench in the Muppet workshop, sketching out designs and constructing elaborate puppets for Jim's Broadway show. It was a task well suited for Goelz—but Jim would soon find a better way to utilize Goelz's considerable talents by putting a puppet at the end of his arm.

With new designers, countless yards of fabric, mounds of fake fur, and bins bursting with noses, eyes, and mustaches, the Muppet workshop had quickly outgrown its space on the second floor of Henson Associates. During the spring of 1973, then, Jim had rented—then renovated—a much larger space just up the block at 201 East 67th Street for the sole purpose of relocating the workshop. Moving the workshop gave Jim the opportunity to spread his designers and builders out across a large space they had entirely to themselves, while also giving the business offices some much needed breathing room just down the street at 227.

In late May 1973, following an appearance with Kermit and Cookie Monster at the Emmy Awards, Jim took thirteen-year-old Lisa and twelve-year-old Cheryl on a vacation to London and Copenhagen. For nearly two weeks, Jim and his daughters relaxed at the stately Grosvenor House in London's opulent Mayfair district, toured old castles in the English countryside, then traveled by boat across the North Sea to Copenhagen. Jim found the choppy waters oddly soothing, and would stand on deck with the girls endlessly watching the diving seagulls as the boat rocked in the waves. Jim's interest in the foaming, softly churning water was, thought Cheryl, a reflection of his growing fascination with his own subconscious—a topic she and Jim discussed earnestly and that Cheryl had lately been exploring in her own poetry. "I was starting to tap into that, to figure out that [water is] a great metaphor for the subconscious," Cheryl recalled. "So I think that's what he was interested in—because my father was very interested in dreaming and keeping dream diaries, and the subconscious."

Perhaps Jim was also quietly trying to make sense of the disorder that had lately crept into his personal life. More and more, Jim and Jane were living at increasingly different speeds. Partly, it was a matter of personalities. "Dad was driving fast cars and zipping around the country roads in our town," said Lisa, "while Mom had developed the habit of driving very slowly with a line of eight to ten cars behind her." Even when walking the streets of New York, Jim and the older children would stroll at a rapid pace, leaving Jane half a block behind to walk more slowly with Heather and catch up at the next intersection. It was an apt metaphor for the current state of their always complex relationship.

Jim and Jane remained devoted to each other—they had built a company together, had five children, and still shared similar artistic sensibilities—but lately their differences in demeanor and temperament were becoming sharper and more accentuated. Jim was genuinely calm, almost stoic in his demeanor—"I think . . . he was setting an example to instill in us [kids] more calmness and peacefulness," said Lisa—while Jane, on the other hand, openly felt, discussed, and displayed her feelings. The contrasting ways in which each of them expressed their emotions, then, inherently bred conflict. "He was so repressed and kind of internalized about [his] emotions," recalled Lisa, "and my mother . . . is very articulate about emotions and really feels them. And if she gets sad she gets *very* sad; if she gets angry, she gets *very* angry. They didn't mesh that way."

That difference alone could often make communication difficult. Jim never liked confrontation anyway—he had subjected Diana Birkenfield to the silent treatment over a sharply worded memo—and if Jane became upset or emotional with him, Jim would simply tune her out, which made Jane that much more frustrated. It was a self-perpetuating cycle that was doomed to keep the two of them from openly communicating. "His repressive silence would really make her angrier and would ramp her up," said Lisa—and the more Jane wanted to hash things out, the quieter Jim got.

Perhaps in the same search for peace, Jim was also continuing to actively explore other New Age concepts that fascinated him, enrolling in a Transcendental Meditation class and reading intensely about reincarnation, alternative existences, and parallel lives. "I think my father was *very* intrigued by this idea of the parallel life," said Cheryl, "and whether that parallel life *is* the dream world, or that parallel life is literally a parallel life—like maybe with a girlfriend or maybe with some other life other than the one you happen to be living where there are . . . five kids and your wife who you don't communicate with. . . . I think my dad was intrigued by that notion."

And then in June 1973, things got even thornier: Jane discussed with Jim what he came to call her "DECLARATION OF INDEPENDENCE," writing the phrase in his journal in all capital letters, a sure sign that she had gotten his attention. Whether it was frustration over being marooned in the suburbs with five children while Jim worked in the city all hours of the day and night, sadness over her marginalization as a partner in the business she had helped create, or disappointment that Jim seemed more interested in spending time with the Muppet performers than with her, Jane had clearly had enough; she was no longer inclined to go quietly along. "I think probably in the long run both of us wanted to do things our own way," said Jane.

"I probably just kept things inside for so long until [I said] 'Hey, look, I have a life, too. It's just not about you and your career. It's about me, too,'" said Jane. "He just assumed that I was either interested in what the children were doing, or I was interested in what *he* was doing, and that was what wives do. . . . The problem, really, was that we just didn't usually talk about these things." Indeed, even as Jane had laid things out, Jim still refused to engage. Apart from his all-caps note in his journals, Jim responded to Jane's declaration with silence. He'd let Jane keep doing the talking—and that would only deepen the chasm between them.

Despite their increasingly different speeds, Jim and Jane would continue to do the things married couples do—indeed, Jane was always "fiercely loyal" to Jim, noted Cheryl, "even when she was mad at him"—putting on her best face as they traveled to the Emmy Awards together, attended conferences, and even celebrated their anniversary each year. But Jim and Jane continued to move at different speeds, and as time went on and the children grew, their emotional distance—like that span of sidewalk between them as they walked the streets of New York—would only widen.

Things were much more firm in Jim's professional life—at least at the moment. For much of 1973, Jim was aggressively pitching his Broadway show to several television networks, trying to gauge their interest in filming the live stage show for a television special he was now calling *An Evening with the Muppets*. Jim was so certain the live show would come together that he had already reserved Alice Tully Hall for three weeks starting in June 1975, with an option for a fourth. Jim estimated the show he was envisioning would cost roughly $350,000 to open, then $35,000 per week after that—and in his pitch to ABC, he even proposed to share the profits from the show with the network in exchange for their backing, sweetening the deal by recalculating the start-up costs at a discounted $275,000.

Making things even more attractive for investors, Jim had recently secured the services of writer Larry Gelbart—a good fit, as the two shared similar comedic sensibilities and a fondness for variety shows. He had also reached an agreement with Pat Birch, the Tony-nominated choreographer for *Grease,* to assist with directing and staging, and had piqued the interest of Emanuel Azenberg, who had overseen several of Neil Simon's plays, about taking on the role of producer. For the music, Jim had contracted with a San Francisco organization called Imagination, Inc., putting them to work almost immediately on the hymnal music for the subversive "Religious Piece." Everything seemed to be going smoothly—until all of a sudden it wasn't.

Jim's major creative catch, Larry Gelbart, suddenly found the bulk of his time taken up by a new television show he had helped develop for CBS called *M*A*S*H,* which would win Gelbart an Emmy the following year. "Gelbart out of B'way," Jim wrote gloomily in his journal, though there would be no hard feelings, as Gelbart would helpfully provide Jim with other contacts as he tried to hold the show together. Next, the collaboration with Imagination, Inc. for music turned into a creative mismatch, and Jim released the company from its obligations in late spring 1973, bruising the ego of Imagination, Inc.'s Walt Kraemer. "You're a better artist than you are a client," Kraemer wrote to Jim. "I admittedly gave little thought to how we were ever going to work nose-to-face on a project of this scope. . . . I have no hard feelings because I am still proud of the work we did."

Jim tried to put the best face on things, assuring investors that he had either Joe Raposo or Billy Goldenberg lined up to provide the music, and brought in Marshall Brickman, who had co-written *Sleeper* with Woody Allen, to help write additional material. The ever-loyal Jerry Juhl also vowed to stand by, ready to draft new Muppet sketches whenever Jim might ask. But despite Jim's best efforts— and his unwavering belief in the strength of the show—the project was disintegrating quickly. Jim would reluctantly shelve the show by autumn 1973, though for the rest of his life he would never entirely let go of the idea of putting together an elaborately produced live stage production.

With the prospects of the stage show fading, Jim redoubled his efforts to interest networks in several new television specials. Most were Muppet holiday-related specials—Halloween, Thanksgiving, New Year's Eve—but there were also the usual fascinating non-Muppet-related proposals, including the creepy, *Twilight Zone*–ish *The Monsters Inside Jason's Brain,* another variation on Jim's fascination with illusion and reality, and *The Island,* an artsy piece proposing to tell the same story from four different points of view.

Jim's method for pitching Muppet projects required both enthusiasm and stamina. As he had done when wooing Jerry Juhl and Bernie Brillstein a decade earlier, Jim preferred to pitch by doing, and would not only describe the show but also perform Muppet skits for pin-striped network executives, many of whom sat by blank-faced as Jim, Oz, and Nelson chattered back and forth, often with puppets on each arm. It was a process Oz found excruciating. "We would carry these big, heavy motherfuckin' black boxes in cabs to go across town to try to sell the show to network executives," Oz said, his voice rising at the memory even forty years later. "We'd perform it, and someone would say, 'That's great! Bob'—or some other fuckin' guy—'has to see this!' So then we'd do it some more." The problem, said Oz, was that no matter how many times they performed, they never seemed to have the person in the room who could actually approve a project.

Eventually, however, Jim found a particularly perceptive audience in a young network executive at ABC named Michael Eisner, who listened closely, laughed appreciatively, and—unlike many of the executives who had so frustrated Oz—could actually green-light a project. And as Jim and his team packed up their boxes to leave,

Eisner gave them the go-ahead for a Muppet-related pilot. At last, Jim had yes for an answer—and now that he had ABC on board to produce a pilot, Jim was certain a weekly Muppet television show was a sure thing.

He would be wrong.

CHAPTER EIGHT

THE MUCKING FUPPETS

1973–1975

Jim's Land of Gortch cast from the first season of Saturday Night Live.
Left to right: King Ploobis, Wisss, the Mighty Favog, Scred, Queen Peuta, and Vazh.
SNL's *human cast members hated giving up on-screen time for the Gortch sketches
almost as much as* SNL's *writers loathed writing them.*

"THE TIME IS RIGHT FOR A VARIETY SHOW HOSTED BY DOGS, FROGS AND monsters," wrote Jim in his first official pitch for a Muppet-based television show. In the late 1960s, after nearly a decade of appearances on other people's variety shows, Jim was convinced the Muppets could more than hold their own for thirty minutes each week—and in the summer of 1969, he had prepared his first formal proposal, packaging it under a hand-lettered, full-color cover page, announcing "THE MUPPET SHOW [—] a concept for a half hour PRIME TIME BIG BUDGET SHOW STARRING THE MUPPETS."

Even in its earliest stages, Jim knew precisely the audience he wanted for *The Muppet Show*. "The show is aimed at the adult or young-adult audience—but it is a show for the whole family," he wrote. "The humor and writing will be adult, but children always enjoy the puppets, and the show will present nothing in bad taste to offend kids." He was also certain of the format. The show would be "a loose assemblage of bits and pieces," wrote Jim, "incorporating a guest star each week who does musical numbers with and without the Muppets, comedy bits with some of the puppet characters, etc." While Jim was proposing Danny Kaye as a first guest, he was also willing to forgo the idea of a guest star altogether, offering to host the show himself "in a low-key, unperformer way *a la* Ernie Kovacs."

Jim's first draft was heavily influenced by the variety shows of the time, which relied on set pieces and recurring characters, in the same vein as *Laugh-In*'s "joke wall" or "Here Comes the Judge" skits. Jim, then, proposed a number of regular segments—which he helpfully illustrated with full-color cartoons—including Kermit as a late night talk show host named Jackie Kavson, presiding over panel discussions that erupted into fistfights, and a skit featuring a prissy "critic at large" named Elmont Fidge who reviewed books and films with bawdy titles like *The Orgy Next Door*. Some of these bits, explained Jim somewhat clumsily, "have a satiric point of view, but they often exist only for the sake of pure comedy entertainment."

Jim would tinker with his proposal over the next few years, describing shows built around guest stars like Paul McCartney or Stan Freberg, drafting detailed budget spreadsheets (Jim thought episodes would cost roughly $32,350 to produce—a number far below the $125,000 he would eventually spend on each installment of *The Muppet Show*) and elaborating at length on why the Muppets were uniquely suited for a show of their own. "Puppets are fortunate—they can do and say things a live performer wouldn't touch with a stick," Jim explained. Later, he would enthusiastically—though not very helpfully—gush, "The Muppets, more than any other puppets, are more real than the real thing." Ultimately, Jim's early *Muppet Show* proposals were more passion than polish—but once Jim opened his black boxes and began performing his way through Muppet skits he had only described on paper, his vision was clear, his enthusiasm infectious. In his April 1973 meeting with Jim, it had been impossible for Michael Eisner to say no. With Eisner's approval, ABC would back a pilot for a weekly Muppet series.

Now that he had ABC's support, Jim sat down in July to discuss ideas with Jerry Juhl, television writer Jerry Ross, and former *Jimmy Dean* scribe Will Glickman. Jim had his mind set on a Muppet Valentine's Day show—yet another one of the holiday-themed specials he had been pitching for the last two years—and met with his writers regularly throughout the fall of 1973 to review early drafts of the script. By early September, Jim had even landed an A-list guest, twenty-eight-year-old actress and singer Mia Farrow, who willingly agreed to serve as the Muppets' very first human costar. Things were moving quickly—and yet, typically, Jim was juggling several other obligations, making it difficult for him to get his pilot before the cameras as quickly as he wanted.

Of particular importance—though Jim had no way of knowing just how important at the time—was a two-week stint in London to film the television special *Julie on Sesame Street* with Julie Andrews. Jim had first worked with Andrews in early 1973, serenading her with Rowlf on her weekly series *The Julie Andrews Hour*. Andrews's series was highly acclaimed, but with a poor time slot—it was up against *The Mary Tyler Moore Show*—it was doomed to cancellation after only a little more than a year. Still, sympathetic executives at ABC offered Andrews the opportunity to star in five more variety shows over the next two years, this time permitting her to tape them in her native England and ceding production over to ATV (Associated Television) and ITC (Incorporated Television Company), overseen by British producer, media mogul, and impresario Lord Lew Grade. *Julie on Sesame Street* would be Andrews's first special for Grade—and on October 20, three days after recording a few songs for his Muppet pilot, Jim was off to London to work with Andrews.

For two weeks, Jim—along with Oz, Spinney, Nelson, and much of the *Sesame Street* crew—zipped back and forth between the Cavendish Hotel and Grade's ATV Studios in London's Borehamwood district, piling the entire team into several cabs each day for the thirty-minute trip north. *Julie on Sesame Street* featured the Muppets in nearly every segment—there would be only a brief interlude for Andrews to sing a duet with guest Perry Como—and Jim and his team worked almost constantly, rehearsing their singing and dancing all day, then filming into the evenings. There were plenty of charming moments, from Kermit singing "Bein' Green" with Andrews to rows and rows of dancing grouches in trash cans, though Jim had scuttled an idea for a similar performance featuring multiple Big Birds, politely but firmly explaining to Andrews's producers that "Somehow it seems to make a rather unique large bird not quite so unique."

Between tapings, Jim managed to catch Joe Raposo at the Dorchester hotel for lunch, and spent time at the home of Mia Farrow and husband, André Previn, for some last-minute discussions with the Muppets' now visibly pregnant costar. When taping with Julie Andrews wrapped on November 5, Jim wasted no time returning to New York and his own project. But his hard work in London had landed him squarely on the radar of producer Lew Grade, who later admitted that he had been "struck with [Jim's] originality and humor." Quietly, the savvy Grade, who was always on the prowl for talent, made a note to discuss Jim and the Muppets with his ITC producers.

Taping on Jim's pilot—which he was calling *The Muppets Valentine Show*—began at ABC studios on December 3, 1973. Jim spent three days taping Farrow's segments, then returned to the studio a week later to complete two Muppets-only pieces. Final editing took place in early January 1974—and just like that, Jim had completed his pilot. To celebrate, Jim threw a party at his home in Bedford where he screened the pilot for his guests, then immediately took off on a fifteen-day press tour to promote the show in Baltimore, Philadelphia, Cleveland, San Francisco, and several other major television markets, including an appearance on *The Tonight Show*. As usual, Jim was up against the puppetry prejudice, constantly reminding reporters that the Muppets were for more than just children. "We made this special to appeal to all ages, because a lot of people just think of us as a company that does shows for children because of all the *Sesame Street* shows," Jim told *The Hollywood Reporter* patiently. "We want to maintain a separate image. Not all of our shows are for children."

With *The Muppets Valentine Show,* Jim was clearly still feeling his way around for a format, placing the core of the show on a set that looked like an overgrown conservatory, and populating it with an assortment of monsters, most of them holdovers from *The Great Santa Claus Switch.* There were also several new humanoid characters, including George the Janitor and the detonator-wielding Crazy Harry (here called Crazy Donald, a nod to the explosion-loving Don Sahlin), both of whom would eventually make their way onto *The Muppet Show.* For the hosting duties, Jim turned things over to another new character, the vaguely human Wally, a sunglasses-wearing hipster who managed the Muppet cast while banging out stage directions on a typewriter. Kermit was there, too, but largely as a supporting character: while he did get to star in his own musical number—where he pedaled across the stage on a bicycle, a trick that would wow audiences several years later—he was otherwise blended into the crowd.

Only two weeks after completing final edits, *The Muppets Valentine Show* premiered on ABC on January 30, 1974. Reviews were overwhelmingly positive—"absolutely delightful," bubbled *Variety*—and most seemed to acknowledge that the special played well across all age groups. The show impressed executives at ABC, including network president Martin Starger, who called Jim into his office in March for a conversation about other projects. While the weekly series Jim wanted wasn't yet on the table, Jim was still hoping to be given the opportunity to put into production several more holiday-themed shows he had outlined. Jim left the meeting in Starger's office without a firm deal in place, but each promised to keep the discussions going. It was enough for now.

Late in the spring, Jim took the family on another car trip, spending Easter in North Carolina with his Aunt Attie and Uncle Jinx, along with cousins Will and Stan and their families. Attie, Betty Henson's oldest sister, was nearing seventy now, but remained in good health and spirits—and for Jim, it may have briefly seemed like those days in Hyattsville again, with the families crowded around the dinner table, swapping stories and jokes. It was also a reminder to Jim of just how alone his father must have been in Albuquerque following the death of Betty Henson nearly two years earlier.

Recently, however, Paul Henson had been spending more and more time with Attie and Betty's youngest sister, Bobby, now nearing sixty, who was also living alone following her divorce. Paul and Bobby's relationship wasn't necessarily romantic, but the two had known each other for nearly forty years—and with each now living alone, it seemed somehow appropriate for the two of them to take care of each other. On May 22, as Jim, Jane, Lisa, and Cheryl looked on, Paul and Bobby were married in Albuquerque. While Jim acknowledged the marriage was one of convenience, he was pleased his socially inclined father would again have the companionship he craved and needed. For his part, Jim would continue his habit of regular visits, affectionately referring to the new couple as "Dad and Bob."

Back in New York, Jim was having—by his definition, at least— a relatively leisurely summer, auditioning performers at the new workshop in late May, discussing toys with Fisher-Price executives in June, and in July overseeing a segment for the national tour of the Ice Follies that featured several of his *Sesame Street* characters. Jim was particularly excited about the Ice Follies project; after being approached by Ice Follies representatives with the idea, Jim had eagerly handwritten a twenty-nine-page script for the show, including lyrics for several songs. He was also intrigued by the mechanics of recreating characters that had only been seen in a smaller, hand puppet size as full-sized, figure-skating walkarounds. Working with designer Bonnie Erickson and the Muppet workshop, "we blew them up so they were exactly in scale," Jim said proudly. When the segment finally debuted at an Ice Follies show in Sacramento that August, the crowd greeted the characters with thunderous applause—"one of those great roars of appreciation," recounted Jim. "It was really neat to see it."

Most days, Jim would drive into the city to check in at the Muppet workshop, arriving about ten in the morning, loping up the long stairway and quietly calling out "Hi, guys!" as he entered the main room. Most mornings, he would briefly gather the designers and builders around him to discuss individual puppets and projects before heading up the street to his office, half a block away. While Sahlin and Goelz could almost always be found tinkering with something, Sahlin had, for a while, turned the entire workshop into a whirring, clicking mouse terrarium, with wires and pulleys stretched across the ceiling and down the walls. "Bonnie Erickson's boyfriend worked for Sloan-Kettering Hospital, and he would liberate mice every now and then, save them from being experimented on, and give them the dubious advantage of surviving in our shop," said Goelz. Sahlin had set up an elaborate elevator system by which mice could be dropped on the benches of unsuspecting Muppet builders; later, he built an aerial highway made of wires and Slinkies, allowing mice to clamber over cupboards, desks, and light fixtures. "It was like a mouse freeway," said Goelz—and more than once, Jim entered the workshop to find Sahlin bent over a table, working intently as a mouse sat perched on top of his head.

There were spiritual matters to tend to that summer, too. Over the past several months, Jim had been reading the metaphysical *Seth Material*, written by spiritualist Jane Roberts, who claimed to be channeling a male personality that called itself Seth. In her books—and through Seth—Roberts explored life after death and the pros and cons of reincarnation, with the underlying message that "You create your own reality." That intrigued Jim—it was a message that must have resonated with a man who regularly spent his days creating completely new personalities at the end of his arm—and on July 30, he drove to Elmira, New York, to pay his respects to Roberts and her husband. "I find this inspired material very beautiful," Jim said of the *Seth Material*. "It puts everything into a harmonious totality that I just love." Jim's interest in other realities was no surprise to Jon Stone. "He was always interested in getting beyond," said Stone. "I think he saw his mind as a sort of prison. He was always kind of outside of it, trying things that the rest of us just . . . keep going with our blinders on, down our own little path, and he was out in the woods somewhere. He was great." Oz, too, understood, and listened patiently but skeptically as Jim enthused about Roberts and Seth. "I didn't believe a word of them," said Oz, "but Jim truly believed in other realms. His willingness to believe gave him a kind of noble cause. There's a nobility in the Muppets, and Jim brought that."

That nobility was genuine, for Jim saw virtue and worth in nearly everyone. His own generosity, in fact, could be staggering.

When Bernie Brillstein went through a divorce in 1974—and lost nearly everything in the settlement—Jim immediately loaned the agent $100,000 and told Brillstein there was no need to hurry to repay him. "That's Jim Henson," said Brillstein. "He was *grand* in this strange, quiet way. His love was unbounded." Jim's faith in his fellow man was unbounded, too. Jim rarely, if ever, locked his car—and if anything were ever stolen, he would simply shrug and say "someone must have needed it." Even after his wallet was stolen from the front seat of his Jaguar—yet another in a long line of flashy cars—Jim refused to get angry; instead, he saw it as another teachable moment, and Brian Henson remembered his father launching into a mock sermon at the breakfast table, speaking in inflated tones on the value of forgiveness: "My car was broken into and things were stolen," Jim told his family, speaking in the voice he would always use for his most self-important characters, "but I realize I have a very wonderful life, I have plenty of money, and whoever it was who stole my wallet needs it more than me, so I find it in my heart to forgive them." While their father might "make fun of himself a little bit" at these moments, said Brian, "his intention was to teach a lesson."

In August 1974 came the word that Jim had been waiting for: ABC had agreed on a development deal for several programs, including an after-school special, a ninety-minute movie of the week, and exclusive use of the Muppets on ABC for a period of time. While ABC hadn't opted for a weekly Muppet series, Jim had deftly persuaded the network to give him another shot at it, clearing the way for a second pilot. Jim, in fact, had already prepared an outline for a show he was calling *The Muppet Nonsense Show*. "It would be a half hour show, with no guest star," Jim wrote, "a lot more zany comedy, more magazine-type pieces [and] continuing characters that the audience will get to know and love."

With the deal in place, Jim was determined to get his second pilot in front of the cameras as soon as possible. Jim immediately put the Muppet designers to work on several new puppets he'd drawn, handing Bonnie Erickson pages of character sketches scribbled in his distinctive swooping style. One new character was a grinning piano player that Jim had based on the flamboyant New Orleans musician Dr. John, who had charted in 1973 with "Right Place Wrong Time." Dr. John personified the kind of laid-back, hep-talking bandleader that had appeared all the way back in Jim's proposals for *Zoocus* in 1960, and Jim's first drawing for the character boiled the performer down to the basics: a wide, grinning mouth over a scrap of beard, sleepy eyes, and a bulbous nose holding up wire-rimmed glasses. Erickson assigned the design of the character to a new member of the Muppet team: Michael Frith, a brilliant, thirty-two-year-old illustrator with a wickedly droll sense of humor. Frith—who had been an art director and editor at Random House, where he had overseen much of Dr. Seuss's work—wasn't a puppet builder, but he had a knack for taking Jim's energetic drawings and fleshing out their personality in beautiful full-color sketches that builders could use for further inspiration. Working off Jim's drawing, Frith sketched out a slightly more polished version of the character, giving him long rubbery arms, a potbelly, and a tall, feathered top hat. Across the top of the page, he scrawled out a potential name: Leon "Doctor" Eltonjohn Dontshoot (The Piano Player). However, given the character's wide grin and glinting gold tooth, Jim had a different, and simpler, name in mind: Dr. Teeth.

Another new character, too, could also trace its origins almost as far back as *Zoocus*. In Jim's outline for *The Muppet Nonsense Show* was a regular skit featuring a frazzled foreign chef who "create[s] new dishes—with subtitles in various languages. . . . In the end, the dish explodes, walks away in disgust, or even eats him." At the USDA show in Hamburg in the early 1960s, Jim and Jerry Juhl had performed *Sam and Friends'* Omar as a live hand puppet creating a messy chef's salad as he ranted in mock German—a bit Jim loved, but had kept out of his repertoire for nearly a decade. Now he would bring it back, though for the *Nonsense Show,* the Chef, and his mock language, would be Swedish. Jim initially named the character *Jarnvagskorsning,* a Swedish word that translated roughly as "railway crossing," then decided that the name, while funny, was too hard to remember or pronounce. In his earliest appearances, then, Jim would refer to the character as "The Swedish Meatball," and then simply as "The Swedish Chef."

Despite the relative simplicity of the puppet—it was essentially a head with two empty sleeves through which a second performer could insert both hands—the Swedish Chef was one of the last Muppets completed before filming on the pilot began in November 1974. It had been only three months since ABC had approved the pilot, and in that time Jim had been in motion almost constantly, overseeing the writing duties with Marshall Brickman—his collaborator on the unrealized Broadway show—and *Sesame Street* writers Jon Stone and Norman Stiles, as well as visiting the workshop every day to check on Muppet production.

There was a quick break in September for Jim to celebrate the Muppet team winning its first Emmy for their work on *Sesame Street*—a major accomplishment to be sure, though Jim was typically low-key about it, grinning somewhat stiffly in his tuxedo as he accepted the award along with Oz, Nelson, Spinney, Hunt, and Brill. Three weeks later, Jim and the Muppet team took nearly a week to travel to London for an appearance on *The Herb Alpert Show,* dancing two enormous Boss Men Muppets to Alpert's "Spanish Flea." But the rest of the time, "[he] was in the office every day, and he was always either upstairs or he'd come down and work the shop," recalled Bonnie Erickson. "Even to the end . . . Jim came in and worked on the Swedish Chef and I sort of finished for him."

Jim's work extended beyond the office and workshop; in preparation for his performance as the Swedish Chef, Jim was even working in his car, practicing his mock Swedish during his daily drives from Bedford into New York City. Jim had installed a cassette deck in his Jaguar on which he could both play and record tapes, and each day he would listen to a cassette prepared for him by writer Marshall Brickman—who could bring Jim and Oz to tears with his ability to mock foreign languages—instructing him on how to speak mock Swedish. After listening to Brickman's tape, Jim would then record himself—speaking into a full-sized microphone he had clipped to the dashboard—and play back his performance, trying to get it right. "I used to ride with him a lot," said Brian Henson. "And he would drive to work trying to make a chicken sandwich in mock Swedish or make a turkey casserole in mock Swedish. It was the most ridiculous thing you had ever seen, and people at traffic lights used to stop and sort of look at him a little crazy."

In mid-December, Jim spent six days taping his second pilot—which he was now cheekily calling *The Muppet Show: Sex and Violence* in an almost cathartic defiance of his kids' stuff reputation—bringing in ten puppeteers, including Jane and several designers from the workshop, to perform more than seventy Muppets. Unlike the more deliberately paced and sweeter *Valentine Show*, the snappier, snarkier *Sex and Violence* bounced itself around a number of running gags, ranging from the homespun to the slightly surreal. Notably, *Sex and Violence* also marked the debut of a number of characters who would later move into the upper tiers of the Muppet pantheon. Besides Dr. Teeth and the Swedish Chef, Jim introduced the rest of the Electric Mayhem Band—the lanky bassist Floyd, the laid-back guitarist Janice, the silent, sax-playing Zoot, and the wild drummer Animal—as well as Sam the Eagle ("who represents the older establishment values," wrote Jim) and the curmudgeonly Statler and Waldorf, grumbling from oversized chairs in a parlor as a grandfather clock ticked loudly in the background. A prototype of Miss Piggy was even there, too, a carryover from the Herb Alpert special taped in London earlier that fall, and used here as a supporting member in the movie parody "Return to Beneath the Planet of the Pigs." "These are all characters that the audience will get to know and love—or hate—over a period of time," wrote Jim.

While Jim didn't necessarily have any characters to hate, he did have one to yawn at—a milquetoast, vaguely amphibious character named Nigel who, unfortunately, Jim had placed in the role of emcee. "He's a lot like me," said Jim, though apart from the voice, that really wasn't the case. Nigel was an admitted "middle of the road" character, but lacked any real personality—a failing that was especially obvious when the blasé Nigel was played up against Oz's Sam the Eagle or Nelson's Floyd. Kermit, meanwhile, had again been relegated to the background cast, appearing only in a dance sequence. According to co-writer Jon Stone, the decision to bench Kermit had been deliberate on Jim's part. "Jim wanted to get out of performing a little bit," said Stone. "At Jim's request, we did not use Kermit, because he wanted to establish somebody else to be able to do it on a day-to-day basis and free him up to do his daydreaming and fantasizing and all that other stuff he did." Regardless, the decision to put Nigel at the helm was a mistake—one that Jim would come to appreciate only after it was too late to remedy.

Jim completed the first edit of *Sex and Violence* during the first week of 1975 and sent a rough cut to network executives for review. As he waited for the network's response, Jim went skiing with the family in Vermont, then drove to Washington to accommodate a distinguished request: the Smithsonian Institution was preparing an exhibit for the upcoming Bicentennial, and had asked if Jim would donate the original Ernie and Bert Muppets. Jim was proud to oblige—and the two Muppets proved so popular that what was originally to be a four-year stay turned into a nearly fifteen-year residency for the Muppet duo. At the conclusion of the "We the People" exhibit in 1980, the museum wrote to Jim begging to keep Ernie and Bert a little while longer. A longtime fan of the museum—he would even propose an after-school special called *Kermit at the Smithsonian*—Jim was happy to gratify the request. The Muppets would remain on display for another ten years.

Jim had scheduled another family vacation at the Snowmass resort in Aspen, Colorado, in early February, but dutifully scrapped his plans after receiving an unexpected phone call from director Blake Edwards, who wanted Jim to "come over [to London] for lunch" to discuss his participation in another television special with Julie Andrews, Edwards's wife. Jim flew to London early on February 8, arriving just in time for the promised lunch. He later admitted to being awed by the courteous manner in which Edwards and Andrews received him, dispatching a limo to pick him up at the airport, then bringing him to their home for lunch and tea. Andrews also promised to make up for Jim's canceled Snowmass trip by arranging a ski vacation for the Hensons in Gstaad, Switzerland. "I . . . was just knocked out by the whole experience," Jim admitted later. He would make certain to treat his own guests with a similar courtesy once he had a show of his own.

After agreeing to participate in Andrews's upcoming special, Jim flew back to New York to corral his family for the Gstaad ski trip—but his schedule over the past few weeks had been grueling, and he was exhausted. As he drove home, he fell asleep at the wheel of his Jaguar, smashing it against a guardrail when he missed the exit ramp for Bedford. Fortunately, he walked away unhurt—and a few days later he and his family departed for Gstaad.

Jim's family returned from Switzerland without him, as he detoured back through London to spend several days taping Muppet segments for the Julie Andrews special. After wrapping on March 6, Jim flew back to New York to make his final edits on *Sex and Violence*. Work on the Julie Andrews special had put him behind schedule; he now had less than two weeks to complete editing before ABC aired the show—and he had run into a minor problem.

After reviewing a rough cut of the pilot in early January, ABC executives had written Jim with a number of suggested changes. Early on, Jim had run into trouble over the title *Sex and Violence* for his pilot, as nervous network officials had surveyed potential viewers and fretted to Jim about their findings. In particular, they were concerned about the title for the special, which, they found, had "produced substantial negative reaction." But Jim wouldn't budge. Besides the obvious nose thumbing at his squeaky clean reputation, Jim thought the title was just plain *funny,* and that anyone complaining didn't get the joke. "My 14-year-old daughter Lisa saw it, and throughout the show she kept asking 'Where's the sex?'" Jim explained somewhat incredulously. "As for violence, there probably wasn't enough to fill a thirty second spot announcement for *Kung Fu.* . . . The special's title . . . was a humorous hook. While the show depicted some of the current attitudes toward sex and violence, our purpose was to poke fun at them." While he would eventually agree to make several other changes the network had suggested—removing a brief sequence where he appeared on camera to introduce the show, for instance, and shortening Dr. Teeth's musical number—the title would stay.

Overall, he was pleased with the final version—"freak city!" he laughingly called it—and he was anxious to hear what viewers and reviewers thought. Diligently, Jim made the rounds with the press to promote the show in the days leading up to its debut. He was chatting about puppetry and television in a much more thoughtful and relaxed manner than in the past; at other times, he tried almost too hard to make the case for puppets as art. "Puppets are by their very nature symbolic, so any time you use them, you're doing something symbolically," he told one interviewer pensively. "An audience will go away with their own message. But this is not a 'messagey' show," he added quickly, "it's a fun show."

And still, he continued to stress his credentials as an adult entertainer. "A lot of our work has always been adult-oriented, so we'll be working a lot with those aspects of the Muppets," he explained to *The Hollywood Reporter.* "Through this pilot, we hope to be able to demonstrate that puppetry can be very solid adult entertainment." Privately, in fact, Jim felt he was already pulling his comedic punches, after toning down some of his jokes out of deference to his reputation as a children's entertainer. "He had lots of changes which were necessary, I think, in order to achieve the success he had," said Richard Hunt. "[With the] Muppets . . . there was a sense of that perverted humor. . . . And he backed off that."

Reviews of *Sex and Violence* were uneven, though Jim was likely relieved to see *Variety* call it "zippy" and "good fun for children and adults who are on the in." But rather than relying solely on newspaper reviews to determine whether he had succeeded, Jim had commissioned his own viewer survey, polling homes in New Jersey, New York, Los Angeles, Chicago, Atlanta, and West Virginia. Perhaps Jim was hoping to use the viewer comments as leverage in his negotiations with ABC for an ongoing series; if so, he was surely disappointed. "There was a mixed reaction with regard to the material," the survey reported. "A number of people felt that some of it was not funny. Some thought it was too far out."

Whatever it was, ABC executives decided it hadn't worked; there would be no weekly Muppet series, at least not on ABC. But Jim was typically resolute; if ABC wasn't interested, he'd try someplace else. "Perhaps one thing that has helped me in achieving my goals is that I sincerely believe in what I do, and get great pleasure from it," said Jim. Even the showbiz-hardened Bernie Brillstein could get caught up in that kind of dogged determination. "We thought it was gonna be great, we knew it was," Brillstein said. And yet, one door after another was closed in his face. The response, said Brillstein, was always the same: "We don't do puppets at night." "Puppets are funny things," Jim said later. "They seem to win the hearts of both small and grown-up kids, but the networks have never been eager to buy it."

Still, Jim felt he was getting close; it was just a matter, he thought, of patience and personnel. At the moment, there was a noticeable hole in the administrative structure at Henson Associates following the uncomfortable but amicable departure of Diana Birkenfield in February 1974—and for over a year now, Jim had been without a full-time producer to assist in the development and management of his projects. Although he had the devoted Brillstein looking out for him on both coasts, Jim knew he needed a producer inside Henson Associates who could help him steer his dreams of a weekly Muppet show out of choppy waters and into the safe port of prime-time television. He needed someone who knew and understood the media, was savvy in business, and, ideally, shared his sense of humor and low-key management style—who could, as Al Gottesman put it, "translat[e] Jim's philosophy and essential ethic about work and the quality of what he wants to produce" into the actual practice of helping to run a business.

The more he thought about it, the more Jim thought he knew exactly who he needed. As he prepared to travel to Burbank in March 1975 for an appearance on *The Tonight Show* with Johnny Carson, he placed a call to David Lazer, the dynamic IBM executive with whom Jim was still making short films, and asked to meet him at the Beverly Wilshire hotel. Jim suggested the two of them attend the Carson taping together, then discuss a bit of business over lunch the next day.

Jim made his appearance on *The Tonight Show* in his version of dress attire, wearing a suede jacket over a dark turtleneck and dark trousers, his hair curling down onto his shoulders and his beard slightly shaggy. While he still looked vaguely uncomfortable, once he began performing Kermit, no one noticed Jim anyway: all eyes, including Carson's, were on the frog. When asked about his role in the *Sex and Violence* special, Kermit complained that he had only "one lousy line!"—perhaps a winking acknowledgment by Jim that he had made a mistake in sidelining Kermit in favor of Nigel—and bristled in mock offense when Carson asked him about his love life. "Listen, I work on *Sesame Street*. You don't ask a frog questions like that!" Kermit replied. "Do you ask Captain Kangaroo about his sex life?" The line got a big laugh, but after the taping, Jim was upset about his performance, calling it only "fair."

Jim continued to fret into the evening, groaning and *hmmm*ing in his hotel suite and appealing to Lazer for reassurance. With the three-hour time difference between the East and West coasts, Jane would be able to watch Jim's taped performance on *The Tonight Show* in New York even before Jim could watch it in Los Angeles. Jim eyed the clock, and at the appropriate time dialed home to discuss his appearance on Carson with Jane. "He was very interested in her opinion," said Lazer. "I liked that." Despite their widening differences, Jim still relied on Jane for emotional support and professional perspective; when it came to assessing Muppet performances, her instincts were almost always dead-on.

The next afternoon, over Mexican food at Señor Pico, Jim asked Lazer if he would "ever consider joining" Henson Associates. Lazer was stunned. "That was a dream," he said later. "I remember having a fork [in my hand] and it froze . . . it was such a shock. And I said, 'Oh my God! Oh, probably!'" As Lazer got into his cab for the airport, Jim leaned in the car window. "I'm very serious, Dave. I want to hear soon. I want you." Three weeks later—following a trip to Miami, where Jim had to soothe the hurt feelings of Lazer's employers at IBM—Lazer was Jim's new producer. His impact would be felt almost immediately.

With his impeccably tailored suits, bright red ties, and loosely curled head of hair, the New York–born Lazer looked as if he had stepped out of a central casting call for the role of Smooth Businessman—a stark contrast to Jim, who was still wearing his flare-bottomed slacks, brightly colored shirts, and at times a colored scarf under a leather jacket. As a master of promotion, sales, and public relations, Lazer was determined to bring the same polish to Henson Associates that he had brought to the IBM product line— and as far as Lazer was concerned, the product at Henson Associates wasn't the Muppets; it was Jim.

To Lazer, Jim was more than just Muppets; he was a creative force, on a par with Walt Disney, whose name epitomized a high caliber of entertainment that transcended any particular medium. "We had to work on Jim's image, for his own sake first," said Lazer, "and then let the *world* know this man has such character." That was easier said than done; despite the fact that it was Jim's name over the door, Jim had never thought of himself as the face of the corporation. That had to change. "Jim was considered an act, instead of who he was," said Lazer. One of Lazer's first missions, then, was to turn his boss from merely one of Henson Associates' performers into *Jim Henson.*

Not that he was going to change Jim *too* much—and Lazer had some lessons of his own to learn about Jim's way of doing business. At Lazer's first staff meeting, Jim had asked his new producer to make a brief presentation, and Lazer—brought up in an executive culture of flip charts and handouts—completely baffled the Muppet designers and performers with his endless handouts and lists of people, profiles, products, and personalities. "People were laughing and snickering," Lazer remembered. "I was a suit . . . coming through a creative world. But," he added rakishly, "I was a *maverick* suit." Taking the hint, Lazer threw his flowcharts into the middle of the table and continued talking as if nothing had happened. Afterward, Jim sympathetically pulled him aside.

"It's not the same, is it?" he said.

"Oh no," said Lazer. "It's better."

Jim was delighted with that sort of response. His instincts about Lazer had been correct; he would fit in nicely.

In late July 1975, Jim spent two weeks in California to tape performances on several variety shows, including two appearances on *Cher* for CBS. Jim's time with Cher would be notable more for what went on between takes than for what appeared on the show itself; Cher and her executive producer at CBS, George Schlatter, in fact, would play an important role in bringing *The Muppet Show* to television.

At the urging of Brillstein, Jim had intended to approach Schlatter to discuss the possibility of CBS picking up a regular Muppet series—and now that he was in Los Angeles, Jim, Brillstein, Lazer, and Schlatter huddled to discuss their options. While Schlatter couldn't necessarily approve a show, he *could* help actively promote it at CBS—but he needed more than just Jim's written pitches or copies of the two failed ABC pilots to make his case. He needed something dynamic to take to the network that would show, not just tell about, Jim's inventiveness and enthusiasm. Jim—who had spent much of the first decade of his career promoting other people's products—thought he had a solution.

He would make a commercial.

Not just a regular commercial, but a lengthy *Muppet Show* pitch reel—one that would highlight some of the Muppets' strongest performances, spotlight the versatility of the Muppets, and, ideally, do so in a way that conveyed Jim's unique, and slightly skewed, brand of humor. Lazer was excited about the idea and suggested that the pitch reel mention by name the network executives who would be watching it and making the decision—a trick he had often incorporated into his presentations at IBM. Schlatter—the father of *Laugh-In* and a writer with a wicked sense of humor—volunteered to help Jim with the script. Even better, he also offered to make time available during the *Cher* taping to allow Jim to tape a few segments with Kermit interviewing Cher and her daughter, Chastity, to give executives an idea of how the Muppets might interact with human guest stars—an offer both Cher and six-year-old Chastity were happy to accommodate. The segment with Cher, in fact, ended up being particularly feisty, full of double entendres (many of which were fed to Jim by Schlatter, squatting on the floor beside him), which resulted in both performers laughing so hard that Jim eventually broke character.

On August 31, 1975, a little more than two weeks after his initial meeting with Schlatter, Jim was in the studios at Bevington Stage in Los Angeles to film the framing sequences for his *Muppet Show* pitch. Most of the twenty-five-minute pitch would involve Kermit introducing clips of Muppet appearances, mainly highlights from the two Muppet pilots and assorted variety shows, as well as snippets of Kermit's conversations with Cher and Chastity. But the most memorable moment of the reel would turn out to be its final two and a half minutes, a new sequence written by Jim and Schlatter featuring a smooth-talking Muppet salesman performed by Jim who becomes more and more manic as he makes his pitch for *The Muppet Show,* eventually building to a frothing, enthusiastic crescendo worthy of Guy Smiley:

> Friends, the United States of America *needs The Muppet Show*—and you should *buy this show*! . . . Buy the show and put it on the air and we'll all be famous! . . . and we'll all get temperamental and hard to work with, but *you won't care*! Because we'll all make a lot of money! . . . and *you'll* be happy! And Kermit's *mother* will be happy!

Then, as a heavenly choir swelled, came Jim's comedic promise of huge ratings:

> And God will look down on us! And smile on us, and He will say, *"Let them have a forty share!"*

Even God, however, wouldn't get the last word—and with the CBS logo rising like the sun in the background, Kermit wandered into the shot and stared straight into the camera to ask, "What the hell was that all about?"—a joke Jim had written at the last minute, scrawling the line in pencil across the bottom of his script. After viewing the pitch reel with his fellow CBS executives, Perry Lafferty—one of the executives mentioned by name in the pitch reel—called Brillstein with congratulations. "If they don't buy this," Lafferty told the agent, "they're crazy."

And yet, remembered Lazer glumly, "it didn't sell." Standing partly in Jim's way—at least at CBS—was the recently enacted Prime Time Access Rule (PTAR), a policy implemented by the Federal Communications Commission to encourage more diverse and independent television programming. Prior to enactment of the rule in 1971, the major television networks had essentially barricaded themselves inside the prime-time viewing hours—generally 7:00 to 11:00 P.M. Eastern Time—which all but banished independent and local programming to early afternoons or late nights, where viewers and ratings were scarcer. Starting in September 1971, however, the PTAR required networks to open up the first hour of prime time to non-network programming "so that [independent] producers may have the opportunity to develop their full economic and creative potential under better competitive conditions than are now available to them."

That may have sounded like an open door for the Muppets, but Jim's real problem was a 1975 rule change within PTAR, which exempted Sunday nights from the restriction—exactly the spot where CBS was considering placing *The Muppet Show*. With the FCC exemption allowing the network to fill the entire Sunday night block with its own programming, CBS opted to move its floundering news program *60 Minutes* into the first hour instead. That move quickly established *60 Minutes* as the network's Sunday night flagship, but doomed the prospects for *The Muppet Show* on CBS. (At least, said Brillstein later, the Muppets had lost to the best.) While disappointed, Lazer thought the pitch reel had still done "something good for us. It said, 'We . . . have what it takes to do it.'" It was "a wonderful goddamn thing," agreed Brillstein—and he would continue to show the reel to anyone who would watch.

At the same time Brillstein was circulating the *Muppet Show* pitch reel, he was also lining up an opportunity for Jim and the Muppets to become a regular part of a new late night sketch comedy series being developed by another of Brillstein's clients, a thirty-year-old producer and former *Laugh-In* writer named Lorne Michaels. "He described the show, and I really loved it," said Jim. In August, then, Jim began meeting regularly with Michaels's writers in preparation for the weekly late night series Jim referred to on his desk calendar only as the "NBC Show," but which Michaels was calling *Saturday Night*—and then, eventually, *Saturday Night Live*.

Saturday Night Live was a comedy variety show, but, as envisioned by Michaels and his scrappy team of writers, one unlike any variety show that had ever been seen before. "We wanted to redefine comedy the way the Beatles redefined what being a pop star was," Michaels said later. The very idea of it—an unpredictable live show unafraid of taking on politicians, presidents, or pop culture—terrified the network even months before it ever went before the cameras. "NBC was so scared of what Lorne . . . was doing that they insisted on Jim Henson and the Muppets [to] soften it," said Brillstein. Jim's inclusion, in fact, had been one of the network's non-negotiables. "In the first contract for *SNL,* there were three essential factors," said Brillstein, who had brokered the deal with NBC: "Lorne Michaels, Jim Henson and the Muppets, and Albert Brooks's [short] films."

For his part, Michaels was delighted to have Jim's involvement. "I'd always liked and been a fan of [the Muppets] and Jim's work," Michaels said. "When we were starting *Saturday Night,* I knew that I wanted as many different styles of comedy as I could possibly have, and I knew some of what the ingredients would be. . . . I just assumed that the Muppets under Jim would be able to do one segment a week."

Nestled safely in the deep end of late night television, Jim wanted to do something dramatically different with his segments, as far removed from the look and feel of *Sesame Street*—which, he knew, was still what audiences thought of when they heard the word *Muppets*—as he could possibly get. For Jim, the characters themselves were always the easy part: he knew he wanted monsters of some sort, scrawling out rough descriptions of five characters for a segment he was initially thinking of calling "Muppet Night Creatures." But the universe in which these characters would exist was more problematic—a matter Jim had struggled with in both of his *Muppet Show* pilots, neither of which had clearly established where things were taking place. Jim made a long list of potential settings and scenarios—a TV game show or sitcom, a therapy session, a rock group—before finally settling on a vaguely described "Mystic set up." Eventually, Jim would hammer out a typed proposal for his segment and set it in "a place called Gortch," describing the world rather unhelpfully as looking "either like another planet, or earth, sometime thousands of years in the future." The workshop began hurriedly constructing new Muppets—with an eye on character designs by Michael Frith, who had translated Jim's rough descriptions into beautiful, brightly colored drawings—and Jim checked in on their progress most mornings, even as he dashed off to the UNIMA conference in Detroit or business meetings in L.A. "He was the hardest-working person I've ever met in my life," said Dave Goelz.

At noon on Wednesday, October 8, Jim and his team entered the soaring building at 30 Rockefeller Plaza and headed for Studio 8H, where they would participate in the read-through for the first show with the entire *SNL* cast, an immensely talented—and largely unknown—set of young performers skilled in improv and hungry for success. On Friday night, the Muppet team attended a party thrown by cast member John Belushi, mingling casually with the show's eclectic crew of writers and performers and sizing each other up. After three days of rehearsal, one thing was clear: "They had their style, we had ours," said Oz—a distinction that would only become more and more obvious in the coming weeks.

Saturday Night Live, as even Jim was calling it by now, made its debut on October 11, 1975. For that first show, Jim and the Muppet crew had arrived at NBC at 1:00 P.M. for a walk-through with the entire cast—including guest host George Carlin and musical guests Janis Ian and Billy Preston—that lasted until after 4:00. Following dinner, there was a dress rehearsal in front of the studio audience beginning at 7:30, with cameras finally rolling live at 11:30 P.M. Lazer, sticking to his vow to promote Jim as more than merely an act, had arranged for Jim to have his own private dressing room, placing him in room 8H3 right next to comedian Andy Kaufman, who was also appearing on the first episode.

The Muppet sketch—referred to as "The Land of Gortch"— was featured during *SNL*'s second half hour, coming in right after the commercial break that had followed the "Weekend Update" mock news segment. Jim's monstrous new Muppets—including the gruff but stupid King Ploobis, his earnest sidekick Scred, and a mystic stone oracle called the Mighty Favog—were all beautifully built and masterfully performed, but it was clear, even from the very first episode, that something wasn't working. The sketch was too long, and most of the jokes fell flat—and things would only worsen as time went on. Oz grumbled that a new puppeteer, a stand-up comedian named Rhonda Hansome, performing the saucy Vazh, was throwing off their rhythms and ruining their timing, but Jim knew immediately that the main problem was with something over which he had absolutely no control: the writing.

Under Writers Guild rules, only writers hired for *SNL* could write *SNL* sketches—and it was quickly apparent that the Muppets and *SNL*'s writers weren't a good fit. "Somehow what we were trying to do and what [the] writers could write for it never jelled," said Jim later. "When they were writing for us, I had the feeling they were writing normal sitcom stuff, which is really boring and bland." Oz thought it had more to do with a mismatch between the basic comedic DNA of the Muppets and *SNL*. "I think our very explosive, more cartoony comedy didn't jive with their kind of Second City, casual, laid-back comedy," said Oz, "so the writers had a lot of trouble writing for us. They weren't used to that kind of Muppet writing."

Jerry Juhl, watching from California, understood that Jim was "very frustrated" that he had little input into the scripts. The *SNL* writers, thought Juhl, "didn't have any real handle" on Jim's concept. "Jim would come in with ideas, and sit with them, and give them wonderful ideas, and they wouldn't know how to fly with them." Lorne Michaels thought part of the problem lay in the skit's underlying concept. "It was a very, very difficult premise that Jim had created," said Michaels. "We didn't know what the rules of the world were yet." As a result, no one wanted to write for the Muppets. "Whoever drew the short straw that week had to write the Muppet sketch," said writer Alan Zweibel. The frustration of the *SNL* writers was often palpable; during one meeting in Michaels's office, volatile head writer Michael O'Donoghue angrily wrapped the cords of the venetian blinds around the neck of a Big Bird doll and stalked out of the room. "I won't write for felt," he declared blackly.

Compounding the problem was that many of *SNL*'s writers were also performers on the show—and every minute of airtime devoted to the Muppets meant one less minute that could be spent on cast members, who were rapidly developing their own personalities and break-out characters. "They weren't interested in the Muppets because it kept them off the air," Juhl said plainly. "The Muppets were known, but they weren't," agreed Oz. "So they wanted every moment they could get." Even John Belushi, who was otherwise friendly with the Muppet performers, would sneer derisively about giving up his airtime to the "mucking Fuppets."

Despite the grumbling, Jim had nothing but good things to say about *Saturday Night Live*. He and Michaels liked each other, and Jim showed up without complaint for blocking and rehearsals every Thursday and Friday, then spent most of his Saturdays dutifully performing someone else's scripts until 1:00 A.M. "Lorne Michaels loved them," said Lazer, "but it was not a good feeling, going there . . . knowing you weren't loved there—they were just putting up with you." Still, it wasn't all bad. "The good part," said Oz, "was that every Saturday was very exciting . . . meeting and seeing the beginnings of Andy Kaufman, and the great little films of Albert Brooks, and . . . John [Belushi] and Chevy [Chase] and Danny [Aykroyd]. . . . A live show on Saturday night is always exciting."

It could get exciting for reasons that went beyond mere performing. The *SNL* cast and writers were notable not only for their talent on-screen, but also for their rowdy weekly wrap parties, where prodigious amounts of drugs and alcohol were sometimes consumed—a practice that could continue on into the working week. Cocaine was a particularly attractive substance to those working on a late night show, as the user could often go for days without sleep. However, *SNL* writer Al Franken—who usually ended up working on the Gortch sketches, with his writing partner, Tom Davis—recalled that while a few writers and performers used hard drugs, for the most part marijuana was the drug of choice. Indeed, with its smoking craters, booze-guzzling Muppets, and explicit references to drugs and sex, there was a distinctive whiff of pot influencing the Gortch skits—and even though Jim and his team had little or nothing to do with the writing of their segment, viewers were nevertheless convinced that Jim, and the Muppet performers, had to be on drugs.

While Jerry Nelson and Richard Hunt were known to sneak away to pass a joint back and forth, the Muppet crew was, for the most part, fairly straitlaced. Oz wasn't a partier at all—he found large gatherings too noisy—and Jim, while he might enjoy a glass of wine or two from time to time—and maybe, said Nelson, "a little grass"—rarely ingested anything more potent than aspirin. He had, however, tried LSD exactly once—and, if asked, would probably confess that it had been something of a disappointment.

In the late 1960s, as he pursued his dreams of a psychedelic nightclub and immersed himself more and more deeply in the counterculture, Jim had become fascinated with the idea of mind-altering drugs. Many of the musicians he had spoken with for *Youth 68* had publicly admitted to dropping acid—and had just as openly praised the alleged positive effects it had had on their art and creativity.

While Jim's artistic vision was already expansive enough, he was intrigued by the possibilities of stretching it even further. He was determined, then, to take an acid trip, but confessed to friends that some of the reports he had heard about bad trips had scared him, and he was worried he might set himself on fire or jump out a window. Finally, he decided to try it in the company of his closest friends—in this case Oz, Don Sahlin, Jerry Nelson, and Jerry Juhl—nestled in the relative warmth and comfort of the Muppet offices. "I remember Jim sitting at his little desk in that Eames chair of his, looking at his sugar cube laced with LSD," said Oz, who left shortly thereafter with Juhl, leaving Jim alone with Nelson and Sahlin to contemplate his cube. "I took it," Jim reported later, "and I waited . . . and nothing happened." Only slightly disappointed, he wished Sahlin and Nelson good night and drove home. If Jim's experiment with drugs had been a failure, one thing was clear: Jim didn't need chemicals to take his mind to new worlds; his mind was already there.

The world he had created for *SNL,* however, wasn't showing any signs of life. Even Brillstein admitted that the Gortch idea "was not a great thing"—a criticism at which Jerry Nelson always bristled. "I always loved [Scred]," said Nelson, who thought the characters had real potential if given the chance—it was Nelson, in fact, who fought to have Scred sing "I Got You Babe" with guest host Lily Tomlin, dogging the idea through the show's weeklong writing sessions. It turned out to be one of the sweeter moments of the show, and a highlight even among *SNL's* strong first season of skits. Regardless, while Brillstein knew that "Lorne, being Lorne, didn't want to fire them," it was clearly time to find something else. As it turns out, they didn't have to look long; Lord Grade, through his lieutenants at ATV and ITC, was looking for *them.*

Sometime in 1975, CBS executive Thomas Miller, a devoted Muppet fan, was scouting for original programming that could be shown on CBS-owned and -operated stations—the so-called O&Os—and had reached out to Abe Mandell, the New York–based president of Grade's ITC Entertainment, to practically *beg* Mandell to invest in a Muppet series. Mandell appealed in writing to Grade—and Grade, who had already been impressed by Jim's ATV appearances with Julie Andrews, enthusiastically directed Mandell to approach Jim to "see if he would do a TV series for me in England." Mandell and Brillstein traded calls for some time—Brillstein typically played hard to get, letting Mandell chase him "all over the country"—until eventually they agreed to discuss the matter at Mandell's home in Larchmont, New York.

Sitting down to chat with Brillstein and Lazer, Mandell led off by explaining that he and Grade "always felt Henson would be interested in the right prime time Muppet vehicle," and expressed amazement that no network had added the Muppets to their prime-time schedules. Mandell noted that they were specifically "looking for a series for . . . the primetime access period," that first hour of prime time that the FCC had pried away from the networks for independent and local programming. That meant Mandell—and Grade—wanted to produce and market the show not for any of the major networks, but independently, allowing Grade's ITC production company to market the show to local stations looking to fill the 7:00–8:00 P.M. access period or earlier. In the case of the Muppets, Mandell was already prepared to take the show directly to five of Miller's CBS O&Os located in the key markets of New York, Los Angeles, Chicago, Philadelphia, and St. Louis. But this wasn't a network show, Mandell stressed; this was a whole new concept called *prime-time syndication*.

Brillstein didn't blink, but he may have flinched. He knew Jim was skeptical of syndication—the television equivalent of free agency—which provided no real guarantees; after a significant financial investment, a show could be picked up by five stations, or fifty, or zero. Brillstein knew he would have to talk to Jim about it, but he thought Jim might be persuaded if Grade and ATV would agree to provide Jim with the resources he needed to produce the kind of show Brillstein knew he was capable of creating. At the moment, most weekly shows were budgeted at $80,000 per episode; Brillstein would make sure ATV did better than that—but before he could open his mouth to discuss the higher rate, Mandell said they needed one more thing: a new Muppet pilot to take to the CBS O&Os. Brillstein roared with laughter. "I said, 'I've saved you a lot of money,' " Brillstein told Mandell, " '[because] I have the best [twenty-five] minutes of film you've ever seen in your life!' " As he and Lazer got up to leave, Brillstein promised to send over the *Muppet Show* pitch reel for Mandell to watch, after which he and Mandell would speak again. Now that ATV wouldn't have to produce a pilot, Brillstein was certain he could negotiate a higher weekly rate.

The pitch reel was immediately dispatched to Mandell; the next day, Mandell phoned Brillstein with the news: "We have a deal."

Still, Brillstein didn't want to commit until he had a firm number from ATV on the budget. After back-and-forthing with Brillstein, Mandell finally called Lord Grade in London, where the producer agreed to raise the budget for the first season to $3 million. With twenty-four episodes per season, that gave Jim $125,000 to spend per episode, making it one of the most expensive half-hour series produced for syndicated television at that time. The only condition Grade had imposed on the deal was that Jim had to tape his show at Grade's ATV Studios in London. Brillstein—without even checking with Jim first—eagerly agreed. The deal was done.

Vibrating with excitement, Brillstein immediately called Jim. "We finally did it!" the agent shouted into the phone. Brillstein waited for Jim to inquire about the details, certain he would ask how much they were getting per episode. But Jim didn't—and his response made the crusty Brillstein smile even twenty years later: "I love you," Jim said.

The details could be discussed later—and on the morning of Saturday, October 18, Jim met with Mandell to run through the fine print. The details were already spectacular: less than twenty-four hours after reaching their agreement with Jim, Mandell had sold *The Muppet Show* to all five CBS O&Os, who wanted it in their lineups for the 1976–1977 season, starting in September. Following the meeting with Mandell, Jim headed over to Rockefeller Plaza to join the Muppet team in rehearsals for *Saturday Night Live*. During a break, he pulled Oz to one side. "We're doing twenty-four half-hour shows," he told Oz excitedly, "*guaranteed!*"

Four days later, Jim and Mandell stood side by side at a cocktail party and press conference held at the posh "21" Club on West 52nd, where reporters had been told to come prepared "for a major announcement." With Kermit on his arm and flashbulbs popping, Jim quietly reported the news of his deal with Grade—and was stunned when the room erupted into applause. Mandell touted the show as a "network-budgeted, high quality series . . . designed as the perfect all-family vehicle," while Jim reassured reporters that he would continue to perform on *Sesame Street* and make guest appearances on other shows "as the opportunities arise." Kermit nodded at the end of Jim's arm. "We'll do anything for money," said the frog.

At last, Jim had the opportunity to pursue his dream; and yet he was concerned that his new obligations—he would have to leave for London to begin production in May 1976—meant letting down Lorne Michaels. Brillstein was prepared to begin the messy formal process of getting Jim out of his contract with NBC, but Jim wanted to discuss the matter with Michaels personally. Michaels—who was already weathering increasingly heated calls from *SNL*'s writers to dump the Muppets from the show's lineup altogether—could afford to be gracious and magnanimous, releasing Jim from his contract without penalty, even making clear that Jim had complete ownership of the characters he had created for *SNL*. "I always figure people stay if they want to stay," said Michaels diplomatically. "[The Muppets] had the opportunity to do their own show. You never stand in the way of somebody." Jim—who also knew the Muppets' days on *SNL* were numbered—was equally magnanimous in his praise of Michaels. "I really respect Lorne," he said later, "[and] at no time did I ever lose my respect for the show. I always liked what they were doing. We parted on very good terms."

Well, mostly. Years later, Jim took great pleasure in displaying a copy of a postcard the Muppet team had sent from London to the cast of *Saturday Night Live,* pasting it to a piece of paper under block letters asking WHERE ARE THE MUCKING FUPPETS? "Dear Gang," the postcard read, "We're having a wonderful time here in England. We're doing our own show and it's a big hit."

Within a year, Jim and the Muppets would be the biggest act in England; in less than two years they would take the United States by storm. And before the decade was over, *The Muppet Show* would be the most popular show in the world.

Mucking Fuppets indeed.

CHAPTER NINE

MUPPETMANIA

1975–1977

The second season (1977–1978) cast of performers on The Muppet Show.
Clockwise from bottom left: Dave Goelz, Jerry Nelson, Jim,
Frank Oz, Richard Hunt, and Louise Gold.

IT MAY SEEM EXTRAORDINARY THAT A TELEVISION SERIES FEATURING A gonzo daredevil who eats a tire to "Flight of the Bumblebee" would have appealed to a British lord—but Lord Lew Grade was an extraordinary man. Born Louis Winogradsky in Russia in 1906, Grade's family immigrated to London's East End in 1912, where he went to school and spent several years working in his father's constantly struggling embroidery company. In 1926, Grade broke into show business, wowing British vaudeville audiences by frantically dancing the Charleston on narrow tabletops—a stunt worthy of the Great Gonzo himself.

When perpetually swollen knees ended his dancing career, Grade became a theatrical agent, landing bookings for A-listers like Judy Garland and Danny Kaye at venues like the Palladium or on British television variety shows. Unlike many agents who had cut their teeth on theater bookings, Grade was quick to embrace the new television medium, and in 1954—the same year seventeen-year-old Jim Henson was first performing with his Muppets on the *Junior Morning Show* in Washington, D.C.—Grade founded his own TV company, which eventually became the juggernaut, Associated Television, or ATV.

Grade himself was as familiar to British audiences as his booming network, frequently photographed at premieres emerging from his Rolls-Royce Phantom with smoke from one of his enormous cigars curling around his piebald head. A "British Louis B. Mayer," Oz called him, and the comparison was apt—for Grade was not only an old-fashioned showman, but a shrewd businessman as well. In fact, his offer to produce *The Muppet Show* had both fiscal and artistic benefits. ATV's Elstree studios were sitting largely empty and unused in London, a red mark on ATV's books. So with Jim committed to producing twenty-four episodes at Elstree—and with five CBS stations in the United States already obligated to pick up the series—*The Muppet Show* would ensure the lights stayed on at Elstree.

For Jim, the prospect of picking up and moving to London was no more daunting than the snap decision to move from D.C. to New York had been nearly fifteen years ago. After learning of the deal that would bring *The Muppet Show* to London, one of Jim's first phone calls was to Jerry Juhl out in California to ask the writer if he would pack up and follow him out to England. Jim couldn't offer Juhl the head writer job—one of the few conditions on which Grade and Mandell had insisted was that Jim hire an experienced television variety show writer as his lead writer. It was a slight that Jim knew would bruise Juhl's feelings, and Jim—always one to avoid hurting feelings as much as he could—had written out a list of sympathetic talking points to use during his phone call. The approach worked, and Juhl, who had dutifully made the move from D.C. to New York with Jim in 1963, promised to join the Muppet team in London in 1976, where he would serve—for a while, grudgingly—under lead writer Jack Burns, an experienced stand-up comic who, along with his partner, Avery Schreiber, was a veteran of perhaps as many variety shows as Jim.

In early November 1975, Jim began meeting regularly with Burns and Juhl in Los Angeles and New York to go over the dynamics and structure of the show—including nailing down the important but always problematic question of where, exactly, the show would be taking place. As Juhl remembered it, after several days of "talking around ideas" they finally settled on a "show-within-a-show" format, in which the Muppets would be working each week to put on a vaudeville show in an old theater, with action taking place both onstage and backstage. It was a format, said Juhl, that "[none] of us were convinced . . . was gonna work."

Jim, however, liked it—and with some help from Bernie Brillstein, who set the writers up in an office near the Beverly Wilshire, Burns and Juhl began hammering out scripts for the first few episodes, which Jim was planning to put before the cameras at Elstree in January 1976, only a few short weeks away. In early December, Jim flew to London with Brillstein and David Lazer to look over the facilities at Elstree and prepare a number of offices and workspaces that had been set aside by the studios specifically for Henson Associates—including an area for a fully functional Muppet workshop where puppets could be designed, built, and repaired on site, rather than in the workshop in New York at least a day's flight away. Satisfied, Jim came home for Christmas and a bit of skiing in Vermont. On January 11, 1976, he returned to London to begin work on the first two episodes of *The Muppet Show*.

Although Jim had an agreement in place that guaranteed him twenty-four episodes for the first season, much was riding on the first two episodes of the show, which were essentially considered pilots for the new series. While Brillstein had five local CBS stations on the hook to broadcast the series, there was no guarantee the show would be picked up beyond those five. What was needed, then, were one or two strong episodes that either Brillstein or Abe Mandell at ITC could circulate to promote and sell the series. More than anything, the first two episodes were Jim's chance to spot-check his new format, get a feel for several new characters—namely Fozzie Bear,

Gonzo, and Scooter—and show his new partners at ATV what he could do.

One of the first real challenges, however, was finding guest stars. As a syndicated show targeted at the pre-prime-time access hour— and a puppet show at that—*The Muppet Show* had at the outset what many booking agents likely regarded as two strikes against it. Appearing outside of prime time, their client would already likely have a smaller viewing audience; worse, in syndication—still viewed as the wasteland of television—they might have no audience at all. Further, the pay wasn't great; most of the budget for *The Muppet Show* was wrapped up in design and production, which didn't leave a lot left over to entice guests. Most would be paid a flat rate of $3,500 for their appearance—"very, very little money," said Lazer.

It was left largely up to Brillstein to make the pitch and appeal to clients and agents. For the first two shows—and much of the first season, in fact—Brillstein dug into his personal Rolodex and called in a few favors, courting and finally landing dancer Juliet Prowse for the first show and actress Connie Stevens for the second. "The first . . . guests were . . . friends of mine who did favors," said Brillstein. "We couldn't get anyone else. . . . They did the show for me." Taping for both episodes went quickly—each show was filmed in less than a week—and on February 14, Jim returned to the United States to screen the two pilots with Abe Mandell and ITC executives in New York.

Things didn't go well. "We got a blood bath," said Lazer flatly. "They hated them." In Mandell's opinion, the pilots were "too British" and exactly what Grade didn't want. "Grade had told us, 'Don't be British,'" said Oz, and even Juhl admitted the shows "were all wrong." Most likely, the two episodes were just too talky, with an overly long opening credit sequence that Jim wisely cut down. Regardless, said Lazer, "Jim was pissed at them!" Jim stalked out of the screening in silence and started walking with Lazer back toward the Muppet offices when, after only a few blocks, he suddenly started laughing. The tension was broken, and Lazer pulled Jim into the bar at the Drake Hotel where the two commiserated over Bloody Marys at eleven in the morning. "It's not the end of the world," Jim reassuringly told Lazer between sips, and resolved to go back and re-edit the show, and even refilm several Muppet sequences. Jim "was hurt . . . his guts are on the screen," said Lazer. But Mandell had also picked up on what Lazer thought was a larger problem with the pilots. "In truth, the characters hadn't gelled then," said Lazer. "Character voices weren't good. And so we went back, rehuddled, and did it again."

Jim had taken a risk in building *The Muppet Show* around an entirely new cast of Muppet characters. There was a chance that viewers who knew the Muppets largely through *Sesame Street* might tune in to *The Muppet Show* expecting to see familiar faces and, seeing none, would tune out and never come back. Trying to manage such expectations, Jim had brought in Ernie and Bert for an appearance in the second episode, as if to reassure *Sesame Street* fans that they were peeking into the windows of the right house, even if they didn't recognize most of the other occupants. Jim also put an established character at the head of the show, wisely placing the reliable Kermit the Frog in the eye of the Muppet hurricane.

If there was a problem with any of the characters in the pilot episodes, however, it was with the one envisioned as Kermit's sidekick: the joke-telling, ear-wiggling, much abused stand-up comic Fozzie Bear. "We knew we wanted to have a stand up comedian," said Jim. "We had in mind a Red Skelton–type of character that was a bundle of anxieties off stage and a gung ho story teller up front." Unfortunately, in the early episodes, "Fozzie was a disaster," said Juhl. "We said . . . 'this is a bad comedian,' and so we put him onstage and let him be bad . . . and it was embarrassing." Worse, the razzing Fozzie received at the hands of the curmudgeonly Statler and Waldorf, heckling from the balcony, only made the character seem more pathetic, rather than funnier. "Fozzie did help make Statler and Waldorf because he was good to heckle," said Juhl, "but what we did to him in those first few shows was terrible. We just humiliated the poor guy."

Fozzie was intended to be Oz's main character, and the perfectionist Oz was frustrated that he couldn't get a handle on the bear. "Frank was dying, because he knew it was bad and didn't know what to do with it," said Juhl. Jim promised to keep tinkering with the puppet to see if perhaps a change in design might spark something, similar to the way in which the slight change in Big Bird's eyes and plumage had helped Caroll Spinney get a firm hold on that character's core personality. Juhl, meanwhile, blamed himself and the writing team for the character's rough start. Writing scripts in California for a show produced in London, said Juhl, was like "working in a vacuum. There was no interplay with the performers, there was no sense of fun and excitement. . . . Jim and I knew there was a possibility that we would just start over again in London." For Juhl, that interaction with the Muppet performers was crucial to the creative process. Once he was on the ground in London, watching rehearsals and working among the performers, Juhl thought he might finally "find that bear as a character."

In the meantime, he and Burns would keep producing scripts and sketches as quickly as they could, in the hope that once the Muppet team relocated to London in May to begin producing shows in earnest, there would be enough material available to produce one show per week. Until then, Jim still had plenty to do that spring, taping inserts for *Sesame Street,* traveling with the family to Hawaii and Japan, and making a few more appearances on *Saturday Night Live.* Jim convinced *SNL*'s writers to let him script one of the Muppets' final appearances on the show, turning in a clever, and uncredited, script in which the Muppets finally realize they're puppets and pack themselves away in a trunk—a nice bit of closure for *SNL*'s problematic puppets.

Jim left for England on May 5, 1976, taking his time by traveling on the ocean liner *Queen Elizabeth 2* with Jane, Jack Burns, and several Muppet performers. London would be Jim's home for six months of the year now, so he had made arrangements to move into a flat in Harley Gardens, in the fashionable Kensington district. Jane would remain with Jim in London for only a few weeks, helping him settle in and decorate his flat before returning to New York. The Muppet performers, meanwhile, were scattered around central London in hotels or flats that Jim had helped them find and, in some cases, had negotiated an affordable rent. Each year, in fact, Jim would send each Muppet performer a brief questionnaire, asking where in London they wanted to live and what kind of accommodations they needed (most asked for a "real shower"), and would then make the appropriate arrangements. "[Jim was] accused of spoiling everyone," laughed Lazer.

Not that any of them were going to be spending much time in their flats anyway. During each season of The Muppet Show's five-year run, Jim would produce one show each week for twelve weeks—usually from early May until late July or August—then, after a brief break, shoot the remaining twelve episodes of the season from September through November. Such a schedule meant that on almost any given day, the Muppet team could be working on at least three shows at one time—filming the current episode, doing editing and postproduction on the previous week's show, and writing and building sets for upcoming episodes.

Fortunately, Grade was committed to providing Jim with everything he needed to produce The Muppet Show without ever having to set foot outside of ATV's Elstree studio complex. In fact, the facilities at Elstree were some of the best in the United Kingdom—fifteen acres of stages, editing rooms, warehouses, and offices, all professionally laid out, splendidly equipped, and superbly maintained solely for television production. At the center of the compound were four massive studios, and Jim and the Muppets had been assigned Studio D, perhaps the best of the four. It was immediately adjacent to an editing area and the closest to Elstree's main office building, an L-shaped, six-story, glass-fronted structure called the Neptune House, a tip of the hat to Neptune Studios, which had constructed the first film studio at Elstree back in 1914. Grade had set aside part of the third floor of the Neptune House for Henson Associates, giving Jim a place to set up offices for himself and Lazer, as well as conference areas and rooms for Juhl and the writing team—"The Muppet Suite," as Jim would call it.

For most of the 1960s, the cavernous Studio D at Elstree had been the home to the popular Morecambe and Wise variety show, filmed in front of a live studio audience of about 350 people, sitting in a raised, auditorium-like seating area along one wall. Normally, the spacious rooms under the seats were used for storing large equipment—but Jim had other plans for the space, and cleared them out to make room for a Muppet workshop, just steps away from the studio floor. "We were setting up with this room that had nothing in it but a bunch of black cases that we brought over," said Bonnie Erickson, who had been assigned by Jim the task of setting up and overseeing the Elstree workshop. Erickson had converted the cramped but cozy space into a veritable Muppet factory, pushing in workbenches and tables and lining the walls with makeshift metal shelves sagging under the weight of boxes filled with costumes, fur, feathers, and eyes. Here Muppets could be quickly built, repaired, clothed, or modified without the need for materials from New York or even the costume or prop shop at Elstree. "We prided ourselves on the fact that nobody from the set shop or from the costuming took any time away from the shooting schedule, because we knew how valuable that time was," said Erickson.

Time was indeed a precious commodity, for Jim and the Muppet team were working at a breakneck pace. A typical work week began at 10:00 A.M. on Sunday, when the Muppet team—writers, performers, builders, and musicians—would gather in Elstree's Rehearsal Room 7/8 on the fourth floor of the Neptune House for the first read-through of the script with the guest star. It was Jim's policy that guest stars would be treated well, and therefore it only made sense that they be placed in the care of the suave, smooth-talking Lazer, who made sure guests were ferried around London in style—often in Lew Grade's own limousine—and stayed in first-rate hotels. Especially in that critical first season, when Jim felt the guest stars were "slightly sticking their necks out" working on an untested show for not much money, he wanted as few surprises for them as possible. For that reason, Lazer would often go to the guest's hotel the night before the read-through to personally deliver the script and address any questions or concerns.

At the read-through, the crew sat facing each other at long Formica-topped tables pushed into a loose rectangle, reading the script aloud and in character, with Burns or Juhl reading out the scripted stage directions. Folding himself into one of the rehearsal room's hard plastic shell chairs, Jim would scribble notes on his script as he read aloud his parts—sliding easily into the characters of Kermit or Dr. Teeth or the Muppet Newsman—and noting where additional puppets might be needed to fill in a crowd scene, or where an ad-libbed line worked better. Juhl, long used to watching Jim and Oz "talk around" a *Sesame Street* script, actively encouraged ad-libbing among the Muppet performers, as he thought such spontaneity gave him additional insights into the characters that made them that much more interesting to write. "Let's leave that in," Juhl would say excitedly as he scratched out the old line in his script and replaced it with the ad-lib.

Once the read-through was finished, the performers and musicians would head for what they called "The Music Hall," which was actually just the far end of the rehearsal room where a Bosendorfer piano, painted battleship gray, squatted among a scattering of chairs. Here they would rehearse any songs for the coming week, enthusiastically performing their own routines or practicing harmonies as they backed up the guest star. While Jim could barely read treble clef and only tinkle at the piano—and often joked that he could barely sing—his passion more than made up for his lack of technique. During rehearsals, Jim would always sing with gusto, gleefully announcing a key change by calling out *"Modulate!"*—a habit that so amused Frank Oz that he would incorporate it into the personality of the unconventional Muppet musician Marvin Suggs.

Music would be an important part of *The Muppet Show,* and Jim chose the songs to be performed on the show with the same relish with which he had once chosen records for *Sam and Friends.* Each week he would sort eagerly through Tin Pan Alley sheet music and old songbooks—including old favorites *Songs of the Pogo* and A. A. Milne's *Pooh Song Book*—as well as scouring the current Top 40 charts for songs with unusual or catchy hooks. Consequently, *The Muppet Show*'s first season alone featured an impressive array of songs reflecting Jim's quirky musical sensibilities, rolling through traditional tunes like the vaudeville-era "You and I and George," A. A. Milne's rollicking "Cottleston Pie," Latham and Jaffe's novelty tune "I'm My Own Grandpa," and Gilbert and Sullivan's "Tit Willow" (a selection that prompted a confused Sam the Eagle to ask, "Is it cultural?").

When it came to popular music, Jim's personal tastes had mellowed slightly with time; while he may have looked like he would be right at home lounging in a beanbag chair listening to 1970s stadium rock through oversized headphones, he actually preferred so-called adult contemporary artists like Jim Croce, James Taylor, and Billy Joel. Still, even when selecting songs from the mellower side of the Top 40, Jim could make some surprising choices, pulling deep cuts and obscure B-sides rather than the more familiar chart toppers. After listening to Barry Manilow's 1976 album *This One's for You*, for example, Jim opted to use "Jump Shout Boogie" for *The Muppet Show* rather than any of the album's four Top 40 hits.

After Music Hall and a break for lunch, rehearsal and blocking would take up the rest of the day—but Jim was always in and out of the rehearsal room, huddling with the writing team during lunch in the canteen, running over to the editing room to check on the progress of last week's episode, or in the Muppet workshop consulting on costuming needs. "[Jim] worked the hardest of anybody," said Lazer. "He was in the writers' meetings, he was in the performers' meetings, in the scenery meetings. He was in every possible meeting, constantly." By the time the lights went out at Elstree at 7:00 P.M. on Sunday night, the Muppet team had been at work for nine hours. And that, said Juhl, was "a light day."

On Monday began what the Muppet crew affectionately termed "Band Day," which started in the morning with the ATV studio musicians—conducted by Jack Parnell, a former big band drummer and bandleader who had served as ATV's musical director for twenty years—recording the music for that week's songs. During these sessions, the band would also record several isolated music tracks—just drums or bass or piano or sax—that each puppeteer who performed a musician would be given to listen to on their own. This way Jerry Nelson and Richard Hunt, for example, could familiarize themselves with the bass or the lead guitar solos so they could make their performances that much more convincing. Jim, for one, took great pride in his ability to make Rowlf or Dr. Teeth convincingly play the piano, listening to their performances on the tape deck in his car on his way into Elstree each morning. "I'm really enjoying it," he reported. "I haven't played piano for years."

Once the band had completed its work, the Muppet performers would gather in the main band room to begin recording their vocals. While all dialogue on the show would be performed live during the taping of the show, the songs would almost always be recorded in advance to ensure the song would sound the same—and the Muppet performers' voices would remain intact—over multiple takes. Recording sessions could last anywhere from an hour to half a day— but Jim used much of the day to meet with Burns, Juhl, and the rest of the writing team to review scripts and talk through ideas for upcoming episodes.

The Muppet writers each had different strengths and writing styles that would shape both the show and the characters—sometimes through trial and error—as the show progressed from year to year. Writer Don Hinkley had a knack for puns and verbal wordplay— and was, in the minds of many, the funniest guy in the room—while quick-writing Mark London, a veteran of *Laugh-In,* was a workhorse who wrote straight-ahead comedy routines, like the soap opera spoof "Veterinarian's Hospital." Head writer Jack Burns understood how to put together a show, though he tended to think of episodes as a series of roughly strung together vignettes, with no underlying story gluing the episode together. Instead, regular routines like "Veterinarian's Hospital" or "At the Dance," in which couples waltzed past the camera and told jokes, were mostly just pushed together, giving the shows a rhythm, but no cohesion. That would change in the second season, with the removal of Burns and the promotion of Juhl to head writer. Juhl's first order of business: "We phased out that ballroom dancing thing," said Juhl, "partly because everybody hated to write for it, and everybody hated to perform it . . . it was boring kind of writing. Pointless one-liners. No character and no motivation of any kind."

For Juhl, the former Muppet performer, it was character and motivation that mattered more than puns or vaudeville-style jokes— a predilection Jim and the puppeteers appreciated. "What he always seemed to do best was to watch . . . us develop our characters and then write along those lines," said Hunt. In the writing room, however, Jim was adamant that "these puppets are not just characters up there telling jokes. If you just stand there and tell jokes," he continued, "the whole thing will die. The humor only holds if there's visual interaction between the characters."

That visual interaction, however, was sometimes difficult for Jim to articulate. "How the characters play a particular moment on a punch line is very visual," Jim would insist. "The whole concept of the comedy take is totally visual. Even deadpan comedians are very visual." And yet, Jim couldn't always explain exactly what he meant by *visual*. Jim knew when sketches or jokes worked—and when they didn't, he usually knew why—but expressing his views in the writers' room could often be excruciating for everyone involved. "He would drive [the writers] crazy," said Juhl, "because he would know that what was on the page wasn't what he wanted. But he couldn't quite *know* what he wanted—or if he did know what he wanted, he wouldn't quite know how to tell you." And so writers' meetings could stretch on, sometimes for hours, with bursts of enthusiastic conversation followed by long periods of silence as Jim tried to come up with just the right way to describe what he was looking for.

Often, the biggest source of disagreement was over what Juhl called "the implied joke," in which a joke is set up on-screen, "and then the punch line happens off camera . . . somebody walks out and you hear the whole thing collapse." Jim thought that was throwing away a perfectly good punch line. "We can show that!" he would insist, appealing to the writers with his huge hands spread outward—and then he and the writing team would go around and around again. "There would be fairly heated arguments," said Juhl. "We would try to make the case that actually *not* seeing it would be funnier. And he *hated* that argument. He could see the logic in it, but he didn't want to give in to it." Jim would only slouch lower in his chair and *hmmmm*; an implied joke, he thought, was not only a waste of a joke, but a waste of the puppets themselves. "Most TV humor is verbal. Somebody says something to somebody and somebody else replies," he explained. "But with puppets, you do a funny kind of character, and that's the joke. That's where the humor arises. Often, the best pieces don't look like *anything* on paper."

Now that they were all working together in London, Jim and Juhl, as promised, had slowly but surely helped Oz get a better handle on Fozzie Bear. Jim had directed the Muppet builders to modify the puppet, slightly changing Fozzie's color to a brighter orange, removing the unreliable mechanism that wiggled Fozzie's ears, and remodeling the mouth to get rid of the downturned corners that gave the early version of the character a perpetual grimace. From a writing perspective, said Juhl, the real trick was to take "Fozzie's ineptness . . . [and] make that entertaining and wonderful." Oz, too, was beginning to change the way he performed the character, and at Jim's urging had somewhat modified the voice, sliding up to a slightly higher register and a more excited delivery. Oz had also decided that Fozzie, rather than being a victim, was just "a simple guy who wants to be funny and loved."

Yet, Fozzie continued to struggle as the fall guy—until the character suddenly and wonderfully fell into place. In a sketch worthy of Abbott and Costello, Fozzie asks Kermit for help in telling a joke, convincing the frog to act as his straight man. "When you hear me say the word '*hear*,'" Fozzie tells Kermit carefully, "you will rush up to me and say, 'Good grief! The comedian's a bear!'" Kermit agrees— and over the next ninety seconds, Fozzie's best-laid plans come quickly unraveled:

> FOZZIE: Okay, here we go . . . ready? . . . (*faces audience*)
> Now then: Hiya hiya hiya! You're a wonderful looking
> audience, it's a pleasure to be here. I—
> KERMIT (*rushing in*): Good grief! The comedian's a bear!
> FOZZIE: Not yet!
> KERMIT: But you just said "here" . . .
> FOZZIE: That was the wrong "hear"!
> KERMIT: Which is the right "hear"?
> FOZZIE: The *other* "hear"! Go, go . . . (*pushing Kermit off-
> stage*) Okay—hey hey folks! This is a story you guys'll
> *love* to hear. . . .
> KERMIT (*rushing in*): Good grief! The comedian's a bear!
> FOZZIE: Will you stop that?!?
> KERMIT: But you said "hear"!
> FOZZIE: Not *that* "hear"!
> KERMIT: Well which "hear"?
> FOZZIE: *Another* "hear"!

KERMIT: How am I gonna know?!?
FOZZIE: You'll know when you hear!
KERMIT: Good grief! The comedian's a bear!

And so on, at which point the punch line—"No he's-a not! He's-a wearin' a necka tie!"—is nearly beside the point. While it was a defining moment for the character, it very nearly didn't make it before the cameras. It had been written quickly—"We sent the material down on the floor just a few minutes before they were gonna tape it," recalled Juhl—and taped toward the end of the day when Jim and Oz had little time to rehearse. After reading through it once, Jim and Oz put Kermit and Fozzie on their arms, and completed the complicated sketch in one remarkable take. "They just played the hell out of it," said Juhl admiringly, "and suddenly Fozzie was *wonderful*. I remember that moment and saying, 'Now *there's* a character there!' "

It was indeed a wonderful moment—but it wouldn't have worked without Kermit, played by Jim at his most delightfully and arm-wavingly frantic, frazzled, and frustrated. Many television critics, writing of Kermit during that pivotal first season, thought Kermit was already one of Hollywood's great straight men—"funny not because of what he does," wrote one reviewer, "but because of what others do around him, and because of the aplomb with which he bears their doings." That was true to some extent, but Kermit was more than a mere straight man; he was the sun around which the entire Muppet solar system revolved. "He relates to the other characters on many different levels," said Juhl. "More important, they *have* to relate to him. Without Kermit, they don't work. Nothing could happen without him. The other characters do not have what it takes to hold things together."

The same could be said of Jim, although Jim was always wary of letting the press view him and Kermit interchangeably. "There's a bit of me in Kermit," Jim conceded. "Kermit's the organizer, always desperately trying to keep things going while surrounded by all these crazy nuts," he explained to London's *TV Times*. "I suppose he is not unlike me and it's not unlike the way the place operates around here." Mostly, Jim saw both himself and Kermit as the steady eye of the *Muppet Show* hurricane, the center around which the storm wildly raged and revolved—though steady didn't necessarily mean *staid*. "Me not crazy?" Kermit once exclaimed. "I hired the others!" Jim, too, often saw himself as the ringleader of a group whose members unapologetically referred to themselves as "a bunch of goddamn lunatics!"

To Jim, *The Muppet Show* would always be his version of Walt Kelly's *Pogo,* with the mostly patient Kermit anchoring an eclectic cast of misfits. But even those unacquainted with Kelly's world could immediately grasp the formula Jim had put to work. "It's *The Mary Tyler Moore Show,*" said *Sesame Street*'s Jon Stone. "It's the central, neutral type figure trying to bring order out of chaos. . . . It was a pretty good formula." Such a formula, then, usually included a love interest for the main character, and *The Muppet Show* was no exception—though as the show was originally envisioned, it wasn't supposed to be that way.

The rise of Miss Piggy from nameless background dancing girl to full-fledged movie star is a story straight out of Hollywood legend—except it actually happened. Piggy had made her first appearance as a nameless character on *The Herb Alpert Show,* then showed up as an incidental character in the *Sex and Violence* pilot, one of several beady-eyed pigs who appeared in the "Return to Beneath the Planet of the Pigs" sketch (Bonnie Erickson, who designed the first Piggy, had jokingly named her "Miss Piggy Lee" as an homage to singer Peggy Lee). For the first episodes of *The Muppet Show,* the puppet was slightly redesigned and given larger eyes—she would be one of the few Muppets with full-color irises—and sent to the chorus line, where she danced during the opening credits and appeared in a few sketches. She was considered such a minor character, in fact, that for much of the first season she didn't even have a regular performer assigned to her, and was passed back and forth between Frank Oz and Richard Hunt with little concern about consistency in voice or mannerisms.

Even as the puppet was being passed around, however, there were glimpses of the character in the making. "Sometimes a character will start from something we write, and someone will do something very funny with it," said Juhl. "Or sometimes the guys just start ad-libbing something and it starts with them." In Miss Piggy's case, it was a bit of both, as Frank Oz took a simple stage direction written on the page and ad-libbed it into a memorable, almost iconic, moment. "I was working as Miss Piggy with Jim, who was doing Kermit, and the script called for her to slap him," said Oz. "Instead of a slap, I gave him a funny karate hit. Somehow, that hit crystallized her character for me—the coyness hiding the aggression." That karate chop, agreed Juhl, made all the difference. "The place fell apart. It was like just instantly you knew that you gotta see this again."

Piggy would continue to be traded between Oz and Hunt for a while longer, but gradually she became Oz's character alone. "Miss Piggy was to have been a minor character," noted Jim, "but Frank Oz gave her such a strong personality that she immediately became one of the principals." That also meant that Fozzie, who was originally intended as Oz's main character, was relegated to the supporting cast as Piggy became his primary character, in the same way that Rowlf couldn't share as much screen time with Kermit, since Jim performed both puppets. "Rowlf could have been one of the stars of the show if only we could have had him interacting on a regular basis with Kermit and Piggy," said Juhl. "But from a practical point of view, it just wasn't possible." ("Poor Rowlf," Jane said with a sigh.)

Oz quickly became immersed in Piggy and her personality. "She takes over," Oz told reporters. "She has become so real to me. In fact, when I talk about her my voice changes and I move my vocal gears and become her, using her voice and even adopting her personality." ("But let's get it straight that I'm *straight*!" Oz told one London gossip columnist with just a hint of exasperation.) While watching the six-foot-two Oz perform as a female character was second nature to the Muppet performers, for some *Muppet Show* guests, it took some getting used to. During the first table read-through with British comedian Spike Milligan, when Oz began speaking in Piggy's voice, Milligan stood up, pointed incredulously at Oz, and exclaimed, "It's a man?!?"

Writing for Piggy, said Juhl, was "real, real tough." "The whole *Muppet Show* conceit is based on this concept of family," Juhl explained. "Piggy stands aside from all of that. Piggy demands things that are quite outside of the family. . . . You're walking a fine line with that character. If she isn't a bitch, she isn't funny. But you've got to feel the other side." Oz, though, was confident he could play her just right, and had crafted an elaborate backstory ("She grew up on a small farm; her father died in a tractor accident, her mother wasn't that nice to her . . .") to help him better understand, and therefore better perform, the character—including her love for Kermit, setting up one of Hollywood's great one-sided love affairs. "She's sensuous and she's been hurt a lot," said Oz. "She loves the frog—my God how she covets that little green body!—but the frog doesn't love her."

Richard Hunt had no patience for crafting those kinds of elaborate background stories for his characters, calling it "endless [and] fairly pointless." Hunt didn't immerse himself in characters; Hunt *played* them, taking great relish in putting on voices and performing in broad gestures, the same way children delight in putting on a neighborhood circus. That wasn't to say that Hunt couldn't find parts of himself in his characters. Hunt's main character, the eager-to-please Scooter, wasn't all that different from Hunt. "He was this little, little kid," said Hunt of Scooter, "and that was me when I first walked in." Scooter's moderate pestering of Kermit and others wasn't that far removed from Hunt, either. "I was a pain in the ass!" said Hunt, though Jim would generally allow Hunt to hover and chatter over his shoulder for a while before finally saying in mock frustration, "Richard, shut up and go away!"

The Muppet Show's other major character, the enigmatic Gonzo the Great, was assigned to Dave Goelz, who was still doing his best to resist Jim's efforts to remove him permanently from the Muppet workshop to become a full-time performer. "I was so upset when Jim took him to be a puppeteer!" said Bonnie Erickson, who needed in the workshop every skilled hand she could get. "He was really so talented." Despite Jim's confidence in him, Goelz was still unconvinced he had what it took to be a performer. "I was very insecure, because I really had no business being in the entertainment industry," said Goelz. "I had no training of any kind, except two little sessions with Jim and Frank, so I felt very unqualified." But as Jim seemed to inherently understand—even if Goelz didn't—that was just the sort of perspective necessary to create the character. "Gonzo believes he is a worthless creature," said Goelz. "He knows and believes it, but he wants to prove he has worth." So did Goelz.

As originally written by Juhl, Gonzo was "a loser who did these horrible acts and thought they were great art." Jim had selected al-most at random the sad-eyed, bent-nosed Cigar Box Frackle from *The Great Santa Claus Switch*, retrieving the character from a box in New York and telling Goelz, "This could be Gonzo." For the first season, then, Goelz played Gonzo as "this little dark frightened char-acter," but remained frustrated with his own performance, which he thought was boring even to the Elstree crew. "They loved watching Jim and Frank work," said Goelz. "When I came onstage, I could hear the newspapers come up."

That would change late in the first season when a simple "No!" from Gonzo helped Goelz find himself—and thus the character. At first, the insecure Goelz would only feebly croak out "*no,*" and "Jim kept saying, 'Well, do it again. Make it big!' . . . And I couldn't do it," said Goelz. "We did take after take after take, and Jim was so pa-tient. I finally just went, '*Nnnnoooo!*' And I could hear the newspa-pers all come down. . . . I got a laugh from the crew." Gonzo—and Goelz—had finally gotten excited about something—and "when you got excited," discovered Goelz, "it was good."

With a new enthusiasm, Goelz rebuilt Gonzo to remove his per-manently sad eyes and replaced them with an eye mechanism that allowed the character to open his eyes for a wider range of emotion. Now, said Goelz, "Gonzo can still get very, very depressed, but he has moments of high, intense excitement." Jim's faith in Goelz, and Gonzo, had paid off. "As *I* got confidence, *he* got confidence," said Goelz of Gonzo. And both would regularly get laughs from the Elstree crew.

Rounding out the the top tier of the Muppet performers was Jerry Nelson, who had taken a leave of absence during *The Muppet Show*'s first season to spend some additional time with his teen-age daughter and was unable to commit to a full season. Conse-quently, Nelson was not assigned any of *The Muppet Show*'s central characters—a necessary but inadvertent slight that would later cause some hard feelings. Instead, Nelson would become the team's invalu-able utility player, making even minor or one-note characters, like Lew Zealand, Crazy Harry, or Uncle Deadly, memorable, while his gravelly singing voice would establish the Electric Mayhem's bass player Floyd as the epitome of Muppet cool. Nelson's performance mentality was halfway between Oz's and Hunt's; each character, explained Nelson, "is an aspect of my own personality. The Muppets are roles I assume, rather than puppets I manipulate."

Performing and filming the Muppet segments would begin in earnest on Tuesdays. On that day, the Muppet team would spend the entire day taping the sketches featuring that week's guest star, then continue on with Muppet-only segments on Wednesday and Thursday. Spending all day Tuesday with the star could be "really tough" though it depended largely on the guest star. Fifth season guest Tony Randall would be one of the few problematic guests, micromanaging Muppet performances and growing increasingly pushy as the filming progressed. "Some [guests] relate to us more easily than others," Jim explained earnestly to *The Christian Science Monitor*. "A person who is cool personally can play marvelously well with the Muppets."

Working with the Muppets, said Jim, was an opportunity for guests "to work in a sort of fun land, a Never-Never Land," where the atmosphere was laid-back, a sense of humor was mandatory, and the dress code was casual. In the first few years of *The Muppet Show*, before he began wearing stylish sweaters or tucking colorful scarves around his neck, Jim was at nearly his shaggiest, his long hair falling against his denim collar and his beard a bushy bib that he absent-mindedly stroked while *hmmmm*ing his way through a problem. Lazer, in his impeccably tailored Jaeger suits, then, was there to provide a dose of showbiz conventionality. "Although he never told people what to wear . . . some part of [Jim] liked that I was wearing a tie and jacket," said Lazer. "We had all these major stars coming in, and they needed to zero in on one person who was familiar . . . because they were coming into a strange world!"

And yet, it was Jim who the guests couldn't stop watching. "The women stars fell in love with Jim," said Lazer, "[and the] male stars couldn't stop talking about him." Guests wanted nothing more than to please Jim—to make him laugh or to see him enthusiastically raise his eyebrows in approval of their performance. But Jim related particularly well with his female costars, who were drawn not only to his talent but responded strongly to his charisma and inherent Southern-bred sweetness. "They clicked with him," said Lazer. "In the beginning they weren't sure. And then as soon as they watched him in operation . . . he was in such control, and so gentle . . . and he would direct them, and they would just listen to anything he said. They trusted him." When first-season guest Ethel Merman struggled slightly with a feathery costume during a complicated sketch, Lazer approached the singer between takes to offer his assistance. Merman shooed him away. "Listen," she said, "you tell that Jim Henson that if he wants me to wear a feather up my ass, I'll do it for him!"

Following the taping of the show, Jim would take each guest, along with much of the Muppet crew, out for dinner. Lazer called them "wrap parties," though they were usually just large dinner parties with copious amounts of wine—and Jim joked that he only knew enough about wine to order exactly one kind of red and one kind of white. Even after their appearance on the show, no guest would ever be truly forgotten; Lazer kept a running list of the home addresses and birthdays of all his guest stars, and after the publication of a book about the making of *The Muppet Show,* Jim went out of his way to ensure that every guest received a copy. "I've heard stories about other shows that thrive on the tension that exists between the stars, or between the star and the producers, but that wouldn't work for us," said Jim. "If we didn't manage to maintain a friendly atmosphere, we'd be in deep trouble." As Lazer put it: "Unless our guests go home telling everyone that they had a great time doing *The Muppet Show,* then I haven't done my job."

While Brillstein had called in favors to secure guests during the early part of *The Muppet Show*'s first season, "as the show kept gaining in popularity," said the agent, "we had a waiting list." The success of the first fifteen shows in particular—featuring a wide range of talents such as Peter Ustinov, Rita Moreno, Joel Grey, and Lena Horne—went a long way toward sealing *The Muppet Show*'s reputation as a hip hit. "The calls started coming in," said Lazer. Not only was the show a success, but word had spread quickly that "we took such good care of the stars . . . we gave them a chance to do what they wanted to do. If they ever wanted to sing, we'd give them a chance to sing. Or be a comedienne if they were straight, or whatever." Only on *The Muppet Show* could Sylvester Stallone sing and dance with a lion or Beverly Sills hang a spoon from the end of her nose—and bring in big ratings to boot.

Even Lord Grade was impressed. "The atmosphere and excitement during the making of these shows was electric, and in a very short while we had international celebrities clamoring to do the guest spot," recalled Grade. Grade even loved dropping by the set every once in a while to watch the Muppet team at work, strolling the studio and casually asking, "Everything all right, boys?"

Most sets for *The Muppet Show* were "platformed up," elevated about four feet off the ground on stilts, with plenty of low walls, boxes, stairs, or doorways for the performers to poke puppets into. Most of the budget for *The Muppet Show,* in fact, went into sets, which had to be carefully designed and constructed so that the Muppets could interact seamlessly with the human guest star. Doors and stairs for the Muppet theater's backstage set, for example, had to be built at a scale small enough for Muppets, but not *too* small or the guest stars couldn't use them. And since most sets were mainly just backdrops and low walls for the puppeteers to poke puppets between, movable platforms had to be built for the guest stars to stand on during any scenes in which they had to interact with the Muppets.

Down on floor level, things were perhaps even more hectic. As they performed, puppeteers had to step over cables snaking across the floor, and around the struts elevating the sets over their heads. Sketches that involved cars or motorcycles or any moving vehicle required another group of performers to push the vehicle, elevated on a raised platform, across the studio floor while the puppeteers walked along behind it performing—and "everybody," directed Jim, "has to see a monitor." At almost all times, all eyes were on one of the countless monitors placed strategically around the floor of the studio, so it was always possible to see how the puppets looked on camera, no matter which way the performers were facing.

Amid the chaos in Studio D, Jim was calm, cool, and clearly in charge, mapping out shots with cameramen, consulting with the writers over script changes, or huddling with *Muppet Show* directors Peter Harris and Philip Casson, who alternated directing duties from week to week. Unlike Jon Stone, who preferred directing the

Sesame Street Muppets down on the main floor in the thick of things, Harris and Casson were more comfortable directing from the glassed-in booth overlooking the studio floor, patiently broadcasting instructions over the studio's squawky sound system, or calling down directions for floor managers Richard Holloway or Martin Baker to convey to the crew. Jim had initially wanted to direct *The Muppet Show* himself, but discovered that trying to direct while performing the show's central character only slowed things down. Instead, said Jim, "I settle for a set of headphones so I can make a suggestion once in a while," communicating directly with Harris and Casson through a headset with a microphone covered with green foam carved to look like Kermit.

While the bulk of the responsibility for keeping things running smoothly fell largely to Jim, he never made it look like work. "Everything was play for him," said Juhl. "Work was play. That was the thing that we all plainly understood." Agreed Oz, "Jim wasn't a workaholic. Our job was playing." For Jim that meant encouraging the team—from the Muppet performers to the lighting crew—to ad-lib or interject ideas, and maintaining an overall atmosphere of collegiality in which everyone's performance and opinion was valued. "We know each other so well that we can kind of bounce off each other when we're working together," explained Jim. "This working relationship . . . has a kind of marvelous chemistry to it, and I think it's terribly important that when we're working in the studio, we work with this kind of affection and high spirits."

And spirits were high indeed. The Muppet performers would constantly joke and banter without ever breaking character, their puppets jabbering at each other with eyebrows waggling and arms waving. "Even when they're not shooting, they keep talking [in character]," said impressionist Rich Little, a second season guest. "It's incredible. . . . After a few minutes at the studio . . . the Muppets become real." Even those who worked with the Muppets daily found it a bit disorienting. Watching the performance from the booth, director Peter Harris would notice Jim's head in a shot and would call out, "Sorry, Jim, we have to go again"—and Kermit, rather than Jim, would turn to the camera and respond. "In the end you just talk to Kermit," said Harris. "It's a very weird experience."

Other times, Oz and Goelz would grab the struts elevating the Muppet sets and send themselves racing across the studio floor in rolling chairs, cheered on by cameramen and Muppets alike. Jerry Nelson would sprawl in the theater seats over the Muppet workshop and strum a guitar, one eye on the monitor, waiting to be called in to perform. Richard Hunt, the always willing master of ceremonies, was in everybody's face—and no one, not even the guest star, was off-limits. "If he was driving to work and he passed the limo with the guest in it, he would roll down the window and . . . just yell and go crazy," said Goelz fondly. "All the guests who went away from the show remembered Jim and Frank and Richard Hunt—and that was because Richard's personality was so big."

But the best moments, as nearly everyone agreed, were when Jim laughed. "He laughed until he cried," said Oz. "It didn't matter if we were taping or prerecording for a TV show or a record, we would just end up cracking each other up. He had to wrangle us, yes, but other times he was the instigator." More often than not, it was performing with Oz that got Jim laughing the hardest, the two of them collapsing in fits of laughter as they performed Kermit and Fozzie— or Kermit and Miss Piggy—and tried desperately not to break character.

"Frank and Jim were incredible at getting the play started," said Lazer. "The combination of Jim and Frank was just magical," added Goelz. "Jim had this light playful side, and Frank had the underpinnings, the drama, the backstory, the depth of character—and the two just meshed perfectly." For Richard Hunt, it was like watching "the 70s and 80s Laurel and Hardy. . . . It was hysterical."

And yet, when Oz wasn't performing, he was "this very intimidating figure," said Brian Henson. "He really was kind of like Sam the Eagle—he was dark and brooding and if Frank was coming down the hall, you got out of the way!" Juhl remembered Oz as "incredibly moody" during those years. "Frank has this incredible thing," said Juhl. "He is quite clearly the best puppeteer in the world, and he fights it." Discussing Oz's moodiness with Juhl, Jim would merely shake his head in genuine pity. "That's just such a shame, you know," he told Juhl. "Everything is happening right now, this is just an incredibly exciting time in our lives. . . . I wish Frank could enjoy it."

254 | JIM HENSON

The highlight of the week—indeed, the one time when it was certain that every member of the Muppet team and the ATV crew would be watching—was the moment Jim and Oz, usually performing as Kermit and Fozzie, stepped in front of *The Muppet Show*'s trademark red curtain to film two short promotional spots for the week's episode. There were no scripts for these ten- to twenty-second segments; the name of the game was to improvise the piece, with Oz doing his best to surprise and provoke a response from Jim—or, better yet, make him laugh. It was thrilling, said Hunt admiringly, "the way they could second-guess each other. . . . They would laugh so much that they would end up crying. . . . It got to a point where they couldn't really talk, but they were still going. . . . Frank was capable of reducing Jim to giggles, and vice versa."

Even the very proper English crew at ATV grew to love working for Jim and with the Muppets—especially after Jim came to understand and appreciate the quirks of working with a British crew. Tea time was strictly observed—a tradition Jim found charming and willingly embraced. The canteen at Elstree was also equipped with a fully stocked bar, where some of the British crew would polish off one or two shandies during lunch before returning to the studio floor in what one insider diplomatically described as a "more relaxed" state. It was a custom Jim neither questioned nor complained about, as long as the work got done.

If there was anything distinctly British that would plague Jim during his five years at Elstree, however, it was the British union's strict requirement that the studio lights at Elstree be turned off at exactly 8:00 P.M. Unlike American or Canadian studios, where filming could continue into the early hours of the morning until the work was completed, British studios stationed union representatives on the set at all times to ensure work ended promptly at the required hour. "We could be in the middle of a number," said Lazer, "and it was 'Lights out!' and [they'd] walk off." Consequently, if the Muppet team was still filming after 7:30, Jim would assign a crew member to watch the clock, calling out after each take the minutes remaining before eight. As the clock ticked, either Jim or Lazer would negotiate for additional time—which, if granted, would be parsimoniously doled out in five-minute increments. By Lazer's account, the Muppet team was left standing in the dark "probably ten times"—enough, he said, "to make you crazy."

Filming the Muppet-only segments usually took two days—especially if the union's lights-out policy had left them unable to finish the first day on time—and for Jim, Thursday was often the busiest day of the week, though not because of filming. Mostly, he was in meetings, discussing upcoming shows or music or scripts, meeting with set builders, or in the workshop checking on the progress of any new puppets—and "once [the meetings] started," said Juhl, "they didn't stop." Meetings would continue over lunch—"we have to eat anyway," Jim would say with a shrug—either at Signor Baffi's, an Italian restaurant across the street with famously slow service, or back in the Muppet Suite where trays of lukewarm grilled cheese and bacon sandwiches and even warmer bottles of beer would be delivered from the canteen and lined up on the side tables. No matter how many meetings he attended during the day, Jim could almost always concentrate intently on the task in front of him, getting down to business so quickly that Burns, Juhl, and the writing team often couldn't turn the pages of their scripts fast enough to keep up.

Still, there were days when Jim was so pressed for time that he couldn't always prepare for meetings. He was reluctant to let on that he was unprepared—more than anyone in the room, he understood the consequences of wasted time—and with every head in the room turned toward him, he would quietly eat his sandwich and flip through the pages of his script. And suddenly, said Juhl, "he'd start improvising this piece of material . . . it was blowing jazz. He would start free-associating." At times like this, no idea was too outrageous, whether it was penguins singing "Lullaby of Broadway," a killer lamb attacking the Muppet newsman, or a Chopped Liver monster antagonizing the cast of the "Pigs in Space" sketch. "He'd just start calling for things, and people would start writing them down," said Juhl, "and the whole show . . . was done that way." Only Jim could make such madness seem so routine. "He had," said Juhl, in perhaps the most apt description of Jim, "a whim of steel."

Even with the meeting over, there would usually be someone try-ing to talk with Jim during his walk to the elevator and the forty-five-second elevator ride down three floors. As Jim walked toward the studio floor—and he never rushed, but would simply walk at a rapid clip, taking long loping strides—members of the Muppet staff would walk backward in front of him, trying to finish their conversa-tions before Jim ducked into Studio D.

When filming finished that evening, Jim would attend more meetings—often with Lew Grade or Muppet staff from the New York workshop—in his office in the Muppet Suite, or over dinner, finally wrapping up at midnight. He would return to Elstree early Friday morning to review edits with his directors—including the in-sertion of two additional minutes of material for the U.K. version of the show, since British television had fewer commercials—and spend time in the Muppet workshop. At the end of the day, he and Lazer would discuss next week's show over dinner. "My work schedule here is extremely full," Jim wrote in his private diary. "Work days usually start when I get up and go late into the evenings—shooting days end at 8 PM and often I'm meeting someone for dinner—business mostly. I go to ATV virtually every day . . . weekends I drop by the editing and sound dubbing."

And so it would go, twenty-four weeks a year. It was a grinding, grueling schedule—and Jim loved every minute of it. "One of Jim's real talents was that he had the ability not to take most things more seriously than they deserved," said Juhl. "And that means that most things are pretty funny. I think that's what got him through the kind of schedule he had. . . . While he was doing it, he always knew that it was just a Muppet show. And he could keep things in that kind of perspective."

It was more than just keeping things in perspective; Jim just flat-out loved to work. As he confided in his diary:

I don't resent the long work time—I shouldn't—I'm the one who set my life up this way—but I love to work. It's the thing that I get the most satisfaction out of—and probably what I do best. Not that I don't enjoy days off—I love vacations and loafing around. But I think much of the world has the wrong idea of working—it's one of the good things in life—the feeling of accomplishment is more real and satisfying than finishing a good meal or looking at one's accumulated wealth.

Still, Jim's ideas of vacations and "loafing around" were becoming more and more ambitious with his increasing success. That first summer in London, Jim flew his family and several members of the Muppet team—including the boisterous Richard Hunt—to Athens, where Jim had reserved a boat and crew for a week's worth of cruising the Greek islands. Jim found even his extraordinary patience quickly tested by the ship's bullheaded Greek captain, who refused to bow to any of Jim's polite requests to put up the sails and visit certain islands, and instead went chugging slowly around with the diesel engine belching purple smoke. Brian Henson remembered his dad being frustrated, yet refusing to put his foot down. "Oh well," Jim would say with a shrug. "That's what it is."

Other times, Jim would make short sprints to Europe with one or more of the kids, taking sixteen-year-old Lisa and Brian with him to Paris in early August of 1976 to sightsee and visit the French abstract puppeteer Philippe Genty, or traveling to Morocco for five days with Lisa, Cheryl, and Brian. Those trips, said Brian, were "fantastic." Looking back, said Cheryl, she could see that her father perhaps felt "a little bit burdened" with family and that the trips were his way of "keeping it all together." "He wanted everyone to be happy," said Cheryl, "he wanted everyone to be included, and I think he really also was making an effort to be a family man."

Jim completed work on the first half of *The Muppet Show*'s first season on August 13, 1976. With the first fifteen episodes complete, he returned to New York on August 16, and went immediately into the studio to spend a week working on Muppet inserts for *Sesame Street,* for which Jim and the Muppet team had been awarded two more Emmys over the summer. Three weeks later, the promotional tour for *The Muppet Show* was in high gear, with Jim crisscrossing the country to appear on *Merv Griffin, Dinah Shore,* and *The Tonight Show,* and chatting amiably over the phone with reporters in

St. Louis, Cleveland, and San Diego. Already there was a buzz of excited anticipation; before even a single episode had aired anywhere in the United States, *Backstage* was already lauding it as "one of the fastest selling half-hour series" of all time.

Indeed, Brillstein and Mandell had worked hard to sell the series, showing the two pilot episodes to any station programmer who would listen, and aggressively promoting the series at the 1976 conference for the National Association of Television Program Executives. "Seeing was believing," Mandell said later. "The station executives were genuinely entertained." After that, *The Muppet Show* had picked up stations at an almost exponential rate, growing quickly from the initial five CBS O&Os in late 1975, to 112 stations by May 1976, including 87 of the top 100 markets in the United States. By the beginning of the 1976 television season in September, *The Muppet Show* had been picked up by a record 162 U.S. television stations—making it available for viewing in a staggering 94.6 percent of American households—as well as in a wide number of international markets, including Germany, France, the United Kingdom, and Taiwan.

The first episode of *The Muppet Show* went on the air in New York on channel 2 at 7:30 P.M. on Monday, September 20, 1976. With a batch of fifteen shows to choose from, most stations chose to start with the episode featuring Rita Moreno—a strong episode featuring a notable moment when Moreno performed "Fever" with Animal backing (and interrupting) her on drums. Local reviewers were enthusiastic—"If you have a child, or ever were one," wrote the *Chicago Tribune,* "you ought to watch," while the *Louisville Times* raved simply, "Long Live the Muppets!"—but though it was widely watched, the show wasn't an immediate hit. More typical was the review in *Variety,* which liked the first episode, but found the humor rather ho-hum, astutely noting that the material "bore more of the [head writer] Jack Burns touch . . . than the wry, whimsical Henson type of humor fans are more familiar with."

Jim wasn't concerned. "We are well on our way to a smashing success," Jack Burns had written to Jim in a private memo at the end of July, and Jim was inclined to agree—though he didn't always agree with *everything* Burns wanted to do with the show. Jim had scuttled a suggestion from Burns that the writers play up catch-phrases and specific quirks to help viewers more quickly differentiate between characters—that was trying too hard, in Jim's opinion—and would ignore Burns's objections to refilming the show's opening credits. While Jim and Burns respected each other, friction between the two was increasing. Besides serving as head writer, the strong-willed Burns was also serving as a producer during the first season—and that, said Lazer, "was hard for Jim . . . Jim needs to be in *the* role." Burns would eventually be fired by Bernie Brillstein, after Jim complained tactfully to the agent that Burns "gives me a stomach-ache." But "it was never personal," said Oz, and Jim would continue to collaborate with Burns on other projects over the next decade.

Jim flew back to London on September 23—turning forty years old on the airplane as it crossed the Atlantic overnight—and returned to work at Elstree to shoot the final nine episodes of *The Muppet Show*'s first season, working nonstop right up until the day before Thanksgiving. Two days later, he was back in New York in time to oversee the company Christmas party at the upscale Rainbow Room at 30 Rockefeller Center before spending a quiet New Year's Eve with the family in Ahoskie, North Carolina. All in all, it had been a good year.

Nineteen seventy-seven began with Jim working on what would become one of his best-loved projects, a musical Christmas special based on Russell and Lillian Hoban's 1971 children's book *Emmet Otter's Jug-Band Christmas*. Jim was an early fan of the book, featuring Emmet and his widowed mother, each of whom sets out to win a talent show's $50 prize—and gamble each other's most prized possessions in the process—so each can buy the other a Christmas present. Jim had successfully snagged the rights from the Hobans and in 1976 assigned Jerry Juhl the task of adapting the story for an hour-long special. Juhl completed his first draft by fall, turning in an inspiring, fully realized treatment on November 1. As he and Jim worked their way through several drafts of a script, Jim would keep most of Juhl's outline intact.

Emmet would also require several original songs—and given the importance of the songs to the story, Jim had opted to go after an established pop tunesmith who shared his own quirky, Tin Pan Alley tastes. Songwriter Paul Williams—who had penned the Top 10 hits "An Old Fashioned Love Song" for Three Dog Night and "We've Only Just Begun" for the Carpenters—had come to London in June 1976 to appear as a guest star on *The Muppet Show,* and he and Jim had gotten on so well they agreed to find another project on which to collaborate. Jim thought *Emmet* was a good fit for their combined sensibilities—and after reviewing Juhl's treatment, Jim had tried to connect with Williams in person, narrowly missing him in California five days before Christmas. Just after the New Year, however, Jim finally caught up with Williams and explained the project to him over dinner in Los Angeles. "It felt like the warmest, funniest thing to tune in to," said Williams. "Something in me lit up when I was exposed to anything Jim Henson did. So when they asked me to come over, I was really happy to do it."

At the same time, Jim had the New York workshop creating an entirely new cast of Muppets—based largely on the Hoban drawings—and designing and building not only some of their most picturesque sets, but also some of the first radio-controlled puppets. It was a project both designer Don Sahlin and technowizard Faz Fazakas devoured, building puppets of different sizes with different functions, and creating an ingenious device—based on a remote-control system developed by NASA engineers—in which a puppet's mouth could be manipulated remotely by a radio control device resembling an electronic mitten. Jim's favorite, though, was a mechanized Emmet who could actually row and steer a boat in the water. Jim couldn't keep his hands off of it. "Oh, I *love* this thing!" he would say as he leapt for the controls.

The Muppet team spent the first few days in March 1977 recording the songs for *Emmet Otter* in Los Angeles, performing in the recording studio backed by Paul Williams and his road band. All agreed that the songs were extraordinary. Once again, Jim had seemed almost intuitively to find the best person for his particular project—a knack that, in this particular case, at least, amazed the notoriously skeptical designer Michael Frith. "When [Jim] chose Paul Williams to do the music for *Emmet Otter,* did he know what a brilliant, brilliant contribution Paul was gonna make?" Frith said later. "There's just one wonderful song after another." "We all *love* the music in this show," Jim wrote to Williams immediately afterward, "and think it all works fantastically well." While it was the hymnal "Where the River Meets the Sea" that gave *Emmet* heart, Jim's guilty pleasure was the hard-rocking song Williams had written for the rival River Bottom Nightmare Band, which Jim, Oz, Nelson, Goelz, and Hunt performed with snarling relish. Laughed Williams, "I think there's some little piece of Jim Henson's soul that just wanted to be in . . . some nasty rock and roll [band]!"

Filming began in earnest on March 13, 1977, when Jim and his crew took over one of the larger television studios in Toronto. Here the Muppet designers—keeping an eye on drawings by Frith—had constructed most of *Emmet*'s world, including an enormous Frogtown Hollow set, with a real river snaking through it. The lighting crew had set up a sunrise and sunset that ran on regularly timed cycles throughout the day, leaving the sets aglow in soft morning purple and, later, blazing evening orange. Real grass, covered in artificial snow, was used to dress the set, though to Jim's amusement, the studio lights were so warm that the grass began to turn green and sprout through the fake snow. It was big and impressive, and Jim was clearly proud of it, slowly strolling the set's quaint Main Street in his leather jacket and wide-brimmed hat, looking as if he had stepped directly onto his set from a spaghetti western.

Other sets were just as painstakingly designed. "*Emmet Otter* was the first time we got into elaborate sets where we had floors in the interiors and we could take a wide shot with characters coming up through holes in the floor, and we'd remove parts of the floor and have the characters moving through space in waist shots," said Jim. "That was the most elaborate production we'd gotten into at that point." Said Jerry Nelson, who performed Emmet, "This was a way of working that we had done before, but never on the scope of this production—particularly because there was a huge, fifty-foot-long river."

The puppetry itself was typically flawless, with a few flashy moments: there was Kermit pedaling a bike again, as well as Muppets driving snowmobiles and jalopies, and the *How'd they do that?* moment utilizing Fazakas's remote-controlled singing and rowing Emmet—an illusion "so perfect and so beautiful," said Frith admiringly, "because you knew darn well—at least at some subliminal level—that there was no puppeteer down there in the river with his hand up inside this rowboat doing that!" The performers also had more to be particular about than any previous Muppet production; for the first time, said Jim, "we were looking for realistic movement and animals that looked like animals. They still had cartoon-like features, but we were looking for three-dimensional animals out in the real world." With this in mind, Jim would film certain sequences over and over again if he didn't think they were convincing enough, or if he decided a character was moving too much like a puppet and not enough like a real animal. "Working as I do with the movement of puppet creatures, I'm always struck by the feebleness of our efforts to achieve naturalistic movement," said Jim later. Consequently, when a puppet bird flew "too straight," Jim rolled tape over and over again until he had it right, at last remarking quietly, "Very nice."

Shooting for *Emmet* lasted twelve days, followed by eight more days of editing at the end of March. Jim had invested over $525,000 of his own money on *Emmet* and he and the Muppet performers were rightfully very proud of the project. "Everything about that production was magic," said Nelson; Goelz, who had played Emmet's porcupine friend Wendell, called it "one of the highlights of my career." And yet, incredibly, after completing the final mix in April, Jim couldn't spark the interest of a single television network. Brillstein would make the rounds, eventually getting it aired on Canadian television in December 1977, but Jim would have to wait more than a year before *Emmet Otter* made its American debut— and even then it would only show up on HBO, a subscription cable channel with a minuscule viewership at that time.

In the meantime, Jim spent the rest of the spring zipping between New York and London, meeting with the Muppet designers in the Elstree workshop, presiding over a company meeting at Tavern on the Green, cutting together an official *Muppet Show* record, and marking Kermit the Frog's birthday with a celebratory appearance on *Dinah Shore*. At home, he had finally relented to thirteen-year-old Brian's pleas for a motorcycle, and had decided that both he and

Brian would each get bikes and learn to ride together. Unfortunately, Jim's knowledge and passion for cars didn't carry over to motorcycles, and he ended up purchasing a gigantic bike with a tiny engine built for rough-and-tumble enduro racing. Brian, who had simply wanted a dirt bike, could barely sit astride it, and Jim's own enthusiasm waned quickly. "I don't think he ever rode the bike," Brian recalled with a laugh.

On May 8, 1977, Jim headed for London to begin production on the second season of *The Muppet Show*, once again taking the *Queen Elizabeth 2* from New York—and paying to take most of the members of *The Muppet Show*'s creative staff with him. Jim was positively beaming as the ship pulled out into the open waters of the Atlantic. "It was such a good time for him," said Juhl. Whether it was a good time for everyone else, however, the writer couldn't say. Juhl, who had spent his 1971 vacation writing scripts and outlines with Jim, understood all too well Jim's inability to sit still. "We have all these days when there is nothing happening out at sea . . . and we worked like fools!" said Juhl. "That's a typical Jim Henson vacation."

In the six months Jim had been away from London, *The Muppet Show* had slowly but steadily been building a following with British audiences. In 1976, the Rita Moreno episode had been submitted by ATV as a nominee for the prestigious Golden Rose of Montreux Award—perhaps the most important international festival in television—and had won, beating out entries from twenty-nine other countries. That had given the show the gloss of critical and artistic gravitas it needed to catch the eye of the press, but more than anything, British viewers themselves had been loyal and patient. To build an audience, Jim said, "we needed time"—and the TV audience in Britain had stuck with the show week after week, even as local programmers, in a move reminiscent of WRC's treatment of *Sam and Friends* over a decade ago, bounced the show from time slot to time slot.

Initially, *The Muppet Show* had been consigned to England's "family time," airing on Saturdays at 5:15, a relatively dead zone of

TV time—and yet, as a reporter from the *Evening Standard* was quick to note, every television set on display at Harrod's department store was tuned to *The Muppet Show,* with a throng of shoppers and employees crowded around to watch. Sensing they had a winner, the network moved the show to Sunday evenings, traditionally a ratings stronghold, though *The Muppet Show*'s 7:00 P.M. time slot still put it well outside peak viewing hours. Nonetheless, it became the number two show in the United Kingdom, only narrowly trailing the hugely popular *Bruce Forsyth and the Generation Game*. Its following was so large and loyal, in fact, that when Granada TV in Manchester moved the show from Sunday evening to the less popular Saturday night, network executives were disparaged in the *Evening Mail* as "Muppet Murderers" and the program was wisely moved back to its Sunday time slot.

As a result, when Jim arrived back in London that May, *The Muppet Show* was already being watched weekly by 15 million faithful Britons. Fan mail poured into the Muppet Suite at Elstree, burying Jim's desk until his return. *The Muppet Show Album,* scarcely a month old, was speeding up British music charts, and would knock *The Beatles Live at the Hollywood Bowl* from the number one spot by summer (meanwhile, back in the United States, the album would never even crack the Top 100, reaching only 153). And like the Beatles whom he had displaced on the music charts, Jim suddenly found himself—and the Muppets—in the middle of a fan and media frenzy that surprised even him. "It's like they're creating this 'Muppetmania' thing," Jim said with just a hint of exasperation. But what did he expect? "The show was a big smash hit," said Jerry Nelson plainly. The first week back at Elstree, the shuttle bus Jim used to ferry the Muppet team around the area—emblazoned with *The Muppet Show* logo on the sides—was mobbed by fans at a traffic light. In Parliament, several members of the House of Commons would "rendezvous secretly" each Monday morning "to discuss the weekend show." It was even reported in the *Daily Express* that the entire staff of the Russian embassy in London would gather around the embassy's lone TV to watch the show, peering in on Kermit and the Muppets at a time when most Western television shows were prohibited in the Soviet Union.

"It's fantastic the way the Muppets have really taken off," Jim told the *Daily Mirror*—but British journalists were just as interested in the Muppet performers, profiling Jim and "the Muppet Men" as if they were pop stars. Jim was demure about his own celebrity. "I don't think or talk about superstars," he told one journalist. "A lot of the credit for the Muppets must go to Lew Grade for putting money and faith in us." But once the subject of money had been broached, Jim was typically reluctant to discuss numbers, and parried efforts to speculate on how much he and the Muppets might be worth. "Really, money doesn't concern me at all. I'm only worried about getting each show right."

Regardless of Jim's deflection on the matter, it wasn't just the show that was successful; Muppet-related merchandise was booming in the U.K. as well—during the first four years of the show, British merchandising alone would take in more than $25 million. As was his habit with any Muppet-related *Sesame Street* merchandise, Jim took it upon himself to act as his own quality control, personally authorizing the licenses for any Muppet products himself, signing off on puzzles, jack-in-the-boxes, and T-shirts, but rejecting other products with artwork or materials he considered "shabby." "I feel I owe it to the many people who think of the Muppets as personal friends to keep the standards high," Jim explained. "The most common comment people make [is] that Kermit . . . and all the other Muppets seem to be real people. That is very gratifying to me, but it also means I have a big responsibility. . . . After all, they've become real people to me, too, and I like them too much to let anyone take advantage of them."

The huge success of the show also made the job of landing guest stars that much easier. By the second season, said Jerry Juhl, "there were times when the stars would call *us*. It was the thing to do." Letters from agents and publicists flooded into Lazer's suite at Elstree or Brillstein's office in California, every one offering their client as an ideal guest, and assuring Jim that their client "adored" the Muppets. Some of these appeals were successful; Brillstein booked Kenny Rogers as a guest during *The Muppet Show*'s fourth season after receiving an imploring telegram. There were also intriguing offers from nontraditional entertainers like the opera singer Régine Crespin, who wanted to be on the program ("I love that show!" she gushed) and the humor writer Erma Bombeck. And each week, Jim and Lazer would make lengthy—and expensive—long-distance phone calls to Brillstein to gauge the agent's reaction to the countless letters and telegrams and postcards. "Bernie was a rock, an anchor for show business for us," said Lazer. "He kept us real. We were in London and he would [tell us] what's entertaining now, what the networks want."

Jim also wrote down his own list of dream guests—and urged the Muppet writers and performers to do the same—filling pages and pages of his yellow notepads with columns of names. On one page, Jim put together a list of puppeteers and personal influences he wanted on the show, including two—Señor Wences and Edgar Bergen—that he eventually got, as well as some tantalizing possibilities in those he didn't, such as Bil Baird, Shari Lewis, Burr Tillstrom, and Stan Freberg. On another sheet, Jim took great care to note potential female guest stars, drawing up a long and somewhat quirky list that included Mae West, Mia Farrow, Princess Anne, Kim Novak, and Katharine Hepburn. At the bottom of the page, written in giggling afterthought, Jim had added Liberace's name to the list. As it turns out, it was one of the few names on this particular wish list he actually booked, with the pianist appearing during *The Muppet Show*'s third season. "Everybody had only the nicest things to say about him," Jim wrote of Liberace in his diary, though he confessed he was shocked to learn what a "surprisingly bad pianist" he was.

The dream lineup assembled by the Muppet performers and writing staff was no less quirky, though slightly hipper than Jim's somewhat stodgy list. The performers asked for interesting, slightly dangerous actors, artists, and musicians to work with, putting Dustin Hoffman, David Bowie, Salvador Dalí, Michael Caine, and Robert DeNiro near the top of their list. The writers, meanwhile, aimed even more adventurously, proposing Frank Zappa, Meryl Streep, the entire Monty Python troupe, and staggeringly, a reunited Beatles. Lazer, in fact, was convinced the Beatles could be persuaded if their schedules could be accommodated—and with Jim's encouragement, he made a serious though unsuccessful run at each member of the Fab Four, nearly securing Ringo Starr and getting at least a passing interest from Paul McCartney, who was, his representatives promised Lazer, "a great fan of the show."

Still, there were more than enough big names moving through Elstree during *The Muppet Show*'s five-year run; the second season alone featured Zero Mostel, Milton Berle, Steve Martin, John Cleese, Peter Sellers, and—in one of the most anticipated shows of the season—ballet virtuoso Rudolf Nureyev, who gamely danced with a gigantic pig in a Muppet production of "Swine Lake." "As the show kept gaining in popularity, we had a waiting list," said Brillstein. "Jim was the king of London. . . . It was a great time."

That summer, too, Jim moved into a flat on the serendipitously named Frognal Gardens, a shady, bending street lined with quaint Georgian row houses in London's Camden district, just south of Hampstead Heath. It was an area Jim came to love, strolling the steep streets, and walking or flying kites in the enormous, rambling, grassy Hampstead Heath, which came to be a special retreat for him. Some nights, if he wasn't working too late, he would put on a tuxedo and spend the evening at one of the exclusive clubs to which he belonged, often taking Lazer or any interested *Muppet Show* guest with him to have dinner and play craps or blackjack until late into the night. "He *loved* all that James Bond kinda stuff," recalled Cheryl Henson.

While Jim wasn't normally a high-stakes gambler, he could be a gutsy player—and one evening, during a hot streak playing craps, he chose to let his money ride for much of the night and ended up winning $10,000. For Jim, though, the gambling experience itself—putting on a tuxedo, walking into a smoky club, and sidling up to the craps table—was more exciting than the outcome; losing didn't matter, and any winnings were cheerfully regarded as a kind of unearned income. "It's a kind of equanimity that he really cultivated," said Lisa Henson, "so that if he lost money, it would mean nothing." Still, watching Jim build a big pot could be nerve-racking. Lisa recalled another evening when Jim spent most of the night at the blackjack table, building a sizable pile of chips—"and I just took the chips off the table," she said, "and he was like, 'Oh, come on!' and I said, 'All right, you can keep gambling with what you have, but I'll be taking this for later!'" Rather than pocket the money for himself, then, gambling winnings were usually reserved for upscale staff retreats or entertainment for the Muppet crew—in the case of his $10,000 gambling windfall, Jim banked the money until Christmas, using it to pay for a lavish Christmas party for Henson Associates.

Jim also loved the restaurants in the Hampstead area. He wasn't much of a cook—peanut butter sandwiches and tomato soup were the extent of his culinary skills—so he ate out nearly every evening. Eventually, said Lisa, he knew "every single restaurant in Hampstead," and could steer visitors to the best restaurant, pub, or bakery for anything from crepes and pastries to French or Italian food. And there was always dessert; Jim *loved* dessert, and would end every meal by asking the waiter to bring over the dessert tray, where he would waggle his long fingers at every item. "What's that thingy?" he would ask playfully.

Despite being an ocean away from his family, Jim was an intensely devoted father—and every night, almost without fail, he would call Bedford at 6:00 P.M. New York time, so he could speak to each of the Henson children before he went to bed at midnight. "There was no question that he was totally part of our lives and our scene," said Jane, "even though he wasn't physically there." During summer breaks or school holidays, Jim would almost always have one or more of the children stay with him in London, taking them to the studio during the day and out to dinner meetings with him in the evening. Whichever child happened to be in London with him, said Lazer, "was his absolute favorite at that moment. [He had] total focus and concentration on that child."

"We all enjoyed being around him, and one of the best ways for us to be around him was to work with him," said Cheryl Henson, who spent several summers working in the ATV workshop, "because when he was working, he was always at his peak." For Jim, having his children with him was never an inconvenience. "That's great fun for me," he wrote, and he would eagerly jump into projects and other schemes with them, even committing to "go vegetarian"—at least for a while—at the encouragement of Cheryl, who had been impressed by vegetarian Bernadette Peters during her August 1977 appearance on *The Muppet Show*.

Jim returned to New York in early September 1977, just in time to spend several days taping inserts for *Sesame Street*—as he had assured Cooney and the media, the show would always be a priority—before dashing off to Los Angeles to attend the Emmy Awards. In its first season, *The Muppet Show* had been nominated in three categories—including Outstanding Comedy-Variety Series—and won one, earning Rita Moreno an Emmy for her guest appearance. Not a bad showing for a show in its first season, but privately Jim was a bit disappointed. "Up for 3," he wrote in his journal, "—only Rita won—sigh."

Regardless of the Emmy Award losses, *The Muppet Show* had grown steadily in popularity in the United States during the five months Jim had been in London, continually picking up viewers and winning over critics. Jim, too, was becoming nearly as well known as his creations. After making appearances to promote the Muppets on *The Tonight Show* or *Merv Griffin,* Jim suddenly found himself being stopped by fans as he walked in Central Park or ate in restaurants near the Muppet workshop—and had to admit he liked it. "If some people recognize me, that's enough to flatter my ego," he said sheepishly.

Suddenly, the Muppets were everywhere—in every newspaper, on every television, in every city, in every market. By Lazer's account, the Muppets were already being seen by 125 million viewers in 103 countries—and it was only their second season. Whatever channel they were on, in whatever market, they were unbeatable. When channel 11 in Chicago tried to launch a new local children's music show and put it up against the powerhouse *Muppet Show,* the reviewer at the *Chicago Sun-Times* snickered, "Dumb, dumb, dumb."

And it wasn't just children who were fans. The American Guild of Variety Artists gave the Muppets their "Entertainer of the Year" award—where they were lauded by Edgar Bergen as "the most elegant and sophisticated creation of the puppeteer's art"—while the National Association for Better Broadcasting hailed *The Muppet Show* as the year's "most creative, entertaining and refreshing new program." American soldiers and their English counterparts adopted Muppets as their mascots, flying banners emblazoned with Kermit or Miss Piggy. *People* magazine and *Good Morning America* sent reporters to shadow Jim in the workshop, dazzled by the relatively small crew that built and performed the magical Muppets.

Lazer could barely contain his glee. "[Critics] didn't feel this show could bridge the gap between kids and adults. But we knew it could. We knew it." Brillstein, too, was nearly vibrating with excitement, and wrote Jim a heartfelt note to let him know how pleased he was for him. "I guess the reason for this letter is simply to tell you that I love you," wrote the agent, "and I'm very proud of what you've accomplished . . . you're terrific and I am proud to be part of the amazing success you're having."

Jim, too, was pleased, but circumspect. Since the early 1960s, he had been drafting, drawing, writing, and pitching various iterations of *The Muppet Show,* from the rough sketches of *Zoocus* in his notebooks and the unrealized pitch for *Johnny Carson and the Muppet Machine* to the proposals and outlines that eventually became the *The Muppets Valentine Show* and *Sex and Violence.* Now that he finally had *The Muppet Show,* he was ready to move on.

Jon Stone, who was still working with Jim on *Sesame Street,* thought he understood Jim's creative wanderlust. "He was restless," said Stone. "And Jim would've been restless if he'd lived to a hundred and nine. . . . He would never be satisfied to stay where he was. He was always pushing the limits." Added Lazer, "He'd want to move on to another phase. . . . That's what kept him doing this. . . . If he didn't have that other thing, he would be bored. But he never stopped thinking or going beyond."

To Jim, then, the next step was obvious. He had conquered television; now he was going to make a movie.

CHAPTER TEN

LIFE'S LIKE A MOVIE

1977–1979

Frank Oz, Jim, Dave Goelz, and Jerry Nelson perform on their backs
in the baking sun for 1979's The Muppet Movie. *
Jim was delighted by its success.*

ON A BRISK NOVEMBER MORNING IN 1977—THE TUESDAY JUST BEFORE Thanksgiving—Jim left his flat in Frognal Gardens and slid into the backseat of a hired car for the twenty-minute ride to Elstree. He and the Muppet crew were in the middle of a hectic week; on Monday evening, they had made a triumphant appearance at the prestigious Royal Variety Performance ("Last night," Jim had written with near audible glee in his private diary, "I met the Queen of England—*ta dah!*"). Now they would spend the next three days packing in tapings for two episodes of *The Muppet Show* before taking a short break for Thanksgiving—and on Thanksgiving Day, a gigantic Kermit the

Frog balloon would glide over the crowd during the Macy's Thanksgiving Day Parade in New York. As the car moved north through London, Jim's driver asked, "Did you ever, in your wildest dreams, think you would have success like this?"

Jim had no doubt about his answer. "The honest answer to this," he explained later, "which I do occasionally admit, is that yes, I've always known that I would be very successful in anything I decided to do—and it turned out to be puppetry. And not only am I not surprised, but I'm disappointed that it's taken this long, and I haven't begun to be as successful as I will be."

That response would have been no surprise to Jane, who had been impressed by Jim's quiet resolve and self-confidence since the very beginning. "Jim's way of operating and his way of thinking was extraordinary," said Jane. "I met him when he was eighteen and it was already in place. . . . And even by eighteen he was convinced he was going to be successful." And yet, "his dilemma," said Jane, "was, 'Why is it taking so long to be successful?'"

Like his protagonist in *Time Piece,* Jim still felt he was racing against a ticking clock to get everything done. As Jon Stone had said, Jim would have been restless if he'd lived to be 109—and one had only to look at Jim's schedule that winter to see a man trying to do it all. During eight weeks in London, Jim had wrapped up work on eleven episodes of *The Muppet Show,* participated in the Royal Variety Performance, and taped new television specials with Julie Andrews and Bob Hope. On December 16, he flew back to New York long enough to host two Christmas parties, went skiing for five days, then spent ten days in early 1978 working on inserts for *Sesame Street.* "Jim was the hardest working man I have ever met," said Muppet performer Caroll Spinney, who was also astounded at how little sleep Jim seemed to need. Spinney recalled once leaving a party with Jim in the wee hours of the morning, and asking whether he was at all concerned about getting up in time to make a 9:00 A.M. taping. Jim laughed; he'd be ready, he told Spinney, because he had a breakfast meeting to attend first. "He loved what he did so much, I don't think he thought of it as work," said Spinney. "It was the way he lived. . . . He was like a juggler who could keep twenty things in the air at the same time."

By late 1977, one of those things was a movie—and not just "*The Muppet Show* on film," as Jim put it, but rather "the flip side of *The Muppet Show*." Instead of bringing a live guest into the world of the Muppets, Jim explained, "we are taking the Muppets out into the real world." It was an ambitious idea. Puppets had played supporting roles on the big screen before—puppeteer Lou Bunin had provided the puppetry and stop motion effects for a 1950 version of *Alice in Wonderland,* while Bil Baird had performed the memorable marionette sequence in *The Sound of Music.* But no one had ever filmed a full-length movie with puppets as the main characters, interacting with real people in the real world. "Jim was a dreamer," said Jerry Juhl, and yet "he was pragmatic enough to make the dream happen."

Fortunately for Jim, Lord Grade was much the same way—and when Jim approached the ATV chief in late 1977 to discuss the possibility of financing a Muppet movie, he found Grade remarkably receptive. Grade, said Bernie Brillstein, "was the only one who understood" Jim's conviction that the Muppets could work on the big screen, and listened and nodded enthusiastically as Jim made his pitch. It wasn't until Jim mentioned the budget he had in mind that Grade finally arched an eyebrow. At a time when most Disney movies were budgeted at just over a million dollars, Jim was asking for $8 million for his film. As always, Jim's "whim of steel" was tough to resist. "Lew Grade, being a true gentleman, went ahead with it," said Brillstein admiringly.

What Grade didn't know was that Jim already had in the planning stages not just one movie, but *two*—and typically, Jim would juggle both projects at once. Even as he set to work on a rough story outline for *The Muppet Movie* with *Muppet Show* writer Jack Burns, Jim had already been talking for months with British fantasy artist Brian Froud about collaborating on some sort of yet-to-be-determined fantasy film. While *The Muppet Movie* would be the priority, the fantasy film would be Jim's pet project, a creative sandbox where he hoped to build and play and extend puppetry beyond the Muppets.

It had started with a drawing. "I saw Brian Froud's work in a couple of books, and I loved what he did," said Jim. Froud—a puckish, bespectacled Englishman with a mop of curly hair—didn't so much draw as he *conjured,* sketching out beautiful, ethereal worlds populated by trolls and fairies and elves and ogres, all penciled in a highly detailed, sumptuous style with a vaguely Victorian shimmer. Froud honestly believed in fairies, and it showed; his work was brimming with mood and atmosphere, and Jim was enchanted with Froud's vision—he had been particularly taken with a drawing of a young adventurer gazing up into a waterfall cascading over a carved troll—and couldn't wait to start bringing his drawings to life. "The thought of being able to take those designs and convert them into three dimensions," Jim said, "was really exciting."

Even before meeting Jim, Froud was already considering doing some sort of project featuring tangible versions of his illustrations, and puppetry seemed the ideal art form to bring his visions to life. Jim had brought Froud to the Muppet workshop at Elstree over the summer so he could see how the Muppet builders worked, and Froud had been immediately intrigued by the Land of Gortch puppets performed on *Saturday Night Live,* with their mossy bodies and glistening taxidermy eyes. It was enough to convince Froud that Jim was his man. "Make deal with BRIAN FROUD to do great film," Jim wrote excitedly in his journal in August 1977. The enthusiastic agreement that would eventually spawn *The Dark Crystal* was in place.

Things would begin to take a bit of shape in early 1978, when Jim and Froud began an extended series of morning meetings in New York to try to determine what their movie would be about. "I'm very enthused," wrote Jim in his diary. Rather than trying to develop a story first—never Jim's strongest suit—he was more interested in fleshing out the underlying concept, as well as the look and feel of the world and the characters inhabiting it. He found a willing collaborator in Froud, who filled the backgrounds of his art with intriguing, often unnoticed, details. "When I talked to Brian about the possibility of handing him the whole conceptual side of the project—so that he would be responsible for the look of all the characters and sets, the whole world—I think he found that a delightful challenge." That approach, while artistically satisfying, still didn't result in much beyond a vague description of "a pantheistic world in which mountains sang to one another and forests were alive."

With that sort of worldview, then, it was perhaps fitting that it was a snowstorm that finally nudged Jim into drafting the first rough story outline for the film. In early February, as Jim and sixteen-year-old Cheryl were preparing to leave for London on the Concorde, a massive snowstorm dumped two feet of snow on New York, stranding the two of them at John F. Kennedy Airport. "I was trying to figure out how I could find a few days to work on [the story outline]," Jim recalled later, "and there it was!" He and Cheryl checked into the Howard Johnson's motel next to the airport and spent two days writing. "I really had a delightful time working on the concept—and talking it over with Cheryl," wrote Jim in his diary, "and it all jelled during that time, so that I'm quite happy with the way it has begun taking shape." It was only a skeleton of a story, but he and Cheryl had fleshed out some of the basic plot elements, including the central idea "for the evil characters to be a split from the good characters." "All kinds of things came together," wrote Jim. They had even come up with a name for the film: *The Crystal*. It was a good start.

Jim finally made it to London by Valentine's Day, commuting from his flat in Frognal Gardens to the workshop at Elstree in a brand-new Kermit-green Lotus with a license plate reading KERMIT, a gift to him from Lord Grade to celebrate their success. "I love it!" Jim wrote excitedly in his diary. "I've always enjoyed cars—and I enjoy being in love with my car." It was lean and low-slung, and Jim "looked like he belonged in that car," said Lazer. "He loved it."

In New York, builders were at work on a new full-body walk-around Muppet for *Sesame Street*, a large shaggy dog named Barkley, while in London, production was ramping up for the third season of *The Muppet Show*. The success of *The Muppet Show* had meant more than just fame or high ratings; it also meant the workshop at Elstree was becoming a destination, almost a kind of Mecca, for Muppet fans. "Unlike other TV studios, [ATV is] all quite open," said *Muppet Show* director Peter Harris, "and we've had parents bringing their kids in to watch it all happening." Tours of Studio D and the Muppet workshop became so popular, in fact, that Jim had to put up a sign in the workshop politely asking visitors not to "fondle, molest, handle, touch or tweak" any of the two hundred Muppets hanging neatly on pegs around the room ("They *hate* being tweaked," joked Jim). On any given day, there could be several different versions of Kermit being clothed or repaired on workbenches, which led more than one tourist to ask which puppet was the *real* Kermit. "They're *all* the real one," Jim would grin in response.

While he tolerated visitors to the set, producer David Lazer would wince when tourists began taking photos of Muppets hanging lifelessly on the studio walls. He didn't like for people to see the puppets looking, as he called it, "dead." That never bothered Jim, who could still toss a Muppet on a bench or the floor as easily as he had tossed members of the *Sam and Friends* cast into the Henson toy boxes. Caroll Spinney remembered being shocked when Jim once pulled Ernie off his arm and casually cast the character aside. Spinney scooped up the discarded puppet, cradled it in his arms and assured Ernie that Jim "hadn't meant" to do it. When Spinney explained to Jim that he *always* apologized to a dropped puppet, Jim could only smile; to Jim, they were simply tools of their craft. "I'm not sentimental about them," he told Spinney.

In the past year, workshop staff had grown from twelve designers and builders to more than twenty, split between New York and London. The London workshop was now overseen by Amy van Gilder, a vivacious designer and builder who had been assigned the post following the departure of Bonnie Erickson, who left to form her own company. It had been an emotional farewell for Erickson. "I cried; Jim didn't," she said later, laughing. For Jim, it was just the natural progression of things—people came, people went. "This is what you need to do," he told her, "and we're not going to lose touch." They never did. "Jim always said that you are where you are because that's where you need to be," said Erickson, "and if you need to move on, you will move on. . . . He was not worried that people went off to do their own thing because he knew that other people were coming in. He felt it was really important to have fresh, new ideas."

The new year would bring another loss that was more heartbreaking. On February 20, forty-nine-year-old Don Sahlin was found dead in his ransacked New York City apartment. Police never determined if Sahlin had been the victim of a crime; instead, the cause of death was listed as fatty liver—but either conclusion was puzzling. Muppet builders had long grown used to Sahlin's habit of leaving the Muppet workshop each day at 4:30 and climbing into a cab at the end of the block, then enigmatically returning to the workshop hours later. When asked where he went, Sahlin would only insist it was a personal matter. "Don was extremely private," said Dave Goelz. "He was always claiming [health issues], but it seemed like a joke."

Lazer, who had taken the call from Sahlin's family in the Muppet Suite, delivered the news to Jim as gently as he could. "He just stared at me," said Lazer. "His jaw dropped, his mouth just opened, and he stared." As the news spread through the Muppet organization, everyone seemed to naturally gravitate toward the workshop that Sahlin had called home. Oz remembered Jim and the Muppet team lingering in the workshop in stunned silence. "I was standing there crying, I was really angry," said Oz. But Jim didn't cry. Lazer thought perhaps Jim didn't want to be seen crying in front of staff—"He thought maybe showing feelings was like a weakness at times," offered Lazer—but that wasn't it, either.

Oz—who knew Jim perhaps better than anyone—understood. "Jim said, 'It's okay, we'll see Don again,'" said Oz, "and he really believed it." It was yet another facet of Jim's self-proclaimed ridiculous optimism. "In some ways, he didn't allow himself to *not* be an optimist," said Jane—and Jim took comfort in the firm belief that, somehow or other, whether on another plane of existence or perhaps in another life, he and Sahlin would work and play together once more. "I'm sure he will go on and do many more things," Jim wrote of Sahlin in the days following his death, "and I'm sure we will be together again sometime—for there is certainly a loving and creative bond between us." Four days later, Jim, Lazer, Oz, and Goelz took the Concorde from London to New York to attend Sahlin's funeral, returning to London that same evening. Shortly thereafter, Jim would honor Sahlin by dedicating one of the memorial benches in Hampstead Heath to the Muppet builder's memory. Life would go on, but Sahlin's death, said Oz, "was a huge, massive impact for us personally and professionally."

Production on *The Muppet Show*'s third season began in London in early April. The Muppet cast had expanded again, with the addition of the characters like the boomerang-fish-throwing Lew Zealand—performed by Nelson in what he called his "Frankie Fontaine voice"—and the earnest Beauregard the janitor, a character Goelz loved, but whose passive nature frustrated Muppet writers. With the Muppet cast growing, Jim had also decided to hire additional performers—and late in the second season had brought in a young English actress named Louise Gold, who had interviewed with Jim at the encouragement of her agent, who thought her dynamic voice might make up for her initial lack of puppetry skills. He was right, though Gold always joked that she had been hired mainly because, at five foot nine, she was one of the few women tall enough to perform alongside the taller male performers. Nevertheless, Gold took to puppetry quickly, performing right hands with Jim before moving on to characters of her own before the season was over, including Annie Sue, Miss Piggy's adoring—and aspiring—rival with the big singing voice.

Like Fran Brill on *Sesame Street*, Gold had immediately fit in with the *Muppet Show* performers. "Everyone here's lovely," she told the British newspapers, admitting that "puppeteering is a very difficult craft to do really well." Her major strength as a performer—and one of her most endearing traits—was an ability to see almost anything, including herself, as slightly silly, an outlook she shared with Jim. "She was just out there and ready to make fun of herself," said Brian Henson, "and she was adorable."

Another new performer, hired just before work began on the third season, was an eighteen-year-old puppeteer and Muppet enthusiast from Atlanta named Steve Whitmire, who, at the urging of Caroll Spinney, had boldly cold-called the New York Muppet workshop and landed an audition. As it turned out, Jane Henson had been on her way south to inspect the Kermit the Frog balloon being constructed for the 1977 Macy's Thanksgiving Day Parade, and offered to meet Whitmire at the Atlanta airport for an audition and interview. Whitmire showed up with a cardboard footlocker full of puppets he had performed on Atlanta television—reminiscent of Jim, who had lugged black boxes of Muppets from one job to another—but "there really was no place [to talk]," recalled Jane, "so we sat down in a little café kind of place, and he pulled out a puppet."

With diners and coffee drinkers looking on, Whitmire and his puppet began chatting with several delighted children seated nearby. "I was just so impressed with the way he handled the situation," said Jane, who recommended that Jim personally interview the young puppeteer. Jane's instincts—as usual—were right, and after a brief interview with Jim, Whitmire was hired and dispatched to London to join *The Muppet Show* team in the spring of 1978. Like Gold, he would spend time performing right hands and background puppets before being given recurring characters like Miss Piggy's dog, Foo Foo, and Rizzo the Rat.

Jim believed that puppetry—especially the Muppet brand of puppetry—required the same kind of serious time and training that great actors devoted to their craft. "Muppet operators must be good actors, good technicians, preferably good singers . . . and occasionally good dancers. It's like being a television star by proxy." Jim was committed to the idea of his performers learning by doing, serving apprenticeships of right hands and background characters, then being handed more and more responsibilities and visible roles as their skills improved. "One thing about being a puppeteer is it really takes a long time to learn how to do it," said Jim. "And people who join us, you usually have to do it for about a year before the puppetry gets sort of good enough to be able to handle major parts." Ultimately, said Jim, "I like working collaboratively with people. I have a terrific group of people who work with me, and I think of the work that we do as 'our' work."

By the third season of *The Muppet Show*, however, more and more of the media's hurricane was revolving around the show's break-out star—Miss Piggy—and, consequently, on her performer, Frank Oz. Oz claimed he scarcely noticed the attention lavished on Piggy—"I had other characters to do, after all," he said coyly—and Jim, too, seemed unfazed, generously praising Oz as "probably the person most responsible for the Muppets being funny." But for some Muppet performers, long used to the collegial atmosphere Jim encouraged on the set, it was tough to see one puppeteer promoted above the rest.

Richard Hunt, who had worked alongside Jim and Oz for eight

years, admitted to hurt feelings. Both Oz and Jim, he thought, were "distancing themselves" from the rest of the performers as the Muppets grew in popularity. "It was very hard on us," said Hunt, "especially Jerry [Nelson, who] was very equal with them" as a performer on *Sesame Street*. At one point, Nelson had even confronted Jim at a party, demanding to know why he wasn't being used more—a question Jim left hanging in the air. (Lazer later said it was because Nelson—at times emotionally ragged and admittedly drinking too much while coping with the challenges of raising a child with cystic fibrosis—had a tendency to "freeze a little bit.") For his own part, said Hunt, "I knew I was a great supporting player . . . but Jim and Frank had separated themselves and that in turn was at the expense of some of the others." Still, Hunt tried to be diplomatic. "Jim owned the company, and Frank was an essential. . . . You can't focus on everyone."

Oz understood the bruised feelings. "I was the workhorse, the go-to guy," he said. "I would say to Jim, 'You've got to give stuff to the other guys!' I worked really hard—Jim and I worked hard—but I sometimes felt I was getting all the work, and I know the other guys did, too." Performances aside, there were other divisive differences as well. For one thing, Oz had the additional perk of receiving a "creative consultant" credit on *The Muppet Show*, which meant, as Oz described it, "I didn't write, but I got to sit in on all the writing sessions and meetings and didn't get thrown out. And I would let them know when I thought something didn't work." That was putting it mildly. "He would sit right with the writers . . . and he would just slash line after line to condense it," said Lazer, "and the writers resented it, but they knew it was for their own good, too, because if the character was great, they were great."

In many respects, the elevation of Oz was due to Lazer, who made the decision to provide Oz with his own dressing room, as well as with his own separate performance credit, tagging "and Frank Oz" at the end of the alphabetical list of Muppet performers in *The Muppet Show*'s closing credits. "The other people resented it," Lazer admitted later, but he never regretted the decision. Oz was responsible for too many of the major Muppet characters, and Lazer "wanted to give Frank this kind of respect." Hunt may have rolled his eyes, but he eventually came to understand that treating Oz with a certain level of respect didn't mean Jim didn't value the rest of his team. "There's a sub-level that makes you think that, 'Well, these are the *important* ones, and we're just here,'" Hunt said later. "It took me years to realize the untruth of that."

Ultimately, thought Lazer, the dynamics between the Muppet performers were much like the dynamics between the Muppets themselves. "[The Muppets] may be fighting with one another and have interpersonal problems, but they were always united in their support of one another," said Lazer. "And this is what Jim does. There's always a little hell going on, because everyone's vying for Jim's attention. But somehow, when he pulled it together, we'd support one another and we'd go on."

And go on they did, sprinting through a frantic spring schedule in which they completed eight episodes of *The Muppet Show* in six weeks. As the show entered its third season, the Muppets were more popular than ever, and ITC's Abe Mandell gleefully reported that *The Muppet Show* had now been sold in 106 countries, with a total audience of 235 million (a number Henson Associates willingly circulated, even as some privately joked that Mandell would soon be claiming a viewership larger than the world's population). It could even be seen by millions of viewers inside the Soviet sphere, including Hungary and Romania, where the show ran with subtitles, and East Germany, which dubbed the episodes in the native language ("I hope they manage to make the jokes funny," Jim said nervously. "A language gap is always a problem.") "[It's] almost certainly the most popular television entertainment now being produced on Earth," declared *Time* magazine matter-of-factly, and called Jim "the rarest of creatures in the imitative and adaptive world of entertainment: an originator." To others, he was, quite simply, "the new Walt Disney." Jim would likely have argued that he wasn't—at least not yet. Disney had conquered film, then moved into television. Jim had conquered TV, but had yet to make the leap onto the big screen. But now, with work on the first half of the third season of *The Muppet Show* completed in mid-May, Jim's march toward the movie screen wouldn't take much longer.

Earlier in the spring, Jim had brought in Jerry Juhl to polish Jack

Burns's rough movie script, hoping that by stirring the two together, the final mix would capture both Burns's rat-a-tat joke sensibilities and Juhl's warmth for the characters. Paul Williams, too, had been pressed back into service, though after his positive experience of working with Jim on *Emmet Otter,* it didn't take much persuading for Jim to get Williams on board. "Working with Jim Henson was probably the easiest collaboration of my life," said Williams later. "[He] had a sweetness about him, and I don't think he ever got emotionally pulled off course. But I've also never worked with anybody who spent less time over my shoulder." Jim never even insisted on hearing demos of the songs as Williams wrote them, merely shrugging that he would "hear them in the studio" when he showed up to record them. Williams's only other request, then—and one that Jim willingly granted—was that he be permitted to work with composer Kenny Ascher, allowing Williams to fully devote himself to writing the songs while Ascher undertook the more time-consuming task of scoring them.

Throughout May and June, Jim jetted back and forth between Los Angeles and New York, sometimes twice a week, to finalize the script, oversee production of the sets in California, and meet with director James Frawley, who had spent several days with Jim in London early in the spring to get a feel for the Muppet sensibilities. Jim had wanted to direct *The Muppet Movie* himself, but had been grudgingly persuaded by the argument that it was better to have an experienced director at the helm of the Muppets' first foray into film. "Up until that time they had never shot film. They had only shot tape, and they had never shot outside the studio," said Frawley. "So [Jim] knew that he needed somebody who was a filmmaker and knew what to do with the camera." Juhl—who had swallowed his own pride when the more experienced Burns had been installed as head writer of *The Muppet Show* in its first season—understood Jim's disappointment at being bumped in favor of Frawley. "[It] was actually a very frustrating experience for him in that he wanted to direct," said Juhl. "*So* much. It drove him crazy."

Regardless, Frawley—who had headed up several small comedies like *The Big Bus* and *The Christian Licorice Store*—was a fine choice. With a visual sensibility similar to Jim's—he had cut his

teeth directing episodes of *The Monkees,* where he employed the
same sort of quick-cut editing style Jim had used on *Time Piece*—
and a low-key sense of humor honed by several years in an improv
troupe, Frawley and Jim were a good fit. "He felt pretty good about
my sense of humor," remembered Frawley. "It seemed like a good
combination of talents for his Muppets. I had a very childlike approach to my work, and the Muppets fit in well with that."

One of the first orders of business was to see how the Muppets
would look when they were filmed outside, in the real world, under
natural light instead of the more controlled, and forgiving, environment of the television studio. On a gray, drizzly spring day, Jim, Oz,
and Frawley piled into Jim's car and drove north into the English
countryside, pulling over to film anything remotely interesting. With
Frawley's camera rolling, Jim and Oz poked Kermit, Fozzie, Piggy,
and Animal up into the low branches of trees, peeked them around
corners, sat them behind the wheel of the car, and chatted with real
cows, who stared at Kermit so intently that Jim broke down in giggles. "We're taking the characters out of the show and bringing them
into the real world," Jim later explained. "Nobody has ever done
anything like this using our technique." After reviewing the nearly
fifteen minutes of footage, they proclaimed themselves "very excited" with the results. It was going to work—just as Jim had known
it would.

During the final week of June 1978, Jim hopscotched across the
country one more time, attending Lisa's high school graduation ceremony in New York—she had already been accepted to Harvard, an
accomplishment Jim noted proudly in his journal with the appropriate number of exclamation points—then spent two days in Lubbock,
Texas, at a Puppeteers of America convention, before finally arriving
at Bernie Brillstein's beach house in Los Angeles just in time to celebrate the Fourth of July. The next morning—a bright and sunny
Wednesday—cameras rolled on *The Muppet Movie.*

For eighty-seven days over the summer and fall of 1978, Jim and
the Muppet performers sweated in the sun on locations in California
and New Mexico, rolling around on their backs on furniture dollies

or chairs with the legs cut off and wheels attached—almost anything that would roll and keep them out of the view of Frawley's cameras. While the big screen allowed the Muppets the space to move about freely in the real world—many times out in the open where even their lower bodies could finally be seen—keeping the Muppet performers hidden from view required them to squeeze into even tighter and more claustrophobic spaces than ever. For some scenes, rectangular pits would be dug in which the puppeteers would stand to perform. Other times, the pits would be covered with a piece of plywood—which would then be covered by sand or dirt—and the puppeteers would stick their arms up through holes in the wood, watching themselves on monitors from their shallow underground crypt. As a first-time director of puppeteers, Frawley was surprisingly in tune with the physical demands placed on the performers. Jim, who had once made a particularly inconsiderate director stand holding his arm over his head for ten minutes to understand the pain involved in performing, found a sympathetic ally in Frawley, who would call out "Muppets relax!" between takes so the puppeteers could rest their aching arms and shoulders. "If you don't dig sore arms," said Richard Hunt, "don't work with puppets."

In Frawley's view, the most difficult sequences were those in which the Muppets drove or rode in cars. "[The Muppets] had never been shot outdoors, or in a car or real locations," said Frawley, "and we pretty much had to invent it as we went along. Every shot had never been done before, because nobody had taken Fozzie Bear and Miss Piggy and Kermit and put them in a Studebaker." With four puppeteers and their monitors scrunched together in the front seat just under the dashboard, there was no room for a driver—so Frawley's solution was to rig the car so it could be driven from the trunk by a stunt driver who watched the road on a monitor.

But it was Jim—in what Frawley called "the single most difficult sequence to execute"—who ended up in the most cramped spot of all. In one of the film's most memorable moments, a long swooping camera shot eases out of the clouds over a swamp, floats down through the trees, and eventually closes in on Kermit, sitting on a log in the middle of the swamp, strumming a banjo and singing "Rainbow Connection"—a pitch-perfect tune written by Williams and

Ascher, who had been directed by Jim to give Kermit a song similar to "When You Wish Upon a Star" from Disney's *Pinocchio*. The take is seamless, slowly closing in on Kermit surrounded by water, in another of those *How'd they do that?* moments that Jim loved. In a similar scene in *Emmet Otter,* when Emmet and his mother had sung as they rowed a boat downriver, Jim had used remote-controlled puppets. In this case, however, the puppetry is so flawless—Kermit is clearly *not* radio-controlled—that it seems the only way it could possibly have been accomplished would be for Jim to have performed Kermit from underwater.

As it turns out, that's just what he did.

In a water tank on a movie studio backlot, Jim had created an enormous and entirely convincing swamp set, with real trees—shipped in from the Georgia bayous—drooping their branches into a massive tank full of muddy-looking water. Jim's idea was to sink a custom-made diving bell into the tank, lower himself inside, then perform Kermit up on the surface by sticking his arm up through a rubber sleeve in the top of the diving bell. It almost worked perfectly—but not quite. For one thing, the water in the studio tank was only four feet deep, while the diving bell being constructed—which Jim had initially intended to sink into a real swamp, before abandoning the idea—was nearly five feet tall. Rather than reconfigure the entire set with a deeper tank, Jim simply directed the construction crew to remove eighteen inches from the diving bell. It was going to make a tight fit that much tighter, but Jim wasn't worried. "Well, if I can fit," he said with a shrug, "I'll do it."

Once the diving bell was secured in place underwater and Kermit and his log were arranged on top, Jim lowered himself into the cramped space, folding himself inside swami-style, with his legs crossed, his knees up, and a monitor and a copy of the script cradled between his legs. When the top of the tank was closed and sealed, Jim could reach up through the rubber sleeve and slide his right arm inside Kermit while operating Kermit's banjo-strumming left hand with a wire rod snaked down into the diving bell. Even though oxygen was being pumped in through a hose and Jim was always in contact with the surface through his headset, it was like being buried alive—"no place for someone with claustrophobia," Jim said. Thirteen-year-old

John Henson, visiting the set for the day, thought "it was a bit frightening" watching his dad go into the tank and disappear beneath the surface of the water. At one point during the five days it took to film the sequence, Jim was sealed underwater for over three hours—and when he was finally helped out, it took some time before he could get his legs to straighten out again. But that was Jim's way, said Goelz. "[He] would never ask us to do anything that he hadn't done himself or wasn't willing to do himself."

Generally, Jim's philosophy was "simple is good"—though Jim's definition of *simple* could swing wildly. For the scenes in *The Muppet Movie* in which Kermit rides a bicycle, the simple marionette control system—used reliably on *The Muppets Valentine Show* five years earlier—was deemed unconvincing, and was scrapped in favor of a combined marionette and radio control mechanism. Perhaps more notably, in a scene in which Animal ingests one of Dr. Bunsen Honeydew's InstaGrow pills and erupts, larger than life, through the top of a building, Jim had insisted on having a gigantic Animal puppet head built, which Oz could manipulate, rather than using the regular-sized puppet on a miniature set. "We always used to kid Jim that after telling everybody 'simple is good,' he would turn around and try to produce the most complicated work in the world," said Juhl, "and just about wipe out all of us—him most of all—in the process."

The performers were genuinely excited by the prospect of working with many of the twenty-four celebrities making cameo appearances in the film, including Orson Welles (playing "Lew Lord," a nod to Lord Lew Grade), Mel Brooks, Bob Hope, Madeline Kahn, and Richard Pryor. The real thrill for the Muppet crew, however, was working with one—or maybe it was two—of Jim's boyhood idols, Edgar Bergen and Charlie McCarthy. At the behest of his daughter, Candice, Bergen had been a guest on *The Muppet Show* during its second season, where his presence alone had been nothing short of An Event. For puppeteers, Bergen was their Elvis, the one who had made their craft cool and who had inspired many of them in their chosen career. "Everybody was eagerly awaiting him," said Lazer. "I never saw our puppeteers or Jim or Frank in such awe." Watching Bergen perform, said Juhl, was like going "right back to our childhoods. It was wonderful. . . . And then, of course, the relationship between him and Jim was very special." Jim and Bergen working together, said Juhl, was "like passing on the mantle" from Bergen to Jim and the next generation of puppeteers.

Bergen wasn't well during the shooting of *The Muppet Movie*, but happily made a cameo appearance with Charlie McCarthy as judges at a beauty pageant won by Miss Piggy. It was the last footage that would ever be shot of Bergen, who died on September 30, 1978, at seventy-five. Jim spoke fondly of Bergen at his funeral that fall—"We take up where he left off, and we thank him for leaving this delightful legacy of love and humor and whimsy"—and would dedicate *The Muppet Movie* to Bergen's memory. Later, Bergen's widow, Frances, and daughter, Candice, presented Jim with a framed photograph of Bergen and Charlie engraved, "Dear Jim—Keep the Magic Alive."

As if to confirm Bergen's faith, in mid-September, *The Muppet Show*—nominated for five Emmy Awards in its second season—took home the Emmy for Outstanding Comedy-Variety or Music Series. "Received EMMY," Jim wrote in his journal, drawing a bold box around the four capital letters, and he, Lazer, Oz, and Goelz accepted the trophies on behalf of the team, beaming proudly in black tie. If the size of its viewing audience hadn't made the case already, the Muppets were now officially the best thing on television.

The Emmy excitement carried over onto the movie set where, as was their habit, the Muppet performers remained in character between takes—and Frawley more than once caught himself issuing directions to Kermit and Miss Piggy, rather than Jim or Oz, as he squinted through the camera eyepiece. Disagreements were minor and, for the most part, usually artistic in nature. At one point, Jim and Oz had gotten into a slight dustup regarding *The Muppet Movie*'s villain, a smarmy Colonel Sanders–wannabe named Doc Hopper, who aggressively pursues Kermit as the mascot for his chain of fast food frog legs restaurants. Jim was convinced that, deep down, Hopper wasn't a bad guy and that somewhere along the way, Hopper should be redeemed. "Even the most worldly of our characters is innocent," Jim had once said. "Our villains are innocent, really—and it's that innocence, I think, that is our connection to the audience." While that was likely true in most cases, Oz—who was nearly as cynical as Jim was idealistic—didn't take long to consider his response. "Bullshit," he said. Hopper would remain unredeemed.

That character point, however, was small compared to what was, quite literally, one of the biggest problems in the movie: personnel. For *The Muppet Movie*'s musical finale, Jim planned to feature more than 250 Muppet characters, representing nearly every puppet available in the New York and London Muppet workshops. When filming large crowds of Muppets on television—such as the theater audience of *The Muppet Show*—Jim had usually peppered the set with a number of motionless puppet extras, propped up in the background on wire frames or stuffed with wadding, to fill the spaces while the puppeteers performed around them. On the big screen, however, there would be no unmoving extras allowed; Jim wanted every one of his 250 puppets moving and singing, which would require a considerably higher number of hands than the core group of Muppet performers could provide.

Undeterred, Jim put out a casting call through the Los Angeles Guild of the Puppeteers of America, and managed to wrangle nearly 150 performers to supplement the Muppet team, Henson family, and film crew. Puppeteers reporting to CBS Studio Center's Stage 15— including director John Landis and a young Disney animator named Tim Burton—were handed one, sometimes two Muppets to perform, and given a number that corresponded to a chalked spot on the floor of an enormous pit, seventeen feet across and six feet deep, that had been constructed on the soundstage. Each performer found his or her appropriate space on the floor of the pit, and when Frawley called out "Muppets up!" up came a sea of colorful Muppets— including King Ploobis from *Saturday Night Live,* several characters from *Sesame Street,* and the entire River Bottom Nightmare Band from *Emmet Otter*—making up the largest puppet cast ever assembled on film.

By late October, most of the film work for *The Muppet Movie* was complete. That left Jim just enough time to return to London to tape six more installments of *The Muppet Show* before Christmas, including an exceptional episode guest-starring singer and activist Harry Belafonte. As a longtime admirer of Belafonte—Jim and Jane had attended one of his performances in Washington, D.C., on one of their early dates—Jim had worked hard to woo the showman, offering him significant creative input, and taking time off during the shooting of *The Muppet Movie* to meet with him personally. Belafonte, too, wanted his appearance to be exceptional, and proposed to Jim that the show might provide an opportunity "to take a look at the lore and history of other worlds, other places." In early November, Belafonte and the Muppet team created one of *The Muppet Show*'s most remarkable and memorable moments, a lively five minutes of song and dance to Belafonte's "Turn the World Around," celebrating the oneness of everything. Belafonte later referred to his *Muppet Show* experience as "sheer joy," and would remain friendly with Jim for the rest of his life.

With four episodes still to be completed for *The Muppet Show*'s third season in late 1978, Jim opted to spend the holidays back in the United States, throwing a Christmas party for the Muppet crew at the posh Player's Club in Manhattan, performing with Joe Raposo at a White House children's party, then skiing for several days in Vermont before heading back to London with Jane and Lisa just after the first of the year. During the previous fall, Jim had moved out of the flat in Frognal Gardens and was looking for a more permanent residence in the Hampstead area. In the meantime, at the urging of actor James Coburn, who had made a cameo appearance in *The Muppet Movie,* Jim moved into a house in Holly Village—a "darling little castle," Jane called it—owned by Coburn and girlfriend Lynsey de Paul. The Hensons stayed only long enough for Jim to wrap up the four remaining *Muppet Show* episodes—but before leaving in early February, he and Jane scouted several nearby properties as potential homes, eventually submitting a contract for a Victorian-era place in Church Row. To Jim's disappointment and slight confusion, he would lose the house to another bidder at the last minute, but vowed to keep looking.

Back in New York, however, Jim had successfully sealed the deal on a new headquarters for Henson Associates, a beautiful 1929 double townhouse at 117 East 69th Street in Manhattan. Jim had purchased the five-story building for $600,000 in November 1978, but zoning issues had slowed the renovation of the space for several months. For one thing, Jim wanted to substantially reconfigure the basement and first floor to create a spacious, bi-level Muppet workshop, with several skylights letting natural light into what would normally have been an underground area. "I want to have a place for a creative nucleus," wrote Jim—and once the zoning issues for such an ambitious remodeling were cleared, no detail was too small for Jim to lavish with care and attention. Colorful photo murals were installed in waiting areas and on landings. The Henson Associates logo—a large, lowercase HA, with an exclamation point at the end—was inlaid in brass into the marble floor of the main hall. Furniture was handcrafted, drapes were made from tie-dyed canvas or Chinese silks, and walls were painted in bright reds or warm beiges, with gold-toned trim and molding. It was a place as sprawling as Jim, as quirky as his sense of humor, and as colorful as one of his printed shirts. "I didn't want a pretentious space or one with a feeling of opulence," said Jim. "Instead, I wanted a happy, functioning space with character and warmth."

For many, though, the most memorable feature was the gleaming spiral staircase that ran up through the center of the townhouse, circling toward a large stained-glass skylight dubbed "The View from the Lily Pad," meant to reflect what Kermit might see peering up through the trees from the swamp. The staircase was both the spine and the heart of the organization—all offices and conference rooms on each floor radiated off the stairs, and Jim came to regard the open stairwell as a kind of vertical telephone, leaning over the railing from his third-floor office to call to staff on the floors above or below. The staircase, he thought, broke down the "stratification" of being located on different floors—and more often than not, Jim would hold his meetings while standing on the stairs, leaning against the curved railing with his arms folded, nodding and listening.

Formally opening the new Muppet headquarters—or One Seventeen, as it would be casually called, in deference to its street address—was only one part of a busy spring. Jim was in full publicity mode, trying to generate a buzz of anticipation for *The Muppet Movie,* scheduled for release in the coming summer. He had quickly put into production a variety show called *The Muppets Go Hollywood*—essentially an hour-long promotion for the upcoming movie—which had taken all of four weeks to write, rehearse, and tape. In April, the Muppets hosted *The Tonight Show*, and Jim had even arranged for Kermit to make a brief appearance at the end of a Cheerios commercial to remind viewers of the film. That particular bit of self-promotion had raised the hackles of Joan Cooney, who warned Jim—in a scolding reminiscent of the one administered by TV critic Jack Gould regarding Kermit's appearance as a pitchman during *Hey Cinderella!*—that using Kermit in television advertising "could cause us embarrassment [at CTW]." Jim assured Cooney that Kermit's appearance was related solely to the promotion of *The Muppet Movie* and could not in any way be construed as *Sesame Street*–related advertising. Cooney seemed less than convinced, but let the matter drop.

Jim returned to London in late April to begin work on season four of *The Muppet Show*. Mindful that much of his time in the coming year would be occupied with promoting *The Muppet Movie*, Jim worked at a breakneck pace, taping six episodes in less than a month. Some days, he got no sleep at all—and yet, to the amazement of those around him, never seemed to lose his ability to focus intently on a task or keep a level head. While crew members and production assistants were "running around screaming" and wondering how all the work could possibly get done, Jim was "wandering around in the middle of it all, perfectly calm, perfectly content," said Juhl. "If *The Muppet Show* had a basketball team, the score would always be Frog 99, Chaos 98."

As always, even with the hectic pace, Jim thrived on the work. "I love my work and because I enjoy it, it doesn't really feel like work," he said. "Thus I spend most of my time working." His ethic was contagious—"You had to try to keep up with the guy—it seemed only fair," remarked Jerry Juhl—but many of the longest-serving Muppet performers also came to understand that Jim's devotion to his work came at a personal cost. "For such a giving, generous, non-stop creative person, Jim really didn't have any friends," said Richard Hunt. "He was friends with the guys he worked with. . . . But I think he was so much involved in his work that it didn't help [or] allow him the time or the luxury of developing true, deep friendships."

Juhl thought he understood. "It isn't that Jim didn't have friends," he said, "it was just that . . . there was no separation of life and work for Jim. . . . He knew very few people who weren't involved in his projects or involved in his business. And usually what socializing he did almost inevitably he did with people who he was working on projects with." Hunt, who had spent as much time as anyone socializing with Jim outside work, admitted that some of the most meaningful and memorable times spent with Jim were those private moments on the set. Jim and Hunt would often spend hours crammed shoulder to shoulder in a tiny space as they performed Statler and Waldorf heckling from their box seats—"and that's when we would have these talks," said Hunt. As the rest of the crew worked on the stage floor below, Jim and Hunt were in near isolation "in this little enclosed thing with curtains shut, and in a little booth together. We would talk about our families, and our hopes and desires and politics." "[Jim] was very close to us all," said Juhl. "He just conducted his life in a different way than most people did. He just couldn't understand about this whole thing called *work*, and why people didn't like it, and why people thought there was something wrong with working."

In the spring of 1979, Jane Henson—who had *long* accepted that work was Jim's first priority—joined Jim in London, moving into a large, white-fronted Georgian-style townhouse they had recently purchased together on Downshire Hill, just a short walk from Hampstead Heath. It was "a great house," said Jane fondly, with a formal music room and plenty of space for gatherings, though its backyard looked into the offices and down onto the impound lot of a police station. She and Cheryl, John, and Heather would live with Jim in London for a year—Lisa and Brian would stay in the United States to attend school—and while Cheryl worked in the Muppet workshop, John and Heather were enrolled in the American Community School in London, allowing Jim to punctuate his busy workweek with family walks on Hampstead Heath and side trips to the countryside. As Jim and Jane wrapped up the paperwork to purchase the Downshire Hill house, Jim also closed the deal on a former postage sorting facility just across the street at 1B, intending to use it as a workshop for the more realistic puppets and scenery needed for *The Crystal,* which was still in the planning stages.

On May 31, 1979, *The Muppet Movie* made its world premiere at the Leicester Square Theatre in London, at a glittering event attended by British pop stars and Princess Anne. Jim showed up with Jane and John, along with his stepmother, Bobby, all grinning broadly as flashbulbs crackled around them. "Great evening," Jim remarked in his journal with typical understatement. As the movie's opening scene played in the darkened theater, with the camera gliding down through the clouds to find Kermit playing banjo in the swamp, fourteen-year-old John Henson burst into tears. "I cried in the opening," said John later. "I still do. . . . [It was] just so powerful."

Between the new house in Hampstead, the hardworking Muppet workshop at Elstree and now *The Muppet Movie* making its premiere in a London theater, many of the employees in the New York office of Henson Associates were beginning to wonder whether Jim's priorities had shifted to the upstart London division. In truth, they probably had. With *The Muppet Show* still based at Elstree and puppet building on *The Crystal* under way at the Downshire Hill workshop, London had become home for Jim's television and film production—and "everything follows production," said Lazer. Meanwhile, the New York office had evolved into the *de facto* business arm of the organization. Gone were the days when Jim could make almost every major decision personally. "He'd been used to running a very small company where that was part of his job," said Al Gottesman, "but he soon came to realize that he had to trust other people with some of those decisions." Long used to Jim's direct input on almost every major decision, the New York staff was now trying to adjust to its new long-distance relationship.

"Al [Gottesman] was in New York running the . . . licensing, publishing and administration and everything," said Lazer; meanwhile, the London crew was working directly with Jim on television and film projects, building props and performing puppets. While there was still plenty of creative work to be done in licensing and publishing in New York—led largely by the versatile Michael Frith—

many felt that if there was any real fun to be had in the organization, it was going to be had in London with Jim. "There was no one here [in New York] to say 'you did a good job' . . . to praise them and to make them feel part of the whole—part of Jim," said Lazer. "Because they all wanted to be part of Jim's work and needed Jim's *attaboys*."

Wherever Jim was, then, tended to feel special and needed, while wherever he *wasn't* tended to feel neglected—and more often than not, where he *wasn't* was New York. Frank Oz, who had seen Jim's frustration with the New York–London dynamic, only had so much patience with that kind of neediness. "Sure, the more Jim was in New York, the nicer it was for them," said Oz with a hint of annoyance. "But he had overhead. He had to work. And that meant he had to be in London."

Jim tried his best to soothe any bruised feelings—in his view, everyone at Henson Associates, whether they were puppeteers or accountants, was creative and valuable. "We are primarily a company of creative people, whose art we are helping to bring to the world," he explained—and while art may have been the heart of the organization, it was money and merchandising that kept the blood pumping. "We recognize that business enables art 'to happen,' and that business plays an essential role in communicating art to a broad audience," he said. "As both artists and businesspersons, we understand the value of both worlds, and so we bring them together in a way that facilitates the realization of our artistic vision."

Compounding the problem—if you could call it that—was that as the company became more successful, it required even more employees in New York, working in more divisions—personnel, finance, office management—to keep things running. "It seems that I'm bigger now than I thought I would be," Jim told a reporter from *The New York Times,* estimating that his staff numbered "between 40 and 50." Actually, by the summer of 1979, he had seventy-one employees, including eleven puppeteers and thirty designers and builders—and the more employees there were, the less time and attention Jim could bestow on each one. Yet, each "wanted to be part of the family, part of the team," said Lazer. "People needed his approval. Even *I* did." Consequently, anyone who had spoken personally with Jim—who had gotten a moment of the one-on-one interaction so many of them craved—tended to lord it over other staffers. That could make things touchy for Gottesman as he tried to manage the New York office in Jim's own low-key style. "Jim was not preoccupied by office organization charts, so he would call and speak to whomever he wished," said Gottesman. "So there was a little of that tension . . . the person at a meeting who had the most clout at that moment would be the person who said, 'I just spoke to Jim.' "

Whether he liked it or not, with his sweet, soft-spoken demeanor and casual dress, Jim was regarded by his employees as something more than just the boss; they saw him as a friend or even as a father figure. "He could *not* handle it," Lazer said. "That was a heavy responsibility, because he wasn't a daddy." Yet while Jim may not have wanted to be a father figure, he still couldn't help but feel a sense of paternal obligation to his employees and performers—some of whom, like Hunt and Whitmire, had joined the organization while still in their teens. "I think Jim felt . . . that we have a responsibility to each other," said Richard Hunt. "He took it very seriously, his responsibilities toward his employees. When he couldn't help them and he had to let people go, it was devastating." Lazer told Jim he had to change the way he viewed his employees. "Stop calling this company a *family*," Lazer said. "Call it a *team*, because you can fire team members. You can't fire family." That was still easier said than done, especially when it came to employees who really did feel like family—like Richard Hunt.

One evening, while attending a dinner party in London, Hunt had openly bad-mouthed a *Muppet Show* guest star, which caught the ear of a journalist who promptly splattered Hunt's remarks all over London. Lazer was incensed. "It was a major thing . . . Jim was furious," said Lazer, "[because] all of the [goodwill] we had built up all this time with our image and our stars . . . could be lost." While responsibility for firing or discipline generally fell to Lazer, playing bad cop to Jim's good cop, for serious offenses like this—where Jim's own reputation was at stake—Lazer felt Jim was obligated to get involved. In this case, Lazer planned to call Hunt into his office in the Muppet Suite where he intended to bawl out the puppeteer, then turn him over to Jim in the adjoining office for a formal reprimand. With Jim listening from just behind his office door, "I got Richard in," said Lazer, "and I wiped him out." Hunt began sobbing uncontrollably. "I'm sorry, Richard," Lazer said sternly, "but you have to face Jim now." Hunt had barely pushed open the door to Jim's office when Jim rushed over and wrapped him up in a bear hug. "He just couldn't do it," said Lazer. "He couldn't handle confrontations at all."

The New York office would feel a little less neglected in June, when Jim returned to the city, partly to oversee the opening of an exhibit called *The Art of the Muppets* at the Library for the Performing Arts at Lincoln Center, but mostly so he and Oz could promote *The Muppet Movie*. Lord Grade was marketing the film aggressively, pumping $6 million into publicity—if the film bombed, joked Jim, "we'll all lose our shirts"—and Jim and Oz were ferried from one interview to another with Kermit and Miss Piggy on their arms, gamely bantering with reporters. Most questions now were directed at Miss Piggy, who had clearly surpassed Kermit in popularity. Though Oz would usually deftly turn the discussion back to Jim and Kermit, it had become clear, even to Jim, that the Pig had taken on a life of her own. "Piggy's become a phenomenon in the last few years and I think when we introduced her we had no idea she'd take off like she has," said Jim. "It's a personality that Frank Oz has created that people somehow identify with and either love or hate."

The Muppet Movie opened in the United States on June 22, 1979—but Jim was already back in production on *The Muppet Show* in London and thus attended neither the New York nor the Los Angeles premieres, simply noting in his journal that the reception was "Great!" The critics loved it—typical was the review from the eminent film critic Vincent Canby, writing in *The New York Times,* who hailed Jim for successfully blending "unbridled amiability . . . [with] intelligence and wit." Meanwhile, audiences made it one of the most profitable films of the decade, grossing over $65 million in its initial release—not a bad return on Grade's initial $8 million investment.

Its success wasn't surprising; as Canby had noted, the film had both heart and brains—and like *The Muppet Show*, its appeal cut across age groups. *The Muppet Movie* was an affectionate nod to old Hollywood, with running gags and barroom brawls, dance numbers and slow-motion romantic montages, as well as mad scientists, thrown pies, and characters who winked knowingly at the camera. At its center, it was also a buddy movie, a tip of the hat to the Bob Hope–Bing Crosby *Road* pictures, with Kermit and Fozzie encountering each Muppet character—and adding them to their growing entourage—as they drove across the country to Hollywood. Along the way, Kermit dodges Doc Hopper and his plans for turning Kermit into a frog legs pitchman, before finally landing a Hollywood contract—a moment, said director Frawley proudly, "that brings tears to your eyes."

In a way, *The Muppet Movie* was also Jim's story—for Juhl had cleverly embedded elements of Jim's own life and personality into the plot. "I guess you could say that mine has been somewhat of a fairytale story," admitted Jim. "It's been a long career with a steady and slow increase in fame and prosperity. It has really been very gratifying with no real surprises." Like Kermit, Jim had left the swamps of Mississippi for the glitter of television and film, had put together his own "clan of whackos" to work with, and had struggled to break away from the clutches of the advertising business, which didn't want to see him leave. Kermit's motivation in heading for Hollywood wasn't so far removed from Jim's own outlook, either—rather than solely seeking fame and fortune, Kermit sees it as an opportunity to entertain and "make millions of people happy." Finally, in the film's climactic scene—a *High Noon*–type showdown between Kermit and Doc Hopper—Kermit delivers a defiant monologue that so clearly defined Jim's own personal code that Juhl could have lifted it verbatim from any of his countless conversations with Jim over the last two decades:

> Yeah, well, I've got a dream, too. But it's about singing and dancing and making people happy. That's the kind of dream that gets better the more people you share it with. And, well . . . I've found a whole bunch of friends who have the same dream. And it kind of makes us like a family.

For agent Bernie Brillstein, there was never any doubt that he was seeing Jim's story on-screen. "Kermit was Jim," said Brillstein plainly. "Jim believed in the entire world."

Plot aside, everyone, it seemed, was impressed at how convincingly Jim had integrated the Muppets into the real world. "I'm in particular awe of the techniques by which these hand puppets are made to walk, run, sing and play musical instruments," wrote Canby. "As do the other actors in the movie, we very quickly come to accept the Muppets as real people." Jim cheerfully explained that making the Muppets seem real involved "trying to fool the audience into thinking they're living in a whole world and that there's a whole reality to the world. And so it's a kind of game that we play with the audience." Richard Hunt, however, was less elegant in his explanation. "The reason those characters are appealing is because we're good actors," insisted Hunt. But even that, wrote *Chicago Sun-Times* film critic Roger Ebert, was more than he wanted to know. "If you can figure out how they were able to show Kermit pedaling across the screen," wrote Ebert, "then you are less a romantic than I am: I prefer to believe he did it himself."

With his creations moving with a seeming life of their own on the big screen, comparisons with Walt Disney were again inevitable—and now, perhaps, apt. But Jim was still having none of it. "I'm slightly uncomfortable with all the people who want to say things like that about me, because I like Disney, but I don't ever particularly want to do what he did," said Jim. "He built this great, huge empire. I'm not particularly inclined to do that. You get that large a thing going and I'm not sure that the quality of the work can be maintained." He also continued to dismiss questions about the Muppets' net worth. "It's important to me that the audience doesn't think of us in terms of figures," he told *Time* magazine. "I don't want people looking at the Muppets and thinking 'How much are they worth?' It's just not us. It could be destructive."

To celebrate the success of *The Muppet Movie,* Jim threw a costume party at the new house on Downshire Hill, inviting guests to attend in Elizabethan-era attire. Many of the Muppet crew raided the wardrobe department at ATV for their costumes, and showed up at Downshire Hill to find Jim warmly greeting his guests dressed as a king. Fifteen-year-old Brian Henson, taking a quick trip to London during summer break, came straight to the house from the airport and found the party still in full swing well into the evening. Jet-lagged and groggy, he dutifully pulled on a jester costume Jim had put aside for him and joined the party. "We were the best party givers in the world!" crowed Lazer. All that was needed, said Lazer, was "good food and drink," though it was generally Jim's presence that ensured the necessary "happy environment."

Work on the fourth season of *The Muppet Show* continued through the summer, until August 6, when ATV's technicians—always touchy to begin with—suddenly went on strike, following the lead of London's public sector unions, which had successfully leveraged their own strike for higher pay during the previous winter. Jim and the Muppet team had just begun working on an episode with Andy Williams when "the electricians broke for tea," recalled Bonnie Erickson, "and they never came back." Grade's television stations went dark. Anyone tuning in to *The Muppet Show* that week saw only an on-screen apology, promising to resume programming "as soon as possible." Until then, production was indefinitely postponed.

Even as others huffed around him, Jim was unfazed; it was out of his hands, a matter to be resolved by the unions and television company executives. With ATV closed down, Jim left for an extended vacation with his family, spending a week in late August in the British Virgin Islands, before heading with them to the English seaside resort of Blackpool, where the Muppets had been given the honor of turning on the Blackpool Illuminations—a gala known as the Big Switch On—for the spectacle's one hundredth anniversary. The town had gone all out for Jim, integrating the Muppets into the gigantic light display along Blackpool's central promenade, and Jim and Goelz performed as Kermit and Gonzo at the opening ceremonies, throwing the switch together to light up the town. Jim loved it.

With the strike still unresolved in September, Jim returned to the United States for a week to attend the Emmy Awards—where *The Muppet Show* lost to *Steve and Eydie Celebrate Irving Berlin*—and to see fifteen-year-old Brian off to the Phillips Academy in Andover, Massachusetts, where he planned to study physics and astronomy for his last three years of high school. Brian was fascinated with knowing how things worked, tinkering with gadgets and electronics, and building elaborate Heathkit stereos and televisions. At thirteen,

Brian had even constructed a small mechanical puppet in the Muppet workshop, building a puppet potato with a trigger-activated mouth and eyes. "[My dad] was very intrigued that I was inclined in that direction," said Brian. "He was enormously appreciative and loved seeing what I was doing."

Still awaiting the resolution of the London strike, Jim spent much of the early fall traveling with his family, spending several days in Scotland in late September, a "delightful weekend" marred only by the theft of Jim's Nikon camera from the trunk of his typically unlocked car. Several more days were spent in Amsterdam, followed by a road trip to visit Oxford Scientific Films, where Jim spent several hours looking at the magnifying cameras the company used to film tiny subjects, like ant hills, at ground level. "It would look so otherworldly because you're looking at the mosses and the ferns and everything right up close," said Cheryl. "Neat!" Jim wrote in his journal, hoping to find some use for the technology in *The Crystal*.

On October 24, the strike ended as quickly as it had begun, though Grade's channels would find their viewers slow to return after eleven weeks away. Jim immediately returned to Elstree to wrap up work on two unfinished *Muppet Show* episodes, completing both in only four days. On November 2, he headed back to the States, this time stopping in Maryland to receive a Distinguished Alumnus Award from the University of Maryland and to serve as grand marshal in the school's homecoming parade. Wearing a flowered shirt and paisley tie under a corduroy suit, Jim waved Kermit from the back of a convertible, trawling along in a sea of floats filled with papier-mâché Muppets. While he was becoming known around the world, Jim still blushed at the attention lavished on him in his former backyard, mumbling only half-audible responses to shouted questions at a press event.

In early November, the Muppet team spent a week in Los Angeles taping a Christmas special with John Denver, to coincide with the release of a Christmas album Denver and the Muppets had recorded in London during the heat of the summer. Denver had guest-starred on *The Muppet Show* in May, where his easygoing, no-drama attitude—his strongest epithet was usually *golly!*—meshed easily with Jim's own way of performing. Shortly after finishing Denver's

Muppet Show episode, Jim called Denver in Aspen to discuss working on a Christmas album together, the two of them tossing ideas back and forth for hours over the phone and deciding which songs to record. After settling on thirteen tunes—ranging from traditional songs like "The Twelve Days of Christmas" to the Beach Boys' "Little Saint Nick"—Denver recorded the basic tracks at a studio in Los Angeles, then met Jim and the Muppet team in London in late June to record their vocals together. The resulting album, *John Denver and the Muppets: A Christmas Together,* went gold before Christmas 1979, and platinum by early 1980. "I can honestly say that collaborating with Jim Henson and the entire Muppet Gang in putting this recording together was one of the most enjoyable experiences of my career," said Denver.

The television special, taped over a relatively leisurely eight days, featured the Muppets at their sentimental best, softening the trademark Muppet madness in favor of the quieter, more deferential tones suitable for a Christmas special. It was the right choice—the show's finale, with Denver and the Muppets singing "Silent Night" with the children in the studio audience, is genuinely sweet without being saccharine—but to some critics, the Muppets seemed out of character. "It's discouraging to see the Muppets succumb with increasing frequency to sentimental impulses overly exercised in *The Muppet Movie,*" wrote Tom Shales in *The Washington Post,* lamenting that the Muppets had gone for "sanctimoniousness, rather than their playful anarchic streak." Still, Shales had to admit it was "lavish, warm and insanely entertaining," which was probably good enough for Jim. "He was easily proud, actually," said Brian Henson. "He didn't look at things that he'd finished and grimace. He enjoyed what he made. . . . I mean, he *knew* he was good."

In mid-December—after spending Thanksgiving shooting inserts for *Sesame Street,* riding in the Macy's Thanksgiving Day Parade, and presiding over the annual Christmas party—Jim returned to London to spend the holidays with the entire Henson family in the house on Downshire Hill. After the long and somewhat frantic year, Jim was pleasantly relaxed, chatting casually on the phone with Brillstein—who delivered the welcome news that he had placed *Emmet Otter* with ABC for Christmas 1980—and strolling Hampstead Heath, where he would sometimes sprawl out on Don Sahlin's bench, looking out over Parliament Hill in the brisk cold. For the members of the Muppet team spending their Christmas in London, Jim hosted a formal dinner party at the White Elephant on the River, pulling up at the curb in his Lotus, grinning broadly as he entered the club.

Christmas Day in London was sparklingly clear and cold—"lovely," wrote Jim in his journal in typical understatement—and as 1979 came to a close, Jim jotted down several notes in his journal, as if to remind himself of just what a successful year it had been. "*The Muppet Movie* has grossed around 75 million—I *think*," he wrote, slightly hedging his bets (the real number was closer to $65 million). "*The Muppet Movie* album with Atlantic went gold just before Christmas. *John Denver and the Muppets* album has sold over a million—according to John. The Miss Piggy Calendar is out this year. *The Muppet Show* Music Album just came out in England this December. *The Muppet Movie* book is out."

Meanwhile, he still had *The Crystal* in its early stages, and had even started talking with Lord Grade about a sequel to *The Muppet Movie*. It truly had been—as he at last wrote in his journal without a whiff of understatement—"A VERY MAJOR BIG YEAR."

CHAPTER ELEVEN

THE WORLD IN HIS HEAD

1979–1982

Kira, one of the heroes of 1982's
The Dark Crystal, *with a villainous Skeksis.*

WITH THE WORLDWIDE POPULARITY OF BOTH *THE MUPPET SHOW* AND now *The Muppet Movie,* Jim had, it seemed, conclusively put to rest the puppetry prejudice that had plagued him since *Sesame Street.* If there were still critics clinging to the stifling misperception that puppets were purely kids' entertainment, Jim had a universally acclaimed major motion picture, an Emmy, and 235 million weekly television viewers who would likely help him argue otherwise. But the international success of the Muppets on television and the movie screen had created a different kind of perception problem for Jim. True, he was no longer considered a children's performer; instead, to the entire world, he was now "the Muppet Guy."

It was a label Jim had struggled with before. In the late 1960s, as Jim was branching out into various non-Muppet-related projects—television specials, commercials, documentaries, computer graphics—he had deliberately sought to downplay the prominence of the Muppets in the company, even changing the name over the door from MUPPETS, INC. to HENSON ASSOCIATES. "Back in the sixties—when I was working on movies like *Time Piece*—I thought of myself as an experimental filmmaker," Jim said—and to some extent, that was still true. While the Muppets were certainly the most well known, and most profitable, of Jim's projects, Jim never had, and never would, consider himself to be solely about the Muppets.

"When you try to get people in the industry to accept a big idea, it usually takes a long time—months or years," said Jim, who had devoted more than a decade to the task of bringing the Muppets to television and film. "And when they finally say, 'yes—let's go with it,' part of my creative mind is already somewhere else, doing something quite different. I think that's the normal pattern. By the time I'm actually producing something, part of me is wanting to do something else. I don't particularly want to make my life go crazy doing several things at the same time, but it always seems to happen that way."

That "something else" was *The Crystal,* still in its preliminary stages at the Muppet workshop in New York in 1980—but even before deciding on *The Crystal* as his next project, Jim had wanted to make a non-Muppet fantasy film for a long time. In the early 1970s, in fact, he had briefly flirted with the idea of doing an adaptation of J. R. R. Tolkien's *Lord of the Rings* series, but eventually passed on the project after deciding Tolkien's sweeping epic was "too big to handle" in a single film.

In 1975, while paging through a copy of *The Pig-Tale*—an illustrated version of the poem by Lewis Carroll, with lavish drawings by Leonard Lubin—Jim had been struck by one of Lubin's illustrations of a crocodile in sumptuous Victorian attire. "It was the juxtaposition of this reptilian thing in this fine atmosphere that intrigued me," Jim said later—and with that spark of an idea, he began writing a treatment for a fantasy film called *Mithra,* a dry run of the various plot elements that would eventually coalesce as *The Dark Crystal.*

Even in this early treatment, Jim was already certain he wanted the two warring factions—the villainous Reptus and the wizardlike Bada—to have split from a single species, through the influence of a mystical source of power, "perhaps a lodestone," Jim wrote tenuously.

After meeting artist Brian Froud in August 1977, however, Jim had shelved the *Mithra* treatment in favor of working with Froud on their "GREAT FILM" together, building a new fantasy world from the ground up, and concentrating more on the overall look and feel of the film than on the story. "I'm trying to create this film in a different way," Jim wrote in his diary, "hoping to get all the creative elements going on it for a while before tying things down with a script." In early 1978, as Froud sketched in the New York workshop and handed drawings off to Muppet builders to begin crafting puppets, Jim—while stranded with Cheryl at Howard Johnson's hotel during the snowstorm—had scrawled out a rough outline of a plot, lifting a few key elements from the abandoned *Mithra* and finally deciding that the mystical source of power in the land he and Froud were building would be a crystal. Working off his handwritten notes, he quickly put together a sixteen-page treatment of *The Crystal,* and "set some of the [Muppet] builders working on ideas of ways to create characters unlike anything we've ever done before," he wrote in his diary. "It's such a wonderful challenge to try to design an entire world . . . like no one has ever seen before."

For most of 1978, however, Jim's focus was on filming *The Muppet Movie,* though the New York workshop continued diligently sculpting, building, and tinkering with puppets for *The Crystal.* Wizard heads and various potato-like peasants and slaves slumped on benches around the workshop, while handyman Faz Fazakas was building elaborate—and increasingly smaller—remote-control mechanisms to widen eyes, crinkle foam noses, and wrinkle latex foreheads. In October, Jim took a few of the completed figures out in the backyard of his house in Bedford to film them among rocks and trees, subjecting the puppets to the same sort of outdoor screen test he had put Kermit and Fozzie through earlier in the year in preparation for *The Muppet Movie.* He was pleased with the results of the screen test, yet he knew his preoccupation with the look of the film meant he was approaching the project in an unconventional, almost backward way. "Normally you write the script first and design around the story," he explained later. "I wanted to change that and come up with a visual world first, although knowing vaguely the type of story I wanted."

Six months later, there was still no real script to speak of—but in the summer of 1979, Jim flew to New York to pitch *The Crystal* to executives at Paramount anyway, perhaps hoping the success of the recently premiered *Muppet Movie* would convince the studio to invest the $15 million Jim was asking for his next film. He brought with him a beautifully produced formal proposal, printed on milled paper and brimming with Froud's lavish pencil drawings—but typical of Jim's approach to the project, the pitch book for *The Crystal* devoted most of its space to the characters and the world itself. That left just half a page to outline the story, only vaguely described as a "struggle through terrible dangers and hardships" which built to a nonspecific "startling climax." Paramount executives passed.

With Paramount's demurral, Jim decided to once again approach Lord Grade, his reliable patron for both *The Muppet Show* and *The Muppet Movie*. During their initial negotiations for *The Muppet Movie,* Grade had been encouraging, though noncommittal, about financing a non-Muppet feature—but Jim was certain that, with *The Muppet Movie* turning a healthy profit, Grade would be more than willing to back such an ambitious project. Lazer, however, wasn't so sure, and pulled Jim aside for a frank conversation. The success of *The Muppet Movie,* Lazer explained, had ramped up enthusiasm and demand for a sequel. "I felt that if we gave too much time in between Muppet movies, we couldn't keep that audience," said Lazer, "and I knew Lew [Grade] was ready . . . to go for that second Muppet movie immediately."

Jim was deflated. "He was always interested in the idea of going beyond the Muppets," said Cheryl Henson, "[there was a sense of] wanting to find something, wanting to work on something that had more depth to it." "Jim wanted to do *The Crystal,*" said Lazer. "His mind was off Muppets. He wanted to get *The Crystal* done." And Lazer, who understood perhaps better than anyone just how important *The Crystal* was to Jim, instead "gave him every reason we should do another Muppet movie." However, Lazer offered to take up the negotiations with Grade personally, promising Jim that if he would agree to make the sequel to *The Muppet Movie* first, Lazer would ensure that any funding Grade put up for the second Muppet film would be contingent on financing *The Crystal* next. Jim agreed, and Lazer was as good as his word, convincing Grade to lay down not only a hefty $14 million for the next Muppet feature—nearly double what he had invested in *The Muppet Movie*—but also $13 million for *The Crystal*. Grade also agreed that Jim could shoot the movies back to back, beginning work on *The Crystal* immediately after wrapping the Muppet sequel.

Jim was disappointed, but pragmatic—delaying *The Crystal* in favor of the next Muppet film meant he could keep Froud and the team of artists and builders at work in the New York shop, where they could continue to refine the more realistic, and increasingly complex, puppets Froud was designing. "The idea of doing very naturalistic creatures that looked like living things was exciting to me," said Jim. "I could see that it would take an awful lot of technical know-how to make it work, but we had the beginning of a team of people who could tackle that." In fact, several members of *The Crystal*'s design team—including one of its lead builders, a talented sculptor and doll maker named Wendy Midener—were especially knowledgeable in the technical know-how, having worked in tandem with director George Lucas on a lifelike puppet Lucas wanted for his second *Star Wars* film, *The Empire Strikes Back*.

It is not surprising that Jim and Lucas would eventually cross paths. Not only were they artistically cut from the same cloth, but for the better part of a year, they were practically neighbors. "In England, while we were making [*Star Wars*], we worked across the street from [Elstree], which is where Jim Henson's group was [taping *The Muppet Show*], and I got to know him," said Lucas. "We were very much alike: independent, out of the spotlight, obsessed with our own films. And I really admired the Muppets . . . so I asked him if he thought we could get together and create a very realistic-looking puppet." Lucas already had his own team of special effects wizards in place—including master makeup artist Stuart Freeborn, who had designed several large walkaround creatures like Chewbacca—but if a puppet was needed, Lucas wanted to be certain he had the best puppet designers and performers working side by side with his own team at Lucasfilm. Jim, too, was anxious to learn more about the dynamic special effects technology Lucas and his team were known for developing, hoping perhaps to apply some of Lucasfilm's expertise to *The Crystal*. "It became a mutual thing," said *Empire Strikes Back* producer Gary Kurtz, "because they needed some advice on their film and we needed their expertise in the puppet area"—and by November 1978, Jim noted in his journal that he and the Muppet team were "Working with STAR WARS on YODA."

Initially, Lucas had wanted Jim to perform the character. "I thought he was the best puppeteer," said Lucas—but with his already cramped schedule, Jim was concerned he would be unable to give the project the time and attention it needed, and instead recommended Frank Oz for the job. "Jim called me into his trailer . . . and showed me a sketch of Yoda—and it felt right," said Oz. "Sometimes you have to work at something before you have that feeling, but this felt really good." Additionally, said Oz, "it was acting, not just performing"—a skill at which Oz excelled.

Using concept drawings provided by Lucas, Wendy Midener had drawn and sculpted Yoda to make the character work in three dimensions—then watched in mild frustration as Freeborn and the Lucasfilm technicians built what was essentially a clunky and heavy doll, with thick cables trailing out of it to control the various eye, ear, and face mechanisms. "They were building a special effect," said Muppet performer Kathy Mullen, who assisted Oz with Yoda. "But Wendy really did work hard on that to make it work and I'm sure Frank [Oz] was over there a bunch of times to try to get it right. I mean *everybody* worked to try to get it right."

Freeborn and his team continued to tinker with Yoda, but when Oz showed up at the soundstage at Elstree for the first day of filming in August 1979, the puppet, said Oz bluntly, was still "really fuckin' heavy." Rather than carving and constructing Yoda from foam and lightweight materials, Freeborn had built Yoda out of heavy nonpliable rubber, putting extra weight on Oz's wrist and severely reducing the puppet's flexibility. A thick bundle of cables trailed from Yoda's neck to a black control box under the stage, where Midener could operate the controls for Yoda's eyes—but the short length and additional weight of the cables only made the puppet that much heavier and more difficult to manipulate. Meanwhile, Mullen had to brace herself under Oz's right arm to perform the character's right hand and, at times, operate the mechanisms that wiggled Yoda's ears or pulled his mouth back into a slight smile. The stage had been elevated, though just barely—and there was very little room for the three performers to move about as they watched their performance on monitors glowing in the darkness. "It was *very* hard," groaned Mullen.

And yet the experience was a success, not only for the wondrously memorable character that Oz and the Muppet team created for the film, but also because—as Jim hoped—it had served as a creative reconnaissance mission for *The Crystal*'s designers and builders. Yoda had been a kind of dry run for the sort of creatures Jim hoped to populate *The Crystal*'s world with—and by watching and working with Freeborn and his team they had learned even more about how the latest remote control technology could be integrated into a puppet, to blink or narrow eyes or turn up the corner of a mouth to give a character an even more lifelike appearance. Just as important, they had also learned what *didn't* work. For one thing, the puppets—and all their incorporated technology—would have to be lighter and more flexible. Jim would also have to find new ways of keeping three or more performers—and all the necessary cables controlling eyes and ears and smiles—out of sight of the camera, especially if he hoped to have his puppets walking, climbing, and moving about out in the open. "It was just the sort of thing that needed a lot of research, a lot of time and experimentation," said Jim—and now with *The Crystal* temporarily pushed back, time was, for once, a luxury Jim and his team had.

For now, Brian Froud, Wendy Midener—who would marry Froud in May 1980—and the team at the New York workshop would continue their work, blending the lessons learned from their experience with Yoda with their own creative expertise in puppetry design and function. Jim, meanwhile, would start the wheels turning on the next Muppet movie, putting comedy screenwriter Jack Rose—who had penned *Road to Rio,* one of the early Hope-Crosby films Jim loved—to work on a film treatment. Jim was also going to direct both the next Muppet film and *The Crystal* himself—of that, there was no question, and Grade had never even raised the issue—but now that he would be at the helm of his first big screen features, Jim wanted to be sure he had a reliable and experienced cameraman at his right hand. In early 1980, Jim met with—and "loved"—Ossie Morris, an Oscar-winning cinematographer who had been the cameraman of choice for director John Huston, shooting epics like *Moby Dick* and *Moulin Rouge*. Morris could read a script or walk a movie set and know intuitively if what Jim saw in his head would show up on camera, and his sure eye would make him an invaluable member of Jim's production team.

And there was still *The Muppet Show* to attend to. The strike of 1979 had put the Muppet crew behind schedule, with nine episodes of the fourth season remaining to be taped in a little less than seven weeks. Even as the team speedily wrapped up their fourth year at Elstree, they remained one of London's best-loved acts. Muppet fans continued to mob ATV so much that Jim finally had to put a stop to the popular tours of the workshop. Fan mail from around the world still poured into the Muppet offices at Elstree, most of it addressed to the characters themselves, asking for pictures or autographs. Children sent in drawings of their favorite Muppets or boldly invited Jim to dinner at their house, while their parents asked if they might be allowed to purchase a used or broken Muppet. And nearly every working puppeteer, comedy writer, or songwriter, it seemed, sent in a résumé or audition tape, begging, pleading, praying for a chance to work with the Muppets. Jim responded politely to all of them, saying a kind word or two about their material while letting them down as gently as he could. Still, Jim did find a few performers through the mail, including Karen Prell, a young performer from Washington who enclosed several photos of her handmade puppets and asked for an audition.

More and more, Jim was coming to regard London as home—as was Lazer, who had unconsciously developed a whiff of a posh English accent. He loved dining in the city's finer restaurants, gambling in London's most exclusive clubs, and liked being recognized by cooing British admirers as he walked Hampstead's winding streets. And yet, while Jim may have wanted to live in London full-time—and indeed, with the house in Hampstead, it seemed to many that he already did—he literally counted the days he spent in the city each year, making sure he never stayed a day longer than six months, which would put him at the mercy of England's astronomically high income tax rate, which hovered just over 80 percent.

Success had also made Jim somewhat more aware of himself and how he looked, and he had recently taken steps to add a bit of polish to his comfortable, bohemian look. While one of his favorite boutiques would always be Liberty of London, where he would purchase armloads of long-sleeve shirts in colorful florals and paisleys, Jim had finally allowed Lazer to talk him into investing in several bespoke suits, shirts, vests, trousers, and even custom-made boots from London's best tailors in Savile Row, once spending over £1,000—about $6,000 today—on clothing. At six foot one, Jim was mostly arms and legs—his waist was a waiflike thirty inches—and custom clothing meant there would be no more exposed calves when he crossed his legs on television, or wrists poking from the end of a too-short shirt. Agent Bernie Brillstein, for one, thought Jim looked great in his "beautiful suits" and was impressed to see him wearing ties. "*Strange* ties," added the agent, "but ties."

Brillstein was also pleased to see Jim "enjoying money—you know, in a nice way." While Jim had always been fond of showy cars and luxurious vacations, he had lately begun to indulge in art, sculpture, antiques, and furniture, with a particular eye for bold craftsmanship—an expensive habit for which Lazer felt he was partly to blame. One afternoon as he and Jim were window-shopping in London, Jim spotted a beautiful piece of art in a store window. "How much do you think that costs?" he asked Lazer excitedly, and the two spent several moments guessing the price. Finally, Lazer went inside to ask the owner, and learned the piece was available at an astronomical price. Jim arched an eyebrow quizzically at Lazer. "Should I?" he asked impishly. "Jim, if you like it, just do it," said Lazer—and so Jim did, walking out of the store with the package tucked under his arm, beaming happily.

Lazer later said he "felt badly" that he had given Jim the approval he had seemed to be looking for to indulge himself more freely. "I think I should *not* have encouraged him," said Lazer. "He started . . . on a buying thing . . . he felt free." Still, Jim was never entirely careless with his money; when he felt an expensive antique cabinet was overpriced, he quietly had the piece appraised and discovered it was worth less than half of the $19,000 asking price. Looking back, Lazer couldn't bring himself to begrudge Jim's buying sprees *too* much. "I'm so glad he did. He bought houses where he wanted. He lived where he wanted. . . . I'm glad he *lived* while he lived."

Jim completed work on the fourth season of *The Muppet Show* in late February 1980, taping the final episode with guest Diana Ross, who charmed the entire Muppet crew by modestly asking "Was that all right?" after every take. After only a two-week break—during which Jim worked almost constantly, jetting back to New York for several days and then dashing to Paris to promote *The Muppet Movie*—he reassembled the Muppet team back at Elstree to begin work on the fifth season. While *The Muppet Show* was, at that point, arguably the most watched show in the world, Jim had even higher hopes that the show would live on in perpetuity in reruns, thereby providing a steady revenue stream. "The long range product for this show is down the road," he had explained to *Time* magazine, "when it's syndicated [in reruns]."

For that to happen, however, a show generally needed at least one hundred completed episodes that could be put into rotation; by the end of season four, *The Muppet Show* had only ninety-six. Season five, then, would be pivotal, for several reasons—not only would the show reach its critical one hundredth episode, but Jim had also privately decided that the fifth season would be its last. "After five seasons, we're doing other projects," Jim told reporters. As the Muppet team set to work at ATV on the first few shows of season five, Jim was already conferring with Jack Rose and Jerry Juhl about the script for the second Muppet movie. And he wasn't happy with it.

From the beginning, Jim knew he wanted his film to be a homage to early movie musicals, "because I so enjoy those movies. I intended [the second Muppet movie] to have the fun and joy of those earlier films." He also knew he wanted Kermit to be a reporter-turned-detective who would have to compete with a rival for Miss Piggy's affections—but typically, he was having a difficult time articulating the rest of his story, only vaguely directing that it be "joyful" with a "positive attitude toward life," and that it contain "several hilarious sequences [with] big laughs" as well as "some real emotions/relationships." He thought there might be a big chase at the end, and he was certain the movie would end with all the Muppets floating down in "parachutes—everybody sings as they go down."

With such vague directions, it was perhaps little wonder that what he got back from Rose and Juhl wasn't what he thought he'd asked for. "There are a great many problems with this draft," he wrote testily of their script, confessing privately in his journal that things were "not looking good." Frustrated, he asked veteran television comedy writers Jay Tarses and Tom Patchett—who had written for Bob Newhart and Carol Burnett—to meet with him at his house on Downshire Hill to discuss them taking over the scripting duties. In the meantime, he asked fellow *Sesame Street* alum Joe Raposo to begin crafting songs—despite the fact that a plot hadn't yet been confirmed—and hired choreographer Anita Mann for dance sequences that didn't yet exist.

Fortunately, Patchett and Tarses worked quickly, and by early May 1980, Jim had a first draft he could work with, though one sticking point remained: the title. Patchett and Tarses had given their script the throwaway title *Muppet Mania,* but Jim decided to put the question to the Muppet staff, holding a contest to find the best name for the film. Among some of the more interesting or silly suggestions—*The Rocky Muppet Picture Show, A Froggy Day in London*—Jim found a handwritten submission from nineteen-year-old Lisa Henson, suggesting *The Great Muppetcapade.* Written in pencil next to it, as if rolling the words around in her mouth, she had scrawled "escapade? esc*pig*aide? caper?" and then scratched all three alternatives out. Jim circled *The Great Muppetcapade* and the crossed-out word *Caper.* Problem solved. *The Great Muppet Caper* it would be.

Lisa's involvement was critical to another project as well, an "interactive movie" concept revolving around a story they were plotting with Maurice Sendak and Jon Stone called "The Varied Adventures of Mischievous Miles." During a trip to Hollywood to attend the Oscars—where Jim and Oz performed the Oscar-nominated "Rainbow Connection," only to watch it lose the Best Song trophy to "It Goes like It Goes" from *Norma Rae*—Jim and Lisa met with Sherry Lansing at 20th Century Fox to pitch their ambitious idea: a film in which the audience would be asked at intervals to choose the direction of the story. The mechanics were cumbersome—based on choices made by the audience, seventy-two different variations of the film were possible—but Jim was confident he could make it work. "We were really interested in nonlinear storytelling," recalled Lisa. "The concept was you make a movie on a laser disc, and then a computer program would drive it to play different bits of the disc depending on what choice was made . . . but it wasn't possible to do it on a commercial filmmaking level." It would take another decade before the technology could catch up with Jim's idea. "Really, where it all ended up was in video games," said Lisa, "but we didn't know that at the time."

Jim would shelve the interactive movie concept, but work on *The Crystal* continued—and the more time Jim spent building his world in his head, the more he was convinced that the $13 million Grade had offered to finance the film wasn't going to be enough. Grade was scheduled to attend the Cannes Film Festival in mid-May—and had generously offered to pay for Jim and Lazer to spend a few days at the festival as well—and it was here that Lazer planned to make an appeal directly to Grade to up their budget. "Lord Grade's office chartered a flight to take Jim and me to France," recalled Lazer. "Two fabulous suites awaited us, a detailed itinerary, as well as a major dinner reservation . . . Jim was showered with praise and adoration."

Very quickly, however, both Jim and Lazer came to see the dingy crust beneath Cannes' glossy veneer, and Lazer began to lose his nerve about approaching Grade. "I thought it [Cannes] was trashy," said Lazer, "everyone hawking, selling their wares." That first evening, they ran into Liza Minnelli, who invited them back to a yacht party—"[she] was crazy over Jim," said Lazer. That, too, was another letdown—"people drinking and slobbering," shuddered Lazer—and he and Jim ducked out after midnight to walk along the docks on the way back to their hotel. Jim walked slowly and quietly, and Lazer worried that Jim was disappointed with their Cannes experience. Then he realized Jim wasn't even paying attention to their surroundings; he was watching the moon on the water. "[It] seemed to do a shimmer dance on the water just for him," said Lazer. None of the glamour—or grunge—of Cannes seemed to impress or depress him at all. Instead, said Lazer, "he was mesmerized by the beauty, the serenity and the nurturing power of Nature." With a new perspective, a reinvigorated Lazer strolled over to Grade's suite the next morning and persuaded the mogul to increase his investment in *The Crystal* from $13 million to $25 million. "That's the money that really saved the film," said Oz.

A trip to France had saved one of Jim's worlds; a week later, a trip to Scotland would spawn a new one.

On May 24, 1980, Jim flew to Scotland at the invitation of Jocelyn Stevenson, one of Jim's favorite editors and writers from the Children's Television Workshop. Stevenson and Jim had gotten to know each other in the early 1970s when, as a young secretary for CTW, Stevenson had sloshed through a New York downpour to deliver some pages of *Sesame Street* magazine to Jim for approval. As the two of them talked, they learned they shared a similar commitment to the television medium and its potential for quality children's entertainment. "And he just said to me, 'You're really creative,'" said Stevenson. "It was a really big moment for me to have someone . . . see [me] that way. He was really huge in terms of his influence on me."

Now, a decade later, Stevenson had asked Jim to serve as the godfather for her son and dispatched a private plane to pick up Jim, Jane, Cheryl, John, and Heather in London and ferry them to her husband's family estate near Edinburgh, Scotland. When Stevenson's brother-in-law Peter Orton learned Jim was attending the event, he pleaded with Stevenson to seat him near Jim at dinner. "I want to talk with him about an idea I have," said Orton cryptically. Stevenson obliged, and over dinner Orton—a savvy British television executive who had done some international sales work for *Sesame Street*—enthusiastically pointed out to Jim that the worldwide success of both *Sesame Street* and *The Muppet Show* had opened up a unique opportunity. The time was right, said Orton, to produce a children's show aimed specifically at the international market. Jim was intrigued. He would think about it. The seeds of *Fraggle Rock* had been sown.

Returning to London, Jim spent the next eleven weeks taping the last twelve episodes of *The Muppet Show*. The show had come a long way in five years; after the shaky first season when Brillstein had rifled through his client list in search of guest stars, Jim could now get almost any celebrity he wished. "Who excites you?" he would ask his children—and for sixteen-year-old Brian Henson, the answer was easy: Blondie's alluring lead singer, Debbie Harry. "I said, 'She'll be great!'" Brian said later, laughing. "And I was like, 'Well, I don't know if she'll be *great,* but I *love* looking at her!'" Jim booked Harry for the first week in August, when Brian would be in London for summer break—and at the weekly dinner party that Jim always threw for each guest, Brian found himself sitting goopily next to the sultry singer. At one point, Harry excused herself, then strolled across the restaurant and sashayed up an open staircase toward the powder room. Every head turned. Jim looked at Brian and winked. "You were right," he said, and grinned.

On Sunday, August 17, 1980, *The Muppet Show* team gathered in Rehearsal Room 7/8 for the final time. Jim would have no sad faces; it had been a happy five years at Elstree, and Jim wanted their last week to be a joyful one, bringing in dancer Gene Kelly as guest star for a week of singing and dancing. There would be only one small hint of the show's end in the final episode: a running gag in which Scooter performs a Tarot card reading for Beauregard the janitor and incorrectly informs him the world is coming to an end. As far as Jim was concerned, the world *wasn't* ending; he had other projects to attend to, and *The Muppet Show* would live on in reruns.

Still, Jim appreciated that a milestone had been reached, and to mark the occasion he began the week by hosting a dinner party at the White Elephant on Sunday evening, draping an arm warmly around Brillstein and ITC's American executive Abe Mandell, both of whom had come from the States to celebrate *The Muppet Show*'s final week. Gene Kelly finished taping his sequences by Thursday, leaving Jim and the *Muppet Show* team to wrap things up on Friday the 22nd. That afternoon, as the Muppet performers completed the show's final take—a sequence featuring Fozzie and Scooter dodging knives hurled by the myopic Signor Baffi—floor manager Richard Holloway called out, "Ladies and Gentlemen, that's a final wrap!" and was hit in the face with a pie. It was an ending worthy of the Muppets themselves.

There was another party that evening, this time with Lord Grade in attendance, and Lazer handed Jim a pile of congratulatory telegrams that had come into the Muppet Suites over the past week. Despite the strike and their strict lights out policy, the last five years with the Muppet team had been fun for ATV's British staff, and the electricians, cameramen, and lighting crew were genuinely sorry to see Jim and the Muppet team leave. "All at Elstree hope the Muppets will return," said one telegram. "A marvelous five years with marvelous people." Jim appreciated the sentiments, even as he remained unsentimental. "We finished our 120th *Muppet Show* this summer, and that wraps that up—we felt it was a good place to stop it," he said plainly. "We certainly enjoyed it. . . . It was a nice show to do."

Another important chapter came to a close that summer as well: after more than a year of living in London, Jane had decided to return home to New York. Living, working, and traveling with Jim over the last year "was a great adventure for all of us," said Cheryl, "but ultimately it was not [Jane's] life; she felt out of place and she decided to go back." Their year on Downshire Hill in London would be the last time the two of them would truly live together as a couple; the ocean now separating them was a tangible reminder of the gulf that was widening between them. Following Jane's departure, in fact, Jim began quietly seeing other women.

Decades later Jane was still inclined to be understanding. Jim, she said, "really didn't like being by himself"; there had been occasions in the past when he had casually "gone out," as Jane put it, seeking dinner dates or companions for a movie or show after long days of working in the city. Jim was always respectfully discreet—and, the Henson children thought, felt slightly guilty about it. At one point, in fact, Jim had actually tried to discuss things with Jane, no small feat for someone who generally didn't relish talking about his feelings. Jane had become understandably upset, and Jim—who hated hurting anyone's feelings even more than he disliked talking about his own emotions—wouldn't broach the subject again.

Now that Jim was in London alone, however, Jane conceded that there was likely more going on in the London evenings than merely dinner or movies. "We didn't talk about it," she said flatly, "but I certainly knew he went out to dinner with people and *everything*." As always, Jim generally tried to keep a respectfully low profile—and was stunned when he learned one of his relationships had become "somewhat public." "It horrified him," said Jane. "It really did. Because he himself still really did not want that to be his picture, even though it's sort of what life had become. He didn't like that picture." At that point, "I think [Jim] was evaluating his own marriage," said Muppet performer Steve Whitmire, who had enthused about his own marriage during a drive with Jim in the Lotus. Whitmire had married his high school sweetheart, and Jim seemed genuinely interested in understanding the dynamics of their relationship. Finally, recalled Whitmire, Jim quietly said, " 'You know, Jane and I haven't really been living like a married couple for some time.' He didn't elaborate . . . and I thought, 'He's telling me something quite intimate, and I really don't know what to say.' . . . It was mostly quiet."

In late August, Jim headed for Bermuda for a company-wide staff retreat. It was the first time Jim had pulled together his entire staff from both sides of the Atlantic, and the size of the group likely surprised him: eighty-one employees filled the seats around the room. Lisa and Cheryl also sat in on the three-day retreat, where Jim knew he could count on them for honest feedback. Lisa could immediately feel the New York–London tensions that were troubling her dad. "For the life of him, he couldn't get his group to think together as an organism," said Lisa. "Puppeteers, when they perform together, they have that alchemy, like they're all one organism. But in the company there were always a lot of personalities or ego issues and things that were frustrating for him." Jim did his best to mingle with as many people as he could, playing tennis, swimming, and eating with a different group at every meal to ensure everyone got the face time they needed, since Jim's presence—whether he liked it or not—could, as David Lazer pointed out, "make or break someone's day."

All summer long, work had continued on the second Muppet film—now officially *The Great Muppet Caper*—with Patchett and Tarses finishing up their script and Raposo submitting the final songs and musical score for an orchestra to record. Cinematographer Ossie Morris, too, had been busy scouting locations, and even Morris— who had worked on more than ninety films since the early 1930s— had come to feel the odd magnetism of Jim's presence, almost frantically appealing to him to immerse himself in *Caper* as quickly as possible. "I feel a little distant from you and I believe that is shared by the art and production [departments]," wrote Morris.

On Thursday, September 4, 1980—less than two weeks after shooting the final episode of *The Muppet Show*—Jim settled into his director's chair in London's Battersea Park, now at the helm of his first full-length motion picture. "It has taken me twenty years to get [here]," Jim noted, "and I'm delighted to have made it." In a way, Jim had already been directing for years, watching the television monitor as he performed his characters and adjusting on camera as needed. He brought the same mentality to directing film, rarely looking through the camera's eyepiece, preferring instead to rig a small video monitor next to the camera so he could see exactly what the camera was seeing—a complicated and innovative system that made sense to Jim, and which would eventually become a standard technique for filmmakers. "Usually the cameraman insists I look through [the eyepiece]," Jim said, "[and] I say 'I can see it over here.'"

The first scene Jim would film for *Caper* would be another one of those *How'd they do that?* moments that Jim loved to tease his audiences with. In *The Muppet Movie,* critics had been awestruck by the footage of Kermit riding a bicycle. If audiences had been wowed by *one* Muppet on a bike, then, for *Caper,* Jim would put his entire Muppet cast on wheels—"lots of people on bikes" he wrote in his notes—pedaling them through Battersea Park as part of a large musical number.

It was actually sixteen-year-old Brian Henson, spending several weeks working in the London workshop with Faz Fazakas, who had helped figure out how to make it all work. While shutting down *The Muppet Show* had also meant bidding farewell to the Muppet workshop at ATV, Jim had relocated the workshop to 1B Downshire Hill, the abandoned postage sorting facility he had purchased in 1979 across the street from his home. As the team working on the puppets for *The Crystal* began slowly moving in, Jim already had Fazakas working his wizardry for *The Great Muppet Caper*—and Brian, on a break from his classes at Andover, had been assigned as Fazakas's right hand. "My dad wanted me to just figure it out," said Brian.

Ultimately, the trick was pulled off by using a combination of radio-controlled bikes, marionette rigging, and in some cases attaching several bikes together with rods so they could stand upright on their own. Brian served as one of the lead performers for the sequence, wheeling marionette versions of Kermit and Miss Piggy around on Battersea's wide sidewalks as Jim beamed proudly. Watching the scene on playback, Jim nodded approvingly. "Brian, you did a really, really good job there," he said quietly.

As impressive as it was, the bike riding sequence wasn't *The Great Muppet Caper*'s showstopper. From the very beginning, Jim knew he wanted *Caper* to have "something new—something to talk about." As he filled several pages of a notebook with possible ideas, he scrawled out "Kermit swimming," and then, below it, "Piggy/ Ester [*sic*] Williams." That would be it—an elaborate homage to the swimming, diving, and underwater ballet numbers made famous by Esther Williams in the 1940s and 1950s. "If I had to search out any guilty pleasures," Jim said later, "it is that I probably indulged myself in *Caper* in the underwater sequence with Miss Piggy."

However, making a pig swim—especially a Muppet pig—was no easy task. While the puppetry itself would be a challenge, Oz couldn't just take a regular Miss Piggy Muppet and dunk it in a swimming pool. Not only would the puppet's foam head soak up the water like a sponge, but the water eventually would wash away the flocking sprayed on the character, discoloring the puppet and leaving a scrim of flock shavings floating on the surface. Before a single frame of film could be shot, then, the Muppet builders had to figure out a way to design a waterproof, colorfast, flexible puppet for Oz to work with.

Under the direction of Caroly Wilcox, the New York Muppet workshop became a kind of Muppet Labs. After much trial and error, the team settled on carving and constructing the puppet out of compressed urethane foam, which didn't soak up water but did tend to lose its colored flocking when it got wet. Wilcox then spent several weeks looking at different kinds of flocking in various colors, even writing to the American Fish and Chemical Company—which specialized in shoe and leather chemicals—for advice about stronger adhesives to keep the flocking intact. Eventually, Wilcox and her team developed an elaborate recipe for carving, cutting, gluing, flocking, and then baking the individual puppet parts—to cure them and fuse the flocking into place—finally reporting their findings to Jim as the "Piggy Research and Development Department."

There was only one problem: while the new puppet didn't soak up water and held its shape and color beautifully, the material still didn't stretch very well. "So as soon as Frank would open up the mouth and do a nice exaggerated move," said Wilcox, "the corner of the mouth would tear." The solution, then, was to build as many heads as possible—and if the mouth tore during a take, they would replace the entire head with a new one before the cameras rolled again. In the end, nearly forty different Miss Piggy heads—and seven different bodies—would be used during filming. After each take, the Muppet designers took great delight in smashing each discarded head to bits—mostly, said Wilcox coyly, "to get even."

Oz knew of none of the complex science experiments that had put the puppet in his hands—but he wasn't at all surprised that Jim's quiet confidence in Wilcox and her team had inspired them into finding a workable solution. "He had no patience for, 'I can't figure it out,'" said Brian Henson—but the moment anyone started working to find a way around a problem, no matter how ridiculous the approach, "he was there with you."

Now that Jim had a collection of waterproof Muppets on hand, he and Oz were ready to film the movie's most impressive feat of puppetry, spending a week shooting a water ballet sequence that would last only a little over three minutes in the completed film. On a soundstage at Elstree film studios—the same enormous soundstage where Luke Skywalker had recently fought Darth Vader in *The Empire Strikes Back*—Jim had constructed a swimming pool eighty feet long, fifty feet wide, and eight feet deep. For the comfort of Oz and the eighteen swimmers who would be participating in the water ballet, the water was heated to a swampy eighty degrees, "so the whole place," said Jim, "was like a tropical jungle in the sound stage while we were shooting."

Jim had mapped out most of the mechanics of each shot for the sequence—some shots would use a stiff figure with a remote-controlled head, while the final shot of Piggy diving into the water called for a swimmer in full-body costume—but for the most part, Miss Piggy would be a puppet, manipulated underwater by Oz. Wearing a wet suit the same color blue as the walls of the pool—so he would blend with the background if caught on camera—Oz would sink himself down to the bottom of the pool with the help of asphalt blocks. A scuba diver with an oxygen tank sat on the bottom, holding a breathing tube over Oz's face until Jim signaled the beginning of a take—at which point Oz would take a last gulp of air, then they would film Piggy swimming underwater for as long as he could hold his breath. Jim had placed a number of monitors on the bottom of the pool so Oz could keep an eye on his performance, and lined the underwater walls with speakers so Oz could hear the music and Jim's directions. "It was quite elaborate," said Jim. "But it was fun. We had a good time." Oz—who developed a painful ear infection from spending so much time in the water—said "it was difficult at times, but so what? I was with Jim. That was the joy of it."

Filming on *The Great Muppet Caper* lasted twenty weeks, spanning through the fall of 1980 and into early winter of 1981. While a swimming Miss Piggy had been one of the film's flashier moments, there was a quieter scene that would later be especially poignant. As Kermit sat on a park bench overlooking a lake, Jim had filmed Jerry Nelson and his daughter, Christine, walking past. "Look, Dad, there's a bear!" said Christine brightly, pointing to Kermit. "No, Christine, that's a frog," replied Jerry. "Bears wear *hats*." It was a moment Jim had put in just for a bit of fun for Christine. The following September, Christine Nelson would die of complications from cystic fibrosis at age twenty-two. Jim attended the service, his presence quietly reassuring Nelson—but Jim's actions always spoke louder than any words. Several years earlier, when Henson Associates' insurance provider had notified Jim that it would no longer be paying all of Christine's medical expenses, Jim had insisted that Henson Associates change insurance companies to ensure her costs would continue to be fully covered. Nelson had gone to Jim's office and tearfully thanked him in person, nearly choking on emotion. "Jerry," said Jim, smiling, "that's what insurance companies are *for*."

Work was rapidly progressing on the film Jim was now calling *The Dark Crystal*, with *Muppet Show* writer David Odell laboring to turn Jim's story outline into a workable script even as Froud continued drawing—and builders continued building—at the makeshift Muppet workshop on Downshire Hill. A bit of tension was beginning to develop between the Muppet builders in New York, who were doing the work on puppets for *Caper* and *Sesame Street,* and their counterparts in London working on *The Dark Crystal*. "It [*Dark Crystal*] had become overblown," said Muppet performer Kathy Mullen, who was already rehearsing with her puppet for the film. For one thing, the London shop didn't consider their creations to be mere *Muppets;* they were building *creatures*—a distinction Jim supported, but which caused considerable eye-rolling back in New York. Worse, to the annoyance of Caroly Wilcox—who claimed to be working her staff without vacation or overtime pay to meet the demands of *Caper*'s tight shooting schedule—the head of the London shop had a habit of reassigning Wilcox's builders to work on *Dark Crystal* without clearing it with her first.

To many, *The Dark Crystal* had become Henson's Folly—a project that was not only taking up too much of Jim's time and money, but was also squandering the global success of the Muppets on a project that no one but Jim seemed to fully understand or appreciate. "It was the focus, it was the obsession," said Cheryl, who spent months at a time in the London workshop between semesters at Yale. "He worked so hard to try to make other people happy . . . to keep people feeling like they were a part of it. But that was hard to do, because there were a lot of people in New York who did not understand *Dark Crystal*, did not care about *Dark Crystal*. . . . And it was so essential to him to complete it and get it released." Producer

David Lazer understood Jim's obsession with his vision. "He had it in his head, and no one else saw it," said Lazer. "It was that strong."

The triumph that winter, however, was *Emmet Otter's Jug-Band Christmas,* which—after three years of wheeling, dealing, and cajoling by Brillstein—finally aired on ABC the week before Christmas 1980. Jim had been confident that, given a chance, the special would become a holiday staple, and *Variety* readily agreed that it deserved to be "a prospect for perennial usage during the holiday season." Critic John J. O'Connor, writing in *The New York Times,* thought the "charming" special worthy of Jim and the Muppets. Jim's faith in the special had been vindicated, and *Emmet* would be on its way to becoming an annual Christmas favorite.

The first week in February 1981, Jim left blustery, overcast London for the clearer skies of Albuquerque, New Mexico, where he would film the opening sequence for *The Great Muppet Caper*— a scene in which Kermit, Fozzie, and Gonzo float lazily in a hot air balloon as they comment on the opening credits. Jim spent much of the week with Oz and Goelz in a helicopter hovering alongside a radio-controlled hot air balloon a thousand feet in the air, performing their characters by remote control as a cameraman dangled from the bottom of a second helicopter, camera rolling. Other times, Jim would race across the desert with a chase team to steady the balloon as it came skidding in for a landing. After one particularly rough landing, the basket tipped over, spilling out the Muppets and badly scorching Fozzie in the balloon's propane burners. Luckily, Muppet builder Amy van Gilder was on hand to make the necessary repairs, earning a winking credit in *Caper* as the official "Muppet 'Doctor'" for her handiwork. After each day's filming, Jim spent time with his dad and Bob at their home near the foot of the glowing Sandia Mountains, and finally wrapped shooting on *The Great Muppet Caper* for good on February 6.

With *Caper* complete, Jim spent the next month ping-ponging between New York and London, attending meetings on *The Dark Crystal*—now scheduled to go before the cameras in mid-April— and skiing on slushy, muddy slopes in Stratton, Vermont. Then, at the end of March, came three days of pivotal meetings in London's Hyde Park Hotel, where Jim gathered a small group—including Jerry Juhl, creative director Michael Frith, and writer Jocelyn Stevenson—to discuss the international children's show that Peter Orton had suggested to Jim at the christening for Stevenson's son nearly a year earlier.

Since that evening's conversation, Jim had been thinking, brewing, and ruminating over the possibilities. In October 1980, he had discussed the mechanics of the idea with Lazer and a young producer named Duncan Kenworthy, who had overseen the marketing of the Arabic version of *Sesame Street*—then, a few weeks later, had raised the topic with Jane, Brillstein, Oz, and Frith. Those discussions, while useful, had been largely about the business and marketing strategies for breaking into the international market.

Now, in March 1981, Jim wanted to start developing the series itself—an International Children's Show, he was calling it—bringing Frith, Stevenson, Juhl and several others to the Hyde Park Hotel for a three-day brainstorming session. Jim's pitch to the creative team was simple: create a series that might make a difference—hopefully, with a new global reach—in the world at large. ("I want to do a children's television show that will stop war," Jim said cheekily.) With that noble directive on the table, said Frith, "we talked about doing a show . . . demonstrating how, through misconception, we can create problems that not only shouldn't be there, but can be self-destructive—and how, through harmony, we can achieve strength."

From the very beginning, Jim was intrigued with the idea of having three very different kinds of Muppet "species" linked together in some way that set up an unintentional but very necessary balance between them. "Something that [Jim] had been observing a lot in life is that we all live within our world, but there are other worlds going on at the same time," said Jane Henson. "We really don't know how the ants feel . . . but we know our world and we kind of think that that's it. . . . So he felt that he would like to do a show where there were three worlds and the struggle was to know how to keep each world strong, but also cooperate within the worlds. . . . He liked that, using the different worlds."

For three days, Jim and the creative team talked through various ideas, with Juhl and Stevenson scribbling down notes and Frith offering suggestions and drawing rough sketches of smiling, wide-eyed creatures crouched beneath underground water pipes and inside the foundations of houses. When it was over, Jim left with an armful of notes, stroking his beard thoughtfully. "[Jim's] genius," said Stevenson later, "is that he can sit through days of meetings getting completely different views from people—because he brought people in there to have different views, right?—and then at the end, he'd synthesize the whole thing." A week later, Jim did just that, synthesizing as he sat on board a Concorde flight from London to New York, compressing their three days of conversation into a treatment for a show they had decided to call *Woozle World*.

The set up for *Woozle World* was reminiscent of Jim's 1964 pilot *The Land of Tinkerdee*, with a live-action "old codger" and his Muppet dog living in a cluttered room containing a hidden door that led to the Woozles' underground world. But at the heart of Jim's proposal was the complex relationship between three different Muppet species—which, at the moment, Jim and the creative team were calling Wizzles, Woozles, and Giant Wozles—and how the three species might live in harmony, even if they didn't always mean to. "What the show is really about is people getting along with other people," wrote Jim, "and understanding the delicate balances of the natural world. . . . We will make the point that everything affects everything else, and that there is a beauty and harmony of life to be appreciated."

Several weeks later, Jim installed Juhl, Frith, and Stevenson in his house on Downshire Hill where they could begin the demanding task of fleshing out the Woozle world and its inhabitants. "Jim asked Jerry and Jocelyn and me to develop it and gave us his house to work in," said Frith. "And so we just went off there for a couple of weeks . . . and met every day and it was a silly, wonderful, wonderful time. . . . We loved it." One of the very first orders of business, however, was the show's name, since, as Stevenson pointed out, A. A. Milne had already used the word *woozles* in his Winnie-the-Pooh stories. Jim was open to suggestions—he had noted in his handwritten draft that the name would "likely be changed" anyway— and for a while, the group landed on the name *Googlies* for their main characters. But Jim, who thought carefully about the way words sounded and how they tumbled around in the mouth, wasn't happy with that—and after some consideration came back to the name he and Juhl had given their monsters in *The Great Santa Claus Switch* in 1970: the abrasive sounding *Frackles,* which was then softened to the warmer and fuzzier-sounding *Fraggles.*

For the rest of the summer, the Fraggle team built an entire universe with nearly the same fervor with which Jim had constructed the world of *The Dark Crystal,* putting together a comprehensive guide—a sort of Fraggle bible—to the Fraggles and their realm. In an enormous ringed binder labeled *Things We Know About the Fraggles,* the team polished and expanded on the parameters Jim had laid down in the *Woozle World* treatment, transforming the "old codger" and his cluttered room into the kindly tinker Doc (modeled, Juhl admitted, on Muppet technowizard Faz Fazakas) and his workshop, adding a sentient trash heap, and renaming and refining the other species with whom the Fraggles interacted, from the gigantic and dim-witted Gorgs to the tiny, hardworking Doozers. "We sat around and talked about the fact that we wanted to try to create a childhood fantasy world that had the sense of richness that we all felt in the [L. Frank Baum] *Oz* stories from our own childhoods," said Juhl. "Worlds like that are incredibly rich."

Frith, who illustrated and wrote out much of the Fraggle compendium in his beautiful cursive longhand, also tapped into another favorite childhood tale for inspiration: the real-life story of two boys in his native Bermuda who, in 1905, crawled down a hole to retrieve a lost cricket ball and discovered the breathtakingly beautiful Crystal Cave. With that in mind, Frith conceived of moving the Fraggles beyond just the confines of the foundation of Doc's house and deeper into an endless maze of underground tunnels and caves. That concept, too, made it easy to change the name they'd agreed on for the series from the British-tinged *Fraggle Hill* to the spunkier, edgier *Fraggle Rock.*

Jim was delighted with the work. With the comprehensive *Things We Know About the Fraggles* compendium—thoroughly illustrated with Frith's lively drawings—Jim felt certain he could land a network and put the show into production quickly. It was his worldview and philosophy that had driven the project—"*Fraggle Rock* was a true depiction of Jim's feelings of peace and harmony," said Lazer—but for the first time, Jim had been content to encourage, inspire, and motivate . . . then get out of the way and let his creative team take over. "I have wound up doing things in my career that I . . . could never have done on my own, because of Jim," said Juhl. "Jim was very good at doing that to people. I don't have the driving ambitions that he had. . . . [I was very good at] being able to use his ambition to do the creative work that I really wanted to do. . . . I'd always wanted to do something really big and bold in a children's show. . . . He could make that show [*Fraggle Rock*] happen. I couldn't have."

Frith often remarked that Jim had given them a "blank check" to develop the show, but it was really more of a blank canvas—one Jim had woven and sewn, then stretched and nailed over a picture frame that was precisely the size and shape he wanted. Then he had simply stepped back to let the other artists paint—and still, said Stevenson, "he'd make each one of you feel like you've made a major contribution to this. [He had] a really interesting ability to do that." Perhaps even more important, he had given them the luxury of *time*—the one thing he never seemed to have—to thoroughly think the project through. "Nobody's ever developed a television series better than we developed *Fraggle Rock*," said Juhl. "It was a long, very careful process. Jim had very high aspirations for that show and wanted to make sure it was just right."

Even as work was progressing on *Fraggle Rock* at Jim's home in Downshire Hill, Jim was ramping up *The Dark Crystal* at the workshop across the street. Over the last year, Jim had assembled a talented team to work alongside him on the film, giving *The Dark Crystal* the kind of collaborative atmosphere in which Jim thrived. "Creatively, I find I work best if I can work with someone—talking things over as ideas come up," said Jim. "And I do this best with people I'm very comfortable with—there has to be an absolutely pressure-free situation for this to work well."

Froud was one of those with whom Jim was very comfortable. Each thought visually and had a strong sense of design, and the two could communicate with each other in short bursts of only half-formed sentences, each seeming to intuitively know what the other wanted. Froud was the better artist, but just as with *Fraggle Rock*, it was Jim's overarching vision of the project that drove *Dark Crystal*. Still, said Muppet builder Sherry Amott, "there was some difficulty blending together Brian's and Jim's visions, because they often see things differently. Some of the time, it was difficult to know whom to please or how to please both. You wouldn't want to choose one idea over another but merge both into something else. That, I think, was the most challenging aspect of the project."

Besides Froud and the team in the workshop, Jim had brought in Gary Kurtz, fresh off *The Empire Strikes Back*, to serve as a producer, and Dick Smith—the renowned special effects wizard whose makeup had convincingly aged Dustin Hoffman in *Little Big Man*—as a makeup consultant. For the music—to Jim, one of the least appreciated but most important elements of a film—he had personally selected Trevor Jones, an unconventional young composer who had recently scored *Excalibur*, and who was anxious to experiment with new electronic sounds. Jim had also made the unorthodox decision to collaborate on the directing duties as well, asking Frank Oz to serve as his co-director. Oz was stunned; he had never directed before, and asked Jim why he wanted his help. "I think it would be better," said Jim plainly—a response Oz never forgot. "To Jim, that was the most important thing. The quality would be better . . . all he wanted was to work. He just wanted good stuff, that's all."

As the team prepared for the April filming date, Jim loved dropping into the workshop to see what fantastic creature might be in production on any given day. The creatures were large and complex—from the heavy, lumbering, carapace-shelled Garthim to the loping, long-limbed Landstriders—and Jim would regularly remind designers to keep in mind that it was the puppeteer, and not the puppet, that made a performance lifelike. No matter how beautifully constructed or realistic-looking a puppet might be—no matter how full of complicated mechanisms that blinked its eyes or pulled back its face into a smile—if the gadgetry got in the way of the puppeteer, the performance would suffer. "You have all of these techniques, but at the heart of all the mechanics is an actor performing a role, trying to get the subtlety of the movement," Jim explained. "That's the key thing, and all the technology can merely help and expand and give you more dimension." For the creatures of *The Dark Crystal,* then, Jim wanted to ensure that materials were lightweight and flexible, that any cables driving complex eye-blink or face-flexing mechanisms weren't in the performer's way, and—in the case of particularly large figures—that there was room underneath or inside the puppet for the performer to mount or wear a monitor.

Jim's ideal process was to focus the build around the puppeteer. "When we're doing major characters that we know have to be used through the entire film . . . we build a very rough prototype, put it on a person, videotape it, take a look at it, and then do a critique of it," said Jim. "Then we rip the whole thing apart, re-sculpt it, rebuild all the parts, and build it again." At times, it took three or four tries before Jim was happy with it. Heavy costumes had to be mounted on harnesses so the weight was carried on the puppeteer's hips, rather than on the back or shoulders. Jim also wanted to ensure that any large puppet, no matter how elaborate, could be put on easily and taken off quickly. "My father had a unique way of working," said Brian Henson. "He would visualize what you could do with a puppet or a person in costume before working on it. The whole film is a series of experiments in hiding people in costume, and creating movements that no one has ever seen before."

Sometimes, creating those movements required more than just puppetry skills. "We knew when we went into this film that there would be a lot of very difficult and uncomfortable characters to perform," said Jim. "So we looked for dancer/acrobat/mime performers—people who had the physical stamina to hold up and work in hot, uncomfortable positions." The first ads announcing auditions for performers for *The Dark Crystal,* in fact, didn't ask for puppeteers at all, but rather for "Mimes, Dancers and Actors." After selecting his new performers, Jim brought in the European mime artist Jean-Pierre Amiel to lead them through eight grueling months of training to determine how different kinds of creatures might move and to get them into the physical shape necessary to handle what Jim knew would be a demanding shoot. Jim—who never asked of performers anything he wouldn't do himself—thought those performing the quiet, stooped Mystics actually had the toughest job.

"Performers were on their haunches all the way down on their rear end, walking along very bent over," said Jim, "a position I could barely hold."

For Jim, part of the fun of creating a fantasy world wasn't just building the creatures, but creating everything else in the world as well, from plants and trees to swords and spoons. If a chair was needed in the background, for instance, the crew couldn't just grab a chair from the prop department; they had to build a chair that looked as if it belonged in Jim's fantasy world and had been made from materials found there. "I think the idea of conceiving of and building the *Dark Crystal* world from scratch was really appealing," said Jim. Working alongside the puppet designers in Downshire Hill, then, were jewelers, furniture and pottery makers, wood carvers and armor builders—an enormous team of craftsmen that ballooned the workshop staff from its initial seven to more than sixty. "We could never have tried something like *The Dark Crystal* even a few years earlier because, until recently, we didn't have the performers, the puppet builders or the technicians who could handle the problems involved," said Jim. "I think the idea for *The Dark Crystal* came along at about the time we were ready to handle it—which is basically the way things have happened all my life."

At last, on April 15, 1981, Jim began shooting on *The Dark Crystal*—a film he had been aching to make since 1978, and had pushed aside twice in favor of Muppet movies. "He was trying to reach out to do some things that he hadn't been able to do by doing Muppets," said Jane. "He loved the idea of trying for a different reality." So immersed was Jim in this world he was creating, in fact, that he had asked screenwriter David Odell not to write any dialogue for the Skeksis or Mystics. Instead, he wanted his creatures to speak a language all their own. While the film's main characters, the Gelflings Jen and Kira, would speak English, the villainous Skeksis and the wizened Mystics would communicate with a combination of squawks, grunts, groans, moans, and snippets of ancient Greek or Egyptian, making the film even *sound* otherworldly. It was a gamble, but as he stepped onto the soundstage at Elstree to begin shooting, Jim was confident the film's visuals were strong enough to clearly convey the plot and carry the story. "I guess I've always been most intrigued by what can be done with the visual image," he said later. "I feel that is what is strongest about the work I do, even today—just working with the image, the visual image."

Odell had made the best of Jim's story outline, writing a script steeped in fantasy tradition, in which a young hero—decreed by a prophecy to be the savior of his world—sets out on a quest to "heal" a shattered crystal that will magically merge the evil Skeksis and sage Mystics back into a single, magical species, the glowing, godlike UrSkeks. "It has a lot of elements of fairy tales and the standard fantasy elements," Jim said proudly—but Frith, who never flinched from giving Jim his opinion, thought the plot was "awful." *Dark Crystal* was "a story about genocide," Frith exclaimed, shaking his head even thirty years later. "And what you're saying is that you can extirpate an entire race of people and then, because the stars come together right, suddenly you've become some godlike figure and everything's okay." Jim would hear none of it, however; that was thinking about it too much. "We are working with primary images that appear in many stores of folk-lore and mythology," he explained patiently, again stressing the visuals of the film. "I like fairy tales very much. I like what they are and what they do." (Oz was more typically blunt in his response: "Well, we can't all be perfect," he told Frith dryly.)

As they co-directed their lavish fairy tale, Jim and Oz were a study in opposites, and some on the set likened them to Ernie and Bert: Jim in his bright, comfortable colors, grinning as he unconsciously combed at his beard with his enormous fingers; Oz in a fedora, arms folded, eyes narrowed with intensity. Despite their differences in style, he and Oz "had pretty much come to a common feeling about what we wanted," said Jim. "Besides that, we've worked together for over twenty years, so we know each other rather well." Still, having two directors on the set, Jim admitted, could be "a little tricky. . . . Movie units are not used to two people directing them . . . the units had to get used to the idea of running everything by both of us."

Not everyone got used to that idea. One assistant director pulled Jim and Oz aside to inform them that the crew was confused and wanted Jim to direct the film alone. Jim said no—but looking back,

Oz agreed that his involvement probably *was* making things difficult for nearly everyone. "Things were *not* smooth, but it was because of me," said Oz. "Things would have been smoother had I been more mature, but I was completely inexperienced. Jim should really have fired me several times because I was just this young guy who felt slighted because the crew saw Jim as the key guy. I felt I was ignored. People listened to Jim—as it should be. So, I should have been fired—but Jim, God bless him, just supported me. He was always patient. I'm sure I drove him crazy during that time, too, but we loved each other."

The *Dark Crystal* team, from the performers through the technical crew, quickly came to respect the power Jim could convey simply through his presence and respectful silence. "Jim didn't tell you what to do," said Oz. "He just was. And by him being what he was, he led and he taught. But by not answering, sometimes you answered your own question, and you could do more than you thought you could." Jim spent most of his time overseeing the technical side of things, directing elaborate special effects or large, noisy, crowd scenes—he especially relished working on the slobbering, gnashing Skeksis dinner banquet sequence, which had been in his story outline since the very first draft—while Oz worked more closely with the performers. Already notorious for calling for retake after retake on *The Muppet Show*, Oz continued to make similar demands on the set of *The Dark Crystal*. Jim, too, appreciated that several takes might be necessary, particularly when so many performers were trying to stay out of sight. But while Oz wanted takes to be perfect, Jim wanted takes to be right—a subtle, but important difference. "Jim had the head of a producer," said Lazer, "which meant he understood you can only do two or three takes and move on . . . and Frank, if he didn't feel it was right, wanted to continue . . . and sometimes wanted to over-rehearse when Jim didn't."

It was also obvious to Oz that while he and Jim might generally agree on the "common feeling" of the film, the true visionary on the set, from day one, was always Jim. "He saw the movie in his head," said Oz. "I didn't." For Oz, that distinction was never more apparent than during the several days spent filming the movie's climactic scene in which the stone walls of the Skeksis castle collapse to reveal their crystalline inner structure. "He had that all in his head," said Oz. "And he'd be doing a storyboard, and thinking about doing it in sections—and I'm thinking, 'I'm directing here, and I have no fucking idea what Jim's thinking or talking about.' It was his vision totally."

Jim was not only directing, he was performing one of the lead roles as well, taking on Jen, the Gelfling hero who ultimately brings order to the universe when he makes whole the Crystal of Power by merging it with the shard in his possession. Unlike most of the fantastic creatures populating *The Dark Crystal*, Jen bore a vague resemblance to a human child—a particular challenge for both the designers and the performers. "Everyone knows how a human moves and what we look like, so you set certain expectations," said Froud, "and if they are not fulfilled, people are disappointed." For Jim, that meant special care in figuring out how to move the puppet in a convincing or realistic manner. "I've never done any performing that difficult in my life," said Jim. "And the things that were the hardest were really ordinary things. . . . The Muppets can just go bouncing across the room . . . but when you have some characters that you have to believe in as living creatures, the movements are much more complex and subtle. Like, do you cut your eyes before you turn your head or after? Little things like that, things you normally wouldn't think about."

While Wendy Midener and the puppet builders had done their best to keep Jen light and flexible—she had even constructed the puppet around a mold of Jim's right hand—the figure was still heavier and clunkier than Jim would have liked. Kathy Mullen—only the third full-time female puppeteer in the Henson Associates stable—had rehearsed with her Kira puppet all summer, and had gone back to Midener several times for modifications that had significantly reduced the puppet's weight and increased its flexibility. Jim, however, "was just too damn busy to give it that much thought," said Mullen. "I had all kinds of time. . . . But he never did go in and work on it. He just struggled with what he had. And he made it work because he always did—but he made it hard on himself." Eventually, Faz Fazakas modified the Jen and Kira puppets so the delicate facial mechanisms could be operated by radio control rather than with thick cables connected to black control boxes. "I really do believe it saved our lives," recalled Mullen. Freed from the restrictions of the heavy cables, Jim and Mullen could concentrate solely on their performances, and not on the need to work around the technology.

And so it would go for nearly six months, with Jim and Oz—along with cinematographer Ossie Morris and producer Gary Kurtz, who served as the lead director for the second unit—working their way slowly and deliberately through each scene, creeping their cameras carefully through the massive sets sprawled across nine of Elstree's soundstages and out onto the backlot. While there were the usual challenges of filmed puppetry to overcome—even the most expensive, ornate sets were still platformed up, with removable floor panels—the complexity of the puppets, and the sheer number of people required to operate many of the characters, could slow things down considerably. "You see this character walking in the woods and the audience has no idea that there are television monitors, and cables, and radio control boxes, and all these performers swarming around just out of sight," said Jim. "You have to be concerned about keeping the cable crews out of shot . . . it's a slow process." Oz called it "an exercise in logistics"—and after five months of such meticulous filming, even Ossie Morris—who had shot his share of gigantic, sweeping epics—could be heard muttering, "This just never ends, does it?" "It was massive," agreed Oz.

Through it all, Jim continued to meet his obligations for *Sesame Street*—"You went off and built this great career," Joan Ganz Cooney told Jim warmly, "but you remained faithful, and I really appreciate it"—and huddled regularly with the *Fraggle Rock* team as they continued their work on Downshire Hill. In May there was a quick sprint through Spain with John and Cheryl, and then a weekend shooting several commercials for Polaroid. Jim wasn't thrilled with the thought of getting back into doing commercials again, but after several weeks of "grueling work" on *Dark Crystal,* he and the Muppet performers "had a wonderful time" performing their familiar Muppet characters for the Polaroid ads. "It was just so great to get back to those same old guys again," said Jim, "so we could play."

In June 1981, the movie featuring "those same old guys," *The Great Muppet Caper,* opened in the United States, though Jim was still at work at Elstree and could only discuss the film with American reporters via satellite feed. *Caper* marked Jim's first effort as a director, and as he waited for the reviews to come in, it didn't take long before it was clear the film was a rousing success. *Variety* lauded him for his "sure hand in guiding his appealing stars through their paces" and concluded that "no doubt remains that Miss Piggy and Kermit are now film stars in their own right." That assessment of the Muppet stars was shared by Vincent Canby at *The New York Times*— always one of Jim's most devoted admirers—who likened Kermit and Piggy to an old Hollywood power couple. For critic Rex Reed, the film was gloriously sentimental, full of "humanity, tenderness and intelligence" and "a musical in the best tradition"—exactly as Jim had intended.

One of the film's biggest fans was Joe Raposo, Jim's songwriter of choice for the film, whose love song "The First Time It Happens," would be nominated for an Academy Award. In the opening minutes of *The Great Muppet Caper,* Jim had chosen to give Raposo a prominent on-screen credit, with "Music and Lyrics by Joe Raposo" appearing by itself immediately following the film's title card—and Raposo, who knew nothing of the credit until watching the movie in a theater—was nearly moved to tears by the gesture.

Jim completed primary filming on *The Dark Crystal* in early September 1981, marking the occasion with a party for the movie's first unit at Stringfellow's nightclub in London. For the rest of the autumn he would continue to oversee filming by Kurtz and the second unit on various locations around England before hunkering down for the winter with film editor Ralph Kemplen to assemble the final film. With *Crystal* winding down and heading into postproduction, Jim was ready to turn his attention to other projects—mainly *Fraggle Rock*—but he wasn't the only one who was preparing for a change.

After six years at Jim's side, David Lazer informed Jim that he had decided to take an extended leave of absence. Lazer had battled with various aches and pains since childhood—the symptoms resembled Lyme disease—and now, at age forty-three, he was suffering from nearly debilitating arthritis, which had worsened over the last six years of almost nonstop work. Now he wanted to retire to Long Island to recover his health and oversee the construction of a house—and while he would retain his title as executive vice president and promised to continue to assist Jim as a producer for future films, he was removing himself from both the day-to-day operations of the company and television production. Jim took Lazer to a small dinner in London with Brian and Wendy Froud, then put him on a flight for New York the week before wrapping *Dark Crystal*, allowing Lazer to depart quietly, with little fuss or fanfare, just as he had asked—or so Lazer thought. Three months later, on the day after Christmas, Jim and Brian pulled up in front of Lazer's house in a brand-new $35,000 limited edition black Mercedes coupé. Jim and Brian stepped out of the car, which they'd driven shoeless so as not to scuff or muddy up the car's floor mats, and handed Lazer the keys. "[Jim] was just like a little kid, beaming," said Lazer.

As Lazer's replacement, Jim brought back Diana Birkenfield, his producer from the late 1960s and early 1970s who had often rattled him with her frank appraisals of projects. Despite Birkenfield departing under a cloud in 1974, there were no doubts that the renewed professional relationship would work. "Yeah, she was absolutely no bullshit," said Oz, "but she was also very good at her job. For Jim, that was really all that mattered." With Birkenfield in place, Jim could now focus on *Fraggle Rock,* a project that was falling into place with a cheerful efficiency entirely in tune with *Fraggle*'s colorful optimism.

Jim had Brillstein making the rounds among television networks with the comprehensive *Fraggle Rock* proposal, and was so confident the series would sell that he had put the show into preproduction in Toronto without a firm deal in place. Part of the preproduction process involved finding the right performers for each of *Fraggle*'s five main characters, which had been built according to Frith's designs and now sat on workshop tables in New York. In early November, Jim called in all the major Muppet puppeteers and asked them to perform with each Fraggle—and with each other—to see if they could come up with characters. Such freewheeling play had helped define and hone the characters on *The Muppet Show,* and Jim wanted to see how his performers ad-libbed and bounced off of each other. Partly, it had to do with finding the right chemistry between the five main characters, consisting of four distinctive character types—the athlete, the artist, the worrywart, and the indecisive one—revolving around a steady central character. It was the *Pogo* formula all over again, an approach that Jim's fellow *Pogo* fans Frith and Juhl said was intentional. "We said, 'All right, we're going to have five characters . . . each of whom is a different wedge of the pie,'" said Frith. "But when you put them all together, you get the *whole* pie."

More important, for the first time Jim would not be performing any of the show's central characters; with Jim out of the eye of the Muppet hurricane, then, getting the chemistry right was critical. Frith, an admirer of Jerry Nelson and in awe of his singing voice, had always intended for Nelson to serve as the show's anchor in the lead role of Gobo—the role to which he was eventually assigned—but Jim still wanted each performer trying out different characters in case sparks flew among an unexpected combination of puppeteers. Karen Prell, for example, who came into the casting call hoping to land the role of the introspective poet Mokey, found herself assigned instead to the outgoing athlete Red. "But I really have to thank Jim for wanting to try me as Red," said Prell, "because it was obviously the perfect thing to bring out a lot of crazy Red stuff in myself that I guess he could see." Dave Goelz, who was given the role of the fretful Boober, was convinced that Jim and the *Fraggle* writers had known all along which performer would play what role, and merely wanted to confirm their instincts through the auditions. "I think we went through the motions of playing around with the puppets in New York before we went to Toronto to shoot," related Goelz. However, Steve Whitmire, who was handed the amiable but indecisive Wembley, wasn't so sure. "I really pushed to do that character [Wembley], but we did ad-lib sort of improvisations. . . . I'm not sure how that ended up happening the way it did. I think it happened the best way that it could have happened."

In the middle of casting, Brillstein informed Jim that he had found a home for *Fraggle Rock*—but not with one of the major networks. Instead, Brillstein had placed the series with the subscriber cable channel HBO, which opted to co-produce the show along with Henson Associates, the British television company Television South, and the Canadian Broadcasting Corporation. With only nine million subscribers, HBO's viewership was still small—Jim didn't even have cable, much less HBO, at his home in Bedford—but HBO was aggressively working to expand its subscriber base and promised creative freedom and a high profile for the Fraggles, intending for *Fraggle Rock* to be its first original weekly series—the colorful ancestor to later original series like *The Larry Sanders Show* and *The Sopranos.*

HBO was also hoping to have the series ready for broadcast in early 1983. Since each season would contain twenty-four episodes—and Jim intended for the team to keep to the one-episode-per-week pace they had maintained for *The Muppet Show*—that meant Jim had to begin shooting as quickly as possible. In preparation, the *Fraggle Rock* performers were sent to Toronto to spend several weeks rehearsing and improvising their characters, "just kind of finding out who they were," said Kathy Mullen, who was assigned the role of Mokey.

Jim, meanwhile, returned to a cold and snowy London to oversee work on *The Dark Crystal*, spending several days in January 1982 at Abbey Road Studios with composer Trevor Jones as the London Symphony Orchestra recorded the film's music. Like the puppets in *Dark Crystal*, the music, too, was a fusion of the traditional and the technological, and Jones had brought several unconventional instruments into the session that seemed to embody this approach, carting in a synthesizer and a nineteenth-century double flageolet, a woodwind instrument that produced a droning, otherworldly sound. "I like to think [that what] my music did is bridge the gap between the world that wasn't real and the audience, giving a sense of a real world to something that is totally unreal," said Jones later. "In that process the hardest thing to do was trying to enter the mind of Jim and think of the things he wanted for his film." As so many others had come to understand, Jones could see that Jim saw—and heard—the entire movie in his head. "He knew how great the score would be," said Jones, "he just wanted me to discover it for myself."

Things were far less harmonious outside Abbey Road Studios,

however. That January, Lord Grade had found himself suddenly, almost inexplicably, driven out as the head of his own organization, now broadly known as the Associated Communications Corporation, or ACC. The culprit was a soft-spoken but ruthless Australian entrepreneur named Robert Holmes à Court, a corporate raider who acquired real estate, oil and gas producers, and television and film studios as casually as other businessmen collected cuff links. Over the past eighteen months, Holmes à Court had vacuumed up non-voting shares in Grade's ACC, then worked his way onto Grade's board, where he stealthily acquired more stock. By January 1982, he finally had enough leverage to force Grade from his own company. "It was a clash of an old-style film mogul-entrepreneur with our more disciplined management style," said Holmes à Court.

That sort of management style was bound to grate on Jim, who still preferred doing business with a handshake over a good meal. "Holmes à Court was a cold, carpetbagger businessman," said Oz. "He's just money and power, that's all. And to Lew, that's not what it was about. Jim was like Lew. Their spirits were together." But with Grade out, Jim was forced to deal with Holmes à Court as his new overlord at ACC—and on January 17, Jim and Holmes à Court met at ACC's Great Cumberland Place headquarters near Hyde Park, mostly just so the two of them could size each other up. Jim likely left with a bad taste in his mouth. To Holmes à Court, who knew little or nothing about filmmaking, Jim and his projects were merely lines in an accounting ledger, assets to be traded and sold when they were no longer of interest. Jim was determined to get *Dark Crystal* away from him as quickly as possible.

It was far cheerier back in Toronto, where Jim arrived in early March to oversee the beginning of production on *Fraggle Rock*. Jim would direct seven episodes of *Fraggle* during its first season and occasionally perform several recurring characters—but once the show was up and running, he was content to turn the show almost entirely over to the *Fraggle* team. "*Fraggle Rock* is the first show that I personally didn't have to be involved with every day," Jim said later. "A group split off to do that, and it's worked out very nicely." "He just let it be what it was," said Steve Whitmire.

By letting go, Jim was growing and nurturing the talent within his company—and he was impressed with the work that was being done on *Fraggle Rock*. While Jim had checked over Frith's designs during the show's development, he'd stepped back from trying to influence the overall look or feel, giving Frith a free hand to create a universe in much the same way he'd encouraged Froud to determine much of the look of *The Dark Crystal*. "I think of myself as fairly limited as a designer. Michael is much better than I am," Jim said generously, "and he has been just right for *Fraggle Rock*."

He also loved the technology that was being integrated seamlessly into the Fraggle world, from the tiny, radio-controlled Doozers and their equipment that rolled and rumbled across the set, to the gigantic, walkaround Gorgs with their remote-controlled mouths. "Jim was a huge gadget fan," said Brian Henson. "He just loved them. When the first Sony Walkman came out, he had to go out and buy one straight away. He loved the magical properties of technology." The Gorgs in particular were another leap in puppetry, using the lessons—and technologies—from the *Dark Crystal* experience to allow the puppeteers a much more fluid motion for their performance. "*Dark Crystal* was a $25 million R&D project for *Fraggle Rock*," said Michael Frith, "because all that stuff that we invented for *Dark Crystal* I rolled right into *Fraggle Rock*."

While the Gorgs appeared to be simple walkaround Muppets like Big Bird, there were actually two performers at work: one inside the full-body costume, and a second sitting just off-camera performing the mouth and eyes using a radio-controlled device called a *waldo*. The waldo resembled a high-tech oven mitt—and once Richard Hunt had his hand inside of it, he could bring his thumb and fingers together to remotely open and close the mouth of Junior Gorg ten feet away. Since the performer inside the costume didn't have to work the puppet's mouth, both arms were freed up, making the puppet's movements even more lifelike. "Neat," said Jim appreciatively.

On the occasions when Jim did come in to perform or direct, said Steve Whitmire, "it was very special." Jim loved playing the two characters writers Jerry Juhl and Jocelyn Stevenson had created for him—most likely because each channeled a very specific part of Jim's own personality. Like *The Dark Crystal*'s UrSkeks, magically cleft into two disparate beings, Jim could well have been split into his two *Fraggle Rock* characters: the soft-spoken sage Cantus—who dispensed wisdom in enigmatic, Zen-like nuggets ("There are no rules . . . and those are the rules")—and the energetic, persuasive Convincing John, who could talk the Fraggles into doing *anything*. Cantus in particular became one of Jim's favorite characters to perform. "[Cantus] was great," said Stevenson, "because he was goofy and wise at the same time, kind of like Jim was in real life."

Apart from its noble theme of global community, what truly aimed *Fraggle Rock* directly at the international market was its framing sequence, or the "home base," as Jim called it—the real-world workshop occupied by Doc and his dog, Sprocket, with the small door that opened onto the Fraggles' world. "The idea," said Jim, "was that we would do this home-base segment in different countries, replacing the Doc character with one developed especially for whichever country we were in," and then edit these locally produced sequences back into the master show. In France, then, the Fraggle hole would be in a former bakery overseen by a chef and his dog Croquette, while in England the Fraggles existed in a lighthouse presided over by a crusty sailor known as the Captain.

Fraggle Rock would make its debut on HBO on January 10, 1983, and become an immediate hit, embraced not only by viewers, but by critics, who hailed it as "completely endearing" and "fetchingly whimsical." During its five-year run, *Fraggle Rock* would eventually be broadcast in over ninety countries—many of which dubbed their local language in over Jim's English-speaking version—but Jim even managed to break into a foreign market no one ever expected: the Soviet Union. In 1989, at Jim's urging, the Soviet Union's governing television body *Gosteleradio* televised an episode of *Fraggle Rock* and was stunned when it drew "unprecedented" ratings and more than three thousand fan letters. Intrigued, *Gosteleradio* added both *Fraggle Rock* and *The Muppet Show* to its fall broadcast schedule, making them the first Western television series to air on Soviet television. It was groundbreaking, goodwill television—or, as Jim called it with typical understatement, "a very nice project."

On March 19, 1982, Jim was finally ready to unveil the first full edit of *The Dark Crystal* at a special sneak preview in Washington, D.C.

The purpose of the preview, wrote Jim in a memo to his staff, was "to make final decisions regarding the editing of the film as well as the audio and the music." He had spent the last few weeks dubbing sound for the film, and he was still certain that having the Mystics and Skeksis speak their own foreign language was the right decision— that the visuals and the performance alone would be enough to clearly tell the story.

Michael Frith wasn't so confident. Months earlier, while he and Juhl were still in London working on *Fraggle Rock,* Jim had excitedly asked the two of them to watch one of the first segments he had edited together, the enormous and loud Skeksis banquet scene that Jim absolutely loved. Frith and Juhl sat in the darkened screening room and watched as the Skeksis cackled and hooted at each other in their own language, a scene that seemed to be "going on forever," Frith lamented. Afterward, Frith walked down to the reception area where Jim was slouched down on a sofa, hands folded across his stomach, waiting for Frith's verdict. "What did you think?" Jim asked brightly. "Jim, there's one thing I just have to say," Frith began slowly. But Jim was already sinking down farther into the couch, pulling a sofa pillow down over his ears in mock surrender. "I know what you're going to say!" Jim laughed. "I'm not listening! *I'm not listening!*"

"He knew," said Frith. "I said, 'Jim, I have *no idea* what that scene was about. You've got to have them talk or at least give them subtitles.' . . . But he believed that the story would unfold and be clear through the actions and the personalities of the characters." On the day of the Washington preview, Jim still believed it—and he had proudly invited his father to attend the showing of what he regarded as "close to being an epic" film as he might get. "He was so proud of it," said Cheryl. "He had his father come up to see it. And the audience hated it."

"Not great," Jim reported in his private journal after the preview—and that was putting it mildly. The audience was baffled. As the theater emptied, Jim slowly stood up and walked out, stunned. He had made "a big miscalculation that you could understand a story with just visual language," said Lisa Henson. "[He thought] you could watch it like an opera . . . and you would be able to understand the story even if you only understood snippets of dialogue and language. And this was completely wrong. People wanted to understand every word of it." Executives at ACC and Universal—which had picked up the film's distribution rights—were similarly confused. An earlier private screening for film company executives hadn't gone well, either. "The movie went off," said Oz, "and there was dead silence."

Jim was crushed. "He felt the studio was trying to make it into something that they felt the audience would want—and I don't think that Jim was too interested in working for that," said Jane. "He sincerely did not believe that you . . . get an audience by trying to please them; you get an audience by doing good work." But in its current state, The Dark Crystal seemed to ACC and Universal to be nothing more than a $25 million art film, an expensive failed experiment. Cheryl remembered being "very anxious" for her father. "[There was] that sense of dismay," said Cheryl, "and I think that it was very hard for my father—and he rose above it."

There was nothing to do but go back and redub the entire movie with English dialogue. Screenwriter David Odell was dispatched to begin the difficult task of drafting dialogue that not only conveyed the plot, but also matched the mouth movements and gestures of the puppets. "It was a huge overhaul," said Lisa, and for weeks, Odell hunched over a videotape of the film in a hotel toom, "running a tape backwards and forward," recalled Odell, "counting lip flaps to see where we could put dialogue that would sync with the action." Odell completed the task by early June, and Jim sprinted to London to begin the final mix for The Dark Crystal, recording new character voices with English actors—including Barry Dennen and Billie Whitelaw, who had chewed the scenery as The Omen's demonic nanny—and then spent several weeks synchronizing the voices with the visuals. In mid-July, four months after the disastrous Washington preview, Jim headed back to the States, bound for Detroit, where he would again try Dark Crystal before an audience.

"A bit better," Jim wrote afterward in his journal, but as he left the preview he was becoming more discouraged by the moment. While the dubbed language had taken care of the main problem, Holmes à Court's bankers were meddling in things now, asking for more changes, this time relating to the story and to what Jim regarded as the underlying philosophy of the film. The Mystics, they thought, were "too boring"; they recommended that Jim reduce their screen time and devote more attention to the Skeksis, which the audience seemed to like. Jim *hmmmm*ed politely, then sank silently into his seat. "He felt that the movie was about a balance," said Jane, "and when they wanted to take out a lot of the Mystic stuff . . . and made it much too heavy on the Skeksis, it turned it into a different and darker thing. . . . Because Jim was actually much more interested in the Mystic side of it."

That kind of pressure was almost more than he could bear—but when ACC insisted on participating in the editing process, Jim decided he'd had enough. "I can't work like this," he said flatly. "I've got to get these guys out of here." "There was really only one thing he could do," said John Henson. The moment he returned to the Henson Associates offices at One Seventeen in New York, Jim called Bernie Brillstein. "I'm going to buy back *The Dark Crystal*," he told the agent.

Brillstein was stunned. "How much?" he finally stammered into the phone, and was further shocked when Jim explained that he was planning to take all the cash he had on hand—about $15 million, most of it revenue from Muppet merchandise—and make Holmes à Court an offer. "You're crazy," Brillstein exploded. "Anyone who invests in their own movie is nuts!" But Jim wasn't hearing it. "Bernie, I don't like what they're doing with it," he said—and the two of them went back and forth for several minutes, their voices growing louder and louder, their sentences more clipped.

"And then," recalled Brillstein, smiling at the memory years later, "he hits me with it, the son of a bitch—and I love him." Quietly, Jim reminded Brillstein of their conversation from fifteen years earlier, when Brillstein had urged Jim to license his Muppet characters for merchandising. *If it works like I think it's gonna work,* Brillstein had said then, *you will be financially independent and you can use the money for your own independence.* He was buying his independence and creative freedom. "You told me I could do this," said Jim calmly.

"What do you say?" recalled Brillstein. "He nailed me." Jim was determined, but Brillstein was still nervous about the deal. As far as he was concerned, it was just Jim's whim of steel again, and Brillstein spoke at length with both Al Gottesman and David Lazer, still in retirement on Long Island, to see if there was any way to talk Jim out of it. It was clear there wasn't. "That was a business decision no one could dissuade him from," said Gottesman. Even Jane, who was conservative when it came to financial decisions—especially those requiring such leaps of faith as gigantic as this one—knew it was useless to try to talk Jim down. The movie meant too much to him. "When he had made up his mind," said Lazer, "there was no deterring him. Money couldn't deter him. People's opinion couldn't do it. He went ahead and did what he felt was right. And most of the time, he was right."

In less than a month, Jim owned *The Dark Crystal*. While he would still have to deal with Universal as the distributor, he had gotten himself entirely away from Holmes à Court and ACC, paying $15 million cash to relieve the mogul of Grade's initial $25 million investment. It was an enormous risk not only for Henson Associates but for Jim personally—and John Henson remembered being terrified as a teenager that the family was going to lose everything. "It was a huge gamble," said Cheryl. Despite the hand-wringing around him, Jim had remained unflappable during the entire transaction; it had seemed only logical. "It was a good deal," he told Oz.

After much back-and-forthing with Universal, the studio finally agreed to release *The Dark Crystal* nationally the week before Christmas 1982. In the months leading up to the December release, Jim was determined to build a buzz about the film, making a presentation at the World Science Fiction Convention in Chicago, producing a behind-the-scenes documentary, and opening *Dark Crystal*–related exhibits at the Craft Gallery in Los Angeles and at New York's Lincoln Center Library. Most ambitious, perhaps, he had also asked the costumers in the London workshop to create a *Dark Crystal* Clothing Collection—described by its designers as "dramatic haute couture"—to be sold exclusively through four high-end boutiques, including Jim's favorite, Liberty's of London. The fashion line ended up being more notable for its flashy window displays, which used puppets and props from the film, than for its sales—but for Jim, who appreciated craftsmanship and design, the fun had been more in the doing than in the selling.

In early December, Jim, Oz, and producer Gary Kurtz began a worldwide press tour to promote *The Dark Crystal,* set to premiere in New York in mid-December. Anticipation for the film was high— Jim's name was enough to stir up interest in almost any project—but as he made the rounds with television reporters and newspaper writers, it was becoming clear he had a problem. After watching clips of Skeksis and Mystics and Gelflings, reporters were baffled. "What happened to the Muppets in your new movie?" was the typical question, and rather than talking about the film, Jim found himself instead trying to manage expectations. "They're not there," he explained patiently, "and that is one of the reasons I'm doing some PR on this movie . . . so that people won't go expecting one thing and see something else. . . . There are two totally different dimensions going on here."

Still, when Jim could finally turn the conversation to the film, his excitement was palpable. He loved when interviewers were dazzled by the creatures they saw and demanded to know how Jim had done it. "We're not telling!" Jim grinned. "This is a very exciting time to be making movies," he said. "With all of the developments in special effects—make up, opticals, matte work—I think we can create just about anything on film that the imagination can conceive. So I hope I'll be able to continue working in this area, because I'm having a great time."

The Dark Crystal premiered in New York on December 13, 1982. The early reviews weren't promising. *The New York Times*'s Vincent Canby, who wanted desperately to like the movie, couldn't muster up much enthusiasm for what he called "a watered down J. R. R. Tolkien." Canby quickly zeroed in on the problem: "A lot of obvious effort has gone into this solemn fairy tale," he wrote, "but all of it has been devoted to the complicated technical problems. . . . [The] story by Mr. Henson, is without any narrative drive whatever. It's without charm as well as interest." Worse, he found the characters "unexceptional" and designed without any sense of "humor or wit."

Still, it wasn't all bad. Following its December 17 nationwide opening, a reviewer for *The Washington Post* was so awed by the film's visuals he could hardly bother to concern himself with the story, noting, "Jim Henson and his colleagues have reached a point where they can create and sustain a powerfully enchanting form of cinematic fantasy." *The Boston Globe* found it "enjoyable [and] imaginative," while *Variety* was generally positive, saying the story was "sketchy" but "well handled."

The mixed response was typical. "*The Dark Crystal* really polarized opinion," said Brian Henson. "People who liked it, loved it. But others were not so keen." Generally, though, the reaction from moviegoers was a disinterested shrug. While *Dark Crystal* was impressive—"ambitious" was the word used most often to describe it—it just wasn't much fun. "I find that often the most effective things we do are simple," Jim had once said, "and that elaborate production does not always add to the entertainment value of the film." That was the biggest problem with *The Dark Crystal;* for the first time, Jim had let spectacle get in the way of the story. His vision had come first, the story second—and the audience, usually willing to meet Jim more than halfway, had been unforgiving.

Still, *Dark Crystal* performed steadily and respectably, grossing $40 million during its initial nine-week release, well over the $15 million Jim had paid Holmes à Court for it. The gamble had paid off—but for Jim, *The Dark Crystal* had never been about profit and loss; it was about vision and inspiration, and the fact that audiences didn't or couldn't appreciate it hurt him terribly. "I felt sad for Jim," said Oz. "I helped him with *Dark Crystal*, and I learned an incredible amount, but it wasn't my vision. I just felt bad for him."

"I thought I had failed miserably and I just couldn't watch it," said Kathy Mullen, who had spent six months performing Kira. Over time, however, she came to appreciate what had been accomplished. "What you have here is something that could never have been done before and will never be done again," she said. "It stands alone as the only all-hand-puppet, all-live-action extravaganza ever made. . . . Today you'd rely on computers or visual effects to accomplish all that we did. But back then, everything on the screen— *everything*—was handmade. . . . That makes *The Dark Crystal* a unique artifact from a unique moment in media history. I think that's a phenomenal thing."

Oz, however, thought it was even simpler than that. "The most impressive thing is that *it was done at all*. It came from Jim's head and it actually happened. Yeah, it didn't go over quite the way Jim wanted. But he's a phoenix," said Oz, "he rose again."

CHAPTER TWELVE

TWISTS AND TURNS

1982–1986

Jim with the heroes of 1986's Labyrinth.

"WE HAVE BEEN VERY PLEASED WITH THE RESULTS OF *THE DARK CRYS-tal*," wrote Jim in early 1983—and with good reason. Despite Universal's marked lack of faith and a tepid response from critics, *Dark Crystal* ended up being one of the most successful films distributed by the studio in 1982, eventually grossing over $60 million worldwide in less than a year. Part of its success was likely due to Jim's active promotion, especially in the foreign market; in the first three months of 1983, Jim traveled to Italy, England, Germany, France, Spain, Japan, and Australia ("first time," Jim noted in his journal) to chat about the film.

If Jim had been frustrated by moviegoers who didn't seem to appreciate the art of *The Dark Crystal,* he found a much more receptive audience among science fiction and fantasy fans who more fully understood just how groundbreaking the film was. In France, *Dark Crystal* was awarded the best film at the Avoriaz Fantastic Film Festival, while the Academy of Science Fiction, Fantasy and Horror Films presented Jim with its prestigious Saturn Award for Best Fantasy Film—not bad for a year in which it was competing with heavy hitters like *E.T.: The Extra Terrestrial* and *Blade Runner.* For Jim, the critical acclaim was even more gratifying than the financial success. "[*The Dark Crystal*] was a huge undertaking—a vision I had," he wrote, "and one which ultimately has helped to carry our art form to a more sophisticated and technically advanced stage. The most important thing, however, is to love what you're doing and to go after those visions, no matter where they lead."

Although his schedule in early 1983 sent him leaping from continent to continent for press junkets for *Dark Crystal* and to Toronto to work intermittently on *Fraggle Rock,* for the first time in more than seven years Jim had neither a weekly series nor a film in production. For all his involvement with *Fraggle,* its day-to-day operation was left largely in the hands of producers Diana Birkenfield and Larry Mirkin. That left him time to do a bit of skiing and dog sledding in Aspen in January, followed by a two-day vacation with family at the recently opened EPCOT theme park at Walt Disney World, a place Jim quickly came to love.

As she watched Jim interact with the cast of *Fraggle Rock* that winter, Diana Birkenfield—who had only recently returned to Henson Associates after seven years away—thought Jim had changed much in the last decade. *The Muppet Show* had made both Jim and his characters internationally famous; wherever he went now, he was recognized—and, indeed, was slightly flabbergasted if he was *not.* While living in London, he flitted from private club to private club, drove to the theater in his low-slung Lotus, hosted loud dinner parties, and joyously flew kites on Hampstead Heath. Those experiences, that lifestyle, had made him more cultivated and—though he might argue otherwise—trendier and hipper.

And he even *looked* hipper. While Jim would always enjoy bright colors and would continue wearing fashionably cozy and flashy Missoni sweaters, he had lately begun dressing entirely in white, wearing white linen pants and comfortable jackets with no tie, with white canvas shoes. He had even become a "white meat vegetarian," eating only vegetables with white fish or chicken, and drinking *kir* or white wine. His beard was more tightly trimmed now, shaped closer to his face, and his hair, lightly flecked with gray, was cut shorter, and often swept back, falling just onto his collar and exposing a very visible widow's peak. He had to wear glasses every now and then, too, sporting chic, rectangular lenses in tortoiseshell frames that shaped his face and made him look studious.

There were some who grumbled that he looked and acted as if he had "gone Hollywood"—an accusation Jerry Juhl thought was inevitable for anyone who happened to make films. "In this business, there is nothing more compelling, more exciting [than] . . . feature films," said Juhl kindly. "There's something seductive about the process. . . . I think Jim really felt it. He really loved it. And got caught up in it." Bernie Brillstein thought it was more about celebrating and enjoying success and fame. "He loved the good things," said Brillstein. "And he loved to be in the world of celebrities."

Yet, when it came to family, Jim remained as grounded as ever. A devoted and diligent son, he had always made an effort to visit his father whenever he could, dropping into Albuquerque on his way to California, and was now traveling regularly to and from Ahoskie, North Carolina, where he was having a house built for his dad and Bobby. But it was the five Henson children who would always be the most important part of his life—he frequently alluded to them as his proudest accomplishment—and Jim would work with some, and travel and vacation with others.

And then there was Jane. Their marriage had grown increasingly fractious over the last decade; further, it had become well known that Jim had dated several women while in London—including some of his own employees—and Jim did little to deny or defend his reputation for a wandering eye. Even in the Muppet workshops, there would always be whispering about which female employee Jim might favor at a given moment, though such conversations rarely erupted into the open. Still, Jim was mindful of Jane's feelings, doing his best to do his going out—as Jane still called it—as discreetly as he could. Discussing it with Jane wasn't his style, and hurt feelings weren't Jim's way; instead, he merely compartmentalized his life into two distinct pieces, Work Jim and Home Jim, with one on each side of the Atlantic. "He wanted my mom to be happy," said Cheryl, "and he wanted it all to be okay, so he wound up living a London life and a New York life."

Now, however, with *Dark Crystal* completed and the London workshop idle, Jim's London life had come to an end. After years in the house in bustling and picturesque Hampstead, it was time to return to the suburbs of Bedford, New York—and to Jane. One afternoon, Jane came home to find Jim looking wistfully at his surroundings and at the life they had built in Bedford. "I can't come back here," he told Jane quietly. In fact, he told her, he had already found himself an apartment on the nineteenth floor of the upscale Sherry-Netherland hotel in Manhattan. "Fine," said Jane, mistakenly thinking Jim was merely looking for a place in the city where he could stay when he was working, instead of camping in the top-floor suite of One Seventeen as he usually did. Over omelets the next morning, Jane asked Jim how they would decorate the new apartment. "I thought we were sort of still doing things together, like we did in the house in London," said Jane. But Jim just shook his head. "This time," he said softly, "I'm doing it by myself."

Refusing Jane's help with the decorating was an indication of the state of their marriage—and was likely as confrontational as Jim was ever going to get about it. "It was the first time that had ever happened," said Jane. "It felt very poignant." Yet, Jim *still* wasn't ready to ask for a divorce. "Jim wanted to be separated *and* married," Jane said. "He wanted to do both. He didn't really *not* want to be married." The truth was, Jim loved the idea of family. "He could have asked for a divorce at any time, but he didn't, and neither did I," said Jane. "He held the family together. He liked to come home to a house and kids and pets."

After much discussion, however, Jim and Jane agreed to legally separate—a "handshake of a separation," Jane would call it—something that would permit Jim to "have an above-board independent life," said Lisa Henson, allowing him to openly have other relationships, without the associated guilt he always felt. Typically, Jim favored keeping the proceedings as quiet as possible, asking Al Gottesman and Karen Barnes—two of Henson Associates' most trusted and discreet attorneys—to represent him and Jane in the negotiations. It was an ill-advised jumbling of private and professional affairs, tangling company business in Jim and Jane's private disagreement—and things "escalated quickly," remarked Jane, with the most contentious point being Jane's rightful share in Henson Associates. It was "painful and inevitable," recalled Lisa, and the finalized agreement would separate Jane not only from Jim, but from the company she had helped him found and build more than two decades ago.

The formal separation would remain in place for the rest of Jim's life—and the stack of legal papers would eventually tower to nearly a foot high, with an eye toward divvying up the company and permanently dissolving their marriage. Heather Henson, then twelve, remembered being "really upset" and burst into tears when she learned her parents were separating and heading toward divorce. "There was a part of me that wanted them to stay married, even though all this hoo-hah was going on," said Heather later. For now, Jim and Jane would officially separate, and Jane and Heather would remain in the house in Bedford while Jim moved out of the suburbs and into his Fifth Avenue apartment in the sky. As if modeling himself on the UrSkeks in *The Dark Crystal,* he was at last merging his two separate selves—Work Jim and Home Jim—into a single Jim Henson.

As the weather warmed, Jim had two major projects under way. The first was another Muppet-related movie—at the moment titled simply *Muppet Movie III*—that he was planning to put before the cameras in late spring. Jim had decided to serve as a producer of the film, along with David Lazer, but had placed the directing duties squarely in the hands of Frank Oz. "I was looking at the year ahead and I thought my own life was going to be very busy," said Jim, "and I thought maybe this is a time to have Frank try directing one of these. . . . He went into shock first, then said he wanted a couple of days to think about it." Oz didn't need long to tell Jim yes. "I had learned a lot about directing by co-directing with Jim on *The Dark Crystal*, and I think he just felt at this point he could trust me not to fuck it up," said Oz. "I think by producing it with Dave, Jim could be a part of it and still do other things he wanted to do."

What Jim really wanted to do was his *other* project—another sprawling, ambitious collaboration with Brian Froud, based on an idea the two of them had cooked up in a limo as they left a lackluster showing of *The Dark Crystal* in San Francisco. As the limo pulled away from the theater, Jim and Froud stared at each other in stunned silence. Then Jim started giggling. "The next one will be *so much better!*" laughed Jim, and excitedly began describing several Eastern and Indian folktales he had heard from Lisa, who was studying mythology at Harvard. Jim pictured colorful gods soaring across the sky—but Froud was quiet; that sort of folklore, he told Jim, wasn't really his forte; he much preferred goblin stories. Jim brightened. "Great!" he said—but explained that he didn't want to repeat what he thought had been *The Dark Crystal*'s most fatal flaw. "This time," he told Froud, "I want *people* in the film."

While the lack of live actors actually wasn't *Crystal*'s biggest problem, the suggestion of a human cast was enough for Froud to begin to address what really *had* been the film's main weakness: the story. "I immediately pictured a baby surrounded by goblins," said Froud, "[and] I told Jim that traditionally goblins steal babies." Jim nodded and *hmmm*ed thoughtfully. "That's the beginning of our story," he told Froud, "but what else?" Froud was stumped, but suggested that perhaps a maze "would make a really good metaphor for the soul's journey."

Jim was intrigued by Froud's suggestion, and while promoting *The Dark Crystal* in Japan, he began filling pages of a notebook with notes for a film to be called *The Labyrinth*—or, perhaps, *The Maze* or even *The Labyrinth Twist*. Jim's first outline involved two of his favorite archetypes, a king and a jester, working their way through a maze filled with elaborate traps and exotic monsters. Even at this stage, Jim already had a strong sense for the look of the film, sketching out a giant Buddha statue trapping the heroes in a cage, rooms filled with snakes, and an island with a trapdoor in it. He also knew he wanted a carved door that somehow came to life, as well as an Escher-like sequence in which it was impossible to tell up from down—both images that would end up in the final film. While there were also some darker sequences—he envisioned a room full of jewels that would bleed if one was picked up—Jim very deliberately wanted to include plenty of humor, an ingredient critics had found distinctly lacking in *The Dark Crystal*.

At the end of March, Jim flew to London to meet with Froud and Dennis Lee, the Canadian writer and poet who co-wrote songs for *Fraggle Rock,* to see if they could tease a coherent story from Jim's notes. "What is the philosophy of [the] film?" Jim asked them. He was interested in exploring deeper themes of "attitudes toward God, religion, and women," and wanted audiences constantly questioning their perceptions of size, shape, and reality. "We played around with various story lines," said Froud, "then I created some paintings just to give a general feel to the approach and style of the film." One of Froud's first paintings was a piece called *Toby and the Goblins,* featuring a baby smiling happily amid a sea of grinning, leering, and skeptical monsters. Jim loved it—it would "define and inspire" their work over the next three years—and hung the original painting in his house on Downshire Hill. Lee, meanwhile, would begin trying to compress their conversations and notes into a viable first draft.

As Jim and Froud talked over their next big project, Oz had been hard at work on the script for the next Muppet film, overhauling the first screenplay submitted by *Muppet Caper* writers Jay Tarses and Tom Patchett—initially titled *The Muppets: The Legend Continues*— which Oz had dismissed as "way too over jokey." "I asked Jim if I could take a stab at it," said Oz, "and I think Jay and Tom were both probably very unhappy that I did. But it just didn't have the *oomph* of the characters and their relationships." Jim encouraged the tinkering; Oz, said Jim, was "very precise in terms of his characters and what they're all about and thinks through that depth of why they are and where they came from . . . and all of that creates wonderfully real characters." But capturing that spark of the characters—that *oomph,* as Oz called it—was the most important, and most difficult, part of any Muppet project. "There's a sense of our characters caring for each other and having respect for each other," agreed Jim. "A positive feeling. A positive view of life. That's a key to everything we do. . . . Sometimes we're too heavy in terms of ourselves and trying to carry an idea, and telling kids what life is about. I often have to tell myself that, too."

While Oz put the final touches on the script, the New York workshop was constructing dozens of new Muppets for the movie, including a roller-skating Miss Piggy, a water-skiing Gonzo, and radio-controlled versions of nearly every major character. (As the workshop assembled multiple versions of Miss Piggy, Oz made certain he was always present when builders attached her eyes, just as Jim had insisted on doing twenty years earlier when overseeing Don Sahlin's construction of Rowlf.) The Muppet builders had continued to refine the technology now being used on *Fraggle Rock,* making mechanisms increasingly smaller and allowing puppeteers to remotely control more and more functions of the puppet with the waldo mitt. When using the waldo, there was no need to find a way to keep the puppeteer crouched out of sight; instead, a remote-controlled Kermit could now be propped up on a bench out in the open, while Jim sat several yards away using the waldo to radio-control Kermit's mouth and head.

The third Muppet movie—now titled *The Muppets Take Manhattan*—began filming in New York City on May 31, 1983. "We did our first film in Los Angeles, and our second in London," noted Jim. "I thought it would be nice to do the next one in our hometown." All shots of the Muppets in Manhattan, then, were done on location, with the Muppet performers wheeling around on their backs on rolling carts in Times Square or Central Park. Even uninterested New Yorkers, long accustomed to seeing film crews in their city, would stop to watch the filming—their eyes locked on Kermit and Miss Piggy, rather than on Jim and Oz rolling around underneath—and beg to take pictures or just touch the puppets. Jim didn't mind a bit. "We got a very nice, happy feeling from people in the streets," he said.

Shooting on location also required the Muppet workshop to set up camp close by where they could quickly make any needed repairs, dividing duties between a puppet and costume shop to address puppet-related mishaps, and a mechanical shop to fix technical problems. Working in the mechanical shop that summer was nineteen-year-old Brian Henson, who had recently left his classes at the University of Colorado at Boulder, where he had been studying astrophysics and art. Brian had entered the university intending to make a career in film, with a focus on special effects, a craft he had learned to love from Don Sahlin and Faz Fazakas. "I thought, 'Well, getting a degree in physics actually lends itself to that,'" said Brian. But he found his time taken up more and more by his film work—"I just kept getting movies," he recalled—that he eventually abandoned school altogether in favor of working in the Muppet workshop, reporting directly to Fazakas. He wouldn't stay there long; the following year, he would take on his first non-Muppet role when he was tapped by the Walt Disney Company to perform one of the lead puppet characters in *Return to Oz*.

While Frank Oz was, for the first time, sitting alone in the director's chair, he knew "it was under an umbrella of safety, because I had Jim and David Lazer's full support. . . . But it wasn't a pure handoff," said Oz. "I made all the decisions, but it was still Jim and Dave protecting me, and coming to me to say, 'Frank, we can't afford this.' So it wasn't me doing everything on my own out in the world." The Muppet performers, however, braced themselves. Now that Jim was no longer regularly at Oz's side to temper Oz's notorious tendency for multiple takes, Oz would often nitpick a scene to the point where the performers could no longer tell the difference between takes.

Even Jim could get irritated by Oz's admittedly "dictatorial" manner, growing angrier and angrier one evening as Oz kept the performers around for a seemingly endless round of retakes. "I fucked up," said Oz. "I was like, 'I'm the boss and I can keep everyone around,' and I made Jim stay on the set when he really didn't need to be there." Typically, Jim never got visibly angry, merely setting his mouth in a tight line beneath his beard. But "Jim was steaming," remembered Oz. "He was incredibly angry, and he got so powerfully silent. I don't even remember what he said to me, I just remember that blistering silence. I apologized, and Jim was very forgiving." Jim shrugged it all off. "We sort of go up and down as all relationships do, but we have a great deal of respect for each other."

The Muppets Take Manhattan featured yet more innovative puppetry—including a complicated sequence choreographed by Jim in which several rats take over a kitchen—but some of the most notable moments came from Oz's script. Jim was particularly pleased with Oz's treatment of Kermit, who was given "an opportunity to stretch," said Jim cheerily, "to become a little bit more interesting instead of just . . . the more limited personality that he is most of the time." In fact, it didn't take much squinting at Kermit in The Muppets Take Manhattan to see where Oz had poked a bit of gentle fun at elements of Jim's own personality. Not only did Kermit get to play several different kinds of characters, from a big-shot Hollywood producer to an advertising man—two roles Jim had played in real life—but there was even a moment when he finally got to lose his temper with the entire Muppet cast. "Tell us what we should do!" Fozzie implores of Kermit at one point. "I don't know!" Kermit explodes. "How should I know? Why are you always asking me anyway? Can't you take care of yourselves?? I don't know what to do next!"

Steve Whitmire thought that was probably a moment of pure catharsis for Jim, who rarely, if ever, lost his patience with the Muppet performers. "He'd say, 'I can't be expected to watch everything,'" said Whitmire, "which is very much the same moment when Kermit turns and really screams at everybody and says, 'Why do you expect me to have all the answers?'" But that was about as irritated as Jim would ever get. "You've got Jim . . . and all of us crazies around him at different levels of ability, different levels of knowledge, different capability as performers, and him trying to hold it all together," explained Whitmire, "but by and large . . . I never saw him lose his temper. . . . He had a real knack for getting to the problem without scratching open the scab."

The moment in the film that created a buzz, however—especially after word of it leaked to the press before the film's release—was its final scene, in which Kermit and Miss Piggy are married in a lavish wedding ceremony that may or may not have been merely part of a Broadway musical. To keep the sequence a secret—at least for a while—the wedding had been filmed on a closed and sweltering hot soundstage at Empire Stages in Long Island City, where 175 puppeteers crammed themselves under a chapel set to perform the three hundred puppets attending the Kermit-Piggy nuptials. When word of the wedding scene—and its ambiguous nature—leaked out, reporters began frantically lobbing the same question at Jim and Oz over and over again: *Are they married or not?* But neither Jim nor Oz would provide any clear answers, engaging instead in an elaborate bit of performance art to keep the press guessing. "I'm just an actor," Jim would have Kermit entreat to reporters, "and when two actors marry onstage, they're only acting!" *Not so fast,* Oz as Piggy would respond, and point out that the actor presiding over the on-screen ceremony was a real minister—which was true—and thus the two of them had been officially married. Reporters left more confused than ever, and Jim loved every moment of it. "The argument will continue on, hopefully into . . . I don't know what." He grinned. "We'll wait and see."

Still, while the *Maybe it was real* wedding scene got people talking, it was a dream sequence that would truly have audiences roaring with enthusiasm. Even Jim knew the sequence was something special, as the only production note he wrote in his private journal during *Manhattan*'s entire fifteen-week shoot came with three weeks left in filming, when he jotted down "SHOOTING MUPPET BABIES IN MOVIE."

The three-minute musical number, featuring baby versions of the entire Muppet cast—including a sailor-suited Kermit, a diaper-clad Rowlf, and Miss Piggy in an enormous bow—was one of the toughest sequences to film, requiring a combination of marionettes, radio-controlled figures, and specially designed baby Muppets with "short, stubby arms and legs," which made them "very difficult" to operate. Keeping the performers out of sight often required careful positioning of the camera and a few well-placed props to hide the holes that were cut into the set, just wide enough for the Muppet performers to stick their arms through. "It becomes quite a game, working out all of these things," said Jim. "To me, one of the more enjoyable things is to try to figure out how to stage sequences like this." What had inspired the Muppet Babies, Oz wasn't certain—

"Things spring up in your head, and you never know where they come from, you know?"—but the sequence would end up as one of the most memorable of all Muppet moments, and would soon take on a life of its own in a form that surprised even Jim.

While he had only grudgingly ceded the directing duties on *The Muppet Movie* to James Frawley five years earlier, Jim found that for *The Muppets Take Manhattan* he was delighted not "to worry about it. . . . I was able to relax and kid around, and in between takes, I could talk to people and make phone calls and enjoy a cup of tea." Filming in New York had its advantages, too. "Being able to go home in between takes or at the end of the day . . . was a lot of fun." In the evenings, then, Jim would retreat to his apartment in the Sherry-Netherland, which was being gutted and put back together and re-decorated by an expensive architectural firm. It would take more than a year before Jim would pronounce the work finished. With its pastel-tinted walls, expensive sculpture, custom-made etched glass, and hand-carved furniture, everything in Jim's apartment was richly detailed and interesting to look at—an architectural embodiment of Jim's unique design aesthetic: art noveau, with a dash of whimsy. The dining room furniture, carved by artist Judy Kensley McKie, featured wide-eyed rabbits peeking playfully around the backs of the chairs, while in the bedroom, alongside sculptures and carved furni-ture, lounged a puppet built by Rufus Rose, the puppeteer who had performed Howdy Doody. Like the house on Downshire Hill, Jim's homes were always his oasis in the middle of a bustling city—and the Sherry-Netherland apartment in particular would always be his glowing, cozy sanctuary in the sky.

Other days, when he wasn't needed on-set at Empire Stages, Jim had begun working on a project that was small but close to his heart: a series of one-hour specials he was calling *Jim Henson Presents,* showcasing puppeteers he admired from around the world. With his continued involvement in both the Puppeteers of America and UNIMA, Jim took puppetry even more seriously than many of the Muppet performers, and he intended for *Jim Henson Presents* to be a kind of international puppetry primer, spotlighting both perform-ers and their performances. In late July, Jim spent two days inter-viewing and filming Bruce Schwartz, who performed in a style influenced by the Japanese Bunraku, at the Dance Theater Workshop in New York. In the coming months and years, he would tape five more specials, including programs featuring Australian shadow puppeteer Richard Bradshaw, Dutch puppeteer Henk Boerwinkel—who chatted earnestly with Jim about using puppets to create "magical realism"—and eighty-three-year old Russian performer Sergei Obraztsov, who, perhaps more than any other puppeteer, had inspired Jim in the art and craft of puppetry.

For Jim, the more he learned about different styles of puppetry, the more excited he got—and the more he wanted to incorporate those kinds of puppetry into his work. "Puppetry is a very wide field," he explained. "It encompasses a lot of different ways of operating hand puppets and marionettes and rod-control figures and people in black. There are many, many different techniques and . . . I feel that we can use them all. We try to use a lot of them. I believe in using any technique that will work. . . . I'm not a purist in terms of what puppetry is, or what it should or shouldn't be."

For someone who once considered puppetry merely a "means to an end," Jim had become one of the leading authorities on—and chief promoters of—one of the world's most ancient arts. Recently, in fact, he had established the Jim Henson Foundation to promote and develop the art of puppetry in the United States—to this day, still the only grant-making institution with such a mission. "Jim started the Foundation . . . so that an artist would have a bit of money and breathing space to develop his own vision," said fellow UNIMA member Allelu Kurten, "without having to give up or copy some one else's."

It was the copying, in fact, that bothered Jim the most. "We see frequently puppets which have the overall 'Muppet look,' but which do not look like our individual Muppet characters," he wrote in *Puppetry Journal*. "We feel that the people creating these puppets should create, as we did, their own concepts and not use ours." If puppetry was going to grow and expand as an art form, it needed to move beyond the Muppets—which, given their popularity, was easier said than done. Jim was fine with performers using the look of the Muppets for inspiration—just as he had been inspired by the design and working styles of Burr Tillstrom and Obraztsov—but encouraged puppeteers to "find their own unique style of puppetry. . . . It seems to me that each of us expressing our own originality is the essence of our art and professionalism." The foundation, then, was Jim's effort to encourage such originality—and in the first year alone, the foundation awarded $25,000 in grants to performers and organizations, including $7,500 to a young puppeteer named Julie Taymor, who would later win a Tony Award for her groundbreaking puppetized version of the musical *The Lion King* on Broadway.

On other days, Jim was in Toronto, meeting with his writers on *Fraggle Rock*, or in London, where he had decided to begin building the various creatures and props that would be needed for *The Labyrinth*—or, at least, the building would start once the script was finished. In the meantime, there was more than enough work to be done hammering the old workshop at 1B Downshire Hill into shape. In early July, Jim moved Muppet builder Connie Peterson—who had been part of Caroly Wilcox's ambitious Piggy Research and Development Department—from the New York shop over to London, where she was put in charge of turning the trash-filled former postal sorting facility into a fully functional, state-of-the-art workshop.

"Getting started was really difficult—it was hard to know where to grab hold of the project," said Peterson. "The situation was made harder due to an architectural modification of our building . . . before our arrival. The main work space was filled with an impenetrable pile of stuff from the front of the building to the back . . . ranging from heavy machinery to feathers and sequins all jumbled together and coated with construction dust." The job also required some politicking with the neighbors and local council, since the workshop was the only industrial building in a residential area, and tended to vent slightly noxious fumes from time to time. Faz Fazakas, too, was dispatched to Downshire Hill to help establish the electromechanical side of the workshop, and spent weeks measuring floor thicknesses to determine the best locations for all the heavy equipment needed for metalwork. Under the watchful eye of Duncan Kenworthy—who often joked that part of his job was to "be Jim when Jim wasn't there"—Peterson and Fazakas would spend the rest of the year banging the London workshop into shape.

Jim spent his forty-seventh birthday at the wrap party for *The Muppets Take Manhattan,* earnestly toasting Oz for completing his first film as director—and now that Jim had opened that door for Oz, he was going to find it impossible to close. Two years later, Oz would be asked to direct the musical comedy *Little Shop of Horrors* for Warner Brothers, on his way to a successful career as a film director, racking up a run of well-received, eclectic hits like *Dirty Rotten Scoundrels* and *What About Bob?* "I was always chomping at the bit to go beyond the Muppets," said Oz, "but Jim was amazing, because he never said, 'Hey, you can't leave me! I gave you all this stuff and you learned so much from me.' Instead, he said, 'Of course you've got to go do that.' He was always amazing that way."

Jim was earnestly watching another blooming career that autumn as well. In June, twenty-three-year-old Lisa graduated from Harvard with two distinctions: not only was she graduating *summa cum laude,* but she had also served as the first female president of *Harvard Lampoon.* Now she was spending her summer preparing to attend film school, and after a series of strenuous interviews—during which she discussed at length the interactive movie concept she and Jim had pitched several years earlier—she had been accepted to a school in London. As she prepared to attend classes in the fall, however, she was offered a position at Warner Brothers by executive vice president (and Harvard alumnus) Lucy Fisher—and off Lisa went to Warner Brothers, never to look back. Over the next ten years, she would serve as a production executive and later a vice president for the studio, overseeing blockbusters like *Lethal Weapon* and *Batman.*

Jim devoted much of the fall to tinkering with various television projects, including a music education program and a children's television series he and Lisa had kicked around called *Starboppers,* notable more for the technology he was proposing to use than for its underlying concept. In its early draft, *Starboppers*—a terrible name, but Jim could never come up with a title he liked better—followed the adventures of several star-hopping aliens, with personalities based on the Freudian ideas of id, ego, and superego. More exciting, however, Jim was planning to film his characters against a green screen, then insert them into entirely computer-generated environments. He had even approached Digital Productions, a Los Angeles–

based computer animation company, about using their powerful Cray X-MP supercomputers to create the virtual backgrounds. Unfortunately, Jim could never get the idea to catch fire with a network, but he loved the technology—he had been playing with computer animation since even before *Sesame Street*—and was determined to find a use for it.

While he awaited Dennis Lee's first draft of *Labyrinth*, as he was now calling it, Jim was excitedly looking for a screenwriter with whom he could collaborate on the script. Very briefly he had considered enlisting the help of Melissa Mathison, who had written *E.T.* for Steven Spielberg, but then abandoned the idea, deciding that if he was hoping to give *Labyrinth* the more lighthearted, comedic edge that had been missing from *The Dark Crystal,* he was better off collaborating with a comedian. An early fan of *Monty Python's Flying Circus*—he would regularly note on his desk calendar the dates and times when the show was airing on PBS—Jim was particularly impressed with Terry Jones, one of the group's most versatile members, who seemed to share his penchant for fantasy and folklore. Jones had co-directed and co-written the Arthurian spoof *Monty Python and the Holy Grail,* had written a serious, literary analysis of the knight in Chaucer's *Canterbury Tales,* and had recently published a children's book called *The Saga of Erik the Viking,* which Jim greatly admired. In late fall, he approached Jones about collaborating on *Labyrinth*—"a really marvelous idea," fellow Python member and former *Muppet Show* guest John Cleese told Jim approvingly—and was delighted when Jones said yes. "Your contributions to *Labyrinth* will surely make the script jump to life," Jim wrote Jones.

At the end of December, after nine long months of waiting, Jim finally received a treatment of *Labyrinth* from Lee, who had transformed Jim's rough story outline and his own meticulous notes into a ninety-page novella. In early 1984, Jim handed Lee's novella and an enormous pile of Froud's drawings ("I filled sketchbook upon sketchbook," admitted Froud) over to Jones to begin the task of writing the screenplay. While Lee's novella provided a guiding track of a plot, Jones didn't find it of much use, calling it a "poetic novella [that I] didn't really get on with." Instead, he was much more inspired by Froud's drawings of monsters and goblins. "I sat at my desk with

Brian Froud's drawings stacked on one side of the desk and writing away sort of to see what would happen," said Jones. "And every time I came to a new scene . . . I looked through Brian's drawings and found a character who was kind of speaking to me already and suddenly there was a scene." Jones would complete his draft by early spring, at which point Jim would pass it off to another writer for revisions—and then another—cooking up an increasingly murky screenwriter stew that would send the *Labyrinth* screenplay veering through nearly twenty-five revisions and rewrites over the next two years.

With *The Muppets Take Manhattan* due to premiere in July 1984, Jim and the merchandising department at Henson Associates spent their spring reviewing agreements on toys and other movie-related tie-ins, including deals with Frito-Lay, McDonald's, General Mills, and even Oral-B, which would be marketing a line of Muppet toothbrushes. While the Muppet films had always generated a good share of revenue for the company with related merchandise, *The Muppets Take Manhattan* would prove particularly profitable because it had something going for it the other two Muppet films didn't: Muppet Babies. To Jim's surprise, lucrative offers came in from companies wanting to produce items targeted specifically toward families with infants and toddlers, including Procter & Gamble, which wanted the Muppet Babies to help sell Pampers diapers. Jim arched an eyebrow coyly. "You're going to let kids shit on my name?" he asked in mock annoyance—then agreed to the deal.

The most successful Muppet Babies–related product wasn't in stuffed animals or diapers, but in a market Jim had intentionally long avoided: Saturday morning cartoons. "I'd always stayed away from Saturday morning, not really thinking it was an area in which I would feel comfortable working," said Jim. Jerry Juhl, too, was wary of putting animated Muppets on Saturday morning television, as he was concerned whether this was "the right way to meet our characters for the first time." But Jim eventually shrugged off that particular concern. "If the kids are already watching on Saturday morning, then *we* should be there, too," he told Juhl, "and maybe we could do something different." When he was approached by executives from Marvel Productions—the animation wing of Marvel Comics—and CBS television about developing an animated Muppet Babies series, Jim was willing to listen, bringing in Michael Frith and several others for an all-day "concept meeting" in March.

It was important to Jim that the Muppet Babies—like Fraggle Rock—"have a nice reason for being." Where Fraggle's overarching theme was one of harmony and understanding, Muppet Babies "can be used to develop creativity," Jim told his writers. "I think we can try to do something rather important with this show. There is almost no 'teaching' of creativity that I know of. . . . We can . . . show the Muppet Babies using their individual creativity in how each one can do the same thing differently. There is no right or wrong to it." In the same way five different people could look at an ink blot and see something different, Jim wanted Muppet Babies to examine how different creative approaches could all solve the same problem—by "trying many different approaches, trying something no one has ever tried before, and not being satisfied with the way it's always been."

With that objective as its guiding principle, then, Jim agreed to create a joint production with Marvel that allowed Henson Associates to maintain quality control of the project while handing off the majority of the day-to-day work to Marvel's writers and animators. With both Jim and Marvel on board, CBS gave its enthusiastic backing, paying $250,000 per show for the initial thirteen episodes, and putting it at the center of its Saturday morning lineup. Frith was enlisted as a "creative consultant," overseeing not only the look and design of the series, but reviewing scripts and story ideas with the same fervor he had devoted to Fraggle Rock, and sending the same kind of detailed—and entertaining—notes back to Marvel's story writers that Jim had once sent to Jerry Juhl. The commitment paid off: when the first episodes went on the air in September 1984—only six months after closing the deal—Muppet Babies was an immediate critical and commercial success, winning its time slot, pulling in huge ratings (though it usually finished second to another CBS juggernaut, Pee-wee's Playhouse), and winning the Emmy for Outstanding Animated Program for the first four years of its seven-year run. It would also spawn a cringe-inducing sub-industry of Your Favorite

Characters as Children! cartoons like *Flintstone Kids* and *A Pup Named Scooby-Doo,* none of which had quite the spark of *Muppet Babies*—probably because they didn't aspire to Jim's lofty objectives.

Fraggle Rock and *Muppet Babies* were colorful reflections of Jim's own personal principles—and lately, Jim was becoming more personally and publicly involved in a number of causes. Though never overly political—in fact, he rarely voted—Jim's own leanings were firmly Democrat, and the issues with which he chose to involve himself—and the Muppets—were markedly left of center. He was particularly passionate about ecology and the environment, embracing conservation, wildlife preservation, and clean air and water. "At some point in my life," said Jim, "I decided, rightly or wrongly, that there are many situations in this life that I can't do much about: acts of terrorism, feelings of nationalistic prejudice, cold war, etc. So what I should do is concentrate on the situations my energy can affect." In 1983, then, he had agreed to produce several public service announcements for the National Wildlife Federation, filming Kermit and Fozzie in Central Park talking about clean water as they fished junk out of a pond, and in March 1984, Kermit delivered the keynote address at the National Wildlife Federation's annual meeting. Several years later, Jim would get similarly involved with the more politically inclined Better World Society, an organization founded by media giant Ted Turner to educate the media on global and social issues. In 1989, Kermit even served as "spokesfrog" for the organization, and Jim would direct several thoughtful public service announcements to promote conservation and arms reduction, scoring serious social and political points in a typically colorful and agreeable Muppet style.

Jim was most fired up when it came to the environment. Nature was both his muse and his solace. It "recharged and re-inspired" him. "The beauty of nature has been one of the great inspirations in my life," wrote Jim. "Growing up as an artist, I've always been in awe of the incredible beauty of every last bit of design in nature. The wonderful color schemes of nature that always work harmoniously are particularly dazzling to me." Whenever he could find a rare moment of quiet or solitude, he would fling himself down on the ground and stare up into the sky, dreamily losing himself in the clouds, the sun, the moon, or whatever happened to cross his line of sight, just as he had done as a boy in Leland. "One of my happiest moments of inspiration came to me many years ago as I lay on the grass, looking up into the leaves and branches of a big old tree in California," wrote Jim. "I remember feeling very much a part of everything and everyone."

Jim traveled widely in the weeks leading up to the release of *The Muppets Take Manhattan*—usually with one or more of the kids in tow—interviewing puppeteers on camera for *Jim Henson Presents* with John, taking Heather to London and New Orleans for a symposium, then heading to Connecticut in time to proudly attend Cheryl's graduation from Yale on a rainy Saturday in May. As always, Jim talked with each of his five children about his work, gauging their reactions to ideas and seeking their opinions on just about anything. And their honesty, while refreshing, could sometimes be frustrating—especially when Jim had his mind made up about something, as he had, at the moment, about one of the key roles to be cast in *Labyrinth*.

In the early discussions on *Labyrinth,* Jim had assumed that Jareth, *Labyrinth*'s charismatic goblin king, would be performed as another elaborate puppet, similar to the Skeksis in *The Dark Crystal*. After further thought, however, he decided to make Jareth one of the roles filled by a live actor. Initially, he considered offering the role to either Simon MacCorkindale, who had just played one of the heroes in the fantasy film *The Sword and the Sorcerer,* or to Kevin Kline, at that time one of New York's most respected and energetic stage performers. And then, said Jim, "while we were considering various and sundry actors, we thought to make Jareth a music person, someone who could change the film's whole musical style."

For Jim, the choice for Jareth was obvious: Sting, the brooding front man from the New Wave group the Police. But both Brian and John Henson stridently protested that decision, arguing in favor of one of their idols, the innovative and enigmatic rock 'n' roller David Bowie—who also happened to be a proven actor—as the better choice. John, in fact, went immediately to the Sherry-Netherland to make the case to his dad directly, arguing that Sting was simply "happening *now*, whereas David Bowie is an artist, he's got longevity. You don't want to go with *Sting*," John told Jim adamantly, "you want to go with *Bowie*."

Jim may have been intrigued with the idea, but he wouldn't commit. Instead he arranged to meet with Bowie in New York, mainly just to size the singer up, but brought along a handful of Froud's drawings, Terry Jones's recently completed first draft of the script, and a videotape of *The Dark Crystal*. "Jim . . . outlined his basic concept for *Labyrinth* and showed me some of Brian Froud's artwork," recalled Bowie. "That impressed me for openers, but he also gave me a tape of *The Dark Crystal*, which really excited me. I could see the potential of adding humans to his world of creatures." As the conversation continued, Jim was convinced Brian and John were right. When the meeting ended, Jim gave Bowie a copy of Jones's script to take with him. "If you like the script," he said quietly to Bowie, "would you consider being Jareth and singing and writing songs for him?" Bowie was encouraging. "I'd always wanted to be involved in the music writing aspect of a movie that would appeal to everyone," said the musician, "so I was pretty well hooked from the beginning."

On July 13, 1984, *The Muppets Take Manhattan* opened in the United States. For the most part, postproduction on the film had gone smoothly, but up until nearly the last minute, one contentious point remained: Oz's on-screen credit. Oz, who had directed the film, significantly rewritten the script, and performed several main characters, wanted *The Muppets Take Manhattan* to be credited as "A Frank Oz Film." "I thought it was fair," said Oz, "or, at least, my ego wanted that." But Jim kept putting Oz off, casually dismissing him with, "We'll see." Finally, a month before the film's release, Oz received a gift from Jim and David Lazer: a beautiful mantelpiece clock with "A Frank Oz Film" inscribed on top. "That's when I knew," said Oz. The final cut of the film would, indeed, be credited as "A Frank Oz Film."

The response from critics to *The Muppets Take Manhattan* was largely one of amused toleration. In the *Chicago Sun-Times,* Roger

Ebert noted the film's central plot was "not original" but was, none-theless, "a good one." Most agreed the film was funny, though some-what lacking in the normal Muppet madness—a criticism Oz thought was fair. "It doesn't have enough lunacy," said Oz. "I think the story is your basic old-fashioned story, and it was a well-crafted thing because of that. But it didn't have flights of fantasy like *The Muppet Movie*. I just wanted to make sure that the Muppets' char-acters came out, and their relationships, that's all." Only *The Wash-ington Post* seemed truly unimpressed, griping under the headline "The Muppet Mope" that Kermit and Miss Piggy's staged marriage was "a terminally sappy idea to begin with" and that the Muppet Babies were "grotesquely cute." But Jim was pleased, and the film performed well enough, grossing $25 million on Jim's $8 million in-vestment.

Meanwhile, in London, Connie Peterson, Faz Fazakas, and Dun-can Kenworthy had finally knocked the workshop at 1B Downshire Hill into shape—but with *The Dark Crystal* long finished and Jim still months, if not years, away from beginning work on *Labyrinth*, the lights at Downshire Hill were off, Faz's heavy machines silent. Jim had been reluctant to dismiss the eclectic staff of sculptors, jew-elers, armorers, silversmiths, and puppet makers who had given *The Dark Crystal* its distinctive look and feel—nor did he want to merge them into the New York workshop alongside the Muppet builders who derisively referred to the London craftsmen as the staff on "that brown film." Instead, Jim wanted to keep them together, preferably in the same place, until he was ready for them to start the build for *Labyrinth*. But with nothing to do, there was no way to hold the crew together, and most of the staff had moved on—some to Elstree to work on Disney's *Return to Oz*, others to California, where they had built and performed Jabba the Hutt for George Lucas.

Earlier in the spring, however—at about the time Jim and Marvel were discussing the Muppet Babies in New York—Duncan Kenwor-thy had read a script by TV writer Dennis Potter called *Dreamchild*, a faux-biographical drama about the elderly Alice Liddell, who, as a child, had inspired Lewis Carroll's *Alice's Adventures in Wonder-land*. As the aged Liddell recalls her friendship with Carroll through flashbacks, she encounters grotesque versions of some of Wonderland's inhabitants, including a terrifying Gryphon and a truly insane-looking Mad Hatter—and Kenworthy thought the London workshop would be the perfect place to build such fantastic puppets. "I was always keen to try and get the company working in drama," said Kenworthy, "and *Dreamchild* really was the perfect combination of realism and fantasy." Jim, too, loved Potter's story, and with Universal Studios backing the film and footing the bill, Jim gave the okay to reassemble the London team and begin production on the creatures needed for *Dreamchild*—"the first time my father had considered doing puppets for other people," said Brian Henson.

Under the direction of sculptor and designer Lyle Conway, who had sculpted the heads for the Skeksis and Mystics for *The Dark Crystal*, the crew at Downshire Hill worked quickly—and on a shoe-string budget—to produce six large puppets in only fourteen weeks. To keep costs down, there was little radio control involved in the figures; most were operated much as Yoda had been, with a mass of cables snaking out of the puppets' necks, requiring large teams of puppeteers to operate the controls manually. When shooting began on *Dreamchild* on July 16—only three days after the premiere of *The Muppets Take Manhattan*—eleven puppeteers were needed to operate the complex facial movements of the Mad Hatter. "The Mad Hatter's face was all over the place, and he looked absolutely insane," said Kenworthy gleefully. "It was great."

Jim had left most of the work to Conway and his team, but he was delighted with the results. Not only had the team learned to work quickly and efficiently, stretching the budget as far as they could, but with every project the puppets were getting more complex, the mechanics smaller and more precise, and the resulting movements more subtle and realistic. In fact, with their seamless splicing of traditional puppetry with high-tech gadgetry, it probably wasn't even accurate to refer to the figures as *puppets* anymore. "The characters are just not Muppets at all," said Jim. "We hesitate to call them puppets even. . . . Instead, we're trying to go toward a sense of realism—toward a reality of creatures that are actually alive and we're mixing up puppetry and all kinds of other techniques. . . . You're trying to create something that people will actually believe."

Partly to assuage the British unions, which insisted that crafts-men be engaged in some sort of identifiable trade, the workshop had begun referring to their complex puppets as *animatronics*— a term lifted from Walt Disney, who called the animated figures that moved and sang in attractions like Pirates of the Caribbean *Audio-Animatronics*. The distinction was small, but critical: while a Disney Audio-Animatronic moved in a preprogrammed manner to a prere-corded soundtrack (hence the need for the prefix *Audio*), with ani-matronics, it was the puppeteer, and not a computer program, who controlled every aspect of the figure. No matter how complicated it might be, the puppet was still just an extension of the live performer, with the gadgetry serving to enhance the performance rather than defining it. "I feel I've always done well at using the technical aspects of the medium to expand what we can do," said Jim. "I find that combination of art and technology pretty exciting."

But as much as Jim liked the word *animatronics* (and there would be some in-fighting in the London workshop over who had first ap-plied the term to their craft) it was just a bit too technical, too process-oriented. Nonetheless, "people say, 'you really should have a term for that,'" Jim said, "but at the moment we're saying *crea-tures*." This name would stick, and from here on the London work-shop would be known as the Creature Shop. That gave the London shop a personality and mission very different from its New York counterpart—which, Jim hoped, would help clarify whose project was whose and reduce some of the tensions between the two work-shops. New York was "more oriented to the Muppets," explained Jim, while the Creature Shop was "more high tech . . . more into re-alistic detail, and so forth."

Regardless of whether it was *creatures* in London or *Muppets* in New York that were being built and performed, there was one term that Jim expressly would *not* allow to be used to describe his performers—and that was the word *Muppeteer*. While the media and others used the term freely to describe Jim's occupation, Jim thought it was just a bit too gimmicky. In 1984, when the Apple com-puter company sent Jim a mock-up of a page from its annual report proudly hailing Jim as an Apple user and listing his occupation as "Muppeteer," Jim scratched darkly through the term and wrote

"Muppet performer" beneath it. He was a *performer* or a *puppeteer.* Not a *Muppeteer.*

With a bit of rare downtime in the summer of 1984, Jim took an extended vacation—which for him meant four days—chartering a yacht with Cheryl, Heather, and John, and cruising the waters off the coast of Antigua. But even as Jim basked in the Caribbean sun, he had Al Gottesman and other executives hard at work back in New York trying to close one of the most important deals of his career.

Ever since Robert Holmes à Court's acquisition of ACC in early 1982, Jim had been wary of the mogul and the way he did business, and was determined to shake himself free of ACC's grasp. Jim had managed to buy *The Dark Crystal* out from under Holmes à Court in late 1982, but that still left ACC owning the first two Muppet movies (*The Muppets Take Manhattan* had been financed independently, and thus remained free of ACC's grip), several Muppet-related television specials, and, most gallingly, all 120 episodes of *The Muppet Show.* While Holmes à Court had washed his hands of *The Dark Crystal*—and indeed, was likely glad to be rid of it—the Muppet properties were of a different caliber altogether. Not only was *The Muppet Show* already in syndication, earning a steady flow of revenue, but—even more irksome to Jim—ACC received 10 percent of the net income generated by Muppet-related merchandising.

Being handcuffed to Holmes à Court was beyond frustrating. For the better part of the year, then, Jim and Holmes à Court had tangled on the phone—and, from time to time, in person—with Jim trying to convince Holmes à Court to release *The Muppet Show* from his clutches, and Holmes à Court either complacently demanding an exorbitant price for the show or ignoring Jim's pleas altogether. "The terms that I mentioned were not designed to commence negotiation," Holmes à Court had written Jim curtly in March, cutting off any further discussion—a patronizing response that likely set Jim's teeth on edge. While Duncan Kenworthy ran the numbers to determine a fair price for buying back just *The Muppet Show*'s distribution rights—about $1.5 million, Kenworthy thought—Jim was upping the ante, putting together an offer that would not only rescue *all* of the Muppet properties in ACC's claws, but also close down ACC's share in merchandising.

Never sell anything I own, Jim had insisted to Bernie Brillstein two decades earlier, and he intended to take his own advice. On August 17, 1984, after weeks of heavy negotiation, Jim acquired all of his Muppet properties from Holmes à Court for $6.5 million, agreeing to pay ACC $5 million up front, then $750,000 for the next two years. It wasn't an extraordinarily large amount—and according to Kenworthy, there was plenty of money on hand from merchandising—but just as he had done with *The Dark Crystal,* Jim had seen the value in securing his own creative and artistic freedom—and, as it turns out, his future. "We would have no company today if he hadn't done that," said Lisa Henson twenty years later, "and *he* wouldn't have had that much of a company, either. How many people take that gamble? [How many] invest in their own interests?" For Holmes à Court, the Muppets had been little more than a stock option; for Jim they were the foundation on which he could continue to build a company and a legacy. "He knew it had long-term value," said Lisa admiringly. Al Gottesman, who had helped close the deal, called the effort "simply heroic."

Relieved, and feeling slightly victorious, Jim headed for Europe with Cheryl, first to Dresden to attend the UNIMA Puppet Festival, then on to Edinburgh, where he spent several days rewriting the script for *Labyrinth.* Only seven months in, the screenplay already had multiple fingerprints on it—Jim had given Jones's first draft to *Fraggle Rock* writer Laura Phillips—and now Jim was tinkering with the script as well. At its core, the plot of *Labyrinth* was simple: Sarah, the fourteen-year-old heroine of the story, wishes her baby brother would be whisked away by goblins—and when the Goblin King makes her wish come true, Sarah has thirteen hours to rescue her brother from the Goblin's labyrinth. But Jones and Phillips had approached that basic plot differently.

Jones had written an episodic, *Alice in Wonderland*–type story that was funny and contained some of the story elements Jim had already envisioned—the Escher room, the talking door knockers, comic relief sidekicks—but only lightly touched on the personality and motivations of Sarah, the heroine of the story. "[It was] about the world," said Jones, "and about people who are more interested in manipulating the world than actually baring themselves at all." Laura Phillips, on the other hand, excelled at writing relationship-oriented stories, and had written a character-centered treatment that more fully fleshed out Sarah, but downplayed the humor and relied less on the kind of strong visual sequences Jim preferred. But Jim liked parts of both scripts, and was hoping he could split the difference and compress the strengths of both Jones's and Phillips's scripts into a single screenplay. Everyone agreed to keep working.

With both scripts in a constant state of flux—and neither quite getting a firm grip on the heroine—it was clear that casting the role of teenage Sarah was going to be critical. Jones, in fact, had argued that a good actress was vital, as she could express through her performance much of what he had intentionally left unwritten on the page. "We've got a live actress playing the part," he told Jim, "and she can convey a lot of this in her manner and by the way she talks and walks." Finding the right young actress, however, would take nearly ten months. Jim had started monthly auditions in London beginning in April 1984, and by July his first choice was the "dark and cynical" seventeen-year-old British actress Helena Bonham Carter. As more actresses read for the part, however—Sarah Jessica Parker, Laura Dern, Mia Sara, Mary Stuart Masterson—Jim was convinced that the role should go to an American. By late December 1984, he had narrowed the list down to five actresses he considered his leading candidates—including Ally Sheedy and Jane Krakowski—but after looking at their screen tests, decided to open auditions again.

On January 29, 1985, fifteen-year-old New Yorker Jennifer Connelly—a former child model who had appeared in films by Italian directors Sergio Leone and Dario Argento—auditioned for Jim at One Seventeen, and was pronounced "just right for the role" almost the moment she walked in. Jim signed her for the part within a week, and immediately moved her and her mother to London, where she would stay for the duration of her work on *Labyrinth*. David Bowie, too, who had continued to follow the various iterations of the script, formally signed his deal two weeks later. In the meantime, the Creature Shop was now working full-time on the assortment of monsters and other creatures needed for the movie, and had filmed several of the main characters together to establish the relative sizes for the gigantic, full-body puppet Ludo, the dwarf Hoggle, and the foxlike, dog-riding knight Sir Didymus.

With production ramping up quickly—though the script still remained a problem—Jim excitedly presided over a massive *Labyrinth*-inspired masked ball in mid-February. Starting with the Elizabethan costume party he had hosted at Downshire Hill in 1979—the precursor for the masked balls he would begin hosting regularly in 1983—Jim's costume parties had gotten increasingly larger and louder over the last three years, and now sprawled through the gigantic, four-story-high Starlight Room on the fiftieth floor of the Waldorf-Astoria hotel. Jim loved dressing in costume, strolling the ballroom in a feathered mask, dark cape, and goblin armor borrowed from the Creature Shop, shaking hands with Andy Warhol and other celebrity guests. "Puppets are a lot like masks," Jim once noted. "Children—and adults—can perform without inhibitions and without being seen. That sort of helps to foster true expression." The Muppet staff, already expressive and uninhibited enough, took great joy in putting together elaborate costumes, hoping to disguise themselves to the point where Jim couldn't figure out who they were.

With a glass of white wine in his hand, Jim moved among his staff proudly, asking about children and grandchildren, and wrapping his long arms around them as they posed for pictures. "I have a good group of people that work with me," Jim said. "I don't do everything myself." The masked balls were a conscious effort to thank the group for their work. While Jim had gotten better about openly appreciating the efforts of the staff, he was still less effusive in his praise of his employees than David Lazer—who was constantly encouraging Jim to "hand out the 'attaboys'"—would have liked. In Jim's mind, the fact he had chosen to hire a particular person was already proof of how much he valued them, and their work was the validation of that decision. "He didn't wonder if his own work was good, so he didn't have to be extracting and pulling approval and praise out of people," said Lisa, "but that meant when other people needed his praise and tried to pull it out of him, he didn't always respond well to that." But he was trying—and the masked balls, he hoped, were one way of showing how much he appreciated and valued them.

That didn't mean staff were making it any easier for him. While Jim had hoped that the formal creation of the Creature Shop would put an end to the turf wars that seemed to continually erupt between the New York and London workshops, there was still muted grumbling among the New York staff that Jim preferred the Creature Shop to the Muppet workshop—especially as his time became more and more wrapped up in projects requiring the Creature Shop's work. And it didn't help when *Dreamchild,* on its release in 1985, provided a prominent on-screen credit for JIM HENSON'S CREATURE SHOP.

So powerful was the pull of Jim's personality that even those Jim worked with outside the company craved his time and approval— and sulked when Jim moved on to projects that no longer required their services. At one point, when Jim decided to start working with a new music producer for a new series of *Sesame Street* records, his former producer wrote Jim a long, agonizing letter of protest. Jim was genuinely baffled that his decision had been taken so personally. "If you like one person, does that mean that you dislike someone else?" Jim asked. "I work with a great many people all the time, and as one goes through life, you work with one person for a while and then you work with someone else. This feels healthy and correct to me. As we do this, we try to treat people fairly and with respect for what they've done." Jerry Juhl, though, thought he understood the former producer's plight. "When you first encounter the kind of energy that Jim brought, and the kind of desire he had for you to give things to a project, you became so caught up in it that you were really at a loss when he moved on."

In late February, only a month and a half away from the April 15 date when he planned to begin filming *Labyrinth,* Jim brought in screenwriter and comedian Elaine May, who had done some touch-up work on the screenplay for *Tootsie,* to make a pass at the *Labyrinth* screenplay as well. Jim left her with Jones's and Phillips's scripts, along with his own treatment and a pile of notes from *Labyrinth*'s executive producer, George Lucas, in the hopes that somewhere in the mess May would be able to find and define the characters of Sarah and Jareth.

As May went to work, Jim headed for Toronto for a "Future of Fraggles" meeting with the creative team of *Fraggle Rock,* now in its third season and still a solid hit for HBO. As he had with *The Muppet Show,* Jim was determined not to let his TV series wear out its welcome—and *Fraggle*'s creative team was already putting the same kind of thought into ending the show as they had put into its development, brainstorming ways to bring the series to a close while also leaving room for a possible *Fraggle Rock* spinoff. While writers Jerry Juhl and Jocelyn Stevenson wanted a final episode that would "dramatize the fact that the hole in Doc's workshop is not the only entrance to the magic"—that the Fraggle world is actually accessible *anywhere*—Jim wasn't so certain he wanted a solid sense of closure for the series. From a purely practical standpoint, that made the series less tenable in syndication, as a final episode implied a particular order in which shows had to be broadcast—an unattractive option for local syndicates, which wanted to show the episodes in any order they chose.

He was more excited, however, by the idea of doing a *Fraggle Rock* spinoff series. In a memo to the creative staff, Jim described a show built around Uncle Matt and two new Fraggle characters, who "travel around the world in a nutty hot air balloon," wrote Jim enthusiastically, "landing in new places each week . . . possibly on a quest to gather music." Jim had even planned out the technical tricks he wanted to put to work each week. "We could radio-control Uncle Matt and the female Fraggle on a bicycle with a sidecar . . . and the Doozers might follow along in their radio-controlled vehicles." Jim left the meeting with no real decisions made, only writing down that "everyone wants 120 [episodes]"—which would leave the show on for another two years.

Jim headed for London at the end of March to begin rehearsals for *Labyrinth* out at Elstree movie studios. Bowie wasn't available yet, and wouldn't be until June, but the puppeteers welcomed the rehearsal time. "It takes a lot of rehearsing . . . and getting to know each other's timing," explained Jim. "Even if you have the characters together, the puppeteers start working with them and they find out problems. . . . So there's a great deal of sort of last minute adjusting, figuring out what it's all going to be before you start to shoot."

While wireless radio control had replaced the clunky and heavy cable-controlled mechanisms—thanks largely to the efforts of the Creature Shop's new gadget guru, Tad Krzanowski, who replaced the retiring Faz Fazakas—many of the characters still required a small fleet of puppeteers to operate, with different performers controlling eyes, chins, cheeks, and eyebrows. Brian Henson, who was performing the dwarf Hoggle, led a team of five puppeteers—including little person Shari Weiser, who performed the full-body Hoggle costume—and spent months trying to get the smallest movements just right. "Everyone has to work closely and smoothly with one another when Hoggle is being operated," said Brian. "We all have to think the same way, even though we're doing very different jobs."

Jim was still tinkering with the script right up until nearly the last minute, huddling with Elaine May at Downshire Hill only five days before shooting was to begin. Jim was delighted with May's contributions—he felt she had done a good job "humanizing" the characters—and would leave her changes intact. That made the final screenplay an amalgam of contributions from May, Laura Phillips, Jim, Dennis Lee, Terry Jones, and even executive producer George Lucas—talented chefs all, but a far too crowded kitchen. While the final film would credit the script to Terry Jones, based on a story by Jim and Dennis Lee, Jones "didn't feel that it was very much mine. I always felt it fell between two stories, Jim wanted it to be one thing and I wanted it to be about something else."

There was another writer, however, who would also feel he deserved a writing credit—and without it, was determined to stop the film altogether. When he learned the plot of *Labyrinth* in late 1985, writer Maurice Sendak—a friend of the Hensons for over a decade—had his attorneys fire a warning shot across Jim's bow, cautioning him that the plot of *Labyrinth* sounded a bit too much like his 1981 book *Outside Over There*, in which a young girl named Ida must rescue her younger sister after she is kidnapped by goblins. Further, Sendak had learned that Jim was calling some of his characters "wild things," which Sendak thought was a bit too close to *Where the Wild Things Are*. Sendak's lawyers advised Jim to cease production on the film, and warned that a longer list of grievances would follow.

Cheryl remembered her father being "stunned" by Sendak's accusation. While Jim was likely familiar with the book—Cheryl owned a copy, and Jim had seen Sendak's original drawings for the book during a visit to the author's Connecticut home—the idea of poaching Sendak's work was a ridiculous affront to Jim's own work ethic; anyone who knew Jim understood that he simply wasn't wired that way. "Jim was hurt," said Lazer. "If things had been reversed, he would say, 'Oh, go use it.' . . . But he didn't consciously steal anything." However, there may have been other issues surrounding Sendak's charges than the prickly writer let on; while Sendak was friendly with Jim, he was closer with Jane—and there were some who thought Sendak's charges might have been an expression of righteous indignation over Jim's decision to separate from Jane. Whatever the cause, Jim responded by renaming his *wild things* as *Fireys* in the final film, and would give Sendak a special acknowledgment in the credits. Sendak withdrew his objection, though he would grumble about it for years.

Filming for *Labyrinth* finally began on April 15, 1985—a massive, $25 million project that sprawled across Elstree's nine soundstages. "It's a big one," Jim told the American Film Institute. "I think it would be very difficult to do any of those major fantasy, in-studio productions for under 20 million." Executive producer George Lucas was also on hand the first day, and surprised the entire crew by arranging for Darth Vader to stroll onto the set and present Jim with a good luck card.

For the first time, Jim would not be performing a major character in one of his films, allowing him to devote his full attention to directing. Early on, he found that Jennifer Connelly needed some coaxing to interact naturally with puppets. "In the beginning it was hard because . . . it's just strange thinking about the fact that you really are talking to a puppet," said Connelly. Eventually, the illusion became real to her—just as Jim knew it would. "The puppeteers make them so lifelike," said Connelly, "and you can really learn to relate to each one of them." Jim was delighted with her attitude both on and off camera; he got along with her well, in no small part because she didn't crave the constant reassurance so many around Jim seemed to need. "I found I could talk very straight to her," Jim said. "I didn't have to tiptoe around her feelings or anything like that."

Bowie, who reported to the set in early June, also had to learn how to act with *Labyrinth*'s elaborate puppets. He found himself especially troubled by scenes with Hoggle, whose mouth opened and closed in front of him, but whose voice came from Brian Henson, sitting just offstage, speaking into a microphone and performing Hoggle's mouth remotely with a waldo. "Once I'd overcome the disorientation," laughed Bowie, "we all got along great!" "[Bowie] has been wonderful to work with," Jim wrote privately, "and has added a truly magical spark as Jareth." Jim also respected Bowie's songwriting, giving Bowie—as he had Paul Williams—"a completely free hand" with the songs.

While Bowie winkingly described Jareth as "a spoiled child, vain and temperamental, kind of like a rock 'n' roll star," Jim found Bowie himself to be anything but spoiled or temperamental. "[He's] a very normal well-grounded straightforward person," said Jim. John Henson, who visited the set with a friend, was starstruck by Bowie, who greeted the twenty-year-old while still dressed as Jareth. When Bowie, finally out of makeup, sought John out at the end of the day, prowling the Elstree lobby in a bright red jacket, John was so awed by the sight of the musician that he and his friend ducked out of the studio without being seen. "Supposedly, David Bowie went around looking for us for about an hour after," said John sheepishly. "But we were gone!"

For his part, Bowie was impressed by Jim, who seemed constantly in motion, yet oddly unaffected by his own crazy schedule. "Jim is undoubtedly the most unflappable guy I've ever encountered in any profession," said Bowie admiringly. "I just can't believe his capacity for work. For instance, he would finish shooting for the week on *Labyrinth* in London, catch an airplane to New York, work . . . over the weekend, then catch a plane back to London Sunday night and be at the studios early on Monday morning. . . . He's desperately work-conscious but he seems to love it all. His calm spirit made the whole film a pleasure to work on, not just for me, but for the entire cast and crew."

Live actors aside, Jim was, as always, interested in doing new or unexpected things with puppetry. While the animatronic creatures were impressive in themselves, Jim had two more memorable sequences in mind, one that would involve the largest and heaviest mechanical puppet he'd ever created, and another that relied on nothing more complicated than the gloved hands of his performers.

"Late in the story, what we wanted was for our hero to come up against some huge obstacle," Jim explained. The result was a creature Jim called Humongous, a fifteen-foot-tall, armored warrior that stepped from the ornate carvings on a door. *Labyrinth*'s special effects team—led by George Gibbs, who had done mechanical effects for George Lucas—constructed an enormous puppet with a mechanical skeleton that used hydraulics to slowly walk and raise its arms. The gigantic figure could be operated remotely by a single performer wearing a robotic sleeve that controlled the skeleton's arms, and using levers and switches to pivot and bow the figure at the waist. Despite its lumbering appearance, "this was the most complicated thing we'd ever built," Jim enthused, requiring computers to translate the motions of the operator for the hydraulics raising and lowering the mechanical arms of the skeleton. "To just stand there and have this large thing walk towards you is one of the most awesome sights in the world," said Jim.

Equally as impressive, though far simpler, was a sequence Terry Jones had written in which Sarah falls down a Shaft of Hands— a narrow chute lined with gnarled hands that grab at her as she falls past. "I suddenly had this idea of *oooh!* all these hands . . . and they all grab her . . . [and it] sounds pretty spooky," said Jones. "And then I thought it would be very nice if the hands started talking to her." Jones thought this might involve performing the hands in a Señor Wences–like manner, with each hand making a mouth by curving the thumb against the closed fingers. But Jim had something better, and creepier, in mind.

As Jim saw it, multiple puppeteers could use their hands to form faces, with one performer making eyes, another making a fist for a nose, while another formed a mouth with one or both hands. Standing on-set, Jim ran a group of performers through possible hand motions, relying largely on Brian Henson and Kevin Clash, a dynamic young puppeteer borrowed from *Sesame Street,* to help make the faces and choreograph the performance. The result was both spooky and funny. "It's certainly one of the most bizarre and unusual sequences I've ever used in a movie," said Jim. Jones, too, was delighted. "When you've had an idea which you thought was a pretty good idea, and then you see it done and it is so much better than you ever imagined. . . . It was one of those magic moments, I think, when I actually saw it."

Brian Henson, who shared his father's love of technology and ambitious puppetry, loved every moment of it, whether he was making mouths of his hands in the Shaft of Hands, puppeteering one of the countless background goblins at Jareth's castle ("real crazy!" laughed Brian), or leading his team through a performance on Hoggle. But it was also hard work, the hours were long, and Brian was coming to more fully appreciate the work ethic that made his father . . . well, Jim Henson.

For one thing, it was never about money. After several long and grueling days of filming, Brian—who was now working as a paid performer—raised the issue of overtime. "I never leave the studio before around 10:30 P.M.," Brian pointed out to his father, "[and] I never put in for overtime." Jim considered for a moment, then smiled wryly. "When you're in your twenties, don't ever put in for overtime and don't ever ask for a raise," he told Brian warmly. "Just do the best work you can do. Impress the heck out of people." Brian understood immediately. "He wanted to see me develop my experience and become really excellent and not get greedy," said Brian. "That way, I'd know that I'd earned whatever I had."

Jim wrapped shooting on *Labyrinth* on September 6, marking the moment with a small party at Downshire Hill (the final wrap party, which he had hosted on-set a week earlier, had drawn over a thousand attendees). Across the street at 1B, Connie Peterson was preparing to close down the Creature Shop—but Jim was determined not to let the workshop lie fallow between projects again. "Rather than laying everyone off, Jim wanted to start a permanent workshop, where research and development could be continued," said Duncan Kenworthy. At Jim's direction, Kenworthy rounded up *Labyrinth*'s core group of designers, builders, and craftsmen—a close-knit group of about ten—and installed them as the Creature Shop's first permanent staff. This wasn't Jim being sentimental, but practical. "By keeping a group of people together, we are staying closer to what we've always done with the Muppets, where we had our own builders," Jim explained. "That way, you can make it better every time and build on your past work."

As for finding the right person to run the Creature Shop, Jim's decision-making process epitomized his management style. "He had tried to approach the problem from an engineering and creative perspective, although without much success," remembered Brian Henson. Then Kenworthy suggested John Stephenson, who had been a designer for *Labyrinth*—but Stephenson was also a good friend of Kenworthy's, and Kenworthy worried "it would have almost been nepotism to have offered him the job." Jim stroked his beard thoughtfully. "We should all be so lucky as we go through life working only with friends," he said. Stephenson was hired immediately.

When it came to working with friends, Jim, too, considered himself lucky. In early October, he rented a yacht to spend a week cruising the waters just off the south of France with a group of colleagues, including Bernie Brillstein, who was loudly and joyously celebrating twenty-five years of working with Jim. "He was the first one to take me on a yacht," said Brillstein. "That was Jim! He was something." A yacht trip, in fact, was typical of the kind of vacation Jim loved. "He was a modest guy in some ways," said Heather Henson. "In other ways, he was *completely* over the top."

"He was very conservative, but there was this whole other side of him," agreed Brillstein. "He just loved to laugh. He got the joke. He always got the joke." Lately, in fact, Jim had become a much more engaged practical joker, actively taking up the mantle since the death of Don Sahlin, and showing a knack for somewhat prurient pranks. "My dad was *naughty*," laughed Brian Henson. "He had a wicked sense of humor and he loved to do naughty things . . . and he certainly had that *glint* in his eyes."

A favorite target was Duncan Kenworthy, whose very proper British chain Jim delighted in yanking. One Saturday morning, Jim asked Kenworthy to join him for a meeting with a Swedish filmmaker who hoped to hire the Creature Shop to construct realistic-looking animals for a foreign film called *Animal Farm*—though as the pitch unfolded, and the director described a story of a nubile young girl who spent her summer tending to animals on a farm in the country, it was clear the filmmaker was *not* planning to film the George Orwell novel. Kenworthy was ready to dismiss the project outright, but noticed Jim listening with real interest. "Why not just use real animals?" Jim asked earnestly. The foreign filmmaker shrugged. "The sex scenes will be more difficult to do with real animals," he explained. A horrified Kenworthy nearly erupted in outrage at the idea of building creatures for an X-rated film, but Jim merely kept nodding and *hmmm*ing. "It sounds like an art film," said Jim to Kenworthy, "and I think it could be interesting. Besides, don't we need the money for the Creature Shop?" Kenworthy blanched. "It all sounds tawdry to me," he finally spluttered—and Jim exploded into his high-pitched giggle, unable to contain himself any longer. Laughter erupted from just outside the room, where Muppet performers had been hidden just out of sight, witness to—and videotaping—the entire elaborate prank.

Jim continued editing *Labyrinth* into the winter—often working alongside an editor with the serendipitous name of John Grover—and regularly reviewed rough cuts of the film with George Lucas. In early January 1986, Jim put Digital Productions—the computer animation firm with whom he had discussed the *Starboppers* project—to work on the film's opening credits, a two-and-a-half-minute sequence featuring a computer-generated white owl soaring over a labyrinth and across the credits. While computer-generated images (CGI) had been used in films before—most notably in 1984's *The Last Starfighter,* which featured CGI spaceships (also produced by Digital Productions)—*Labyrinth*'s opening sequence marked the first time a realistic, real-world animal had been created and animated in the computer. The result, said Jim later, "was really quite beautiful."

As he put the finishing touches on *Labyrinth,* Jim checked himself into the Colombe d'Or hotel in France to spend a weekend banging out a proposal for IBM Europe, whose CEO had dangled a tantalizing offer for Jim to come up with a television project he might do if "money were no object." Jim's response, for a show called *Muppet Voyager*, was typically high-minded. "Television is one of the greatest connectors around," he wrote. "The world is an immense network of human relationships, and peace and the resolution of conflict can only come through greater awareness of our connections. I think it's possible to change the world by reinforcing our inter-connectiveness, the spirit of one family of man, to the children of the world." Building on the objectives of *Fraggle Rock*, Jim envisioned a series centered around an intergalactic documentary film crew, reporting back to their home planet about life on Earth—much as Traveling Matt had reported back to the Fraggle residents on his adventures in "outer space"—while making the point that all life on the planet is connected. The project never got beyond an illustrated proposal, but Jim was serious about ensuring he had a meaningful presence on television—especially since *Fraggle Rock* was coming to an end.

Due to some difficulties with HBO—Jim would never let on exactly what had happened, but there were murmurings that *Fraggle* had been collateral damage in another battle over exclusive content for the network—it had been decided that *Fraggle Rock* would end after ninety-six episodes. While that was four shy of the one hundred usually needed for syndication, cable television was making it increasingly easier to syndicate shows with fewer episodes. However, Jim still wanted *Fraggle* to run for five seasons, which meant stretching the final twenty-six episodes out over two years. So while Jim and the *Fraggle Rock* team would be filming the final episode in Toronto in May 1986, the episode itself wouldn't air until March 1987—nearly a year later.

In the year since their "Future of Fraggles" meeting, Jerry Juhl and Jocelyn Stevenson had overseen the writing of a final arc of stories that brought some closure to the story of the Fraggles and their relationship with the Gorgs, the Doozers, and even Doc, who, in one of *Fraggle Rock*'s most memorable moments would finally discover the Fraggles. While Jim had initially resisted a final episode, he agreed with producer Larry Mirkin's assessment of the final story arc: "Those last four shows are just beautiful." "We who were totally involved in the creation of the world through the years, came to feel so strongly that we wanted a sense of . . . not ending, but a sense of roundness and finality to the series," said Juhl. "We tied up the threads."

And so, Jim had returned to play the minstrel Cantus in the second-to-last episode, dispensing his usual nuggets of cryptic wisdom in a typically calm manner as he helps the Fraggles find their way. While Jim wasn't directly involved in the final episode, Jerry Juhl's script seemed to capture much of Jim's own view of the universe. "Everyone is magic," the Trash Heap oracle tells Gobo. "The silly creatures are sometimes just too silly to remember that. . . . You go to him and you say this . . . 'You cannot leave the magic.'" In the end, Doc and Sprocket move to a new home far out in the desert, sadly leaving their beloved workshop and the Fraggles behind—only to discover a new Fraggle hole has magically appeared behind a box in their new home. "I think we all cried when we watched it," said Jerry Nelson. As the Fraggles sang and danced in Doc's new apartment, a final, loving dedication appeared at the end of the closing credits: "THIS SHOW IS FOR DON SAHLIN."

Following the taping of the final episode in May, Jim threw a wrap party for the entire *Fraggle* team. "This whole project has been a joy from the beginning," he told the crew earnestly. "It's fun when you start off trying to do something that makes a positive statement . . . that brings out the best in a lot of people. [*Fraggle Rock*] is something that's going to stay around and something that all of us are going to be proud of for a long time. And that's really nice." *You cannot leave the magic.*

Despite his intentionally arm's-length engagement with the show, *Fraggle Rock* had been something special for Jim—a higher calling for television as well as an embodiment of his own views of what was right about the world. "Jim wanted to make a difference," said Jerry Juhl later. "He knew that television shows do not bring peace to the world, but he wasn't so cynical to say we can't think about it. There was a kind of idealism there that could seem naive and childlike, but that didn't mean it couldn't come true."

That idealism—that ridiculous optimism—carried over to *Labyrinth* as well. As Jim made the rounds with the press in the weeks leading up to the film's June 27, 1986, release, he was brimming with excited anticipation and was clearly proud of the movie. "When I go see a film, when I leave the theater, I like a few things," he explained. "I like to be happier than I was when I went in. I like a film to leave me with an 'up' feeling. And I like a picture to have a sense of substance. I like it to be about life, about things that matter to me. And so I think it's what we're trying to do with this film, is trying to do a film that would make a difference to you if you saw it."

At first, it seemed the reviews would bear out Jim's high expectations and enthusiasm. Nina Darnton of *The New York Times* hailed *Labyrinth* as "fabulous" and "a remarkable achievement" marred only by what Darnton thought to be a weak performance from Connelly. That, unfortunately, was as good as it was going to get. *Chicago Sun-Times* critic Roger Ebert, always an admirer, tried hard to make lemonade from what he found to be a most bitter lemon. "[It's] obviously made with infinite care and pains, and it began with real inspiration [with] impressive production that is often good to look at," said Ebert sympathetically. "Yet, there's something missing. It never really comes alive." Nick Roddick, a critic for *Cinema Papers*, also tried gamely to point out *Labyrinth*'s merits. "[It] has quite a lot going for it," wrote Roddick, "but it all somehow fails to gel. . . . It's all admirably clever rather than compulsive watching." Perhaps, the critic gently suggested, Jim's talents were "not the stuff of adult fantasy."

More typical, however, were reviews like the one in *Variety*, which took a nearly morbid glee in dashing Jim and the film repeatedly against the rocks. "A crashing bore," the reviewer sneered, unimpressed by puppets he found "terminally cute with no real charm" and which "become annoying rather than endearing." Even Connelly was "stiff and childish." (Despite early criticism of her *Labyrinth* performance, Connelly would go on to have a very successful acting career; in 2002, she won an Academy Award for Best Supporting Actress for *A Beautiful Mind*.) Meanwhile, over at the *Chicago Tribune*, critic Gene Siskel was positively cranky. "Jim Henson knows what he's doing with his Muppet characters on TV and in the movies," wrote Siskel. "But he's completely at sea when he tries to create more mature entertainment." *Labyrinth* was "quite awful," its creatures were "visually ugly," and Jim had stooped to "one of the sleaziest gimmicks a film can employ" by placing a baby in peril as the center of the plot. All in all, thundered Siskel, the film was "an enormous waste of talent and money."

While critics were split on what it was about *Labyrinth* that annoyed them the most—was it trying to be a music video? Was it supposed to be scary?—most agreed that the biggest problem was the story. There had been too many hands at work on the screenplay, and it showed; the resulting patch job had turned the movie into a "series of incidents," wrote Ebert. "Sarah does this, she does that . . . until at last nothing much matters." In the end, "it doesn't have a story that does justice to the production." *Variety* sniffed that the story "loses its way and never comes close to the archetypical myths and fears of great fairy tales. . . . [It's a] silly and flat excursion to a land you can't wait to leave."

While that was probably all fair criticism, the real problem—as Jim had feared from the beginning—was with the character of Sarah. Despite the best efforts of Phillips and May, Sarah remained an empty, slightly brusque character, whose motivations were suspect and who didn't seem to have evolved or grown by the end of the film. Jerry Nelson summed up the problem perhaps most succinctly: "I didn't give a fuck whether she got her brother back or not. I just didn't like her at all. . . . You had to care about her, and you had to care about her getting her brother back. And I just didn't." Neither did audiences. After a relatively strong opening weekend, *Labyrinth* began losing money so rapidly that distributor Tri-Star Pictures pulled the film from theaters after three weeks. In the end, *Labyrinth* only grossed $12 million on its $25 million budget—a "costly bore," snarked *Variety*.

Jim was devastated by the response. "I was stunned and dazed for several months trying to figure out what went wrong—where *I* went wrong," he said later. "[It] was a real blow," added Jane Henson. "He couldn't understand it." "I think that was the closest I've ever seen him to turning in on himself and getting quite depressed," said Brian Henson. "It was rather a bad time." Arthur Novell, Jim's publicist, thought the response took a physical toll as well. "[It was] really despair," said Novell. "He changed physically . . . the beard got lighter. . . . He had great hopes for *Labyrinth*. The buildup toward it was so heavy and strong and positive, and he got bit by it. He was stung by the criticism. But it was *never* about the money. It wasn't about . . . what he lost, what he spent."

As with *The Dark Crystal*, it had been all about artistic vision and artistic integrity. *Labyrinth* was "absolutely the closest project to him," said Jane, the one in which he had invested most of his creative capital—and to have audiences reject it felt to Jim like they were rejecting *him* personally. "That movie looked exactly the way Jim wanted," said creative consultant Larry Mirkin. "Everything you see on the screen looks exactly the way Jim imagined it." But as Oz noted, apart from the grousing of a few perpetually unhappy critics, the problem really wasn't with Jim's vision; it was with the storytelling. "Take a look at *Labyrinth* and forget the story for a moment," said Oz. "The images you get are abso-*fucking*-lutely amazing. Absolutely amazing. That's Jim's production design and that's what his love was. It was just staggering the work he did. But as a story, it just didn't hold up."

"Life is a kind of labyrinth," Jim had once mused, "with all its twists and turns, its straight paths and occasional dead ends." For the moment, *Labyrinth* itself was one of those dead ends—and so, it seemed, were movies. He had wandered down a blind passage into a stone wall—but a bit of offhanded good advice at a party, courtesy of a drunken Jerry Nelson, would help set him back on course again. "You know," slurred Nelson, draping an arm warmly around Jim's shoulders, "you should stick with television."

CHAPTER THIRTEEN

STORYTELLER

1986–1987

Jim directing the "Heartless Giant" episode of
The Storyteller *in 1988.*

As *LABYRINTH* FADED FROM MOVIE SCREENS IN THE SUMMER OF 1986, Jim—after the brief period of hand-wringing that had so alarmed some of his colleagues—became increasingly pragmatic about the movie's fate. He took full responsibility for the film's tepid reception, acknowledging that it "wasn't the movie audiences were waiting to see." It would be easy to blame bad distribution or a poor release date, he told *The Hollywood Reporter*, but "obviously, the picture was not in tune with our audience completely, or they would have found us wherever we were." Typically, he refused to take up much time second-guessing the film's misfortune. For Jim, who had seemed to so effortlessly walk away from the world's most popular television show at the height of its success to pursue a new venture, it was easy to move beyond the relative failure of *Labyrinth* and on to newer, exciting projects. "I work in one capacity for a while, and then it's time to jump over to some other kind of thing," he said earnestly, explaining that he already had in mind "a handful" of other projects. "To me, it's just fun."

Fun, in fact, was the name of the game for Jim's first post-*Labyrinth* project, a one-hour television special taped in February 1986 for HBO and the BBC called *The Tale of the Bunny Picnic*. Jim had undertaken the project due in no small part to the encouragement of Cheryl, who thought that after *The Dark Crystal* and *Labyrinth*—"these huge, grandiose visions"—it might be fun to get back to doing "something with cute, fun, funny puppets and do it as a family show." The story, too—in which the well-meaning but overly imaginative Bean Bunny tries to warn his fellow rabbits about a nearby dog—had been inspired by a bit of real-life cuteness, dating back to *The Muppet Show* years in London when Jim and the Muppet performers would regularly picnic out on Hampstead Heath at dusk. As the puppeteers sprawled on the ground to eat, groups of rabbits would emerge from the brush to forage in the shadows—and Jim came to refer to these excursions to the heath as "bunny picnics." One particular evening, as rabbits shuffled about in the grass—"looking to all the world like they were gonna have a meeting or convention or something," remembered Jim—a dog raced over, barking madly. "The rabbits, of course, disappeared in a flash," said Jim, "[and] Cheryl and I thought it might be fun to make up a story about what had just happened. And from that notion came *The Tale of the Bunny Picnic*."

Bunny Picnic was a bit of warmhearted, homespun fare cut from the same cloth as *Emmet Otter* or *The Muppet Musicians of Bremen*, intentionally cute and with lively songs by the *Fraggle Rock* team of Philip Balsam and Dennis Lee. After more than a year of seeing themselves as backbenchers to the Creature Shop, the builders in the Muppet workshop leapt into the new production with relish, building fluffy, fuzzy, huggable rabbits, dogs, and other animals, based on designs by children's illustrator Diane Dawson Hearn. For

the Muppet workshop, "it was really fun to make puppets again"—
and Jim delighted in the two weeks he spent in London in February
directing and performing. He enjoyed working in television again—
but after spending the last five years immersed in fully realized worlds
of goblins, Mystics, and Gelflings, there now had to be more to television than just the bright colors and soft edges of the Muppets.
"Having done the Muppet stuff so beautifully, [and] having nothing
else to explore or prove there," said Jerry Juhl, "[Jim] wanted to
move on."

There was an employee moving on at that time, too, leaving
David Lazer—who would always be involved with the management
of the company, despite his best efforts to stay retired—with a sticky
personnel issue at Henson Associates. Following the promotion of
Jim's longtime assistant Mira Velimirovic in January 1986, Jim had
been planning to hire thirty-year-old Mary Ann Cleary—who had
worked for Henson Associates several years earlier, and in whom Jim
had always had more than just a professional interest—as his new
assistant. Lazer, astutely gauging the likely outcome of Jim's proposed arrangement, called publicist and close personal advisor Arthur Novell and judiciously asked him to arrange a lunch date for
Jane and Mary Ann. "See how Jane reacts to all this," suggested
Lazer.

The arranged lunch was amicable enough, recalled Novell, but it
was clear that Jane and Mary Ann "were sizing each other up." Later,
Jane would only coyly describe her lunch conversation with Mary
Ann as "interesting"—and Jim, perhaps preferring not to chum the
waters any further, opted for Cheryl as his assistant instead, hiring
her in February 1986. By the end of the summer, however, following
a working vacation through Egypt, Japan, and Indonesia, Cheryl left
to study textiles at the Fashion Institute of Technology in New York,
leaving the position once again vacant. This time, Jim quietly installed Mary Ann as his assistant, and within two months—just as
Lazer predicted—Jim and Mary Ann were vacationing together on a
yacht cruise in Sardinia with Bernie Brillstein and other friends, celebrating Jim's fiftieth birthday. But Lazer, and others, had rightly
sensed that this new relationship would be more than just a casual
office romance or fling.

It was easy to see Jim's attraction to Mary Ann. "She was spirited, outgoing, and attractive," said Al Gottesman matter-of-factly. Good-looking and lithe, with an easy smile and a shaggy mane of sandy blond hair, Mary Ann was, in many ways, what Jane was not. Mary Ann, who had initially had little physical attraction to Jim— she had spurned his advances several years earlier—soon found herself drawn in by the sheer power of his personality, that same undefinable trait that even the most seasoned Hollywood veterans found irresistible. She was charmed by his ease in conversation, and would watch in adoring fascination as he punctuated his sentences with a quick sweep of his hands or a flutter of his long fingers. "Jim really used his hands," said Mary Ann. "They were very powerful and present, as much as any other attribute. A puppeteer's hands." In no time, she and Jim would be practically inseparable.

That fall, Jim already had a more ambitious television project under way—an anthology show as gorgeously designed as *The Dark Crystal* and with the same kind of fairy tale–*cum*–music video look and rhythm he had tried, with only some success, to instill in *Labyrinth*. The basic idea had come from Lisa, who had studied folklore and mythology at Harvard. Lisa had written a long treatment for a show presenting what she called the "unfamous" versions of fairy tales "that really capture the flavor of how these stories were told and could be told with visuals that feel more authentic." Jim had taken to the idea immediately, sending graduate students fanning out to academic libraries to photocopy old Russian folktales, Celtic and Japanese fairy tales, Italian myths, and heroic tales—and the more stories he read, the more excited he became. "Most folktales . . . are really very good, very solid, gutsy material that is really quite adult and sometimes quite violent," he said later, "and we were intrigued with the idea of treating the material honestly, the way it was meant to be treated."

As Jim and Lisa talked through the concept and began putting more ideas down on paper, Lisa suggested that the best way to tell the old stories might be to have them dramatically narrated by a storyteller. What made folklore truly special, she explained, were "the words, and the sound of a man's voice telling a tale and evoking a host of images." With that description, Jim could immediately see the visual possibilities—and when he called Duncan Kenworthy to propose that the Englishman oversee production of the show in London, he excitedly described a man sitting by a fire telling stories of fantastic creatures he was certain the Creature Shop could bring convincingly to life. Once the reliable Kenworthy had agreed to serve as his producer, Jim was certain the look and feel of the show—which he was proposing to call *The Storyteller*—would be just as he wanted. However, there were still two critical pieces that had yet to fall into place.

Jim intended to treat *The Storyteller* much as he had *Fraggle Rock;* while he would serve as executive producer, establish the overarching look and feel for the series, and direct an episode from time to time, for the most part he planned to leave the show in the hands of his creative team, including Kenworthy and, ideally, a director with a distinctive style. However, finding a director suited to Jim's vision of *The Storyteller* wouldn't be easy—after all, how exactly did one film something in an "oral tradition" where the voice evoked images? The answer, suggested Jim, was already at work in music videos, where lyrics often *suggested* a story against which the accompanying video established its own narrative. Jim had done something similar with *Time Piece,* using quick cuts and seemingly unrelated images to convey a story with a percussive soundtrack behind it. In the fledgling modern music video era—the upstart MTV channel had been launched only five years earlier—no one made music videos that were more interesting or visually compelling than Steve Barron, a twenty-nine-year-old Irishman who had directed Michael Jackson's groundbreaking "Billie Jean" and the cutting-edge "Take on Me" for the Norwegian band a-ha. "He was the absolute top of the heap," said Lisa—and with only minimal prodding from Kenworthy, Barron signed on as Jim's primary director.

The most important part of *The Storyteller,* however, was the stories themselves. From the start, Kenworthy was enthusiastic about the work of thirty-two-year-old English playwright Anthony Minghella, who had written a thoughtful British television miniseries called *What If It's Raining,* which explored the effects of separation and divorce on an English family. At Kenworthy's prompting, Jim had invited Minghella to lunch to discuss writing *The Storyteller*, a summons Minghella excitedly accepted simply because he wanted to meet Jim. Over lunch, recalled Minghella, "[Jim] told me he had an idea for a series which they'd been exploring for a while, which involved a man by a fire telling stories." But *"nobody,"* said Minghella, "wants to look at a man telling stories. . . . I just didn't get it." The writer politely declined.

And yet, the image Jim had enthusiastically described, of the storyteller sitting with his dog before a roaring fire, stayed with him. "This was something I learned about Jim later," said Minghella. "He had a brilliant sense of the possibilities of something without ever really being able to articulate those possibilities." Kenworthy was still convinced Jim and Minghella would be a good fit, and after several false starts, arranged for them to spend an evening listening to actual storytellers weave folktales. "I was even more convinced then that it wouldn't work out," said Minghella, but he agreed to write a pilot episode anyway, eventually turning in an intelligent script based on the Brothers Grimm tale "Hans My Hedgehog," about a half man, half hedgehog who can only be freed from his curse by true love.

As the Creature Shop went to work building the necessary characters—including the man-hedgehog Hans, a giant chicken, and the Storyteller's dog—Jim and Kenworthy assembled their cast, bringing in English actor John Hurt to take the critical role of the craggy and enigmatic Storyteller. Jim was paying for the pilot himself, and Kenworthy did his best to keep an eye on the bottom line, regularly alerting Jim to any potential cost overruns. Keeping with its music video mentality, *The Storyteller* would feature computer-generated backgrounds and animation, requiring long and expensive computer time to render. Most of the budget busting, however, was on the part of the Creature Shop, which was trying to maintain motion picture standards on a television budget. Kenworthy grumbled to Jim about what he called the Creature Shop's " 'sculpted foot syndrome,' where the level of finish on everything is pitched at feature film standard." With the pilot for *The Storyteller* already budgeted at a whopping $943,000 for a thirty-minute program, Kenworthy promised to keep the production on budget. Still, Jim went through his own script to see if there were any places where an otherwise elaborate or expensive visual effect might be eliminated, writing "SHOW THIS" on some pages and "DO WE NEED THIS?" on others.

It didn't get any cheaper once director Steve Barron began shooting at Lee International Studios in London on August 26. Barron was a tough director, with high expectations of himself and his performers—including Brian Henson, performing the role of the Storyteller's straight-talking dog—and Barron would work the cast and crew ten hours one day, then edit for fourteen hours the next. "I really don't think we could sustain the effort on a weekly basis," Kenworthy confessed to Jim. But Jim was delighted with the results and proudly pronounced the effort as "some of the prettiest television we've ever done." Making the most of Jim's artistic vision, director Steve Barron's rock 'n' roll rhythms, and Anthony Minghella's poetic scriptwriting, *The Storyteller* was a simple concept, sumptuously done. Now Jim just needed to find a television network that believed in it as much as he did.

For much of the fall, Jim was sorting out private matters. While he loved his apartment at the Sherry-Netherland, for tax reasons he had recently closed on a second apartment, a Southern-style structure at 633 Steamboat Road, overlooking Smith Cove in Greenwich, Connecticut. The apartment at Steamboat Road would become his official home address, and for the rest of his life accountants at Henson Associates would carefully track Jim's schedule to ensure he spent the appropriate number of days in Connecticut to qualify for Connecticut residency, and its marginally lower tax rate.

As he had done at the Sherry-Netherland, Jim tore down and rebuilt the interior of the Steamboat Road apartment, then called a professional—this time designer Connie Beale—to assist with the decorating. Like many of Jim's most fulfilling projects, the work with Beale was a true collaboration. Where Beale's tastes were more traditional, Jim leaned ethnic and international, and the resulting décor was an eclectic but tasteful merging of artistic temperaments. Jim loved spending the afternoon shopping with Beale, discussing

decorating over lunch, then buying handmade furniture from antiques stores or browsing for sculpture, fabrics, and art at Elements
in Greenwich or Julie's Gallery in New York. Jim filled his rooms
with Windsor chairs, African masks, and Indonesian cabinets—but
his favorite place in the apartment was the back room with its floor-
to-ceiling windows, where he would sprawl on the sofa beneath a
sculpture of herons, and watch the waves out in Smith Cove.

One thing Jim didn't have in his apartment—either at Steamboat Road or the Sherry-Netherland—was memories. "As much as
he loved objects," said Cheryl, "he didn't care about holding on to
things." When Jim had moved out of the house in Bedford, then, he
had left behind not only Jane, but nearly everything else—from furniture and floor coverings, to school report cards and souvenirs—
and simply started over again, building a new life in a new apartment
with new *everything*. Jane, meanwhile, after spending the past year
living in Bedford with fifteen-year-old Heather, had decided to move
into a house of her own, carefully packing up boxes of painted
wooden toys and handmade Christmas ornaments and rearranging
old furniture in her new house in Greenwich. Their new homes, as
much as anything, symbolized their differing approaches to their relationship with each other as well as their perspectives on life in general: Jim was always looking forward, excited about new things and
the future, while Jane carried the weight and obligations of the past.
Perhaps tellingly, their homes in Greenwich were less than three miles
apart; even legally separated, Jim and Jane could never be entirely
removed from each other.

As Thanksgiving neared, Jim was in discussions with Brandon
Tartikoff, the enthusiastic head of programming for NBC, to gauge
the network's interest in *The Storyteller*. The response was encouraging. "[Tartikoff] loves it," Jim told Kenworthy. "Or at least loves it
enough to broadcast it in January so that he can find out if the *audience* loves it." While a favorable reception from an audience might
eventually assure the show a spot as a regular prime-time series, Jim
wasn't ready to call it a sure thing, especially with a series as unconventional as *The Storyteller*. And now that Tartikoff had opened the
door, Jim wanted another series ready to pitch to NBC in the event
Storyteller failed to take hold.

Jim was an enormous admirer of comedian Paul Reubens's frantic Saturday morning *Pee-wee's Playhouse,* which, apart from being funny, liberally combined live actors with playful chromakey effects and computer animation. "I thought it was just terrific," Jim had written to Reubens appreciatively after the show's premiere in 1986. "We've been waiting for someone to come along and put a lot of this stuff together like you did." Jim thought he could have even more fun with the technology than Reubens—and since early summer he had been kicking around an idea for a fast-paced, sketch-driven comedy called *IN-TV* that would utilize all the technology Jim had at his disposal—from computer graphics and chromakey to Muppets and animatronics—to poke fun at the medium of television itself.

At the heart of *IN-TV* was a clever concept: each week, a live guest star would get sucked into the television set and would have to work his way back out again, usually by moving from one bad television channel to another. It was a fun idea, giving Jim an opportunity to satirize the seemingly endless parade of upstart cable channels and lame public access shows that were common in the early days of cable. Jim had a number of new characters in mind, though not much else, but he was excited about it—and when Jim was excited about a project, no detail was too small for his attention. He designed the IN-TV logo himself, and brought in respected music producer Phil Ramone to collaborate on original songs for a new Muppet band. He was so pleased with how things were proceeding, in fact, that he presented Ramone with a thank-you gift—a $2,900, thirty-five-inch Mitsubishi television—along with a note thanking Ramone for his music and assuring the composer with typical optimism that "we're going to have great fun doing some wonderful television that should look good on this set."

Jim spent the first part of December promoting *Labyrinth* overseas—like *The Dark Crystal* before it, *Labyrinth* would perform strongly in the international market—traveling with Heather and Mary Ann to Germany and London, where the British press swooned adoringly as Jim introduced the lumbering Ludo to Princess Diana at the royal premiere. There were more parties and premieres in Amsterdam, Madrid, Paris, and Copenhagen before they finally returned home just before Christmas. While the pre-holiday skiing in Vermont was "great," Christmas itself was a somber affair. Jim spent the week between Christmas and New Year's Day silently helping Jane pack up the last of their belongings in the Bedford house—and all the boxes, of course, would go to Jane's new place, not Jim's. It was a "broken-family Christmas," said John Henson. "It was really devastating."

The first two weeks of 1987 were spent rehearsing and preparing for the *IN-TV* pilot, which Jim was moving forward with despite some apprehensions about the show's script, by *Mork and Mindy* scribe David Misch. While Jim could usually tell intuitively when a script wasn't working, he didn't always know *why*. Creative consultant Larry Mirkin—who Jim relied on to give him a straight read on scripts to help figure such things out—told Jim he thought the script was a disaster, "consistently dark, victimized, and pessimistic," and flat-out unfunny. Despite Mirkin's misgivings, Jim and the Muppet performers spent three days taping Misch's messy script anyway, which Jim eventually edited down into a ten-minute pitch reel and renamed *Inner Tube*. Bernie Brillstein was assigned the job of selling the show to NBC—or any other network for that matter—but found no takers. Frustrated, Jim would spend the better part of the year trying to figure out what to do with it.

While *Inner Tube* sputtered, *The Storyteller*—which finally made its debut on NBC on the evening of Saturday, January 31, 1987—was a qualified success. While it failed to crack even the top thirty in the ratings for the week, *The Storyteller* was an immediate critical hit—and, in fact, would go on to win the Emmy as the Outstanding Children's Program. It would also earn Jim some of his best reviews in years. "It's time to stop thinking of him simply as the man who created the Muppets," said an impressed *Hollywood Reporter,* finally conceding a point Jim had been trying to make for two decades. "When a show arrives under the auspices of Jim Henson, we can be pretty sure we won't be disappointed," wrote Walter Goodman in *The New York Times*. "If it [*The Storyteller*] were turned into a series, that would be a real happy ending." *USA Today,* meanwhile, hailed it as "one of Jim Henson's finest moments on TV."

Jim was justifiably proud of *The Storyteller,* which he regarded as something of an artistic higher calling. "It is our responsibility to keep telling these tales—to tell them in a way that they teach and entertain and give meaning to our lives," he said later. "This is not merely an obligation, it's something we must do because we love doing it." A delighted NBC offered to pick up *The Storyteller* as a weekly series, and Jim approached Anthony Minghella about writing new episodes. The inscrutable Minghella, who had initially been skeptical about his ability to write for the series, found himself caught up in Jim's energy and enthusiasm. With Jim, said Minghella, "it's very hard to just visit. You tend to lose your return ticket when you go on the journey [with him]. I wrote the pilot and then discovered, of course, that it was a fascinating subject and the possibilities of it were enormous. [Jim] was absolutely right. There was a series there and, in fact, we could go on making it for the rest of our lives."

Even with *The Storyteller* now fully in production—and the problematic *Inner Tube* on the back burner—Jim continued to develop and pitch one television series after another. One of them—*Puppetman*, a live-action sitcom about a group of puppeteers working on a daily children's television show—actually made it as far as the pilot stage, though abysmal ratings doomed it from being picked up as a regular series. Others—like *Muppet Voyager*, still languishing in outline form in Jim's desk drawer, or *Read My Lips*, a comedy series co-written by Muppet performer Richard Hunt about puppets who come to life after they've been put away for the night—never made it much beyond the written page. Jim had always kept a breakneck pace—multiple projects were the rule, rather than the exception—but lately some of the projects had a slight whiff of indifference to them, as if Jim were simply launching a handful of darts at a dartboard, hoping for any of them to hit. "I think Jim felt . . . he was responsible [for us]," said Richard Hunt. "And he would go out of his way to keep creating new work so that these people had something to do." And if Hunt or any of the Muppet performers or writers questioned the artistic merits of a project, Jim would simply fold his arms and sigh knowingly. "Richard, please," he would say quietly. "I'm *trying*."

And he *was* trying. Jim took seriously the management of his

*Lord Lew Grade (second from right, with wife Kathie, David Lazer, and Jim)
believed in Jim and the Muppets from the very beginning and ensured that Jim
had the resources he needed to make* The Muppet Show *successful. With a budget
of $125,000 per episode, it was one of the most expensive
syndicated shows of its day.*
(Courtesy of The Jim Henson Company)

Jim's beloved Kermit-green Lotus, a gift from Lord Grade.
(Courtesy of The Jim Henson Company. Kermit the Frog © Disney)

Writer Jerry Juhl was one of Jim's most important and trusted creative collaborators. Starting in the 1960s, Juhl guided the Muppets from television to the movie screen and played a critical role in countless projects, including the development of Fraggle Rock.
(COURTESY OF THE JIM HENSON COMPANY)

Jim and Jane at a formal dinner honoring Lord Grade in London. While their relationship had always been a true creative partnership, differing priorities—and vastly different communication styles—would eventually fracture their marriage.
(COURTESY OF HENSON FAMILY PROPERTIES)

Filming the Muppets was both a high- and low-tech creative endeavor. Above, Jim, always the gadget freak, performs Kermit remotely with the help of a waldo, while below, he performs on his back while being pushed on a rolling cart.

The Dark Crystal (1982) *was Jim's most ambitious project to date, a richly designed universe requiring complicated and physically demanding puppetry. Here Jim and performer Kathy Mullen bend and squeeze themselves out of camerashot as they perform Jen and Kira, the film's heroes.*
(COURTESY OF THE JIM HENSON COMPANY. PHOTO: MURRAY CLOSE)

Jim and the cast of Fraggle Rock. *Airing on HBO from 1983 to 1987, the show was the network's first original series—the colorful ancestor to shows like* The Sopranos *and* Game of Thrones.
(COURTESY OF THE JIM HENSON COMPANY. PHOTO: JOHN E. BARRETT)

Creative director Michael Frith wa Jim's most versatile and brilliant co tors, influencing everything from p. design and publishing to Muppet P and Disney rides. He would play a in shaping the world of Fraggle Ro
(COURTESY OF THE JIM HENSON COMPANY PHOTO: STAR BLACK)

Jim with the intentionally monstrous cast of 1985's Dreamchild, *an outside project that helped launch the successful and highly respected Creature Shop in London.*
(Courtesy of The Jim Henson Company)

loved performing the sage Cantus on the set of le Rock. "[Cantus] was great," said one Fraggle *writer, "because he was goofy and wise at the same time, kind of like Jim."*
(Courtesy of The Jim Henson Company. Photo: Fred Phipps)

Jim on the set of Labyrinth *with executive producer George Lucas in 1985. "We were very much alike," said Lucas. "Independent, out of the spotlight, obsessed with our own films."*
(Courtesy of The Jim Henson Company)

Brian Froud (left) with Labyrinth *writer (and Monty Python member) Terry Jones. Jim loved Froud's bold artistic sense, which forged the look of both* The Dark Crystal *and* Labyrinth. (COURTESY OF THE JIM HENSON COMPANY)

Jim with David Bowie and Jennifer Connelly on the set of Labyrinth *in 19 The movie was, according to Jane, "absolutely the closest project to him, and he was devastated by its failure at the box office.* (COURTESY OF THE JIM HENSON COMPANY. PHOTO: JOHN BROWN)

Agent Bernie Brillstein, Jim, and actor John Hurt, in full makeup, on the set of The Storyteller. *Though low-rated, the sumptuously produced TV series was a critical hit and won Jim another Emmy.* (COURTESY OF THE JIM HENSON COMPANY.)

Twenty-three-year-old Brian Henson performed the dog on The Storyteller one of many projects in which Jim ar the Henson children would perform participate. "One of the best ways fo us to be around him," said daughter Cheryl, "was to work with him." (COURTESY OF THE JIM HENSON COMPANY.)

Happiness: Jim plays with breadsticks over dinner. "Jim really used his hands," said Mary Ann Cleary. "They were very powerful and present . . . a puppeteer's hands."
(PHOTOS BY AND COURTESY OF MARY ANN CLEARY)

Jim on vacation with Mary Ann in France.
It was his first real relationship since his separation from Jane.
(Photo by and courtesy of Mary Ann Cleary)

The major Muppet performers, on the steps of the circular
staircase at One Seventeen in 1989. Clockwise from bottom
center: Jim, Frank Oz, Dave Goelz, Richard Hunt,
Steve Whitmire, and Jerry Nelson.
(Courtesy of The Jim Henson Company. Photo: Richard Termine)

company—and his nearly 150 employees—personally writing chatty quarterly reports to the entire staff, organizing company orientations, and even submitting himself and several managers to the Myers-Briggs test to identify their management styles. Jim's Myers-Briggs results labeled him, to perhaps no one's surprise, as an idealist. As he made a list of his business objectives, Jim wrote near the top, "work for common good of all mankind" and "use of technology and business for common good." The "common good," as he saw it, was "growth and development of children . . . sharing wealth . . . respect[ing] work—nature—environment." But running the company was taking increasingly more and more of his time, draining his energy from the creative projects he considered his *real* work for the common good. "I've never particularly wanted to have a large organization," Jim confessed to one reporter. "The trick is to try to stay small enough to be creative but still be able to do all the projects we want to do—and not to get so big where you just spend your time managing people and trying to keep everybody working." And *trying*.

At times, the pressures were more than he wanted to handle. He was easily frustrated with internal squabbles; Henson Associates' legal department, in fact, could often be particularly exhausting. "The lawyers would all fight with each other," remembered Jane Henson, and then would call in Jim to resolve the dispute. Jim—who wouldn't even argue with his own wife—refused to engage, and simply backed out of the room with his big hands up, palms out. "You resolve it," he begged them. "I have to go to London." And then, said Jane, "he'd just get on a plane and go," whether he actually had business in London or not. "It was fight or flight," said Jane, "and he'd choose flight."

That summer, however, there really was business taking him overseas and away from the worries of the company. In July, Jim spent twenty days in Charleville-Mézières, France, teaching a puppetry workshop to twenty-one students—"many of whom," Jim wrote playfully, "will not speak English." With Brian and Cheryl assisting, Jim strolled the classrooms at the Institut International de la Marionnette, teaching puppet building, Muppet-style performing, and going over the basics of lip-synching, singing "Frère Jacques" as a roomful of students waved a sea of Muppets over their heads, staring intently at monitors.

From France, Jim returned to the familiar grounds of Elstree film studios in Borehamwood, where the Henson Organization—the British arm of Henson Associates—had taken over three soundstages, along with several offices in the studio's centrally located John Maxwell Building, to film four new episodes of *The Storyteller*. After the successful premiere episode in January, Jim had been approached by a number of young directors interested in working on the show—"It's almost like the early days of *The Muppet Show*, when top stars would beg to be guests," said producer Duncan Kenworthy—but after handing directing duties over to Steve Barron, Charles Sturridge, and Jon Amiel, Jim was itching to get back in the director's chair himself. And once he was back within the comforts of Elstree, Jim took the helm of the episode "Soldier and Death," an adaptation of a Russian folktale in which a soldier uses a magic sack to capture Death. Jim had a ball.

Financially, however, *The Storyteller* was barely keeping its head above water—while Jim was now financing the series with money from NBC and the independent British television company TVS, *The Storyteller* was running a deficit. So troublesome was the series to produce, in fact, that Jim and NBC had agreed that it would be impossible to produce as a weekly series; instead, *The Storyteller* would air on the network as a series of half-hour specials, shown on a sporadic basis. But that wasn't really an ideal setup, either—and on August 22, Jim met with Brandon Tartikoff to suggest that installments of *The Storyteller* might be incorporated into a weekly themed anthology series Jim was proposing, called *The Jim Henson Hour*. Tartikoff liked the idea well enough that he asked Jim to prepare a proposal and a pitch reel—which NBC would pay for—that Tartikoff could then take back to the network brass.

As Jim saw it, *The Jim Henson Hour* would be "in the same grand tradition" as *The Wonderful World of Disney*, a weekly anthology in which Disney appeared on camera to introduce an assortment of features, from cartoons and nature films to short movies and behind-the-scenes documentaries. "Each week," Jim explained, "we'll tell a different story: some with puppets, some with people, and most with a mix of the two." For *The Jim Henson Hour,* Jim was proposing four different themed shows, shown in a regular rotation. The first week of each month, then, would be devoted exclusively to *The Storyteller,* allowing Jim to put the show on a regular monthly schedule as part of his own series. And since he would now have an hour to fill, Jim could produce hour-long installments of *The Storyteller*—something he was longing to do, as current episodes were only thirty minutes—slowing down and spreading out "to allow ourselves to take advantage of the rich imagery" of folktales.

For the second week of each month, Jim was hoping to salvage the remains of *Inner Tube* and reshape them into something called *Lead-Free TV.* The concept was still relatively the same—a cast of new Muppets and a guest star interacting across television channels—but for Jim, it was still more about playing with the new technology. "In the many years we've been on television, the capabilities of TV itself have changed dramatically," he pointed out enthusiastically. "Using state of the art technology we can create settings that exist only as electronic information." With new technology at his disposal, Jim envisioned *Lead-Free TV* as "*The Muppet Show* of the future!"

The third week of each month would be devoted to "Picturebook Specials"—spotlighting more homespun fare like *Emmet Otter's Jug-Band Christmas* or *The Tale of the Bunny Picnic*—while the fourth episode in the monthly cycle would be "The Next Wave," shows that would have "unlimited potential," Jim said, "because we will allow ourselves to do almost anything." Jim already had plenty of ideas for his "Next Wave" specials, including a celebration of the upcoming twentieth anniversary of *Sesame Street,* a Miss Piggy special, and a behind-the-scenes documentary on the Muppets. "We're tremendously excited about these shows," he enthused.

On September 25, 1987—the day after his fifty-first birthday, and only a little more than a month after discussing the idea with Tartikoff—Jim stepped before the cameras to tape his host segments for the pitch reel for *The Jim Henson Hour.* Dressed casually in a black-and-white-patterned jacket over a collared shirt, Jim looked remarkably at ease as he strolled onto a set designed and constructed to resemble an idealized version of the Muppet workshop. It was a perfect setup. "I thought that was a wonderful way of doing *The Jim Henson Hour* because that's the way it happens," said Muppet performer Kevin Clash. "What I love and always have loved about . . . Jim Henson started in this workshop. . . . That's the way that you do it. That says *Jim* to me." It was perhaps no wonder that Jim looked so comfortable; this was home, in the workshop—or at least a reasonable facsimile—and Jim played his role as a cheerful and thoughtful host enthusiastically. "Imagination is what this show is all about," he said warmly, bantering with Gonzo, Animal, Miss Piggy, and Kermit ("you, as usual, have your hand in almost everything here," joked Kermit) and grinning broadly as he played at the controls of a computer and teased an animatronic gryphon. "We think it's an hour families will want to spend together watching quality television," he concluded. "What more can I say?"

As he sent the pitch reel off for editing, Jim reported that its filming had gone "quite well." He found it was fun to play with the Muppet gang again—and with Frank Oz back performing Animal and Miss Piggy, even for a moment, it was almost like old times, when Jim could play with the guys and not worry so much about running a company. Juhl, too, after writing almost exclusively for *Fraggle Rock* for the last four years, discovered he enjoyed writing for the familiar characters again. Feeling nostalgic, Juhl had written what Jim considered a "lovely" Christmas show, in which the casts from the three major Muppet productions—*The Muppet Show, Sesame Street,* and *Fraggle Rock*—gathered at Fozzie's mother's house for the holidays. The resulting special, *A Muppet Family Christmas,* would be one of Jim's favorites.

Taped quickly in late September and early October at Glen Warren Productions in Ontario, *A Muppet Family Christmas* was a true homecoming. Not only was Oz back ("He doesn't do a lot of puppeteering anymore," said Jim. "So this was very much a reunion."), but so were *Muppet Show* alumni Peter Harris and Martin Baker, as well as Caroll Spinney, just starting his twentieth consecutive season on *Sesame Street,* whom Jim greeted with a warm, "Hello, Muppets

West!" With Juhl's lovingly written script, Harris's tight direction, and top-notch performances from every Muppet performer, *A Muppet Family Christmas* stands as one of Jim's finest, and most underappreciated, productions. As the characters from the various Muppet universes encounter each other, many for the first time, the hourlong episode is full of remarkable moments: Ernie and Bert bantering with Doc; Kermit and Robin entering a Fraggle hole and learning how the Fraggles give presents; Rowlf speaking "dog" with Sprocket ("Woof woof! Yeah! Bark bark!"). Jim even makes a cameo in the closing moments, watching over the Christmas celebration from the kitchen with Sprocket. "Well, they certainly seem to be having a good time out there, Sprocket," Jim says. "I like it when they have a good time."

Viewers and critics had a good time, too. When it aired that December, *A Muppet Family Christmas* was warmly received by reviewers and easily won its time slot. The Muppets, who hadn't appeared in an entirely new production since 1984's *The Muppets Take Manhattan,* were back in the news again—and as Jim cheerfully made the rounds with the press, he seemed genuinely stunned to find his characters were not just enjoyed, but "cherished"—and moving with a seeming life of their own toward an iconic status. "There's a nice, naive quality to this family of characters," Jim explained helpfully, speaking so softly that one reporter's voice-activated tape recorder kept shutting off. "I think people relate to their childlike quality, because everybody has that in themselves."

To the delight of the press, Jim also announced that he was at work on another Muppet movie, which he hoped to start shooting in early 1989. For much of the year, he had been mulling over various proposals and brainstorming with Juhl and other Muppet writers. Some ideas sparked his interest—for a while, he seriously considered "taking them [the Muppets] on an archeological adventure to discover their roots"—while others were dismissed outright, including a suggestion that Miss Piggy might get pregnant. Jim had blanched at that one, calling it a little too "specific and explicit." But Jerry Juhl had recently handed in a movie treatment that Jim *loved*—and which had been inspired, in part, by a private conversation in which Oz had groused to Jim and Juhl about the growing costs of projects at Henson Associates. If they were going to make another Muppet film, Oz said testily, they would have to "figure out a way to do a really low-budget kind of thing." That was all Juhl needed. Hunching over his Macintosh computer in his home office in California, he quickly pounded out a treatment for a film called *The Cheapest Muppet Movie Ever Made*.

In Juhl's first treatment, Kermit allows Gonzo to write and direct a bad adventure movie called *Into the Jaws of the Demons of Death*—with "this cheesy, terrible plot," as Juhl put it, "that made absolutely no sense whatsoever, about something being stolen that led to a chase around the world." In his enthusiasm, Gonzo spends his entire budget on an impressive opening credits sequence, then has no money left for the rest of the film. As the movie proceeds, the film quality gets worse and worse, eventually eroding into black-and-white Super 8 film, then a slide show, and finally just storyboards—until Gonzo sells out to corporate sponsors and finishes the movie in a beautiful, high-definition, widescreen format.

Jim was delighted with the treatment, and put Juhl to work writing a full script, which he turned in as Jim was wrapping up *A Muppet Family Christmas* in Ontario. Jim, Juhl, and Oz passed the script back and forth, and even Oz—always prickly about the treatment of the characters—thought it was an exciting project. "It's going to be the kind of movie the audience wants the Muppets to do," he told Jim. "Just a little crazy and a whole lot of fun." As it was written, *The Cheapest Muppet Movie Ever Made* actually wouldn't be cheap to make—Juhl's script called for erupting volcanoes and exploding islands, and for Meryl Streep to play Miss Piggy's stand-in—but the idea was funny and Jim thought he could manage things on a budget of $8 million. He and Juhl would keep playing with it.

That autumn, Jim flew to Los Angeles to make an appearance with Kermit on a Dolly Parton television special on October 21—but more important, he would be meeting the next day with Tartikoff and NBC executives to make the pitch for *The Jim Henson Hour*. Besides the pitch reel, Jim brought with him a densely written proposal—unlike many of his proposals, this one had no illustrations—behind a cover

with a sharply designed JIM HENSON HOUR logo, featuring Jim's signature prominently tilted across the page in bright Kermit green. Jim
leapt into his pitch with gusto, touting *The Jim Henson Hour* as "a
rich and mysterious, wonderfully imaginative hour . . . for the whole
family to enjoy," and which put "the best of everything" he did in
one complete package. The executives listened intently, and Tartikoff promised to get back to Jim soon.

What Jim was hoping he had conveyed to the network, perhaps
more than anything else, was just how much he still loved and believed in television. While he had branched out into movies over the
last decade, television was still his artistic and creative oasis. It was
the medium he knew and understood the best—and it was a medium
he still thought could do much for the common good. "We should be
creating a kind of basis for TV which will be good for us and for
kids," Jim said. "There's too much negative thinking in the world.
Why don't we try dealing with the happier side instead?"

He would expand on those views a month later in front of a
large and enthusiastic crowd gathered in Los Angeles to honor him
as an inductee to the Television Hall of Fame. Jim had "mixed feelings" about being singled out for the award, which honored "persons
who have made outstanding contributions in the arts, sciences or
management of television." "I like working collaboratively with
people," he once said. "I have a terrific group of people who work
with me, and think of the work that we do as 'our' work." Nonetheless, he knew the award was "certainly an honor"—plus he was
being recognized alongside several performers he admired, including
Johnny Carson, Bob Hope, and the late Ernie Kovacs. Jim gamely
accepted his Hall of Fame award on November 15, but his speech
that evening said much about how he regarded his work, his colleagues, and his responsibilities to the common good:

> All the work that I do in television is very much a group effort.
> It's a lot of us that do this. It's these talented people that make
> it possible for me to do the things that give me the credit for
> doing a lot of good stuff on television, and I would really like
> to thank those people. Television is already one of the most
> powerful influences on our culture, but because it is so power-

ful, there's a great deal of responsibility that goes with that. And I think those of us that make programs, particularly for children, have to be aware of what we're putting out there. I think this is what is fun for me, and why I am very grateful for this very special honor . . . it makes my work—or rather my *fun*—so gratifying.

Finally, in the third week of December 1987 came the news Jim had been waiting for: NBC had agreed to produce a half season of weekly episodes of *The Jim Henson Hour*, to begin airing in January 1989, a little over a year away. "It's very exciting," wrote Jim in a memo to the entire Henson Associates staff, "but a bit scary because there is so much to do." Beneath the enthusiasm, however, was a slight annoyance: as a condition of its approval, NBC had insisted on major changes to the show's format. While Tartikoff had told Jim from the outset that he could rotate among the four themed hours one after another, just as Jim had proposed, NBC executives had pushed back against that approach. Instead of a comprehensive, themed hour, the network insisted on two fifteen-minute sections for the first half hour—made up of Muppet moments, short *Lead-Free TV* bits, or other skits—while the second half hour would be one long piece, such as an installment of *The Storyteller* or another original feature.

There were still some visible remnants of the original proposal; once a month, Jim could produce an hour-long special, such as a *Storyteller* or one of his "Next Wave" projects, like the *Sesame Street* twentieth-anniversary show he was still hoping to produce, or a proposed hour-long musical special featuring the Electric Mayhem in Mexico. For the most part, however, NBC had taken the unique ingredients Jim had provided in his original proposal and asked him to blend them together into a garbled chop suey. Jim tried to put the best face on it, eventually explaining publicly that it had been a mutual decision. "We were working on *Storyteller* and coming up with a concept for a very electronic variety show," Jim told the *Austin American-Statesman* later. "And we also had a series of specials we were putting together. So, we came to NBC with this concept of putting all these things into one show. We thought it'd be nice to kind of pull it all together." Nothing about that statement was necessarily untrue, but it didn't accurately reflect Jim's more cohesive starting point.

Still, it wasn't like Jim to complain; he was pleased to at last have a spot secured in the NBC lineup, and for now that was enough. Now he had a year to "pull it all together." Doing so, however, would prove tougher to do than Jim had ever imagined.

CHAPTER FOURTEEN

A KIND OF CRAZINESS

1987–1989

Jim and the Muppet cast of the ill-fated Jim Henson Hour *(1989).*
"Most things didn't work on that show," said Jerry Juhl. "It was
a huge frustration and a great sadness."

As 1988 BEGAN, JIM PUT HIS WRITERS TO WORK BRAINSTORMING AND
writing short pieces to fill the first half hour of the newly reformat-
ted *Jim Henson Hour*. "[I was] in a meeting with NBC yesterday,"
Jim told his team in late January, "[and] they seemed to be quite
happy with the direction this is all going." At the moment, however,
even Jim wasn't quite sure what direction that might be. Jim still
believed the *Lead-Free TV* concept was an ideal format for satirizing
cable television, but the writing remained a problem—he had already rejected a similar concept called *Pirate TV* for being too
"nasty." He also insisted that the Muppet segments be somewhat

educational, and proposed skits in which the Muppets somehow explained the federal debt, the ozone, or the legislative process.

Coming up with features for the second half hour was a bit easier, and a lot more fun. Besides *The Storyteller*, Jim was thinking about an origin storytelling of the discovery of Fraggle Rock called *The Saga of Fraggle Rock*. There was also *Inside John*, another variation on Jim's Limbo concept, in which the various parts of a seventeen-year-old boy's brain try to wrest control of him throughout a typical day. And then there were proposed stories of enchanted bowling balls, extraterrestrial mailmen, and adaptations of Madeleine L'Engle's science fiction novel *A Wrinkle in Time* or the works of A. A. Milne, as well as an ambitious outline for a show called *ASTRO G.N.E.W.T.S.* that blended puppets with animation, computer graphics, and video effects. All would be false starts, but ideas, as always, were never a problem.

And then there was the question of the "home base" for the series, the room or set from which Jim would host the show. Figuring out where a show was located was always a problem for Jim; he had misfired with the vague sets in his two early *Muppet Show* pilots before finally getting it right on *The Muppet Show* itself. *The Jim Henson Hour*'s pitch reel had been set in a *faux* Muppet workshop— still the best idea—but he wasn't happy with the look or feel of that, either; he wanted something more dynamic and high-tech—and ideally, he wanted something computer-generated.

Typically, even as he struggled to find some sort of structure for *The Jim Henson Hour*—which, given its current amorphous state, should probably have been his priority—Jim had decided to speed up production on yet another project, a film based on Roald Dahl's 1983 children's book *The Witches*, which Jim had decided to executive-produce. It was a project he'd had simmering on the back burner, under the watchful eye of Duncan Kenworthy, for more than a year—and it had been a problem almost from day one, due largely to the involvement of the highly irritable, seventy-one-year-old Dahl. Jim and Dahl had gotten off to a bad start, with Henson Associates' and Dahl's lawyers squabbling over the costs of optioning the book for film. "I don't like this," Dahl had sulked to Jim. "If there is going to be any ill-feeling, I would rather the film was not made." Jim had done his best to smooth things over, promising the writer that while there *had* been some problems with financing, it was "for very valid reasons, and it shouldn't become personal." "It is one of my favorite projects in a long time," Jim assured Dahl, "and I'm going to try very hard to produce a film which we can all be proud of."

The Witches would be another opportunity for Jim to rally the Creature Shop into action—always one of his favorite sandboxes in which to play. To direct, Jim had lined up Nicolas Roeg, the edgy and somewhat unpredictable English director of eclectic films like *The Man Who Fell to Earth*. Jim had initially recruited Roeg as a director for *The Storyteller* before offering him *The Witches*—a job Roeg was delighted to accept—but Roeg, too, would eventually become antagonistic, caught between Jim's and Dahl's creative whirlwinds and grousing about executive interference. Dahl was also unimpressed with Roeg. "I will tell you I was devastated when I learned you were not directing it yourself," Dahl wrote to Jim.

Pricklier than Dahl or Roeg, however, were the witches themselves. Wiccans across the country—already smarting over Dahl's book for what they considered its negative portrayal of witches—admonished Jim in a letter-writing campaign when they learned he was adapting the book for the big screen. Jim tried to appease their concerns, but only got caught up arguing semantics over the terms "black magic" or "evil witch" with the head of the Witches' League for Public Awareness, based in Salem, Massachusetts. Finally, Jim simply pleaded for patience. "While I am not an advocate of any one religion, I feel close to many of the concepts of the Wicca way of thinking," he wrote, "and for these reasons, I will try not to do anything that will harm any of you."

By late January, Jim had an agreement for *The Witches* in place with Lorimar, where Bernie Brillstein had recently been installed as CEO of the film division, and in early February had dinner with Anjelica Huston and secured her as his leading lady—a decision, for once, that Dahl was happy with. He would not stay happy for long.

At the same time, Jim had his own unhappy news to deal with: *The Storyteller* was doomed. After three installments, the show remained a critical darling, but a ratings disaster—and NBC's confidence in the show was rapidly eroding. After some discussion with the network, Jim decided to hold on to the two unaired episodes of the series, and scrapped plans to expand *The Storyteller* into one-hour installments. "NBC is worried about the appeal of the show," Jim wrote in a memo to the entire Henson Associates staff. "I am not worried about this, but I don't mind dropping the [planned one-hour episodes] at this point. We'll do something else instead." Despite the best face, he was more disappointed than he let on. "I think they're the best television shows ever made," he confided to *The Washington Post*.

While he understood NBC's impatience—gone were the days when a series like *The Muppet Show* could be given breathing room to find its way—he was certain there was still a place for television shows that took their time and rewarded patient viewers with high production values and top-notch storytelling. Jim, in fact, was among the first to realize that cable television—with its niche channels and willing, paying audience—was an ideal market for original, made-for-cable films. "When the cable is hooked up to enough homes," mused Jim, "then we'll be able to make films just for the video and the cable market. Certainly, that will come." But, he hastened to add, without high-definition picture quality and the capability to show films in a widescreen format, it was still "so much more interesting" to work on feature films. Once again, Jim had seen the potential in a new technology, even if the technology itself hadn't yet caught up with his plans for it.

Even with NBC's lack of faith, Jim still had enough confidence in *The Storyteller* to put into production the remaining four episodes NBC had approved, with the intention of marketing them internationally and using them for *The Jim Henson Hour*. In late February, he went back to Elstree to spend a week directing an installment of *The Storyteller* called "The Heartless Giant," a bittersweet story of friendship—and betrayal—in which a young prince frees an imprisoned, heartless giant, then becomes his servant to help him find his missing heart. "I love working on this show," Jim told his staff—and he also loved the underlying morality of the old folktales, which fell directly in line with his own views of the common good. "In broad strokes," explained Jim, "the message I try to bring across is the positives of life and a positive attitude toward the goodness of mankind."

After completing his episode of *The Storyteller,* Jim headed for France to meet with Jerry Juhl and Larry Mirkin and have a frank conversation about *The Jim Henson Hour*—and to spend a few days with Mary Ann at the swank L'Hôtel in Paris.

The daytime hours were for work. Juhl and the writing team—mainly Mirkin and Jocelyn Stevenson—were still frustrated by the dilemma NBC had created by insisting on jumbling together all four elements of Jim's initial proposal. Juhl thought he understood what NBC was getting at—"*The Disney Hour* [*sic*] consisted of a lot of things Walt Disney thought were worthy of him and his audience [and] that's what this is," explained Juhl—but the scattered format remained a problem. Jim was confident they could hold the fragments of the show together by putting Kermit—the reliable eye of the Muppet hurricane—in a television control room, overseeing things much as he had done on *The Muppet Show.* On the technical side, Jim thought hiring a regular director to preside over the look and feel of the series might also give the show a more cohesive structure, and picked through a list of suggestions that included Sam Raimi—whom Lisa Henson was dating at the time—and Brad Bird before finally deciding on former *Muppet Show* director Peter Harris. Jim pronounced himself "delighted" with the involvement of Harris. "I'm feeling quite good about the show," Jim said.

The rest of the time in Paris was devoted to romping with Mary Ann, goofily posing for pictures for each other, gazing at the scenery ("Isn't this a *romantic* view?" Jim would say dreamily), and frolicking in bed in their exclusive Parisian hotel. Jim loved being giddily in love—and now, in Mary Ann, it seemed he had found a sexual warmth and an intimacy that he had long been missing. Nineteen years Jim's junior, Mary Ann made him feel younger and more vibrant—and some thought Jim had intentionally sought out such reassurance. Turning fifty had been hard for him—and now at fifty-one, he was starting to feel his age. His feet, already aching from the years of standing to perform, had grown increasingly stiff and sore—finding the most comfortable shoe had lately become something of a Grail-type quest. His teeth also bothered him constantly, and, more upsetting, he'd developed a slight tremor in his hands—an affliction that had also plagued his father, but which was particularly worrisome for a puppeteer.

Mary Ann, then, was just the kind of willing partner he wanted and needed in his adventures, both inside the bedroom and beyond. Mary Ann dove eagerly into Jim's noisy exploits right along with him, whether it was swimming, yachting, horseback riding, or taking the kind of long hikes Jim loved. For her part, Mary Ann would later take him to his first nude beach in Palm Beach—an experience, she said, that made Jim almost giddy with joy—indulge his tastes for caviar and *kir*, or tease him gently about his hair, encouraging him to brush it back from his forehead or wear it in a tight ponytail.

"I think he was very much in love," said Richard Hunt. "Jim was a romancer. . . . It wasn't just some fling." Heather Henson—who perhaps more than any of the Henson children had observed first-hand her parents' relationship and Jim's dating habits—thought Mary Ann was good for her father as well. "I was really quite fond of her," said Heather. "By the time Mary Ann came around, I was actually happy to have him seeing someone stable." It was Jim's first real relationship since his legal separation from Jane, and while he had always enjoyed the company and the aesthetics of beautiful women, he was now in a committed relationship with one . . . or at least as committed as Jim could be. "I don't think he ever wanted to marry anybody else," said Brian Henson. "Besides," he added, "if you're not divorced from your last wife, you can never get married again."

Mary Ann wasn't bothered by Jim's lack of interest in marriage, but she *was* annoyed by his desire to keep their relationship from becoming public. Despite admitting to the press that he and Jane were separated, Jim was still reluctant to have his relationship with Mary Ann out in the open. While Jim loved taking Mary Ann on exotic vacations—boat cruises in Italy, glamorous hotels in Paris, romantic sprints to England—she soon came to realize that Jim was deliberately keeping her out of sight. Whether Jim liked it or not, his efforts made little difference; Henson Associates was already a hotbed of gossip about her—and it didn't help that in the past year Mary Ann had been promoted into production, a move that led to some snickering and hard feelings about the cause of her ascent within the company. "I found Mary Ann kind of calculating," said one longtime Henson employee, while another thought "she was an aggressive person, out for herself."

The gossip alone might have been bearable, but by refusing to carry out an open relationship, Jim was hedging his bets—as if by not admitting he was with Mary Ann, he was free to discreetly play the field. To some extent that was true; after he escorted the willowy actress Daryl Hannah to one of his opulent masked balls—where the two of them dressed as Beauty and the Beast—gossip columnists had assumed they were linked romantically. There was actually nothing romantic there—Jim had gotten to know Hannah and her sister Page, and considered them friends—but he had no intention of correcting such a misperception, telling his publicist that "it's great for my reputation!" It was all more than Mary Ann could stomach—and that summer, she angrily left Jim, and the company, to move back to her hometown in Florida.

For one of the few times in his life, Jim responded to and fully engaged in a conflict—something he had always been loath to do, whether it was with Jane or with Henson Associates attorneys. "It was hard on him," said Richard Hunt, "but it was also good for him." Against the counsel of David Lazer, Jim wrote Mary Ann long, apologetic letters, trying to explain himself. He warned that he still considered their relationship to be no one's business, but promised he would no longer write or call and would let their separation remain permanent if she so chose. Perhaps to his surprise, baring his soul—engaging in the conflict—had an effect: he and Mary Ann reconciled, and now that she was no longer an employee of the company, or living in New York, Jim was less reticent about being seen openly with her. While the crisis had been averted, Jim and Mary Ann's relationship would continue to wind its way through smoldering hot peaks and frigid valleys over the next two years.

In April 1988, Jim headed for Norway to oversee production on *The Witches*, ready to go before the cameras despite being bogged down by budget problems and creative spats. Like *Labyrinth*, the script for *The Witches*—by director Nic Roeg's frequent collaborator, Allan Scott—had been tinkered with and revised until the very last moment, with Jim still passing notes to producer Mark Shivas (mainly about use of words like "bitchy" and "pooper scooper") in the weeks leading up to the April 12 filming date. The larger problems, however, were still with Roald Dahl, whose griping and threats about the script would continue well up until the film's release.

Early on, Dahl had complained to Duncan Kenworthy that he was not being kept sufficiently in the loop about the development of Scott's script. "I do think it would be courteous if you kept me informed," Dahl wrote Kenworthy. "You would surely rather have me on your side than against you." Thus rebuked, Kenworthy shipped off a copy of the script to Dahl, who immediately wrote back with his comments—mostly unhelpful remarks like "AWFUL" and "STUPID AND USELESS"—and insisted, in black ink scrawled across the bottom of the page, that someone "PL[EASE] SHOW TO JIM H."

Jim, who was at that time swamped with work on *The Witches* and *The Jim Henson Hour*, unintentionally—and unwisely—left Dahl to stew. He was much more engaged with what was going on in the Creature Shop, where designers were working not only on craggy witches, but on one of their toughest assignments yet: lifelike mice. As the central plot of *The Witches* involved turning children—including the main character—into mice, it was critical that the Creature Shop figure out how to design a mouse that could act. The solution was to build mice in three different scales: one a remote-controlled mouse built close to actual size, which couldn't do much more than scurry; another three times larger, crammed with enough mechanics to give it lifelike movements in long shots; and finally, one about the size of a small hand puppet, with fully functional legs, ears, whiskers, mouth, and face that could be performed in close-ups. Jim loved working with his "Mouse Unit," even as they struggled to get the fur looking just right at each of the different sizes. "Things have been a little bumpy," he admitted.

Things would get even bumpier as filming went on, thanks mainly to the dyspeptic Dahl, who hit the ceiling when he learned that the script being filmed had tampered with the ending of his original story. In Dahl's book, the young hero remains a mouse, happy in the knowledge that, as a mouse, he will likely die in less than ten years. Scott, however, had written a more upbeat ending in which the main character was changed back to normal by a sorceress—and Dahl was apoplectic. Frustrated by Jim's lack of response to his earlier letters, Dahl fired off a missive to Roeg instead, complaining that such an ending was "OBVIOUS. It is also TRITE." In his original story, explained Dahl, "the boy is happy as a mouse. He tells us so." Dahl further admonished Roeg for "tampering with a very successful plot. . . . I may not know as much about making films as you, but I know a hell of a lot about plot and about how to end a story. . . . Your ending is wrong." Dahl was informed that Jim had asked for *both* versions of the ending to be filmed, so he might determine which one worked better in the context of the film— a stipulation that only made Dahl angrier.

The Witches was quickly becoming a nightmare. Dahl was incensed, Roeg felt compromised, and Jim was caught in the middle, trying hard to respect and manage the artistic views of both the writer of the source material and his film's director. The budget continued to be a problem, too, though Jim had managed to convince Warner Brothers—which was in the process of acquiring Lorimar— to take a more active role in the film's production. "It is essential that they are enthusiastic about it," Jim wrote in an internal memo, and noted only half jokingly that it helped having his oldest daughter working as an executive at Warner Brothers.

All of those problems with *The Witches* would screech to a sudden insignificance on an evening in late April, when twenty-three-year-old John Henson, driving at a speed of nearly one hundred miles per hour, flipped his Toyota truck on the Bruckner Expressway in the Bronx. John was thrown out the driver's window, bounced over a concrete median—tearing muscles and badly injuring his legs in the process—and landed on his back in oncoming traffic. Jim, who had been in London editing *The Storyteller* with David Lazer when he learned of the accident, shakily booked the first available flight to New York. The trip seemed to take an eternity, and Jim was visibly distraught. "David, I don't know what I would do if something happened to one of my kids," he confessed during the flight. "I would have to go first." Lazer, who had watched Jim with his children since the mid-1960s, understood Jim's anguish. "He gave the kids undivided love," Lazer said later. "He was crazy about them— each one individually. . . . They must have felt it." For John Henson— who would recover from his injuries—there was never any doubt. "I just felt that he was an amazing dad," said John later. "Whether he was physically there or not, I felt like he was *always* there."

Lately, too, it seemed he was always in the offices at One Seventeen, presiding over personnel compensation committees, strategic planning sessions, and attending one budget presentation after another. For the most part, the company was on secure ground, with money coming in from multiple sources. Since buying back *The Muppet Show* from Holmes à Court, Jim had negotiated a deal with Ted Turner to show both *The Muppet Show* and *Fraggle Rock* exclusively on his WTBS and TNT cable channels for four years—an agreement that netted Henson Associates more than $20 million—and he was still hoping to develop the lofty *Muppet Voyager* concept with Turner's backing as well. Merchandising from *Sesame Street* was always reliable, as was revenue from almost any *Muppet Babies*–related product. A series of direct-to-video Muppet projects also continued to roll out at a steady pace, including the popular Play-A-Long series in which young viewers were encouraged to sing, tell jokes, or draw with the help of the Muppets (one video showed Jim teaching viewers how to skip stones on a lake in Central Park—a skill he was grinningly proud of, as he could skip a stone a long way). Finally, there was a series of videos in the works based on tales from Mother Goose, helmed by twenty-five-year-old Brian Henson, making his directorial debut for Henson Associates.

More discouraging, however, were the reports from the countless "management consultants" who had been hired to look at the structure of the organization. "I think we are going to see some real positive changes in the way I—and we—run the company," Jim optimistically told his staff. He knew his own weaknesses as a manager and administrator. "I tend to avoid confrontation and I tend to push and see only the good aspects of a particular thing," Jim said later. "I'm a very human person." He gamely continued to hold team-building events, regular company meetings, and staff retreats, but the management structure seemed irreparably broken. While the air of collegiality he instilled on a movie or television set might produce wonderful results on the screen, as a business practice it tended to leave holes in the chain of command. Decisions couldn't be made, because no one wanted to be in charge. As a result, more and more decisions would get pushed up to Jim, who would simply delegate them back down the line to management.

No project would be more emblematic of Henson Associates' broken decision-making process than *The Jim Henson Hour,* which Jim was preparing to put before the cameras at the end of July. For perhaps the first time, the disarray had crept into a creative project. "It was frustrating because we just didn't have the time and we were trying to do a lot," said writer Larry Mirkin. "We were very stretched just in terms of trying to be on top of everything." Mirkin and Jerry Juhl were still struggling with the scripts, trying to find an internal structure for the show, but "it was *so* difficult," said Juhl. "Jim had so many ideas . . . so many things he wanted to do. He was given the opportunity of doing this show and he wasn't content with doing one show. He wanted to do *more* than one television series." Despite Juhl's misgivings, Jim was confident the show would work. He was certain of it.

Money, it seemed, was no object. The computer-generated opening credits—a beautiful opening shot of a gryphon contemplating a crystal ball, followed by a sequence with Muppets, boats, books, and fish swirling in a computer-generated maelstrom—cost nearly half a million dollars to produce, an enormous amount that exceeded the total budget of many half-hour television shows at the time. It had also eaten up a great deal of time to put together and edit. "This is great," Mirkin conveyed to Jim after watching the credits, "but I'm worried about the remaining twenty-two minutes." Jim merely shrugged and grinned. "Look," he told Mirkin happily, "nobody's ever done this before." For Jim, that was almost always enough.

While Jim had filmed the pitch reel for *The Jim Henson Hour* with himself as the host, he was skeptical about appearing on camera for the show itself. "I always prefer to be slightly behind camera," he said. He hoped Kermit would serve as the host for the series, providing continuity between skits and sequences. But Brandon Tartikoff wanted Jim out in front—the series had his name on it, after all, and his presence would give the series a consistency. "It seemed the logical thing for this type of show," Jim conceded later—and in mid-July, at the urging of publicist Arthur Novell, Jim was put in the hands of a voice coach and a professional hairstylist. His hair, now a silvery gray, was blown dry and swept back, his beard neatly trimmed along the curve of his jawline. He would have to learn to speak louder, and to keep his hands away from his face, where he was used to curling his long fingers around his mouth as he spoke.

More problematic, he also had to learn to stand comfortably, without folding his arms or fidgeting. Peering at Jim through the lens of the camera, director Peter Harris thought he looked "stiff" and asked that he be given someone or something to interact with. For no other reason "except [that it] was kind of wonderful," the Thought Lion—a beautiful, enormous, fully functional, white animatronic lion, which had been sitting in the corner of the Creature Shop since its use in an episode of *The Storyteller*—was brought in to serve as Jim's mostly silent sidekick. "There was no reason for it at all" except for "innocence and optimism," said Juhl, but it gave Jim something to talk to—without folding his arms—and he liked it.

Over six days in late July and early August, Jim taped a rough cut of the pilot episode of *The Jim Henson Hour*, shooting several segments with vocalist Bobby McFerrin—whose international breakout hit "Don't Worry, Be Happy" was still several months from release—as well as a number of short Muppet sketches. For nearly a month, he would cut and edit the various pieces together before finally shipping it off for Tartikoff to look at. Even then, Jim still wasn't entirely happy, and pleaded with Tartikoff to view it as "a work in progress." He knew it still seemed randomly pieced together, a problem he thought could be solved by "establish[ing] a type of theme for each half hour." And while he made clear that the writers and performers were "still getting a sense of the characters and how they should interact," he also admitted that several characters and sketches hadn't worked at all, and would be cut from the final show. (Frank Oz, who often seemed to develop characters at will, was still pursuing a directing career and was increasingly unavailable.) Ultimately, Jim told Tartikoff, "whenever possible, *The Jim Henson Hour* should be breaking new ground." He would continue to recut it, even as he continued filming new episodes in late September and early October.

At the same time, Jim had in production a number of specials he was hoping could be incorporated into the second half of *The Jim Henson Hour*. The most important was a celebration of *Sesame Street,* which would be marking its twentieth anniversary in 1989. Jim had been trying for years to produce a *Sesame Street* special— a decade earlier, he had unsuccessfully proposed a behind-the-scenes documentary—but now, with Joan Cooney's approval, he finally had a one-hour retrospective under way. For Jim, working on the special was a pleasant reminder not only of *Sesame Street*'s growing and lasting impact, but it also gave him an opportunity to reflect on the show that had made the Muppets a household word. Every six months or so, Jim and the Muppet performers still regularly made time—usually about a week each year—to perform their inserts for *Sesame Street*. And they still loved it. "[It's] still so much fun to do," he told Cooney. "The show, from the beginning, was a good idea. It's been a delightful thing to be a part of for all these twenty years . . . and I think it will be around in another twenty years. I'll be sitting in my rocking chair, and I'll still be doing Ernie."

He was having just as much fun working and performing on another special, a "Damon Runyon with dogs" film noir parody called *Dog City,* which had been in development for over a year. With expressive Muppet dogs inspired in part by C. M. Coolidge's painting *Dogs Playing Poker,* and elaborate, detailed sets, *Dog City* had some of the highest production values of any Muppet production—"I just love it," said Jim. So much, in fact, that he took his time directing it, lingering on the Toronto set for more than eighteen days—about twice as long as usual—bumping several other production companies who were waiting for studio time. Whether he was performing *Dog City*'s main villain, or staging elaborate puppet car chases, gunfights, and billiard games, Jim just didn't want the fun to stop. "He was just having such a wonderful time," said Juhl. "It was the kind of puppetry stuff that nobody had ever done before, and Jim did it."

Jim spent late 1988 reviewing the first rough edits of *The Witches,* screening it with test audiences in London and Los Angeles, and making careful notes for director Nic Roeg on where he could trim down scenes Jim thought were too frightening. Jim still hadn't decided on the ending, however, merely noting in his journal that the film "need[ed] work"—Dahl would have to wait. He also visited with Industrial Light and Magic, George Lucas's groundbreaking special effects company, to discuss special effects for *The Cheapest Muppet Movie Ever Made,* which he was determined to put into production in 1989. Meanwhile, he was continuing to stitch together a number of installments of *The Jim Henson Hour,* and sent another episode to Tartikoff for review over the Christmas holidays. The new shows, thought Jim, were "looking good," and Tartikoff seemed pleased—yet Jim couldn't get a commitment from NBC on when the series would premiere. Initially, the network had told Jim to prepare for a January 1989 start, but had then delayed the series until March, and then finally decided on April.

It was frustrating, but "given the extra time," Jim said later, "we took it"—and spent much of it in a computer lab at Pacific Data Images (PDI) in San Francisco. Jim was still fascinated with the possibilities of computer animation; in the mid-1980s, he had tried to develop a television special on computers with Chris Cerf, and had explored the possibilities of creating a computer-generated Kermit. For several years, then, Jim had been studying ways to develop a kind of virtual puppet, a computer-generated figure that could be manipulated by a performer in real time and interact with live actors and puppets. Now the technology had finally caught up with the idea—and with the help of PDI, Jim had set up a system wherein a waldo, which usually remotely controlled an animatronic figure, was wired instead into a computer to control a low-resolution computer-generated image.

For *The Jim Henson Hour,* the technology was used in the creation of a vaguely birdlike, bouncing, hovering shape-shifting CGI Muppet called Waldo C. Graphic, which Jim put in the hands of veteran performer Steve Whitmire. The computer image of Waldo would be overlaid on video images of other live performers—and Whitmire, working in the traditional Muppet style, could watch the low-resolution Waldo move on-screen as he performed, talking and interacting virtually with other performers. Once the low-resolution image was recorded, it would be sent to PDI where the character would be rendered in high resolution; once complete, the final version would then be matted back into the original scene. A complicated process that "worked out quite nicely," reported Jim.

Jim put the technology to work in the background, too. In early February 1989, he began shooting an environmentally themed special initially titled *Snake Samba* (Jim would rename it *Milton's Paradise Lost* before finally settling on *Song of the Cloud Forest*) about an endangered golden frog searching for a mate in the rain forest. Jim wanted the backgrounds to look like primitive South American art, almost abstract, with intensely bright colors. Using the state-of-the-art PaintBox graphics program, Jim turned drawings and designs by Cheryl into fully realized virtual backgrounds. It took several tests before he was happy with it, but Jim loved playing with the technology. "It's so incredible," he enthused. "I love the things that you can do with it." The only real problem was the cost. "It's quite expensive, and the tricky thing is to try to get it down to the point where we can afford it on a television budget."

To Jim's dismay, budgets, not backgrounds, would take up more and more of his time in the coming months. In London, the Creature Shop had been hired by Mirage Enterprises to create the title characters for *Teenage Mutant Ninja Turtles*—a live-action adaptation of the successful independent comic and Saturday morning cartoon— and was having an absolute blast. Meanwhile, Jim was stuck in New York attending Henson Associates board meetings, discussing business plans, squinting at new logos, and sitting in on endless rounds of planning meetings and budget review sessions. There were some eye-rolling discoveries as Jim and his business managers scoured their ledgers; one executive had been taking regular trips to France with his wife on the company's dime, while an art director was paying for expensive monthly haircuts with his corporate credit card ("Maybe if it was a *better* haircut," Jim offered wryly). "I think we are getting a handle on the status of the company, and it's coming together nicely," he wrote to staff with forced enthusiasm. "I really appreciate the way everyone is pitching in to help." He even sat through his own appraisal process, "a very healthy exercise," he assured his employees.

Even *The Witches* had become more bogged down than usual in personalities and drama. "It hasn't been an easy film," said Jim with a sigh, who now found himself "a bit in the middle" of a spat between Nic Roeg and Warner Brothers over edits in the film. Jim had finally settled on the more conventional ending, in which the young hero is changed from a mouse back to a human, and now he and Roeg were putting together a final cut to be delivered to Warner Brothers. Then, of course, Dahl was certain to check in with his response to the film—and Duncan Kenworthy was already bracing for the explosion.

On Friday, April 14, the first episode of *The Jim Henson Hour* finally made its debut on NBC. Jim was disappointed in the time slot he'd been given; he wanted the Sunday evening spot that had traditionally been occupied by various iterations of Walt Disney's one-hour show. While *The Jim Henson Hour* had no real competition in the lineup—it was opposite the sci-fi love story *Beauty and the Beast* on CBS and the sitcom block *Perfect Strangers* and *Full House* over on ABC—Friday night was traditionally a dead zone, especially for family-themed fare. "They put us in a time slot that they [NBC] had been consistently not doing very well in," Jim said later. It was not an encouraging start.

As he had promised Tartikoff, Jim was now structuring the first half hour of each show around a specific theme; for the premiere, it was science fiction, with comedian Louie Anderson appearing in sci-fi parodies like "My Dinner with Codzilla" or "Space Guy." Throughout, Jim tried to hold everything together by interspersing "MuppeTelevision" sequences—a high-tech version of *The Muppet Show* (and the last remaining vestiges of the *Inner Tube/Lead-Free TV* concept) featuring Kermit in a control room crammed with television monitors where he "has to pick and choose the stuff he thinks we'll enjoy." One had to wonder about the frog's decisions; most sketches fell flat. For the second half hour, however, Jim was on sturdier footing, filling the thirty minutes with "The Heartless Giant," the episode of *The Storyteller* he had directed more than a year ago. When that finished, Jim came back on camera to cheerfully wrap things up.

Jim knew it wasn't his finest moment. Only hours before the program aired, in fact, Jim had told an audience at the American Film Institute that the "biggest problem" with the show was the opening thirty-minute "variety show" portion. "Variety is not easy to do and no one is doing it successfully right now—and we may not either. But variety is a very difficult thing to get a handle on and make it work."

Unfortunately, in the minds of most critics, he *hadn't* made it work. While everyone still loved *The Storyteller,* most agreed that the rest of *The Jim Henson Hour* was a disaster. "Fixing what's wrong . . . would be simple as microwave pie," wrote Tom Shales in *The Washington Post.* "All NBC has to do is throw out the first half and keep [*The Storyteller*]. A *Jim Henson Half-Hour* would be plenty." Matt Roush, writing in *USA Today,* was kind enough to concede that the first half hour had been "different," noting that "such originality, even if flawed, should be encouraged"—but Shales was having none of it, insisting that the opening thirty minutes was "sadly frantic drivel." Even Jim himself drew critical fire for being "astonishingly dull" in his on-screen appearances. "Henson should sit there," sniffed Shales, "and the lion should talk."

The reviews also made clear that Jim had a new and potentially more devastating problem on his hands: for the first time, the critics were disappointed in the Muppets themselves. Those who tuned in expecting to see the regular cast of *The Muppet Show* saw only Kermit and briefly Gonzo; the rest were new characters, designed by Frith and Kirk Thatcher and performed largely, though not entirely, by the second generation of Muppet performers. Shales thought the new Muppets were "ugly"—but more critically, no one thought the MuppeTelevision segments were very funny or even all that interesting. The Muppet segments—which had always seemed to come to Juhl and the writing team so effortlessly—simply sputtered, dragged down by slow pacing, heavy dialogue, and a distressing desire to be hip. Roush thought the segments resembled "the lame parts of *Saturday Night Live* scaled for kids. Judged by Henson's typically high standards, MuppeTelevision is an undeniably creative mess." This wasn't *The Dark Crystal* baffling audiences or *Labyrinth* landing with a thud; this was a project with Kermit at the center—and for the first time Kermit was flopping.

There were some kinder reviews—the *Los Angeles Times* called it "a bright addition to prime time"—and Jim was certain that, given time, the show might find its way and begin to right itself. But after only three low-performing weeks in which *The Jim Henson Hour* failed to make a dent in the ratings, NBC was running out of patience. Lord Grade had given Jim the time he needed to find his way with *The Muppet Show* in the 1970s—but as Michael Frith pointed out, "that was then, and this is now. Very few shows are given that luxury."

Jim built the fourth episode around *Dog City,* which ended up being little watched but highly acclaimed, and would win him an Emmy for Outstanding Direction the following year. By May 14, for the fifth installment, he finally managed to land the coveted Sunday evening time slot that had traditionally been held by Disney—an episode titled, fittingly enough, "The Ratings Game." It would end up the lowest rated episode of *The Jim Henson Hour* so far, finishing 72nd of 77 shows for the week. The following week, Tartikoff gently informed Jim that after the network aired the episodes it had ordered, NBC would be canceling the series. "I'm sorry the Sunday experiment didn't work out," Tartikoff told Jim in a handwritten note. "I am proud of the painstaking care and love and innovations you and your group put into the show. I just wish more people could have seen what we did."

Jim was "hurt" and "embarrassed" by the network's decision, recalled Bernie Brillstein. Jim told staff he was "disappointed" and called the cancellation "a major aggravation"—for him, a strongly worded indictment. "I don't particularly like the way NBC handled us," he wrote in one of his quarterly reports, "but what the hey, that's network TV." Jim still believed the series "was really coming together nicely. . . . I'm sure that we would have made it even better in subsequent seasons." Larry Mirkin thought so, too. "We were very ambitious," said Mirkin, "we just didn't have enough time. I think we could have sorted it out but we weren't allowed to do that." NBC, however, wasn't even willing to give the remaining episodes a chance, banishing four installments—including the episode featuring *Song of the Cloud Forest*—to the wilderness of the summer schedule, where they sank to the bottom of the Nielsen ratings. The last two episodes would be pulled from the network's schedule entirely.

Jerry Juhl wasn't certain that the show would ever have been salvageable, no matter how much time they might have spent on it. There was "a kind of craziness about that project that we could never put our finger on," Juhl said. One of *The Jim Henson Hour*'s underlying problems was a familiar one that had plagued Jim since the days of *The Dark Crystal:* namely that new technology—the visual effects, the virtual backgrounds, the CGI Muppets—had gotten in the way of storytelling or character development. "He was in love with technology and future-thinking stuff," said Henson Associates producer and creative consultant Alex Rockwell, "and so, when he revisited the Muppets on *The Jim Henson Hour,* he wanted to bring that sense of futuristic techno-hipness into the show [and] the marriage of those technological visuals and CGI with the Muppets didn't work that well." In the case of the CGI character Waldo, even Jim agreed he was "one of those characters I don't think we ever really got a handle on in terms of how to use him. . . . He hasn't really gelled as a major contribution to the show except technologically, I suppose."

At the heart of it, however, the real problem with *The Jim Henson Hour* was that it had a massive identity crisis. "It was like the show didn't know what it wanted to be," said Juhl. "This was Jim trying to do a whole lot of things at once, and it always puzzled us, and we couldn't talk him out of it. . . . Most things didn't work on that show. It was a huge frustration and a great sadness." Rockwell called it "a chaotic hour" that took a physical toll as well. "It was rigorous to make . . . because one minute you're shooting the Muppet stuff in Toronto and then you're up in Nova Scotia doing one of those Creature Shop stories," said Rockwell. "It was really exhausting, and Jim's energy got pretty diffused—unlike on *The Muppet Show,* where it was so focused."

Oz, too, thought the disarray in the show was reflective of Jim's increasingly divided attention, split between the creative work he enjoyed and the obligations of "flying around and getting money for the overhead." "Whatever Jim did, even some of the things that failed, there was always amazing stuff in it," said Oz. "But *The Jim Henson Hour* just didn't have the usual Jim focus. It was more like a grab bag of the brilliant things he's done."

Running the company was slowly sapping his creative energy, making it more difficult for Jim Henson to do the things that made him Jim Henson. *The Jim Henson Hour* was proof of that. Jim knew the strain was showing, both in the way the company was run and in the on-screen product. "I know that this period of time has been somewhat filled with a sense of uncertainty and an apparent lack of direction," he wrote in a memo to his entire staff, "but I want to say that we are working and looking at various alternatives, and we should have a resolution in the not too distant future."

Resolution was closer than he let on; he was already pursuing a course of action that, he hoped, "releases me from a lot of business problems. As anyone in the business knows, you spend a great deal of your time raising financing, finding distributors and all." If everything worked out as planned, he explained, "I'll be able to spend a lot more of my time on the creative side of things." That spring, as he and Rockwell rode in the back of a town car in Toronto, Jim reached for the enormous brick of a cellular telephone he kept under the seat. He had talked with Brillstein and Lazer, he told Rockwell, and they both agreed with his decision. Now he was going to make a phone call to put the plan into motion.

He was going to sell his company to Disney.

CHAPTER FIFTEEN

SO MUCH ON A HANDSHAKE

1989–1990

Agent Bernie Brillstein (left) and producer David Lazer were two of Jim's closest and most trusted colleagues and business advisors. Brillstein, however, was largely sidelined during the Disney negotiations, while Lazer continued to argue that Disney was getting Jim too cheaply.

FOR DISNEY CEO MICHAEL EISNER, THE VERY IDEA OF JIM HENSON joining the Walt Disney Company was a match "made in family entertainment heaven." For Jim Henson, it was a lifelong dream come true. "The first film I saw was *Snow White*," Jim noted, "and ever since then, I've had a secret desire to work with this great company."

Jim may have loved Disney's animated features—"outside of my own films, these are the only ones I buy for my video library," he wrote privately—but he was an even bigger fan of the Disney theme parks. Disneyland and Walt Disney World were, he said, "two of my favorite places," and he had made regular vacations to the two parks for decades, even making a point to visit the newly opened EPCOT center in early 1983, within months of the park's grand opening. Putting himself and the Muppets in the hands of Disney, then, would, in a sense, be like going on an extended vacation—one in which he would be expected to work and create, certainly, but then that was just the kind of vacation Jim liked best.

While Jim was working in the spring of 1989 to put his company in the hands of Disney, five years earlier things had very nearly gone the other way. In 1984, Disney had been on the verge of a hostile takeover at the hands of financier Saul Steinberg, who intended to dismember the company and sell its assets. With Disney's stock plunging, Jim had asked Bernie Brillstein to make some discreet inquiries about Jim either stepping in as Disney's new president or buying the company outright. The discussion went nowhere, due largely to bad timing; the Disney ship was in the process of righting itself, and later that year Paramount executives Michael Eisner and Jeffrey Katzenberg, along with Warner Brothers vice president Frank Wells, were chosen by a new Disney board to steer the company. Jim let the moment pass with no regrets, said Brillstein, "but a seed was planted about how perfect a Disney/Henson pairing might be."

Still, Jim had a good relationship with Eisner, who had given the go-ahead for the first two *Muppet Show* pilots while working as an ABC executive in the early 1970s. Shortly before starting work on *Labyrinth* in late 1984, Jim had called Brillstein and asked the agent to set up a meeting with Eisner, now Disney's CEO, and Katzenberg, the head of production. Jim's projects were getting "very expensive" to produce, said Brillstein, and Jim wanted to discuss the possibility of Disney financing and distributing projects for Henson Associates —or, better still, having Disney buy Henson Associates outright. Brillstein called to set up the meeting, enthusiastically telling Eisner, "I have the best thing in the world for you: Jim Henson." Jim and Lazer flew to California for a private dining room at Chasen's restaurant in West Hollywood ("like a Mafia dinner," joked Brillstein). This time, however, finances doomed any agreement. In 1984, the Muppets were entering a post–*Muppets Take Manhattan* holding pattern—and Jim was still negotiating with Holmes à Court to bring the Muppets back home—making their earning potential, in Eisner's assessment, "very soft." "The Muppets' world renown wasn't enough to carry the deal," said a somewhat annoyed Brillstein, "so Disney passed." But Brillstein assured Jim that if he wanted to sell his company to another major studio—and in fact, Disney rival MCA was interested—he could make it happen. But Jim refused; he wanted Disney, or no one.

Now, five years later, Jim had decided to try again—and in early spring 1989 had casually reopened discussions with Eisner. From a purely financial standpoint, Jim's company was on sturdier footing than it had been on that day at Chasen's in 1984. All of his properties were now safely back in his hands. *Muppet Babies*– and *Fraggle Rock*–related merchandise was steadily filling the company coffers, Muppet videos were selling well internationally, and *The Muppet Show* was in regular rotation on cable. The company had come a long way in the last five years, as Jim had expanded the company more broadly beyond television and into motion picture production.

As a reflection of the company's growing film presence, Jim was in the process of changing the name of the company from Henson Associates to Jim Henson Productions, which made the company sound more like a major film studio than the small, independent organization of around 150 employees it actually was. He had even recently unveiled a new logo, built around his stylized signature (in Kermit green) with a swooping J and dramatically crossed H. Jim called it "disarmingly simple"—and perhaps intentionally, it also looked a lot like the logo for the Walt Disney Company, which was centered on Walt's own widely recognized signature.

Clad smartly in its new logo, Henson Associates—it wouldn't officially be Jim Henson Productions until November—had become a major player with an international reputation, entirely worthy of Disney's growing company and legacy. But Jim felt he was bringing to Disney more than just a financial asset or a valuable stock option; he was bringing them a creative commodity that they couldn't put a value on—for no matter what the transaction or the logo on the letterhead, Disney wouldn't just be getting the Muppets or Henson Associates or Jim Henson Productions; they'd be getting *Jim Henson*.

And Disney could use him. As Jim and Eisner casually chatted that spring, Disney, despite its new administrative stability, was still feeling its way creatively. In early 1989, the seemingly unstoppable string of Disney blockbusters—beginning with the ambitious animated musical feature *The Little Mermaid*—was still to come; the 1988 hit *Who Framed Roger Rabbit* was the first real smash for the company in years. But with *The Little Mermaid* still months away from its November 1989 release—and no certainty for how it would be received by audiences—Disney needed not only reliably bankable characters to add to its slowly expanding character base, it needed a blast of creative energy and talent as well. Jim was their man. "It was *never* just selling the Muppets," said Frank Oz. "It was always in conjunction with him being there as the main creative guy, who could help the company. Jim felt he could *be* Walt Disney."

And so, Eisner had been not only responsive, but enthusiastic when Jim had called him from the car in Toronto and asked to meet at the Hotel Bel-Air in Los Angeles on May 22. Over breakfast that morning, Jim told Eisner he had made up his mind, and laid out his intention to sell his company to Disney. For Eisner, there was never any doubt that Jim Henson was exactly what the Walt Disney Company needed. "It's special because you get a guy like Jim, who brings a new creative vitality to the company," said Eisner. "That's really the reason for the whole deal—plus you get the Muppets."

As much as Disney wanted and needed Jim Henson, Jim, too, needed Disney. "On a personal level," wrote Jim, "I think this move will enable me to free up my life and to focus more time on the creative and conceptual aspects of our work, and less time worrying about the business and financial side of everything." It wasn't that Jim wasn't up to the task of running his own company; more than anything, it was a matter of how much of his precious time and energy he wanted to devote solely to business. "It's not easy on an organization when you're doing a lot of other activities," Jim told the American Film Institute. He knew his extended absences had taken a toll on morale in the New York office in particular, where personalities often clashed and jurisdictions overlapped. "When I went off to do *Labyrinth* . . . it pulled me away from my core business, which has been in New York, and it became a major draw there on energy," he admitted.

Despite Jim's best efforts, the company, said David Lazer, "was getting unwieldy, and there were personnel problems and all kinds of stuff." Brillstein, who had sat in on a few of the endless meetings with Jim and his managers at Henson Associates, had seen firsthand how "people would go to Jim directly about everything, and he hardly had the time." "He was a very *good* businessman," said producer Larry Mirkin, "but that isn't what he cared about. He cared about the work, he cared about what it meant in the world, and he cared about making the art grow and develop." Going with Disney, then, would be the first step in lifting the administrative yoke of running a company from Jim's shoulders—"the organizational albatross," as Brillstein called it, "that drained his creative energy." And he was getting tired; he had been splitting his time between the creative work that was so much fun and the tedium of running his own company since he was seventeen years old. With Disney's money and machinery behind him, he could finally be creative full-time. "He was an artist first and foremost," said Brillstein appreciatively, "and he needed to concentrate on his work and come up with magnificent ideas like he always had."

Disney would be good for the Muppets as well. If there was any organization that knew how to preserve and promote iconic characters beyond the lifetimes of their respective creators, it was the Walt Disney Company: at the moment, the company was tending not only to the classic Disney characters created during Walt's lifetime, but it was also successfully serving as caretaker to Disneyfied versions of characters from A. A. Milne's Winnie-the-Pooh books. For Jim, finding such a suitable home for the Muppets was important. The failure of the Muppet sequences in *The Jim Henson Hour* had spooked him—and if he couldn't always tend to their well-being, he wanted to ensure they were with someone else who would. "Looking way back down the road to when I stop sitting in my rocking chair and working Kermit the Frog, I really like the idea of characters living on in the Disney parks," said Jim. "It's a wonderful future for these characters. It's as close to an eternal life as a little green frog can get."

After Jim and Eisner finished their breakfast meeting at the Bel-Air, the two men shook hands—always enough for Jim to seal any deal. They had made a gentleman's agreement with each other, and that was enough; the details could come later. "This was so much on a handshake between Michael and Jim that whatever [the deal said] didn't matter," said Brillstein. "Jim loved Michael and trusted him a lot. And Michael understood Jim. He just really got it." That evening, Jim made an appearance on *The Arsenio Hall Show,* strolling casually onstage to a jazzy version of the *Sesame Street* theme, and looking not at all like a man who had just put in motion a life-altering business transaction.

Two days later, Jim met Mary Ann and Brillstein at the La Costa Hotel and Spa to spend several days swimming, enjoying massages, and celebrating. Jim was clearly delighted with his pact with Eisner, giggling happily as he sipped one whiskey sour after another in the hotel lounge. "[It was] just great," said Brillstein. Fully relaxed, Jim returned to New York to meet privately with his attorneys and business managers to begin the process of sharing information with Disney to pave the way for the sale of the company. Jim personally wrote a seven-page letter to Eisner outlining the structure of the company and its various departments (to his own surprise, he discovered during a company inventory that over two thousand Muppets were in storage), while his management team circulated internal memos marked PRIVATE AND CONFIDENTIAL. At the moment, Jim was keeping things as quiet as possible; outside of the Henson family, only a small group of advisors and employees—the "JHP 'deal team'"— were aware of Jim's plans for the company.

Outside the company, however, there was one person who Jim insisted had to be made aware of the negotiations: Joan Ganz Cooney. From the very beginning of his discussions with Eisner, said Cooney, "Jim had been adamant that Disney could *not* have the *Sesame Street* Muppets." In one of his first letters to the Walt Disney Company, in fact, Jim's manager of strategic planning, Charles Rivkin, expressly warned Disney that not only were the *Sesame Street* characters off-limits, but so was the shared revenue stream generated by *Sesame Street*–related merchandise. "In none of the information previously sent to you are *Sesame Street* revenues included," wrote Rivkin, then underlined the next part emphatically: "nor is it our intention to include this part of our company in any combination with Disney." Jim assured Cooney that he regarded *Sesame Street* as a "holy place" and that he was confident Disney had no intention of asking for it in the negotiations. (Ironically, Disney's internal memos referred to its acquisition of Jim's company as "Project Big Bird," giving the transaction a code name based on a Muppet the company was never going to get.)

Even as lawyers and accountants bustled behind the scenes, creative business continued at One Seventeen. "In general," Jim told his staff, "things have been pleasantly active over the last few months." While *The Jim Henson Hour* had been pulled from the NBC lineup in May, the network had promised to air the remaining episodes in July, so Jim was putting the final touches on *Song of the Cloud Forest* as well as on a behind-the-scenes documentary *The Secret of the Muppets,* each of which would be incorporated into a later *Jim Henson Hour. The Witches,* too, was finished—"and looking quite nice," Jim added—and was now awaiting a commitment from Warner Brothers on a release date. In the meantime, the Creature Shop's other project, *Teenage Mutant Ninja Turtles,* was filming in North Carolina, with Brian Henson heading up the puppet team. Jim was thrilled with the work, and thought *Turtles* contained some of their best animatronics yet. "The lip articulation is the most advanced we've ever had," he enthused. "We're definitely breaking new ground here."

There was new ground to be broken, too, he thought, with a new gadget that he found absolutely fascinating: the handheld minicam. The Handycam, Jim explained enthusiastically, was a marked improvement over the "enormous, heavy beasts" normally used in television production—and was so light and easy to use, in fact, that anyone could make a video or a television show. Jim wasn't quite sure what to do with it yet—he and John Henson would create playful short videos together, looking for the right idea—but he was intrigued with the possibilities of putting filmmaking technology into the hands of anyone and everyone. "We're going to see a whole new and different kind of television," Jim said, astutely predicting the democratization of video technology that would make YouTube possible twenty-five years later. As always, Jim had seen the potential in a technology well before the technology could catch up to it.

After work, Jim would walk the few blocks from One Seventeen to his apartment at the Sherry-Netherland. More and more now, Mary Ann was making extended trips from West Palm Beach to the city, where they would spend their evenings eating dinners of fish or pasta ordered from the Sherry-Netherland hotel room service—or walking a few blocks to the fashionable China Grill restaurant—before heading out for a movie or a show. Jim was still an avid theatergoer, and living in the city meant he could attend shows regularly, whether it was concerts at the Brooklyn Academy of Music, dances at Lincoln Center, or any of the countless Broadway shows he loved. His tastes in theater were varied and interesting; one night it might be heady fare like Wendy Wasserstein's *The Heidi Chronicles*, the next a musical like *Anything Goes!*—though if he had to pick a favorite show, it was probably the musical *Les Misérables*, which he had seen several times, always tearing up at Jean Valjean's heartfelt solo, "Bring Him Home." Jim truly loved living in the city, though his growing fame was making it more and more difficult for him to move about freely without being swamped by requests for his autograph or badgered by shouted demands to "Do Kermit!"

The first week in July, following two nonstop weeks of back-and-forthing between New York and Los Angeles to meet with Eisner and Katzenberg, Jim left for Hana, Hawaii, with Mary Ann for what he hoped would be a romantic weeklong getaway. Instead, the week was a bust. Uncharacteristically, Jim was moody and brooding—or at least as moody as he could be—fussing about their nineteen-year age difference, which normally never bothered him very much. "Where are we going with this?" he would ask, and then would sigh with a sad uncertainty, lamenting that he was too old to settle down and start a family with her. For her to have the kind of life she deserved, he said, he would have to let her go, and she would have to move on. At the end of the week, they agreed to separate.

Once again, they would not remain apart long—as Richard Hunt had noted, they always seemed to be on again, off again. A little more than a month later, Jim met Mary Ann in New Mexico, where she was now living, to survey a parcel of land he wanted to buy, with the intention of building either a house or perhaps even a small spa and hotel. They were staying in separate casitas at the Rancho Encantado resort, and following their long day of looking at property, Jim dropped by Mary Ann's room with caviar and wine. As they sat on the portal of the casita dining on caviar and watching the sun set over the cottonwoods, Jim turned suddenly to Mary Ann and sank to his knees in front of her, his eyes glistening with tears. "For whatever we become," he said warmly, raising his wineglass to her, "for the love we will always have for each other, and for the friends we will always be." By the end of the evening, they were back together.

Discussions with Disney continued on through July. While Jim was still trying to keep things quiet, the company was vibrating with internal gossip and rumor. On July 26, 1989, Jim sent a memo to his entire staff begging for patience. "I know that this past period of time has been a difficult one for everyone," he wrote. Apologizing that "things are not resolving as fast as we thought," he vowed to "let everyone know what's happening as soon as we can. . . . Thanks for your patience and understanding and, once again, I'm sorry for these last few months of uncertainty." Over the next several weeks, he met privately with Joan Cooney and Frank Oz to keep them apprised of the discussions, and made a quick trip to London to update Kenworthy and a few others in the overseas arm of the company. But news was starting to trickle out; "Disney Said to Be Wooing Henson," wrote the Minneapolis *Star Tribune* in mid-August, while the *Houston Chronicle* speculated—correctly—that "Disney May Be Courting Miss Piggy's Company." Both companies could only decline to comment; it was time for Jim and Eisner to make their decision official, and then make it public.

On August 24 at 9:15 A.M.—a sunny Thursday morning—Jim and Disney president Frank Wells, flanked by a small group of staff, boarded a Learjet at JFK Airport, bound for Orlando, Florida. On their arrival at 11:30, they were whisked away in two cars to Disney-MGM Studios, the newest of the three Disney theme parks at the Walt Disney World resort, for a quick meet-and-greet with Disney staff in the park's Animation Building. For the next six hours, Jim and his staff casually toured Disney-MGM and the Magic Kingdom, then were escorted to the opulent, red-gabled Grand Floridian hotel to check into their suites and change clothes for the evening. At seven, Katzenberg met Jim in the hotel lobby and took him back to Disney-MGM to watch the final run-through of an Indiana Jones stunt show that would be opening the following morning. As Jim entered the show's amphitheater, Eisner and Wells came over to greet him, followed by Jim's former collaborator George Lucas, who was serving as executive producer of the stunt show. Jim shook all their hands warmly and looked over the attraction, which resembled the set of an adventure film. Standing next to Lucas, arms crossed as they surveyed the enormous set, the two of them could have been working on *Labyrinth* again. It truly felt as if he had come home.

Just after dark, Jim and the three Disney chiefs headed for the Portobello Yacht Club, an Italian restaurant in the newly opened Pleasure Island section of the resort. With the other eight spots at their large dinner table occupied by executives and attorneys from the Walt Disney Company and Henson Associates, this would be very much a business dinner. Starting at 9:15, as waiters whirled in plates of pasta and glasses of wine around them, both sides got to work.

Discussion went on late into the evening; lights went off at the restaurants and shops out on Pleasure Island. Finally, just after midnight, the two companies reached an agreement—legally speaking, an agreement-in-principle—that would permit the Walt Disney Company to acquire Henson Associates and allow Jim to enter into a long-term exclusive production agreement with the Walt Disney Company. At 12:30 A.M.—it was now the morning of Friday, August 25—Jim signed his name on the agreement's final page. Smiling, he said his good nights and retired to his suite at the Grand Floridian. "Jim Henson's wish, desire, dream was to be with Disney," said Brillstein. With Jim's signature, that dream was on the verge of coming true. "The Disney deal," as Jim would always refer to it in his correspondence, was under way.

Jim arose early to have breakfast with Bob Mathieson, the executive in charge of the Walt Disney World theme parks, then headed for Disney-MGM for the official dedication of the Indiana Jones Stunt Theatre, avoiding any press who may have questioned him about his presence at Disney. After an early afternoon tour of EPCOT, he was taken to the airport and flown back to New York, arriving home at the Sherry-Netherland apartment on Friday evening. Incredibly, the media had picked up no trace of his trip to Orlando or of the agreement. That was just as he wanted it; he and Eisner intended to announce the deal at a nationally televised press conference to be held at Disney World on Monday morning.

On the morning of Sunday, August 27, then, he and Cheryl were driven to Teterboro Airport in New Jersey and headed for Orlando aboard one of Disney's sleek Gulfstream 3 corporate jets. Jim spent a long afternoon chatting with Katzenberg in the Disney chairman's Grand Floridian hotel suite, then went to dinner with Cheryl, Eisner, and a few others at the Portobello Yacht Club. The next morning, he was up and out of the Grand Floridian by seven and on his way to meet Eisner at the entrance to the Animation Building at Disney-MGM Studios, where they would announce their agreement live on ABC's *Good Morning America.* Standing with Eisner and walk-around versions of Kermit, Miss Piggy, and Mickey and Minnie Mouse, Jim was visibly excited. As a subtle show of corporate respect, Jim had worn—under his colorful purple-and-blue-striped jacket—a red tie printed with pictures of Mickey Mouse, while Eisner, looking very much in charge in his dark suit, added a blue tie emblazoned with images of Kermit the Frog. "I think hooking up with Disney creates such a wonderful force," Jim enthused, grinning broadly. Eisner thundered excitely at the crowd, "Mickey Mouse has a new sibling, and he's going to have to get used to it!" As flashbulbs exploded, Kermit, Piggy, Mickey, and Minnie all gave an approving thumbs-up.

Away from the television cameras, Jim was more effusive as he explained to the press why he had chosen to sell his company. "I feel I have reached a certain level with my own company," he explained, "but what really intrigues me is to find out how much more we can accomplish by joining forces with an organization as effective and far reaching as the Disney company." He was excited by more than just his new creative freedom; he was optimistic about the future of the Muppets, too. With Disney's deep pockets and enormous marketing and merchandising machine behind them, the Muppets could be promoted around the world, giving them the kind of international prominence that Henson Associates could never buy. "I think Michael Eisner and Jeffrey Katzenberg have been brilliant in their handling of the Disney company," Jim continued. "I look forward to seeing what we can do together." For his part, Eisner was delighted to have both Jim on their team as "a creative designated hitter" and the Muppets filling out their character roster. "There are only a few characters in the world who have the kind of appeal [the Muppets have]," explained Eisner. "And they're all evergreen," added Katzenberg. "You're dealing with material that does not age. . . . There could not be a more productive association for our company."

Still, not everyone was happy about it, due mainly to confusion over how the transaction would affect the *Sesame Street* Muppets. Despite Jim's best efforts to make it clear that the *Sesame Street* characters were *not* included in the deal, some critics fretted that Disney's acquisition of the Muppets meant that Ernie and Bert would soon be selling Disney toys and clothing. Jim finally drafted a letter, to be published under Kermit's signature, in yet another attempt to correct the record. "Just thought I'd let you know that our friends from *Sesame Street* . . . are expressly *not* part of the agreement with The Walt Disney Company," wrote Jim-as-Kermit. "All of the *Sesame Street* friends will remain right there at home on *Sesame Street,* under the watchful eye of the Children's Television Workshop and Mr. Jim Henson." Still, misunderstandings over the status of the *Sesame Street* Muppets would be a continuing source of anxiety during the negotiations.

Joan Cooney, however, was genuinely delighted for Jim. She understood exactly why he had made the decision to sell the company. "He will no longer have to be raising money for his movies and trying to find air time on television," she told *USA Today*. "I can't imagine that he would have [sold to anyone else]. It is a marriage made in heaven." As always, Jim promised Cooney that she could count on his continued involvement with *Sesame Street*—he'd already joked that he and Oz would be performing Ernie and Bert when they were eighty—and assured Cooney, with a twinkle in his eye, that he would insist his lawyers insert language into his Disney contract guaranteeing that he would spend two weeks of each year working on inserts for the show. "He *never* spent two weeks a year with *Sesame Street,* but he just *loved* putting that into the contract!" laughed Cooney. "We could not ask for a more supportive friend."

As described in the agreement-in-principle, the transaction would be fairly straightforward: in exchange for $150 million in Disney stock, Jim would sell all of his copyrights to the Walt Disney Company, including all of the Muppets (with the exception of those from *Sesame Street*), *Fraggle Rock,* all three Muppet films, *The Dark Crystal,* and *Labyrinth.* Once in Disney's hands, the company could freely use the characters in merchandising, videos, theme parks, publishing, or in any of the countless other media under the Disney imprint. Additionally, Jim himself would be attached exclusively to Disney for fifteen years (Eisner had joked that he hoped it would be "for life"), but would still have the opportunity to pursue his own projects through his own independent production company, with offices in New York, London, and Los Angeles (in fact, Jim already had producer Martin Baker scouting for office space in California). It was a corporate structure, said one confidential Henson Associates memo, that should ideally "[give] Jim the maximum operating flexibility with the minimum financial risk."

Still, the agreement-in-principle was only a road map; there were a number of small but important details that would have to be carefully worded and resolved on the way to the final agreement. Jim had interviewed four law firms to represent his interests, and had liked each of them so much he had engaged all four, though much of the work was left to the powerhouse firm of Skadden, Arps, which specialized in mergers and acquisitions. The attorneys would have their hands full, especially as Disney had a reputation for hard-knuckled negotiating. It had yet to be decided, for example, whether Jim Henson Productions would operate as a kind of subsidiary of Disney, or whether it would be a truly independent production company. The distinction was important: as a subsidiary, Disney would own the company and pay Jim a salary and a share of the company's profits, while as a completely independent production company, Jim would own and fund the company and receive production and development fees from Disney. Negotiators were already working to find a middle ground between the two alternatives—but whatever the final compromise, Jim was insistent that Disney at least pay the dreaded over-head costs for his production company.

Another sticking point related to the use of the Muppets them-selves. Jim hoped he would be permitted to retain some sort of lim-ited control over the use of the "Muppets as puppets"—that is, in any production that required the use of puppeteers to perform the Muppet characters. Put simply, Jim wanted to be involved in the se-lection and hiring of puppeteers. As Jim was constantly reminding anyone who would listen, characters didn't come easily; many took years to develop. Sometimes it was a matter of finding the character through something as intensive as the writing process, or as wonder-fully impromptu as an ad-libbed aside. Other times, an old puppet in the hands of a new performer could create miracles, such as when Richard Hunt—frustrated with a fuzzy red *Sesame Street* monster named Elmo—hurled the Muppet at Kevin Clash and asked him to do something with it—and a lovable, huggable star was born. "A lot of times, you go through a lot of experimenting and moving around before it all [comes together]," Jim said. Performers were crucial; he didn't want Disney treating puppeteers, or their puppets, inter-changeably. Early on, Katzenberg had promised to put in writing the rates at which the performers would be paid—and even suggested that some of them be put on the Disney payroll—but had backped-aled immediately, refusing to speculate on whether Disney could ac-tually legally make such a commitment. But Jim wanted a guarantee his performers would be taken care of—and, perhaps more impor-tant, that their craft be respected. Without them, Disney was simply getting a toy box full of puppets.

Jim had a similar concern about the integrity of the Muppets in licensing and merchandise. "Much like Disney," he explained to Eis-ner, "we have a reputation in the consumer products community as a licensor with very exacting quality control procedures." Jim had al-ways taken licensing seriously, putting in place a rigorous review process for every kind of Muppet merchandising or for the use of Muppet likenesses; now he wanted a guarantee that he could pre-approve quality standards for any of Disney's Muppet merchandise—or, at the very least, that Disney would "treat our characters with the same high quality standards that apply to their own characters." He wasn't being unreasonable, he thought; rather, he simply wanted to maintain his hard-earned reputation for quality, the trust he'd earned from consumers who could be certain that Muppet products weren't junk. "That was Jim's mandate," said Lazer. "He only wanted quality things out there."

And then there was Kermit the Frog. While Jim was prepared to hand over all of the Muppets to Disney, he didn't intend for Kermit to go with them unconditionally. He was too important. "Kermit should be treated in the negotiations as a separate issue," recommended a confidential Henson Associates memo. "Since Kermit the Frog is so closely associated with Jim Henson, *Jim must have control over the use of Kermit.*" For Disney, however, getting the Muppets without the free use of Kermit was like getting the cast of *Peanuts* without Snoopy. For the moment, Kermit was in a kind of legal limbo as both sides tried to figure out, Solomon-like, how to split the million-dollar baby.

Still, regardless of the issues that had yet to be resolved, Disney—and particularly Eisner—knew they were getting a lot for their $150 million. Eisner acknowledged that the company was paying "a lot of money" but added that, from a purely financial point of view, with "the established franchises and the upside of new Jim Henson products, we will earn a really good return on our investment." On Wall Street, Disney stock crept slightly upward the day the deal was announced, but astute analysts understood the deal was about more than money. "It's a strategic acquisition," said one trader. "It almost doesn't matter if they paid too much or too little." For Jim, though, it was never really about the money. "Jim is ambitious in expressing himself, not in wanting a lot of money or fame," Oz told one reporter. "If that was all, he could kick back and relax now. But he wants to play and have fun and do good stuff."

Jim also understood that his success—and the success that had made Henson Associates such a desirable commodity for Disney that they were willing to invest $150 million in it—had been a collaborative effort. "It's not just me doing this stuff," he once said. "It's a lot of us creating it, writers and designers and puppeteers." Despite his frustration with the personality conflicts that had become a regular part of running his company, Jim was always sincerely fond of his colleagues, collaborators, and staff. "[It's] the people who have made this company such a delightful place for me," Jim told Eisner. "As you well know, it all begins with them and their loyalty and dedication." Once the deal went through, then, Jim wanted to show his appreciation for that loyalty and dedication.

For several weeks he'd been scribbling what came to be called "The List"—the names of people who Jim believed had played a significant role in the success of the Muppets or had brought value to the company over the last thirty years. Next to each name was a dollar figure, running from thousands all the way up into the millions. "He really wanted to do right by everybody," said Lisa Henson. "This was money he wanted to get into people's hands" as a show of his appreciation. In the past, Jim had been generous about rewarding a number of key writers, producers, and performers with shares in merchandising profits, or awarding partial ownership of a project. Several years earlier, for example, Jerry Juhl had been struck speechless when he learned that Jim had given him a percentage of the profits from the lucrative *Muppet Babies* merchandising. "After twenty-five years, you can still surprise me, chief!" Juhl told Jim warmly. "[Jim] really wanted this deal to be a good thing for everyone," said Mary Ann Cleary. "He seemed only thrilled to be sharing his bounty with everyone that had made contributions to the success of the company."

Jim took great pleasure in The List, carrying it around with him and taking it out from time to time to add another name or adjust a dollar figure. It gave him the opportunity to do a personal inventory of his relationships with his collaborators, and think about what others had done with him and for him over the last three decades. "He tried to be very benevolent with everybody," said Dave Goelz— and yet there were some who still felt, fairly or not, that he had never been generous enough in his praise for their efforts. With The List, Jim felt he was in some way atoning for what he considered his greatest weakness as an employer and manager: no matter how hard he tried, he had not always made his employees happy. The bonuses, he hoped, would finally soothe some of the bruised egos at Henson Associates, providing the fiscal equivalent of the backslapping "attaboys" that Jim never really bestowed. For the most part, though, Jim

448 | JIM HENSON

took genuine glee in working on his list. For someone who enjoyed giving gifts as much as Jim did, it was going to be a fun way to spend his own money.

If asked, however, Jim would often enthuse that the most exciting part of the Disney deal was neither the money nor the production company he would oversee; it was the chance to develop rides and attractions for the Disney theme parks. As recently as 1987, Jim had been seriously exploring the idea of a Muppet-themed amusement park, even commissioning concept art for a park called Muppetville before conceding that "Disney does it so well that we could never do it better." Now, however, he was being given a corner of the fledgling Disney-MGM Studios in which to develop Muppet-themed rides, attractions, and restaurants, with Disney's wildly creative and innovative Imagineers at his full disposal. This was a playground far more fun to play in than even his Creature Shop. "The idea of working our characters into the Disney parks!" Jim gushed. "I can't wait! This is going to be such fun."

By the beginning of September, in fact, Jim was already enthusiastically at work on his first project for the park, a 3-D Muppet movie he'd pitched to Eisner at dinner the night before their joint announcement. Jim had been intrigued by 3-D films for years; while he could never get the technology to work correctly for the "interactive film" he'd been hoping to make, he thought a 3-D movie might provide a similarly immersive experience for audiences—but there, too, the technology left something to be desired. By the early 1980s, 3-D film technology had improved markedly since its gimmicky, eye-straining heyday in the 1950s, but Jim still wasn't impressed enough with it to use it for a Muppet project, telling one 3-D producer, "If you've seen a process that works, I'd love to have my people see it."

Typically, he finally saw it at Disney, which had premiered Michael Jackson's science-fiction-themed 3-D film *Captain EO* at EPCOT in 1986. That movie—in which smoke and laser effects inside the theater were seamlessly synced with events on-screen—was hailed as one of the first "4-D" film experiences, an artistry Jim admired. He loved the idea of giving the audience a more complete experience, but wanted to take the concept to a manic extreme worthy of the Muppets. Instead of smoke belching and lasers flashing, then, Jim wanted walkaround Muppet characters running frantically down the theater aisles and soap bubbles floating from the ceiling—and when audiences ducked one of Fozzie's squirting flowers, Jim wanted them to get wet. "He was *very* excited" about the idea, said Alex Rockwell, who had helped Jim develop the concept with Muppet writer Bill Prady. On September 11, 1989, Jim and Rockwell flew to California to discuss the movie with Disney Imagineers, meeting them in their exalted Glendale offices, a compound so secure that Jim needed a security clearance to enter the grounds. For two hours, Jim was given a full tour of the facility, then spent the rest of the afternoon discussing 3-D movie ideas with the Imagineers— the first of many energizing meetings Jim would have with the Imagineers over the next eight months. "Oh, they had so much fun in those meetings," said Rockwell. "He was in heaven. Heaven, heaven, heaven."

Back in New York, Jim was also holding regular meetings with Michael Frith and his creative team—usually including Alex Rockwell, Chris Cerf, Kirk Thatcher, and Bill Prady, among others—to brainstorm ideas for Muppet rides. Jim's favorite attractions in the Disney parks were the Pirates of the Caribbean ride—the reliable favorite in which passengers float through scenes filled with comic, Audio-Animatronic pirates—and the lesser-known River of Time, a quiet boat ride through moments in Mexican history, housed in the Mexico pavilion at EPCOT. Both were dark rides in which riders floated through the attraction in boats, looking at Audio-Animatronic figures, so it is perhaps of little surprise that the first attraction Jim wanted to design was a massive dark ride filled with scenes featuring Audio-Animatronic Muppets. Jim thought it would be funny to parody Disney-MGM's centerpiece dark ride—a slow cruise through great moments in film called the Great Movie Ride—with an attraction of his own called the Great Muppet Movie Ride. "It'll be a backstage ride explaining how movies are shot," said Jim, giggling, "but all the information is wrong!" Michael Frith went quickly to work, pencil flying as he drew Muppet parodies of famous films.

It wasn't all creative fun, however. Until the Disney deal was finalized, Jim was still responsible for running his company and for putting things in order to ensure a smooth transition to Disney's ownership. Part of the transition process involved downsizing staff—a heartbreaking task that Jim left largely to Lazer, though he took the time to write glowing letters of recommendation himself, including a letter for the regular morning housekeeper at One Seventeen, a woman everyone called simply Tainy. After a quick trip to California in mid-September—where he picked up an Emmy for directing the *Dog City* episode of *The Jim Henson Hour*—Jim spent several days almost exclusively in the company of Lazer and Brillstein, talking quietly over meals at the Sherry-Netherland, trying to deal with transition issues and discussing the ongoing negotiations with Disney.

The first week in October, he was back for an extended stay in Los Angeles to personally continue the conversation with Katzenberg. On October 3, Jim had formally set up the West Coast arm of Jim Henson Productions, running the company out of a set of offices in the Disney Tower in Burbank. He was also renting a house—for $15,000 a month—on a relatively remote stretch of the Pacific Coast Highway just north of Malibu, moving into a mission-style home jutting out of the bluffs just above Nicholas Canyon Beach. It was nearly fifty miles from the house into his offices at Disney, but Jim savored the drive, conducting business on his clunky cellular phone as he cruised into Burbank in a rented white convertible Volkswagen Cabriolet or, later, his own cream-colored Mercedes. And Jim loved driving *fast,* roaring down the Pacific Coast Highway with the top down, blaring the local Top 40 radio station. The speeding tickets piled up, but Jim paid them all with a shrug; he *liked* speeding.

His schedule was packed—but Jim was fully engaged again, in a way he hadn't been since well before *The Jim Henson Hour.* Put simply, said John Henson, "at the end of the day, what he was really excited about was working with the Disney company." Over lunch, Jim would talk with the head of the Disney Channel about creating original content for cable, while at dinner he would meet with the president of Touchstone Pictures, a Disney film company that produced more adult-oriented fare. In between, he would attend countless meetings with Imagineers to discuss the 3-D movie and the Great Muppet Movie Ride. Weeks earlier, *USA Today* had noted admiringly that Disney, by aligning itself with Jim, had purchased "creative vitality." It certainly seemed so; Disney Imagineers admired both his enthusiasm and his seemingly endless stream of ideas. "[Jim's] natural curiosity and openness and receptiveness to new ideas made him a perfect fit to work with Imagineering," said one Imagineer. "The room always lit up when he was around."

On his way back to New York, Jim stopped for several days in New Mexico to visit Mary Ann. "The trips were often whirlwinds," said Mary Ann. Ever since their reconciliation, she and Jim had tried to continue seeing each other as regularly as possible, but with Jim's schedule they often had to cram as much activity as they could into three or four days. Jim liked casually strolling the galleries and museums in Santa Fe or riding horses along the arroyos near Albuquerque—and if there was time, they would get in a ski trip to Taos, or take long drives to Chimayó to explore spiritual sites. Jim, thought Mary Ann, was always "light [and] relaxed," in New Mexico.

Things weren't as light and relaxed back in New York, however, where Jim spent two days being briefed by his attorneys on the status of the Disney deal. On the evening of October 17, Jim boarded an all-night flight for London, where he would spend a week with producer Martin Baker meeting with Disney executives at Shepperton Studios—and he wasn't happy. Jim "was frustrated," said Brillstein, "as Disney fought over every single point." The day after his arrival at Shepperton, Jim fired off a note to Lazer, enclosing a draft of a letter he wanted to send to Eisner and Katzenberg, "communicat[ing] to both . . . my concern about our relationship." While Jim never raised his voice in meetings, his draft letter to the Disney chiefs had a markedly sharp timbre to it. "I feel we are getting started in a way that is not going to work for me in the future," Jim warned:

> The tone of the negotiations does not seem to me to be the
> way two parties should be relating to each other if they intend
> to go into a long term relationship. Jeffrey [Katzenberg] has
> said that this is what our respective lawyers are supposed to
> do—to fight like hell and give in as little as possible; but some-
> how this doesn't seem correct to me. The kind of deal I like is

one in which both parties try to arrive at a fair settlement and everyone walks away satisfied. I really don't intend to do battle with you guys for the next fifteen years. My impression is that Disney is standing firm on all issues, assuming that my company is committed to this deal and thus we will eventually cave in. This is not a wise assumption.

He was further annoyed by his treatment at the hands of Disney's accounting department, which was haggling over the costs he was billing for the 3-D film. Jim had asked for $1.2 million—most of which, he reminded them, would be paid to the puppeteers—and he was "disturbed" that Disney considered his fee for directing (which was "a couple hundred thousand dollars") to be "too high and precedent breaking." As their first major collaboration, he warned, "this doesn't bode well for the future." "I think I can make major contributions to the Disney company," Jim concluded, "but if I'm going to have to spend my time defending my value to you, or in combat with your business affairs people, it's good to know this now, because perhaps we would do better to go our separate ways."

Lazer—who called himself "the peacemaker" in the discussions— was eventually able to talk Jim down and the storm passed. But it was clear, only a month into talks, that it was going to be a long negotiation. "It was a tough process," said Henson Associates attorney Peter Schube. "[Disney] was very aggressive and very thorough . . . [but] no one should have been surprised. . . . This was not a bait and switch. This was not anything other than them being who they promised and announced themselves to be." For Jim, though, the tone of the negotiations mattered as much as the content. Jim might have been a realist when it came to business, said Steve Whitmire, "but I think his idealism wasn't able to deal with this cutthroat world . . . where suddenly everything is about being a commodity and it's about buying and selling."

Jim spent much of the autumn bouncing across from coast to coast, meeting with Imagineers in Los Angeles one week, then spending the next week walking his corner of Disney-MGM Studios in Orlando, pointing out potential locations for Muppet attractions. To his delight, Jim found Disney's Imagineers—unlike their counterparts in the accounting department—to be willing conspirators in almost any plan, no matter how ridiculous, or expensive, an idea might be. "He loved the fact that the bar for excellence was set so high inside the theme parks," said Schube. "Jim loved to solve really hard problems in the production work that he did . . . [and] Disney does that all day long in the theme parks. That's all they do . . . and he loved how well they did it." During one walk through the park, Jim and Michael Frith pointed out to an Imagineer a set of power lines that were visible as visitors entered the area where the Muppet pavilion would be located and mused that it was unfortunate there wasn't a facade or a small building blocking the wires from sight. The Imagineer never even blinked. "When do you need it?" he asked.

Back in New York, he had another construction project that was a bit more problematic, but just as much fun; his apartment at the Sherry-Netherland was again being refurbished, mostly to deal with problems caused by a crumbling inner wall. It was an expensive mess—Jim would spend nearly $140,000 on renovations—but he made the most of the chaos, bringing in subcontractors to install new fixtures, repaint, and clean all the carpets and marble surfaces. His collection of antiques had continued to grow over the years; he had recently added a carved chess set, which he intermingled with an ancient imperial Roman perfume bottle, a carved Egyptian cat dating back to 500 B.C., and a two-thousand-year-old grinning terracotta pig from Syria. On one wall, a brass elevator door from Selfridge's department store in London hung alongside a Mystic cloak from *The Dark Crystal*. Comfortable and quirky, the apartment would always be a warm and welcoming place.

That December, Jim couldn't resist throwing one more of his large, elaborate Christmas parties for his staff. Jim was notably relaxed, perhaps appreciating this would be the last Christmas party he would host before the company's absorption into Disney. But in the throes of his Christmas cheer and benevolence, he made a regrettable error, and informed a few partygoers of the existence of The List and—even more critically—exactly how much money he would be giving them when the Disney deal finally went through. "It was like he was Santa for the night," recalled Mary Ann, but not everyone took the news with the gratitude Jim expected. Some grumbled they should have received more; others were miffed when they learned of the amounts others would receive compared to their own. Jim was stunned by the reaction. "It was a little bit heartbreaking," said Lisa Henson, "because he was giving money from the bottom of his heart."

Christmas itself, however, was a much happier affair, as Jim spent several days with Lisa, John, Heather, and Mary Ann at Walt Disney World. Each morning, Jim and the kids would dive eagerly into the parks, enjoying the rides but taking the time to savor the small things—the hedges clipped to resemble Disney characters, the inside jokes etched in the windows overlooking Main Street—that made up "the Disney experience." "My dad liked *everything*," said Heather, "the atmosphere, walking around . . . he was so in awe." He loved the parks, and was looking forward "to having his characters be so alive and well maintained" as the other iconic characters in the parks. On Christmas Day, Jim participated in his first Disney Christmas Parade, singing "Sleigh Ride" with Kermit from the top of a float, and then diving into the crowd with Kermit in his reporter outfit to interview parade watchers for television. John Henson remembered his father being truly happy that day. "I gave him a bottle of white zinfandel wine [as a Christmas gift,] and he was just so appreciative of it. He was so thankful." It would be Jim's last Christmas.

In the second week of January 1990, Jim began production on the Muppet 3-D film—to be called *Muppet*Vision 3D*—shooting the majority of the movie on the gigantic Stage 3 at Disney Studios in California, where 20,000 *Leagues Under the Sea* had been filmed thirty-six years earlier. "He was more relaxed in a lot of ways," said Muppet performer Jerry Nelson. "I think it was because he thought he had found the solution to not having to chase the money . . . that he would just have these projects and be able to create stuff." And yet, said Nelson, the more he talked with Jim about the details of the deal, the more he worried it wouldn't be everything Jim wanted it to be. Jim was growing more concerned, for example, that his production company, regardless of its structure, would be anything but independent once it was under the Disney umbrella. "I think they would not have let him just do projects as he wanted," said Nelson. "I think their production people would've just gotten in the way of all of it. . . . It would not have been a company that Jim was running."

Jim's larger concern, however, was still for his performers. There had been no resolution on whether Jim would be permitted to participate in the selection and training of puppeteers, or whether his performers would be seamlessly transferred over to Disney. "I don't think they understood it took Jim years to get a single puppeteer up to speed," said Joan Cooney. Jim was growing particularly irritated with Katzenberg, who he found condescending toward the puppeteers and contemptuous of the art of puppetry. Even inside the Disney organization, Katzenberg was famously haughty and combative; Roy Disney—Walt's nephew and vice chairman of the company—found him rude, arrogant, and dismissive of the concerns of artists. In 1987, *The Wall Street Journal,* with grudging admiration, described Kaztzenberg as "the most brutal, the stingiest, most compulsive—and possibly the best—deal maker in town." Such a style may have gotten results, but "that's not the way Jim operated," said Lazer, who spent countless evenings on the phone with Jim, trying to smooth things over after one of Jim's encounters with the abrasive Katzenberg. "Many times, the deal was off," said Lazer, "and I brought it back to life again." Lazer's advice: talk with Eisner. "Every time he would go see Eisner, it got better," said Lazer. "Eisner made it better."

Still, even Jim's relationship with Eisner could get prickly from time to time. The point of contention was usually the same: *Sesame Street.* Jim had continued to assure Joan Cooney that Disney wouldn't acquire the *Sesame Street* Muppets in the deal, and had even personally informed Eisner that pursuing such a negotiation would be "a non-starter." During one lunch meeting with Cooney and Eisner, however, Jim became visibly annoyed when Eisner even *mentioned* the words *Sesame Street.* "There you go again," said Jim curtly. Eisner let the matter drop.

Also rocky was Jim's relationship with Mary Ann. The two of them had been together almost constantly since Christmas, and in mid-January they were staying in Jim's house in Malibu while Jim worked on *Muppet*Vision 3D*. With his regular team of performers all in one place again, Jim threw a party at the house, beaming happily as he moved comfortably among friends—including a number of women, noted Mary Ann, who seemed to know their way around Jim's kitchen. "I felt like the writing was on the wall," said Mary Ann.

Shortly thereafter, Mary Ann returned to New Mexico. Jim didn't try to follow. "After a few weeks, we decided to let go," she recalled, "and he said he would give me the space I needed. It was hard but very loving." Several weeks later, however, Jim went out of his way to bump into her as she left a lunch meeting in Los Angeles, giving her an enormous hug as she waited for a car. If Jim was hoping for reconciliation, he was likely surprised by the cold reception. That evening, Mary Ann angrily called Jim at home, and shouted, "I was five weeks into building my own life again!" There would be no argument, however; Jim simply listened quietly and hung up—then called back the next evening. But her anger was too much for him, and when she finally asked Jim not to call again, he complied. "Later on, I felt badly, because even if you thought you were justified, it was hard to stay mad at Jim," said Mary Ann. "But he understood."

While Jim understood, it was painful for him *not* to be in a relationship—especially as he looked around him as his children and co-workers entered into serious relationships or marriages of their own. Lisa, now nearly thirty and a successful film executive, was in a long-term relationship with director Sam Raimi. Cheryl, too, was in a committed relationship, while twenty-six-year-old Brian Henson would soon marry costume designer Ellis Flyte. Frank Oz had been married since 1979 and was raising children, while several Muppet office romances had bloomed into matrimony: besides Brian Froud's marriage to Wendy Midener, creative director Mike Frith had married performer Kathy Mullen. It made Jim feel lonely and old—and he sometimes wondered aloud if he would ever truly be in love again.

And then there was Jane. Despite their differences, "they were always very civil except when they weren't," reported Brian Henson. Jim trusted her to deliver an honest opinion, and the two of them would go to lunch or dinner regularly, where they would talk about the children and the company. More often now, Jim would lay out the details of the Disney discussions and ask her opinion. Jane would listen patiently, offering advice only when asked. She understood his frustration with Katzenberg. "Jim didn't really want to work with somebody who had no respect for what he did," said Jane. But she also knew Jim wanted the deal to work out. "He could see the possibilities of what could be done if he could be part of that big company."

If Katzenberg was giving Jim headaches, he was nothing compared with Roald Dahl, who was positively fuming over *The Witches*, finally released in the middle of February 1990. Things had been quiet over the past few months while the film went into postproduction and final editing; but Dahl had finally seen the completed movie with an audience, and was "appalled" at what he considered "the vulgarity, the bad taste and the actual terror displayed in certain parts of the film." Dahl fired off an angry letter to Duncan Kenworthy (since "Jim . . . does not seem to answer any of my letters" he complained) and demanded that his name, and the name of the book, be removed from the credits of the final film. If Jim refused to comply with this request, warned Dahl, "then I shall obviously have to do my best with press conferences, etc. to ensure that children don't go and see the film." Kenworthy refused to rise to the bait, merely responding that he was "saddened" to receive Dahl's letter, and noting that the film had played well in test screenings. He assured Dahl that he would pass his letter on to Jim.

Jim responded to Dahl a week later, suitably apologetic, but tactfully ignoring Dahl's threat. "I'm sorry that we didn't stay in closer touch with you through the process of making the film," wrote Jim. "We certainly had our problems, and perhaps you could have helped us through some of the rocky patches to a final product that you would be happier with." Nonetheless, Jim liked the final film, and would stand by it. "It's such a delightful book that you've given us to work with," he told Dahl diplomatically. "I hope you will forgive us for falling short of your expectations." Though he would never be happy with the film, Dahl grudgingly withdrew his threat.

Jim was spending more and more time at the Disney facilities in Orlando now, tending to his corner of the park, examining walkaround Muppet costumes, and recording voice tracks to be used inside of Disney World's elaborate transportation system. As much as he enjoyed the Grand Floridian, he wanted a home of his own in the area, and had recently put in the paperwork to purchase a house overlooking Lake Down in the town of Windermere, an affluent suburb thirty minutes north of Walt Disney World. Jim had so enjoyed decorating his Steamboat Road home in Connecticut with Connie Beale that he hired her to help with his new home as well, flying her to Orlando regularly to shop for furniture and fabrics.

Negotiations with Disney dragged on through the spring, with no end in sight, though there had already been one casualty: Bernie Brillstein. Disney lawyers were insisting that Disney have the exclusive authority to sell and distribute Jim's projects—and that meant Brillstein could no longer serve as Jim's representative. Jim had flown to California to discuss the matter with Brillstein personally, breaking the news to the agent at his home. Brillstein understood. "Everyone who knows the Disney Company knows that they think they're smarter than anyone who was ever born," said Brillstein. But what Jim did next stunned him.

Brillstein's name was at the very top of The List—the first name Jim had written down when assessing who had been vital to his success, and with little wonder: Brillstein had been watching out for Jim—and vice versa—for thirty years. "We've had a great, great time," Jim told Brillstein. "I wanted to tell you myself, because I love you and you deserve it." Jim handed Brillstein a check for $7 million—he promised another $3 million when the deal went through—and offered to pay the agent $500,000 annually in perpetuity to serve as his personal advisor. Brillstein was speechless. "Jesus Christ," he finally croaked as he took the check. "Our bond was the unspoken certainty that we belonged together," said Brillstein later.

Through it all, Jim continued working on *Muppet*Vision 3D*, as well as a live stage show for Disney-MGM called *Here Come the Muppets* and the television special *The Muppets at Walt Disney World*. There were some inside the organization who wondered why Jim would keep doing work for Disney without a formal agreement in place. Duncan Kenworthy thought it was typical not only of Jim's work ethic, but Jim's faith in Eisner. "Jim didn't say, 'We're not going to do anything until the Disney deal is signed,'" recalled Kenworthy. "He said, 'Hey guys, this is about relationships.' Besides, he couldn't sit on his hands for eight months. He just pitched in."

It wasn't just Disney getting work out of him; Jim was still actively pursuing and promoting projects for Henson Associates and the Creature Shop, most of which he would own as part of his production company once the agreement was complete. In early March, Jim began meeting with Henson Associates staff about a second series of *Storyteller* episodes based on Greek myths, and put the final touches on a family special called *Living with Dinosaurs*, about an asthmatic boy with a talking stuffed dinosaur, that had been intended as an installment of *The Jim Henson Hour*. By the end of the month, he was out promoting *Teenage Mutant Ninja Turtles*, which opened strongly on March 30 and earned rave reviews for the Creature Shop's expressive turtle costumes.

Jim was spending so much time at his California production company, in fact, that he had decided to purchase the Malibu house he had been renting for the past year. He now had homes in Malibu, Florida, New York, Connecticut, and London—"one home per child," he joked. The place in Malibu was particularly good for Jim—tucked up on the bluffs near Nicholas Canyon Beach, far removed from the bustle of Burbank, with no other homes around, it seemed, at times, to be in the middle of nowhere. He had recently taken up yoga, and in the mornings he would set up his yoga mat on the rear deck and go through his sun salutation poses as he looked out over the Pacific Ocean. "It just made him so happy," said Cheryl. Other times, he would simply sit quietly as he watched the ocean stretch out toward the horizon—"just a few minutes in meditation and prayer each morning," he said. "I find that this really helps me to start the day with a good frame of reference. As part of my prayers, I thank whoever is helping me—I'm sure somebody or something is—I express gratitude for all my blessings and I try to forgive the people that I'm feeling negative toward. I try hard not to judge anyone, and I try to bless everyone who is part of my life, particularly anyone with whom I am having any problems."

That spring, Jim made the short flight from Burbank up to Sacramento, then drove up the coastline to visit Jerry Juhl at his home a hundred miles north of San Francisco. The two walked and talked among the giant redwoods for a while, then returned to Juhl's home office to discuss *The Cheapest Muppet Movie Ever Made,* which Jim was still determined to make once the Disney deal was complete. It was a project the two of them loved to talk about—and Jim would spread the storyboards out on the floor of Juhl's office where, in no time, the two of them would be giggling uncontrollably as they tossed around one idea after another. "I thought he was more relaxed and happier, sort of more content with what was happening than I'd seen him in a long time," said Juhl. "Really happy."

Lazer thought so, too. In April, he briefly joined Jim down at Disney-MGM, where Jim excitedly described a new attraction he wanted to build: a fully operational television studio in which park visitors could watch the Muppet performers at work on whatever production happened to be under way at the time. As he showed Lazer around the rest of the Muppet area—making big sweeping motions with his hands as he pointed out where the Great Muppet Ride would be or where he wanted to set up the Great Gonzo's Pandemonium Pizza Parlor—Lazer thought that "Jim was never happier in his life. . . . Anything he wanted to do, he could do," said Lazer. "I never saw this friend of mine so happy."

By the end of April, then, Jim was determined to get the Disney deal done. There was still the major issue of the status of the Muppet performers to resolve—the big question was whether Disney would buy out any performers it *didn't* put on its own payroll—but Jim was getting tired of the haggling. "Disney focused on *everything,*" said one Henson insider. "You'd have to call Michael Eisner and say, 'This is where it's gone with your zealous robots.' Every single issue was pushed as a deal point by Disney. As opposed to focusing on the big points, they focused on everything." It was a war of attrition, and no detail was too minute. Even the small service elevator at One Seventeen had drawn fire from the Disney lawyers, who pounded away at Jim's legal team for weeks, arguing over elevator permits and inspection records. Henson Associates attorney Peter Schube still grimaced at the negotiations even twenty years later. "[Henson Associates] was extremely solid," said Schube. "We had been well served by the very best outside lawyers, particularly in the field of copyright and trademark, for as long as there had been a company. But we were a closely held, nonpublic company, operating out of a brownstone. There's always something that can be ginned up if an army of Disney lawyers is charged with finding things." As one Muppet writer put it, "Disney is a corporate entity and Jim and the Muppets have a very fuzzy, Grateful Dead kind of sensibility." It was that underlying difference in corporate personalities, said Schube, "that drew the process out, and created frustration on both sides. They had a way of doing things that were meaningful to them. Jim had a goal that was meaningful to him—but Disney's way of doing things sort of pushed that goal further and further out."

Lazer was still arguing that, even at $150 million, Disney was getting Jim too cheaply. Some even thought that Jim was willing to let an unfavorable deal move forward simply so he could place the Muppets safely in the hands of Disney—and then, once his fifteen-year exclusive obligation expired, he would leave the Muppets behind and move on to something completely different. "Of all the people in the world, Jim could actually probably do that," said Larry Mirkin, "because he would just say, 'You know, let's do something new.'"

"That goddamned deal!" Jim was now calling it, using an expletive so rare, said Michael Frith, that "I'll never forget my surprise and, frankly, shock when he said it. . . . It came from a place of *deep* hurt and frustration." It saddened Jim, recalled Jane, when "things just didn't work out between people or projects . . . he never really knew how to deal with [that disappointment] because, in some ways, he didn't allow himself *not* to be an optimist." But Jim had given Eisner his word—and he was confident he and Eisner could work things out.

"Don't worry," he told Brillstein, reminding the agent that there was still something bigger than merely legal negotiations holding the deal together: "My handshake."

CHAPTER SIXTEEN

JUST ONE PERSON

1990

ON FRIDAY, APRIL 27, 1990—A LONG DAY THAT BEGAN WITH A 5:30 A.M. taping of the *Today* show—Jim left for Orlando to spend several days filming Disney commercials with the Muppet team. Negotiations between Disney and Henson Associates continued even as Jim worked, and on May 1 he met with Lazer, Martin Baker, and planning director Charles Rivkin over dinner at the Grand Floridian—a meeting serious enough that they resumed it over breakfast the next morning. Jim would be leaving Orlando for Los Angeles later that afternoon—but when he returned to New York in a week, he wanted to get everything in order to close the deal.

"He was ready," said Brillstein. In fact, Jim had already called the agent and told him he wanted to plan on setting aside a few days to go on a yacht trip "with the boys." "We're gonna celebrate the Disney deal," he told Brillstein excitedly. "Pick people who are fun!"

Late in the afternoon of Friday, May 4, Jim met Kevin Clash and Arthur Novell at Paramount Studios in Hollywood to tape an appearance on *The Arsenio Hall Show*. Jim wasn't feeling well; somewhere along the way, he had picked up what he thought was a trace of a cold, perhaps even a mild case of strep throat, admitting to Novell that he was tired and his throat was slightly sore. "He insisted it would go away," said Novell—as Clash remembered, he said "it wasn't anything extreme"—and Jim ambled out onstage that evening in gray slacks and a colorful sweater, his hair newly trimmed, grinning happily. But things were clearly off. Placing Kermit on his arm, he bantered with Hall about the Kermit–Miss Piggy relationship, struggling at times to come up with a clever retort. With his voice somewhat thicker than normal, Jim so noticeably stumbled over his own ad-libbed punch lines that even Hall joked about Kermit's faltering speech. "I would've said I had a frog in my throat," Kermit responded a bit lamely, "but I won't say that." Following a commercial break, Clash came on to perform his hip Muppet musician Clifford, sparring nimbly with Hall for the final five minutes. Jim sank back into the couch, legs crossed, quietly stroking his beard.

At dinner afterward, Jim thanked Clash for helping make the appearance a success. "It was funny how much he was disappointed by his performance," said Clash. "He loved what I did with Clifford but he wasn't happy with what he did—and I think that had to do with him not feeling really good." Later that evening, Jim was scheduled to sit for an interview with Tom Snyder for ABC Radio. Novell, concerned about Jim's sore throat, offered to bring some antibiotics he had in a suitcase in the back of their town car. "No, leave it," Jim told Novell. "I'll be okay."

Contrary to rumors that persisted long after Jim's death, Jim's Christian Science upbringing had *not* given him a lifelong aversion to doctors or medication. Although Jim always respected the Christian Science point of view, he had long abandoned its practices as a way of life. "I think it's not particularly necessary to lead a religious life," he once wrote. "People progress just as well in music, or art, or math or science or gardening or whatever. It all seems to work as well and the process is good." While Jim rarely took anything stronger than aspirin or Advil, the truth was that he rarely went to doctors—or rarely took medication—because Jim rarely got sick. "Jim was very stubborn about sickness," said Alex Rockwell. "He basically didn't tolerate it." And, said Rockwell sincerely, "his schedule didn't allow for it."

"He was always quite robust and healthy," said Brian Henson, a contention supported by nearly everyone who worked closely with him. "He just wasn't an unhealthy guy," said Steve Whitmire. "He was happy and he was healthy." So healthy, in fact, that anytime Jim came down with *anything*—especially if it was serious enough to disrupt his work schedule—he made a note of it in his private journal, writing "I get the flu," over five days in February 1985 or, more seriously, "Went to Washington for holiday; Got pneumonia upon return," in early 1968. But illness for Jim was atypical— and when he did get sick, he preferred to simply weather the storm, recovering quietly at home, without a fuss, and dosing himself with aspirin and his favorite comfort foods, usually tomato soup and peanut butter sandwiches. There was nothing unusual or sinister, then, in his refusal of Novell's offer of antibiotics. "Typical Jim," said Novell with a sigh two decades later. "Very much so."

Jim remained in California for several more days, staying at the house in Malibu, before finally heading back to New York on Tuesday, May 8. He was feeling better—and on his way to the Los Angeles airport, he stopped in to see Bernie Brillstein, whose father had passed away a week earlier. Jim hadn't been able to attend the funeral, and wanted to offer his condolences. Jim wrapped Brillstein in one of his big hugs. "I love you," he told the agent. "I'll see you when I get back." He was going to North Carolina to visit his dad and Bobby, he said—he was especially determined to see his father, who was in the early stages of Alzheimer's disease—but then he was returning to Los Angeles to see Eisner and sign the deal. "I don't give a shit what happens," Jim laughed, using another rare epithet. "We'll sell it!" On his way out the door, Jim casually asked Brillstein's receptionist out for a date. Then, with a wave goodbye, he was gone.

May 9 was always an important date for Jim. In 1955, it had been the day *Sam and Friends* had debuted in Washington—and since then, it had served as a kind of unofficial birthday for both Kermit the Frog and the Muppets. More important, however, it was also Lisa Henson's birthday—and today, as she turned thirty, Warner Brothers announced that she had been promoted to executive vice president. Jim was so proud. He sent flowers.

On the morning of Saturday, May 12, after two days of seemingly nonstop meetings at One Seventeen, Jim and Cheryl boarded a USAir flight at LaGuardia Airport, and touched down in Norfolk, Virginia, a little after 10:00 A.M. Jim wasn't feeling well again; while he didn't have a fever, his throat was still sore, his nose was running, and he had picked up a slight cough. "It seemed like a cold or flu," said Cheryl. But he felt well enough to carry his own bags and drove their rental car the seventy miles south from Norfolk to rural Ahoskie, North Carolina, where they checked into a motel near Paul and Bobby's home.

Jim and Cheryl spent the rest of Saturday with Paul and Bobby, playing croquet on the lawn, sipping tea with lots of ice, and chatting casually in the kitchen. "This was a place where Jim was always at home, embraced with love and easy companionship," said Cheryl. After dinner, Jim—along with an assortment of cousins and extended family—retired to the Hensons' screened-in "secret porch," watching the sun go down as they swapped stories and swayed silently in gliders or creaked in rocking chairs. "We just laughed and had a wonderful time," said Bobby. Jim was "a little sniffly," she recalled, but would never say he was sick. Rather, he said he "just didn't feel good"—which was more than anyone had ever heard him complain about his health.

Sunday morning, however, Jim said he felt worse, and went back to bed in his motel room, sleeping in until nearly lunchtime. Around noon, his cousin Stan Jenkins came to pick up Jim and Cheryl to drive them back out to Paul and Bobby's for lunch. Jim mentioned during the short car ride that he still wasn't feeling well and had taken Advil—and Stan, a physician, advised Jim to see a doctor the moment he was back in New York (it would later be incorrectly and unfairly reported that Stan had examined Jim and missed the warning signs of pneumonia, an accusation that haunted Stan for years). Jim tried to eat, but had little appetite. His cough had worsened, sometimes rasping so violently that he coughed blood—something he disclosed to no one at the time, preferring not to worry his family. By late afternoon, Jim shakily mentioned that he might try to catch an earlier flight back to New York. There were other factors to consider, too; beginning at ten the next morning he was scheduled to spend all day in a recording session for a Disney show, and wanted to make sure he, and his voice, were rested enough. Bobby, who thought Jim "looked kind of bad," told him to go. "Nobody knew that Jim was that ill," Bobby said. "I knew he'd been tired. I chalked it up to that."

What no one suspected was that Jim was in the early stages of pneumonia brought on by a rare group A streptococcal bacterial infection—an infection that may possibly have invaded Jim's system as he struggled with the mild case of strep throat during his *Arsenio Hall* appearance in early May. The question of how and why such a rare and terrible infection should strike an otherwise healthy, robust person remains one of the great, unjust mysteries of Jim Henson's life. All that is known for certain is that as he left Paul and Bobby's that afternoon, the streptococcal bacteria were already slowly spreading through Jim's lungs and organs.

Jim and Cheryl drove back to Norfolk, where they were able to swap their 9:45 P.M. flight for an earlier one, and arrived back at LaGuardia early Sunday evening. "He was really tired," said Cheryl. As they walked through the airport, Jim cleared his throat and tested his voice in anticipation of the recording session the next morning, repeating, "Hi, ho, Kermit the Frog here!" several times, trying to shake the same thickness that had fogged his voice on *Arsenio Hall* a week earlier. A car service drove both Jim and Cheryl home, dropping Jim off at the Sherry-Netherland first. As

Jim climbed out of the car, he told Cheryl he was going straight to bed.

Only he didn't. John had been staying with him at the Sherry-Netherland for some time—it was John, in fact, who was helping Jim train Disney performers to play the role of Sweetums for the *Muppet*Vision 3D* show—and when Jim came in the door, John was racing around the apartment, experimenting with a small Steadycam. Always the gadget junkie, Jim couldn't resist taking the camera, and went whizzing around the apartment with it until his knees suddenly buckled. John took the camera away and led his father to the bedroom. "Dad, you're sick," John said. "Sick people lie in bed. They don't run around trying Steadycams. Go lie in bed." Jim finally crawled into bed, and John sat down next to him, rubbing his back, until Jim fell asleep.

Jim awoke on Monday morning "feel[ing] lousy"; his voice was wrecked, and he was starting to have trouble catching his breath, both symptoms of the bacterial pneumonia that was now rapidly eating away at his lungs. Jim called his assistant, Anne Kinney, and asked her to cancel not only his 8:30 breakfast meeting, but also the all-day recording session for the *Muppets on Location* that was starting at ten. "This was big news," said Kinney; Jim had never missed a recording session before, much less canceled one. Jim may have had a whim of steel, but to the Muppet performers, he was also their iron man, never absent. "No one could remember Jim ever calling in sick," said Dave Goelz. Kinney stopped in later that morning to check on Jim and deliver some soup; at the same time, Jane called the apartment and spoke briefly with him. She had been upset with Jim about something the night before, and had called Cheryl, looking for him so they could discuss it—but Cheryl had informed her that Jim was sick in his apartment, trying to sleep, and advised her to wait until morning to call him. Now, as she spoke on the phone with Jim, Jane became concerned. "He said he'd had a very rough night," recalled Jane.

Late in the afternoon, Jane dropped by Jim's apartment to check on him, bringing along a pot of chicken soup. Jim had just gotten out of a warm bath and was getting ready to go back to bed—anything, he told Jane, to stop his heart from beating so fast. "I probably should have realized how serious that was, and he should have, too," said Jane—but Jim insisted he merely needed to sleep. "Do you want me to stay?" Jane asked quietly. Jim nodded. "I wish that you would."

Jane firmly shooed John out of the apartment—"she basically kicked me out"—and put Jim to bed. But he couldn't sleep; in addition to his rapid heartbeat, he was coughing violently and having difficulty catching his breath. Jane sat with him, speaking to him quietly and trying to get him to relax. Toward evening, Cheryl stopped in with more soup ("*Everyone* was coming in trying to give him chicken soup," said Jane). Cheryl thought her father looked terrible, and considered staying the night—but Jane had already sent John away, and was insisting that she "did not want anyone else around." Cheryl lingered for a while, but eventually complied with Jane's wishes and went back to her apartment, where she called Lisa in California. "I'm really worried," she told her older sister.

Over the next few hours, Jane settled into Jim's guest bedroom, but spent most of the night making tea and sitting with Jim in his bedroom as he sipped it delicately. "We just talked," said Jane. "There was no discussion of broken marriage or anything like that. We were just there together." None of the Henson children was surprised Jim had asked Jane to stay with him. "He and Mom were always just really fond of each other," said Brian Henson. Agreed Cheryl, "she was his best friend for so much of his life. He loved her and wanted her to be happy. He just couldn't make her happy himself. . . . Of course it is complicated; life is."

Around 2:00 A.M., Jim's breathing became more labored; it hurt his abdomen to cough, and with each raspy bark he was coughing blood. Jane had finally had enough, and insisted on calling a doctor, but Jim refused. "Just rub my back," he said, rolling over onto his stomach. "Try to calm down my breathing." As Jane massaged Jim's back, he laughed weakly. "Maybe I'm dying," he said darkly. But by 4:00 A.M., even Jim could no longer joke about his condition: his heart was racing, and he was struggling for breath. "Okay," he finally told Jane. "I'll go to the hospital"—but he made the request grudgingly. "He really didn't want anyone else to be disturbed by his pain," said Jane.

However, now that Jim was ready to go to the hospital, Jane suddenly didn't know what to do. "We really didn't know anything *about* hospitals," she said later, almost apologetically. Jim suggested she call the reliable—and discreet—Arthur Novell, who was managing a press event out in San Francisco that evening. While Novell never considered himself to be Jim's "fixer," Jim held him in high regard as a confidant whom he could trust implicitly. "In every family," said Anne Kinney wryly, "there are some people that can *manage* things." Additionally, Novell knew his way around New York and its operations with a savvy that rivaled any cabdriver or politician. If there were anyone in the Henson organization who could get Jim to a hospital quickly and quietly—even all the way from San Francisco—it was Novell. Jane made the call.

It was just after 1:00 A.M. in San Francisco when the phone rang in Novell's hotel suite. "I'm here with Jim at the apartment," Jane blurted out immediately.

"Is everything all right?" asked Novell.

"No," said Jane. "Here's Jim."

Jim came to the phone, breathing heavily. "I'm very sick," he said quietly.

The normally unflappable Novell felt the ground drop out from underneath him. "It was so out of character for him to even utter those words," he said. Novell ran through several quick potential courses of action in his head, then told Jim he would make some phone calls. "Jim, it'll be okay. I love you," Novell assured him.

Jim thickly murmured his thanks, then added quietly, "Arthur . . . just look after them for me."

Novell's eyes stung with tears. "In the back of my head," he recalled later, "I said, 'I'm losing Jim.' "

Novell's phone calls produced results almost immediately. A private car was dispatched to meet Jim in front of the Sherry-Netherland. The driver had been instructed to bring along a wheelchair to carry Jim down to the lobby, but Jim—who had gotten fully dressed and cleaned up—insisted on taking the elevator down nineteen floors and walking out to the car himself, even pleasantly waving to the doormen as he crawled into the backseat beside Jane. The car sped for New York Hospital on East 68th Street, less than two miles away, but the driver, unfamiliar with the layout of the hospital, pulled up at the main entrance, instead of the emergency entrance tucked between two buildings around the corner. "We'll just get out here," Jim said—"Jim never wanted to put anybody out," said Novell—and walked the half block to the emergency room where he slumped into a chair. As he was whisked away into the examination room, he raised a hand and waved weakly to Jane. "See you later," he croaked, trying to smile. "I feel like I'm in good hands." He was formally admitted into New York Hospital at 4:58 A.M., the morning of Tuesday, May 15.

At the time of his admission to New York Hospital, Jim's blood pressure was normal and he wasn't running a fever—but his heartbeat was irregular, and preliminary blood tests showed his kidneys were failing rapidly. At 6:00 A.M., Jane called Cheryl, who arrived to find Jim on a gurney with an oxygen mask strapped to his face, and held his hand as he waited to be examined by a team of critical care specialists. By 6:30, specialists had determined Jim was suffering from severe pneumonia and kidney failure and recommended he be moved immediately to the Intensive Care Unit. Shortly thereafter, he slipped into unconsciousness.

By 8:00 A.M., Jim could only breathe with the assistance of a breathing tube; by 10:00, doctors noted that he was not responding to any stimulation at all—"no movement, no response," except to "deep pain." The antibiotics being pumped into his system had little effect. In the five hours since entering the hospital, Jim's body had almost completely shut down. He would never regain consciousness.

At One Seventeen, phones had been ringing all morning. Cheryl had phoned both Anne Kinney and David Lazer to let them know of Jim's condition, and Lazer had sped from Long Island to the hospital, where he went into executive mode, briskly making phone calls from the pay phone outside Jim's room and displaying the calm that had made him *The Muppet Show*'s prince regent. The first call was to Bernie Brillstein, waking the agent up in California to let him know what had happened. "I'm here at New York Hospital," Lazer told Brillstein. "Jim just came in. I just came here. He may not make it."

Brillstein was stunned. "You're kidding."

It fell to Anne Kinney, manning the phones at her desk outside Jim's third-floor office at One Seventeen, to pass the word on to employees and the Muppet performers throughout the day—and their responses were much the same as Brillstein's. "I couldn't believe it," said Dave Goelz. "Jim was so vital and indestructible." "I lost it. I pretty much cried myself to sleep," said Kevin Clash, who was so stunned he nearly wandered away from his apartment without wearing shoes. Steve Whitmire, notified in Atlanta by Frank Oz, found it "hard to even hear it." Oz himself was typically blunt: "God, it was awful."

And it *was* awful. Around noon, when physicians inserted a feeding tube into Jim's stomach, a massive amount of blood was extracted, indicating that Jim was bleeding severely in his stomach and intestines. Then, at 12:55 P.M., he went into cardiac arrest. "It happened insanely fast," said John Henson, who had walked to the hospital from One Seventeen. Doctors were able to revive him, but "they were saying he'd be a vegetable," said John. "I went back to [One Seventeen] and just stared at the wall. I couldn't believe it was happening."

Throughout the late afternoon and evening, family and a few close friends came to stand vigil outside Jim's room. After Jane, Cheryl, John, and David Lazer, Lisa, who had the farthest to go, was actually the next to arrive, having taken the first available flight from Los Angeles. All she could think about during her flight, she said later, was "that he would want to see his grandchildren. I kept repeating, 'you want to see your grandchildren, you want to see your grandchildren,' like a mantra. . . . But I never even spoke to him. He was already unconscious and on life support by the time I got to see him." The flowers Jim had sent to celebrate her promotion were still fresh and colorful on her desk at Warner Brothers.

Heather, attending school at the Rhode Island School of Design, was making her way down from Providence and would arrive late in the evening. Brian, meanwhile, had been in England working—and despite scrambling to make arrangements to get to New York as soon as possible, he would arrive too late to see his father alive. Frank Oz had also come to camp in the hospital, as had Jerry Nelson, Michael Frith, and Kathy Mullen. Steve Whitmire and his wife, Melissa, who had taken the last flight from Atlanta that evening, would arrive shortly after midnight. All of them took turns sitting by Jim's bed, holding his hand and talking to him.

Around 11:00 P.M., Jim's condition worsened. His blood pressure plunged, requiring physicians to administer CPR. He then went into full cardiac arrest—his second heart attack in ten hours—though doctors managed to revive him yet again. His chest tube was replaced with a larger one, and a second tube was inserted in his left side to increase the drainage from his lungs. With his breathing dangerously weak, he was placed on a jet ventilator to increase his oxygen intake.

Finally, just after 1:00 on Wednesday morning, Jim's blood pressure bottomed out; his heart had stopped beating. A medical team rushed to his bedside to administer CPR and inserted a chest tube, which immediately gushed enormous amounts of blood and fluid, indicating massive hemorrhaging in his chest and lungs. Doctors continued applying CPR without success, then used a defibrillator to try to shock his heart into starting. Jim's body tensed, then sagged; the charge to the defibrillator was increased and tried again, three more times. Jim jerked sharply each time; more blood and fluid erupted through the tubes in his chest. Then he slumped back, and went limp.

Jim Henson died at 1:21 A.M. on Wednesday, May 16, 1990. He was fifty-three years old.

The official cause of death was septic shock due to group A streptococcus. Jim's organs, particularly his lungs, were so infiltrated with toxin-spewing bacteria that his internal systems had collapsed. Physicians later speculated that had Jim checked into the hospital on Monday morning, perhaps even at the time he first noticed his heart beating too fast, the antibiotics might have saved him—or, perhaps not. In many cases, the toxins produced by streptococcus are so powerful that they begin deteriorating organs and tissue before patients show any outward sign of sickness. Doctors later determined that even at the time Jim checked into the hospital, an "overwhelming infection" had been coursing throughout his body for at least three days. "There had already been extensive damage done," said Dr. David M. Gelmont, who had been the attending physician. "It just raced quickly through his body."

The Henson family was summoned by doctors, who gently broke the news, then escorted the family into the room to see him. Jim "was so bloated, he didn't even look like himself," said Jane. John lay across his father's body and hugged him. "I love you, Daddy," he whispered, then left the room, sobbing uncontrollably. Heather, the last of the Henson children to arrive—and who "had wanted *so* much for Jim to get through it," said Jane lovingly—was steered gently to Jim's bedside by Jane, who put her mouth close to Heather's ear. "Let him go," Jane said softly. "Just say goodbye and let him go."

Out in the waiting area, Oz quietly informed the others of what had happened, then he and Lazer disappeared to start making phone calls. It was hard to even cry, remembered Steve Whitmire. "A few tears were around," he said, "but everyone was just stunned. We just couldn't believe this had happened." Jerry Nelson sat and tried to console John, who was staring at the carpet, crying and gasping uncontrollably. "He was really devastated," said Nelson. "All the kids were."

All night long and into the morning, word spread through the Henson organization. Kevin Clash remembered receiving a call at 5:00 A.M. giving him the news. Dave Goelz, who caught a plane from California after learning Jim was ill, called the hospital during his layover in Chicago. "A custodian answered," said Goelz. "He said no one was around. That's when I knew Jim had died." *Sesame Street* performer Fran Brill heard the news that morning from a casting director as she waited her turn to audition for a voice-over. "My heart stopped," she said.

By daybreak, performers and employees began trickling into the offices at One Seventeen. "I remember growing up, when there's a loss everybody comes to the house and you eat and you just stay around," said Clash. "The offices became a house. . . . I remember . . . doing nothing else but going over to [One Seventeen] and staying there until the afternoon or early evening and then going home—and doing that for five days. We couldn't do anything else." By late morning, every space at One Seventeen was packed with friends, colleagues, and co-workers, most of whom could do little more than try to comfort one another, hugging each other and dabbing their eyes with tissues as Muppets stared lifelessly from tables in the workshop. Jim's third-floor office, however, sat respectfully empty. "Everybody was walking wounded," said Cheryl later. "Everyone felt so close to my dad . . . everyone had a very intense, personal relationship with my father." Later, a hand-drawn card was placed on the grand piano in the townhouse's main library, a sympathy card from the Imagineers at Disney, who had loved playing in Jim's world as much as he had in theirs. On the front, a despondent Kermit the Frog sat on a log in front of a blazing sunset, a discarded banjo behind him, his head in his hands; next to him sat Mickey Mouse, with a consoling arm draped around Kermit's shoulders. No words were needed.

The Henson family had retreated to Jim's apartment—dazed, shocked, and trying to rest. Several lawyers from the Henson's legal team knocked on the apartment door, wanting to discuss the impact of Jim's death on the still unsigned Disney deal—an expected, though ill-timed, interruption that the recently arrived Brian Henson dealt with by listening patiently and intently as the lawyers explained their concerns. "We were thrown into having to deal with the legal complexity before we had time to breathe much less mourn," remembered Cheryl. "It was all devastating . . . [but Brian] was relatively clearheaded, and together with Lisa dedicated themselves to figuring it out." The attorneys had one other bit of business to conduct as well, handing over a sealed envelope from the law firm of Kleinberg, Kaplan, Wolff & Cohen. There were no legal documents inside, only two letters addressed to the Henson children.

They were from Jim.

Dated March 2, 1986, they were letters he had written during a quick weekend visit to France while mixing audio for *Labyrinth*—the same weekend, in fact, when he had written the buoyant *Muppet Voyager* proposal for IBM Europe. Jim had filed the letters with his personal attorneys, and asked that they be delivered to his children in the event of his death. Now, suddenly—remarkably—in the middle of sadness and chaos, it seemed Jim was there again, calmly taking charge. "Today I am sitting here in the lovely room of La Colombe d'Or in St. Paul de Vence," Jim had written, "with lovely thoughts about life . . . and thinking I should write this note sometime . . . also of death":

> *I'm not at all afraid of the thought of death, and in many ways, look forward to it with much curiosity and interest. I'm looking forward to meeting up with some of my friends who've gone on ahead of me, and I'll be waiting there to say hi to those of you [who] are still back [here].*
>
> *Since I consider death a rather joyous step forward into the next stage of things, I'd like to lay out a few thoughts as to what might happen when I leave this place.*
>
> *I suggest you first have a nice, friendly little service of some kind, hopefully using the talents of some of the good people who have worked with me over the years. It would be nice if Richard Hunt, if he's still around, would talk and emcee the thing. It would be lovely if some of the people who sing would do a song or two, some of which should be quite happy and joyful. It would be nice if some of my close friends would say a few nice, happy words about how much we enjoyed doing this stuff together—and it would be good to have some religious person read a few quotes by some of the great teachers to remind us how this is all part of what is meant to be.*
>
> *Incidentally, I'd love to have a Dixieland band play at this function and end with a rousing version of "Saints" . . .*
>
> *Have a wonderful time in life, everybody. It feels strange writing this kind of thing while I'm still alive, but it wouldn't be easy to do after I go.*
>
> > *With all my love to you all,*
> > JIM (DAD)
>
> *(P.S. I suppose I should say a word about what happens to my old body. In truth, I don't really care. Hopefully, make as little of it as possible. One way would be to cremate and then*

*distribute the ashes somewhere pleasant. . . . Be sure not to
waste money on an expensive casket or any of that garbage.)*

Suitably directed and inspired by Jim's own words, longtime producer and collaborator Martin Baker went to work coordinating a memorial service, set for Monday, May 21, that would comply with Jim's wishes. The days immediately following Jim's death were "a traumatic period, as you can imagine," said Duncan Kenworthy. "[But] one of the things that kept us all going was the memorial service. . . . We had from Wednesday until Monday to pull it together."

Everyone, it seemed, had an idea for the format and content of the memorial service. "All these people were coming," remembered Jane, "and they all wanted to do things." Planning the memorial, said Kenworthy, "was a wonderful microcosm of *us*. There we were, disagreeing in many ways, having very strong views, trying not to say, 'What would Jim have done?'" Things suddenly fell together when Jane casually suggested that they "just let it happen like a show . . . a 'Jim Show.'" "As soon as it was said that way," said Jane, "then everybody knew what they were doing. Nobody had to wonder what their part was."

The service, a "celebration of Jim Henson's life in song and remembrances," would be open to the public—a fitting decision, but one that was certain to ensure a large crowd. It was decided, then, that the memorial would be held at the Cathedral of St. John the Divine in New York, a soaring Episcopal church on Manhattan's Upper West Side that could hold nearly five thousand. The service would be silly and sad and bright and reassuring—at Jim's direction, no one was to wear black—and Jane and Martin Baker met regularly with eighty-nine-year-old Episcopal bishop Paul Moore to make certain that the church would be comfortable hosting such an unconventional ceremony. "Is this going to be all right in your church?" Jane asked respectfully. The thoughtful, liberal Moore merely smiled warmly. "Oh yes," he told them.

Monday, May 21, dawned dreary and rainy in New York City. As it neared the memorial service's noon starting time, a light drizzle was still falling; the sidewalk outside the cathedral was dotted with puddles that children in yellow rain slickers splashed through as their parents led them up the steps and into the cathedral's enormous nave. As each guest entered, they were handed a long wand—actually a puppeteer's arm rod—with a bright foam butterfly attached at the end, one of the thousands put together by the Muppet Workshop over the last three days.

Inside, photos of Jim and his various creations looked down from the walls and the back of the altar; at Jane's insistence, the cathedral was filled with brightly colored flowers. As expected, the place was packed nearly full—so full, in fact, that many parents sat with their children in the main aisle, their arms wrapped around stuffed Ernies or Big Birds. "I would think all the people who work for me should be invited," Jim had specified in one of his letters, "plus my relatives, friends, lovers, etc." And so they were—Novell took particular delight in seating several of Jim's girlfriends together in the same row—plus so many others. George Lucas sat among the Muppet performers and staff, as did Disney chiefs Frank Wells and Michael Eisner. ("[Eisner] was crushed," said Brillstein, who had flown to New York with the Disney CEO.) Joan Ganz Cooney—who said she had felt "wasted" in the days following Jim's death—sat nearby as well, along with most of the writers and performers from *Sesame Street*.

It was the theme to *Sesame Street,* in fact, that the audience would hear first, followed by "Rainbow Connection," played on the cathedral's enormous pipe organ. The family came in next, trailing behind the Dirty Dozen Brass Band, playing a slow traditional New Orleans dirge—you could take Jim out of the South, but you could never entirely take the South out of Jim. As Jim had requested, Richard Hunt—already showing symptoms of the HIV virus that would take his life less than two years later—acted as an informal emcee, opening the memorial by reading aloud from some of the countless letters that had poured into One Seventeen over the last five days. "That was just amazing," said Kevin Clash. "Letters from a truck driver and a little boy in Ohio or the president. It was amazing . . . just amazing."

There were plenty of other amazing moments over the next two and a half hours. Louise Gold, in the big voice that the Muppet performers loved, sang "Bring Him Home," the song from *Les Misérables* that Jim adored—a feat that still had Fran Brill in awe decades later. "I remember admiring Louise Gold so much for getting up and singing that beautiful song," said Brill, "and thinking, 'How did she do that?'" Gold's serenity also impressed Jerry Nelson as the two of them sang the hymnlike "Where the River Meets the Sea," from *Emmet Otter*. "I remember coming close to breaking on that," said Nelson. "Louise held me together there with it." Harry Belafonte performed "Turn the World Around," the same song he had performed so memorably on *The Muppet Show* more than a decade earlier. As if on cue, the moment Belafonte's song ended, sunlight came streaming in through the big stained-glass windows. Foam butterflies danced and fluttered in the colored light inside the cathedral. There was an audible gasp. It was "a sight I'll never forget," said one audience member.

As Jim had asked, friends said "a few nice, happy words about how much we enjoyed doing this stuff together." Jerry Juhl warmly recalled how "Jim taught us many things: to save the planet, be kind to each other, praise God, and be silly. That's how I'll remember him—as a man who was balanced effortlessly and gracefully between the sacred and the silly." Frank Oz spoke of the joy in making Jim laugh, and of the love and care Jim had put into making and giving him an elaborate Christmas gift. Oz understood "the generosity of [Jim's] time to do this when he was so busy. . . . I think that's when I knew that he loved me and I loved him." Breaking down, Oz left the stage in tears.

After Oz's speech, a lone piano played a long, melodious introduction to "Bein' Green." Then, from the rear of the church, came Caroll Spinney as Big Bird, wearing a Kermit-green bow tie, lumbering slowly up through the audience to the central stage, where he tearfully sang Joe Raposo's heartfelt song. "Somehow," said Spinney later, "I managed to do it without crying." As the final chord faded, Big Bird looked skyward. "Thank you, Kermit," he said. (Brillstein, who was the next speaker, brightened the moment when he ad-libbed, "Jim told me, 'Never follow the Bird!'")

Perhaps predictably, one of the most remarkable moments in-

volved the Muppet performers—Oz, Nelson, Goelz, Hunt, Whitmire, and Clash—singing, hugging, crying, and laughing as they
worked their way through a long medley of some of Jim's favorite
songs. Most were the old vaudeville tunes or the songs of *Pogo* or
A. A. Milne—"Lydia, the Tattooed Lady," "Cottleston Pie," "Halfway Down the Stairs"—that Jim and his family had sung around the
Henson family piano and had eventually found their way into *The
Muppet Show*. The six performers sat on stools, without puppets,
until the very end, when Richard Hunt slid Scooter onto his right
arm and began singing the opening bars of "Just One Person," from
the 1975 musical *Snoopy,* a song the group had first performed on
The Muppet Show in 1977. It was a song Jim loved, with a simple
message that seemed to sum up his own joy in collaboration:

> *If just one person believes in you—*
> *Deep enough, and strong enough, believes in you,*
> *Hard enough, and long enough—*
> *Before you knew it, someone else would think:*
> *"If he can do it, I can do it."*

At the second verse, Hunt was joined by Nelson performing
Gobo, his character from *Fraggle Rock*—then, on the third verse,
with Whitmire, performing Wembley. As the piano swelled into the
final verse, Clash joined with Elmo, and Oz with Fozzie Bear—and
suddenly the stage was full of Muppet performers, standing beneath
a large photograph of Jim as they waved their characters in the air
and sang:

> *And when all those people believe in you—*
> *Deep enough, and strong enough believe in you,*
> *Hard enough and long enough—*
> *It stands to reason you yourself will start to see*
> *What everybody sees in you . . .*
> *And maybe even you*
> *Can believe in you, too.*

Standing amid the sea of her fellow performers, Fran Brill, with
her Prairie Dawn Muppet from *Sesame Street* on her arm, was so
overcome with emotion she could barely perform. "I know I couldn't

sing," she said later. "I think my mouth tried to move, but I was just crying so much I could not sing." It didn't matter; the audience was already on its feet, cheering and crying.

Finally, the Dirty Dozen Brass Band leapt into a rousing performance of "When the Saints Go Marching In"—just as Jim had asked—and "we all marched out of the cathedral smiling, singing, crying," said Caroll Spinney. Jim's "nice, friendly little service" had been, as *Life* magazine put it, "an epic and almost unbearably moving event."

Six weeks later, on July 2, 1990, a similar memorial service was held at St. Paul's Cathedral in London, where *Fraggle Rock* writer Jocelyn Stevenson delivered one of the day's most poignant, elegant, and memorable speeches:

> When Jim left the planet so suddenly, all of us who loved him, worked with him, were inspired by him, gathered in New York City. We were like dandelion seeds clinging to the stem and to each other. And on May 16th, [the day Jim died] the wind began to blow.
>
> There's no stem any more. We're all floating on the breeze. And it's scary and exhilarating, and there's nothing we can do about it. But gradually, we'll all drift to the ground and plant ourselves. And no matter what we grow into, it'll be influenced by Jim. We're Jim's seeds. And it's not only those of us who knew him. Everyone who was touched by his work is a Jim-seed.

Jim was not interred at the Cathedral of St. John the Divine, nor at St. Paul's Cathedral—these were memorials, not funerals. In fact, his body wasn't there at all. Four days after his death, Jim's body—as he had specified—was cremated at Ferncliff Cemetery crematory in Ardsley, New York. (His death certificate, to his likely delight, listed his occupation as "Creator, Producer.") His ashes were stored in an urn and put in the care of John Henson, perhaps the most spiritual or ethereal of the Henson children, who then spent more than a year trying to determine the most appropriate place to scatter the ashes. In one of his letters to the children, Jim had suggested "a pretty river or freshly plowed field or the ocean," adding that "the thought of burial in a pretty place also appeals to me." The more he thought about it, then, the more John thought he finally knew the place.

Several years earlier, Jim and John had been driving near Taos, New Mexico, when Jim had pointed to a small cluster of foothills. "See those hills over there?" he asked John, smiling into the sunlight. "I feel like I'm supposed to live there. I really feel like that's the place I'm supposed to be." "I could never figure out exactly which one [of the foothills] he was talking about," John said later—but then he remembered a bit of advice from his father. "I try to tune myself in to whatever it is that I'm supposed to be," Jim had once written, "and I try to think of myself as a part of all of us—all mankind and all life." John thought if he and the family went out to visit the Taos area again, he might be able to "tune in" to the precise spot Jim had pointed out—that place Jim felt he was "supposed to be." They would scatter the ashes there.

In May 1992, then—exactly two years after Jim's death—John drove his mother and his brother and sisters through a dried-up New Mexico riverbed, scouring the mountains around Taos until he spotted an oddly shaped foothill. "It just looked like a pyramid in the middle of nowhere," remembered John. The family left their SUV and began their journey across the desert toward John's pyramidal foothill, when Jane suddenly sat down on a boulder and declared she had walked far enough. John delicately reached into the urn and handed his mother a handful of Jim's ashes; then the Henson children began the slow ascent up the foothill. (Lisa later joked that she was fairly certain "we hiked up onto somebody's personal property. I would never be able to find it again if my life depended on it.") As they reached the top, John spotted small dark crystals scattered across the ground, glinting blue in the sunlight. "This is it," he said excitedly.

The Henson children took a moment to quietly remember their father—"to make peace with ourselves," said John, "and remember our time with Dad"—then threw his ashes into the warm New Mexico wind, scattering them like the delicate dandelion seeds Jocelyn Stevenson had spoken of at the London memorial service.

Jim Henson's physical body was gone, and yet that powerful

presence—that undefinable *something* that compelled men to seek his appreciation and approval, and that women found somehow irresistible—would always remain. Anyone who had ever smiled as Ernie tried to play a rhyming game with Bert, or laughed as Kermit had chased Fozzie off the stage, arms flailing, had felt it. Anyone who had ever wished they could explore a Fraggle hole, save the world with a crystal shard, or dance with a charismatic goblin king had been touched by it.

It was there now still, in the last words Jim had passed on to his children—the words in the second letter he had written in his hotel room in France that day in 1986. They were words of reassurance for his children, but anyone reading them would be reminded of the power of his presence, and that "ridiculous optimism" that Jim infused in everything he did and in every life he touched. For the last time, then, with his own words ringing happily, almost audibly, from the page, Jim stepped calmly into the center of a hurricane of sadness and uncertainty to assure his children that everything was going to be all right. The presence was still there. Just like Kermit. Just like always:

> First of all, please don't feel bad that I'm gone. While I will miss spending time with each of you, I'm sure it will be an interesting time for me, and I look forward to seeing all of you when you come over. . . .
>
> I feel life has been a joy for me—I certainly hope it is for you. . . . Life is meant to be fun, and joyous, and fulfilling. May each of yours be that—having each of you as a child of mine has certainly been one of the good things in my life. Know that I've always loved each of you with an eternal, bottomless love. A love that has nothing to do with each other, for I feel my love for each of you is total and all-encompassing. This all may sound silly and over the top to you guys, but what the hell, I'm gone and who can argue with me?
>
> . . . To each of you I send my love. If, on this side of life, I'm able to watch over and help you out—know that I will. If I can't, I'm sure I can at least be waiting for you when you come over.

And finally, for his children, and for anyone touched by his life, his work, or his extraordinary imagination—those *Jim-seeds* that Jocelyn Stevenson had spoken of so lovingly—Jim offered a final benediction:

> *Please watch out for each other and love and forgive everybody. It's a good life, enjoy it.*

Love,
JIM

LEGACY

In the end, the Walt Disney Company would end up owning the Muppets—but it would take nearly fifteen years to get them. In the weeks and months following Jim's May 1990 death, negotiations between the two companies intensified—Disney CEO Michael Eisner even vowed to Bernie Brillstein that he was "gonna make this deal go through and happen in memory of Jim"—but discussions, and relations, eroded rapidly. With Jim no longer there to be the "creative vitality" acquired in the deal, Disney went looking for other assets within the Henson organization, and began sniffing around the *Sesame Street* Muppets again. This time, it was the Henson children who held firm; *Sesame Street* was still a nonstarter. Negotiations continued into the winter, but with no resolution. In December 1990, both sides walked away.

Ultimately, what scuttled the agreement was not the fact that Disney was no longer getting Jim in the deal—nor was it because Disney was trying to roll the *Sesame Street* Muppets into the transaction. Rather, it was "death and taxes," related Henson attorney Peter Schube. Jim's death and the subsequent, staggering estate taxes put both sides in such a complicated and untenable position that neither could make the deal work to anyone's benefit. Just as critically, the tone of the discussions—always important to Jim—had become toxic. While there would be a tight-lipped agreement that would allow Disney to complete and retain *Muppet*Vision 3D,* the excitement, the camaraderie Jim relished, was gone. "It finally became a situation where there was not enough joy left in the transaction for anybody," said Schube. "There was no joy left in it for Disney and there was not enough joy left in it for the family."

And so the deal evaporated—and with it The List. Although there were some who grumbled—a few people had even made some expensive purchases in anticipation of the expected windfall—most felt as Bernie Brillstein did: "Believe me," said the agent, "I'd have gladly given up the money to have him back."

The company, and the Muppets, remained in the control of the Henson children for the next decade, while Kermit the Frog was, quite literally, put in the able hands of Muppet veteran Steve Whitmire. With Brian Henson at the helm—joined later by Lisa—The Jim Henson Company, as it would finally come to be called, continued to produce noteworthy Muppet films and specials—many with the help of the Walt Disney Company—and expanded into children's television, but it was becoming "harder and harder for independent companies like ours," said Brian Henson—and in 2000, the company, including its *Sesame Street* assets, was sold to EM.TV & Merchandising, a German media group. Over the next three years, however, EM.TV's stock soured, and by 2003, the Hensons were able to buy their own company back again—minus the *Sesame Street* Muppets, which EM.TV had sold to CTW (now Sesame Workshop), the "natural home for those characters," said Lisa.

Finally, in February 2004, the Muppets were sold to Disney. While The Jim Henson Company would hold on to the Creature Shop, the Fraggles, *Labyrinth,* and *The Dark Crystal,* the Muppets were finally with Disney—just where Jim had wanted them. "We are honored that the Henson family has agreed to pass on to us the stewardship of these cherished assets," said Michael Eisner.

The Muppet legacy was secure—and Jim Henson's own legacy seems to grow with each passing year, as each generation comes to discover—and in some cases rediscover—Jim and his work and claim both as their own. The first generation of children raised with Grover and *Sesame Street* grew up and raised their own children on the same familiar street with the old familiar friends. *The Dark Crystal* and *Labyrinth*—as Jim had known they would all along—found wide and devoted audiences, who savor and appreciate the films with the same adoration and intensity Jim put into making them. And the Muppets themselves—successfully and lovingly returned to the movie screen by Disney in 2011—only continue to grow brighter, more colorful, and more beloved.

Jim Henson's legacy, however, will always be more than merely Muppets. In 1993, Jane Henson founded the nonprofit Jim Henson Legacy, a tribute celebrating Jim's countless contributions to the worlds of puppetry, television, motion pictures, special effects, and media technology. Still, Jim's legacy extends beyond those creative efforts—even beyond the foundation he established to promote the art of puppetry, still running strong today.

Simply, Jim Henson's greatest legacy will always be Jim himself: the way he was, and the way he encouraged and inspired others to be—the simple grace and soft-spoken dignity he brought to the world (and expected, sometimes fruitlessly, of others), as well as his faith in a greater good that he believed he and his fellow inhabitants of the globe were capable of. "Jim inspired people to be better than they thought they could be," said Bernie Brillstein warmly, "and more creative, more daring, more outrageous, and ultimately more successful. And he did it all without raising his voice."

In show business in particular, where so much depends on the ruthless art of the deal, Jim's generosity and genuine respect for talent—as well as that faint aura of Southern gentleman that always seemed to linger about him—made for an unconventional way of doing business. "In this industry, people love you because you have something to give them, and they stop loving you if they feel that they don't have any more they need from you," said *Storyteller* writer Anthony Minghella. "With Jim, there was never any suspicion that his affection was predicated on what he might be able to take from you." Muppet performer Jerry Nelson thought there was a quiet majesty in the way Jim lived and worked. "I see Jim's life as a very Zen kind of thing," said Nelson. "I never heard him say rude or bad things about other people. He lived, I think, by example. To show other people how to be by who you are."

Sometimes, said writer Jerry Juhl, Jim set that example by appreciating life's absurdities. "Jim had a sense of humor that just sorted out life," said Juhl. "And, you know, too much of life for most people is involved in picking what are really fairly petty things and turning them into deep tragedies and horrible melodramas. Jim always cut through that." Even in business, "he could integrate play into the process," said Dave Goelz. "As a parent, one of my goals is to see whether I can raise my children to survive in the world without losing that childlike innocence, trust, optimism, curiosity and decency. I am certain it is possible, because Jim was the living embodiment of it." Indeed, it was that ridiculous optimism—that ability to look at life through a lens that seemed to bring out the brightest colors in nearly everything—that *Sesame Street* performer Fran Brill wanted to emulate in her own life as well. "Even today, many, many years later, if I'm in a difficult position, I say to myself, 'How would Jim have handled this?'" said Brill. "I just felt like if I tried to handle things the way he did, it might be easier to get through life sometimes."

While Jim's positive demeanor was exceptional, his talent remains extraordinary, and his imagination explosive—sometimes literally. "He was a creatively restless individual always looking for something new," said Lisa Henson. "Not just a new project, but a new way of *achieving* a project. He rarely repeated himself. It was not interesting to him to keep doing the same thing." Brian Henson admired his father's "mind-set"—a work ethic that valued both creativity and collaboration. "That's probably what he taught me more than anything," said Brian. "I learned from him to be very, very pre-pared and then very, very flexible—to know exactly what you're going to do, until somebody has another idea . . . because that's the way to work, you know."

As longtime collaborator and *Sesame Street* head writer Jon Stone put it, "Jim didn't think in terms of boundaries at all, the way all the rest of us do. There are always these fences we build around ourselves and our ideas. Jim seemed to have no fences."

His energy and enthusiasm—his sheer joy in his work—were boundless as well. "I often tell people . . . 'if you think it's fun to watch these things,'" said Muppet designer Bonnie Erickson, "'you should have been there *making* them.'" Jim's excitement, said Min-ghella, was "so overpowering, you could just tell he was a man who had not lost an ounce of enthusiasm for anything he was doing." Frank Oz thought it was more than just enthusiasm; he called Jim "an extraordinary appreciator":

> Many people see Jim as an extraordinary creator; I realize that I see Jim first as an appreciator. He appreciated so much. He loved London. He loved walking on the Heath. . . . He ap-preciated his family and his colleagues and his Muppet family. And he appreciated the performances and design of a puppet. He appreciated the art objects that he might buy. He appreci-ated the detail in a Persian rug. He appreciated . . . just beauty. I really don't believe that Jim could have been such an extraor-dinary creator if he hadn't been such an extraordinary appre-ciator.

Perhaps more than anything, however, it was that sense of pur-pose, that basic decency, that made Jim and his life and work so remarkable—and makes it just as remarkable today. "Underneath the zaniness, or perhaps standing next to it, there was a sense of de-cency that the characters had about the world and to each other," said Jerry Juhl. "That's one of the real legacies that Jim left. I think it's one of the reasons he's so loved today, because he could be a pop culture figure doing mass entertainment, and he could explore the edges of crazy, goofy comedy. But at the core, there was always a sense of social values and decency." As creative consultant Alex

Rockwell remembered, "He often started from the position of, 'Let's do something that's going to make the world a better place.' . . . The work was always about fun and creativity and inventiveness, but he really cared in a genuine way that it also had a value system."

Always, then, the work had to matter—because to Jim, the *world* mattered. "I know that it's easier to portray a world that's filled with cynicism and anger, where problems are solved with violence," Jim once said. "What's a whole lot tougher is to offer alternatives, to present other ways conflicts can be resolved, and to show that you can have a positive impact on your world. To do that, you have to put yourself out on a limb, take chances, and run the risk of being called a do-gooder."

Jim was always willing to take that risk, thought Richard Hunt. "He wasn't a saint, but he was as close as human beings get to it." That had made Jim's passing so much harder—and yet, said Hunt, "part of me feels . . . that Jim had done his work on earth. . . . He had done an amazing amount of work. He'd given an amazing amount of himself, and in turn to each person who was affected by him."

In her New York apartment, Cheryl Henson still keeps a small photograph of her father, taken during his years in London while working on *Labyrinth*. In the photo, Jim is walking away from the camera, clutching a walking stick as he strides up a path toward Hampstead Heath—perhaps headed out to one of the Bunny Picnics he so adored. With a blanket tucked casually under one arm, he is relaxed and carefree, looking happily up the hill in front of him with no intention of looking back. "That's how I think of my dad after he died," said Cheryl. "It was time for him to go. He's going off on his own."

"We all have jobs," said Richard Hunt, "and he'd done his. He'd done it well." What Jim Henson did so well was always more than just Muppets. It was more than Fraggles or Gelflings or goblin kings. Like Jim himself, what Jim did was wonderfully complex, though not complicated—and elegant in its simplicity. "When I was young," wrote Jim, "my ambition was to be one of the people who makes a difference in this world. My hope still is to leave this world a little bit better for my being here."

And he did.

ACKNOWLEDGMENTS

Every biographer has the unique privilege and responsibility of living with their subject—and their subject's family, friends, colleagues, and co-workers—during the course of researching and writing about their life. It has been my great good fortune, then, as I wrote about a truly extraordinary life, to spend five years with some very remarkable people.

First and most important, this project would never have been possible without the gracious support and encouragement of the Henson family: Jane, Lisa, Cheryl, Brian, John, and Heather Henson. Enthusiastic as well as endlessly patient, all six were generous with their time and genuinely thoughtful, reflective—and, as you might expect, *funny*—during our countless interview sessions, emails, and phone conversations. They also kindly assisted me in reaching out to other performers, employees, friends, and family members whose input was critical to this book. It has been my privilege to have Jim's family directly involved with this book, and to have them share their stories and memories with me. Jane Henson's death in April 2013 after a courageous fight with cancer was a genuine loss, and I'm so grateful for the time I spent with her, tape recorder rolling, to talk about Jim's life and her own. I'll miss her. A lot.

I also miss Jim Henson, and want to thank him, wherever he is (and he was always certain he'd be *somewhere*) for the pleasure of working on this project. While it may sound goopy and New Agey, there really were times when I sincerely felt his presence as I turned over page after page of his handwritten notes, touched his personal leather-bound copy of a script, or even watched someone's face light up as they recalled a memory of working with him or making him laugh. I wouldn't presume to say he was guiding this project, but he really did seem to somehow always be there, calmly guiding, inspiring, and making everything better. Thanks, Jim.

The Jim Henson Legacy—an organization established in 1993 by Jane Henson with Al Gottesman, Arthur Novell, and Dick Wedemeyer to preserve and perpetuate Jim's countless contributions to puppetry, film, special effects, and culture—also provided invaluable support and critical guidance. My deepest thanks go to the inimitable Arthur Novell—if this book can be said to have a spiritual father, he's it—whose advice, keen instincts, and sense of humor could always be counted on. Al Gottesman, attorney extraordinaire, ran the traps necessary to grant me access to countless unseen documents, and provided critical insight into the inner workings of Jim's company; meanwhile, the good-humored Bonnie Erickson guided me not only through Henson history, but also gave me a crash course in the art and craft of designing and making Muppets.

A mere "thank you" hardly seems adequate to express my appreciation for the enthusiasm and very thorough support I received from Karen Falk, archivist for The Jim Henson Company—the company's official name since 1997—at its Long Island City facility. Talented, infinitely patient, and hugely organized—she can find *anything* quickly—Karen not only helped me pore through the archives, but also gamely helped lug archival boxes, change copier paper, and track down photo credits. She also allowed me to barrage her with emails at all hours of the day, and always responded quickly and thoroughly. You're the greatest, Karen.

I'd also like to thank the staffs at The Jim Henson Legacy and The Jim Henson Company, who not only provided invaluable assistance, but graciously allowed me to share their space and get in their way as they worked. In particular, I'd like to extend a special thanks to Gigi Bewabi, Rhoda Cosme, Carla Dellavedova, Nicole Goldman, Ashley Griffis, Joe Henderson, Hillary Howell, Jill Peterson, Peter Schube, Craig Shemin, and Nathaniel Wharton.

One of the real thrills of this book was meeting and talking with the Muppet performers and creative staff. I am especially indebted to Jim's closest friend and collaborator, Frank Oz, who graciously made himself freely available to me not only in person, but also enthusiastically (and usually hilariously) responded to countless emails and phone calls asking for "just *one* more minute" to answer a question. I'm deeply saddened by the loss of performer Jerry Nelson, who passed away in late 2012 as this book was being completed, but I'm extremely grateful for the time I had with him at his home in Cape Cod, and thank his wife, Jan, for sharing him. I also appreciate the time I was given by Dave Goelz and Steve Whitmire, not only for their insights and perspectives, but also because they allowed me the pleasure of watching them perform on-set (and my thanks to the members of OK Go, who also permitted me to be there). I'm also very thankful for the time, courtesy, and insights I received from the wonderful and talented Martin Baker, Diana Birkenfield (whom we also lost in 2012), Fran Brill, Christopher Cerf, Kevin Clash, Michael Frith, Brian and Wendy Froud, Louise Gold, Peter Harris, Susan Juhl, Duncan Kenworthy, Rollie Krewson, Larry Mirkin, Kathy Mullen, David Odell, Bob Payne, Alex Rockwell, and Jocelyn Stevenson. I also appreciate the courtesy extended by the families of Bernie Brillstein, Richard Hunt, Jerry Juhl, and Anthony Minghella, all of whom graciously permitted me to use unpublished archival interviews conducted by others.

Further, I am grateful to the following for their time, courtesy, assistance, expertise, and/or insights: Tommy and Barbara Baggette, Bob Bell, Stephen Christy, Mary Ann Cleary, Joan Ganz Cooney, Mark Evanier, Christopher Finch, Royall Frazier, Stan and Hunter Freberg, Judy Harris, Joe Irwin, Dr. Stanley and Tomma Jenkins, Gordon E. Jones, Mac McGarry, Ken Plume, Nick Raposo, Lynnie Raybuck, Jessica Max Stein, and Susan Whitaker. For background on Leland, Hyattsville, and Jim's family and ancestry, I am indebted to Dot Love Turk, Daryl Lewis, Jody Stovell, Rick Williams, Sr., the Hyattsville Preservation Society, Colleen Formby at the Hyattsville

Library, Sarah Moseley, Mayor John Brunner, Iowa State University archivist Michele Christian, and Vin Novara and Anne Turkos at the University of Maryland. For their assistance with images and other archival matters, my sincere thanks to Susan Tofte and Jennifer Wendell at Sesame Workshop, Madlyn Moskowitz and Tina Mills at Lucasfilm, and Debbie McClellan and her team at Disney. At the Center for Puppetry Arts in Atlanta, Vincent Anthony, Jeremy Underwood, Brad Clark, Liz Lee, and Meghan Fuller were exceptionally helpful.

I also want to acknowledge a few members of the Henson family who made me feel welcome as I took the time of another family member: Lisa Henson's husband, David Pressler, and their children, Julian and Ginger; Cheryl Henson's husband, Ed Finn, and their children, Elizabeth and Declan; and John Henson's wife, Gyongyi, and their children, Sydney and Katrina. Thanks for your patience and courtesy.

I also want to extend my appreciation to Eric Burns, Edward Crapol, Christoph Irmscher, Kate Eagen Johnson, and Ted Widmer (all of whom know why), as well as Jill Schwartzman, Brian Shirey, and Charles J. Shields—who *also* all know why.

At Random House, I am particularly thankful for my editor, Ryan Doherty, whose enthusiasm for this project was truly inspirational, and whose guidance and editorial talent helped make this book better and clearer. I also appreciate the support of Richard Callison and Jennifer Tung, and the talents of David Moench and Quinne Rogers. The copyediting team of Frederick Chase and Beth Pearson went above and beyond in keeping this book as clean and free of mistakes as possible. Any errors or inaccuracies in this book remain mine and mine alone.

A very special thank-you to my agent, Jonathan Lyons, whose expertise helped guide this book through its fledgling state, and who still guides and encourages me to this day. He and his wife, Cameron, made me feel like one of the family during my countless trips to New York, and I am grateful for their personal and professional friendship.

On a personal note, I am thankful for the family, friends, and colleagues who encouraged and supported me during the five years I was at work on this dream project, who always asked, "How are things going?" and understood when I had to decline invitations with, "I can't; I'm writing." My deepest thanks, then, to my parents, Larry Jones and Elaine and Wayne Miller, and my awesome, Muppet-loving brother, Cris. My warmest appreciation to Mike and Cassie Knapp, Frank and Jane Schwartz, Dave and Trish English, Joe and Angie Marella, Raice and Liselle McLeod, Dave and Gail Noren, Mike and Marron Lee Nelson, Daniela Moya-Geber, Carmen Berrios, Nancy Aldous, and Joyce Fuhrmann.

Finally, none of what you now hold in your hands could have been accomplished without the love and support of the two most important people in the world to me—my wife, Barb, and our daughter, Madi. Their enthusiasm and excitement for this project—even as I disappeared downstairs into my office to write for days and weeks on end—made missing family dinners or weekend volleyball tournaments a bit more bearable. More important, their love and laughter always gave me something warm and wonderful to come up the stairs to each evening. Barb and Madi—and yes, even Grayson the dog—this is your book, too, for I couldn't have done it without you. I love you guys. Now get the dog off the couch.

—*Damascus, Maryland, February 2013*

Several frequently cited names and sources appear in these notes in shortened form, including on first reference. A key appears below, but a few sources merit special mention.

First, much of the research for this book was conducted in the private archives of The Jim Henson Company in Long Island City, New York. Most referenced materials from these archives are denoted with the prefix JHCA and some sort of a short identifying tag—usually indicating a folder or, in some cases, an archival box—in accordance with the archive's internal filing system. Additionally, a number of private materials—which do not reside in the company's archives—were graciously provided for my usage by the Henson family, through their counsel. These items are denoted as "Henson Family Properties."

One of the most helpful documents in the archives is the private journal of Jim's that he began in 1965, in which he would note key dates and events in his life. This journal, with a striped red cover on which he inked the words "THE MUPPETS," has since come to be called "Jim's Red Book." It will hereafter be cited as "JH RB" in these pages.

Jim Henson rarely sat for extensive interviews, but one of the best was conducted by Judy Harris, whose complete, unpublished

1982 interview can be retrieved on her website at http://users.bestweb .net/~foosie/henson.htm. I am very grateful to Judy for permitting me to quote freely from this interview, which is cited in these notes as "Harris." Additionally, in the mid-1980s, Jim again permitted himself to be interviewed at length—likely by author Christopher Finch, though memories are hazy—and then had his answers transcribed into a twenty-three-page document filed in the archives as "Jim Henson Quotes." This document will be cited as "JH Quotes."

Finally, two of the most important books on Jim Henson and his work are Christopher Finch's 1993 *Jim Henson: The Works, the Art, the Magic, the Imagination* and his 1981 *Of Muppets and Men: The Making of The Muppet Show* (see the Selected Bibliography). Finch's books contain not only valuable information but also provide crucial firsthand accounts of Jim and the Muppet performers at work. These books are cited in these notes as *WAMI* and *OMAM*, respectively.

Unless otherwise indicated, interviews were conducted by the author.

Key to Shortened or Abbreviated Names and Sources

BB = Bernie Brillstein
Being Green = Jim Henson and the Muppets and Friends, *It's Not Easy Being Green (And Other Things to Consider)*
BH = Brian Henson
CH = Cheryl Henson
DL = David Lazer
FO = Frank Oz
Harris = Jim Henson interview with Judy Harris, 1982
JH = Jim Henson
JHCA = Jim Henson Company archives
JH Quotes = "Jim Henson Quotes" (JHCA family box)
JH RB = Jim Henson's Red Book (JHCA 9177)
JJ = Jerry Juhl
JS = Jon Stone
LH = Lisa Henson
OMAM = Christopher Finch, *Of Muppets and Men: The Making of The Muppet Show*
WAMI = Christopher Finch, *Jim Henson: The Works, the Art, the Magic, the Imagination*

Chapter One: The Delta

3   **The town of Leland**   Dorothy Love Turk, *Leland, Mississippi: From Hellhole to Beauty Spot* (Leland Historical Foundation, 1986), 3–12.

4   **In 1904**   Amy Lipe Taylor, *The Delta Branch Experiment Station: 100 Years of Agricultural Research* (Mississippi State University, 2004), 13.

4   **One of Jim's favorite family stories**   The author is grateful to the Henson family, through Henson Family Properties, for providing audio recordings of Jim interviewing Betty and Paul Henson, Sr., on August 6, 1972, and Mary Ann Jenkins, Bobby Henson, and Paul Henson, Sr., on Deccember 30, 1981. Unless otherwise noted, these recordings served as this chapter's primary source of quotes and stories regarding Jim Henson's ancestry (hereafter cited as "JH audio interviews").

5   **Albert and Effie would eventually settle**   The Twelfth Census of the United States (1900) shows the Hensons living in the township of South Wichita, Lincoln County, Oklahoma.

5–6   **Over the next four years**   Paul Henson's 1928 thesis was titled "Yield Studies of Seventy-Five Hybrid Strains of Soybeans." The author is grateful to Iowa State University for providing a copy of this document.

6   **One afternoon, while eating his lunch**   Tomma S. Jenkins, email to Heather Henson, September 9, 1998.

6   **Oscar Hinrichs**   Rick Williams and Rosanne Butler, "Journals of a Confederate Mapmaker," Boston Map Society newsletter 18 (October 2006). See also Rosanne Butler, "Information About Oscar Hinrichs and Family," December 2006 (JHCA 20028).

7   **Less than a year later**   Hinrichs's suicide note was published in the September 25, 1892, *Washington Post* as "A Strange Document."

7   **Born in Kentucky**   See Twelfth Census of the United States for Jefferson County, Kentucky.

8   **For the next few years**   The Thirteenth Census of the United States (1910) shows the Browns—including Mary Agnes and Betty—living in Memphis City, Shelby County, Tennessee, where Maury's profession is listed as "chief clerk, railroad office." In 1920, the Browns—now including youngest daughter Bobby—were in New Orleans, while the Fifteenth Census (1930) puts them in Hyattsville, Maryland.

8   **"I just thought we had the happiest home"**   JH audio interviews.

8   **At some point**   Jane Henson interview.

8   **"perfectly awful"**   JH audio interviews.

9   **"upbeat all the time"**   CH interview.

9   **spring of 1930**   Anne Turkos, Archivist, University of Maryland, email to the author, October 25, 2010.

10   **Near record harvests**   Turk, *Leland, Mississippi: From Hellhole to Beauty Spot*, 84.

10   **a four-room house**   Donald H. Bowman, *A History of the Delta Branch Experiment Station, 1904–1985* (Mississippi State University, 1985), 19.

10   **Milk was delivered** Turk, *Leland, Mississippi: From Hellhole to Beauty Spot,* 83.

10   **with Dear and Bobby close at hand** An announcement in the December 11 *Washington Post* indicates that Sarah and Bobby Henson had returned home after being in Leland for "more than a month." See social page announcements relating to Hyattsville, *Washington Post,* December 11, 1932.

10   **Paul Ransom Henson, Jr.** While many sources, including *WAMI*, state that Paul Henson, Jr., was two years older than Jim—which would mean he was born in 1934—Paul Henson was born in 1932. Paul's birth was announced in the November 6, 1932, *Washington Post* (see social announcements for Hyattsville, *Washington Post,* November 6, 1932). Further, his obituary in the April 16, 1956, *Evening Star* gives his age as twenty-three, consistent with a late 1932 birth.

10   **small, sad-eyed boy** *WAMI,* 2.

10   **regular and extended trips** For evidence of the Hensons' frequent visits to Maryland over several months, see "Bridge Is Given for Mary Carr at Hyattsville," *Washington Post,* September 30, 1934; "Hyattsville Reception Honors Mrs. Sturgis, Retiring Principal," *Washington Post,* October 14, 1934; and "Bridge Is Given by Mrs. Brown at Hyattsville," *Washington Post,* January 13, 1935.

10   **thunderstorms still rumbling** "Harvesting Season Passes the Peak; Cotton Picking Was Halted in Leland This Week by Scattered Showers," *Leland Enterprise,* September 25, 1936.

11   **The following morning** *The Leland Enterprise* of Friday, September 25, 1936, reports, "Mr. and Mrs. Paul Henson are receiving congratulations on the arrival of a son at the Hospital Wednesday." Given that Wednesday would have been the 23rd, and not the 24th, there may have been some confusion over the date on which Betty Henson entered the hospital, and when she actually gave birth to Jim. Despite the newspaper's erroneous report, there is no controversy over Jim's birth date. The Jim Henson Company Archives contains Betty Henson's medical records, confirming date and time of birth, birth weight, and attending physician (JHCA 8699).

11   **4012 Tennyson Road** The author is grateful to former University Park mayor John Brunner for tracking down this information and providing a copy of the deed for this property. Prior to purchasing the home on Tennyson, the Hensons rented a house on Shepard Street.

11   **a thriving downtown** *Hyattsville: Our Hometown* (City of Hyattsville, 1988), 37–42.

11   **newly established Bureau of Plant Industry** "The History of USDA" slide show, http://www.ars.usda.gov/Aboutus/docs.htm?docid=19854.

11   **publishing his findings** P. R. Henson, M. A. Hein, M. W. Hazen, and W. H. Black, "Cattle Grazing Experiments with Sericea Lespedeza at Beltsville, Maryland," *Journal of Animal Science* 2 (1943): 314–20.

11   **"Jim hardly ever"** John Culhane, "The Muppets in Movieland," *New York Times,* June 10, 1979.

11 **while he would later cite** St. Pierre, 18.

12 **"None of us"** Gordon Jones interview.

12 **"there were snakes"** Tommy Baggette interview.

13 **"I was a Mississippi Tom Sawyer"** Don Freeman, "Muppets on His Hands," *Saturday Evening Post*, November 1979.

13 **When pressed** Gourse, 48.

13 **"Jimmy Childress was going to be Jimmy"** Royall Frazier interview.

13 **a religious survey** Turk, *Leland, Mississippi: From Hellhole to Beauty Spot*, 37.

14 **"Over the years"** JH, from the unpublished "The Courage of My Convictions," circa 1986 (JHCA 16422). In the mid-1980s, Jim was asked to write a short piece for a book on spirituality. Neither the book nor Jim's five-page piece was published.

14 **"He was not an evangelical"** Gordon Jones interview.

14 **"Jim found it"** Royall Frazier interview.

15 **On the corner** Turk, *Leland, Mississippi: From Hellhole to Beauty Spot*, 94.

15 **"We'd always go on Saturday"** Tommy Baggette and Gordon Jones interviews.

15 **"A child's use of imagination"** *Being Green*, 110.

15 **"The good guy had a birthmark"** Gordon Jones interview.

16 **regular trips from Maryland** While many biographies state that Dear was a resident of Mississippi, this is not the case. Pop and Dear lived in the same house on Marion Street in Hyattsville from 1923 until 1955, when they moved into a nearby apartment.

16 **"[He's] the one who taught our mother"** JH audio interviews.

17 **"the Brown girls were never allowed to forget they were Southerners!"** Ibid.

17 **"He was convinced"** Jane Henson interview.

17 **"a little bit more of a nerd"** Melissa Townsend, "An Interview with Kermit Scott," *Delta Magazine*, January/February 2006, 30.

18 **"[He] would do things like that"** Gordon Jones interview.

18 **"He'd reach out his handkerchief"** Royall Frazier interview.

18 **It was no accident** Gordon Jones interview. Tommy Baggette recalls another skit night at which Jim and other troop members performed a puppet show, using puppets purchased from a toy store in Greenville. However, Baggette could not recall any specifics about the show or Jim's performance, while others interviewed for this book could not recall performing a puppet show at all. Gourse, 53–54.

18 **"were very quiet people"** Gordon Jones interview.

18 **During the almost weekly summer fish fries** Tommy Baggette interview.

18 **"absolutely delightful"** Gordon Jones interview.

19 **"His mother was great for jokes"** Royall Frazier interview.

19 **"Both of us nearly got killed"** Townsend, "An Interview with Kermit Scott."

19 **While Jim and Paul were four years apart** Finch, in *WAMI*, describes Paul as "a shy, precocious boy," while Jim's friends recall that Paul, though four years older than most of them, was, according to Frazier, "not very big." *WAMI*, 2; Royall Frazier interview.

19   Jim would always be a gadget freak   JH audio interviews.
19   "You could get one radio station"   Royall Frazier interview.
19   "Early radio drama"   St. Pierre, 18.
19   Fibber McGee and Molly   While interviewing his parents in 1972, Jim talked briefly about radio shows he remembered (JH audio interviews).
19   But most of all   Culhane, "The Muppets in Movieland."
20   "I wasn't thinking," "Edgar Bergen's work"   Ibid.
20   The family purchased   While Jim's address—and tax district—was University Park, Jim would always write his address as Hyattsville, which is how it appears on both his passport and his University of Maryland transcript.
20   "I was really sad"   Gordon Jones interview.
21   retire to the porch   CH interview.
21   "There was so much laughter"   JH, quoted during JH audio interviews.
21   "Fifteen or twenty people would be there"   *Being Green,* 112.
22   "drove 'em all crazy"   Culhane, "The Muppets in Movieland."

Chapter Two: A Means to an End

23   a log cabin near Beaver, Utah   *The Encyclopedia of Television,* 2nd ed., ed. Horace Newcomb (New York: Museum of Broadcast Communications, 2004), 854–55.
24   while tilling a potato field   Neil Postman, "Philo Farnsworth," *The Time 100: Scientists and Thinkers,* March 29, 1999.
24   "There you are"   Ibid. See also *The Encyclopedia of Television,* 854.
24   prohibited his own family   "Biography of Philo T. Farnsworth," The Philo T. and Elma G. Farnsworth Papers, University of Utah, Marriott Library, Special Collections.
24   "the simultaneity of television"   Settel, 53.
24   "I loved the idea"   *WAMI,* 4–5. See also JH Quotes.
24   the boxy Admiral   For typical newspaper advertisements for televisions in 1950, see display ads in *The Washington Post,* September 1, 1950.
25   "I badgered my family"   *WAMI,* 4. Emphasis in original. There are some differences of opinion as to exactly when the Henson family purchased its first television. Alison Inches speculates it may have been 1949 (see Inches, 14), while others suggest 1950. For purposes of this chapter, I have deferred to the timeline provided by Jane Henson for the program for the September 26, 2006, presentation at the University of Maryland, *Jim Henson: Creativity and Other Inspirational Stuff / Jane and Friends: The College Park Legacy—A Casual Conversation with Jane Henson,* which sets the date at 1950.
25   There were four television channels   Federal Communications Commission, "History of Communications," http://www.fcc.gov/omd/history/tv/1880-1929 .html.
25   more time watching TV   *WAMI,* 4.
25   "I immediately wanted to work in television"   Ibid., 5.

26   **Ernie Kovacs**   Jim's enthusiasm for Kovacs is described in ibid., 4.

26   **"I don't think I ever saw"**   JH, interviewed by Judy Harris, "Jim Henson," http://users.bestweb.net/~foosie/henson.htm. This is hereafter cited as Harris.

27   **In March of that year**   *Christian Science Monitor,* March 17, 1950, B13.

28   **"Walt Kelly put together a team of characters"**   Gerald Volgenau, "Henson's Offstage Voice Surprises Muppet Family Christmas Visitor," Knight-Ridder News Service, December 16, 1987.

30   **Paul to the University of Maryland**   "Naval Officers Killed in Crash," *Evening Star* (Washington, D.C.), April 16, 1956. Paul would also briefly attend Principia College before transferring back to Maryland.

30   **"He always wanted to fly"**   Tommy Baggette interview.

30   **"I hit a bad lob"**   Joe Irwin interview.

31   **based on Jim's beloved Pogo**   Bob Payne interview.

31   **"When I was old enough"**   WAMI, 7.

31   **"You're not fooling anyone"**   Thomas C. Reeves, *The Life and Times of Joe McCarthy* (Lanham, Maryland: Madison, 1997), 635.

32   **little trouble getting dates**   Joe Irwin interview.

32   **he pleaded with his mother**   Jane Henson interview.

33   **"I would have a nice little proper date"**   Joe Irwin interview.

33   **"youngsters twelve to fourteen"**   See *Evening Star* (Washington, D.C.), May 13, 1954.

34   **"When I was a kid"**   WAMI, 8–9.

34   **a small, skinny hand puppet**   Ibid., 8. Jim later added as an afterthought that he might also have built "a couple of birds."

35   **"Three of the program's participants"**   Harry MacArthur, "On the Air," *Evening Star* (Washington, D.C.), June 25, 1954.

35   **Meachum even landed**   Roy Meachum, August 26, 2003, post on kidshow .dcmemories.com: "Jim Henson, Jane [*sic*] and Russ were hired to cover records on *Saturday,* the show's name. It ran from March through August. *Saturday* was a spinoff to *Roy Meachum in the Morning.* That show ran from June 1953 to March 1954."

35   **"It was interesting"**   WAMI, 8–9.

35   **his performance had caught the eye**   Jim's move from WTOP to WRC involves a bit of detective work, intuition, and supposition, as nearly all accounts differ. According to one story, Roy Meachum phoned Kovach to recommend Jim. (See Chuck Knight, "Sam and Friends," *Old Line,* May 1958, 25.) That differs slightly from the version Michael Davis reports in *Street Gang,* 75–78, in which Kovach—during his unsuccessful recruitment of Meachum—spotted Jim at *Junior Morning Show* and then later recruited him to join the cast of *Afternoon.* Given that *Junior Morning Show* only lasted three episodes—and that Meachum immediately hosted another show on which Jim worked—it seems likely that Kovach approached Meachum during his run on *Saturday.* From there, it follows that he brought Jim to WRC to do other work first, before finally inserting him into the *Afternoon* cast. That version of events more consistently aligns

with Jim's own recollections that he went to WRC and began working on "these little local shows" before finally landing *Afternoon*. It also fills in a roughly seven-month gap in the story reported by Davis—the time in which Jim, by his own admission, worked alone. This information is further supported by *Jim Henson—the Early Years on WTOP and WRC* (K. Falk JHCA 2010).

35 **put through a brief audition** *WAMI*, 15.

36 **"I took the puppets over to NBC"** Ibid., 9.

36 **stammer and giggle** Jane Henson interview.

36 **"The three of us had lunch"** J. Pendleton Campbell, *On the Edge of Greatness (But No Cigar): An Autobiography of Radio and Television Performer Joe Campbell* (Xlibris, 2003), quoted in an email from Bob Bell to Karen Falk, "New Revelations: Jim Henson and Circle 4 Ranch" (JHCA).

36 **work solo for the next eight months** Ursula Keller, " 'Muppets' Win Way," *Christian Science Monitor*, December 15, 1959, 14.

37 **"I was very interested in theatre"** Harris.

37 **University Theaters' publicity director** Knight, "Sam and Friends."

37 **designed and printed posters** Harris; interview with Anne Turkos, archivist, University of Maryland.

37 **"My first year"** Harris.

37 **"[My] puppetry teacher said"** Ibid.

37 **Jane Nebel** Description of her family and quotes are from Jane Henson interview.

40 **"Back in those days"** Harris.

40 **"They would have a cooking segment"** *WAMI*, 15.

41 **2:15 P.M.** "TV Highlights," *Washington Post and Times-Herald*, March 7, 1955, 35.

41 **"51% ownership of muppetts [*sic*]"** See "Jim Henson—The Early Years on WTOP and WRC" (K. Falk JHCA 2010).

41 **"It was really just a term"** Harris.

42 **"As I try to zero in"** *Being Green*, 25.

42 **"just by sitting down"** Lawrence Laurent, "The Straight Man Totes the Load," *Washington Post and Times-Herald*, May 15, 1955.

42 **"integrated chaos"** Ibid.

43 **"The work I did in those days"** Harris.

43 **"in his stumbling unsure way"** Lawrence Laurent, "They Call It Plain Old 'Muppetmania,' " *Washington Post*, October 23, 1977.

43 **"Jim Henson was a very nice young guy"** Jim Naughton, "Jim Henson and Friends: Where It All Began," *Washington Post*, May 17, 1990.

43 **"The kid is positively a genius"** Laurent, "The Straight Man Totes the Load."

43 **"to do spots for children"** *WAMI*, 15.

44 **"We very often would take a song"** St. Pierre, 37.

44 **"I guess it had a quality of abandon"** *WAMI*, 15.

44 **"falling down"** Naughton, "Jim Henson and Friends: Where It All Began."

44 **"Those kids knocked us all out"** Ibid.

44 **a prime piece of TV real estate** While it is usually reported that Jim received

the pre–*Huntley-Brinkley* 6:25 P.M. slot concurrently with the 11:25 P.M. one, that cannot be the case, as *Huntley-Brinkley* would not debut until October 29, 1956—seventeen months after the debut of *Sam and Friends*. And once it did appear, it aired at 7:45 P.M. While Jim would soon receive an early news hour slot, it was initially as part of the *Footlight Theatre* lineup. There would be quite of bit of tinkering with the WRC schedule before Jim finally landed both the pre–*Huntley-Brinkley* spot and the pre-*Tonight* show slot. See the next chapter for more details.

44   "A choice time slot"   *WAMI*, 15.

CHAPTER THREE: *SAM AND FRIENDS*

45   "Harkness; Wthr. Sports; Muppets"   "Monday TV Programs," *Washington Post and Times-Herald*, May 8, 1955.

46   "I made him originally"   Phil Geraci, "Sam's Best Friend," *Sunday Star Magazine* (Washington, D.C.), December 8, 1957.

46   "are actually within him, within Sam"   Jane Henson interview.

46   slowly dying of heart failure   JH audio interviews.

47   "Kermit started out as a way of building"   *WAMI*, 19–21.

48   "milky turquoise," "I didn't call him a frog"   Harris.

48   "Those abstract characters"   Ibid.

49   similar to a habit Burr Tillstrom   A May 23, 1949, feature in *Life* contains a photograph of Tillstrom watching his performance on a television monitor, with the rather tangled caption, "To watch operation, Tillstrom uses backstage TV screen on which he sees how puppets look to camera."

49   "you can actually see what you are doing"   Donna Hudgins, "The Ancient Art of Puppetry . . . Hidden Hands That Teach," *Fifteenth Dimension*, January 1970.

49   "You'd perform but you'd also be the audience"   Jane Henson interview.

50   "After you go through working"   Harris.

50   "What Jim came to love"   Jane Henson interview.

50   "Many of the things I've done"   *Being Green*, 54.

51   "Burr Tillstrom and the Bairds"   Eleanor Blau, "Jim Henson, Puppeteer, Dies; The Muppets' Creator Was 53," *New York Times*, May 17, 1990.

51   "We pretty much had a form"   Harris.

51   "Very early on"   JH Quotes.

51   "[They were] puppets that didn't look like puppets"   JJ, archival interview (Henson Family Properties).

51   "the most brilliant newcomer"   Bernie Harrison, "On the Air: Gobel Persuades Chicago Buddy to Try TV Again," *Sunday Star* (Washingon, D.C.), July 3, 1955.

52   "It was so short"   Layne Mandell Bergin, quoted by Bob Bell, http://kidshow.dcmemories.com/sam4.html.

52   by his own count   Geraci, "Sam's Best Friend."

53   "a way that one"   Inches, 27.

53   "like catching flies"   Jane Henson interview.

53 **It had taken Paul** "Naval Officers Killed in Crash," *Evening Star* (Washington, D.C.), April 16, 1956.

54 **"When I first started working"** Harris.

54 **"I was a kid"** Ibid.

54 **"He had a warm glow"** Amy Aldrich, "The Muppets Take Disney World." Originally slated to appear in the March 1990 issue of the University of Maryland's *Inquiry* magazine, neither the magazine nor the article was ever published. The article may be found at http://www.newsdesk.umd.edu/images/Henson/Articles/InquiryArticle.html.

55 **"All the time I was in school"** St. Pierre, 41.

55 **"I had assumed at that point"** JH, the American Film Institute Elton H. Rule Lecture Series in Telecommunications, seminar with Jim Henson, May 6, 1986 (JHCA 7974).

55 **angry phone calls and letters** Bernie Harrison, "On the Air: WRC Lifts Whammy on Our Sammy," *Evening Star* (Washington, D.C.), August 31, 1955.

55 **"Don't be too grateful"** See the collection of *Sam and Friends*–related clips (JHCA *Sam and Friends* folder).

55 **WRC bounced its newscast** See the daily TV listings in *The Washington Post* for May 1955 through May 1956.

56 **The car veered off the road** "Naval Officers Killed in Crash." See also "Ensign Dies in Crash," *Washington Post and Times-Herald,* April 16, 1956.

56 **After receiving the phone call** Jane Henson interview.

56 **"never got over"** Arthur Novell interview.

56 **"The way of carrying on would be to keep a smile on your face," "good company," "He shared so much"** LH interview.

57 **"When his brother died"** FO interview.

57 **"His intention of working"** Jane Henson interview.

57 **"a rightness"** Ibid. "Boy, no matter what I say it's going to be wrong," said Jane Henson, trying to describe Jim's religious views. "It's sort of like, however things went, that was right."

57 **"I believe that we form our own lives"** JH, "The Courage of My Convictions."

58 **"that whole Footlight Theatre was *so* contrived"** Jane Henson interview.

58 **pirate named Omar** See "Man of Many Voices" promo for WRC, circa 1956 (JHCA).

58 **"He just drove it home"** JH audio interviews.

58 **"After all"** *WAMI,* 21.

59 **"He posed himself beside these signs"** Joe Irwin interview.

59 **"Producers got in touch"** Jane Henson interview.

59 **"Producers were impressed"** See *Sam and Friends*–related clips (JHCA *Sam and Friends* folder).

59 **"This could be their big break"** *Evening Star,* circa September 1956 (JHCA *Sam and Friends* folder).

60   "There were times"   Harris.

61   **That didn't make his schedule less hectic**   Jane described a typical day to Katharine Elson, "For Jane and Jim, Muppets Set a Merry Pace," *Washington Post and Times-Herald,* February 17, 1957. Geraci, "Sam's Best Friend," also describes a typical daily schedule for Jim.

61   **it was his intention**   Geraci, "Sam's Best Friend."

62   **"In his spare time"**   *WAMI,* 18.

62   **"At that time"**   JH Quotes.

62   **"The atmosphere in the studio"**   Jane Henson interview.

62   **"We'd use a lot of records"**   Jane Henson, remarks at MuppetFest 2001.

62   **"I think we were working"**   Ibid.

63   **"I take it all back"**   Stan Freberg to JH, telegram, 1957 (JHCA SF 8928).

63   **"who has a knack"**   "New Lineup at WMAL," *Sunday Star* (Washington, D.C.), August 18, 1957.

63   **"In the early days of the Muppets"**   St. Pierre, 40.

63   **"We'd try some really way-out things"**   J. Y. Smith, "Jim Henson, Creator of Muppets, Dies at 53," *Washington Post,* May 17, 1990.

63   **"I remember one strange thing"**   JH Quotes.

63   **"I was convinced"**   Smith, "Jim Henson, Creator of Muppets, Dies at 53."

64   **"We have so few local shows"**   "Televue Mailbag," *Sunday Star* (Washington, D.C.), September 22, 1957.

64   **"This is one case where I'm certain"**   Ibid.

64   *The Huntley-Brinkley Report*   Barbara Matusow, *The Evening Stars: The Making of the Network News Anchor* (Boston: Houghton Mifflin, 1983), 69–73.

65   **"We got the *Huntley-Brinkley* audience"**   Jane Henson, remarks at MuppetFest 2001.

65   **"very shy, a retiring sort of person"**   Naughton, "Jim Henson and Friends: Where It All Began."

65   **Jane designed most of her own clothes**   Elson, "For Jane and Jim, Muppets Set a Merry Pace."

65   **"Why are you having *your* picture taken with all *my* puppets?"**   Jane Henson interview.

65   **Jim would usually slouch way down**   Ibid.

66   **involved with other people**   Ibid. Jane's relationship is also mentioned in Elson, "For Jane and Jim, Muppets Set a Merry Pace," while Jim's engagement can be found in "Engagement Announcements," *Washington Post and Times-Herald,* December 22, 1957.

66   **"a cheerleader type"**   Jane Henson interview.

Chapter Four: Muppets, Inc.

67 The John H. Wilkins Company Liz Hillenbrand, "Enthusiasm About Coffee Seems Natural to Wilkins," *Washington Post and Times-Herald,* November 18, 1956.

68 fifteen ten-second coffee commercials Knight, "Sam and Friends."

68 "really pretty corny" Naughton, "Jim Henson and Friends: Where It All Began."

68 "We took a very different approach" Inches, 44.

69 Jim really *didn't* like Wilkins coffee Jane Henson interview.

70 "The commercials were an immediate hit" Harris.

70 "sitting through" George Kennedy, "The Rambler Learns About Muppetry," undated newspaper clipping (JHCA 14-1092).

70 "This is the biggest thing" Ibid.

70 "He had the creative ability" Naughton, "Jim Henson and Friends: Where It All Began."

70 "the last inch of winding band" For an example, see the advertisement in *Washington Post and Times-Herald,* November 25, 1958, A8.

70 more than 25,000 pairs Stacy V. Jones, "Patents Granted for TV Ad Puppets," *New York Times,* September 19, 1959.

70 "I'm sure it cost them more" Jane Henson interview.

71 "The funniest thing we have seen in many a moon" See fan letter to Community Coffee Company, November 16, 1959 (JHCA 14-0156).

71 "[The commercials] got a lot of talk" Harris. See also Nash contracts (JHCA 14-0192).

71 "That was almost the first voice stuff" Harris.

71 a future as a painter Elson, "For Jane and Jim, Muppets Set a Merry Pace."

72 "continue with the Muppets" Knight, "Sam and Friends."

72 "I decided to chuck it all" JH Quotes.

72 "The station prevailed" Harris.

72 "He already knew what he was wanting!" Bob Payne interview.

72 "He had this bar inside him" Ibid.

72 "wandered over to Europe" Harris.

73 "But I know the kind of adventures" Joe Irwin interview.

73 "In Europe" Smith, "Jim Henson, Creator of Muppets, Dies at 53."

73 "absolutely marveled," "[Audiences] were very involved" Joe Irwin interview.

73 "That was the first time," "When I traveled around" Harris.

73 "They were very serious about their work" JH Quotes.

74 "It was at that point" Ibid.

75 "ridiculously overcomplicated" WAMI, 25.

75 "just a little bit" Lawrence Laurent, "Story Is Next Lad to Accept the 'Challenge,'" *Washington Post and Times-Herald,* September 2, 1956.

75 "When he came back from Europe" Jane Henson interview.

75 "I remember an elevator ride" Ibid.

76   "they weren't dates"   Ibid.

76   "had an artistic bent"   Joe Irwin interview.

77   "We were very fond"   Jane Henson interview.

77   "From Samson to Delilah"   Inches, 22.

78   "I started painting"   JH Quotes.

78   "about two or three"   Jane Henson, remarks at MuppetFest 2001.

78   "Jim never had me do voices"   Jane Henson interview.

80   "Money cannot measure success"   Keller, " 'Muppets' Win Way," 14.

80   "My impression"   Matt Neufeld, "Jim Henson Made the World Laugh," *Washington Times,* May 17, 1990.

81   "What with the Rolls"   *WAMI,* 25.

81   his job was recruiting   Brillstein, 48.

82   "Burr, give me a break"   BB, archival interview (Henson Family Properties).

82   "I didn't want to"   Ibid.

82   "In walked this guy"   Brillstein, 53–54.

83   sign a contract   One such contract, dated October 12, 1961, was discovered among the files for *Mad, Mad World* (JHCA 02-0873).

83   "Acts as oracle"   Inches, 31.

84   "Sam is back!"   See the display ad in the September 12, 1960, *Washington Post and Times-Herald* for a typical example.

86   "marvelous, very outgoing"   Harris.

86   "I never wanted to be a puppeteer"   FO, interviewed by Kenneth Plume, "Interview with Frank Oz," http://www.ign.com/articles/2000/02/10/interview-with-frank-oz-part-1-of-4 et seq.

86   "Our house was like a salon"   FO interview.

86   At age fourteen   Ibid. See also Erika Mailman, "Muppet Man Oz Got Start at Children's Fairyland in Oakland," *Contra Costa Times* (California), September 17, 2010.

86   which, predictably, he won   FO interview. Sadly, Oz can no longer recall what routine he performed.

87   "they weren't like anything else!"   FO interview.

87   "He was this very quiet, shy guy"   FO, interviewed by Kenneth Plume.

87   "shy, self-effacing boy"   Ibid.

87   "Sunday Painter"   Jane Henson interview.

87   "He said, 'The ending is weak!' "   FO interview.

87   "He was really still at home"   Harris.

87   "somebody or something"   *Being Green,* 44.

87   "I think it was an accident"   Harris.

88   "I never used to go"   FO, interviewed by Kenneth Plume.

88   "The Muppets already had a cult following"   *WAMI,* 19.

88   "The things he brought out"   Ibid.

89   "This guy was like a sailor"   Ibid.

89   "develop and expand"   Barbara J. Witt to JH, July 10, 1961 (JHCA 14-0867).

90   "If . . . one or two of these bits"   "Proposal for USDA Food Fair," September 20, 1961 (JHCA 14-0867).

90   "a rather ingenious set of mechanical puppets"   Ibid.

91   "revolutionary"   Ibid.

91   "a spectacular feat of entertainment"   Wilbert Schaal to JH, November 30, 1961 (JHCA 14-0867).

92   "the average European impression"   Bonnie Aikman, "DC Studios," *Sunday Star TV Magazine* (Washington, D.C.), March 4, 1962. While the Henson Archives contain minimal information on these animatronic puppets—only a drawing of the cigar-smoking man exists—Jane remembered them clearly, as did several others, and the *Washington Daily Star* reported briefly on them in its TV magazine.

93   "It was really just half-an-hour"   *WAMI*, 31.

93   "You'd see him on little grassy knolls," "We frogified him"   Ibid., 31, 37.

CHAPTER FIVE: A CRAZY LITTLE BAND

95   youngest performer to hold   Eide, Cook, and Abrams, 57. As of 2012, Jim still holds the record for serving as the youngest president of the organization.

96   "For puppeteers"   JJ, archival interview.

96   "When you try to sell anyone on puppets"   Gerald Nachman, "How the Muppets Got That Way," *New York Post*, January 24, 1965.

96   "We have a witch who is delightful"   "Notes on On-Cor Idea" (JHCA 14-0194).

97   Ralph it would be, then   Ralph Freeman to JH, February 20, 1963 (JHCA 14-0198). Jim had appeared on the *Today* show on February 7, 1963, using Ralph and Baskerville in the sketch "Dog Music." Following the skit, host Hugh Downs engaged the Muppets in conversation, during which they discussed Ralph's name. "Quite a few of our people saw Ralph and Baskerville on NBC the other day," Freeman wrote, "and got a big kick out of Hugh Downs' question as to how Ralph got his name."

97   "I would generally do a little scribble"   Inches, 50.

98   "That single decision"   *WAMI*, 32.

98   "The Magic Triangle"   Ibid.

98   "He always wanted me there"   Ibid.

98   "had more to do with the basic style"   Ibid., 26.

98   "He knew then"   BB, archival interview.

99   "tossed into a cupboard"   JH, "My Life with Rowlf (Or Something Like That)" (JHCA 14-0746, Production Box 57).

99   "We were never told"   Joan Crosby, "Jim Henson and Rowlf Know Just What's What, Where They're Going," *Hartford Times* (Connecticut), February 29, 1964.

99   "Anyone in this business of television"   "Neighbors from *Sesame Street*: A Visit with Jane and Jim Henson," *Greenwich Social Review* 23, no. 8 (November 1970).

99   "totally typical of the way Jim worked"   JJ, archival interview.

99   "wonderful old apartment building"   JJ, interviewed by Paul Eide, "In the Company of Genius," *The Puppetry Journal* 57, no. 1 (Fall 2005): 4.

100   **In the main room**   FO interview. See also *WAMI*, 35, and JJ, archival interview.

100   **"[Our] spaces never looked like offices"**   JJ, archival interview.

100   **"very serious," "Having your young son"**   FO interview.

101   **"This is the room where Jim"**   *WAMI*, 35.

101   **"But I didn't come to New York to go to school"**   FO interview.

102   **"began looking at ol' JD," "check out"**   Dean, 77, 80.

102   **ABC was bombarded**   "Pooch Came for a Visit . . . and Hasn't Left Yet," ABC Feature Press Release, October 14, 1963 (JHCA 14-0746 Production Folder).

103   **"These were old-school guys"**   FO interview.

103   **"We would spend all week working"**   JH Quotes.

103   **"really quite simple"**   JH, "My Life with Rowlf (Or Something Like That)."

103   **"is not to do too much"**   FO interview.

104   **"As we first had Rowlf set up"**   Aldine Bird, "Public Writes, 'Rowlf' Stays" (JHCA, assorted press clippings, Jimmy Dean box).

104   **"I treated Rowlf like he was real"**   Dean, 80. Emphasis in original.

104   **over two thousand fan letters**   George T. Miller, "Woofing with a Rag Dog," *New York Times,* April 5, 1964.

104   **"It's been interesting for me"**   JH, "My Life with Rowlf (Or Something Like That)."

104   **"He's free-form"** Richard Gehman, " 'Lemme Do It Mah Way': Jimmy Dean Knows What He Wants—and Usually Gets It," *TV Guide,* circa 1963.

104   *"He knew what he was wanting!"*   Bob Payne interview.

104   **"a rascal," "That was completely unexpected!"**   FO interview.

105   **"He was not interested in kids' stuff," "I probably felt a lot more uncertain"**   JJ, archival interview.

105   **"I would have been just as happy"**   James W. Young to Roy Dabadie, June 18, 1959 (JHCA 14-0156).

105   **"it's taken years off my life"**   James W. Young to John F. Hoag, September 18, 1959 (JHCA 14-0182).

106   **"business operations, including supervision"**   Agreement with Alden Murray, December 15, 1961 (JHCA 14-0868).

106   **"Could you please return"**   JH to Roy Dabadie, January 2, 1963 (JHCA 14-0156).

106   **"It was slapdash"**   Transcript of conference call regarding "The Greenwich Years" exhibit, January 20, 1994 (JHCA).

106   **"Until we had the Muppets"**   William F. Wright to Russell McElwee, July 7, 1964 (JHCA 14-0152).

107   **"We'd usually stay in this little hotel"**   FO interview.

107   **"Part of what makes the Muppets work"**   Ibid.

107   **"false start":**   See various camera reports (JHCA 9913).

108   **"they *soaked* Wontkins in it"**   FO interview.

108   **"some pretty high-powered"**   JJ, archival interview.

108   **"I thought I'd better do something"**   JJ, interviewed by Paul Eide, "In the Company of Genius," 4–5.

108–09 "The house in Greenwich," "close enough to be shooed off" LH interview.

109 "sitting with a storyboard pad" JJ, *The World of Jim Henson* (documentary), 1994.

109 "came just completely full-blown" Jane Henson, *The World of Jim Henson* (documentary).

109 "Jim wasn't a puppeteer" JJ, archival interview.

110 "the story of an Everyman" "A Description of *Time Piece*" (JHCA 14-0855).

110 "We didn't know what was going on," "There was this storyboard" "The Greenwich Years" exhibit.

110 "dropping clocks in mud" JJ, archival interview.

111 "We were all over the place" "The Greenwich Years" exhibit.

111 "All those *Time Piece* shots," "a personal piece," "It came totally from Jim" Ibid.

111 "all [the] different places" *The World of Jim Henson* (documentary).

111 "repeated cuts from realistic scenes" "A Description of *Time Piece*."

111 "was maybe about a second" *The World of Jim Henson* (documentary).

111–12 "I was . . . playing," "Richard Lester did *A Hard Day's Night*" JH Quotes.

112 "*Time Piece* is about time" JJ, *The World of Jim Henson* (documentary).

112 "A lot of people want to say something" Nachman, "How the Muppets Got That Way."

112 "the possibility of filmic stream of consciousness" "A Description of *Time Piece*."

112 "rather weird little movie" Invitation to *Time Piece* premiere (JHCA *Time Piece* box).

112 "It was Jim pushing the form" *The World of Jim Henson* (documentary).

113 "I don't think there's anything" Laurence D. Kramer, United Artists, to Harry Ufland, William Morris Agency, May 20, 1965 (JHCA *Time Piece* box).

114 "He thought our senses of humor would mesh" Jerry Nelson, "Jerry Nelson (In His Own Words)—From 'Halfway Down the Stairs,'" http://e.domaindlx .com/jerrynelson.

115 "approach things in a calm and kind way" CH interview.

115 "He just went ashen" FO interview.

115 "A terrible day" JJ, archival interview.

115 "I sat in front of that mirror" FO interview.

116 "The gal started walking away," "Jim was fearless" "The Greenwich Years" exhibit.

116 "When he had a vision in his mind" Jerry Nelson interview.

116 "That's one of the times" "The Greenwich Years" exhibit.

116 "Working at the Muppet office was always fun" FO interview.

117 "I loved the way Don played" *WAMI*, 26.

117 "With typical speed and efficiency" JH to Franklin Cosmen, Celanese Chemical Company, October 16, 1964 (JHCA 8684).

117 "The Muppets were known" BH, interviewed by Kenneth Plume, August 9, 2000, http://movies.ign.com/articles/035/035899p1.html et seq.

117   "it wasn't all that big"   Jerry Nelson, "Jerry Nelson (In His Own Words)— From 'Halfway Down the Stairs.'"

117   "We were just kind of this crazy little band"   "The Greenwich Years" exhibit.

118   "They thought the Muppets were a rock group," "a serious conversation," "didn't look very clean cut either"   Ibid.

118   "Someone would have an idea"   FO interview.

118   "I hated those costume things"   "The Greenwich Years" exhibit.

118   "I was blind"   FO interview.

119   "sense of humor and crazy nuttiness"   DL, archival interview (Henson Family Properties).

119   "ecstatic"   JH RB, March 25, 1966 (JHCA 9177).

119   "We made Rowlf a . . . bungling salesman"   DL, archival interview.

119   "Machines should work"   See the 1967 short "Paperwork Explosion," http://www.youtube.com/watch?v=_IZw2CoYztk.

119   "dinky little offices," "There was this aura of calmness"   DL, archival interview.

120   "We'd do our little bit"   Jerry Nelson, interviewed by Kenneth Plume, March 1, 1999. See http://www.ign.com/articles/2000/02/10/interview-with-jerry-nelson-part-1-of-4 et seq.

120   "Next thing you know"   Gehman, "'Lemme Do It Mah Way.'"

120   "whatever that is"   JH RB, August 27, 1965.

120   "from 'A frightening look'"   "A Description of *Time Piece.*"

120   "such fun!"   Jane Henson interview.

121   "which lessened the dramatic impact of my leaving"   FO, email to the author, March 28, 2011.

121   "I reported for duty" "I came back up the stairs"   FO interview.

121   "Frank Oz is not drafted!"   JH RB, February 18, 1966.

121   "Jim would call me up"   Jerry Nelson, interviewed by Kenneth Plume, "Still Counting: An Interview with Jerry Nelson," Muppet Central, http://www.muppetcentral.com/articles/interviews/nelson1.shtml et seq.

121   "Johnny is not one of those people"   JJ, archival interview.

121–22   "fair," "Fairly good"   See JH RB entries for December 31, 1965, and December 12, 1965.

122   "Our material does have a certain similarity"   Nachman, "How the Muppets Got That Way."

122   "expecting it to lead somewhere," "We had nothing to do"   WAMI, 40.

122   "affectionate anarchy"   FO interview.

123   "people at the studio," "crazy Muppet people"   WAMI, 40.

123   "What's interesting"   Diana Birkenfield interview. The pipes can still be seen today as part of the NBC tour at Rockefeller Center.

123   "Good puppetry has a broad range"   Joan Crosby, "Jim Henson and Rowlf Know Just What's What, Where They're Going," *Hartford Times* (Connecticut), February 29, 1964.

124   "He always had those fancy new cars"   LH interview.

124 "Except for *Jimmy Dean*" *WAMI*, 47.

124 "a new concept" Brochure for Cyclia, circa 1967 (JHCA Cyclia folder).

124 "The idea began" *WAMI*, 46.

125 "a definite prestige atmosphere" Brochure for Cyclia.

125 "I shot thousands and thousands of feet" *WAMI*, 47.

125 "you couldn't shoot just random stuff" FO interview.

126 "as long as there were no more than three instruments" Joseph Karow to JH, October 10, 1966 (JHCA Cyclia folder).

126 "Nearly bought ABZ" JH RB November 1966.

126 "We went to the El Morocco" "The Greenwich Years" exhibit.

126 "It could well be" JJ, archival interview.

126 "Jim went where the excitement was" FO interview.

127 "You would think that he would be tired" LH interview.

127 "There was a lot of making things" CH interview.

127 "Jim loved to come home" Jane Henson interview.

127 "He was very matter-of-fact about it" LH interview.

127–28 "an embracing environment" CH interview.

128 "There were times" Ibid.

128 "was like my surrogate grandmother" LH interview.

128 "Jim and I would sit and think up anything" "The Greenwich Years" exhibit.

128 "This guy Henson's" Howard Morris to BB, May 19, 1967 (JH 5780).

128 "strange electronic pulses and rhythms" See Jim's proposal for "Inside My Head: A Concept Outline for a One Hour Experiment in Television," circa 1968 (JHCA *Inside My Head* folder).

129 "to communicate the ideas of Youth" Proposal for "A Collage of Today" (JHCA 14-0886).

130 "We worked twenty hours a day" Barry Clark to David Granahan, May 7, 1968 (JHCA 140882).

130 "Back in the sixties" JH Quotes.

130 "We got into" JJ, archival interview.

131 "Visually the program" John Voorhees, "TV Can Be Art Form," *Seattle Post-Intelligencer*, April 23, 1968.

131 "No television program" Ralph Gleason, "NBC's Portrait of Our Youth," circa 1968 (JHCA Youth '68 box).

131 "one of the most inspired programs of this season" "Youth 68," *Variety*, April 24, 1968.

131 "excellent" See various viewer mail (JHCA Youth '68 box). Also R. L. Conner to KNBC, April 21, 1968 (JHCA 14-0886).

132 "a novelty act" Jerry Nelson interview.

132 "a few larger projects," "attempt a feature film" Barry Clark to David Granahan, May 7, 1968 (JHCA 14-0882).

132 "a weird kind of dark ritual look" JJ, archival interview.

132 "original, surrealistic comedy" See JH, JJ original screenplay for *The Cube*.

Also "'The Cube,' Original Surrealistic Comedy by Jim Henson and Jerry Juhl, Set for 'NBC Experiment in Television,'" NBC Press Release, January 21, 1969 (JHCA *Cube* production box).

133 **"I see no hope for it"** Tom Egan to BB, November 4, 1966 (JHCA *Cube* production box).

133 **"After *Time Piece*, Jim often got frustrated"** FO interview.

133 **"[Jim's] inspiration"** *WAMI*, 44–45.

134 **"Congratulations"** A. Kleihauer to KNBC-TV, February 25, 1969 (JHCA *Cube* production box).

134 **"We were in an era"** JJ, archival interview.

134 **"A dramatic highlight of the season"** Ben Gross, "A Fascinating TV Play, 'The Cube,' Makes a Hit," New York *Daily News,* circa February 1969.

134 **"excellent," "provocative," "a challenge and a pleasure"** See assorted correspondence, JHCA *Cube* production box.

134 **"it must have been intended"** "Television Reviews," *Variety,* February 25, 1969.

134 **"the most disciplined attention"** F. Dionne to JH, February 22, 1969 (JHCA *Cube* production box).

134 **"Dear Mr. Dionne"** JH to F. Dionne, March 13, 1969 (JHCA *Cube* production box).

135 **"That's actually very Jim!"** FO interview.

135 **"work Jim"** LH interview.

135 **"That isn't something"** Jane Henson interview.

135 **"I used to always think"** JH Quotes.

135 **"demonstrate the technique and approach"** Robert Reed to JH, January 13, 1968 (JHCA 14-0874).

135 **"just decided he didn't want to do it"** "The Greenwich Years" exhibit.

136 **"This is completely wrong"** See draft contract with Young & Rubicam, March 3, 1969 (JHCA 14-0190).

136 **"Tape Pilot Shows"** JH RB, July 9–18.

Chapter Six: *Sesame Street*

137 **"I think there was a kind of collective genius"** *WAMI*, 74.

138 **"We discovered we had a tremendous empathy"** JS, archival interview (Henson Family Properties).

138 **"to create a successful television program"** Borgenicht, 9.

138–39 **"I want this show to jump and move fast"** Beatrice Berg, "Goodbye Bang, Burn, Stab, Shoot," *New York Times,* November 9, 1969.

139 **"I talked to [Joan Cooney] for fifteen minutes"** JS, archival interview.

139 **"I hadn't remembered the name at first"** Davis, 150.

140 **"There was a huge ambivalence there"** JJ, archival interview.

140 **"Jim got involved right away"** "Jim Henson Productions Legacy Meeting— Jon Stone and Jerry Nelson Discuss the Beginnings of Sesame Street, May 26, 1993" (JHCA interviews box).

141   "This was an educational children's show"   JJ, archival interview.

141   "this future amorphous television show"   "Jim Henson Productions Legacy Meeting."

142   "He said, 'So, Brian'"   BH interview.

143   "I fought like hell"   JS, archival interview.

143   "if nobody came up with a better idea"   Davis, 156–57.

143   "The design was so simple"   *WAMI*, 61.

144   "We played with who did what"   FO interview.

144   "it's a total coincidence"   "Jim Henson Productions Legacy Meeting."

145   "I don't like it"   John Culhane, "Report Card on Sesame Street," *New York Times*, May 24, 1970.

145   "We had been told by all our advisors"   *WAMI*, 71.

146   "to have a character that the child could live through," "Big Bird, in theory, is himself a child"   JH, *Henson's Place: The Man Behind the Muppets* (documentary).

146   "Oscar is there"   JS, archival interview.

147   "an experimental production"   Spinney, 20.

147   "I couldn't see my films"   Ibid., 21.

147   "Jim never just wanted to chat"   Ibid.

147   "I saw your show"   Ibid., 25.

148   "I wasn't in California very long at all"   Eide, "In the Company of Genius," 5.

148   "When Big Bird was being developed"   *WAMI*, 57.

149   "Fortunately"   Spinney, 41.

149   Oscar's Salt of the Sea   Located at 1157 Third Avenue, just around the corner from the Muppet office. The name of the restaurant has often been mistakenly recalled as "Oscar's Tavern." The Jim Henson Company Archives contains a number of doodles drawn on napkins from the restaurant. Borgenicht, 107–8.

149   "It would lift up"   JS, archival interview.

150   "Left hands are much stupider"   Davis, 187.

150   "I hoped I had the right voice," "That'll do fine"   Spinney, 53.

150   which Jim later admitted   Ted Gottfried, "The Mastermind of the Muppets," *Plain Dealer* (Cleveland), September 11, 1975.

151   "stocking puppets"   Jack Gould, "This 'Sesame' May Open the Right Doors," *New York Times*, November 23, 1969.

151   Washington, D.C., City Council approved a resolution   Elizabeth Shelton, "Sesame Street Opens," *Washington Post*, November 11, 1969.

151   "It's clever and witty and charming"   "Sesame Street Swings," *Detroit Free Press*, November 24, 1969.

151   "an undisputed hit"   Jack Gould, "TV: Important Breakthroughs for Sesame Street," *New York Times*, December 10, 1969.

151   "I didn't know what success meant"   Joan Ganz Cooney, archival interview.

151   "only Jim"   FO interview.

152   "Apparently, the Children's Television Workshop"   Jack Gould, "'Hey, Cinderella' Given as A.B.C. Classic," *New York Times*, April 11, 1970.

152   "For the past ten or twelve years"   Davis, 212–13.

153   "extreme sensitivity to commercialization"   Irving Schlessel to Richard C. Waldburger, Esq., August 14, 1970 (JHCA 14-0190).

153   "We were really checking the clocks"   DL, archival interview.

153   "The attitude you have as a parent"   *Being Green,* 113.

154   "Jim was intrigued with his children"   Ibid., 109.

154   "Lisa has great taste"   Harry Harris, "Muppet Master Lauds Sesame Street," *Philadelphia Inquirer,* November 9, 1969.

154   "odd, because we're really not kid oriented"   Frank Langley, "The Moog Makes the Muppets," undated clip, *Sesame Street* early publicity folder (JHCA 06-0389, folder 2).

155   "I forgot about the party"   "Jim Henson Productions Legacy Meeting."

155   "Puppetry is different"   "He's His Own Best Audience: Muppeteer Jim Henson Watches TV While He Works," *TV Guide,* August 6, 1972.

155   "We look for a basic sense of performance"   Harris.

156   "but puppeteers do their own voices"   Srianthi Perera, "An Interview with Fran Brill," *Arizona Republic,* January 8, 2008.

156   "That was very much criticized"   Joan Ganz Cooney, interview on Archive of American Television website, http://www.emmytvlegends.org/interviews/people/joan-ganz-cooney.

156   "She brought a sharpness"   FO interview.

156   "analogous to a family of boys"   Fran Brill, email to the author, July 24, 2011.

156   "When I was eighteen"   Richard Hunt, archival interview.

156   "God, he was a comedic force"   FO interview.

157   "It was one of the most exhausting times I ever had"   Caroly Wilcox, archival interview (JHCA 10356).

157   "He'd be in the back working"   FO interview.

157   a beautiful short film   A perpetual *Sesame Street* favorite, the song in the film—sung by Juli Christman—was written by Alan Scott, Marilyn Scott, and Keith Textor.

157   "My dad made the whole thing himself"   LH interview.

157   "I like both a lot"   Maurice Sendak to JH, September 15, 1970 (JHCA 14-0787).

158   "Yanked by the suits at CTW," "the representative of the audience"   JS, archival interview.

158   "Jim never considered anything to be 'done'"   Spinney, 41.

158   "What the hell is that?"   Spinney, 59.

158   "He's not a villain, not horrible"   Ibid., 54.

158   "There's no heart of gold"   JS, archival interview.

159   "he didn't really enjoy it"   "Jim Henson Productions Legacy Meeting."

159   "they're just handed to me"   Robert Higgins, "The Muppet Family and How It Grew," *TV Guide,* May 16, 1970.

159   "There was a big three-hole binder"   JJ, archival interview.

159   "two weeks to a month"   Higgins, "The Muppet Family and How It Grew."

160   "Jim was an extraordinarily serious, yet silly man"   Gikow, 43.

160   "Ready to wiggle some dolls?"   FO interview (and verified by pretty much every Muppet performer).

160   "like a day off . . . that was my holiday"   "Jim Henson Productions Legacy Meeting."

160   "He loved the one-on-one aspect of directing"   FO interview.

160   "The most sophisticated people I know"   JH Quotes.

160   "Often, the material that we were given"   WAMI, 59.

161   "Performing the Ernie and Bert pieces"   Gikow, 46.

161   "We respected the writers' jokes"   FO interview.

161   "The best thing of all"   Borgenicht, 183.

161   "And what are we teaching?"   FO interview.

161   "I can't imagine doing Bert now"   Gikow, 47.

161   "They're Jim and Frank"   JS, archival interview.

162   "There are certainly elements of our own personalities"   Gikow, 47.

162   "We were two people"   FO interview.

162   "it was a magical coming together"   JS, archival interview.

162   "to be a kind of Kermit spokesperson"   Ibid.

162   "Kermit is the closest one to me"   Tom Shales, "Ta-Dahh! It's Jim Henson, Creator of Kermit the Frog and King of the Muppets," Washington Post, January 25, 1977.

163   "I live kind of within myself"   ABC Television Network promotional materials, February 10, 1975 (JHCA Sesame Street box).

163   "an explosion of energy"   FO interview.

163   "On Sesame Street, the monsters"   JH Quotes.

164   "Blue Monster"   "In Just an Hour a Day, Fewer Learning Cavities," Life, October 31, 1969.

165   "I noticed the purity of the dog"   FO interview.

165   "really enabled me to get a real feel"   "Jim Henson Productions Legacy Meeting."

165   "Jim loved complicated puppetry"   Joan Ganz Cooney, Archive of American Television interview.

165   "Every time we built"   JH Quotes.

165   "It wasn't much fun for Richard"   Jerry Nelson, interviewed by Jessica Max Stein, http://jessicamaxstein.com/2010/05/jerry-nelson-interview-part-i.

165   "He was like a puppy"   Ibid.

166   "I always used to do Jim's right hand"   Richard Hunt, archival interview (Henson Family Properties).

166   "blue sky!"   Fran Brill interview.

166   "we'd give the puppeteer a concept or a problem"   "Jim Henson Productions Legacy Meeting."

166   "I'm working with Ernie"   Gottfried, "The Mastermind of the Muppets."

166   "Family, school and television"   Higgins, "The Muppet Family and How It Grew."

166 **"TV is frustrating"** Foxy Gwynne, "Jim Henson and His Muppets," circa 1972 (JHCA *Sesame Street* box).

167 **"Kids love to learn"** Higgins, "The Muppet Family and How It Grew."

167 **"It's why the show is a success"** JJ, archival interview.

167 **"He loved to perform with Frank and Jerry"** Gikow, 183.

167 **"destroyed God knows how much"** "How Cookie Monster Destroys Work Habits of George Plimpton," *Wall Street Journal*, April 22, 1971.

167 **"profusion of aims"** "Who's Afraid of Big, Bad TV?," *Time*, November 23, 1970.

167 **"nondemocratic and possibly dangerous for young Britons"** "BBC Finds Sesame St. Not Ducky," *New York Post*, July 7, 1971.

167 **"Jim's contribution was absolutely essential"** "Jim Henson Productions Legacy Meeting."

167 **"Jim Henson's Muppets"** Jack Gould, "TV: 'Sesame Street' Begins Its Second Semester," *New York Times*, November 11, 1970.

168 **"I think it wasn't until *Sesame Street*"** JH Quotes.

168 **"When *Sesame Street* came on"** Harris.

168 **"I just stopped doing that stuff"** Ibid.

168 **"my goals have changed"** JH to Robert H. Steen, Quaker Oats Company, May 18, 1971.

168 **"hauled in $350,000 in '69"** Higgins, "The Muppet Family and How It Grew."

168 **"really ugly"** Gwynne, "Jim Henson and His Muppets."

169 **"Foundation support is impermanent"** Gikow, 264.

169 **"If I have a song to sing"** JH, "The Producer's Point of View," *Action for Children's Television* (Avon, 1970), 25–26.

169 **"I told him"** BB, archival interview.

170 **"You can't take advantage of the love"** "Jim Henson and His Magic Muppet Empire," *Philadelphia Inquirer*, December 3, 1987.

170 **"If Jim or the Muppets"** Ibid.

170 **"Here's what you have to do"** BB, archival interview.

170 **"I said no"** Joan Ganz Cooney, Archive of American Television interview.

171 **"Our bottom line consideration"** "Jim Henson and His Magic Muppet Empire."

171 **"receive the widest possible distribution"** Leonard Sloane, "Toys Are Talk of Sesame Street," *New York Times*, July 31, 1971.

171 **"more Muppets or more educational value"** Al Gottesman interview.

172 **"Jim was incredibly proud"** JJ, archival interview.

172 **"His means of expression"** FO interview.

Chapter Seven: Big Ideas

173 **"We can do anything you like"** JH to Bill Persky, October 22, 1970 (JHCA 14-0370).

174   "I'd sit there"   JS, archival interview.

174   "We need a song for a frog"   Davis, 256.

175   "I really found it so difficult"   "Girl with a Heart of Goldie," *New Jersey Record*, February 7, 1971.

175   "one day he was working"   See Jim's mid-1970s pitch for the unrealized television documentary *The Autumn Years* (JHCA 13501 Misc).

176   "delightful visual treat for the kids"   *Variety*, December 23, 1970.

176   "It was their show"   See assorted reviews, 1970 (JHCA *Great Santa Claus Switch* folder).

176   "Henson deserves credit"   *Variety*, December 23, 1970.

176   "Time is slipping away"   John T. Ross to JH, October 5, 1970 (JHCA *Frog Prince* box, Prod. 17281).

177   "We just can't get into that"   Sid Adilman, *Toronto Telegram*, March 26, 1971.

177–78 "Jim Henson's Muppets are so humorously conceived," "both kid and adult appeal," "Jim Henson's Muppets are so good"   See the memo "Frog Prince Reviews" from John Frango and Mike Yuro to Bill Frantz et al., June 16, 1971 (JHCA *Frog Prince* box, Prod. 17281).

178   "Good, solid entertainment"   "Neighbors from *Sesame Street:* A Visit with Jane and Jim Henson," *Greenwich Social Review*, 22–25.

178   "Jim was going crazy"   JJ, archival interview.

179   "big, busy, colorful"   "Night Club Reviews," *Variety*, June 30, 1971.

179   "brought down the house"   Norma Lee Browning, "Slight but Super," *Chicago Tribune*, June 21, 1971.

179   "We tried to put together material"   "Henson's Muppets Star Along Las Vegas Strip," *Greenwich Times* (Connecticut), June 21, 1971.

179   "jarring"   "Night Club Review International," *Hollywood Reporter*, June 23, 1971.

179   "I don't particularly like," "Working here [in Vegas]"   "Henson's Muppets Star Along Las Vegas Strip."

180   "We spent half our time"   JJ, archival interview.

180   "a great success"   Gwynne, "Jim Henson and His Muppets."

180   "My dad . . . always remained faithful"   LH interview.

180   "Jim was loyal to puppetry"   FO interview.

180   "The more I was associated with puppets"   Ibid.

181   "When I hear the art of puppetry discussed"   *Being Green*, 32.

181   "That was a big difference"   LH interview.

181   "It's nice for the children"   Gwynne, "Jim Henson and His Muppets."

181   "I was driving early"   BH interview.

182   "At home, we had all kinds"   *Being Green*, 128.

182   "He loved to take a chair"   Ibid., 2.

183   "It took him a while to get comfortable"   FO interview.

183   "I've . . . sat on the panel as myself"   Don Freeman, "Henson Is Shy Actor," *World* (Monroe, Louisiana), June 28, 1977.

183   "He was nervous about going on"   JJ, archival interview.

183 **"It's something I've always faced"** Don Freeman, untitled radio/TV column, *San Diego Union,* March 17, 1975.

184 **"Puppeteering covers a wide range of stuff"** Ibid.

184 **"it would not be supposed"** See JHCA ideas folder.

184–85 **"We know that many people will bring children"** JH, "Some Thoughts on 'The Muppets in Concert' Proposed for Alice Tully Hall—Early Fall, 1973" (JHCA 14-0107).

185 **"This is a very unusual evening of theater"** Ibid.

185 **"We loved the idea of Rowlf"** FO interview.

185 **"I'm not a real dog"** See JJ script for "Pirandello Meets Rin Tin Tin" (JHCA 14-0103).

185 **"You will pay no attention to them"** See "The Muppets Get It Together, Run Down: First Half" (JHCA 02-0564).

186 **"present a series of contrasting moods and scale"** JH, "Some Thoughts on 'The Muppets in Concert' Proposed for Alice Tully Hall—Early Fall, 1973."

187 **"He thought that we were applying"** JH Quotes.

187 **"The character comes first"** Gottfried, "The Mastermind of the Muppets."

187 **"[Jim] was the art director"** Caroly Wilcox, archival interview (JHCA 10356).

188 **"[Jim] felt concerned"** Al Gottesman, archival interview (JHCA 10368 trans).

188 **"the one property I've wanted to do"** See "List of Projects," early 1970s (JHCA 14-0467).

188 **"I was very good"** BH interview.

189 **"I was a strange kid"** John Henson interview.

189 **"[He and John] certainly cared for each other"** Jane Henson interview.

189 **"increas[ing] a child's psychological awareness," "a family mood with characters," "by which time it is hoped"** G. S. Lesser, *Affect Show* draft, July 19, 1972 (JHCA 14-0028).

189 **"character that always sees things in abstract symbols"** See Jim's notes for the *Affect Show* (JHCA *Affect Show* folder).

189 **"meaningful"** Diana Birkenfield, memo, "My Thoughts on Your New Show for CTW," circa 1972 (JHCA *Affect Show* folder).

190 **"I'd say to him"** FO interview.

190 **"stand up to him and get angry at him"** Al Gottesman interview.

190 **"In my opinion"** Birkenfield, "My Thoughts on Your New Show for CTW."

191 **"Diana was just a bit too relentless for Jim," "powerfully silent"** FO interview.

191 **"Diana vs. Bernie"** JH RB, July 27, 1973.

191 **"Talked to Diana Birkenfield"** JH RB, February 6, 1974.

191 **"These things were never personal"** Ibid.

192 **"I think it's fascinating"** LH, email to the author, August 8, 2012.

192 **"My parents weren't really big on funerals"** CH interview.

192 **"Mom passed on"** JH RB, October 21, 1972.

192 **"account of life in the next stages of existence"** Ruth Montgomery, *A World Beyond* (New York: Fawcett, 1985).

192   "My dad would never, ever be snippy"   CH interview.

193   "I've read and studied"   JH, introduction, "The Courage of My Convictions."

193   "the innocence and the simple optimism"   JJ, archival interview.

193   "very strongly"   Richard Hunt, archival interview.

193   "One of the extraordinary things about Jim"   *WAMI,* 59.

194   "I believe that life is basically a process of growth"   *Being Green,* 125.

194   "awkward mess"   JH RB, May 1972.

194   "We've got to stay together for the children"   Al Gottesman interview.

194   "I looked underwater"   LH interview.

195   "Like every other first-day skier"   *WAMI,* 55.

195   "He really didn't like to do something"   Jane Henson interview.

195   "We were all about the same level"   BH interview.

195   "[Driving] across country"   LH interview.

195   "I'm not an ecology nut"   George Maksian, "Jim Henson Fights Trash with Trash," *Los Angeles Times,* March 26, 1973.

196   "fascinated with the design process," "like an assassin"   Dave Goelz interview.

197   "I was starting to tap into that"   CH interview.

198   "Dad was driving fast cars"   LH, note to the author, August 9, 2012.

198   "I think . . . he was setting an example"   LH interview.

198   "He was so repressed"   Ibid.

198   "His repressive silence"   Ibid.

198   "I think my father was *very* intrigued"   CH interview.

199   "DECLARATION OF INDEPENDENCE"   JH RB, June 11, 1973.

199   "I think probably in the long run"   Jane Henson interview.

199   "I probably just kept things inside for so long"   Ibid.

199   "fiercely loyal"   CH, email to the author.

200   "Gelbart out of B'way"   JH RB, February 17, 1973.

200   "You're a better artist than you are a client"   Walt Kraemer to JH, May 10, 1973.

201   "We would carry these big"   FO interview.

CHAPTER EIGHT: THE MUCKING FUPPETS

203   "The time is right"   Proposal for *The Muppet Show,* circa 1969 (JHCA 14-0467).

204   "Puppets are fortunate," "The Muppets, more than any other puppets"   See various *Muppet Show* proposals (JHCA 14-0650, 14-0467).

206   "Somehow it seems to make"   JH to Gary Smith, ATV, September 25, 1973 (JHCA 14-0034).

206   "struck with [Jim's] originality and humor"   *WAMI,* 84.

206   "We made this special to appeal to all ages"   Sue Cameron, "Coast to Coast," *Hollywood Reporter,* January 30, 1974.

207   "absolutely delightful"   Review of *The Muppets Valentine Show, Variety,* February 6, 1974.

208 "we blew them up," "one of those great roars of appreciation" Gottfried, "The Mastermind of the Muppets."

208 "Hi, guys!" Dave Goelz interview.

209 "Bonnie Erickson's boyfriend" *WAMI*, 27.

209 "I find this inspired material very beautiful" JH Quotes.

209 "He was always interested in getting beyond" JS, archival interview.

209 "I didn't believe a word of them" FO interview.

210 "That's Jim Henson" BB, archival interview.

210 "someone must have needed it" BH interview.

210 "My car was broken into," "make fun of himself a little bit" Ibid.

210 "It would be a half hour show" See "List of Projects," circa 1973.

211 "create[s] new dishes" See "*The Muppet Show* as a Series," circa 1975 (JHCA *Muppet Show* box).

212 "[he] was in the office every day" Bonnie Erickson, archival interview (JHCA 14213).

212 "I used to ride with him a lot" BH, introduction to *The Muppet Show* DVD. Brian remembers the tapes being recorded by comedian Sid Caesar. Oz, however, was certain it was Brickman who had made the recordings.

213 "who represents the older establishment values" See "*The Muppet Show* as a Series."

213 "These are all characters" Ibid.

213 "He's a lot like me" "Seventy New Muppets Created by Jim Henson Make Their Bow in the Special, 'The Muppets Show,' Airing on ABC, Wednesday, March 19," ABC Press Release, February 10, 1975 (JHCA *Muppet Show* box).

213 "Jim wanted to get out of performing a little bit" JS, archival interview.

214 "come over [to London] for lunch," "I . . . was just knocked out" JH, private diary (JHCA 1597).

215 "produced substantial negative reaction" Memo on "Sex and Violence with the Muppets" [*sic*], Bob Boyett to Gloria Messina, December 6, 1974 (JHCA *Muppet Show* box).

215 "My 14-year-old daughter Lisa saw it" Gottfried, "The Mastermind of the Muppets."

215 "freak city!" Bernie Harrison, "Muppets Special Brings in Spring," *Washington Star*, March 19, 1975.

216 "Puppets are by their very nature symbolic" ABC Television Network promotional materials, February 10, 1974 (JHCA *Muppet Show* box).

216 "A lot of our work has always been adult-oriented" Unidentified clipping, December 6, 1974 (JHCA *Muppet Show* box).

216 "He had lots of changes which were necessary" Richard Hunt, archival interview.

216 "zippy" "Television Reviews," *Variety*, March 19, 1975.

216 "There was a mixed reaction" "REPORT: Consumer Survey taken on the evening of Wednesday, March 19, 1975 after the Jim Henson Special" (JHCA *Muppet Show* box).

216   "Perhaps one thing that has helped me"   *Being Green*, 52.

216   "We thought it was gonna be great"   BB, archival interview.

216–17 "Puppets are funny things"   "Jim Henson's Self-Imposed Fantasyland," *Herald* (Palatine, Illinois), November 12, 1977.

217   "translat[e] Jim's philosophy and essential ethic"   Al Gottesman, archival interview (JHCA 10368 trans).

218   "fair"   DL, archival interview.

218   "He was very interested in her opinion," "ever consider joining," "That was a dream," "I'm very serious, Dave"   Ibid.

219   "We had to work on Jim's image"   Ibid.

221   "Friends, the United States of America"   "The Muppets" pitch reel script, circa 1975 (JHCA *Muppet Show* folder).

221   "If they don't buy this"   BB, archival interview.

221   "it didn't sell"   DL, archival interview.

221   "so that [independent] producers"   "FCC Limits Network Program Ownership," *Los Angeles Times*, May 7, 1970.

222   "something good for us"   DL, archival interview.

222   "a wonderful goddamn thing"   BB, archival interview.

222   "He described the show"   Harris.

222   "NBC Show"   See Jim's daily desk calendar for 1975 (JHCA 9146).

222   "We wanted to redefine comedy"   Shales and Miller, 69.

222   "NBC was so scared"   BB, archival interview. See also interviews with BB at the Archive of American Television.

223   "I'd always liked and been a fan"   Lorne Michaels, interviewed by Judy Harris, unpublished interview, September 1982 (JHCA 21463).

223   "Mystic set up"   See Jim's notes for *Saturday Night Live* (JHCA 14-0755).

223   "a place called Gortch"   See Jim's full proposal for "Land of Gortch" (JHCA 14-0755). While the sketches are usually referred to as "The Land of Gorch," I am holding to Jim's spelling.

223   "He was the hardest-working person"   Dave Goelz interview.

224   "They had their style, we had ours"   FO interview.

224   Oz grumbled   Ibid. Hansome would be replaced by Fran Brill in subsequent episodes.

224–25 "Somehow what we were trying to do"   Harris.

225   "I think our very explosive, more cartoony comedy"   *Star Wars Insider*, 42, 69–70.

225   "very frustrated"   JJ, archival interview.

225   "It was a very, very difficult premise"   Lorne Michaels, interviewed by Judy Harris.

225   "Whoever drew the short straw," "I won't write for felt"   Shales and Miller, 69–70.

225   "They weren't interested in the Muppets"   JJ, archival interview.

225   "The Muppets were known"   FO interview.

226   "Lorne Michaels loved them"   DL, archival interview.

226   "The good part"   *Star Wars Insider*, 42, 69–70.

226 "a little grass" Jerry Nelson interview.

227 **He was determined, then, to take an acid trip** This story was told, and corroborated, by interviews with Frank Oz and Jerry Nelson, as well as archival interviews with Jon Stone.

227 **"was not a great thing"** BB, Archive of American Television interview, http://www.emmytvlegends.org/interviews/people/bernie-brillstein.

227 **"I always loved [Scred]"** Jerry Nelson, interviewed by Kenneth Plume.

227 **"Lorne, being Lorne"** BB, Archive of American Television interview.

227 **"see if he would do a TV series for me in England"** *WAMI*, 84.

228 **"all over the country"** BB, archival interview.

228 **"always felt Henson would be interested"** Abe Mandell, "Creative and Marketing Talents Wed in Selling 'Muppet Show,'" *Variety*, January 3, 1979.

228 **"I said, 'I've saved you a lot of money'"** BB, archival interview.

229 **"We have a deal"** Ibid.

229 **"We finally did it!"** Ibid.

229 **"I love you"** Ibid.

229 **"We're doing twenty-four half-hour shows, *guaranteed*!"** FO interview.

229 **Four days later** "New Comedy-Music Show Set for Prime Access," *Broadcasting*, October 27, 1975; Ruth Thomas, "Muppets to Do Series," *Sunday Spectator*, November 16–22, 1975; "ITC Sells 'Muppet Show' to CBS O&Os," *Variety*, October 29, 1975.

230 **"I always figure people stay"** Lorne Michaels, interviewed by Judy Harris.

230 **"I really respect Lorne"** Harris.

230 **"Dear Gang"** See postcard from "The Muppets" to "Sat. Night Live," circa 1977 (JHCA 14-0757).

Chapter Nine: Muppetmania

232 **"British Louis B. Mayer"** FO interview.

233 **"talking around ideas"** JJ, *Puppetry Journal* (Fall 2005), 6.

233 **"[none] of us were convinced"** JJ, archival interview.

234 **"very, very little money"** DL, archival interview. See also Guests folder (JHCA 14-0661).

234 **"The first . . . guests were"** BB, Archive of American Television interview.

234 **"We got a blood bath," "too British"** DL, archival interview.

234 **"Grade had told us, 'Don't be British'"** FO interview.

234 **"were all wrong"** JJ, archival interview.

234 **"Jim was pissed at them!"** DL, archival interview.

234 **"It's not the end of the world"** Ibid.

235 **"We knew we wanted to have a stand up comedian"** "Jim Henson's Self-Imposed Fantasyland."

235 **"Fozzie was a disaster"** JJ, archival interview.

235 **"Fozzie did help make Statler and Waldorf"** *OMAM*, 39.

235–36 **"Frank was dying," "working in a vacuum," "find that bear"** JJ, archival interview.

237   "real shower"   Living arrangement memos (JHCA 20216).

237   "[Jim was] accused of spoiling everyone"   DL, archival interview.

238   "We were setting up with this room"   Bonnie Erickson interview.

238   "slightly sticking their necks out"   Stephen Webbe, "Muppet Mania," *Christian Science Monitor*, December 1976.

239   "Let's leave that in"   Richard Hunt, archival interview.

240   "[Jim] worked the hardest of anybody"   DL, archival interview.

240   "a light day"   JJ, archival interview.

240   "I'm really enjoying it"   Ruth E. Thompson, "Lavish New Muppet Series Product of Henson's Wizardry with Puppets," *The Leader*, October 31, 1976.

241   "We phased out that ballroom dancing thing"   JJ, archival interview.

241   "What he always seemed to do best"   Richard Hunt, archival interview.

241   "these puppets are not just characters"   JH Quotes.

242   "How the characters play"   Ibid.

242   "He would drive [the writers] crazy," "the implied joke," "We can show that!," "There would be fairly heated arguments"   JJ, archival interview.

242   "Most TV humor is verbal"   Morton Moss, "Muppet Man Henson Tracks Puppets' Humor to Source," *Herald Examiner* (Los Angeles), September 30, 1976.

243   "Fozzie's ineptness"   JJ, archival interview.

243   "a simple guy who wants to be funny and loved"   Jean Rook, "Jean Rook Meets Miss Piggy," *Daily Express* (London), August 19, 1977.

244   "We sent the material down on the floor," "They just played the hell out of it"   JJ, archival interview.

244   "funny not because of what he does"   Bill Marvel, "TV's Captivating Muppets Are . . . The Adult Kids' Show," *National Observer*, May 1977.

244   "He relates to the other characters"   WAMI, 33.

244   "There's a bit of me in Kermit"   Cordell Marks, "The Muppet Men," *TV Times* (U.K.), undated article.

244   "I suppose he is not unlike me"   Martin Jackson, "Now Cool It, Miss Piggy," *Daily Mail* (London), August 1977.

245   "Me not crazy?"   *The Muppet Show*, Season 3, Episode 15.

245   "a bunch of goddamn lunatics!"   FO interview.

245   "It's *The Mary Tyler Moore Show*"   JS, archival interview.

245   "Sometimes a character will start"   David Hawley, "Muppets Pull the Strings on the Children in All of Us," untitled clip, Milwaukee, circa 1977 (JHCA *Muppet Show* box).

246   "I was working as Miss Piggy with Jim"   Culhane, "The Muppets in Movieland."

246   "The place fell apart"   JJ, archival interview.

246   "Miss Piggy was to have been a minor character"   "Henson Muppets Bridge even Barriers of Language," *Greencastle Banner Graphic* (Indiana), February 3, 1978.

246   "Rowlf could have been one of the stars"   WAMI, 119.

246   "Poor Rowlf"   Jane Henson interview.

246   "She takes over"   "The Muppets: TV's Unlikely Superstars," *Knickerbocker News* (Albany, New York), June 15, 1978.

246   "But let's get it straight"   Rook, "Jean Rook Meets Miss Piggy."

246   "It's a man?!?"   FO interview.

246   "real, real tough," "The whole *Muppet Show* conceit"   JJ, archival interview.

247   "She grew up on a small farm"   FO interview.

247   "She's sensuous and she's been hurt a lot"   Rook, "Jean Rook Meets Miss Piggy."

247   "endless [and] fairly pointless," "He was this little, little kid," "Richard, shut up and go away!"   Richard Hunt, archival interview.

247   "I was so upset"   Bonnie Erickson interview.

247   "I was very insecure"   Dave Goelz interview.

247   "Gonzo believes he is a worthless creature"   Marks, "The Muppet Men."

247–48 "a loser who did these horrible acts"   Dave Goelz interview.

248   "This could be Gonzo," "this little dark frightened character"   Ibid.

248   "They loved watching Jim and Frank work"   Dave Goelz, interviewed by Kenneth Plume, "Gonzo Puppeteerism: An Interview with Dave Goelz," Muppet Central website, January 28, 2000, http://www.muppetcentral.com/articles/interviews/goelz2.shtml.

248   "Jim kept saying, 'Well, do it again'"   Dave Goelz interview.

248   "Gonzo can still get very, very depressed"   Marks, "The Muppet Men."

248   "As *I* got confidence, *he* got confidence"   Dave Goelz interview.

249   "is an aspect of my own personality"   *The Muppet Show* newsletter, 1978.

249   "really tough" "Some [guests] relate to us"   Webbe, "Muppet Mania."

249   "to work in a sort of fun land"   "Jim Henson's Self-Imposed Fantasyland."

249–50 "Although he never told people what to wear," "The women stars fell in love with Jim," "Listen"   DL, archival interview.

250   "I've heard stories," "Unless our guests go home"   OMAM, 24.

250   "as the show kept gaining in popularity"   BB, Archive of American Television interview.

250   "The calls started coming in"   DL, archival interview.

251   "The atmosphere and excitement"   WAMI, 84.

251   "Everything all right, boys?"   Jerry Nelson interview.

251   "everybody has to see a monitor"   *Of Muppets and Men: Behind the Scenes of The Muppet Show,* television documentary, 1981.

252   "I settle for a set of headphones"   John Archibald, "Frog in His Throat," *St. Louis Post-Dispatch,* September 16, 1976.

252   "Everything was play for him"   JJ, *Puppetry Journal* (Spring 2001): 11.

252   "Jim wasn't a workaholic"   FO interview.

252   "We know each other so well"   OMAM.

252   "Even when they're not shooting"   Richard K. Shull, "Rich Little Amazed by TV's Muppets," *Muncie Press* (Indiana), June 28, 1977.

252   "Sorry, Jim, we have to go again"   Peter Fiddick, "All Hands on Deck," *Guardian* (U.K.), May 23, 1977.

253   "If he was driving to work"   Dave Goelz interview.

253 "He laughed until he cried"   FO interview.

253 "Frank and Jim were incredible"   DL, archival interview.

253 "The combination of Jim and Frank"   Dave Goelz interview.

253 "the 70s and 80s Laurel and Hardy"   Richard Hunt, archival interview.

253 "this very intimidating figure"   BH interview.

253 "incredibly moody," "Frank has this incredible thing," "That's just such a shame"   JJ, archival interview.

254 "the way they could second-guess each other"   Richard Hunt, archival interview.

254–55 "We could be in the middle of a number," "probably ten times"   DL, archival interview.

255 "once [the meetings] started," "we have to eat anyway," "he'd start improvising this piece of material"   JJ, archival interview.

256 "One of Jim's real talents"   Ibid.

257 "Oh well," "fantastic"   BH interview.

257 "a little bit burdened"   CH interview.

258 "one of the fastest selling half-hour series"   "Muppets Multiply in '83," Backstage, April 9, 1976.

258 "Seeing was believing"   Mandell, "Creative and Marketing Talents Wed in Selling 'Muppet Show.' "

258 By the beginning of the 1976 television season   Backstage, September 24, 1976; "Muppet Access Show on 162 Stations," Variety, September 8, 1976.

258 "If you have a child," "Long Live the Muppets!"   See Chicago Tribune, Louisville Times clips, circa 1976 (JHCA Muppet Show box).

258 "bore more of the [head writer] Jack Burns touch"   Variety, September 22, 1976.

258 "We are well on our way"   Jack Burns, memo to JH, July 9, 1976 (JHCA Muppet Show box).

259 "was hard for Jim"   DL, archival interview.

259 "gives me a stomachache"   Brillstein, 150–51.

259 "it was never personal"   FO interview.

260 "It felt like the warmest, funniest thing"   "Behind the Scenes Documentary," Emmet Otter's Jug-Band Christmas, HIT Entertainment, 2005.

260 "Oh, I love this thing!"   Tom Shales, "Muppets Make Merry and Money," Washington Post Radio Week, February 20, 1977.

260 "When [Jim] chose Paul Williams"   Ibid.

261 "We all love the music"   JH to Paul Williams, April 7, 1977. Emphasis in original (JHCA Misc Files, Emmet Otter JBC Prod 15689).

261 "I think there's some little piece"   "Behind the Scenes Documentary."

261 "That was the most elaborate production"   JH Quotes.

261 "This was a way of working"   "Behind the Scenes Documentary."

262 "so perfect and so beautiful"   Ibid.

262 "we were looking for realistic movement," "Working as I do"   JH Quotes.

262 "Very nice"   Emmet Otter camera notes (JHCA 21473 VT Reel Breakdown #1).

262   "Everything about that production was magic"   "Interview with Jerry Nelson," the Muppet Mindset website, http://themuppetmindset.blogspot.com/2010/11/interview-with-legendary-muppeteer.html et seq.

262   "one of the highlights of my career"   Dave Goelz interview.

263   "I don't think he ever rode the bike!"   BH interview.

263   "It was such a good time for him"   JJ, archival interview.

263   "we needed time"   Webbe, "Muppet Mania."

264   "Muppet Murderers"   Stephen Cook, "The Muppets Rule OK," *Evening Mail* (London), March 9, 1977.

264   15 million faithful Britons   Rook, "Jean Rook Meets Miss Piggy."

264   "It's like they're creating"   JH, private diary, circa 1977.

264   "The show was a big smash hit"   "Interview with Jerry Nelson," the Muppet Mindset website.

264   "rendezvous secretly"   Cook, "The Muppets Rule OK."

264   It was even reported   Rook, "Jean Rook Meets Miss Piggy."

265   "It's fantastic the way the Muppets"   Marks, "The Muppet Men."

265   "I don't think or talk about superstars"   Rook, "Jean Rook Meets Miss Piggy."

265   "Really, money doesn't concern me at all"   Joe Irwin interview.

265    $25 million   Bill Kaufman, "A Prince of a Frog," *Newsday* (New York), August 14, 1977.

265   "shabby"   Cook, "The Muppets Rule OK."

265   "I feel I owe it"   Rubis Saunders, "The Man Behind the Muppets," *Young Miss,* April 1977.

265   "there were times"   JJ, archival interview. Emphasis in original.

266   "I love that show!"   *High Fidelity,* September 1977 (JHCA *Muppet Show* box, press clippings).

266   "Bernie was a rock"   DL, archival interview.

267   "a great fan of the show"   Carol Ross to DL, January 19, 1978 (JHCA TMS Guest Correspondence 11318).

267   "As the show kept gaining in popularity"   BB, Archive of American Television interview.

267   "He *loved* all that James Bond kinda stuff"   CH interview.

267   "It's a kind of equanimity"   LH interview.

268   "every single restaurant in Hampstead"   Ibid.

268   "What's that thingy"   FO interview.

268   "There was no question"   Jane Henson interview.

268   "was his absolute favorite"   DL, archival interview.

268   "We all enjoyed being around him"   Stephanie Harrigan, "It's Not Easy Being Blue," *Life,* July 1990.

268   "That's great fun for me"   JH, private diary, 1977.

269   "Up for 3"   JH RB, September 10–11, 1977.

269   "If some people recognize me"   Harry Harris, "Henson Speaks for Kermit the Frog," *Philadelphia Inquirer,* July 24, 1977.

269   "Dumb, dumb, dumb"   Eliot Wald, "Channel 11's Fall Shots: Late but with Some Power," *Chicago Sun-Times,* October 14, 1977.

269 **"the most elegant and sophisticated creation"** Harris.

269 **"most creative, entertaining"** "KXAS Focuses on Family," *Dallas Times Herald,* September 6, 1977.

270 **"[Critics] didn't feel this show"** David Hawley, "Muppets Pull the Strings on the Children in All of Us," Milwaukee area newspaper, circa 1977.

270 **"I guess the reason for this letter"** BB to JH, November 29, 1977.

270 **"He was restless"** JS, archival interview.

270 **"He'd want to move on to another phase"** DL, archival interview.

Chapter Ten: Life's like a Movie

272 **"Did you ever, in your wildest dreams,"** **"The honest answer to this"** JH, private diary, 1977.

272 **"Jim's way of operating"** Jane Henson interview.

272 **"Jim was the hardest working man"** Spinney, 133.

273 **"*The Muppet Show* on film"** James Frawley, "Directing 'The Muppet Movie,'" *American Cinematographer,* July 1979.

273 **"Jim was a dreamer"** *Being Green,* 18.

273 **"Lew Grade, being a true gentleman"** BB, Archive of American Television interview.

273 **"I saw Brian Froud's work"** JH Quotes.

274 **"The thought of being able"** Ibid.

274 **"Make deal with BRIAN FROUD"** JH RB, August 1977.

274 **"When I talked to Brian"** JH Quotes.

274 **"a pantheistic world"** Finch, *The Making of The Dark Crystal.*

275 **"I was trying to figure out"** JH, private diary, 1977.

275 **"looked like he belonged"** DL, archival interview.

275 **"Unlike other TV studios"** Stephen Cook, "The Muppets Rule OK."

276 **"fondle, molest, handle, touch or tweak"** Hawley, "Muppets Pull the Strings on the Children in All of Us."

276 **"They *hate* being tweaked," "They're *all* the real one"** Shales, "Muppets Make Merry and Money."

276 **"hadn't meant"** Spinney, 135–36.

276 **"I cried; Jim didn't"** Bonnie Erickson interview.

276 **"Jim always said"** *Being Green,* 94.

277 **"Don was extremely private"** Dave Goelz interview.

277 **"He just stared at me"** DL, archival interview.

277 **"I was standing there crying"** FO interview.

277 **"He thought maybe showing feelings"** DL, archival interview.

277 **"Jim said, 'It's okay'"** FO interview.

277 **"In some ways"** Jane Henson interview.

277 **"I'm sure he will go on"** JH, private diary.

277 **"was a huge, massive impact"** FO interview.

278 **"Frankie Fontaine voice"** Jerry Nelson interview.

278   "Everyone here's lovely"   Richard Tippett, "Muppets' Heart of Gold!" *Look-In* (U.K.), circa 1977.

278   "She was just out there"   BH interview.

278   "there was really no place [to talk]"   Jane Henson interview.

279   "Muppet operators must be good actors"   Moss, "Muppet Man Henson Tracks Puppets' Humor to Source."

279   "One thing about being a puppeteer"   *OMAM.*

279   "I had other characters to do"   FO interview.

279   "probably the person most responsible"   *OMAM,* 72.

280   "distancing themselves"   Richard Hunt, archival interview.

280   Nelson had even confronted Jim   Ibid.

280   admittedly drinking too much   Jerry Nelson interview.

280   "freeze a little bit"   DL, archival interview.

280   "I knew I was a great supporting player"   Richard Hunt, archival interview.

280   "I was the workhorse," "I didn't write"   FO interview.

280   "He would sit right with the writers," "The other people resented it"   DL, archival interview.

281   "There's a sub-level"   Richard Hunt, archival interview.

281   "[The Muppets] may be fighting"   DL, archival interview.

281   106 countries, with a total audience of 235 million   Rick Dubrow, "Muppet Show World's Most Successful Show," *Herald Examiner* (Los Angeles), circa 1978.

281   "I hope they manage to make the jokes funny"   Shirley Eder, "Diane's off to the Cabaret," *Detroit Free Press,* September 24, 1977.

281   "[It's] almost certainly"   John Skow, "Those Marvelous Muppets," *Time,* December 25, 1978.

281   "the new Walt Disney"   Times News Service Report, "Henson's Muppets Bridge Even Barriers of Language," *Banner Graphic* (Greencastle, Indiana), February 3, 1978.

282   "Working with Jim Henson"   "Behind the Scenes Documentary," *Emmet Otter's Jug-Band Christmas,* HIT Entertainment, 2005.

282   "hear them in the studio"   Ibid.

282   "Up until that time"   Peter Hertlaub, "Q&A: 'The Muppet Movie' Director James Frawley," *San Francisco Chronicle* (online version), March 2, 2007, http://blog.sfgate.com/parenting/2007/03/02/qa-the-muppet-movie-director-james-frawley.

282   "[It] was actually a very frustrating experience"   JJ, archival interview.

283   "He felt pretty good"   Hertlaub, "Q&A: 'The Muppet Movie' Director James Frawley."

283   "We're taking the characters"   "On the Road with the Muppets," *Variety,* August 20, 1978.

283   an accomplishment Jim noted   See JH RB, September 10, 1978.

284   "If you don't dig sore arms"   "Sore Arms with Puppet Work," *Kansas City Star,* March 12, 1978.

284   "[The Muppets] had never been shot outdoors"   Frawley, "Directing 'The Muppet Movie.'"

284   "the single most difficult sequence"   Ibid.

285   "Well, if I can fit"   *American Cinematographer,* July 1979.

285   "no place for someone with claustrophobia"   Webbe, "Muppet Mania."

286   "it was a bit frightening"   John Henson interview.

286   "[He] would never ask us to do anything"   Dave Goelz interview.

286   "We always used to kid Jim"   *Being Green,* 27.

286   "Everybody was eagerly awaiting him"   DL, archival interview.

286–87 "right back to our childhoods"   JJ, archival interview.

287   "We take up where he left off,"   "Dear Jim—Keep the Magic Alive"   Culhane, "The Muppets in Movieland."

287   "Even the most worldly of our characters"   *Being Green,* 25.

287   "Received EMMY"   JH RB, September 17, 1978.

288   "Bullshit"   FO interview.

289   "to take a look at the lore"   *OMAM,* 101.

289   "sheer joy"   See correspondence (JHCA *Muppet Show* box).

289   "darling little castle"   Jane Henson interview.

290   "I want to have a place"   JH, private diary, November 1977.

290   "I didn't want a pretentious space"   "Home of the Muppets," *Interior Design,* February 1980, 198–205.

291   "could cause us embarrassment"   Joan Ganz Cooney to JH, March 23, 1979 (JHCA *Muppet Movie* box).

291   "running around screaming," "wandering around in the middle of it all"   Culhane, "The Muppets in Movieland."

291   "I love my work,"   *Being Green,* 73.

291   "You had to try to keep up"   Ibid., 57.

291   "For such a giving"   Richard Hunt, archival interview.

292   "It isn't that Jim didn't have friends"   JJ, archival interview.

292   "and that's when"   Richard Hunt, archival interview.

292   "[Jim] was very close to us all"   JJ, archival interview.

292   "a great house"   Jane Henson interview.

293   "Great evening"   JH RB, May 31, 1979.

293   "I cried in the opening"   John Henson interview.

293   "everything follows production"   DL, archival interview.

293   "He'd been used to running"   *WAMI,* 153.

293   "Al [Gottesman] was in New York"   DL, archival interview.

294   "Sure, the more Jim was in New York"   FO interview.

294   "We are primarily a company"   *Being Green,* 87.

294   "It seems that I'm bigger now"   Culhane, "The Muppets in Movieland."

294   "wanted to be part of the family"   DL, archival interview.

295   "Jim was not preoccupied"   Al Gottesman interview.

295   "He could *not* handle it"   DL, archival interview.

295   "I think Jim felt"   Richard Hunt, archival interview.

295   "Stop calling this company," "It was a major thing"   DL, archival interview.

296   "we'll all lose our shirts"   "Muppets, TV Syndicate Boffo, Readying for Their Invasion," *Variety,* October 4, 1978.

296   "Piggy's become a phenomenon"   *OMAM.*

296   "Great!"   JH RB, June 22, 1979.

296   "unbridled amiability"   Vincent Canby, "The Screen: Muppets Go to Hollywood," *New York Times,* June 22, 1979.

296   grossing over $65 million: See Box Office Mojo at http://boxofficemojo.com/movies/?id=muppetmovie.htm for additional details.

297   "that brings tears to your eyes"   Webbe, "Muppet Mania."

297   "I guess you could say"   JH Quotes.

297   "clan of whackos"   JJ, archival interview.

297   "Kermit was Jim"   BB, archival interview.

298   "I'm in particular awe"   Canby, "The Screen: Muppets Go to Hollywood."

298   "trying to fool the audience"   *OMAM.*

298   "The reason those characters are appealing"   Richard Hunt, archival interview.

298   "If you can figure out"   Roger Ebert, "The Muppet Movie," *Chicago Sun-Times,* November 14, 1979.

298   comparisons with Walt Disney   *The Washington Post* hailed *The Muppet Movie* as "the latest in a progression of accomplishments which eventually should put the Muppets on par with Mickey Mouse." Samuel Allis, "Mon Dieu! Mogul Meets the Muppets; Will Success Spoil Their Innocence?," *Washington Post,* June 7, 1979.

298   "I'm slightly uncomfortable"   Culhane, "The Muppets in Movieland."

298   "It's important to me"   Skow, "Those Marvelous Muppets."

299   "We were the best party givers"   DL, archival interview.

299   "the electricians broke for tea"   Bonnie Erickson interview.

300   "[My dad] was very intrigued"   BH interview.

300   "delightful weekend"   JH RB, September 21–23, 1979.

300   "It would look so otherworldly"   CH interview.

300   "Neat!"   JH RB, October 19, 1979.

300   viewers slow to return   Glenn Aylett, "Strike Out," Transdiffusion Broadcasting System, http://www.transdiffusion.org/tmc/thames/strikeout.php.

300   mumbling only half-audible responses   Elisabeth Bumiller, "Homecoming: Muppets and Memories at Maryland," *Washington Post,* November 5, 1979.

301   "I can honestly say"   See John Denver's note to the 1996 Laserlight CD rerelease of *John Denver and the Muppets: A Christmas Together* (Laserlight 12 761).

301   "It's discouraging to see"   Tom Shales, "Fluff That Satisfies," *Washington Post,* December 5, 1979.

301   "He was easily proud, actually"   BH interview.

302   "lovely"   JH RB, December 1979.

302   "*The Muppet Movie* has grossed around 75 million"   JH RB, last entry for 1979.

302   "A VERY MAJOR BIG YEAR"   JH RB, undated, final entry of 1979.

CHAPTER ELEVEN: THE WORLD IN HIS HEAD

304   **"Back in the sixties," "When you try to get people"**   JH Quotes.

304   **"too big to handle"**   JH, American Film Institute seminar, with Jim Henson, Elton H. Rule Lecture Series in Communications, April 14, 1989 (JHCA 7974).

304   **"It was the juxtaposition"**   Anne Tasker, Approved *Dark Crystal* Production Notes (JHCA 14-0260).

305   **"perhaps a lodestone"**   Treatment for *Mithra,* August 4, 1977 (JHCA *Dark Crystal* box).

306   **"Normally you write the script first"**   Tasker, Approved *Dark Crystal* Production Notes.

306   **"struggle through terrible dangers"**   "The Crystal: A Fantasy Adventure Film conceived by Jim Henson, designed by Brian Froud, dimensionalized by The Muppets" pitch book, circa summer 1979 (JHCA 770).

306   **"I felt that if we gave too much time"**   DL, archival interview.

306   **"He was always interested in the idea"**   CH interview.

306   **"Jim wanted to do *The Crystal"***   DL, archival interview.

307   **"The idea of doing very naturalistic creatures"**   JH Quotes.

307   **"In England, while we were making"**   Rinzler, 71.

308   **"Working with STAR WARS on YODA"**   JH RB, November 1978.

308   **"It became a mutual thing," "I thought he was the best puppeteer," "Jim called me into his trailer"**   Rinzler, 71.

308   **"it was acting, not just performing"**   FO interview.

308   **"They were building a special effect"**   Kathy Mullen interview.

308   **"really fuckin' heavy"**   FO interview.

309   **"It was *very* hard"**   Kathy Mullen interview.

309   **"It was just the sort of thing"**   Michael Stein and Jessie Hortsing, "Muppeteer Jim Henson and Star Wars Producer Gary Kurtz Talk About Their Newest Project: *The Dark Crystal,*" *Fantastic Films,* February 1983.

310   **"loved"**   JH RB, January 1980.

311   **"beautiful suits"**   BB, archival interview.

311   **"How much do you think that costs?"**   DL, archival interview.

312   **"Was that all right?"**   Arthur Novell interview.

312   **"The long range product"**   Skow, "Those Marvelous Muppets."

312   **"After five seasons"**   Judith Feingold, "An Interview with Jim Henson," circa 1980, unmarked clipping (JHCA *Muppet Show* box).

312   **"because I so enjoy those movies"**   Production notes, *The Great Muppet Caper* (JHCA *Great Muppet Caper* box).

313   **"joyful"**   JH, "Thoughts on MM2" (JHCA 10616).

313   **"There are a great many problems"**   JH to Martin Starger, February 11, 1980 (JHCA 17932).

313   **"not looking good"**   JH RB, March 1980.

314   **"We were really interested in nonlinear storytelling"**   LH interview.

314   **"Lord Grade's office chartered a flight"**   *Being Green,* 144.

314   **"I thought it [Cannes] was trashy"**   DL, archival interview.

315   **"[It] seemed to do a shimmer dance"**   *Being Green,* 144.

315 "That's the money" FO interview.

315 "And he just said to me" Jocelyn Stevenson interview.

315 "I want to talk with him about an idea I have" Ibid.

316 "I said, 'She'll be great!,'" "You were right" BH interview.

316 world is coming to an end When the fifth season of *The Muppet Show* finally aired, the Gene Kelly episode would actually be televised first, further obscuring the "end of the world" joke.

317 "All at Elstree hope the Muppets will return" Jack Greenwood to John Krawiec, August 1980 (JHCA correspondence box).

317 "We finished our 120th *Muppet Show*" Feingold, "An Interview with Jim Henson."

317 "was a great adventure for all of us" CH, email to author.

317 "really didn't like being by himself" Jane Henson interview.

318 "somewhat public," "It horrified him" Ibid.

318 "I think [Jim] was evaluating" Steve Whitmire interview.

318 "For the life of him" LH interview.

319 "make or break someone's day" DL, archival interview.

319 "I feel a little distant from you" Ossie Morris to JH, July 14, 1980 (JHCA 17934).

319 "It has taken me twenty years," "Usually the cameraman insists" *The Great Muppet Caper*, production notes (JHCA *Muppet Caper* production box).

320 "My dad wanted me to just figure it out," "Brian, you did a really" BH interview.

320 "something new—something to talk about" See Jim's handwritten notes on *The Great Muppet Caper* (JHCA 10616).

320 "If I had to search out" JH, "Guilty Pleasures," November 1982 (JHCA 10242).

321 "So as soon as Frank" Caroly Wilcox, archival interview (JHCA 10356).

321 "He had no patience for" BH interview.

322 "so the whole place," "It was quite elaborate" JH, AFI seminar, April 14, 1989.

322 "it was difficult at times" FO interview.

323 "Jerry, that's what insurance companies are *for*" Jerry Nelson interview.

323 "It [*Dark Crystal*] had become overblown" Kathy Mullen interview.

323 "It was the focus" CH interview.

324 "He had it in his head" DL, archival interview.

324 "a prospect for perennial usage" *Variety*, December 24, 1980.

324 "charming" John J. O'Connor, "TV: Whole New Cast of Muppets," *New York Times*, December 15, 1980.

325 "I want to do a children's television show" Jocelyn Stevenson interview.

325 "we talked about doing a show" Michael Frith interview.

325 "Something that [Jim] had been observing" Jane Henson interview.

326 "[Jim's] genius" Jocelyn Stevenson interview.

326 "What the show is really about" *Woozle World* treatment, April 3, 1981 (JHCA 10650).

326   "Jim asked Jerry and Jocelyn and me"   Michael Frith interview.

327   "We sat around and talked"   JJ, archival interview.

327–28 *Fraggle Rock* was a true depiction"   DL, archival interview.

328   "I have wound up doing things"   JJ, archival interview.

328   "he'd make each one of you feel"   Jocelyn Stevenson interview.

328   "Nobody's ever developed a television series"   JJ, archival interview.

328   "Creatively, I find I work best"   JH Quotes.

329   "there was some difficulty blending together"   Tasker, Approved *Dark Crystal* Production Notes.

329   "I think it would be better," "To Jim, that was the most important thing"   FO interview.

329   "You have all of these techniques"   JH Quotes.

330   "When we're doing major characters"   JH, AFI seminar, May 6, 1986.

330   "My father had a unique way of working"   Finch, *The Making of The Dark Crystal*, 11–12.

330   "We knew when we went into this film"   JH, "Guilty Pleasures."

330   "Mimes, Dancers and Actors"   Advertisement, *Stage and Television Today*, May 29, 1980.

331   "Performers were on their haunches"   *The Making of The Dark Crystal*, documentary.

331   "I think the idea of conceiving"   Stein and Hortsing, "Muppeteer Jim Henson and Star Wars Producer Gary Kurtz Talk About Their Newest Project: *The Dark Crystal*."

331   "We could never have tried"   JH Quotes.

331   "He was trying to reach out"   Jane Henson interview.

331–32 "I guess I've always been most intrigued"   JH Quotes.

332   "It has a lot of elements of fairy tales"   Tasker, Approved *Dark Crystal* Production Notes.

332   "a story about genocide"   Michael Frith interview.

332   "We are working with primary images"   Tasker, Approved *Dark Crystal* Production Notes.

332   "Well, we can't all be perfect"   Michael Frith interview.

332   "had pretty much come to a common feeling"   JH, "Guilty Pleasures."

333   "Things were *not* smooth"   FO interview.

333   "Jim didn't tell you what to do"   *Being Green*, 35.

333   "Jim had the head of a producer"   DL, archival interview.

333   "He saw the movie in his head"   FO interview.

334   "Everyone knows how a human moves"   Tasker, Approved *Dark Crystal* Production Notes.

334   "I've never done any performing"   Stein and Hortsing, "Muppeteer Jim Henson and Star Wars Producer Gary Kurtz Talk About Their Newest Project: *The Dark Crystal*," 55.

334   "was just too damn busy"   Kathy Mullen interview.

335   "I really do believe"   Ibid.

335 **"You see this character walking"** JH Quotes.

335 **"You have to be concerned"** Finch, *The Making of The Dark Crystal*, 60.

335 **"an exercise in logistics," "This just never ends," "It was massive"** FO interview.

335 **"You went off and built this great career"** Joan Ganz Cooney, interviewed by Jim Henson for production of *The Jim Henson Hour,* October 26, 1988 (JHCA 7965).

335 **"grueling work," "had a wonderful time," "It was just so great"** JH, AFI seminar, May 6, 1986.

336 **"sure hand in guiding"** Film Reviews, *Variety,* June 25, 1981.

336 **an old Hollywood power couple** Vincent Canby, "Screen: Miss Piggy Stars in 'Great Muppet Caper,'" *New York Times,* June 26, 1981.

336 **"humanity, tenderness and intelligence"** Rex Reed, "Musical Muppets Merely Marvelous," *Daily News* (New York), June 26, 1981.

337 **"[Jim] was just like a little kid, beaming"** DL, archival interview.

337 **"Yeah, she was absolutely no bullshit"** FO interview.

338 **"We said, 'All right'"** Michael Frith interview.

338 **"But I really have to thank Jim"** Karen Prell, interviewed by Kenneth Plume and Phillip Chapman, "Animateer Karen Prell: An Interview with Puppeteer, Animator and Writer," MuppetCentral, September 11, 1998, http://www.muppetcentral.com/articles/interviews/prell.shtml.

338 **"I think we went through the motions"** Dave Goelz, interviewed by Kenneth Plume, "Gonzo Puppeteerism: An Interview with Dave Goelz," MuppetCentral, January 28, 2000, http://www.muppetcentral.com/articles/interviews/goelz3.shtml.

338 **"I really pushed to do that character"** Steve Whitmire, interviewed by Kenneth Plume, "Ratting Out: An Interview with Steve Whitmire," MuppetCentral, July 19, 1999, http://www.muppetcentral.com/articles/interviews/whitmire1.shtml.

339 **"just kind of finding out who they were"** Kathy Mullen interview.

339 **"I like to think"** "Two Days with Trevor Jones at the Phone," *BSOSpirit,* June 2004, http://www.bsospirit.com/entrevistas/tjones_e.php.

340 **"It was a clash"** "Robert Holmes à Court, 53, Dies; Australian Built Business Empire," *New York Times,* September 30, 1990.

340 **"Holmes à Court was a cold"** FO interview.

340 **as quickly as possible** While Henson Associates business manager Al Gottesman recalled Jim wanting to purchase the film from ACC immediately following the film's premiere in Detroit in July, an April 29, 1982, letter from Holmes à Court to Jim reveals Jim and Holmes à Court had actually been in discussion for some time. See M. R. H. Holmes à Court to JH, April 29, 1982 (JHCA 9756).

340 **"*Fraggle Rock* is the first show"** JH, AFI seminar, May 6, 1986.

340 **"He just let it be what it was"** Steve Whitmire interview.

341 **"I think of myself as fairly limited"** JH Quotes.

341 "Jim was a huge gadget fan"   Bacon, 14.

341 *Dark Crystal was a $25 million R&D project*   Michael Frith interview.

341 "Neat"   This response was typical. See JH RB.

341 "it was very special"   Steve Whitmire interview.

342 "[Cantus] was great"   Jocelyn Stevenson interview.

342 "The idea"   JH, AFI seminar, May 6, 1986.

342 "completely endearing," "fetchingly whimsical"   John O'Connor, "TV Weekend: Five Hours of 'Lazy,'" *New York Times,* February 24, 1984; Tom Shales, "The Fraggle Factor," *Washington Post,* January 10, 1983.

342 "unprecedented"   Associated Press, "Names in the News," April 7, 1989.

342 "a very nice project"   JH, AFI seminar, May 6, 1986.

343 "to make final decisions"   JH memo to Everybody, "Sneak Previews—Dark Crystal," March 10, 1982 (JHCA 9756).

343 "going on forever," "What did you think?"   Michael Frith interview.

343 "close to being an epic"   JH Quotes.

343 "He was so proud of it"   CH interview.

343 "Not great"   JH RB, March 19, 1982.

343 As the theater emptied   FO interview.

343 "a big miscalculation"   LH interview.

344 "The movie went off"   FO interview. Memories are conflicted on when, exactly, executives from Universal first saw the film, with Oz recalling a viewing in Hollywood and Al Gottesman remembering a showing in London.

344 "He felt the studio"   Jane Henson interview.

344 "[There was] that sense of dismay"   CH interview.

344 "It was a huge overhaul"   LH interview.

344 "running a tape backwards and forward"   David Odell, "Reflections on Making The Dark Crystal and Working with Jim Henson," *The Dark Crystal: Creation Myths* (graphic novel) (Los Angeles: Archaia, 2013).

345 "A bit better"   JH RB, July 12, 1982.

345 "too boring," "He felt that the movie was about a balance"   Jane Henson interview.

345 Jim decided he'd had enough   Again, memories are foggy on whether it was his annoyance with Universal or ACC, following the Detroit premiere, that drove Jim to purchase the film from ACC. While Jim was annoyed with Universal, they had no financial investment in the film—at least beyond distribution—so Jim's decision to purchase the film from ACC would have no direct impact on his relationship with Universal, making it unlikely the studio had triggered his response. However, Al Gottesman, whose memory is more reliable on these things, recalled Jim phoning him on the way back from Detroit and saying that Grade [*sic*] and ACC didn't understand his film. Oz, too, recalled it this way.

345 "I can't work like this," "There was really only one thing he could do"   John Henson interview.

345 "I'm going to buy back *The Dark Crystal*"   BB, archival interview.

345–46 Brillstein was stunned, "And most of the time he was right"   This section is based on personal and archival interviews with BB, DL, CH, and Jane Henson.

346   "It was a huge gamble"   CH interview.

346   "It was a good deal"   FO interview.

347   "What happened to the Muppets," "They're not there," "We're not telling!"   John Calloway interview with JH, WLS-TV Chicago, November 23, 1982.

347   "With all of the developments"   JH Quotes.

347   "a watered down J. R. R. Tolkien"   Vincent Canby, "Review: Henson's Crystal," *New York Times,* December 17, 1982.

348   "Jim Henson and his colleagues"   Gary Arnold, "The Finest in Fantasy," *Washington Post,* December 21, 1982.

348   "enjoyable [and] imaginative"   John Engstrom, "'Dark Crystal' Is Fantastic!," *Boston Globe,* December 18, 1982.

348   "sketchy"   "Film Review: The Dark Crystal," *Variety,* December 15, 1982.

348   *The Dark Crystal really polarized opinion"*   Bacon, 15.

348   "I find that often"   JH Quotes.

348   "I felt sad for Jim"   FO interview.

348   "I thought I had failed miserably"   Kathy Mullen interview.

349   "The most impressive thing"   FO interview.

Chapter Twelve: Twists and Turns

350   "We have been very pleased"   JH to Daniel Burge, January 27, 1983 (JHCA 9878).

350   "first time"   JH RB, March 2, 1983.

351   "was a huge undertaking"   JH to Daniel Burge, January 27, 1983 (JHCA 9878).

352   "In this business, there is nothing more compelling"   JJ, archival interview.

352   "He loved the good things"   BB, archival interview.

353   "He wanted my mom to be happy"   CH interview.

353   "I can't come back here"   Jane Henson interview.

353   "handshake of a separation"   Ibid. Despite Jane's kind categorization, the separation was, in fact, very legal.

353   "have an above-board independent life"   LH interview.

354   "escalated quickly"   Jane Henson interview.

354   "painful and inevitable"   Ibid.

354   "really upset," "There was a part of me"   Heather Henson interview.

354   "I was looking at the year ahead"   "Interview with Jim Henson," *The Muppets Take Manhattan* DVD, Special Feature.

354–54 "I had learned a lot about directing"   FO interview.

355   "The next one will be"   Leslie Stackel, "Jim Henson: Master of Muppets," *Starlog,* August 1984.

355   "This time"   Froud, *The Goblins of Labyrinth,* 139.

355   "I immediately pictured a baby"   Ibid.

356   "What is the philosophy of [the] film?"   See Jim's notes on "The Labyrinth" (JHCA 10732).

356   "We played around with various story lines"   *Labyrinth* production notes.

356   "define and inspire"   Froud, *The Goblins of Labyrinth,* 14–15, 140.

356   "way too over jokey," "I asked Jim"   FO interview.

356   "very precise in terms of his characters"   "Interview with Jim Henson," *The Muppets Take Manhattan* DVD, Special Feature.

357   "There's a sense of our characters"   *Being Green,* 91.

357   "We did our first film in Los Angeles"   *The Muppets Take Manhattan* production notes.

357   "We got a very nice, happy feeling"   "Interview with Jim Henson," *The Muppets Take Manhattan* DVD, Special Feature.

358   "I thought, 'Well, getting a degree"   BH interview.

358   "it was under an umbrella of safety," "I fucked up"   FO interview.

359   "We sort of go up and down"   Stackel, "Jim Henson: Master of Muppets."

359   "an opportunity to stretch"   "Interview with Jim Henson," *The Muppets Take Manhattan* DVD, Special Feature.

359   "He'd say, 'I can't be expected'"   Steve Whitmire interview.

360   "I'm just an actor," "The argument will continue on"   Stackel, "Jim Henson: Master of Muppets."

360   "SHOOTING MUPPET BABIES IN MOVIE"   JH RB, August 29, 1983.

360   "short, stubby arms and legs," "very difficult"   FO interview.

360   "It becomes quite a game"   JH, AFI seminar, May 6, 1986.

361   "Things spring up in your head"   FO interview.

361   "to worry about it"   "Interview with Jim Henson," *The Muppets Take Manhattan* DVD, Special Feature.

362   "Puppetry is a very wide field"   Ibid.

362   "Jim started the Foundation"   Allelu Kurten, quoted on the Jim Henson Foundation website.

362   "We see frequently puppets"   JH, "Some Professional Ethics," *Puppetry Journal* (1975): 24.

363   "Getting started was really difficult"   Connie Peterson, quoted on "Jim Henson's Red Book" website, July 6, 2011, http://www.henson.com/jimsredbook/2011/07/06/741983.

363   "be Jim when Jim wasn't there"   Bacon, 14.

364   "I was always chomping at the bit"   FO interview.

365   "a really marvelous idea"   John Cleese to JH, June 1, 1984 (JHCA 8708 corr).

365   "Your contributions to *Labyrinth*"   JH to Terry Jones, October 31, 1983 (JHCA 9888).

365   "I filled sketchbook upon sketchbook"   "Inside the Labyrinth" documentary, transcript (JHCA, *Labyrinth* box).

365   "poetic novella"   Owen Williams, "Dance Magic Dance: 25 Years of Labyrinth," *Empire,* 201, 272.

365   "I sat at my desk"   "Inside the Labyrinth" documentary.

366   "You're going to let kids"   Arthur Novell interview.

366 "I'd always stayed away from Saturday morning"   JH, AFI seminar, May 6, 1986.

366 "the right way to meet our characters for the first time"   JJ, archival interview.

367 "have a nice reason for being"   JH, AFI seminar, May 6, 1986.

367 "can be used to develop creativity"   JH to Michael Frith, "Notes on Marvel Productions, The Muppet Babies," circa 1984 (JHCA 8497).

368 "At some point in my life"   *Being Green,* 159.

368 "recharged and re-inspired," "The beauty of nature"   Ibid., 139.

369 "One of my happiest moments"   JH, "The Courage of My Convictions."

369 "while we were considering"   Adam Pirani, "Part Two: Into the Labyrinth with Jim Henson," *Starlog,* August 1986.

370 "happening *now*"   John Henson interview.

370 "Jim . . . outlined his basic concept"   *Labyrinth* production notes.

370 "If you like the script"   "Inside the Labyrinth" documentary.

370 "I'd always wanted to be involved"   *Labyrinth* production notes.

370 "I thought it was fair," "We'll see"   FO interview.

371 "not original"   Roger Ebert, review of *The Muppets Take Manhattan,* January 1, 1984, http://rogerebert.suntimes.com/apps/pbcs.dll/article?AID=/19840101/REVIEWS/401010362.

371 "It doesn't have enough lunacy"   FO interview.

371 "a terminally sappy idea"   Gary Arnold, "The Muppet Mope," *Washington Post,* July 14, 1984.

371 "that brown film"   Various Muppet performers and builders called it this.

372 "I was always keen"   Bacon, 16.

372 "the first time my father"   Ibid.

372 "The Mad Hatter's face"   Ibid., 17.

372 "The characters are just not Muppets at all"   Harris.

373 "I feel I've always done well"   JH Quotes.

373 "people say, 'you really should'"   Harris.

373 "more oriented to the Muppets"   JH, AFI seminar, May 6, 1986.

374 "Muppet performer"   See Jim's corrections to the Apple copy, 1984 (JHCA general correspondence A-C box).

374 "The terms that I mentioned"   Robert Holmes à Court to JH, telegram, March 28, 1984 (JHCA 8808).

375 "We would have no company today"   LH interview. In the final agreement, Jim purchased all 120 episodes of *The Muppet Show, The Muppet Movie, The Great Muppet Caper,* and the television specials *Of Muppets and Men, The Muppets Go Hollywood, The Muppets Go to the Movies,* and *The Fantastic Miss Piggy Show,* as well as the rights to all original music in all of the above Muppet properties.

375 "simply heroic"   Al Gottesman interview.

375 "[It was] about the world"   Kim Johnson, *Life Before and After Monty Python* (Plexus, 1993), 210.

376 "We've got a live actress playing the part"   See "Jim Henson's Red Book"

website, January 29, 2011, entry, http://www.henson.com/jimsredbook/2011/01/29/1291985.

376   "dark and cynical"   Ibid.

376   "just right for the role"   *Labyrinth* production notes.

377   "Puppets are a lot like masks"   "Jim Henson's Red Book" website, May 7, 2011, entry, http://www.henson.com/jimsredbook/2011/05/07/571983.

377   "I have a good group of people"   JH, AFI seminar, April 14, 1989.

377   "hand out the 'attaboys' "   DL, archival interview.

377   "He didn't wonder if his own work was good"   LH interview.

378   "If you like one person"   JH to Arthur Shimkin, March 11, 1981 (JHCA 17954).

378   "When you first encounter the kind of energy"   JJ, archival interview.

379   "dramatize the fact"   "Fraggle Rock: Notes for Season Four," circa 1984 (JHCA *Fraggle Rock* box).

379   "travel around the world"   JH memo to Management Forum, "Re: After Fraggle Rock," March 14, 1984 (JHCA 8497).

379   "It takes a lot of rehearsing"   "Inside the Labyrinth" documentary.

380   "Everyone has to work closely"   *Labyrinth* production notes.

380   "didn't feel that it was very much mine"   Johnson, *Life Before and After Monty Python,* 210.

381   "stunned"   CH interview.

381   "Jim was hurt"   DL, archival interview.

381   "It's a big one"   JH, AFI seminar, May 6, 1986.

381–82 "In the beginning it was hard," "I found I could talk very straight to her"   "Inside the Labyrinth" documentary.

382   "Once I'd overcome the disorientation"   *Labyrinth* production notes.

382   "[Bowie] has been wonderful to work with"   JH memo to Management Forum, "London Update," July 30, 1985 (JHCA 2460).

382   "a completely free hand"   *Labyrinth* production notes.

382   "a spoiled child," "[He's] a very normal"   Ibid.

382   "Supposedly, David Bowie went around looking for us"   John Henson interview.

382   "Jim is undoubtedly"   *Labyrinth* production notes.

383   "Late in the story"   "Inside the Labyrinth" documentary.

383   "this was the most complicated thing," "I suddenly had this idea"   Ibid.

384   "It's certainly one of the most bizarre"   *Labyrinth* production notes.

384   "When you've had an idea"   "Inside the Labyrinth" documentary.

384   "I never leave the studio"   BH interview.

384–85 "Rather than laying everyone off," "By keeping a group of people together," "He had tried to approach the problem," "it would have almost been nepotism"   Bacon, 19.

385   "He was the first one"   BB, archival interview.

385   "He was a modest guy"   Susan Schindehette, "Legacy of a Gentle Genius," *People,* June 18, 1990.

385 "He was very conservative"   BB, archival interview.

385 "My dad was *naughty*"   BH interview.

385 a meeting with a Swedish filmmaker   This story was constructed from interviews with Duncan Kenworthy, Brian Henson, and Dave Goelz.

386 "was really quite beautiful"   JH, AFI seminar, April 14, 1989.

387 "money were no object," "Television is one of the greatest connectors around"   *Muppet Voyager* proposal (JHCA 21272).

387 "Those last four shows"   Larry Mirkin interview.

387 "We who were totally involved"   JJ, archival interview.

388 "I think we all cried"   Jerry Nelson interview.

388 "This whole project has been a joy from the beginning"   See video footage of *Fraggle Rock* wrap party, http://www.youtube.com/watch?v=C3kUKjym1nw.

388 "Jim wanted to make a difference"   *Being Green*, 152.

389 "When I go see a film"   "Inside the Labyrinth" documentary.

389 "fabulous"   Nina Darnton, "Screen: Jim Henson's 'Labyrinth,'" *New York Times*, June 27, 1986.

389 "[It's] obviously made"   Roger Ebert, review of *Labyrinth*, *Chicago Sun-Times*, June 27, 1986.

389 "[It] has quite a lot going for it"   Nick Riddick, review of *Labyrinth*, *Cinema Papers*, June 1986.

389 "A crashing bore"   Review of *Labyrinth*, *Variety*, June 1986.

389 "Jim Henson knows what he's doing"   Gene Siskel, "Henson's Wizardry Lost in 'Labyrinth,'" *Chicago Tribune*, June 30, 1986.

390 "series of incidents"   Ebert, review of *Labyrinth*.

390 "loses its way"   Review of *Labyrinth*, *Variety*, June 1986.

390 "I didn't give a fuck"   Jerry Nelson interview.

390 "costly bore"   Review of *Labyrinth*, *Variety*, June 1986.

390 "I was stunned and dazed"   Therese L. Wells, "Henson: From Muppets to 'Storyteller,'" *Hollywood Reporter*, January 30, 1987.

390 "[It] was a real blow"   Schindehette, "Legacy of a Gentle Genius."

390 "I think that was the closest"   Harrigan, "It's Not Easy Being Blue."

390 Arthur Novell, Jim's publicist   Markham/Novell Communications Ltd. was Jim's agency of record. Novell was the primary liaison with Henson Associates and would become a trusted confidant.

390 "[It was] really despair"   Arthur Novell interview.

391 "absolutely the closest project to him"   Jane Henson interview.

391 "That movie looked exactly"   Larry Mirkin interview.

391 "Take a look at *Labyrinth*"   FO interview.

391 "Life is a kind of labyrinth"   *Labyrinth* production notes.

391 "You know"   Jerry Nelson interview.

CHAPTER THIRTEEN: STORYTELLER

392–93 "wasn't the movie audiences," "obviously, the picture," "I work in one capacity" Wells, "Henson: From Muppets to 'Storyteller.'"

393 "these huge, grandiose visions" CH interview.

393 "looking to all the world" JH, introduction to *The Tale of the Bunny Picnic*.

394 "it was really fun to make puppets again" CH interview.

394 "Having done the Muppet stuff" JJ, archival interview.

394 "See how Jane reacts to all this," "were sizing each other up" Arthur Novell interview.

395 "She was spirited, outgoing" Al Gottesman interview.

395 "Jim really used his hands" Mary Ann Cleary, email to the author, April 12, 2012.

395 "that really capture the flavor" LH interview.

395 "Most folktales" Wells, "Henson: From Muppets to 'Storyteller.'"

396 "the words, and the sound of a man's voice" Alan Jones, "The Storyteller," *Cinefantastique*, circa 1987.

396 "He was the absolute top of the heap" LH interview.

397 "[Jim] told me he had an idea" Anthony Minghella, archival interview.

397 "'sculpted foot syndrome'" Duncan Kenworthy to JH, July 9, 1986 (JHCA 18521).

398 "I really don't think we could sustain," "some of the prettiest television we've ever done" Diane Haithman, "The Muppet Man Joins His Cuddly Crew; Henson Variety Show Will Debut Tonight," *Los Angeles Times*, April 14, 1989.

399 "As much as he loved objects" CH interview.

399 "[Tartikoff] loves it" Duncan Kenworthy to Brian Froud, November 12, 1986 (JHCA 12140).

400 "I thought it was just terrific" JH to Paul Reubens, September 15, 1986 (JHCA 14067).

400 "we're going to have great fun" JH to Phil Ramone, August 20, 1986 (JHCA 14067).

401 "broken-family Christmas" John Henson interview.

401 "consistently dark, victimized, and pessimistic" Larry Mirkin to JH, "re IN TV," January 2, 1987 (JHCA 14067).

401 "It's time to stop thinking of him" Wells, "Henson: From Muppets to 'Storyteller.'"

401 "When a show arrives" Walter Goodman, "John Hurt Stars in 'The Storyteller,'" *New York Times*, January 30, 1987.

401 "one of Jim Henson's finest moments" Matt Roush, "Henson's 'Storyteller' Is a Beautiful Beast," *USA Today*, January 29, 1987.

402 "It is our responsibility" "A Message from Jim Henson," *The Storyteller*.

402 "it's very hard to just visit" Anthony Minghella, archival interview.

402 "I think Jim felt" Richard Hunt, archival interview.

403 150 employees Francis X. Clines, "Mr. Muppet's Empire Is Thriving," *New York Times*, October 25, 1987.

403 **idealist** JH Myers-Briggs results (JHCA 10249).

403 **"work for common good"** JH notes (JHCA 23509).

403 **"I've never particularly wanted"** Monika Guttman, "Father of Muppets Diversifies," *Kenosha News* (Wisconsin), December 13, 1987.

403 **"The lawyers would all fight"** Jane Henson interview.

403 **"many of whom"** JH, HA Quarterly Report, June 23, 1987 (JHCA 14067).

404 **"It's almost like the early days"** Jones, "The Storyteller."

404 **"in the same grand tradition"** Proposal for *The Jim Henson Hour,* late 1987 (JHCA 15814).

405 **"In the many years we've been on television"** JH, *The Jim Henson Hour* pitch reel, December 1987, http://www.youtube.com/watch?v=oALgQAEH_Ok.

405 **"*The Muppet Show* of the future!"** *Lead-Free TV* proposal (JHCA 15814).

405 **"unlimited potential," "We're tremendously excited"** Proposal for *The Jim Henson Hour,* late 1987 (JHCA 15814).

406 **"I thought that was a wonderful way"** Kevin Clash interview.

406 **"Imagination is what this show is all about"** *The Jim Henson Hour* pitch reel.

406 **"quite well," "lovely"** JH, HA Quarterly Report, September 29, 1987 (JHCA 14067).

406 **"He doesn't do a lot of puppeteering anymore"** "Jim Henson Organizes a Reunion of Muppets," *News-Press/Gazette* (St. Joseph, Missouri), December 1987.

407 **"cherished," "There's a nice, naive quality"** Matt Roush, "Warm Your Spirit in a Muppet Wonderland," *USA Today,* December 1987.

407 **"I think people relate"** Candace Burke-Block, "Kermit, Miss Piggy, Henson, and Company Host Holiday Flick," *Westsider* (Goodyear, Arizona), December 17, 1987.

407 **"taking them [the Muppets] on an archeological adventure," "specific and explicit"** JH to Brian Muehl, January 23, 1987 (JHCA 22024).

408 **"figure out a way"** JJ, archival interview.

408 **"this cheesy, terrible plot"** JJ, interviewed by D. W. McKim and Phillip Chapman, July 24, 1998, http://www.muppetcentral.com/articles/interviews/juhl1.shtml.

408 **"It's going to be the kind of movie"** FO to JH and Jerry Juhl, December 5, 1987 (JHCA 17236).

409 **"a rich and mysterious"** Proposal for *The Jim Henson Hour.*

409 **"We should be creating a kind of basis"** Andrew J. McCarthy, "Muppets on His Mind," *Total Television,* December 1987.

409 **"mixed feelings"** JH, HA Quarterly Report, December 17, 1987 (JHCA 14067).

409 **"I like working collaboratively with people"** *Being Green,* 73.

409 **"all the work that I do in television"** JH, remarks at the Television Hall of Fame induction, November 15, 1987.

410 **"It's very exciting"** JH, HA Quarterly Report, December 17, 1987.

410   **"We were working on** *Storyteller"*   Diane Holloway, "Prime-Time Puppets: Henson and Children's Pals Create an Unusual Mix in Hourlong Series," *Austin American-Statesman,* April 2, 1989.

CHAPTER FOURTEEN: A KIND OF CRAZINESS

412   **"[I was] in a meeting with NBC yesterday"**   JH to Bill Prady et al., January 19, 1988 (JHCA 15815). Prady would go on to develop such top-rated TV shows as *The Big Bang Theory.*

412   **"nasty"**   Mira Velimirovic to JH, April 18, 1988 (JHCA 22030).

413   **"I don't like this"**   Roald Dahl to JH, December 2, 1986 (JHCA *The Witches* production file).

414   **"for very valid reasons," "It is one of my favorite projects"**   JH to Roald Dahl, December 9, 1986 (JHCA *The Witches* production file).

414   **"I will tell you"**   Roald Dahl to JH, February 28, 1988 (JHCA *The Witches* production file).

414   **"While I am not an advocate"**   Amy Ash Nixon, "Witches Worry About Movie; Muppet Creator Working on Film," *Beverly Times* (Beverly, Massachusetts), March 2, 1988. See also JH to Susan M. Baxter, February 11, 1988 (JHCA 8675).

415   **"NBC is worried"**   JH memo, February 3, 1988 (JHCA 20775).

415   **"I think they're the best television shows"**   Patricia Brennan, "Jim Henson: From Muppets to Movies to Medieval Folk Tales," *Washington Post,* October 25, 1987.

415   **"When the cable is hooked up"**   "Jim Henson: The Future of Video and Cable," http://www.youtube.com/watch?v=UoSutaKx0Ag&feature=related.

415   **"I love working on this show"**   JH, HA Quarterly Report, March 16, 1988 (JHCA 14067).

415   **"In broad strokes"**   McCarthy, "Muppets on His Mind."

416   ***The Disney Hour* consisted"**   JJ to Jocelyn Stevenson, Mira Velimirovic, and Larry Mirkin, March 18, 1988 (JHCA 20864).

416   **"I'm feeling quite good"**   JH, HA Quarterly Report, March 16, 1988.

416   **"Isn't this a** *romantic* **view?"**   Mary Ann Cleary interview.

417   **"I think he was very much in love"**   Richard Hunt, archival interview.

417   **"I was really quite fond of her"**   Heather Henson interview.

417   **"I don't think he ever wanted to marry"**   BH interview.

418   **"it's great for my reputation!"**   Arthur Novell interview.

418   **"It was hard on him"**   Richard Hunt, archival interview.

418   **"bitchy," "pooper scooper"**   JH to Mark Shivas, March 17, 1988 (JHCA *The Witches* production file).

419   **"I do think it would be courteous"**   Roald Dahl to Duncan Kenworthy, April 18, 1988 (JHCA 9002).

419   **"AWFUL," "STUPID AND USELESS," "PL[EASE] SHOW TO JIM H."**   Roald Dahl to Duncan Kenworthy, April 28, 1988 (JHCA *The Witches* production file).

419   "Things have been a little bumpy"   JH, HA Quarterly Report, June 24, 1988 (JHCA 14067).

420   "OBVIOUS. It is also TRITE"   Roald Dahl to Nic Roeg, August 2, 1988 (JHCA 9002).

420   "It is essential"   JH, HA Quarterly Report, June 24, 1988.

420   "David, I don't know what I would do," "He gave the kids undivided love"   DL, archival interview.

420–21 "I just felt that he was an amazing dad"   John Henson interview.

421   "I think we are going to see"   JH, HA Quarterly Report, December 17, 1987 (JHCA 14067).

421   "I tend to avoid confrontation"   Matt Roush, "Jim Henson, the Mogul of Family TV," *USA Today*, December 15, 1987.

422   "It was frustrating"   Larry Mirkin interview.

422   "it was *so* difficult"   JJ, archival interview.

422   "This is great"   Larry Mirkin interview.

422   "I always prefer," "It seemed the logical thing"   Haiuthman, "The Muppet Man Joins His Cuddly Crew; Henson Variety Show Will Debut Tonight."

423   "except [that it] was kind of wonderful"   JJ, archival interview.

423   "a work in progress"   JH to Brandon Tartikoff, September 12, 1988 (JHCA 20851).

424   "[It's] still so much fun to do"   Transcript, conversation between Jim Henson and Joan Ganz Cooney, October 26, 1988 (JHCA interviews box).

424   "Damon Runyon with dogs"   JJ, archival interview.

424   "I just love it"   JH, HA Quarterly Report, January 5, 1989 (JHCA 14067).

424   "He was just having such a wonderful time"   JJ, archival interview.

425   "need[ed] work"   JH RB, December 3, 1988.

425   "looking good"   JH, HA Quarterly Report, January 5, 1989.

425–26 "given the extra time," "worked out quite nicely," "It's so incredible"   JH, AFI seminar, April 14, 1989.

426   "Maybe if it was a *better* haircut"   CH interview.

426   "I think we are getting a handle"   JH, HA Quarterly Report, March 21, 1989 (JHCA 14067).

426–27 "It hasn't been an easy film," "a bit in the middle"   Ibid.

427   "They put us in a time slot"   "Dialogue on Film: Jim Henson: Miss Piggy Went to Market and $150 Million Came Home," *American Film*, November 1989.

427   "has to pick and choose"   See Jim's introduction to *The Jim Henson Hour*, April 14, 1989.

428   "biggest problem"   JH, AFI seminar, April 14, 1989.

428   "Fixing what's wrong"   Tom Shales, "Henson's Happy Ending; Futuristic Muppets and the Storyteller Spell," *Washington Post*, April 14, 1989.

428   "different"   Matt Roush, "A Madcap Mix of Jim Henson's Muppetry," *USA Today*, April 13, 1989.

429   "a bright addition to prime time"   Howard Rosenberg, "TV Review: Mup-

pets Maintain Huggability in Jim Henson Hour," *Los Angeles Times,* April 14, 1989.

429   **"that was then"**   Amy Aldrich, "The Muppets Take Disney World."

429   **"I'm sorry the Sunday experiment"**   Brandon Tartikoff to JH, undated note circa May 1989 (JHCA 14-0421).

429   **"hurt"**   Aldrich, "The Muppets Take Disney World."

429   **"disappointed," "I don't particularly like the way"**   JH, HA Quarterly Report, Summer 1989 (JHCA 14067).

429   **"We were very ambitious"**   Larry Mirkin interview.

430   **"a kind of craziness"**   JJ, archival interview.

430   **"He was in love with technology"**   Alex Rockwell interview.

430   **"one of those characters"**   JH, AFI seminar, April 14, 1989.

430   **"It was like the show didn't know"**   JJ, archival interview.

430   **"a chaotic hour"**   Alex Rockwell interview.

430   **"flying around"**   FO interview.

431   **"I know that this period of time"**   JH, HA Quarterly Report, Summer 1989.

431   **"releases me from a lot of business problems"**   "Dialogue on Film: Jim Henson: Miss Piggy Went to Market and $150 Million Came Home," *American Film.*

Chapter Fifteen: So Much on a Handshake

432   **"made in family entertainment heaven"**   "Miss Piggy and Friends Join Mickey Mouse Club; Disney Buys Rights to Muppets," *Houston Chronicle,* August 29, 1989.

432   **"The first film I saw," "outside of my own films"**   JH, handwritten draft of Disney press release, 1989 (JHCA 10366).

433   **"but a seed was planted"**   Brillstein, 327.

433–34 **"very expensive," "I have the best thing in the world for you," "like a Mafia dinner," "very soft,"**   BB, archival interview.

434   **"The Muppets' world renown"**   Brillstein, 327.

434   **"disarmingly simple"**   JH, HA Quarterly Report, June 24, 1988.

435   **"It was *never* just selling the Muppets"**   FO interview.

435   **"It's special because you get a guy like Jim"**   James Cox and Shelley Liles-Morris, "Mickey Buys the Muppets; 'Creative Vitality' of Henson a Lure," *USA Today,* August 29, 1989.

435   **"On a personal level"**   JH, handwritten draft of Disney press release.

435   **"It's not easy," "When I went off to do *Labyrinth*"**   JH, AFI seminar, May 6, 1986.

435–36 **"was getting unwieldy"**   DL, archival interview.

436   **"people would go to Jim directly"**   Brillstein, 328.

436   **"He was a very good businessman"**   Larry Mirkin interview.

436   **"the organizational albatross," "He was an artist first and foremost"**   Brillstein, 328.

436   **"Looking way back down the road"**   JH, handwritten draft of Disney press release.

436 "This was so much on a handshake" Kim Masters, "Disney's Muppet Miasma: Corporate Style, Henson's Death Complicate a Deal in Waiting," *Washington Post,* June 13, 1990.

437 "[It was] just great" BB, archival interview.

437 "JHP 'deal team'" See "Memo re: Disney Transaction, Charlie Rivkin to Distribution List (JH et al.)," June 19, 1989 (JHCA 10574).

437 "Jim had been adamant" Joan Ganz Cooney interview.

437 "In none of the information" Charles Rivkin to Richard Nanula, June 13, 1989 (JHCA 9597).

438 "holy place" Masters, "Disney's Muppet Miasma: Corporate Style, Henson's Death Complicate a Deal in Waiting."

438 "In general," "and looking quite nice," "The lip articulation" JH, HA Quarterly Report, circa summer 1989 (JHCA 15361).

438 "enormous, heavy beasts," "We're going to see" See "Handmade Video" HensonCompany YouTube channel, http://www.youtube.com/watch?feature=player_embedded&v=o51brOuAbcI.

439 "Where are we going with this?" Mary Ann Cleary interview.

440 "For whatever we become" Mary Ann Cleary, email to the author, April 17, 2012.

440 "I know that this past period of time" JH, memo to staff, July 26, 1989 (JHCA 15365).

440 "Disney Said to Be Wooing Henson" *Star Tribune* [Minneapolis, Minnesota], August 17, 1989.

440 "Disney May Be Courting Miss Piggy's Company" *Houston Chronicle,* August 20, 1989.

441 "Jim Henson's wish" BB, archival interview.

442 "I think hooking up" "Mickey Mouse has a new sibling" Adam Yeomans and Vicki Vaughan, "Muppet Merger: Jim Henson Has Hand in Bringing Characters to Walt Disney," *Orlando Sentinel,* August 29, 1989; "Acquisitions, Mergers and Muppets Series," Editorial, *Tampa Bay Times,* August 30, 1989.

442 "I feel I have reached a certain level" JH, handwritten draft of Disney press release.

443 "a creative designated hitter" Patrick Lee, "Disney Invites Kermit, Friends to Join Mickey," *Los Angeles Times,* August 29, 1989.

443 "There are only a few characters," "And they're all evergreen" Richard Stevenson, "Muppets Join Disney Menagerie," *New York Times,* August 29, 1989; Richard Turner, "Kermit the Frog Jumps to Walt Disney as Company Buys Henson Associates," *Wall Street Journal,* August 29, 1989.

443 "Just thought I'd let you know" Anne Kinney to CTW, September 8, 1989 (JHCA 8803).

443 "He will no longer have to be raising money" Cox and Liles-Morris, "Mickey Buys the Muppets; 'Creative Vitality' of Henson a Lure."

444 "He *never* spent two weeks a year" Joan Ganz Cooney interview.

444 "We could not ask" Cox and Liles-Morris, "Mickey Buys the Muppets; 'Creative Vitality' of Henson a Lure."

444 **"for life"** Yeomans and Vaughan, "Muppet Merger: Jim Henson Has Hand in Bringing Characters to Walt Disney."

444 **"[give] Jim the maximum operating flexibility"** "Memo re: Disney Transaction, Charlie Rivkin to Distribution List (JH et al.)," June 19, 1989.

445 **"A lot of times"** JH, AFI seminar, April 14, 1989.

445 **Katzenberg had promised** Lee, "Disney Invites Kermit, Friends to Join Mickey."

445 **"Much like Disney"** JH to Michael Eisner, June 6, 1989 (JHCA 9597).

445 **"treat our characters"** "Memo re: Disney Transaction, Charlie Rivkin to Distribution List (JH et al.)," June 19, 1989.

446 **"That was Jim's mandate"** DL, archival interview.

446 **"Kermit should be treated"** "Memo re: Disney Transaction, Charlie Rivkin to Distribution List (JH et al.)," June 19, 1989.

446 **"a lot of money," "It's a strategic acquisition"** Stevenson, "Muppets Join Disney Menagerie."

446 **"Jim is ambitious in expressing himself"** Aldrich, "The Muppets Take Disney World."

446 **"It's not just me doing this stuff"** *Being Green,* 77.

447 **"[It's] the people"** JH to Eisner, June 6, 1989.

447 **"He really wanted to do right by everybody"** LH interview.

447 **"After twenty-five years"** JJ to JH, January 21, 1986 (JHCA 11027).

447 **"[Jim] really wanted this deal"** Mary Ann Cleary, email to the author, June 5, 2012.

447 **"He tried to be very benevolent"** Dave Goelz interview.

448 **"Disney does it so well," "The idea of working our characters"** JH, handwritten draft of Disney press release.

448 **"If you've seen a process that works"** JH to Robert A. Brennan, November 25, 1986 (JHCA 14067).

449 **"He was *very* excited," "Oh, they had so much fun"** Alex Rockwell interview.

449 **Jim's favorite attractions** Heather Henson interview.

449 **"It'll be a backstage ride"** See Dateline: WDW video promo for Disney-MGM Studios, 1990, http://www.youtube.com/watch?v=7GiDIPEnSsg.

450 **"at the end of the day"** John Henson interview.

451 **"creative vitality"** Cox and Liles-Morris, "Mickey Buys the Muppets; 'Creative Vitality' of Henson a Lure."

451 **"[Jim's] natural curiosity"** Mark Eades, interviewed by Wade Sampson, "The Muppet*Vision 3D Story," Mouse Planet website, May 19, 2010, http://www.mouseplanet.com/9256/The_MuppetVision_3D_Story.

451 **"The trips were often whirlwinds"** Mary Ann Cleary, email to the author, May 18, 2012.

451 **"was frustrated"** Masters, "Disney's Muppet Miasma: Corporate Style, Henson's Death Complicate a Deal in Waiting."

451 **"communicat[ing] to both"** JH to DL and Bob Bromberg, October 19, 1989 (JHCA Disney folder).

452 **"It was a tough process"** Peter Schube interview.

452 **"but I think his idealism"** Steve Whitmire interview.

453 "He loved the fact" Peter Schube interview.

453 "When do you need it?" Michael Frith interview.

453 "It was like he was Santa" Mary Ann Cleary, email to the author, June 5, 2012.

454 "It was a little bit heartbreaking" LH interview.

454 "My dad liked *everything*" Heather Henson interview.

454 "I gave him a bottle of white zinfandel" John Henson interview.

454 "He was more relaxed" Jerry Nelson interview.

455 "I don't think they understood" Masters, "Disney's Muppet Miasma: Corporate Style, Henson's Death Complicate a Deal in Waiting."

455 Roy Disney found him rude Stewart, 123.

455 "the most brutal, the stingiest, most compulsive" Julie Salamon, "Jeffrey Katzenberg: Disney's New Mogul," *Wall Street Journal,* May 12, 1987.

455 "that's not the way Jim operated" DL, archival interview.

455 "a non-starter" Masters, "Disney's Muppet Miasma: Corporate Style, Henson's Death Complicate a Deal in Waiting."

455 "There you go again" Joan Ganz Cooney interview.

456 "I felt like the writing" Mary Ann Cleary, email to the author, May 18, 2012.

456 "they were always very civil" BH interview.

457 "Jim really didn't want to work with somebody" Jane Henson interview.

457 "appalled," "Jim . . . does not seem" Roald Dahl to Duncan Kenworthy, February 2, 1990 (JHCA 9002).

457 "saddened" Duncan Kenworthy to Roald Dahl, February 9, 1990 (JHCA 9002).

457 "I'm sorry that we didn't stay in closer touch" JH to Roald Dahl, February 15, 1990 (JHCA 9002).

458 "Everyone who knows the Disney Company," "We've had a great, great time" Brillstein, 329.

459 "Jim didn't say" Masters, "Disney's Muppet Miasma: Corporate Style, Henson's Death Complicate a Deal in Waiting."

459 "one home per child" Arthur Novell interview.

459 "It just made him so happy" CH interview.

459 "just a few minutes in meditation" *Being Green,* 44.

460 "I thought he was more relaxed and happier" JJ, archival interview.

460 "Jim was never happier in his life" DL, archival interview.

460 the big question Bob Bromberg to JH et al., May 3, 1990 (JHCA 9597).

460 "Disney focused on *everything*" Masters, "Disney's Muppet Miasma: Corporate Style, Henson's Death Complicate a Deal in Waiting."

460 "[Henson Associates] was extremely solid" Peter Schube interview.

461 "Disney is a corporate entity" Masters, "Disney's Muppet Miasma: Corporate Style, Henson's Death Complicate a Deal in Waiting."

461 "that drew the process out" Peter Schube interview.

461 "Of all the people in the world" Larry Mirkin interview.

461 "That goddamned deal!" "I'll never forget my surprise" Michael Frith, email to the author, March 17, 2013.

461   "things just didn't work out"   Jane Henson interview.
461   "Don't worry"   BB, archival interview.

CHAPTER SIXTEEN: JUST ONE PERSON

462   "He was ready"   BB, archival interview.
463   "He insisted it would go away"   Schindehette, "Legacy of a Gentle Genius."
463   "it wasn't anything extreme" "It was funny"   Kevin Clash interview.
463   "No, leave it"   Arthur Novell interview.
464   "I think it's not particularly necessary"   JH, "The Courage of My Convictions."
464   "Jim was very stubborn about sickness"   Alex Rockwell interview.
464   "He was always quite robust and healthy"   BH interview.
464   "He just wasn't an unhealthy guy"   Steve Whitmire interview.
464   "I get the flu"   JH RB, February 21–26, 1985.
464   "Went to Washington"   JH RB, January 1, 1968.
464   "Typical Jim"   Arthur Novell interview.
464   He was feeling better   See Jim's medical records, May 14–16, 1990 (Henson Family Properties).
464   "I love you," "I don't give a shit what happens"   BB, archival interview. See also Brillstein, 329.
465   "It seemed like a cold or flu"   CH, email to the author, April 23, 2012.
465   "We just laughed"   "Family Denies Reports That Henson Was Examined by Doctor in North Carolina," *Sun* (Baltimore), May 18, 1990.
466   "looked kind of bad"   Ibid.
466   "He was really tired," "Hi, ho, Kermit the Frog here!"   CH interview.
467   As Jim climbed out of the car   From this point, unless otherwise noted, the story of Jim's final days has been pieced together using Jim's medical records and interviews with the following individuals (in alphabetical order): Kevin Clash, Michael Frith, Dave Goelz, Brian Henson, Cheryl Henson, Heather Henson, Jane Henson, John Henson, Lisa Henson, Anne Kinney, Jerry Nelson, Arthur Novell, Frank Oz, Alex Rockwell, and Steve Whitmire, as well as archival interviews with David Lazer and Bernie Brillstein.
467   "feel[ing] lousy"   Jim's medical records indicate that he described his condition this way.
467   "No one could remember Jim ever calling in sick"   Dave Goelz, interviewed by Kenneth Plume, January 28, 2000.
467–68 "He said he'd had a very rough night," "*Everyone* was coming in," "We just talked"   Schindehette, "Legacy of a Gentle Genius."
468   "He and Mom were always just really fond"   CH, email to the author, April 23, 2012.
470   "I'm here at New York Hospital"   Brillstein, 335–36.
471   "I couldn't believe it"   Dave Goelz, interviewed by Kenneth Plume.
471   "hard to even hear it"   "Ratting Out," July 19, 1999.

472   **official cause of death**   See Jim's autopsy report (Henson Family Properties).

472–73 **"overwhelming infection," "There had already been extensive damage done"**   Dennis O'Brien, "Henson's Pneumonia Was Swift, Lethal," *Sun* (Baltimore), May 18, 1990.

473   **"He was really devastated"**   Jerry Nelson interview.

473   **"A custodian answered"**   Dave Goelz, interviewed by Kenneth Plume.

473   **"My heart stopped"**   Fran Brill interview.

473   **"I remember growing up"**   Kevin Clash interview.

474   **"Everybody was walking wounded," "We were thrown into having to deal"**   CH interview.

475   **"Today I am sitting here"**   JH, open letter to "Children and Friends," March 2, 1986 (Henson Family Properties).

476   **"a traumatic period"**   Masters, "Disney's Muppet Miasma: Corporate Style, Henson's Death Complicate a Deal in Waiting."

476   **"All these people were coming"**   Jane Henson interview.

476   **"was a wonderful microcosm"**   Masters, "Disney's Muppet Miasma: Corporate Style, Henson's Death Complicate a Deal in Waiting."

476   **"just let it happen like a show," "Is this going to be all right in your church?"**   Jane Henson interview.

477   **"[Eisner] was crushed"**   BB, archival interview.

477   **"That was just amazing"**   Kevin Clash interview.

478   **"I remember admiring Louise Gold"**   Fran Brill interview.

478   **"I remember coming close to breaking"**   Jerry Nelson interview.

478   **"a sight I'll never forget"**   Chris Barry, "Saying 'Goodbye' to Jim," Jim Hill Media, September 7, 2005, http://jimhillmedia.com/guest_writers1/b/chris _barry/archive/2005/09/08/1722.aspx#.

478   **"Jim taught us many things"**   "Henson Memorial: Thousands Celebrate Muppet Creator's Life in Upbeat, Happy Way He Requested," *Newsday*, May 22, 1990.

478   **"the generosity of [Jim's] time"**   See video of Oz's eulogy at http://www .youtube.com/watch?v=zguccnOjnOI.

478   **"Somehow"**   Spinney, 138.

478   **"Thank you, Kermit"**   Spinney's remarkable performance can be viewed at: http://www.youtube.com/watch?v=lrZyMptC2eQ.

478   **"Jim told me"**   Brillstein, 338–39.

479–80 **"I know I couldn't sing"**   Fran Brill interview.

480   **"we all marched out of the cathedral smiling"**   Spinney, 138.

480   **"an epic and almost unbearably moving event"**   Harrigan, "It's Not Easy Being Blue."

480   **"When Jim left the planet"**   *Being Green,* 168–69.

480   **"Creator, Producer"**   See Jim's death certificate.

481   **"See those hills over there?"**   John Henson interview.

481   **"I try to tune myself in"**   JH, "The Courage of My Convictions."

481   **"we hiked up onto somebody's personal property"**   LH interview.

481   **"This is it"**   John Henson interview.

482   "First of all"   JH to Lisa, Cheryl, Brian, John, and Heather Henson, March 2, 1986 (Henson Family Properties).

Epilogue: Legacy

485   "gonna make this deal go through"   BB, archival interview.
486   "death and taxes," "It finally became a situation"   Peter Schube interview.
486   "Believe me"   Brillstein, 333.
486   "harder and harder"   Dan Ackman, "The Muppets Come Home," *Wall Street Journal*, May 13, 2003.
486   "natural home"   Alice Daniel, "The Muppet Family Business," *Success*, 2011.
487   "We are honored"   Peter Grant and Bruce Orwell, "Leading the News: Disney Buys Henson Muppets; Comcast Continues Its Pursuit," *Wall Street Journal*, February 18, 2004.
487   "Jim inspired people"   Brillstein, 338–39.
488   "In this industry"   Anthony Minghella, archival interview.
488   "I see Jim's life"   *Being Green*, 33.
488   "Jim had a sense of humor"   Ibid., 38.
488   "he could integrate play"   Ibid., 130.
488   "Even today, many, many years later"   Fran Brill interview.
488   "He was a creatively restless individual"   Daniel, "The Muppet Family Business."
488   "That's probably what he taught me"   BH interview.
489   "Jim didn't think in terms of boundaries"   *Being Green*, 151.
489   "I often tell people"   Bonnie Erickson interview.
489   "so overpowering"   Anthony Minghella, archival interview.
489   "an extraordinary appreciator"   FO, remarks at the Jim Henson London Memorial, 1990 (*Being Green*, 138).
489   "Underneath the zaniness"   *Being Green*, 148.
490   "He often started"   Alex Rockwell interview.
490   "I know that it's easier"   *Being Green*, 161.
490   "He wasn't a saint"   Richard Hunt, archival interview.
490   "That's how I think of my dad"   CH interview.
490   "We all have jobs"   Richard Hunt, archival interview.
490   "When I was young"   JH, "The Courage of My Convictions."

SELECTED BIBLIOGRAPHY

Bacon, Matt. *No Strings Attached: The Inside Story of Jim Henson's Creature Shop.* New York: Macmillan, 1997.

Bailey, Joseph A. *Memoirs of a Muppets Writer (You Mean Somebody Actually Writes That Stuff?).* New York: Walnut, 2011.

Batchelder, Marjorie. *The Puppet Theatre Handbook.* New York: Harper & Row, 1947.

Borgenicht, David. *Sesame Street Unpaved.* New York: Hyperion, 2008.

Brillstein, Bernie, with David Rensin. *Where Did I Go Right? You're No One in Hollywood Unless Someone Wants You Dead.* Beverly Hills: Phoenix, 1999.

Chester, Lewis. *All My Shows Are Great: The Life of Lew Grade.* London: Aurum, 2010.

Damron, Andra, and the Hyattsville Preservation Society. *Hyattsville.* Mount Pleasant, SC: Arcadia, 2008.

Davis, Michael. *Street Gang: The Complete History of Sesame Street.* New York: Viking, 2008.

Dean, Jimmy, and Donna Meade Dean. *Thirty Years of Sausage, Fifty Years of Ham: Jimmy Dean's Own Story.* New York: Berkley, 2006.

Durrett, Deanne. *Inventors and Creators: Jim Henson.* San Diego: Kidhaven, 2002.

Eide, Paul, Alan Cook, and Steve Abrams, eds. *A Timeline of Puppetry in America*. Minneapolis: Puppeteers of America, 2003.

Eisner, Michael. *Work in Progress*. New York: Hyperion, 1999.

Falk, Karen. *Imagination Illustrated: The Jim Henson Journal*. San Francisco: Chronicle, 2012.

Finch, Christopher. *Jim Henson: The Works, the Art, the Magic, the Imagination*. New York: Random House, 1993.

———. *The Making of The Dark Crystal: Creating a Unique Film*. New York: Holt, Rinehart & Winston, 1983.

———. *Of Muppets and Men: The Making of The Muppet Show*. New York: Alfred A. Knopf, 1981.

Fischer, Stuart. *Kids' TV: The First 25 Years*. New York: Facts on File Publications, 1983.

Froud, Brian. *The Goblins of Labyrinth*. New York: Harry N. Abrams, 2006.

———. *The World of The Dark Crystal*. New York: Alfred A. Knopf, 1982.

Gikow, Louise. *Sesame Street: A Celebration of 40 Years of Life on the Street*. New York: Black Dog & Leventhal, 2009.

Gourse, Leslie. *Jim Henson: Young Puppeteer*. New York: Aladdin, 2000.

Henson Associates. *The Art of the Muppets*. New York: Bantam, 1980.

Henson, Jim, and the Muppets and Friends. *It's Not Easy Being Green (And Other Things to Consider)*. Edited by Cheryl Henson. New York: Hyperion, 2005.

Hill, Doug, and Jeff Weingrad. *Saturday Night: A Backstage History of Saturday Night Live*. New York: William Morrow, 1989.

Hollis, T. M. *Hi There, Boys and Girls! America's Local Children's Television Programs*. Jackson: University Press of Mississippi, 2001.

Holub, Joan. *Who Was Jim Henson?* New York: Grosset & Dunlap, 2010.

Inches, Alison. *Jim Henson's Designs and Doodles: A Muppet Sketchbook*. New York: Harry N. Abrams, 2001.

Lewis, Jim. *Jim Henson's Doodle Dreams*. Des Moines: Meredith, 2008.

Masters, Kim. *The Keys to the Kingdom: How Michael Eisner Lost His Grip*. New York: William Morrow, 2000.

Obraztsov, Sergei. *My Profession.* Translated by Ralph Parker and Valentina Scott. Moscow: Foreign Languages Publishing House, circa 1950.

Rinzler, J. W. *The Making of The Empire Strikes Back.* New York: Ballantine, 2010.

Settel, Irving. *A Pictorial History of Television.* New York: Frederick Ungar, 1983.

Shales, Tom, and James Andrew Miller. *Live from New York: An Uncensored History of Saturday Night Live.* New York: Little, Brown, 2002.

Spinney, Caroll. *The Wisdom of Big Bird (and the Dark Genius of Oscar the Grouch): Lessons from a Life in Feathers.* New York: Villard, 2003.

St. Pierre, Stephanie. *The Story of Jim Henson, Creator of the Muppets.* New York: Dell, 1991.

Stewart, James B. *Disneywar.* New York: Simon & Schuster, 2005.

PHOTOGRAPH CREDITS

Title page: © Bill Pierce. Kermit the Frog © Disney.

Prologue, page xi: Bernard Gotfryd/Premium Archive/Getty Images. Kermit the Frog © Disney.

Chapter 1, page 3: Courtesy of Henson Family Properties.

Chapter 2, page 23: Courtesy of Henson Family Properties. Muppets © Disney.

Chapter 3, page 45: Courtesy of The Jim Henson Company. Muppets © Disney. Photo: Del Ankers.

Chapter 4, page 67: Courtesy of The Jim Henson Company. Muppets © Disney. Photo: Del Ankers.

Chapter 5, page 95: Courtesy of The Jim Henson Company. Muppets © Disney. Photo: Del Ankers.

Chapter 6, page 137: Courtesy of Sesame Workshop.

Chapter 7, page 173: Courtesy of The Jim Henson Company. Muppets © Disney.

Chapter 8, page 203: Courtesy of The Jim Henson Company.

Chapter 9, page 231: Courtesy of The Jim Henson Company. Muppets © Disney.

Chapter 10, page 271: Courtesy of The Jim Henson Company. Muppets © Disney.

Chapter 11, page 303: Courtesy of The Jim Henson Company. Photo: Murray Close.

Chapter 12, page 350: Courtesy of The Jim Henson Company.

Chapter 13, page 392: Courtesy of The Jim Henson Company.

Chapter 14, page 412: Courtesy of The Jim Henson Company. Kermit the Frog © Disney.

Chapter 15, page 432: Courtesy of The Jim Henson Company.

Chapter 16, page 462: Courtesy of The Jim Henson Company. Photo: Lynn Goldsmith.

Epilogue, page 485: Courtesy of The Jim Henson Company. Photo: Kerry Hayes.

PHOTO: STEPHANIE HITCHCOCK

BRIAN JAY JONES is an award-winning biographer and vice president of Biographers International Organization. Jones is a devoted member of the Jim Henson generation, having been two years old when *Sesame Street* premiered in 1969 and nine when *The Muppet Show* debuted in 1976. A former policy analyst and advisor in the U.S. Senate, Jones abandoned politics for the pen in 2008, with the publication of his award-winning biography, *Washington Irving*. He lives with his wife and daughter in Damascus, Maryland. His favorite Muppet is Rowlf (thanks for asking).

ABOUT THE TYPE

This book was set in Sabon, a typeface designed by the well-known German typographer Jan Tschichold (1902–74). Sabon's design is based on the original letterforms of Claude Garamond and was created specifically to be used for three sources: foundry type for hand composition, Linotype, and Monotype. Tschichold named his typeface for the famous Frankfurt typefounder Jacques Sabon, who died in 1580.